C000143457

TEMPUS
SPEEDWAY
YEARBOOK 2006

TEMPUS
SPEEDWAY
YEARBOOK 2006

EDITED BY ROBERT BAMFORD

TEMPUS

First published 2006

Tempus Publishing Limited
The Mill, Brimscombe Port,
Stroud, Gloucestershire, GL5 2QG
www.tempus-publishing.com

© Robert Bamford 2006

The right of Robert Bamford to be identified as the Author
of this work has been asserted in accordance with the
Copyrights, Designs and Patents Act 1988.

All rights reserved. No part of this book may be reprinted
or reproduced or utilised in any form or by any electronic,
mechanical or other means, now known or hereafter invented,
including photocopying and recording, or in any information
storage or retrieval system, without the permission in writing
from the Publishers.

British Library Cataloguing in Publication Data.
A catalogue record for this book is available from the British Library.

ISBN 0 7524 3692 9

Typesetting and origination by Tempus Publishing Limited
Printed in Great Britain

CONTENTS

ACKNOWLEDGEMENTS

Well, here we go again with the third edition of the Tempus Speedway Yearbook. As ever, there are a number of people to thank for their help, so without further ado here is the list, with much appreciation to one and all: Ian Adam, Nick Barber, Richard Crowley, Gordon Day, Frank Ebdon, Matt Ford, Colin Goddard, Mike Golding, Roger Hulbert, Mike Hunter, Nathan Irwin, Tracy Irwin, Jeremy Jackson, Tony Jackson, Dick Jarvis, Pam Johnson, Roger Last, Charles McKay, Peter Oakes, Robert Peasley, Robbie Perks, Lee Poole, Andy Povey, Laurence Rogers, Alun Rossiter, John Sampford, the Satchell clan (Martin, Chezza, Greg and Jordan), Glynn Shailes, George Sheridan, Mike Smillie, Dave Stallworthy, Barry Stephenson, Norrie Tait, Steve Thorn, Peter Toogood, Malcolm Vasey, Bob Wayte and Bryn Williams. I am particularly grateful to Matt Jackson for help with numerous dates of birth and, indeed, to all the riders who were more than helpful with similar information when asked. Statistical genius Mike Moseley has kept me on the straight and narrow as far as the accuracy of averages is concerned and I am deeply indebted for his time and trouble in cross-checking all my figures. I am grateful for the assistance of various photographers, so many thanks indeed to the following for expertly producing all the images contained herein: main photographic content by Mike Patrick (www.mike-patrick.com); other contributions by Les Aubrey, Steve Brock, Ken Carpenter, Nigel Chanter, Ian Charles, Dave Fairbrother, Eddie Garvey, Phil Hilton, John Hipkiss, Hywel Lloyd and Alan Whale. The internet has also proved invaluable in helping to keep up with everything in the speedway world, so grateful thanks to all the webmasters for collectively doing such a marvellous job. I also wish to pay tribute to *Speedway Star* magazine, which has been an excellent and invaluable reference point.

Robert Bamford
31 October 2005

INTRODUCTION

The 2005 season provided much in the way of interesting racing and, in the league programme, an excellent finish. There were no additions to the Elite League, although once again Dame Rumour suggested that there might be in the not-too-distant future. As far as the top-flight title was concerned, the promoters could not have wished for anything better if they had personally stage-managed it. It all came down to a tussle between Belle Vue and Coventry in the Play-Off final and, in two evenings of nail-biting racing, it was the side from Warwickshire who scooped the Championship from their somewhat unlucky rivals. It was certainly a prize for Coventry, not to mention a complete turnaround in their fortunes. In 2004 the Bees were bottom of the Elite League standings, having totalled just 21 points from their thirty-six fixtures, but in 2005 they tallied 59 points from the same number of meetings. The young and attractive line-up, so painstakingly put together by Colin Pratt and Peter Oakes, started quietly but, as the season progressed, struck a rich vein of form and it surprised few folk when they went on to take glory. It has to be said that the signing of Scott Nicholls had much to do with the success of the Bees. It was something of a shock when he requested a transfer from home-town club Ipswich, but his arrival at Brandon gave Coventry's performances some real steel. There was a period when the transfer was on shaky ground, as indeed were the moves of American duo Greg Hancock and Billy Hamill to Oxford; however, in the end all was well.

Coventry did have a few problems though when Swedish ace Andreas Jonsson gave notice that he found British racing together with his other commitments far too tiring and that as a result his health was suffering. Shortly after his departure a replacement was found in Joonas Kylmakorpi and the Swedish-born Finn proved a popular team member, averaging exactly 7.00 from eleven league matches after initially appearing as a guest. Prior to that Billy Janniro, who had been allowed to go on loan to Peterborough, had returned to Brandon when the opportunity presented itself. Young Australian Rory Schlein had adjusted well, after 'doubling-up' the previous year with Belle Vue while setting the Premier League alight with Edinburgh, but unluckily he was sidelined with a compressed fracture of a vertebra. Team changes at Peterborough meant Janniro was available, so the American stepped back into the Bees' nest. Late in the season, Polish stylist Sebastian Ulamek came into the line-up and performed well, achieving a 7.12 average from nine matches. Aside from this, there were great showings from the team's young brigade, namely Chris Harris, Morten Risager and Martin Smolinski, each of whom made strides and gave Coventry the solidity that made them worthy title winners.

Belle Vue shot up the league table under new club owner Tony Mole and promoter/team manager Ian Thomas. Indeed, Mole spent a great deal of money on the Kirkmanshulme Lane racing strip and it paid off handsomely, with few meetings falling victim to inclement weather. The Manchester outfit may have lost out on Rory Schlein but Kenneth Bjerre became a reliable heat leader, and his bad leg injury, broken while racing in his native Denmark, robbed the Aces of his services and cost the side dearly. Many speedway fans, especially those from Belle Vue, were convinced that the loss of Bjerre made the difference between winning and losing the League Championship. The shrewd Thomas had assembled a workmanlike side around 2004 World Champion Jason Crump, who was again as solid as a rock in recording a 10.30 average. Jason Lyons returned and at times showed his known ability, while Andy Smith was another returnee to the Aces' fold and was a real plus factor, bagging 206 points for a solid 6.28 average. Meanwhile, a fabulous signing was that of Simon Stead from sister track Workington. The Premier League had nothing more to teach 'Steady', who rode his heart out on the revamped Belle Vue circuit and also deservedly received caps for his country. The final piece of the jigsaw was the 'doubling-up' of Rusty Harrison. The Aussie grabbed his opportunity with both hands and played his part in the team's overall success.

Poole, the 2004 League Champions, began their defence of the title in ominous form and for a long time they again headed the standings. However, their unbeaten home record was shattered by Peterborough on 15 August, and the unfortunate illness of skipper Ryan Sullivan meant an early curtailment to his season shortly afterwards. The reserve position in the team also gave rise to problems when Edward Kennett was unavailable and it wasn't until speedy Pole Robert Kosciecha was signed near the close of the Elite League programme that there was sufficient strength in that particular department, his arrival coming too late for the Pirates to salvage a Play-Off spot. Fellow Pole Grzegorz Walasek returned to the side for the Craven Shield competition and, although he helped Poole battle through to the final, they were unable to retain the trophy they had won when it was last raced for in 2002. So, all in all, it was a disappointing campaign for a club that had been used to the winning feeling for some considerable time.

One of the season's big risers was Peterborough, whose promotion changed hands from Mick Horton to brother Colin in May. The Panthers strung some superb results together and jumped right up from ninth position in 2004 to third. In the bespectacled Peter Karlsson they had a number one who could win races against any opposition. Both of the Dryml brothers were again in action for the side, although Lukas initially began the season in the colours of Oxford. Ales, the elder of the two, outscored his sibling to average 8.21 and although Lukas had seemingly lost some of his sparkle, he still finished with a creditable 7.06 figure. Forty-four-year-old Sam Ermolenko, in what once again might just have been his last year of racing, proved a steady performer as he posted a 6.84 average, and if it was indeed his final fling he will leave with good wishes for his future from speedway supporters the world over.

At Swindon, club owner Terry Russell shelled out £32,000 for the signature of Lee Richardson and the Robins also introduced spectacular Frenchman Sebastien Tresarrieu and highly rated Swedish teenager Sebastian Alden. Fellow Swede Jonas Davidsson came on board on the eve of the season after compatriot Peter Ljung had had a change of heart about returning to Blunsdon. The side's lynchpin was of course Leigh Adams, who again topped the entire Elite League averages with a whopping 10.47 figure and at last got his reward on the world stage by scooping third spot in the Grand Prix series. Unluckily, mega-popular Dane Charlie Gjedde again suffered injury, but when fit and on-song he was the ultimate crowd-pleaser, raising his average to 8.45. The fact was that Swindon didn't perform particularly well on their travels, while at home it was often a struggle to win. Despite excellent top-end power from Adams, Richardson and Gjedde, there unfortunately wasn't enough support from the back-up department. Mid-season attempts to sign Tomasz Jedrzejak came to nought after the rider's Polish club refused to sanction the move, so in the end Robins promoter Alun Rossiter dispensed with the mechanically challenged Tresarrieu, opting to give Ljung the opportunity of rekindling his British career. Regrettably, the move wasn't a fruitful one and, having been unable to find his scoring touch, the Swede ended the season with a £500 fine and a twenty-eight-day ban after failing to put in an appearance at Oxford for a Craven Shield meeting on 29 September. Prior to tapes-up on Swindon's final league match of the season at Oxford on 20 October, Terry Russell increased his asset base by concluding a deal with Silver Machine boss Nigel Wagstaff for the full transfer of Jonas Davidsson.

Oxford's season was hampered by injury and most notably it affected Billy Hamill, who was injured early on at Swindon courtesy of a snapped chain and was out of action for some weeks as the side propped up the league table. On the other hand, Greg Hancock was an inspirational leader and Travis McGowan grittily plugged away throughout, enjoying a lengthy golden period in the latter weeks of the campaign. Along the way, promoter Nigel Wagstaff made numerous signings in an effort to attain a winning blend, but only when Hamill finally returned and found form did the Silver Machine hit the right note, ending the season by triumphing over Eastbourne and Poole in the Craven Shield final. Aptly, in a nail-biting climax, it was Hamill who won the last heat, with veteran Henka Gustafsson grabbing third place to give Oxford the aggregate success by just a single point from the Eagles. On a night to really savour for the loyal Sandy Lane supporters, in the second part of a double-header the Silver Machine then defeated Wolverhampton in their last Elite League fixture to secure the match points and the aggregate bonus, thereby handing the wooden spoon to unlucky Arena-Essex. No sooner were the celebrations over than Wagstaff announced he was quitting or, as he put it, 'taking a sabbatical', giving the rumour merchants plenty to chew over as to who might be at the helm in 2006.

That Ipswich missed Scott Nicholls was to be expected, but they did have a trio of Polish successes in Piotr Protasiewicz, Robert Miskowiak and late-season acquisition Mariusz Puszakowski. A fourth Pole, Karol Baran, just couldn't settle in British racing, while young Daniel King perhaps didn't make the hoped-for progress, though he did come on in leaps and bounds at Premier League level with Rye House. Such is his ability that he could still make it in the higher sphere of racing. Dependable Dane Hans N. Andersen was an excellent number one, if also a tad controversial at times. However, he was a class act on a consistent basis and it is difficult to see why he wasn't selected as a permanent wild card for the 2006 Grand Prix series. He certainly has all the right credentials and was understandably aggrieved at his omission. It was great to see Chris Louis showing much of his old dash with Ipswich and an average of 8.48 was an excellent reward for his efforts. Diminutive Swede Kim Jansson finished the season with a flourish and could be a most useful performer for the Witches in the future.

Former World Champion Nicki Pedersen was the star performer for Eastbourne, posting an Elite League average of 10.30. Unfortunately, the East Sussex outfit were hit hard by an injury to skipper David Norris due to a bout of delayed and ongoing concussion following a fall at Swindon on 28 April. This was most unfortunate for a rider who had grown so much in stature during 2004 and come back brilliantly from a broken right leg to begin the campaign on fire. Australian Davey Watt came on strongly to average 7.32, having started the season with a string of huge scores from the reserve berth. Meanwhile, fellow Aussie Adam Shields overcame a badly broken collarbone to end the season on a 7.01 average. The Eagles made it to the Play-Offs only to dip out at the semi-final stage. However, they did reach the gripping Craven Shield final, losing out by just a single point to Oxford on aggregate.

At Arena-Essex, promoter Ronnie Russell endured a frustrating time, although in the early weeks of the season he did sign Tony Rickardsson as cover for the injured Mark Loram, giving the multi-World Champion some valuable match practice prior to the commencement of speedway proper in other countries and, of course, the Grand Prix series. When Loram returned his impact was immediate as the Hammers came from 14 points behind to win 48-47 at Belle Vue in one of the shock results of the year. Although the Russian duo of Sergey Darkin and Roman Povazhny supplied Loram with some support, the success in Manchester was to be one of only eleven league wins for the side, as they slid to the foot of the table. Darkin was unlucky to end the season in intensive care following a pile-up involving three other riders at Togliatti in his homeland. On the plus side, Leigh Lanham was finally able to stage his Testimonial at the fourth attempt and he could be proud of his progress over the season, culminating in a 6.12 average achieved through simple hard work. In truth, the team was capable of doing better, although the injury bug certainly didn't help. For Russell, the biggest cause for concern were the club's attendances and it was to his credit that he kept plugging away right to the end, even introducing popular Pole Adam Skornicki for their last seven league matches.

Wolverhampton found themselves in the lower half of the Elite League standings and a serious leg injury to Mikael Max while racing at Malilla in his native Sweden was a huge blow. In contrast to that misfortune, Max's compatriot Fredrik Lindgren came on well and overcame his dislike of the Monmore Green circuit to average 7.48. After a year at Swindon, Steve Johnston arrived at Wolverhampton as the club's skipper and, although a little inconsistent with his scoring, the effervescent Australian still posted a 6.82 average. New to British racing was Polish recruit Krzysztof Pecyna, who tried his heart out and won many admirers on his way to a satisfactory 5.33 average. At the other end of the scale in terms of experience was thirty-eight-year-old American Ronnie Correy, who outstripped the entire league in terms of bonus points, netting a staggering total of 56 on his way to a solid 6.35 average. Although injury restricted David Howe's season, he recovered well from a broken ankle to attain a 7.24 figure. During his absence, Monmore Green favourite Adam Skornicki filled in admirably, his six matches yielding an 8.14 average.

The Premier League enjoyed an excellent season's racing and it was pleasing to see Len Silver's Rye House take the Championship by 4 clear points. Indeed, a visit to their Hoddesdon home was a real value-for-money trip, with Silver and his showman touch always ensuring that patrons enjoyed a grand evening's entertainment. Having earlier won the Premier Trophy, the Rockets were on course to take all four of the major trophies on offer, but they ran out of steam when the influential Stuart Robson sustained a dislocated shoulder and a broken finger in a full-speed smash at Rye House on 23 September. The team soldiered on using rider replacement but, in the finals of both the Knock-Out Cup and the Young Shield, they found King's Lynn too hot to handle. Nevertheless, the Rockets still gained two pieces of silverware and it was a great solidarity that ensured their success, having tracked a side that was perfectly balanced. Indeed, four of the team averaged in excess of 8.00 in the final league figures, namely Robson (9.18), Chris Neath (8.96), Brent Werner (8.53) and Edward Kennett (8.41), while Daniel King (7.55), Tommy Allen (6.44) and Steve Boxall (4.89) more than played their part.

Berwick chased Rye House all the way for the league title, utilising a cosmopolitan line-up that included two riders from the Czech Republic in Adrian Rymel and Michal Makovsky, Pole Adam Pietraszko, Dane Tom P. Madsen and, in their early matches, German Joachim Kugelmann. Another Pole, Piotr Dym, also appeared in their Premier Trophy fixtures. Scott Smith returned to action after missing out on 2004 when he concentrated on business interests and he had a great season to average 7.45. Rymel was the side's top man, averaging 8.86, while Pietraszko (7.84) and Makovsky (7.59) were solid and entertaining performers. Carl Wilkinson came in and did a wonderful job, upping his league average to 7.28, while Chris Schramm also raised his figure to 5.77.

Reading possessed the Premier League's leading rider in Slovenian Matej Zagar, who ended a terrific domestic campaign with a 10.29 average and also displayed his huge talent on the world stage in his home Grand Prix at Krsko on 28 May, when he claimed third place behind Tony Rickardsson and Nicki Pedersen. As a team, the Racers suffered cruel luck with two accidents to Danny Bird, which restricted him to just six official appearances all season (two in the Premier Trophy and four in the league). As a result, Reading were rarely able to track their strongest septet and finished in the bottom half of the table. If fate had dealt them a better hand, then surely they would have been breathing down the necks of Rye House and Berwick. Despite their difficulties, there were a couple of bright spots. Young Czech Zdenek Simota posted a league average of 6.39 and looks to be made of the right stuff, while Frenchman Mathieu Tresarrieu tenaciously achieved a 5.92 figure.

King's Lynn enjoyed a fine season, culminating in their double triumph in the Knock-Out Cup and Young Shield. The pacy Saddlebow Road bowl provided top-class racing and it must have been pleasing for promoter Buster Chapman to see the crowds turn up each week to witness all that is good in speedway. In the loyal and consistent Tomas Topinka, the Stars had the only other rider to enjoy a 10-plus average in the Premier League, the brilliant Czech's final figure being 10.03, as he occupied second place behind Matej Zagar in the overall averages for Britain's second tier. Like good wine, Topinka just seems to get better with age. After being linked with several other teams, Olly Allen unsurprisingly decided to join the Stars in order to 'double-up' with Swindon and, after recovering from an early-season shoulder injury, he went on to reveal much of his old spark in averaging 8.74. A late switch of his Elite League duties saw him sport the colours of Eastbourne, for whom he showed an improvement on his Swindon form. Like Allen, Aussie Troy Batchelor overcame injury to achieve a 7.11 average and played a leading role in the team's cup double in his first season. The youngster appears destined to follow in the footsteps of the many other famous Antipodeans who have graced the sport in Britain. Additionally another Australian, Kevin Doolan, was hit by injury, but he also battled back and was an integral part of the Stars' winning finish to the campaign.

With an average of 9.88, the Isle of Wight were capably led by Craig Boyce, while the all-action Ulrich Ostergaard showed great improvement to post an 8.62 figure. Latterly the cheery Dane particularly enjoyed a 'doubling-up' spell with Swindon, having initially performed a similar role with Eastbourne. Having averaged 4.68 for the Islanders, Tomas Suchanek, a World Cup rider with the Czech Republic, was purchased by Poole and understandably found the going tough in the Elite League. It was perhaps too soon for a move to the higher rung, but in the future he could be a useful asset for the Pirates. Suchanek and fellow Poole rider Krzysztof Kasprzak were involved in possibly the most bizarre ending to a major Championship, when, with the rain teeming down in Wiener Neustadt, Austria, the World Under-21 Final was abandoned. At the time both riders shared top spot on the scorechart with 8 points apiece and the destiny of the title was decided on the toss of a coin, with Suchanek being the unfortunate one to lose out. When Suchanek left for Poole, the Islanders replaced him with Krzysztof Stojanowski, who proved a real find and hit several big tallies on his way to a 7.88 average. The sky is the limit for the young Pole and one cannot help wondering what would have happened had Poole plumped for his signature.

Workington, under new promoter Graham Drury, suffered with injuries to key riders, none more so than long-serving club number one Carl Stonehewer. The Mancunian was doing his usual professional job when he sustained a serious arm injury in a league encounter against the Isle of Wight at Derwent Park on 23 July. James Wright, Scott Robson, Kauko Nieminen and

Kevin Little were among others to miss meetings through injury, although Wright bounced back to end the league fixtures with a superb 7.64 average. Having come up through the Conference League, this was a tremendous achievement in only his second season of Premier League racing and he is definitely one to look out for. Polish racer Tomasz Piszcz was brought in to pep up the side late on and did well, yielding a 7.09 average from seven matches.

It was wonderful for Sheffield to welcome back Sean Wilson and it didn't take the York-born rider long to settle into the groove, as emphasised by a 9.07 average. His winning of the Premier League Riders' Championship at Owlerton showed he is still one of the leading performers at that level, with much still to offer. Andre Compton took over at the head of the Tigers' averages with a 9.45 figure, while Ricky Ashworth had a year of consolidation and doubtless learned a great deal from 'doubling-up' with Poole. Young Ben Wilson continued to make his way in the sport, increasing his average to 6.65, while Canadian Kyle Legault had a steady debut season, posting a 5.80 figure.

Up in Scotland, Edinburgh enjoyed a good year, with Ross Brady overcoming injury to top their league averages on 9.02. The Scot was ably backed by Aussie Rusty Harrison (8.34), who 'doubled-up' with Belle Vue and gained from the experience. Swede Daniel Nermark put his injuries of the past behind him to average 8.12, while Dutchman Theo Pijper enjoyed his best season in British racing to date, ending with an 8.04 figure. After spells with Glasgow and King's Lynn, Australian Matthew Wethers came 'home' to average 7.42, while taking the number of recruits from Down Under to four were Cameron Woodward (7.41) and Robert Ksiezak (2.40). Woodward's season ended in August with a broken wrist, while his compatriot had a late run in the side after overcoming the effects of a broken left leg during the club's Premier Trophy campaign.

Over at Glasgow, Shane Parker was the leading Tiger for the second year on the bounce, averaging 9.81, with excellent top-end support supplied by the stylish George Stancl (8.58). Backing them, Stefan Ekberg registered an 8.25 figure after returning to British racing in mid-season. This was an excellent contribution considering he hadn't appeared on these shores since representing Eastbourne in 1995. Beyond that trio the scoring fell away somewhat, as did results for a side that ruled the roost in Second Division circles just over a decade ago. Ashfield played host to the prestigious Premier League Pairs Championship on 26 June and for most in a large attendance it was a memorable occasion, with Parker and Stancl combining brilliantly to scoop first place. Regrettably though, crowd levels were a cause for concern for the promotion during the season.

Across the Severn Bridge, Newport endured a difficult term. Michael Coles had been a pre-season acquisition but he was hit by personal problems and didn't appear for the Wasps after 20 May. He did make a return to the saddle for three late-season meetings at Exeter, however, and it is to be hoped that he can recommence his excellent service to the sport in 2006. Compounding Newport's problems, Mads Korneliussen and Craig Watson both suffered injuries, with the high-scoring Australian missing all but just two matches of the club's league programme. Neil Collins continued to belie his advancing years at Queensway Meadows though, being thrillmaker-in-chief on his way to 7.56 average. When fit, Korneliussen made a lot of progress, gaining much from his 'doubling-up' duties with Swindon.

Stoke's season was another to be blighted by injuries. The Potters lost the services of Paul Pickering to a serious arm injury in their opening Premier Trophy match at Hull and popular Dane Jan Staechmann was also ruled out for the duration in early May. It wasn't all gloom at Loomer Road though, as Robbie Kessler did a sterling job to average 7.87, while evergreen Alan Mogridge continued to entertain in his own inimitable fashion, posting a 7.75 figure in a year when he also celebrated his double Testimonial.

At Somerset, Magnus Zetterstrom topped the Rebels' averages on 9.43 and enjoyed his first year in the Premier League, helping his side to win the Four-Team Championship while individually triumphing in the Champions' Chase at King's Lynn. Reports suggest the Swede fancies another term with the Highbridge club and there can be little doubting that their supporters would welcome him back. Glenn Cunningham enjoyed his best year for some time to average 8.16, while the ever-popular Paul Fry posted a healthy 7.66 figure despite reaching forty-one years of age as the season drew to its conclusion.

Newcastle had a better season results-wise than in 2004, rising from the basement position to eighth spot. Track specialist James Grieves joined the Diamonds from Glasgow and shot to the head of the averages on 8.65, while Czech racer Josef Franc arrived via Berwick to record a 7.86 figure. Regrettably, the club's third incoming rider, Phil Morris, had a troubled year with injuries and a 6.65 average certainly wasn't a true reflection of his ability. To his credit, the Welshman stated that he hoped to get the opportunity to show what he can really do in 2006.

The Premier League unfortunately had to bid farewell to a couple of their number in 2005. The first was Exeter, whose County Ground raceway had seen several spells of action (1929-31, 1934, 1947-55, 1957-58 and continuously from 1960-2005). The track had survived the threat of closure on several occasions in recent years, but this time there was no halting the developers. A large crowd, reckoned by some to be around the 6,000 mark, turned out to witness the aptly titled 'End of an Era' meeting on 10 October, when former Falcons legends Ivan Mauger and Scott Autrey were in attendance. Fittingly, it was Mauger who rode the final four laps around the County Ground circuit before the lights finally went out. Following the sad passing of long-time Exeter promoter Colin Hill on 30 October 2004, it was Terry Russell who stepped in to allow the Falcons one more year of activity and it is to be hoped that the hard work of people like David Short, Mike Spearpoint and Tony Lethbridge is successful in finding a new home for the team. There is much to be done and perhaps a long time to wait, but hopefully the dream of Colin Hill will one day become a reality. In Mark Lemon, Exeter had a super number one to lead them in their final year, the Aussie finishing with an 8.41 average. Ray Morton came on board in May after being released by Poole and, although the Londoner achieved a higher 8.64 figure, injury restricted him to just a dozen league appearances. Sebastien Tresarrieu also joined the camp and certainly livened things up in averaging 7.09, but there were still the same kind of question marks over reliability that there had been at Swindon earlier in the season.

The situation at Hull was so very different to what it had been the year before when, with Eric Boocock as team manager, the Vikings had won everything there was to win in Premier League speedway. That, however, was 2004. In 2005, Hull seemed to be in almost constant dispute with their landlords, Hull Kingston Rovers Rugby League Club, over unpaid rent and, in the end, Paul Hodder and David Peet had their promoter's licences revoked, the club closing down with two home league matches outstanding versus Glasgow and King's Lynn. On track, in Paul Thorp the Vikings had a rider who again gave his all for the team he had first joined upon their arrival at Craven Park in 1995. He headed their averages on 8.16, while Emiliano Sanchez (7.67), Garry Stead (7.58) and Emil Kramer (7.51) also did all they could to alleviate the supporters' concerns over the club's ongoing problems. There is obviously a desire for speedway in Hull and it is to be hoped that a new venue for the sport can quickly be found within the city.

On the subject of new ventures, there was the news that Tony Mole, the owner of Belle Vue and Workington, was looking to bring speedway back to Birmingham at Perry Barr Greyhound

Stadium. This used to be known as the Alexander Sports Stadium and had previously staged speedway in three separate stints (1928, 1946-57 and 1960). It's a considerable time since the second city last housed the sport at the Birmingham Wheels Project, Bordesley Green in 1986, and it would certainly be a shot in the arm to the Premier League if Mr Mole's plans were to come to fruition. One only need look back at the impact speedway's return had at Birmingham (at the original Perry Barr Stadium in Walsall Road) in 1971 under the John Berry/Colin Barber/Joe Thurley promotion to see how significant it would be. Every fan of our beloved sport must surely wish Tony Mole the best of luck in his efforts.

The Conference League again served up plenty of thrilling racing and, in a close finish, it was Oxford who claimed the Championship just a single point ahead of Wimbledon. This was apt, since Oxford were the only Elite League club to run a team at this level and there is no doubt it paid off for promoter Nigel Wagstaff and his most-able lieutenant Bryn Williams. The Silver Machine Academy lost the services of teenager Ben Barker due to a nasty leg injury at Stoke on 3 August, yet team spirit and an ability to raise their game saw them through to success. In addition, Chris Mills, Craig Branney and Jamie Courtney had a number of outings for the senior side, albeit some as 'guest' appearances, and, while they didn't rack up many points, the experience can have done nothing but good. Having said that, Mills did end the campaign in fabulous fashion, netting 6+1 points in Oxford's final Elite League match of the season against Wolverhampton at Sandy Lane on 28 October.

With a promoter of Len Silver's enthusiasm it isn't surprising that Rye House have a second team, the Raiders, which has helped several youngsters up the rungs of the speedway ladder in recent years. Barry Burchatt, Harland Cook and Gary Cottham continued on their learning curve in 2005, while Silver also had the Conference League Riders' Champion in Steve Boxall. The lad from Canterbury was a regular for the title-winning senior Rockets' side too. Proof indeed that the Conference League is doing a grand job.

As the season reached its conclusion there were doubts over the future of some Conference League clubs, one in particular being the famous Wimbledon team and their plush Plough Lane home. What a great shame it was to learn that this fine old stadium, steeped in speedway history, could possibly be no more. The curtain came down on speedway at the venue on 5 October, with the forty-fourth staging of the prestigious Laurels individual event. Dons' rider Mark Burrows stormed to victory with a 15-point maximum on the night and there couldn't have been a more popular winner. 'Buzz' has served many tracks in a career that began at Scunthorpe in 1984 and his wholehearted efforts did much to help Wimbledon as they worked hard to establish themselves in the Conference League. The speedway grapevine suggests a number of possible venues for the Dons' continuance, although there was nothing concrete at the time of writing. It is to be hoped that Ian Perkin and Dingle Brown are successful in their search.

There was a problem with attendance figures at Armadale and, while John Campbell has pledged to find the Devils a new home, it was nice that they bowed out with victory over Stoke in the Conference Trophy final. There also appear to be difficulties at Weymouth, who were worthy winners of the Knock-Out Cup courtesy of an aggregate success against Mildenhall. On the subject of the Fen Tigers they might also be lost to the Conference League but, happily, for the best possible reason as promoter Mick Horton would like to see his club advance to the Premier League.

Despite its problems the Conference League continues to do a fine job in giving vital competitive racing experience to aspiring speedway riders. Unfortunately at some venues support is down to just the hard core. These teams desperately need support if they are to continue, so it is up to the speedway public at large to give them their backing.

The 2005 season can rightly be said to be the year that British speedway did take a step forward. It was only a small one, though, as there is still much to be done. However, the establishment of the British Academy League under the guidance of Peter Oakes must be regarded as a success. In the past there had been a great deal of talk but little action. Mr Oakes changed all that, with the result that many promising lads were given opportunities that they grasped with both hands. The league consisted of five teams, interestingly named Buffalo, Bulls, Cobras, Dinosaurs and Rhinos, while there were also Play-Offs and a Knock-Out Cup competition for the willing youngsters. Speedway must build on this foundation and it really would be excellent if this could be expanded on, with all the Elite and Premier League tracks staging these kind of meetings as second-half events. It'll be some time before the present crop of youngsters are ready for racing at the highest level, although two riders readily spring to mind who look to be destined for big things. Josh Auty is a young man rich in talent and he triumphed in the Under-15 Championship for the second year running, while also grabbing a team berth at Scunthorpe. The sensational Lewis Bridger was a regular member of the Weymouth line-up and, in a brilliant showing, won the Europress Bronze Helmet at Mildenhall on 2 October.

This elongated introduction has just scratched the surface with the happenings of 2005, so for much, much more please read on and enjoy the pages that follow; it's all in here, well reported and painstakingly researched.

Glynn Shailes and Robert Bamford
31 October 2005

ABBREVIATIONS

GENERAL

AL	Amateur League
BSPA	British Speedway Promoters' Association
CL	Conference League
CLKOC	Conference League Knock-Out Cup
CS	Craven Shield
CT	Conference Trophy
DNA	Did Not Arrive
DNR	Did Not Ride
EL	Elite League
ELKOC	Elite League Knock-Out Cup
FIM	Federation Internationale de Motorcyclisme
KOC	Knock-Out Cup
PL	Premier League
PLKOC	Premier League Knock-Out Cup
R/R	Rider Replacement
YS	Young Shield

AVERAGE TABLES

Mts	Matches
Rds	Rides
Pts	Points
Bon	Bonus Points
Tot	Total Points
Avge	Average
Max	Maximums

SCORE TABLES

DNA	Did Not Arrive
DNR	Did Not Ride
(R)	Replay
R/R	Rider Replacement
15 (5)	Maximum (Applies to any underlined total)

LEAGUE TABLES

Mts	Matches
Won	Won
Drn	Drawn
Lst	Lost
For	For
Agn	Against
Pts	Points
Bon	Bonus Points
Tot	Total Points

RACE POSITIONS

ex	Excluded
f	Fell
ns	Non-starter
rem	Remounted
ret	Retired

RACE SCORES TABLES

F	Fell
M	Excluded, 2 minutes
n	Non-starter
R	Retired
X	Excluded
T	Excluded, tapes

NOTE: In the calculation of rider averages, any tactical ride and tactical substitute points are recorded as those normally given for the relevant finishing position, e.g. 1st = 3 points, 2nd = 2 points and 3rd = 1 point. Appearances are only included in a rider's statistics when he was a member of the side as per the BSPA team declarations. All other appearances are included in the total for guests.

SKY BET ELITE LEAGUE 2005

SKY BET ELITE LEAGUE TABLE

	Mts	Won	Drn	Lst	For	Agn	Pts	Bon	Tot
Belle Vue	36	24	0	12	1,766	1,520	48	13	61
Coventry	36	23	0	13	1,739	1,605	46	13	59
Peterborough	36	21	2	13	1,709	1,598	44	12	56
Eastbourne	36	19	1	16	1,658	1,646	39	10	49
Poole	36	18	1	17	1,666	1,647	37	10	47
Ipswich	36	16	3	17	1,661	1,672	35	9	44
Swindon	36	17	2	17	1,617	1,675	36	7	43
Wolverhampton	36	14	2	20	1,682	1,647	30	10	40
Oxford	36	11	1	24	1,550	1,773	23	3	26
Arena-Essex	36	11	0	25	1,539	1,804	22	3	25

PLAY-OFFS

SEMI-FINALS

Belle Vue	53	Eastbourne	40
Coventry	55	Peterborough	41

FINAL

Coventry	54	Belle Vue	41	
Belle Vue	42	Coventry	47	(Coventry won 101-83 on aggregate)

CRAVEN SHIELD

QUALIFYING TABLES

	Mts	Won	Drn	Lst	For	Agn	Pts	Bon	Tot
Poole	3	2	0	1	149	132	4	1	5
Arena-Essex	3	2	0	1	146	130	4	1	5
Ipswich	4	1	0	3	169	202	2	0	2

	Mts	Won	Drn	Lst	For	Agn	Pts	Bon	Tot
Oxford	4	3	0	1	180	171	6	2	8
Wolverhampton	4	2	0	2	191	183	4	1	5
Swindon	4	1	0	3	168	185	2	0	2

SEMI-FINALS

FIRST LEG (at Peterborough): Peterborough 38, Coventry 36, Poole 34
SECOND LEG (at Poole): Poole 38, Peterborough 35, Coventry 34
THIRD LEG (at Coventry): Poole 40, Coventry 34, Peterborough 34
AGGREGATE: Poole 112, Peterborough 107, Coventry 104

FIRST LEG (at Eastbourne): Eastbourne 37, Oxford 27, Belle Vue 26
SECOND LEG (at Oxford): Oxford 42, Eastbourne 34, Belle Vue 32
THIRD LEG (at Belle Vue): Oxford 38, Eastbourne 36, Belle Vue 34
AGGREGATE: Eastbourne 107, Oxford 107, Belle Vue 92

FINAL
FIRST LEG (at Eastbourne): Eastbourne 41, Oxford 40, Poole 27
SECOND LEG (at Poole): Oxford 39, Poole 35, Eastbourne 34
THIRD LEG (at Oxford): Eastbourne 39, Oxford 36, Poole 33
AGGREGATE: Oxford 115, Eastbourne 114, Poole 95

KNOCK-OUT CUP

ROUND ONE

Wolverhampton	37	Ipswich	53	
Ipswich	55	Wolverhampton	40	(Ipswich won 108-77 on aggregate)
Poole	51	Swindon	41	
Swindon	60	Poole	36	(Swindon won 101-87 on aggregate)

QUARTER-FINALS

Peterborough	56	Eastbourne	37	
Eastbourne	59	Peterborough	36	(Eastbourne won 96-92 on aggregate)
Belle Vue	59	Oxford	35	
Oxford	49	Belle Vue	41	(Belle Vue won 100-84 on aggregate)
Coventry	51	Swindon	41	
Swindon	55	Coventry	39	(Swindon won 96-90 on aggregate)
Ipswich	52	Arena-Essex	42	
Arena-Essex	51	Ipswich	40	(Arena-Essex won 93-92 on aggregate)

SEMI-FINALS

Eastbourne	55	Arena-Essex	40	
Arena-Essex	52	Eastbourne	41	(Eastbourne won 96-92 on aggregate)
Belle Vue	61	Swindon	32	
Swindon	37	Belle Vue	35	(Belle Vue won 96-69 on aggregate)

FINAL

Eastbourne	46	Belle Vue	44	
Belle Vue	53	Eastbourne	37	(Belle Vue won 97-83 on aggregate)

ARENA-ESSEX HUSQVARNA HAMMERS

ADDRESS: Arena-Essex Raceway, A1306 Arterial Road, Thurrock, Essex, RM19 1AE.
PROMOTER: Ronnie Russell.
TRACK LENGTH: 252 metres.
TRACK RECORD: 57.2 seconds – Andreas Jonsson (27 April 2005).
FIRST MEETING: 5 April 1984.
YEARS OF OPERATION: 1984–90 National League; 1991 British League Division Two; 1992–94 British League Division One; 1995 Premier League; 1996 Conference League; 1997–2003 Premier League; 2004–05 Elite League.

CLUB HONOURS

LEAGUE CHAMPIONS: 1991.
KNOCK-OUT CUP WINNERS: 1991.
FOUR-TEAM CHAMPIONS: 1991.

RIDER ROSTER 2005

Sergey DARKIN; Gary HAVELOCK; Paul HURRY; Leigh LANHAM; Josh LARSEN; Mark LORAM; Phil MORRIS; Roman POVAZHNY; Tony RICKARDSSON; Adam SKORNICKI; Piotr SWIST.

OTHER APPEARANCES/GUESTS (official matches only):
Jason CRUMP; Charlie GJEDDE; Steve JOHNSTON; Jason KING; Joonas KYLMAKORPI; Ray MORTON; Scott NICHOLLS; David NORRIS; Adam SHIELDS; Carl STONEHEWER; Ryan SULLIVAN; Shaun TACEY.

SKY BET ELITE LEAGUE

(*Denotes bonus-point victory)

No	DATE	OPPONENTS	H/A	RESULT	Havelock	Povazhny	Lanham	Larsen	Loram	Hurry	Swist	Rickardsson	Darkin	Morris	Skornicki	Others
1	22/3	Poole	H	W61-30	12 (5)	8+3 (4)	10 (4)	7+2 (4)	–	8+1 (4)	5+2 (4)	–	–	–	–	11 (5)
2	25/3	Ipswich	A	L41-53	7 (4)	10 (5)	2+1 (4)	1+1 (3)	–	1 (3)	7 (6)	13 (5)	–	–	–	–
3	30/3	Oxford	H	L41-49	5+1 (4)	5 (5)	5+1 (4)	4+1 (4)	–	7+1 (4)	4+2 (4)	11 (5)	–	–	–	–
4	6/4	Poole	A	L40-55*	6 (5)	1+1 (4)	5+1 (4)	0 (3)	–	6+1 (5)	6+1 (4)	16 (5)	–	–	–	–
5	13/4	Wolverhampton	H	W52-41	9+1 (5)	4+1 (4)	6+1 (4)	6+1 (4)	–	7 (4)	6+1 (4)	14+1 (5)	–	–	–	–
6	18/4	Wolverhampton	A	L47-49*	14+1 (5)	6+2 (4)	7 (4)	2 (4)	–	1+1 (4)	2+1 (4)	15+1 (5)	–	–	–	–
7	20/4	Peterborough	H	W48-42	10 (5)	9 (4)	6+2 (4)	3+3 (4)	–	6 (4)	1 (4)	13 (5)	–	–	–	–
8	21/4	Oxford	A	W48-46	11+1 (5)	4+1 (4)	4 (4)	1+1 (3)	–	7+1 (4)	9 (5)	12 (5)	–	–	–	–
9	25/4	Coventry	A	L40-53	8 (5)	8+1 (4)	4+1 (4)	2 (4)	–	5+1 (5)	0 (3)	–	–	–	–	13 (5)
10	27/4	Coventry	H	L42-51	3+2 (4)	2 (4)	7 (4)	4 (4)	–	10+1 (5)	1 (4)	–	–	–	–	15 (5)

No	DATE	OPPONENTS	H/A	RESULT	Havelock	Povazhny	Lanham	Larsen	Loram	Hurry	Swist	Rickardsson	Darkin	Morris	Skornicki	Others
11	9/5	Belle Vue	A	L30-63	7+1 (5)	3 (4)	7 (5)	1+1 (3)	–	6 (5)	3 (4)	–	–	–	–	3 (4)
12	11/5	Belle Vue	H	L43-47	10+1 (5)	5+1 (4)	8+1 (4)	6+1 (4)		8+2 (6)	1+1 (3)	–	–	–	–	5 (4)
13	18/5	Ipswich	H	W57-39*	5+1 (4)	8+3 (4)	10+1 (5)	7+2 (4)		9+1 (5)	6+2 (4)	–	–	–	–	12 (4)
14	19/5	Swindon	A	L38-53	6 (5)	9 (4)	5+2 (4)	2+2 (4)		4+2 (4)	2 (4)	–	–	–	–	10 (5)
15	25/5	Eastbourne	H	L43-47	4 (4)	R/R	4 (4)	10+3 (7)		7+1 (6)	3+1 (4)	–	–	–	–	15 (5)
16	30/5	Wolverhampton	A	L31-63	0 (2)	5+1 (5)	5+1 (5)	3+1 (5)		5 (4)		–	2 (4)	–	–	11+1 (5)
17	1/6	Coventry	H	L42-51	5+2 (4)	3 (4)	4 (4)	15 (6)		3 (4)		–	3 (3)	–	–	9+2 (5)
18	6/6	Belle Vue	A	W48-47	3 (4)	4+2 (4)	4 (4)	–	14+1 (5)	9+1 (4)		–	10 (5)	4 (4)	–	–
19	8/6	Oxford	H	W47-46	7+1 (4)	7+1 (4)	8+2 (5)	–	10 (5)	6+2 (4)		–	5+1 (4)	4 (4)	–	–
20	16/6	Oxford	A	L41-49	4+1 (4)	12+1 (6)	4 (4)	4+3 (4)	9+1 (5)	3+1 (3)		–	5 (4)	–	–	–
21	18/6	Eastbourne	A	L42-52	3 (4)	15+1 (7)	7 (4)	1+1 (2)	9 (5)	1 (3)		–	6+1 (4)	–	–	–
22	22/6	Peterborough	H	L39-54	7 (4)	7+3 (5)	3 (4)	–	11 (5)	3 (4)		–	–	7+1 (6)	–	1+1 (3)
23	23/6	Peterborough	A	L39-52	8+1 (5)	11 (6)	7+1 (4)	–	9+1 (5)	0 (3)		–	–	3 (4)	–	1 (3)
24	29/6	Wolverhampton	H	L36-60	1 (4)	0 (4)	5 (4)	–	17 (5)	2 (4)		–	10 (5)	–	–	1 (4)
25	6/7	Swindon	H	W53-42	7+3 (4)	3 (4)	13+1 (5)	–	11+1 (5)	8+1 (4)		–	7+2 (4)	4+1 (4)	–	–
26	13/7	Belle Vue	H	L41-51	11 (5)	1+1 (4)	11 (4)	–	9 (5)	–		–	4+3 (4)	3+1 (4)	–	2+1 (4)
27	14/7	Swindon	A	L35-58	4 (4)	4 (4)	5 (4)	–	14 (5)	2 (4)		–	5+1 (5)	1+1 (4)	–	–
28	20/7	Poole	A	L38-52	6 (5)	11 (6)	3+1 (5)	–	13+1 (6)	3+1 (4)		–	R/R	2+1 (4)	–	–
29	22/7	Poole	H	W51-44	12+3 (6)	6+1 (5)	7+3 (5)	–	10+2 (6)	9 (4)		–	R/R	7+3 (4)	–	–
30	17/8	Ipswich	H	W49-41	7+2 (4)	5+2 (4)	10+2 (5)	–	12+1 (5)	4+1 (4)		–	7+1 (4)	–	4+1 (4)	–
31	19/8	Coventry	A	L42-54	9+3 (5)	6+1 (4)	2+1 (4)	–	10 (5)	3+1 (4)		–	7+1 (4)	–	5 (4)	–
32	27/8	Eastbourne	A	L37-56	5+1 (5)	3+1 (4)	5 (5)	–	11+1 (6)	8+1 (5)		–	R/R	–	5 (5)	–
33	29/8	Peterborough	A	L32-61	6 (4)	4+1 (5)	1+1 (4)	–	10 (5)	5+2 (4)		–	2+1 (4)	–	4+1 (4)	–
34	31/8	Swindon	H	W52-42	9+1 (5)	6+2 (4)	8+2 (4)	–	7 (4)	6+3 (4)		–	6+1 (4)	–	10+1 (5)	–
35	7/9	Eastbourne	H	L43-47	5+2 (4)	8 (4)	5+2 (4)	–	7 (5)	5+1 (5)		–	8 (5)	–	5 (4)	–
36	8/9	Ipswich	A	L30-64	3 (4)	1+1 (4)	3 (4)	–	14 (5)	5 (5)		–	4+2 (5)	–	0 (3)	–

DETAILS OF OTHER RIDERS:

Match No. 1: David Norris 11 (5); Match No. 9: Ryan Sullivan 13 (5); Match No. 10: David Norris 15 (5); Match No. 11: Carl Stonehewer 3 (4); Match No. 12: Steve Johnston 5 (4); Match No. 13: Scott Nicholls 12 (4); Match No. 14: Scott Nicholls 10 (5); Match No. 15: Jason Crump 15 (5); Match No. 16: Adam Shields 11+1 (5); Match No. 17: Charlie Gjedde 9+2 (5); Match No. 22: Jason King 1+1 (3); Match No. 23: Jason King 1 (3); Match No. 24: Ray Morton 1 (4); Match No. 26: Shaun Tacey 2+1 (4).

TACTICAL RIDES, AS INCLUDED IN THE SCORES GRID:

Match No. 2: Rickardsson 4 points (TR); Havelock 4 points (TR); Match No. 4: Rickardsson 6 points (TR); Havelock 4 points (TR); Match No. 6: Rickardsson 6 points (TR); Havelock 6 points (TR); Match No. 9: Sullivan 4 points (TR); Povazhny 2 points (TR); Match No. 10: Norris 6 points (TR); Match No. 11: Hurry 4 points (TR); Povazhny 2 points (TR); Match No. 14: Povazhny 2 points (TR); Match No. 16: Shields 6 points (TR); Hurry 2 points (TR); Match No. 17: Larsen 6 points (TR); Hurry 0 points (TR); Match No. 18: Hurry 6 points (TR); Loram 4 points (TR); Match No. 21: Povazhny 6 points (TR); Lanham 4 points (TR); Match No. 22: Havelock 4 points (TR); Loram 4 points (TR); Match No. 23: Povazhny 2 points (TR); Match No. 24: Darkin 6 points (TR); Loram 6 points (TR); Match No. 26: Lanham 4 points (TR); Match No. 27: Loram 4 points (TR); Darkin 2 points (TR); Match No. 31: Havelock 6 points (TR); Loram 6 points (TR); Match No. 32: Loram 4 points (TR); Match No. 33: Loram 4 points (TR); Havelock 4 points (TR); Match No. 36: Loram 6 points (TR); Havelock 2 points (TR).

ARENA-ESSEX: From left to right, back row: Gary Havelock, Leigh Lanham, Phil Morris, Ronnie Russell (Promoter/Team Manager), Paul Hurry, Josh Larsen. Front, kneeling: Piotr Swist, Roman Povazhny. On bike: Mark Loram.

ELITE LEAGUE AVERAGES

Rider	Mts	Rds	Pts	Bon	Tot	Avge	Max
Tony Rickardsson	7	35	86	2	88	10.06	1 paid
Mark Loram	19	97	188	9	197	8.12	–
Gary Havelock	36	160	224	29	253	6.33	–
Leigh Lanham	36	153	206	28	234	6.12	–
Sergey Darkin	16	68	87	14	101	5.94	–
Roman Povazhny	35	155	197	32	229	5.91	–
Paul Hurry	35	148	176	28	204	5.51	–
Josh Larsen	19	76	76	23	99	5.21	–
Adam Skornicki	7	29	33	3	36	4.97	–
Phil Morris	9	38	35	8	43	4.53	–
Piotr Swist	15	61	56	11	67	4.39	–
Guests	14	61	101	5	106	6.95	2 full

(Jason Crump [1]; Charlie Gjedde [1]; Steve Johnston [1]; Jason King [2]; Ray Morton [1]; Scott Nicholls [2]; David Norris [2]; Adam Shields [1]; Carl Stonehewer [1]; Ryan Sullivan [1]; Shaun Tacey [1]).

KNOCK-OUT CUP

(*Denotes aggregate victory)

No	DATE	OPPONENTS	H/A	RESULT	Havelock	Darkin	Lanham	Hurry	Loram	Larsen	Swist	Povazhny	Morris	Skornicki	Others
1	26/5	Ipswich	A	L42-52	10+1 (5)	–	3+2 (4)	7 (4)	–	0 (3)	6+2 (6)	–	–	–	16+2 (8)
2	15/6	Ipswich	H	W51-40*	8+1 (5)	5+1 (4)	7+2 (4)	7+1 (4)	12 (5)	4 (4)	–	8+2 (4)	–	–	–
3	23/7	Eastbourne	A	L40-55	11+2 (6)	R/R	3+1 (5)	6+1 (5)	13 (6)	–	–	7 (5)	0 (3)	–	–
4	21/9	Eastbourne	H	W52-41	7+3 (5)	R/R	15 (6)	8+1 (5)	11+1 (6)	–	–	7+1 (4)	–	4+2 (4)	–

DETAILS OF OTHER RIDERS:

Match No. 1: Joonas Kylmakorpi 14 (5); Jason King 2+2 (3).

TACTICAL RIDES, AS INCLUDED IN THE SCORES GRID:

Match No. 1: Havelock 4 points (TR); Kylmakorpi 4 points (TR); Match No. 3: Havelock 6 points (TR); Loram 4 points (TR).

OTHER MEETINGS

16 March: Air-Tek Trophy (first leg)

    Arena-Essex 53 (Paul Hurry 14+1; Mark Loram 12+1; Gary Havelock 7+2; Josh Larsen 7+1; Leigh Lanham 7; Piotr Swist 4+2; Roman Povazhny 2+1) Eastbourne 37.

19 March: Air-Tek Trophy (second leg)

    Eastbourne 57 Arena-Essex 36 (Paul Hurry 10; Leigh Lanham 9+1; Piotr Swist 8+2; Mark Loram 4; Josh Larsen 3; Gary Havelock 2; Roman Povazhny R/R) – Eastbourne won 94-89 on aggregate.

28 July: Elite League

    Ipswich 24 Arena-Essex 12 (Paul Hurry 6; Sergey Darkin 3; Scott Nicholls 2; Roman Povazhny 1; Gary Havelock 0; Leigh Lanham 0; Phil Morris 0) – meeting abandoned after heat six.

14 September: Craven Shield (first leg)

Arena-Essex 53 (Mark Loram 14+1; Paul Hurry 13+3; Adam Skornicki 8; Sergey Darkin 7; Gary Havelock 6; Roman Povazhny 5+1; Leigh Lanham R/R) Ipswich 40.

27 September: Craven Shield (first leg)

Arena-Essex 52 (Mark Loram 16; Roman Povazhny 9+2; Gary Havelock 8+1; Paul Hurry 7+2; Leigh Lanham 7; Adam Skornicki 5+3; Sergey Darkin R/R) Poole 41.

28 September: Craven Shield (second leg)

Poole 22 Arena-Essex 14 (Roman Povazhny 6; Mark Loram 5; Adam Skornicki 2+1; Gary Havelock 1; Leigh Lanham 0; Paul Hurry 0; Sergey Darkin R/R) – meeting abandoned after heat six. No result counted towards the final table.

29 September: Craven Shield (second leg)

Ipswich 49 Arena-Essex 41 (Roman Povazhny 12+2; Mark Loram 12; Paul Hurry 6; Adam Skornicki 5+1; Gary Havelock 4+2; Leigh Lanham 2; Sergey Darkin R/R) – Arena-Essex won 94-89 on aggregate.

INDIVIDUAL MEETING

5 October: Leigh Lanham Testimonial

QUALIFYING SCORES: Jason Crump 12; Adam Skornicki 10; David Howe 9; Mark Loram 9; Leigh Lanham 8; Paul Hurry 7; Davey Watt 5; Chris Louis 5; Daniel King 2; Shane Parker 1; Gary Havelock 1; Jason King (Res) 1; Brent Werner 0. SEMI-FINAL: 1st Howe; 2nd Loram; 3rd Lanham; 4th Hurry. FINAL: 1st Crump; 2nd Loram; 3rd Skornicki; 4th Howe.

BELLE VUE FONESTYLE UK ACES

ADDRESS: Greyhound Stadium, Kirkmanshulme Lane, Gorton, Manchester, M18 7BA.
PROMOTERS: Tony Mole, Redvers Mole & Ian Thomas.
TRACK LENGTH: 285 metres.
TRACK RECORD: 57.9 seconds – Jason Crump (1 September 2003).
FIRST MEETING: 28 July 1928.
YEARS OF OPERATION: 1928 Open; 1988-90 British League; 1991-94 British League Division One; 1995-96 Premier League; 1997 Elite League & Amateur League; 1998-2005 Elite League.

PREVIOUS VENUE: Zoological Gardens, Hyde Road, Manchester.
YEARS OF OPERATION: 1929 English Dirt-track League; 1930 Northern League; 1931 Northern League & Southern League; 1932-33 National League; 1934 National League & Reserve League; 1935-36 National League; 1937 National League & Provincial League; 1938 National League Division One; 1939 National League Division One & National League Division Two; 1940-45 Open; 1946 National League; 1947-56 National League Division One; 1957-64 National League; 1965-67 British League; 1968-69 British League Division One & British League Division Two; 1970-74 British League Division One; 1975-87 British League.

CLUB HONOURS

LEAGUE CHAMPIONS: 1930, 1931, 1933, 1934, 1935, 1936, 1963, 1970, 1971, 1972, 1982, 1993. Note: The Division Two side were also crowned League Champions in 1968 and 1969.

KNOCK-OUT CUP WINNERS: 1931, 1972, 1973, 1975, 2005.

Note: The Division Two side also won their Knock-Out Cup competition in 1969.

NATIONAL TROPHY WINNERS: 1933, 1934, 1935, 1936, 1937, 1946, 1947, 1949, 1958.

ACU CUP WINNERS: 1934, 1935, 1936, 1937, 1946.

BRITISH SPEEDWAY CUP WINNERS: 1939.

BRITANNIA SHIELD WINNERS: 1957, 1958, 1960.

INTER-LEAGUE KNOCK-OUT CUP WINNERS: 1975.

PREMIERSHIP WINNERS: 1983.

LEAGUE CUP WINNERS: 1983.

PAIRS CHAMPIONS: 1984.

FOUR-TEAM CHAMPIONS: 1992.

RIDER ROSTER 2005

Kenneth BJERRE; Jason CRUMP; Rusty HARRISON; Jason LYONS; Krister MARSH; Steve MASTERS; Joe SCREEN; Andy SMITH; Simon STEAD; James WRIGHT.

OTHER APPEARANCES/GUESTS (official matches only):
Richard JUUL; Claus KRISTENSEN.

SKY BET ELITE LEAGUE

(*Denotes bonus-point victory)

No	DATE	OPPONENTS	H/A	RESULT	Screen	Lyons	Bjerre	Stead	Crump	Smith	Masters	Harrison	Marsh	Wright	Others
1	17/3	Ipswich	A	L41-48	8 (5)	2+2 (4)	7+1 (4)	4 (4)	11+1 (5)	7+2 (5)	2 (3)	–	–	–	–
2	21/3	Swindon†	H	W40-32	5+1 (3)	6+1 (3)	11 (4)	3+1 (3)	8 (3)	6+3 (5)	1 (3)	–	–	–	–
3	25/3	Wolverhampton	H	W53-42	3+1 (4)	9 (4)	13+1 (5)	5+2 (4)	14 (5)	9+3 (5)	0 (3)	–	–	–	–
4	28/3	Wolverhampton	A	W50-40*	7+1 (4)	6 (4)	9 (5)	5+1 (4)	15 (5)	6+1 (5)	2+1 (3)	–	–	–	–
5	4/4	Poole	H	W55-37	6 (4)	5+3 (4)	13 (5)	8+1 (4)	13+1 (5)	10+1 (5)	0 (3)	–	–	–	–
6	8/4	Coventry	A	W53-38	4+2 (4)	6+1 (4)	14 (5)	9+1 (4)	12+1 (5)	8+2 (5)	0 (3)	–	–	–	–
7	12/4	Swindon	A	L44-46*	10+1 (5)	6+1 (4)	4+2 (4)	6 (4)	9+1 (5)	7+1 (5)	2+1 (3)	–	–	–	–
8	13/4	Poole	A	L41-53*	3+2 (4)	4+1 (4)	3+2 (4)	9 (5)	14 (5)	8+1 (5)	0 (3)	–	–	–	–
9	18/4	Ipswich	H	W50-43	3+1 (4)	9+1 (5)	6 (4)	4+1 (4)	12 (5)	10+1 (6)	–	6+2 (4)	–	–	–
10	25/4	Eastbourne	H	W49-41	5+1 (4)	7+2 (4)	10 (5)	5 (4)	10 (5)	8+2 (5)	–	4 (3)	–	–	–
11	4/5	Peterborough	A	L39-52	1+1 (4)	4 (4)	6 (5)	7 (4)	14 (5)	4+1 (5)	–	3+1 (3)	–	–	–
12	9/5	Arena-Essex	H	W63-30	12 (4)	8+2 (4)	11+1 (5)	7+1 (4)	14+1 (5)	8+1 (4)	–	3+1 (4)	–	–	–
13	11/5	Arena-Essex	A	W47-43*	11+2 (5)	9 (4)	4 (4)	5+1 (4)	13+1 (5)	4 (5)	–	1 (3)	–	–	–
14	6/6	Arena-Essex	H	L47-48	8+1 (5)	8 (4)	7 (4)	3 (4)	9+2 (5)	7+2 (4)	–	5 (4)	–	–	–
15	13/6	Peterborough	H	W58-38*	7+1 (4)	7 (4)	8+3 (5)	9+2 (5)	15 (5)	8+1 (4)	–	4+2 (3)	–	–	–
16	16/6	Swindon	A	L39-53	5+2 (4)	3+1 (3)	4+1 (5)	12 (7)	14 (5)	1+1 (3)	–	0 (3)	–	–	–
17	20/6	Swindon	H	W52-41	6+3 (4)	9+1 (4)	5+1 (4)	10 (6)	15 (5)	7+1 (4)	–	–	–	0 (3)	–

No	DATE	OPPONENTS	H/A	RESULT	Screen	Lyons	Bjerre	Stead	Crump	Smith	Masters	Harrison	Marsh	Wright	Others
18	27/6	Eastbourne	A	L37-53	9 (5)	2+2 (4)	8 (5)	9+1 (6)	6 (3)	2 (3)	–	1 (4)	–	–	–
19	29/6	Coventry	H	W49-41*	11 (5)	6+1 (4)	10+1 (5)	7 (6)	11+1 (4)	3 (3)	–	1 (3)	–	–	–
20	4/7	Poole	H	W53-42	10+1 (5)	9+2 (4)	7+1 (4)	6+1 (5)	14 (5)	4 (4)	–	3+1 (3)	–	–	–
21	6/7	Peterborough	A	L42-48	5 (4)	0 (0)	5+1 (5)	15+2 (7)	13 (5)	2 (4)	–	–	2+1 (5)	–	–
22	11/7	Ipswich	H	W64-29	9+2 (4)	9+2 (4)	12+1 (5)	12+1 (5)	13+1 (5)	7+4 (4)	–	–	–	2+1 (3)	–
23	13/7	Arena-Essex	A	W51-41*	7+1 (4)	6+1 (4)	12 (5)	6+1 (5)	14+1 (5)	0 (3)	–	6+1 (4)	–	–	–
24	15/7	Coventry	A	L42-49	6 (4)	4+1 (4)	11 (5)	10+1 (6)	10+1 (5)	0 (3)	–	–	1+1 (3)	–	–
25	18/7	Oxford	H	W63-28	9 (4)	8+1 (4)	11+1 (5)	9+1 (4)	13 (5)	6+3 (4)	–	7+3 (4)	–	–	–
26	20/7	Wolverhampton	H	W58-38	8+2 (4)	6+1 (4)	13 (5)	11+1 (4)	10 (5)	6+1 (4)	–	4+2 (4)	–	–	–
27	21/7	Oxford	A	W52-43*	7+2 (4)	6+1 (5)	7 (4)	14+3 (6)	12+1 (5)	2+1 (3)	–	4+2 (3)	–	–	–
28	23/7	Ipswich	A	W47-43*	9+1 (5)	5+2 (4)	6 (4)	8+1 (5)	13 (5)	6+1 (4)	–	–	–	–	0 (3)
29	25/7	Wolverhampton	A	W51-39*	7+1 (4)	1 (3)	10+3 (5)	18+1 (7)	15 (5)	0 (3)	–	0 (3)	–	–	–
30	8/8	Oxford	H	W52-43	11 (5)	4+2 (4)	3+2 (5)	11+2 (6)	R/R	17+1 (7)	–	–	–	6 (3)	–
31	10/8	Poole	A	L41-53	7+1 (4)	2 (3)	6+2 (5)	5+1 (4)	11+1 (5)	3+2 (4)	–	7 (5)	–	–	–
32	11/8	Oxford	A	W54-41*	11 (5)	4 (4)	6+1 (4)	10 (5)	12 (4)	5+3 (4)	–	6 (4)	–	–	–
33	15/8	Coventry	H	W51-44*	12+2 (5)	12+1 (5)	4+1 (4)	R/R	11+1 (5)	11+3 (7)	–	1 (4)	–	–	–
34	20/8	Eastbourne	A	L43-46	10 (4)	3+1 (4)	8+1 (5)	6+1 (4)	12+1 (5)	4+1 (5)	–	–	0 (3)	–	–
35	22/8	Eastbourne	H	W59-35*	R/R	8+2 (4)	15 (5)	9+4 (5)	11+1 (5)	10+1 (6)	–	4 (3)	–	2 (2)	–
36	31/8	Peterborough†	H	L36-39	1+1 (2)	6+1 (3)	–	7 (4)	10 (3)	0 (5)	–	12 (5)	–	–	0 (2)

†Meeting abandoned after heat twelve, with the result permitted to stand.

DETAILS OF OTHER RIDERS:

Match No. 28: Richard Juul 0 (3); Match No. 36: Claus Kristensen 0 (2).

TACTICAL RIDES, AS INCLUDED IN THE SCORES GRID:

Match No. 8: Crump 4 points (TR); Stead 4 points (TR); Match No. 11: Lyons 2 points (TR); Match No. 16: Crump 6 points (TR); Match No. 24: Stead 2 points (TR); Match No. 31: Screen 4 points (TR); Crump 4 points (TR); Match No. 36: Crump 6 points (TR).

ELITE LEAGUE AVERAGES

Rider	Mts	Rds	Pts	Bon	Tot	Avge	Max
Jason Crump	35	167	413	17	430	10.30	5 full; 3 paid
Kenneth Bjerre	35	162	289	27	316	7.80	1 full
Joe Screen	35	148	251	34	285	7.70	1 full
Simon Stead	35	168	281	33	314	7.48	1 paid
Jason Lyons	36	138	208	37	245	7.10	–
Andy Smith	36	160	206	45	251	6.28	–
James Wright	3	8	10	1	11	5.50	–
Rusty Harrison	21	76	82	15	97	5.11	–
Steve Masters	8	24	7	2	9	1.50	–
Krister Marsh	4	14	3	2	5	1.43	–
Guests	2	5	0	0	0	0.00	–

(Richard Juul [1]; Claus Kristensen [1]).

BELLE VUE: From left to right, back row: Ian Thomas (Promoter/Team Manager), Jason Lyons, Simon Stead, Rusty Harrison, Andy Smith. Front, kneeling: Joe Screen, Kenneth Bjerre. On bike: Jason Crump.

KNOCK-OUT CUP

(*Denotes aggregate victory)

No	DATE	OPPONENTS	H/A	RESULT	Bjerre	Stead	Smith	Lyons	Crump	Screen	Harrison	Wright
1	16/5	Oxford	H	W59-35	12 (5)	6+1 (4)	8+2 (4)	9+1 (5)	11 (4)	10+4 (5)	3 (3)	–
2	19/5	Oxford	A	L41-49*	6+1 (5)	8+1 (4)	5+1 (4)	3+1 (3)	11 (5)	8 (5)	0 (4)	–
3	27/7	Swindon	H	W61-32	11+2 (5)	14+1 (5)	8+2 (4)	7+2 (5)	10 (4)	9+2 (4)	–	2+1 (3)
4	18/8	Swindon†	A	L35-37*	4+2 (3)	8+1 (4)	3+1 (3)	3+2 (3)	9 (3)	6 (4)	2 (4)	–
5	1/10	Eastbourne	A	L44-46	R/R	3+1 (4)	7+2 (6)	9 (5)	16 (6)	8+1 (6)	1 (3)	–
6	3/10	Eastbourne	H	W53-37*	R/R	5+3 (5)	5 (5)	11+1 (6)	16+2 (6)	12 (5)	4 (3)	–

†Meeting abandoned after heat twelve, with the result permitted to stand.

OTHER MEETINGS

18 March: Air-Tek Trophy (first leg)

Coventry 43 Belle Vue 47 (Jason Crump 14; Simon Stead 11; Kenneth Bjerre 7+2; Joe Screen 6+1; Jason Lyons 6; Steve Masters 3; Andy Smith 0).

11 April: Air-Tek Trophy (second leg)

Belle Vue 58 (Jason Crump 12; Jason Lyons 10+2; Kenneth Bjerre 10+1; Joe Screen 9; Simon Stead 8+1; Steve Masters 5+3; Andy Smith 4+1) Coventry 37 – Belle Vue won 105-80 on aggregate.

30 May: Inter-League Challenge

Rye House 48 Belle Vue Select 47 (Joe Screen 13; Jason Lyons 11+1; Simon Stead 9; Rusty Harrison 6+2; Krister Marsh 4+1; Ben Powell 2+1; Luke Bowen 2).

23 June: Inter-League Challenge

Sheffield 47 Belle Vue 49 (Joe Screen 10+2; James Wright 9+3; Simon Stead 8; Rusty Harrison 7+2; Jason Lyons 7+1; Krister Marsh 7; Aidan Collins 1; Andy Smith R/R).

12 September: Elite League Play-Off semi-final

Belle Vue 53 (Jason Crump 17; Joe Screen 12; Jason Lyons 11+1; Andy Smith 8+2; Simon Stead 4+2; Rusty Harrison 1+1; Kenneth Bjerre R/R) Eastbourne 40.

19 September: Elite League Play-Off final (first leg)

Coventry 54 Belle Vue 41 (Jason Crump 21; Joe Screen 9; Andy Smith 4+1; Simon Stead 4; Rusty Harrison 2; Jason Lyons 1; Kenneth Bjerre R/R).

26 September: Elite League Play-Off final (second leg)

Belle Vue 42 (Jason Crump 10+1; Andy Smith 9+2; Joe Screen 9; Simon Stead 7+1; Jason Lyons 4; Rusty Harrison 3; Kenneth Bjerre R/R) Coventry 47 – Coventry won 101-83 on aggregate.

8 October: Craven Shield semi-final (first leg at Eastbourne)

Eastbourne 37, Oxford 27, Belle Vue 26 (Jason Lyons 11; Joe Screen 4; Rusty Harrison 4; Jason Crump 3+1; Andy Smith 3; Simon Stead 1) – meeting abandoned after heat fifteen, with the result permitted to stand.

13 October: Craven Shield semi-final (second leg at Oxford)

Oxford 42, Eastbourne 34, Belle Vue 32 (Jason Crump 11; Simon Stead 10; Joe Screen 5; Jason Lyons 4+1; Rusty Harrison 2; Andy Smith DNR).

17 October: Craven Shield semi-final (third leg at Belle Vue)

Oxford 38, Eastbourne 36, Belle Vue 34 (Jason Crump 11+1; Joe Screen 7; Andy Smith 6+2; Jason Lyons 5+1; Simon Stead 5; Rusty Harrison 0). Aggregate result: Eastbourne 107, Oxford 107, Belle Vue 92.

INDIVIDUAL MEETINGS

7 March: Peter Craven Memorial Trophy

    1st Jason Crump <u>15</u>; 2nd Jason Lyons 14; 3rd Joe Screen (on count-back) 11; Niels-Kristian Iversen 11; Chris Louis 10; Kenneth Bjerre 8; Andy Smith 8; Sam Ermolenko 7; Peter Karlsson 7; Adam Shields 6; Simon Stead 6; Gary Havelock 5; Carl Stonehewer 4; James Wright 4; Ricky Ashworth 4; Steve Masters 0; Rusty Harrison (Res) 0.

1 August: Greggs North-West Junior Championship

    QUALIFYING SCORES: Charles Wright 9; Lee Derbyshire 9; Carl Belfield 8; Adam McKinna 8; Karl Mason 7; Benji Compton 7; Luke Priest 6; John Branney 6; Paul Burnett 5; Byron Bekker 3; Jack Gledhill 2; David Farley 2. FIRST SEMI-FINAL: 1st Derbyshire; 2nd Branney; 3rd Mason; 4th McKinna. SECOND SEMI-FINAL: 1st Priest; 2nd Compton; 3rd Wright; 4th Belfield. FINAL: 1st Compton; 2nd Branney; 3rd Derbyshire; 4th Priest.

COVENTRY BUILDBASE BEES

ADDRESS: Coventry International Motor Speedway, Rugby Road, Brandon, nr Coventry, Warwickshire, CV8 3GJ.
PROMOTERS: Colin Pratt & Jeremy Heaver.
TRACK LENGTH: 303 metres.
TRACK RECORD: 57.4 seconds – Lee Richardson (15 September 2003).
FIRST MEETING: 29 September 1928.
YEARS OF OPERATION: 1928 Open; 1929-31 Southern League; 1932-33 National League; 1934 Open; 1936 Open; 1948 National League Division Three; 1949-56 National League Division Two; 1957-64 National League; 1965-67 British League; 1968-74 British League Division One; 1975-90 British League; 1991-94 British League Division One; 1995-96 Premier League; 1997-2003 Elite League; 2004 Elite League & Conference Trophy; 2005 Elite League.

CLUB HONOURS

LEAGUE CHAMPIONS: 1953, 1968, 1978, 1979, 1987, 1988, 2005.
KNOCK-OUT CUP WINNERS: 1967.
PAIRS CHAMPIONS: 1978 (Shared with Cradley Heath).
LEAGUE CUP WINNERS: 1981, 1985, 1987.
PREMIERSHIP WINNERS: 1986.
CRAVEN SHIELD WINNERS: 1997, 2000.

RIDER ROSTER 2005

Daniel DAVIDSSON; Chris HARRIS; Billy JANNIRO; Andreas JONSSON; Joonas KYLMAKORPI; Scott NICHOLLS; Morten RISAGER; Adrian RYMEL; Rory SCHLEIN; Martin SMOLINSKI; Tomas TOPINKA; Sebastian ULAMEK.

OTHER APPEARANCES/GUESTS (official matches only):

Henning BAGER; Emil KRAMER; Stuart ROBSON; Adam ROYNON; Simon STEAD.

SKY BET ELITE LEAGUE

(*Denotes bonus-point victory)

No	DATE	OPPONENTS	H/A	RESULT	Jonsson	Risager	Schlein	Harris	Nicholls	Davidsson	Smolinski	Topinka	Jarniro	Kylmakorpi	Ulamek	Others
1	25/3	Peterborough	H	L44-51	13 (5)	2+1 (4)	9 (4)	1 (4)	12 (5)	3 (4)	4+1 (4)	–	–	–	–	–
2	28/3	Peterborough	A	L43-52	13+2 (5)	4+1 (4)	8 (4)	2 (3)	9 (6)	6 (5)	1 (3)	–	–	–	–	–
3	31/3	Ipswich	A	L42-51	7 (5)	5 (4)	4 (4)	–	14 (5)	6+1 (5)	0 (3)	6+1 (4)	–	–	–	–
4	1/4	Poole	H	W47-43	9+1 (5)	7+1 (4)	6 (4)	–	10 (5)	5+1 (4)	2+1 (4)	8+1 (4)	–	–	–	–
5	8/4	Belle Vue	H	L38-53	3+1 (4)	7 (4)	0 (3)	8+1 (5)	14 (6)	2+1 (4)	4+1 (4)	–	–	–	–	–
6	14/4	Swindon	A	L41-49	8+1 (5)	8+2 (4)	6 (4)	5+2 (4)	10 (5)	2 (4)	2+2 (4)	–	–	–	–	–
7	22/4	Ipswich	H	L47-49	9+1 (5)	5+2 (4)	5 (4)	8+2 (4)	8 (5)	5 (3)	7+2 (5)	–	–	–	–	–
8	25/4	Arena-Essex	H	W53-40	10+1 (5)	7 (4)	3+1 (4)	8+2 (4)	12+1 (5)	4 (3)	9+1 (5)	–	–	–	–	–
9	27/4	Arena-Essex	A	W51-42*	13+1 (5)	6+1 (4)	7 (4)	6+3 (4)	12+1 (5)	3 (4)	4+2 (4)	–	–	–	–	–
10	5/5	Oxford	A	W54-40	12+1 (5)	9+1 (4)	8+1 (4)	7+3 (4)	9 (5)	–	3+1 (5)	6+1 (4)	–	–	–	–
11	6/5	Oxford	H	W51-43*	11+1 (5)	4+1 (4)	11+1 (4)	4 (4)	11+1 (5)	–	4 (4)	6+1 (4)	–	–	–	–
12	9/5	Wolverhampton	A	L45-48	13+1 (5)	4+1 (4)	6+2 (4)	2 (4)	11+1 (5)	–	3+2 (3)	6 (5)	–	–	–	–
13	11/5	Poole	A	L36-57	R/R	6 (5)	6+1 (6)	4+2 (5)	14 (6)	3 (4)	3+1 (4)	–	–	–	–	–
14	23/5	Eastbourne	H	W52-41	13+1 (5)	3+2 (3)	6+1 (3)	6+2 (6)	14+1 (5)	–	2 (4)	–	8 (4)	–	–	–
15	30/5	Swindon	H	W54-40*	13+1 (5)	–	R/R	14+1 (7)	11 (5)	–	0 (3)	–	6+1 (5)	–	–	10+1 (5)
16	1/6	Arena-Essex	A	W51-42	R/R	–	–	5+2 (5)	18 (6)	–	6+1 (4)	–	11+1 (6)	–	–	11+5 (9)
17	17/6	Peterborough	H	W53-43	13+1 (5)	–	R/R	10+3 (6)	13+1 (5)	–	–	–	7 (5)	–	–	10+5 (9)
18	20/6	Poole	H	W49-44	14 (5)	8 (5)	R/R	10+1 (6)	10+2 (5)	–	3 (4)	–	4+2 (5)	–	–	–
19	23/6	Oxford	A	W52-42	R/R	2+2 (3)	–	14+2 (7)	12 (5)	–	–	–	13+1 (6)	–	–	7+1 (4)
20	29/6	Belle Vue	A	L41-49	R/R	1+1 (3)	–	14+1 (7)	9+1 (6)	–	3+1 (4)	–	6+1 (5)	–	–	8+1 (5)
21	2/7	Eastbourne	A	W51-42*	R/R	6+3 (5)	–	11 (6)	15+2 (6)	–	2 (3)	–	11+2 (6)	–	–	6 (4)
22	4/7	Wolverhampton	A	W55-38	R/R	8+2 (5)	–	9+3 (4)	17 (6)	–	3+2 (4)	–	8+1 (5)	–	–	10+1 (6)
23	11/7	Swindon	H	W51-45	R/R	7+2 (5)	–	10+2 (5)	10+1 (5)	–	8+2 (4)	–	6+3 (5)	10+1 (6)	–	–
24	15/7	Belle Vue	H	W49-42	R/R	7+1 (5)	–	12+1 (6)	15+1 (6)	–	0 (3)	–	5+3 (4)	10+3 (6)	–	–
25	22/7	Wolverhampton	H	W55-39*	R/R	8+2 (5)	–	9 (4)	15+1 (6)	–	6+2 (4)	–	6+4 (5)	11 (6)	–	–
26	25/7	Peterborough	A	L42-48*	–	6+1 (5)	–	12+2 (7)	9 (5)	–	4 (4)	–	5 (4)	R/R	6+2 (5)	–
27	29/7	Oxford	H	W54-39*	–	5+1 (4)	–	11 (6)	11 (4)	–	8+4 (4)	–	8+1 (5)	R/R	11+2 (6)	0 (1)
28	15/8	Belle Vue	A	L44-51	–	5 (5)	–	4+2 (4)	19 (6)	–	3+2 (4)	–	3+1 (5)	10 (6)	R/R	–
29	19/8	Arena-Essex	H	W54-42*	–	–	–	6+2 (4)	15 (5)	–	7+1 (5)	–	6 (4)	6+1 (4)	10+2 (4)	4+1 (4)
30	29/8	Ipswich	H	L44-46	–	2 (3)	–	6 (4)	12 (5)	–	8+1 (5)	–	4+1 (4)	5+1 (4)	7 (5)	–
31	31/8	Poole	A	W47-46*	–	8+1 (5)	–	6+3 (4)	12 (5)	–	7+2 (4)	–	1+1 (4)	7+2 (5)	6 (4)	–
32	1/9	Ipswich	A	W54-40*	–	4+2 (5)	–	9+1 (4)	11+1 (5)	–	7 (4)	–	4+3 (4)	6+1 (4)	13 (5)	–
33	2/9	Wolverhampton	H	W48-41*	–	4+1 (4)	–	10 (5)	7 (4)	–	12+2 (6)	–	4+2 (3)	10+1 (5)	1 (3)	–
34	3/9	Eastbourne	A	W46-43	–	3+2 (5)	–	13+2 (6)	14 (5)	–	7 (5)	–	8+1 (5)	R/R	1 (4)	–
35	4/9	Swindon	A	L43-47*	–	8+1 (5)	–	7 (5)	18 (6)	–	3 (3)	–	5+1 (5)	2+1 (6)	R/R	–
36	8/9	Eastbourne	H	W58-37*	–	3 (4)	–	7+2 (4)	5 (3)	–	10+2 (5)	–	9+3 (5)	12 (4)	12 (5)	–

NOTE: Sebastian Ulamek is not credited with a paid maximum from the home match v. Arena-Essex on 19 August, as he missed a programmed ride in heat thirteen through a two-minute exclusion.

DETAILS OF OTHER RIDERS:

Match No. 15: Simon Stead 10+1 (5); Match No. 16: Stuart Robson 7+3 (5); Henning Bager 4+2 (4); Match No. 17: Simon Stead 7+4 (5); Adrian Rymel 3+1 (4); Match No. 19: Emil Kramer 7+1 (4); Tomas Topinka 4 (5); Match No. 20: Stuart Robson 8+1 (5); Match No. 21: Henning Bager 6 (4); Match No. 22: Joonas Kylmakorpi 10+1 (6); Match No. 27: Adam Roynon 0 (1); Match No. 29: Adrian Rymel 4+1 (4).

TACTICAL SUBSTITUTE AND TACTICAL RIDES, AS INCLUDED IN THE SCORES GRID:

Match No. 1: Jonsson 6 points (TR); Schlein 4 points (TR); Match No. 2: Jonsson 6 points (TR); Schlein 4 points (TR); Nicholls 0 points (TS); Match No. 3: Nicholls 6 points (TR); Topinka 2 points (TR); Match No. 5: Nicholls 2 points (TS); Match No. 12: Jonsson 6 points (TR); Match No. 13: Nicholls 4 points (TR); Risager 2 points (TR); Match No. 28: Nicholls 6 points (TR); Kylmakorpi 4 points (TR).

ELITE LEAGUE AVERAGES

Rider	Mts	Rds	Pts	Bon	Tot	Avge	Max
Scott Nicholls	36	187	429	15	444	9.50	3 full; 1 paid
Andreas Jonsson	16	79	165	14	179	9.06	–
Chris Harris	34	167	270	47	317	7.59	1 paid
Sebastian Ulamek	9	41	67	6	73	7.12	–
Joonas Kylmakorpi	11	56	87	11	98	7.00	1 full
Billy Janniro	23	109	148	33	181	6.64	–
Rory Schlein	14	56	81	7	88	6.29	1 paid
Morten Risager	32	136	171	35	206	6.06	–
Tomas Topinka	5	21	31	4	35	6.67	–
Martin Smolinski	34	137	155	36	191	5.58	1 paid
Adrian Rymel	2	8	7	2	9	4.50	–
Daniel Davidsson	10	40	39	3	42	4.20	–
Guests	10	44	63	13	76	6.91	–

(Henning Bager [2]; Emil Kramer [1]; Joonas Kylmakorpi [1]; Stuart Robson [2]; Adam Roynon [1]; Simon Stead [2]; Tomas Topinka [1]).

KNOCK-OUT CUP

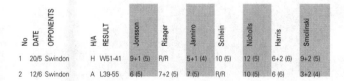

No	DATE	OPPONENTS	H/A	RESULT	Jonsson	Risager	Janniro	Schlein	Nicholls	Harris	Smolinski
1	20/5	Swindon	H	W51-41	9+1 (5)	R/R	5+1 (4)	10 (5)	12 (5)	6+2 (6)	9+2 (5)
2	12/6	Swindon	A	L39-55	6 (5)	7+2 (5)	7 (5)	R/R	10 (5)	6 (6)	3+2 (4)

TACTICAL RIDES, AS INCLUDED IN THE SCORES GRID:

Match No. 2: Nicholls 6 points (TR); Risager 2 points (TR).

COVENTRY: From left to right, back row: Rory Schlein, Martin Smolinski, Andreas Jonsson (on bike), Morten Risager, Daniel Davidsson, Scott Nicholls. Front, kneeling: Tomas Topinka, Chris Harris.

OTHER MEETINGS

18 March: Air-Tek Trophy (first leg)

Coventry 43 (Scott Nicholls 12; Andreas Jonsson 9+1; Rory Schlein 7+1; Martin Smolinski 5+2; Daniel Davidsson 5; Morten Risager 3+1; Chris Harris 2+1) Belle Vue 47.

11 April: Air-Tek Trophy (second leg)

Belle Vue 58 Coventry 37 (Scott Nicholls 13; Andreas Jonsson 10; Chris Harris 4; Daniel Davidsson 4; Rory Schlein 3+2; Morten Risager 2+1; Martin Smolinski 1+1) – Belle Vue won 105-80 on aggregate.

1 July: Elite League

Coventry 14 (Billy Janniro 6; Chris Harris 3; Morten Risager 2+1; Martin Smolinski 2+1; Joonas Kylmakorpi 1; Scott Nicholls DNR; Andreas Jonsson R/R) Eastbourne 4 – meeting abandoned after heat four.

12 September: Elite League Play-Off semi-final

Coventry 55 (Scott Nicholls 14; Joonas Kylmakorpi 13+2; Billy Janniro 12; Morten Risager 6+2; Chris Harris 6+1; Martin Smolinski 4+2; Sebastian Ulamek R/R) Peterborough 41.

19 September: Elite League Play-Off final (first leg)

Coventry 54 (Sebastian Ulamek 11; Scott Nicholls 10+2; Morten Risager 9+1; Billy Janniro 8+2; Joonas Kylmakorpi 7+1; Chris Harris 5+3; Martin Smolinski 4) Belle Vue 41.

26 September: Elite League Play-Off final (second leg)

Belle Vue 42 Coventry 47 (Scott Nicholls 11+1; Chris Harris 9+1; Billy Janniro 8; Morten Risager 6; Sebastian Ulamek 5+1; Joonas Kylmakorpi 4+1; Martin Smolinski 4+1) – Coventry won 101-83 on aggregate.

4 October: Craven Shield semi-final (first leg at Peterborough)

Peterborough 38, Coventry 36 (Sebastian Ulamek 10+1; Scott Nicholls 10; Billy Janniro 6; Joonas Kylmakorpi 5+2; Chris Harris 5+1; Morten Risager 0), Poole 34.

5 October: Craven Shield semi-final (second leg at Poole)

Poole 38 Peterborough 35, Coventry 34 (Scott Nicholls 11; Sebastian Ulamek 8; Joonas Kylmakorpi 6+1; Billy Janniro 4+1; Chris Harris 3+1; Martin Smolinski 2+1).

7 October: Craven Shield semi-final (third leg at Coventry)

Poole 40, Coventry 34 (Scott Nicholls 11; Billy Janniro 7+1; Chris Harris 6+1; Joonas Kylmakorpi 5; Sebastian Ulamek 3; Morten Risager 2+1), Peterborough 34. Aggregate result: Poole 112, Peterborough 107, Coventry 104.

14 October: Midland Cup (first leg)

Coventry 66 (Joonas Kylmakorpi 14; Sebastian Ulamek 12+2; Scott Nicholls 9+1; Billy Janniro 9; Morten Risager 8+3; Martin Smolinski 7+2; Chris Harris 7) Wolverhampton 33.

17 October: Midland Cup (second leg)

Wolverhampton 45 Coventry 51 (Scott Nicholls 13; Morten Risager 10+1; Billy Janniro 8+3; Sebastian Ulamek 7+2; Joonas Kylmakorpi 6+1; Martin Smolinski 4; Chris Harris 3) – Coventry won 117-78 on aggregate.

28 October: Championship Celebration Challenge

Coventry 47 (Martin Smolinski 11+1; Scott Nicholls 9; Billy Janniro 7; Morten Risager 6+2; Sebastian Ulamek 6; Chris Harris 5+1; Joonas Kylmakorpi 3+1) Elite League Select 43 (Adam Skornicki 9; Mark Loram 8+1; Andreas Jonsson 8+1; Simon Stead 7+2; Billy Hamill 7; Morten Risager (tactical opponent) 2+1; Ritchie Hawkins 1+1; Adrian Rymel 1).

EASTBOURNE SCV EAGLES

ADDRESS: Arlington Stadium, Arlington Road West, Hailsham, East Sussex, BH27 3RE.
PROMOTERS: Terry Russell & Jon Cook.
TRACK LENGTH: 275 metres.
TRACK RECORD: 55.1 seconds – Tony Rickardsson (10 May 2003).
FIRST MEETING: September 1928.
YEARS OF OPERATION: 1928-37 Open; 1938 Sunday Dirt-track League; 1939
Open; 1946 Open; 1947 National League Division Three; 1948-53 Open; 1954-57
Southern Area League; 1958 Open; 1959 Southern Area League; 1960-63 Open; 1964
Metropolitan League; 1965 Training; 1969-74 British League Division Two; 1975-78
National League; 1979-84 British League; 1985-90 National League; 1991-94 British
League Division One; 1995 Premier League; 1996 Premier League & Conference League;
1997-2005 Elite League.

CLUB HONOURS

LEAGUE CHAMPIONS: 1938, 1947, 1959, 1971, 1977, 1986, 1987, 1995, 2000.
KNOCK-OUT CUP WINNERS: 1975, 1977, 1978, 1985, 1986, 1987, 1994, 1997, 2002.
PREMIERSHIP WINNERS: 1995, 1996.

RIDER ROSTER 2005

Olly ALLEN; Adam ALLOTT; Dean BARKER; Troy BATCHELOR; Richard HALL; Trevor
HARDING; Steen JENSEN; Andrew MOORE; David NORRIS; Ulrich OSTERGAARD; Nicki
PEDERSEN; Adam SHIELDS; Davey WATT.

OTHER APPEARANCES/GUESTS (official matches only):
Steve BOXALL; Jason CRUMP; Daniel GIFFARD; Charlie GJEDDE; Billy HAMILL; Chris
HARRIS; Rusty HARRISON; Billy JANNIRO; Steve JOHNSTON; Ashley JONES; Peter
KARLSSON; Joonas KYLMAKORPI; Mark LORAM; Jason LYONS; Travis McGOWAN; Joel
PARSONS; Cameron WOODWARD.

SKY BET ELITE LEAGUE

(*Denotes bonus-point victory)

No	DATE	OPPONENTS	H/A	RESULT	Norris	Moore	Barker	Shields	Pedersen	Allott	Watt	Jensen	Ostergaard	Hall	Allen	Others
1	25/3	Poole	A	L44-50	11 (5)	0 (3)	6 (4)	4+1 (4)	14+1 (5)	0 (3)	9+3 (6)	–	–	–	–	–
2	25/3	Poole	H	L44-46	13+2 (5)	0 (3)	0 (1)	6+1 (4)	14 (5)	0 (3)	11+1 (7)	–	–	–	–	–
3	2/4	Peterborough	H	W51-40	11 (5)	3+1 (4)	9 (4)	5+1 (4)	11+1 (5)	–	9+2 (5)	3+1 (3)	–	–	–	–
4	9/4	Oxford	H	W55-39	10 (5)	0 (3)	7+3 (4)	9 (4)	15 (5)	–	11+1 (5)	3 (4)	–	–	–	–
5	16/4	Ipswich	H	W48-45	7+1 (5)	2+1 (3)	7+2 (4)	5 (4)	11 (5)	–	14+1 (6)	2+1 (3)	–	–	–	–

No	DATE	OPPONENTS	H/A	RESULT	Norris	Moore	Barker	Shields	Pedersen	Allott	Watt	Jensen	Ostergaard	Hall	Allen	Others
6	21/4	Ipswich	A	W50-41*	13 (5)	1+1 (3)	4+2 (4)	12 (5)	9+1 (4)	2 (3)	9+2 (6)	–	–	–	–	–
7	23/4	Wolverhampton	H	D45-45	13+2 (5)	3 (4)	3+2 (4)	4 (4)	14 (5)	–	8+1 (5)	–	0 (3)	–	–	–
8	25/4	Belle Vue	A	L41-49	10 (5)	2+1 (3)	5+1 (4)	5+1 (4)	9+1 (5)	0 (3)	10 (6)	–	–	–	–	–
9	28/4	Swindon	A	L44-48	0 (1)	5+2 (4)	1+1 (3)	10 (5)	14 (5)	–	13+1 (7)	1+1 (5)	–	–	–	–
10	2/5	Wolverhampton	A	W47-46*	9 (5)	4+1 (4)	1 (3)	4+1 (4)	15 (5)	–	11+2 (6)	3+1 (3)	–	–	–	–
11	7/5	Swindon	H	W56-40*	6 (3)	5+2 (4)	6+2 (4)	11+1 (5)	13 (5)	–	13+2 (5)	2+1 (4)	–	–	–	–
12	23/5	Coventry	A	L41-52	10 (4)	4+1 (4)	5+1 (5)	5 (4)	3 (3)	–	14+2 (6)	0 (4)	–	–	–	–
13	25/5	Arena-Essex	A	W47-43	10+1 (5)	0 (3)	7+2 (4)	12+1 (5)	–	–	6 (4)	5 (5)	–	–	–	7 (4)
14	4/6	Poole	H	W46-40	9+2 (5)	3+2 (5)	6+2 (4)	4+2 (4)	14 (5)	–	10 (4)	0 (3)	–	–	–	–
15	18/6	Arena-Essex	H	W52-42*	7 (4)	2 (4)	4+2 (4)	5+1 (4)	15 (5)	–	12 (5)	7 (4)	–	–	–	–
16	22/6	Poole	A	L40-50	3 (4)	6+1 (4)	6 (4)	6+1 (5)	10 (5)	–	5 (4)	–	–	–	–	4+2 (4)
17	23/6	Ipswich	A	L38-55	R/R	5+1 (6)	3+2 (5)	10+1 (5)	11 (6)	–	6 (5)	–	–	–	–	3 (3)
18	27/6	Belle Vue	H	W53-37*	R/R	6+4 (5)	6+1 (5)	6 (5)	17 (6)	–	16+1 (6)	–	–	–	–	2 (3)
19	2/7	Coventry	H	L42-51	R/R	5+1 (5)	4+1 (5)	6 (5)	17 (6)	–	10 (6)	0 (3)	–	–	–	–
20	11/7	Peterborough	H	W48-42	R/R	6+1 (5)	9+2 (6)	7+1 (5)	17 (6)	–	6+1 (5)	–	3 (3)	–	–	–
21	16/7	Oxford	H	W57-35	R/R	8+1 (4)	11+2 (5)	11+1 (6)	16+1 (6)	–	9+1 (5)	–	–	2+1 (4)	–	–
22	18/7	Wolverhampton	A	L41-49	R/R	2 (5)	5+2 (5)	6+1 (5)	18 (6)	–	–	–	–	0 (3)	–	10 (6)
23	21/7	Swindon	A	W46-44	R/R	7+4 (5)	5+3 (5)	7 (5)	15 (6)	–	–	–	–	–	–	12 (9)
24	30/7	Swindon	H	W55-39*	9 (5)	8+2 (5)	8+3 (6)	16 (6)	12 (4)	–	R/R	–	–	–	–	2 (4)
25	8/8	Ipswich	H	W58-38*	8 (4)	9+2 (5)	7+3 (4)	11+2 (5)	15 (5)	–	5+1 (4)	–	–	–	–	3+1 (3)
26	12/8	Wolverhampton	H	W49-41	R/R	3 (5)	8+1 (5)	–	–	–	10+3 (5)	0 (3)	–	–	–	28+2 (12)
27	20/8	Belle Vue	H	W46-43	6 (5)	8+1 (6)	5+2 (5)	R/R	14 (5)	–	9 (5)	–	–	–	4+1 (4)	–
28	22/8	Belle Vue	A	L35-59	4 (5)	7+1 (6)	7 (5)	R/R	10 (4)	–	5+1 (6)	–	–	–	2+1 (4)	–
29	25/8	Oxford	A	L41-50*	9+1 (5)	5+1 (5)	12 (6)	R/R	–	–	6+1 (6)	–	–	–	9+2 (5)	0 (3)
30	27/8	Arena-Essex	H	W56-37	10 (4)	3+1 (5)	5+2 (5)	R/R	–	–	12+2 (5)	–	–	–	11+1 (6)	15 (5)
31	1/9	Peterborough	A	L31-62	4 (4)	4+1 (5)	–	6+1 (5)	R/R	–	4+1 (6)	–	–	–	–	13 (10)
32	1/9	Peterborough	A	L43-52	–	6 (4)	–	10 (5)	R/R	–	12 (6)	–	–	–	–	15+3 (15)
33	3/9	Coventry	H	L43-46	5+1 (4)	7+1 (6)	7+2 (5)	12 (6)	R/R	–	12 (6)	0 (3)	–	–	–	–
34	5/9	Oxford	A	L41-49*	R/R	10 (5)	10+3 (6)	11+1 (6)	–	–	2+1 (5)	–	–	–	3+1 (3)	5+1 (5)
35	7/9	Arena-Essex	A	W47-43*	R/R	4 (5)	6+1 (5)	12+3 (6)	–	–	7 (5)	–	–	–	–	18 (9)
36	8/9	Coventry	A	L37-58	R/R	4 (5)	7 (6)	14 (6)	–	–	1+1 (4)	–	–	–	2+2 (5)	9 (5)

NOTE: Match No. 14 originally ended in a 46-44 victory, but was amended following a protest over Poole's use of rider replacement for Matej Ferjan.

DETAILS OF OTHER RIDERS:

Match No. 13: Jason Lyons 7 (4); Match No. 16: Cameron Woodward 4+2 (4); Match No. 17: Cameron Woodward 3 (3); Match No. 18: Joel Parsons 2 (3); Match No. 22: Joonas Kylmakorpi 10 (6); Match No. 23: Joonas Kylmakorpi 11 (6); Troy Batchelor 1 (3); Match No. 24: Trevor Harding 2 (4); Match No. 25: Trevor Harding 3+1 (3); Match No. 26: Mark Loram 16 (6); Chris Harris 12+2 (6); Match No. 29: Steve Boxall 0 (3); Match No. 30: Peter Karlsson 15 (5); Match No. 31: Steve Johnston 9 (5); Troy Batchelor 4 (5); Match No. 32: Steve Johnston 9 (5); Troy Batchelor 4+2 (4); Rusty Harrison 2+1 (4); Ashley Jones 0 (2); Match No. 34: Billy Janniro 5+1 (5); Match No. 35: Jason Crump 17 (6); Daniel Giffard 1 (3); Match No. 36: Billy Hamill 9 (5).

TACTICAL SUBSTITUTE AND TACTICAL RIDES, AS INCLUDED IN THE SCORES GRID:

Match No. 1: Pedersen 4 points (TR); Norris 4 points (TR); Match No. 9: Shields 4 points (TR); Match No. 12: Watt 4 points (TR); Norris 4 points (TR); Match No. 17: Shields 4 points (TR); Moore 2 points (TR); Match No. 19: Pedersen 6 points (TR); Match No. 28:

Pedersen 6 points (TR); Barker 2 points (TR); Match No. 29: Barker 2 points (TS); Match No. 31: Johnston 4 points (TR); Shields 2 points (TR); Match No. 32: Watt 6 points (TR); Shields 6 points (TR); Match No. 36: Shields 6 points (TR); Hamill 4 points (TR).

ELITE LEAGUE AVERAGES

Rider	Mts	Rds	Pts	Bon	Tot	Avge	Max
Nicki Pedersen	26	132	335	5	340	10.30	6 full
David Norris	24	107	193	10	203	7.59	2 paid
Davey Watt	33	177	292	32	324	7.32	1 paid
Adam Shields	31	150	241	22	263	7.01	–
Dean Barker	34	154	200	50	250	6.49	–
Olly Allen	6	27	31	8	39	5.78	–
Andrew Moore	36	160	156	35	191	4.78	–
Troy Batchelor	2	9	8	2	10	4.44	–
Trevor Harding	2	7	5	1	6	3.43	–
Steen Jensen	13	47	26	5	31	2.64	–
Ulrich Ostergaard	2	6	3	0	3	2.00	–
Richard Hall	2	7	2	1	3	1.71	–
Adam Allott	4	12	2	0	2	0.67	–
Guests	19	84	129	6	135	6.43	1 full

(Troy Batchelor [1]; Steve Boxall [1]; Jason Crump [1]; Daniel Giffard [1]; Billy Hamill [1]; Chris Harris [1]; Rusty Harrison [1]; Billy Janniro [1]; Steve Johnston [2]; Ashley Jones [1]; Peter Karlsson [1]; Joonas Kylmakorpi [2]; Mark Loram [1]; Jason Lyons [1]; Joel Parsons [1]; Cameron Woodward [2]).

KNOCK-OUT CUP

(*Denotes aggregate victory)

No	DATE	OPPONENTS	H/A	RESULT	Norris	Moore	Barker	Shields	Pedersen	Allott	Watt	Jensen	Harding	Allen	Others
1	13/5	Peterborough	A	L37-56	R/R	1 (4)	7 (5)	10+1 (6)	–	3 (3)	13+1 (7)	–	–	–	3 (5)
2	21/5	Peterborough	H	W59-36*	12+2 (5)	3+1 (3)	5+2 (4)	11 (4)	14 (5)	–	13+2 (6)	1 (3)	–	–	–
3	23/7	Arena-Essex	H	W55-40	R/R	8 (5)	7+4 (5)	8+2 (5)	15 (6)	–	–	–	2+1 (3)	–	15 (6)
4	21/9	Arena-Essex	A	L41-52*	R/R	0 (4)	5 (5)	10+2 (6)	18 (5)	–	6 (6)	–	–	2 (4)	–
5	1/10	Belle Vue	H	W46-44	R/R	5 (5)	5+2 (5)	10+2 (6)	17 (6)	–	9+2 (5)	–	–	–	0 (3)
6	3/10	Belle Vue	A	L37-53	R/R	5+3 (5)	–	7+2 (6)	11 (6)	–	6 (5)	–	–	3 (3)	5+2 (5)

DETAILS OF OTHER RIDERS:

Match No. 1: Charlie Gjedde 3 (5); Match No. 3: Joonas Kylmakorpi 15 (6); Match No. 5: Daniel Giffard 0 (3); Match No. 6: Travis McGowan 5+2 (5).

TACTICAL RIDES, AS INCLUDED IN THE SCORES GRID:

Match No. 1: Shields 4 points (TR); Barker 2 points (TR); Match No. 4: Pedersen 6 points (TR).

EASTBOURNE: From left to right, back row: Davey Watt, David Norris, Jon Cook (Promoter/Team Manager), Adam Shields, Andrew Moore, Nicki Pedersen, Steen Jensen. Front, on bike: Dean Barker.

OTHER MEETINGS

16 March: Air-Tek Trophy (first leg)

Arena-Essex 53 Eastbourne 37 (David Norris 15; Dean Barker 8+1; Davey Watt 6; Adam Shields 5+1; Steen Jensen 2; Andrew Moore 1+1; Nicki Pedersen R/R).

19 March: Air-Tek Trophy (second leg)

Eastbourne 57 (Nicki Pedersen 15; Adam Shields 14+1; David Norris 9+1; Dean Barker 8+3; Davey Watt 7; Andrew Moore 3+2; Adam Allott 1+1) Arena-Essex 36 – Eastbourne won 94-89 on aggregate.

16 May: Elite League

Eastbourne 1 (Adam Shields 1; Andrew Moore 0; Dean Barker DNR; Nicki Pedersen DNR; Steen Jensen DNR; Davey Watt DNR; David Norris R/R) Ipswich 5 – meeting abandoned after heat one.

1 July: Elite League

Coventry 14 Eastbourne 4 (Dean Barker 3; Steen Jensen 1; Adam Shields 0; Davey Watt 0; Andrew Moore 0; Nicki Pedersen DNR; David Norris R/R) – meeting abandoned after heat four.

12 September: Elite League Play-Off semi-final

Belle Vue 53 Eastbourne 40 (Mark Loram 13+2; Adam Shields 9+1; Dean Barker 8+1; Davey Watt 6; Andrew Moore 4+1; Olly Allen 0; David Norris R/R).

24 September: South Coast Trophy

Eastbourne (52) 2 (Mark Loram 13; Adam Shields 12+1; Dean Barker 8; Davey Watt 7; Olly Allen 6+1; Andrew Moore 5+1; Lukasz Romanek 1+1) Poole (40) 1. NOTE: The meeting was split into three sections for the football-style result.

8 October: Craven Shield semi-final (first leg at Eastbourne)

Eastbourne 37 (Nicki Pedersen 9; Mark Loram 8; Adam Shields 7+1; Andrew Moore 6+1; Davey Watt 5+3; Dean Barker 2+2), Oxford 27, Belle Vue 26 – meeting abandoned after heat fifteen, with the result permitted to stand.

13 October: Craven Shield semi-final (second leg at Oxford)

Oxford 42, Eastbourne 34 (Nicki Pedersen 9; Adam Shields 8; Mark Loram 7; Dean Barker 4+1; Andrew Moore 4+1; Davey Watt 2), Belle Vue 32.

17 October: Craven Shield semi-final (third leg at Belle Vue)

Oxford 38, Eastbourne 36 (Nicki Pedersen 10; Mark Loram 8+2; Dean Barker 6; Adam Shields 5; Andrew Moore 4+2; Davey Watt 3), Belle Vue 34. Aggregate result: Eastbourne 107, Oxford 107, Belle Vue 92.

22 October: Craven Shield final (first leg at Eastbourne)

Eastbourne 41 (Nicki Pedersen 12; Adam Shields 10; Mark Loram 10; Dean Barker 5+3; Davey Watt 2+1; Andrew Moore 2), Oxford 40, Poole 27.

26 October: Craven Shield final (second leg at Poole)

Oxford 39, Poole 35, Eastbourne 34 (Adam Shields 11; Nicki Pedersen 10; Mark Loram 7+1; Davey Watt 3+1; Dean Barker 2+1; Andrew Moore 1).

28 October: Craven Shield final (third leg at Oxford)

Eastbourne 39 (Nicki Pedersen 11; Davey Watt 8+1; Adam Shields 8; Mark Loram 7+1; Dean Barker 3; Andrew Moore 2+1), Oxford 36, Poole 33. Aggregate result: Oxford 115, Eastbourne 114, Poole 95.

IPSWICH EVENING STAR WITCHES

ADDRESS: Foxhall Heath Stadium, Foxhall Road, Ipswich, Suffolk, IP4 5TL.
PROMOTER: John Louis.
TRACK LENGTH: 305 metres.
TRACK RECORD: 57.5 seconds – Jaroslaw Hampel (12 September 2002).
FIRST MEETING: 25 October 1950.
YEARS OF OPERATION: 1950-51 Open; 1952-53 Southern League; 1954-56 National League Division Two; 1957-58 National League; 1959 Southern Area League; 1960-62 National League; 1964 Metropolitan League; 1965 Open; 1969-71 British League Division Two; 1972-74 British League Division One; 1975-88 British League; 1989-90 National League; 1991-94 British League Division One; 1995-96 Premier League; 1997-2005 Elite League.

NOTE: Ipswich also took part in the 1997 Amateur League, sharing their fixtures with King's Lynn and riding under the banner of 'Anglian Angels'.

CLUB HONOURS

KNOCK-OUT CUP WINNERS: 1970, 1971, 1976, 1978, 1981, 1984, 1998.
LEAGUE CHAMPIONS: 1975, 1976, 1984, 1998.
PAIRS CHAMPIONS: 1976, 1977.
INTER-LEAGUE KNOCK-OUT CUP WINNERS: 1977.
FOUR-TEAM CHAMPIONS: 1991.
CRAVEN SHIELD WINNERS: 1998.

RIDER ROSTER 2005

Hans N. ANDERSEN; Karol BARAN; Kevin DOOLAN; Kim JANSSON; Daniel KING; Chris LOUIS; Robert MISKOWIAK; Piotr PROTASIEWICZ; Mariusz PUSZAKOWSKI; George STANCL.

OTHER APPEARANCES/GUESTS (official matches only):
Jon ARMSTRONG; Billy HAMILL; David HOWE; Ashley JONES; Scott NICHOLLS; Tomasz PISZCZ; Adam SHIELDS; Mathieu TRESARRIEU; Davey WATT; Carl WILKINSON.

SKY BET ELITE LEAGUE

(*Denotes bonus-point victory)

No	DATE	OPPONENTS	H/A	RESULT	Andersen	Baran	Jansson	Louis	Protasiewicz	King	Miskowiak	Doolan	Stancl	Puszakowski	Others
1	17/3	Belle Vue	H	W48-41	15 (5)	3+1 (4)	8 (4)	5+2 (4)	9 (5)	5 (4)	3 (4)	–	–	–	–
2	25/3	Arena-Essex	H	W53-41	12+1 (5)	3 (4)	8+2 (4)	10+1 (4)	11+1 (5)	5+1 (4)	4+1 (4)	–	–	–	–
3	31/3	Coventry	H	W51-42	11+2 (5)	5+1 (4)	3+1 (4)	9+1 (5)	10+1 (4)	4 (4)	9 (4)	–	–	–	–
4	14/4	Poole	H	L44-49	11 (5)	0 (3)	6 (4)	6+1 (4)	13+1 (5)	4 (5)	4+1 (4)	–	–	–	–

No	DATE	OPPONENTS	H/A	RESULT	Andersen	Baran	Jansson	Louis	Protasiewicz	King	Miskowiak	Doolan	Stancl	Puszakowski	Others
5	16/4	Eastbourne	A	L45-48	15 (5)	–	5+2 (4)	12+1 (5)	–	2+1 (4)	1+1 (4)	3+1 (4)	–	–	7 (4)
6	18/4	Belle Vue	A	L43-50*	11+1 (5)	2 (3)	3 (4)	7+1 (4)	13+1 (5)	1 (3)	6+1 (6)	–	–	–	–
7	21/4	Eastbourne	H	L41-50	10 (5)	2 (3)	3 (3)	13 (5)	4 (4)	3 (4)	6+2 (6)	–	–	–	–
8	22/4	Coventry	A	W49-47*	14+1 (5)	3+1 (4)	0 (2)	0 (0)	15 (5)	–	13 (7)	4 (6)	–	–	–
9	2/5	Peterborough	H	D45-45	15+1 (6)	2+1 (4)	5 (5)	R/R	11 (5)	1 (3)	11+2 (7)	–	–	–	–
10	5/5	Swindon	A	L44-49	14+1 (6)	4+1 (5)	8 (6)	R/R	5 (4)	–	13+1 (7)	0 (0)	–	–	–
11	12/5	Swindon	H	W55-40*	11+2 (6)	6+1 (5)	12+2 (6)	R/R	9+1 (4)	3+1 (3)	14+1 (6)	–	–	–	–
12	18/5	Arena-Essex	A	L39-57	13+3 (6)	0 (4)	3 (5)	R/R	4 (4)	1 (4)	18 (7)	–	–	–	–
13	30/5	Peterborough	A	W55-40*	14 (6)	–	9+2 (5)	R/R	10+2 (5)	2+2 (3)	12+2 (6)	–	–	–	8+1 (5)
14	6/6	Poole	A	L43-47	11+2 (5)	1+1 (4)	12+1 (6)	R/R	5 (5)	5+2 (5)	9 (5)	–	–	–	–
15	9/6	Oxford	A	L46-48	14+1 (6)	5 (6)	0 (1)	R/R	19 (6)	1 (7)	7+1 (5)	–	–	–	–
16	13/6	Oxford	H	W56-38*	9+3 (4)	4+1 (4)	5+1 (4)	11 (4)	15 (5)	1+1 (4)	11+1 (5)	–	–	–	–
17	23/6	Eastbourne	H	W55-38	11+1 (4)	–	7 (4)	7+1 (4)	13 (5)	4+2 (4)	8+2 (5)	5+1 (4)	–	–	–
18	27/6	Wolverhampton	A	L43-47	8+2 (5)	1+1 (3)	9 (4)	5+1 (4)	12 (5)	–	6 (4)	2 (5)	–	–	–
19	30/6	Swindon	A	L41-52	6+1 (4)	5+1 (4)	10 (5)	5+1 (4)	5 (4)	–	8+2 (5)	2+1 (4)	–	–	–
20	7/7	Peterborough	H	D46-46	15 (5)	0 (3)	4 (3)	11+1 (5)	5 (4)	6+1 (6)	5+1 (4)	–	–	–	–
21	11/7	Belle Vue	A	L29-64	14 (5)	0 (3)	2+1 (4)	3 (4)	3 (4)	–	2+1 (5)	5 (5)	–	–	–
22	13/7	Peterborough	A	L43-50	14+1 (5)	3 (4)	R/R	5+1 (4)	9+1 (5)	–	3 (5)	–	–	–	9 (7)
23	14/7	Oxford	A	W47-45	13+1 (5)	2+1 (3)	–	6+1 (4)	3 (4)	7+1 (5)	8+1 (5)	–	8 (4)	–	–
24	18/7	Swindon†	H	D42-42	9 (4)	–	6 (4)	11+1 (4)	7 (4)	1 (4)	7+2 (4)	–	–	–	1 (4)
25	23/7	Belle Vue	H	L43-47	9+2 (5)	–	4 (4)	12 (5)	5 (4)	6 (5)	6 (4)	1 (3)	–	–	–
26	8/8	Eastbourne	A	L38-58	11+1 (5)	–	2 (4)	11 (4)	6+1 (5)	1+1 (4)	5 (4)	–	2 (4)	–	–
27	11/8	Poole	H	W51-45	8+1 (4)	–	3+1 (4)	11+1 (5)	11+2 (5)	–	8+2 (4)	4+1 (4)	6+2 (4)	–	–
28	17/8	Arena-Essex	A	L41-49	12 (5)	–	0 (3)	11 (5)	6+1 (4)	12+2 (7)	0 (3)	–	–	–	0 (3)
29	18/8	Wolverhampton	H	W51-44*	10+1 (5)	–	7+1 (4)	10+1 (5)	8 (4)	0 (2)	8+1 (4)	–	8+1 (6)	–	–
30	22/8	Wolverhampton	A	L34-59	11 (5)	–	8 (5)	5+1 (4)	4 (4)	–	2+2 (4)	2 (4)	–	–	2 (4)
31	29/8	Coventry	A	W46-44	–	–	9+1 (5)	11+2 (6)	R/R	1 (4)	7+2 (5)	–	2 (4)	–	16 (6)
32	1/9	Coventry	H	L40-54	7+1 (4)	–	4 (4)	6+1 (5)	13 (5)	2 (4)	5 (4)	–	3 (4)	–	–
33	3/9	Wolverhampton	H	W50-42	12+2 (5)	–	4+2 (4)	13+1 (5)	4 (4)	–	8+1 (4)	–	9 (5)	–	0 (3)
34	7/9	Poole	A	W46-44*	6+1 (4)	–	6+3 (5)	10+1 (5)	9 (4)	5 (4)	7 (4)	–	3 (4)	–	–
35	8/9	Arena-Essex	H	W64-30*	13+1 (5)	–	9+1 (4)	7+2 (4)	11+1 (4)	5+2 (4)	8+1 (4)	–	11+1 (5)	–	–
36	6/10	Oxford	H	W54-40*	14+1 (5)	–	14 (6)	14+1 (5)	R/R	3+2 (5)	7+2 (5)	–	–	–	2 (4)

†Meeting abandoned after heat fourteen, with the result permitted to stand.

DETAILS OF OTHER RIDERS:

Match No. 5: Scott Nicholls 7 (4); Match No. 13: Davey Watt 8+1 (5); Match No. 22: Carl Wilkinson 9 (7); Match No. 24: Carl Wilkinson 1 (4); Match No. 28: Mathieu Tresarrieu 0 (3); Match No. 30: Carl Wilkinson 2 (4); Match No. 31: Billy Hamill 16 (6); Match No. 33: Jon Armstrong 0 (3); Match No. 36: Tomasz Piszcz 2 (4).

TACTICAL RIDES, AS INCLUDED IN THE SCORES GRID:

Match No. 4: Protasiewicz 6 points (TR); Andersen 2 points (TR); Match No. 5: Andersen 6 points (TR); Match No. 6: Protasiewicz 6 points (TR); Match No. 7: Louis 4 points (TR); Match No. 8: Protasiewicz 6 points (TR); Andersen 6 points (TR); Heat 10: Andersen 6 points (TR); Match No. 12: Andersen 6 points (TR); Miskowiak 6 points (TR); Match No. 15: Protasiewicz 6 points (TR); Andersen 2 points (TR); Match No. 19: Jansson 6 points (TR); Match No. 20: Andersen 6 points (TR); Match

No. 21: Andersen 6 points (TR); Jansson 0 points (TR); Match No. 22: Andersen 6 points (TR); Match No. 26: Andersen 6 points (TR); Louis 6 points (TR); Match No. 30: Jansson 4 points (TR); Andersen 2 points (TR); Match No. 32: Protasiewicz 6 points (TR); Andersen 2 points (TR).

ELITE LEAGUE AVERAGES

Rider	Mts	Rds	Pts	Bon	Tot	Avge	Max
Hans N. Andersen	35	174	375	35	410	9.43	1 full; 3 paid
Chris Louis	29	126	242	25	267	8.48	2 paid
Piotr Protasiewicz	33	149	272	13	285	7.65	1 full; 1 paid
Robert Miskowiak	36	173	256	34	290	6.71	–
George Stancl	4	18	24	3	27	6.00	–
Kim Jansson	34	143	193	21	214	5.99	–
Mariusz Puszakowski	5	22	28	1	29	5.27	–
Daniel King	27	115	91	19	110	3.83	–
Kevin Doolan	10	39	28	4	32	3.28	–
Karol Baran	20	77	51	11	62	3.22	–
Guests	9	40	45	1	46	4.60	–

(Jon Armstrong [1]; Billy Hamill [1]; Scott Nicholls [1]; Tomasz Piszcz [1]; Mathieu Tresarrieu [1]; Davey Watt [1]; Carl Wilkinson [3]).

KNOCK-OUT CUP

(*Denotes aggregate victory)

No	DATE	OPPONENTS	H/A	RESULT	Andersen	Baran	Jansson	Louis	Protasiewicz	King	Miskowiak	Others
1	4/4	Wolverhampton	A	W53-37	14 (5)	0 (3)	2 (4)	9 (4)	13+2 (5)	1+1 (3)	14+3 (6)	–
2	7/4	Wolverhampton	H	W55-40*	13+2 (5)	6+2 (4)	4+2 (4)	10 (4)	12 (5)	2 (4)	8+1 (4)	–
3	26/5	Arena-Essex	H	W52-42	R/R	0 (3)	12+1 (6)	–	9 (5)	7 (5)	15+1 (7)	9+1 (5)
4	15/6	Arena-Essex	A	L40-51	8 (5)	1 (3)	3 (4)	5+1 (4)	13 (5)	5 (5)	5+2 (4)	–

DETAILS OF OTHER RIDER:

Match No. 3: Adam Shields 9+1 (5).

TACTICAL RIDES, AS INCLUDED IN THE SCORES GRID:

Match No. 4: Andersen 2 points (TR); Louis 2 points (TR).

OTHER MEETINGS

10 March: Air-Tek Trophy (first leg)

Ipswich 44 (Chris Louis 12+1; Piotr Protasiewicz 11+1; Robert Miskowiak 6+1; Kim Jansson 5+1; Hans N. Andersen 5; Karol Baran 3+1; Daniel King 2+1) Peterborough 46.

13 April: Air-Tek Trophy (second leg)

Peterborough 53 Ipswich 43 (Robert Miskowiak 12+1; Piotr Protasiewicz 12; Hans N. Andersen 11+1; Kim Jansson 5; Daniel King 3+1; Karol Baran 0; Chris Louis 0) – Peterborough won 99-87 on aggregate.

16 May: Elite League

Eastbourne 1 Ipswich 5 (Hans N. Andersen 3; Karol Baran 2+1; Kim Jansson DNR; Piotr Protasiewicz DNR; Robert Miskowiak DNR; Jason King DNR; Chris Louis R/R) – meeting abandoned after heat one.

2 June: Jeremy Doncaster Farewell

Potters Turf Select 29 (Jason Crump 8+1; Adam Shields 6+1; Sam Ermolenko 5; Leigh Lanham 4+1; Joe Screen 3; Andrew Appleton 3) Orwell Motorcycles Select 25 (Scott Nicholls 8; Chris Louis 5+1; George Stancl 4; Phil Morris 3+1; Paul Hurry 3+1; Shane Parker 2+1). Second-half Championship final: 1st Crump; 2nd Nicholls; 3rd Lanham; 4th Ermolenko.

28 July: Elite League

Ipswich 24 (Chris Louis 6; Hans N. Andersen 5+1; Kim Jansson 4+2; Robert Miskowiak 4; Daniel King 3+1; Karol Baran 2; Piotr Protasiewicz 0) Arena-Essex 12 – meeting abandoned after heat six.

14 September: Craven Shield (first leg)

Arena-Essex 53 Ipswich 40 (Piotr Protasiewicz 11; Chris Louis 10; David Howe 6; Mariusz Puszakowski 5+3; Kim Jansson 4+1; Robert Miskowiak 2; Carl Wilkinson 2).

21 September: Craven Shield (first leg)

Poole 58 Ipswich 33 (Hans N. Andersen 10; Piotr Protasiewicz 6; Kim Jansson 5; Chris Louis 5; Robert Miskowiak 4; Daniel King 3+1; Carl Wilkinson 0).

22 September: Craven Shield (second leg)

Ipswich 47 (Chris Louis 17; Hans N. Andersen 10+1; Robert Miskowiak 8; Kim Jansson 6; Piotr Protasiewicz 3+1; Daniel King 2; Ashley Jones 1) Poole 50 – Poole won 108-80 on aggregate.

29 September: Craven Shield (second leg)

Ipswich 49 (Hans N. Andersen 14+1; Chris Louis 12+2; Kim Jansson 10+1; Robert Miskowiak 8; Carl Wilkinson 4+1; Daniel King 1+1; Piotr Protasiewicz R/R) Arena-Essex 41 – Arena-Essex won 94-89 on aggregate.

INDIVIDUAL MEETING

13 October: Meridian Lifts 16-Lap Classic

QUALIFYING SCORES: Chris Louis 9; Adam Skornicki 9; Kim Jansson 9; George Stancl 9; Roman Povazhny 8; Robert Miskowiak 7; Kevin Doolan 6; Chris Harris 5; Troy Batchelor 4; Lubos Tomicek 3; Tomas Topinka 2; Shane Parker 1. FINAL: 1st Harris (14); 2nd Doolan (12); 3rd Louis (10+2); 4th Jansson (8+2); 5th Povazhny (6); 6th Stancl (4); 7th Skornicki (2+2); 8th Miskowiak (0). OVERALL RESULT: 1st Louis 21; 2nd Jansson 19; 3rd Harris 19; Doolan 18; Stancl 15; Povazhny 14; Skornicki 13; Miskowiak 7. CONSOLATION FINAL: 1st Parker; 2nd Tomicek; 3rd Topinka; 4th Batchelor.

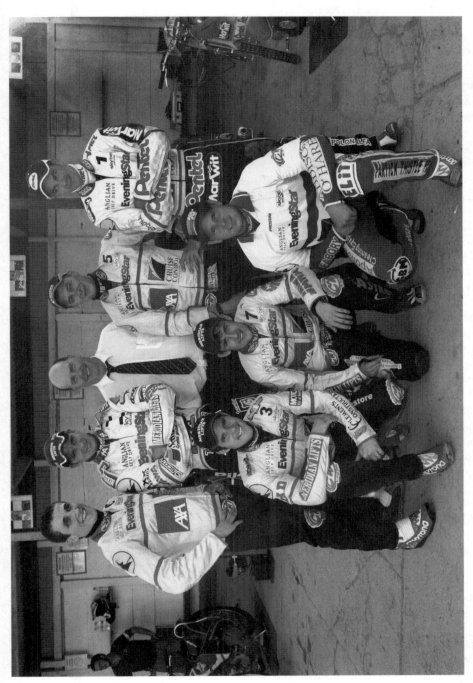

IPSWICH: From left to right, back row: Robert Miskowiak, Hans N. Andersen, Mike Smillie (Team Manager), Karol Baran, Piotr Protasiewicz. Front, kneeling: Chris Louis, Daniel King, George Stancl.

OXFORD SILVER MACHINE

NOTE: The information below relates only to the main Oxford team. For details of the second side, please refer to the Conference League section.

ADDRESS: Oxford Stadium, Sandy Lane, Cowley, Oxford, OX4 6LJ.
PROMOTERS: Nigel Wagstaff & Jim Lynch.
TRACK LENGTH: 297 metres.
TRACK RECORD: 56.2 seconds – Hans Nielsen (13 October 1988).
FIRST MEETING: 8 April 1939.
YEARS OF OPERATION: 1939-41 Open; 1949-50 National League Division Three; 1951-52 National League Division Two; 1953 Southern League; 1954-56 National League Division Two; 1957-64 National League; 1965-67 British League; 1968-74 British League Division One; 1975 British League; 1976-83 National League; 1984-90 British League; 1991-92 British League Division One; 1993-94 British League Division Two; 1995-97 Premier League; 1998-2005 Elite League.

CLUB HONOURS

LEAGUE CHAMPIONS: 1950, 1964, 1985, 1986, 1989, 2001.
NATIONAL TROPHY (DIVISION THREE) WINNERS: 1950.
NATIONAL TROPHY WINNERS: 1964.
BRITANNIA SHIELD WINNERS: 1964.
PAIRS CHAMPIONS: 1985, 1986, 1987.
KNOCK-OUT CUP WINNERS: 1985, 1986 (Shared with Cradley Heath).
LEAGUE CUP WINNERS: 1986 (Shared with Cradley Heath).
PREMIERSHIP WINNERS: 1987.
GOLD CUP WINNERS: 1989.
FOUR-TEAM CHAMPIONS: 1994, 1996.
CRAVEN SHIELD WINNERS: 2005.

RIDER ROSTER 2005

Stefan ANDERSSON; Tomasz BAJERSKI; Craig BRANNEY; Lukas DRYML; Freddie ERIKSSON; Renat GAFUROV; Henrik GUSTAFSSON; Billy HAMILL; Greg HANCOCK; Niels-Kristian IVERSEN; Jesper B. JENSEN; Emil KRAMER; Tobias KRONER; Travis McGOWAN; Tom P. MADSEN; Michal MAKOVSKY; Chris MILLS; Kjastas PUODZHUKS; Pawel STASZEK; Lubos TOMICEK; Brent WERNER.

OTHER APPEARANCES/GUESTS (official matches only):
Jamie COURTNEY; Chris HARRIS; David HOWE; Peter KARLSSON; Scott NICHOLLS; David NORRIS; Luke PRIEST; Lee RICHARDSON.

OXFORD: From left to right, back row: Billy Hamill, Greg Hancock, Henrik Gustafsson. Front: Nigel Wagstaff (Promoter/Team Manager), Jamie Courtney, Travis McGowan, Niels-Kristian Iversen, Freddie Eriksson, Chris Mills, Bryn Williams (Assistant Team Manager).

SKY BET ELITE LEAGUE

(*Denotes bonus-point victory)

No	DATE	OPPONENTS	H/A	RESULT	Hancock	McGowan	Dryml	Iversen	Hamill	Madsen	Jensen	Andersson	Gustafsson	Bajerski	Kroner	Others
1	23/3	Peterborough	A	L42-48	11+2(5)	5(4)	6+1(4)	6+1(4)	11(5)	3(5)	–	–	–	–	–	0(3)
2	24/3	Swindon	A	L43-46	10(5)	8+1(5)	6+2(4)	7(4)	5(3)	5+2(5)	–	–	–	–	–	2(4)
3	25/3	Swindon	H	L41-49	13(6)	6+2(6)	4(5)	9+2(5)	R/R	6+2(5)	–	–	–	–	–	3+1(3)
4	30/3	Arena-Essex	A	W49-41	13+2(6)	10+1(5)	2(4)	15(6)	R/R	9(6)	–	–	–	–	–	0(3)
5	9/4	Eastbourne	A	L39-55	7+1(5)	10(5)	0(3)	10(5)	–	5+2(5)	3(4)	–	–	–	–	4(3)
6	14/4	Peterborough	H	W49-46	9+1(5)	7+1(4)	–	18(5)	–	2(5)	7+1(4)	6(4)	–	–	–	0(3)
7	21/4	Arena-Essex	H	L46-48*	13(5)	2+1(4)	–	13+1(5)	–	5+1(5)	6+2(4)	7(4)	–	–	–	–
8	5/5	Coventry	H	L40-54	10+2(5)	4+1(4)	–	12(5)	–	1(3)	3+1(4)	3(4)	7(5)	–	–	–
9	6/5	Coventry	A	L43-51	10(5)	3(4)	–	15+1(5)	–	4+1(5)	0(3)	0(1)	11+2(7)	–	–	–
10	11/5	Peterborough	A	L30-62	R/R	6+1(6)	–	12(6)	–	3+1(6)	4+1(4)	5(5)	0(3)	–	–	–
11	12/5	Poole	H	W49-41	–	6(4)	–	7+2(4)	–	3(3)	6+1(4)	7(5)	9+3(5)	–	–	11+1(5)
12	1/6	Poole	A	L41-54	11+1(5)	4(4)	–	–	–	–	9+1(5)	0(2)	14(6)	3(4)	–	0(3)
13	2/6	Wolverhampton	H	W50-45	15+2(6)	8+1(5)	–	–	–	–	15+1(6)	R/R	0(1)	7+1(7)	–	5+2(5)
14	6/6	Wolverhampton	A	L38-55	19(6)	1(5)	–	3(5)	–	–	10+2(6)	R/R	–	5(5)	–	0(3)
15	8/6	Arena-Essex	A	L46-47	21(6)	5(5)	–	3(5)	–	–	11+1(6)	R/R	–	6+1(5)	–	0(3)
16	9/6	Ipswich	H	W48-46	12+1(6)	8+2(5)	–	8+1(5)	–	–	10+1(6)	R/R	7+2(4)	3+3(4)	–	–
17	13/6	Ipswich	A	L38-56	–	6+2(6)	–	10(5)	–	–	4+3(5)	R/R	7+2(5)	–	–	11(9)
18	16/6	Arena-Essex	H	W49-41*	14(5)	5+3(4)	–	14+1(5)	6(4)	–	–	–	8+1(7)	–	–	2+1(5)
19	23/6	Coventry	H	L42-52	13(5)	6(4)	–	8(4)	9+1(5)	–	–	–	2(5)	–	–	4+1(7)
20	29/6	Poole	A	L44-46	9+1(5)	8+1(4)	–	8(5)	6+2(4)	–	–	–	7(5)	–	0(3)	6+2(4)
21	7/7	Swindon	A	L38-54	8(5)	8+3(5)	–	12(5)	5+1(4)	–	–	–	4(4)	–	0(3)	1+1(4)
22	14/7	Ipswich	H	L45–47	11+1(5)	14(5)	–	7+1(4)	2(3)	–	–	–	9+1(6)	–	0(2)	2+1(5)
23	16/7	Eastbourne	A	L35-57	14(5)	6(6)	–	5(4)	2(2)	–	–	–	1+1(1)	–	2+1(4)	5+1(6)
24	18/7	Belle Vue	A	L28-63	14+1(6)	4(6)	–	–	R/R	–	–	–	–	–	3(4)	7(14)
25	21/7	Belle Vue	H	L43-52	15+1(5)	6+1(5)	–	10(4)	–	–	–	–	–	–	0(3)	12(13)
26	29/7	Coventry	A	L39-54	16(5)	6+2(4)	–	9(5)	5(4)	–	–	–	–	–	0(3)	3+1(9)
27	8/8	Belle Vue	A	L43-52	15(5)	8+1(4)	–	6+1(4)	10+1(5)	–	–	–	–	–	1(4)	3(8)
28	11/8	Belle Vue	H	L41-54	11+1(5)	12+2(6)	–	10(5)	6(4)	–	–	–	R/R	–	0(4)	2+1(6)
29	15/8	Wolverhampton	A	D45-45	11(5)	9+1(5)	–	8+1(5)	14(5)	–	–	–	R/R	–	–	3(10)
30	18/8	Poole	H	W46-44	R/R	9+2(5)	–	13+1(6)	15+1(6)	–	–	–	–	–	0(3)	9+2(10)
31	25/8	Eastbourne	H	W50-41	–	14+2(6)	–	14(5)	13+1(5)	–	–	–	R/R	–	5(7)	4+2(7)
32	29/8	Peterborough	H	L43-47	13(5)	8+2(5)	–	5(2)	9+2(5)	–	–	–	R/R	–	3(7)	5+1(6)
33	5/9	Eastbourne	H	W49-41	9(5)	13+1(7)	–	R/R	11+3(6)	–	–	–	–	–	–	16(12)
34	6/10	Ipswich	A	L40-54	–	12+1(6)	–	5(5)	R/R	–	–	–	1+1(3)	–	–	22+6(16)
35	20/10	Swindon	H	W51-42	13(5)	10+1(5)	–	4(4)	8+1(4)	–	–	–	12+1(5)	–	–	4(7)
36	28/10	Wolverhampton	H	W47-43*	13+1(5)	7+1(4)	–	8(4)	3(3)	–	–	–	–	–	–	16+2(14)

DETAILS OF OTHER RIDERS:

Match No. 1: Kjastas Puodzhuks 0 (3); Match No. 2: Kjastas Puodzhuks 2 (4); Match No. 3: Chris Mills 3+1 (3); Match No. 4: Chris Mills 0 (3); Match No. 5: Lubos Tomicek 4 (3); Match No. 6: Craig Branney 0 (3); Match No. 7: Chris Mills 0 (3); Match No. 11: Peter Karlsson 11+1 (5); Match No. 12: Jamie Courtney 0 (3); Match No. 13: Michal Makovsky 5+2 (5); Match No. 14: Michal Makovsky 0 (3); Match No. 15: Michal Makovsky 0 (3); Match No. 17: David Norris 10 (6); Lubos Tomicek 1 (3); Match No. 18: Renat Gafurov 2+1 (4); Jamie Courtney 0 (1); Match No. 19: Chris Mills 2+1 (3); Brent Werner 2 (4); Match No. 20:

Renat Gafurov 6+2 (4); Match No. 21: Renat Gafurov 1+1 (4); Match No. 22: Jamie Courtney 2+1 (5); Match No. 23: Lubos Tomicek 5+1 (6); Match No. 24: Lubos Tomicek 3 (5); Jamie Courtney 2 (4); Brent Werner 2 (5); Match No. 25: Scott Nicholls 9 (5); Brent Werner 3 (5); Chris Mills 0 (3); Match No. 26: Emil Kramer 2 (5); Craig Branney 1+1 (4); Match No. 27: Emil Kramer 2 (4); Craig Branney 1 (4); Match No. 28: Lubos Tomicek 2+1 (6); Match No. 29: Lubos Tomicek 2 (5); Jamie Courtney 1 (5); Match No. 30: Chris Harris 6+2 (5); Pawel Staszek 3 (5); Match No. 31: Chris Mills 3+2 (4); Pawel Staszek 1 (3); Match No. 32: Emil Kramer 5+1 (6); Match No. 33: Freddie Eriksson 14 (6); Emil Kramer 2 (3); Chris Mills 0 (3); Match No. 34: Freddie Eriksson 13+3 (6); Lubos Tomicek 6+1 (6); David Howe 3+2 (4); Match No. 35: Freddie Eriksson 3 (4); Chris Mills 1 (3); Match No. 36: Freddie Eriksson 10+1 (5); Chris Mills 6+1 (5); Jamie Courtney 0 (4).

TACTICAL SUBSTITUTE AND TACTICAL RIDES, AS INCLUDED IN THE SCORES GRID:

Match No. 5: McGowan 6 points (TR); Iversen 2 points (TS); Hancock 0 points (TR); Match No. 6: Iversen 6 points (TR); McGowan 4 points (TR); Match No. 7: Iversen 6 points (TR); Match No. 8: Iversen 6 points (TR); Jensen 2 points (TR); Match No. 9: Iversen 6 points (TR); Hancock 2 points (TR); Match No. 10: Iversen 4 points (TR); Jensen 0 points (TR); Match No. 12: Gustafsson 6 points (TR); Hancock 4 points (TR); Match No. 14: Hancock 6 points (TR); Match No. 15: Hancock 6 points (TR); Match No. 17: Iversen 4 points (TR); McGowan 4 points (TR); Match No. 19: Hancock 4 points (TR); Iversen 4 points (TR); Match No. 21: Iversen 2 points (TS); Hancock 2 points (TR); Gafurov 0 points (TR); Match No. 22: McGowan 6 points (TR); Match No. 23: Hancock 4 points (TR); McGowan 2 points (TS); Iversen 0 points (TR); Match No. 24: Hancock 4 points (TR); McGowan 0 points (TR); Match No. 25: Hancock 6 points (TR); Iversen 4 points (TR); McGowan 0 points (TS); Match No. 26: Iversen 4 points (TR); Hancock 4 points (TR); Match No. 27: Hancock 6 points (TR); McGowan 4 points (TR); Match No. 28: Iversen 6 points (TR); Hancock 4 points (TR); Match No. 34: Eriksson 6 points (TR); McGowan 4 points (TR).

ELITE LEAGUE AVERAGES

Rider	Mts	Rds	Pts	Bon	Tot	Avge	Max
Greg Hancock	30	157	347	18	365	9.30	1 full
Billy Hamill	18	77	140	13	153	7.95	–
Freddie Eriksson	4	21	37	4	41	7.81	–
Niels-Kristian Iversen	32	150	267	13	280	7.47	1 full; 1 paid
Jesper B. Jensen	13	61	87	15	102	6.69	–
Travis McGowan	36	177	249	37	286	6.46	–
Henrik Gustafsson	16	72	96	14	110	6.11	–
Lubos Tomicek	1	6	6	1	7	4.67	–
Tomasz Bajerski	5	25	24	5	29	4.64	–
Stefan Andersson	7	25	28	0	28	4.48	–
Renat Gafurov	3	12	9	4	13	4.33	–
Lukas Dryml	5	20	18	3	21	4.20	–
Tom P. Madsen	11	53	46	9	55	4.15	–
Emil Kramer	3	15	9	1	10	2.67	–
Michal Makovsky	3	11	5	2	7	2.55	–
Chris Mills	4	14	7	1	8	2.29	–
Pawel Staszek	2	8	4	0	4	2.00	–
Brent Werner	3	14	7	0	7	2.00	–
Tobias Kroner	12	47	14	1	15	1.28	–
Kjastas Puodzhuks	2	7	2	0	2	1.14	–
Craig Branney	1	3	0	0	0	0.00	–
Guests	25	102	73	13	86	3.37	–

(Craig Branney [2]; Jamie Courtney [6]; Chris Harris [1]; David Howe [1]; Peter Karlsson [1]; Emil Kramer [1]; Chris Mills [5]; Scott Nicholls [1]; David Norris [1]; Lubos Tomicek [6]).

KNOCK-OUT CUP

No	DATE	OPPONENTS	H/A	RESULT	Hancock	McGowan	Jensen	Iversen	Andersson	Gustafsson	Bajerski
1	16/5	Belle Vue	A	L35-59	14+1 (5)	1 (4)	0 (3)	7 (5)	6 (4)	4 (4)	3 (5)
2	19/5	Belle Vue	H	W49-41	11+1 (5)	5+2 (4)	2+2 (4)	11+1 (5)	8 (4)	11+1 (5)	1 (3)

TACTICAL RIDES, AS INCLUDED IN THE SCORES GRID:

Match No. 1: Hancock 6 points (TR); Iversen 2 points (TR).

OTHER MEETINGS

17 March: Air-Tek Trophy (first leg)

> Oxford 47 (Gary Havelock 12+2; Billy Hamill 11+1; Travis McGowan 7+1; Niels-Kristian Iversen 7; Tom P. Madsen 5+1; Lukas Dryml 3+1; Kjastas Puodzhuks 2) Wolverhampton 41.

21 March: Air-Tek Trophy (second leg)

> Wolverhampton 55 Oxford 38 (Greg Hancock 16+1; Niels-Kristian Iversen 7; Lukas Dryml 6; Billy Hamill 4; Tom P. Madsen 2+1; Kjastas Puodzhuks 2; Travis McGowan 1) – Wolverhampton won 96-85 on aggregate.

15 September: Craven Shield (first leg)

> Oxford 41 (Travis McGowan 12+1; Billy Hamill 7; Freddie Eriksson 6+2; Greg Hancock 6+1; Niels-Kristian Iversen 5; Chris Mills 3+1; Henrik Gustafsson 2+1) Swindon 34 – meeting abandoned after heat twelve, with the result permitted to stand.

19 September: Craven Shield (first leg)

> Oxford 48 (Greg Hancock 12; Billy Hamill 11+1; Travis McGowan 10+1; Niels-Kristian Iversen 8+1; Freddie Eriksson 4+2; Henrik Gustafsson 2+1; Craig Branney 1) Wolverhampton 42.

26 September: Craven Shield (second leg)

> Wolverhampton 51 Oxford 45 (Travis McGowan 14; Greg Hancock 13+1; Billy Hamill 13; Freddie Eriksson 2; Lubos Tomicek 2; Henrik Gustafsson 1+1; Luke Priest 0) – Aggregate score 93-93, with Oxford winning the bonus point run-off.

29 September: Craven Shield (second leg)

> Swindon 44 Oxford 46 (Travis McGowan 16+2; Billy Hamill 9+2; Greg Hancock 8+1; Freddie Eriksson 6; Henrik Gustafsson 5; Lubos Tomicek 2; Chris Mills 0) – Oxford won 87-78 on aggregate.

8 October: Craven Shield semi-final (first leg at Eastbourne)

> Eastbourne 37, Oxford 27 (David Howe 8; Travis McGowan 6+1; Lee Richardson 6; Freddie Eriksson 4; Niels-Kristian Iversen 3+1; Lubos Tomicek 0), Belle Vue 26 – meeting abandoned after heat fifteen, with the result permitted to stand.

13 October: Craven Shield semi-final (second leg at Oxford)

> Oxford 42 (Niels-Kristian Iversen 11; Travis McGowan 9+1; Billy Hamill 8+1; Freddie Eriksson 5+2; Greg Hancock 5+1; Henrik Gustafsson 4+1), Eastbourne 34, Belle Vue 32.

17 October: Craven Shield semi-final (third leg at Belle Vue)

> Oxford 38 (Billy Hamill 11; Greg Hancock 8+2; Niels-Kristian Iversen 6+1; Freddie Eriksson 5+2; Travis McGowan 5; Henrik Gustafsson 3), Eastbourne 36, Belle Vue 34. Aggregate result: Eastbourne 107, Oxford 107, Belle Vue 92.

22 October: Craven Shield final (first leg at Eastbourne)

Eastbourne 41, Oxford 40 (Niels-Kristian Iversen 10; Greg Hancock 8+1; Travis McGowan 8+1; Billy Hamill 7+1; Henrik Gustafsson 4+1; Freddie Eriksson 3+2), Poole 27.

26 October: Craven Shield final (second leg at Poole)

Oxford 39 (Billy Hamill 9+1; Greg Hancock 8+1; Niels-Kristian Iversen 8; Henrik Gustafsson 6+2; Freddie Eriksson 5+1; Travis McGowan 3+1), Poole 35, Eastbourne 34.

28 October: Craven Shield final (third leg at Oxford)

Eastbourne 39, Oxford 36 (Niels-Kristian Iversen 9; Greg Hancock 8+1; Billy Hamill 7; Travis McGowan 6+3; Henrik Gustafsson 4+2; Freddie Eriksson 2+2), Poole 33. Aggregate result: Oxford 115, Eastbourne 114, Poole 95.

PETERBOROUGH BARTERCARD PANTHERS

ADDRESS: East of England Showground, Alwalton, Peterborough, PE2 0XE.
PROMOTERS: Mick Horton & Neil Watson, with Colin Horton taking over from his brother, Mick, as club owner and co-promoter in May 2005.
TRACK LENGTH: 336 metres.
TRACK RECORD: 59.3 seconds – Peter Karlsson (8 April 2005 and 23 June 2005) & Bjarne Pedersen (2 September 2005).
FIRST MEETING: 12 June 1970.
YEARS OF OPERATION: 1970-74 British League Division Two; 1975-90 National League; 1991-94 British League Division Two; 1995 Premier League; 1996 Premier League & Conference League; 1997 Elite League & Amateur League; 1998 Premier League; 1999 Elite League; 2000-03 Elite League & Conference League; 2004-05 Elite League.

CLUB HONOURS

FOUR-TEAM CHAMPIONS: 1977, 1978, 1988, 1989, 1992, 1997, 1998.
LEAGUE CHAMPIONS: 1992, 1998, 1999.
KNOCK-OUT CUP WINNERS: 1992, 1999, 2001.
PREMIERSHIP WINNERS: 1993.
PAIRS CHAMPIONS: 1998.
CRAVEN SHIELD WINNERS: 1999.

RIDER ROSTER 2005

Jon ARMSTRONG; Henning BAGER; Daniel DAVIDSSON; Ales DRYML; Lukas DRYML; Sam ERMOLENKO; Ritchie HAWKINS; Billy JANNIRO; Jesper B. JENSEN; Peter KARLSSON; Joonas KYLMAKORPI; Paul LEE; Chris SCHRAMM.

OTHER APPEARANCES/GUESTS (official matches only):
Dean BARKER; Matej ZAGAR.

SKY BET ELITE LEAGUE

(*Denotes bonus-point victory)

No	DATE	OPPONENTS	H/A	RESULT	Karlsson	Kylmakorpi	A. Dryml	Janniro	Ermolenko	Lee	Bager	L. Dryml	Hawkins	Jensen	Davidsson	Others
1	23/3	Oxford	H	W48-42	13+1 (5)	8+1 (5)	6+1 (4)	5+1 (4)	7 (4)	3 (3)	6+2 (5)	–	–	–	–	–
2	25/3	Coventry	A	W51-44	10 (5)	6+2 (4)	11 (4)	7+2 (4)	9 (5)	3+1 (3)	5+4 (5)	–	–	–	–	–
3	28/3	Coventry	H	W52-43*	10+1 (4)	6+1 (4)	15 (5)	5+1 (4)	8 (5)	3+1 (4)	5+3 (4)	–	–	–	–	–
4	2/4	Eastbourne	A	L40-51	12 (5)	9+2 (5)	4+1 (4)	4+1 (4)	5 (4)	0 (3)	6+1 (5)	–	–	–	–	–
5	8/4	Poole	H	L40-50	14 (5)	4+1 (4)	5 (3)	3 (4)	7+1 (5)	0 (3)	7+1 (6)	–	–	–	–	–
6	14/4	Oxford	A	L46-49*	9 (5)	10+2 (6)	9+1 (5)	R/R	6+1 (5)	3+1 (3)	9+2 (6)	–	–	–	–	–
7	20/4	Arena-Essex	A	L42-48	10 (5)	13+1 (6)	R/R	–	5+1 (4)	0 (4)	10 (7)	–	–	–	–	4+3 (4)
8	2/5	Ipswich	A	D45-45	11 (5)	R/R	13+2 (6)	–	6+1 (5)	0 (3)	8+2 (6)	7+2 (5)	–	–	–	–
9	4/5	Belle Vue	H	W52-39	13 (5)	6+2 (4)	11+2 (5)	–	8 (4)	0 (3)	9+2 (5)	5+1 (4)	–	–	–	–
10	9/5	Swindon	A	L44-46	9 (5)	9 (5)	7+1 (4)	–	8 (4)	1 (3)	8+1 (6)	2 (3)	–	–	–	–
11	11/5	Oxford	H	W62-30	11 (4)	R/R	16+2 (6)	–	12+3 (6)	–	12 (4)	5+3 (4)	–	–	–	6+3 (6)
12	18/5	Poole	A	L41-52	11 (5)	3+1 (4)	9 (4)	–	4 (4)	–	7 (5)	7+1 (5)	–	–	–	0 (3)
13	23/5	Wolverhampton	A	L40-55	14 (5)	9+2 (5)	7 (5)	–	2 (4)	3+1 (3)	3+1 (4)	2 (4)	–	–	–	–
14	27/5	Wolverhampton	H	W47-43	12+1 (5)	5 (4)	13 (5)	–	6 (4)	1 (3)	6+1 (5)	4+1 (4)	–	–	–	–
15	30/5	Ipswich	H	L40-55	11 (5)	R/R	11+1 (5)	–	5+2 (5)	–	3 (6)	10+1 (7)	–	–	–	0 (3)
16	13/6	Belle Vue	A	L38-58	7 (5)	R/R	13+1 (6)	–	0 (5)	–	8 (6)	9 (5)	1 (3)	–	–	–
17	17/6	Coventry	A	L43-53	14 (5)	R/R	10 (5)	–	7 (6)	0 (3)	4+1 (6)	8 (5)	–	–	–	–
18	20/6	Wolverhampton	A	L41-55	17 (5)	R/R	0 (5)	–	8 (6)	–	4 (5)	10+1 (6)	2+1 (3)	–	–	–
19	22/6	Arena-Essex	A	W54-39	12 (5)	R/R	–	–	14 (6)	–	13+2 (5)	–	0 (4)	–	–	15+2 (10)
20	23/6	Arena-Essex	H	W52-39*	11+1 (4)	R/R	14+1 (6)	–	9+1 (6)	–	4+2 (5)	11+1 (5)	3+1 (4)	–	–	–
21	6/7	Belle Vue	H	W48-42	10+3 (5)	–	13 (5)	–	6+2 (4)	–	1 (3)	8+1 (6)	–	7+1 (4)	3+1 (3)	–
22	7/7	Ipswich	A	D46-46	14+1 (5)	–	7 (4)	–	5 (4)	–	4+2 (4)	6+1 (5)	–	8+1 (5)	2 (3)	–
23	11/7	Eastbourne	A	L42-48	16 (6)	–	R/R	–	9+2 (6)	–	4+2 (5)	5 (5)	–	7 (5)	1+1 (3)	–
24	13/7	Ipswich	H	W50-43*	12 (4)	–	7 (4)	–	6+1 (4)	–	8+1 (5)	10+1 (5)	–	6+1 (4)	1+1 (4)	–
25	25/7	Coventry	H	W48-42	13 (5)	–	6 (4)	–	9+1 (5)	–	3+1 (4)	12+1 (5)	–	5 (4)	0 (3)	–
26	10/8	Wolverhampton	H	W51-39	13+1 (5)	–	11 (5)	–	5+1 (4)	–	3 (4)	15 (5)	–	4 (4)	0 (3)	–
27	11/8	Swindon	A	L43-47	7+1 (5)	–	5 (3)	–	11 (5)	–	3+1 (4)	7+1 (5)	–	6+2 (4)	4+1 (4)	–
28	15/8	Poole	A	W46-44	9 (4)	–	7 (4)	–	6 (5)	–	2+1 (4)	14 (6)	–	7+2 (5)	1 (3)	–
29	17/8	Swindon	H	W55-41*	9 (4)	–	8+2 (5)	–	12 (5)	–	6+4 (5)	11 (4)	–	6+2 (4)	3+2 (4)	–
30	29/8	Oxford	A	W47-43*	13 (5)	–	5 (4)	–	5+1 (4)	–	5+2 (4)	8 (5)	–	8+1 (5)	3 (3)	–
31	29/8	Arena-Essex	H	W61-32*	12 (4)	–	14+1 (5)	–	11+1 (4)	–	6+2 (4)	9 (4)	–	9+3 (5)	0 (4)	–
32	31/8	Belle Vue†	A	W39-36*	5+1 (3)	–	5 (3)	–	6+1 (3)	–	8+2 (4)	5+2 (4)	–	–	6+1 (4)	4 (3)
33	1/9	Eastbourne	H	W62-31*	12 (4)	–	11+2 (5)	–	14+1 (5)	–	7+1 (4)	8+2 (4)	–	9+1 (4)	1 (4)	–
34	1/9	Eastbourne	H	W52-43*	11 (5)	–	6+2 (4)	–	8+1 (5)	–	8+2 (6)	9+2 (4)	–	7 (4)	3 (3)	–
35	2/9	Poole	H	W48-42*	12 (5)	–	7+1 (4)	–	7+2 (5)	–	8+2 (5)	6+1 (4)	–	5+2 (4)	3 (3)	–
36	5/9	Swindon	H	W53-43*	9+1 (5)	–	8 (4)	–	7+3 (4)	–	9+2 (5)	7 (4)	–	9+1 (5)	4 (3)	–

†Meeting abandoned after heat twelve, with the result permitted to stand.

DETAILS OF OTHER RIDERS:

Match No. 7: Dean Barker 4+3 (4); Match No. 11: Jon Armstrong 6+3 (6); Match No. 12: Chris Schramm 0 (3); Match No. 15: Jon Armstrong 0 (3); Match No. 19: Matej Zagar 8 (5); Billy Janniro 7+2 (5); Match No. 32: Jon Armstrong 4 (3).

TACTICAL SUBSTITUTE AND TACTICAL RIDES, AS INCLUDED IN THE SCORES GRID:

Match No. 4: Karlsson 2 points (TS); Match No. 12: A. Dryml 4 points (TR); L. Dryml 2 points (TR); Match No. 13: Karlsson 6 points (TR); Kylmakorpi 4 points (TR); Match No. 15: A. Dryml 4 points (TR); Karlsson 4 points (TR); L. Dryml 2 points (TS); Match No. 16: L. Dryml 6 points (TR); A. Dryml 6 points (TR); Match No. 17: L. Dryml 6 points (TR); Karlsson 6 points (TR); Match No. 18: Karlsson 6 points (TR); L. Dryml 4 points (TR); Ermolenko 2 points (TS).

ELITE LEAGUE AVERAGES

Rider	Mts	Rds	Pts	Bon	Tot	Avge	Max
Peter Karlsson	36	171	396	12	408	9.54	3 full; 2 paid
Ales Dryml	33	150	287	21	308	8.21	1 full; 2 paid
Jesper B. Jensen	15	66	103	17	120	7.27	–
Joonas Kylmakorpi	12	56	86	15	101	7.21	–
Lukas Dryml	28	132	210	23	233	7.06	1 full
Sam Ermolenko	36	169	262	27	289	6.84	2 paid
Henning Bager	36	175	222	50	272	6.22	1 full; 1 paid
Billy Janniro	5	20	24	5	29	5.80	–
Jon Armstrong	2	9	6	3	9	4.00	–
Daniel Davidsson	16	54	35	7	42	3.11	–
Ritchie Hawkins	4	14	6	2	8	2.29	–
Paul Lee	13	41	17	4	21	2.05	–
Chris Schramm	1	3	0	0	0	0.00	–
Guests	4	17	23	5	28	6.59	–

(Jon Armstrong [1]; Dean Barker [1]; Billy Janniro [1]; Matej Zagar [1]).

KNOCK-OUT CUP

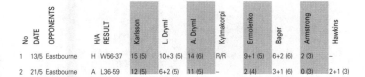

No	DATE	OPPONENTS	H/A	RESULT	Karlsson	L. Dryml	A. Dryml	Kylmakorpi	Ermolenko	Bager	Armstrong	Hawkins
1	13/5	Eastbourne	H	W56-37	15 (5)	10+3 (5)	14 (6)	R/R	9+1 (5)	6+2 (6)	2 (3)	–
2	21/5	Eastbourne	A	L36-59	12 (5)	6+2 (5)	11 (5)	–	2 (4)	3+1 (6)	0 (3)	2+1 (3)

TACTICAL SUBSTITUTE AND TACTICAL RIDES, AS INCLUDED IN THE SCORES GRID:

Match No. 2: A. Dryml 4 points (TR); Karlsson 4 points (TR); L. Dryml 2 points (TS).

OTHER MEETINGS

10 March: Air-Tek Trophy (first leg)

Ipswich 44 Peterborough 46 (Joonas Kylmakorpi 11; Peter Karlsson 10; Sam Ermolenko 9+1; Henning Bager 8+2; Paul Lee 4+1; Ales Dryml 4; Billy Janniro R/R).

4 April: Elite League

Peterborough 10 (Billy Janniro 3; Ales Dryml 2+1; Peter Karlsson 2; Henning Bager 2; Joonas Kylmakorpi 1+1; Paul Lee 0; Sam Ermolenko DNR) Swindon 8 – meeting abandoned after heat three.

PETERBOROUGH: From left to right, back row: Jesper B. Jensen, Lukas Dryml, Henning Bager, Trevor Swales (Team Manager), Daniel Davidsson, Ales Dryml, Sam Ermolenko. Front, on bike: Peter Karlsson.

13 April: Air-Tek Trophy (second leg)

Peterborough 53 (Joonas Kylmakorpi 14+3; Ales Dryml 12+2; Peter Karlsson 10; Paul Lee 9+2; Sam Ermolenko 5; Henning Bager 3+1; Billy Janniro R/R) Ipswich 43 – Peterborough won 99-87 on aggregate.

12 September: Elite League Play-Off semi-final

Coventry 55 Peterborough 41 (Jesper B. Jensen 14; Peter Karlsson 9+1; Lukas Dryml 7+2; Ales Dryml 7; Henning Bager 4+1; Sam Ermolenko 0; Daniel Davidsson 0).

4 October: Craven Shield semi-final (first leg at Peterborough)

Peterborough 38 (Ales Dryml 9+1; Peter Karlsson 8; Henning Bager 7+2; Lukas Dryml 6+2; Sam Ermolenko 5+1; Jesper B. Jensen 3), Coventry 36, Poole 34.

5 October: Craven Shield semi-final (second leg at Poole)

Poole 38 Peterborough 35 (Peter Karlsson 12; Ales Dryml 8; Jesper B. Jensen 6+2; Sam Ermolenko 6+1; Henning Bager 2+2; Lukas Dryml 1), Coventry 34.

7 October: Craven Shield semi-final (third leg at Coventry)

Poole 40, Coventry 34, Peterborough 34 (Peter Karlsson 8+2; Lukas Dryml 7+1; Sam Ermolenko 6+1; Jesper B. Jensen 5+1; Ales Dryml 5; Henning Bager 3). Aggregate result: Poole 112, Peterborough 107, Coventry 104.

INDIVIDUAL MEETING

16 October: ASL Freight Trophy

QUALIFYING SCORES: Jason Crump 14; Hans N. Andersen 12; Sebastian Ulamek 12; Chris Harris 10; Simon Stead 9; Lee Richardson 9; Joe Screen 8; Adam Shields 7; Gary Havelock 6; Matej Zagar 6; Zdenek Simota 5; Sam Ermolenko 5; Henning Bager 5; Shane Parker 4; Kevin Doolan 4; Dean Barker 4. FIRST SEMI-FINAL: 1st Crump; 2nd Ulamek; 3rd Stead; 4th Screen; SECOND SEMI-FINAL: 1st Richardson; 2nd Andersen; 3rd Shields; 4th Harris. FINAL: 1st Crump; 2nd Andersen; 3rd Ulamek; 4th Richardson.

POOLE RIAS PIRATES

ADDRESS: Poole Stadium, Wimborne Road, Poole, Dorset, BH15 2BP.
PROMOTERS: Matt Ford & Mike Golding.
TRACK LENGTH: 299.1 metres.
TRACK RECORD: 57.06 seconds – Ryan Sullivan (16 June 2004).
FIRST MEETING: 26 April 1948.
YEARS OF OPERATION: 1948-51 National League Division Three; 1952-55 National League Division Two; 1956 National League Division One; 1957 Open; 1958-59 National League; 1960-63 Provincial League; 1964 Provincial League & Metropolitan League; 1965-67 British League; 1968-74 British League Division One; 1975-84 British League; 1985-90 National League; 1991-94 British League Division One; 1995-96 Premier League; 1997-2005 Elite League.

CLUB HONOURS

LEAGUE CHAMPIONS: 1951, 1952, 1955, 1961, 1962, 1969, 1989, 1990, 1994, 2003, 2004.
NATIONAL TROPHY (DIVISION TWO) WINNERS: 1952, 1955.
KNOCK-OUT CUP WINNERS: 1990, 2003, 2004.
FOUR-TEAM CHAMPIONS: 1994.
CRAVEN SHIELD WINNERS: 2001, 2002.
BRITISH LEAGUE CUP WINNERS: 2003.

RIDER ROSTER 2005

Ricky ASHWORTH; Matej FERJAN; Tobias JOHANSSON; Krzysztof KASPRZAK; Edward KENNETT; Robert KOSCIECHA; Antonio LINDBACK; Ray MORTON; Bjarne PEDERSEN; Tomas SUCHANEK; Ryan SULLIVAN; Toni SVAB; Grzegorz WALASEK.

OTHER APPEARANCES/GUESTS (official matches only):
Leigh ADAMS; Jason DOYLE; Richard HALL; Billy JANNIRO; Joonas KYLMAKORPI; Mark LORAM; Kristian LUND; Jason LYONS; Glen PHILLIPS; Adam SHIELDS; Zdenek SIMOTA; Shaun TACEY; Sebastian ULAMEK.

SKY BET ELITE LEAGUE

(*Denotes bonus-point victory)

No	DATE	OPPONENTS	H/A	RESULT	Pedersen	Kasprzak	Ferjan	Lindback	Sullivan	Morton	Kennett	Ashworth	Svab	Johansson	Suchanek	Others
1	22/3	Arena-Essex	A	L30-61	10 (5)	7+2 (5)	3 (4)	3 (4)	3 (4)	3 (4)	1+1 (4)	–				
2	25/3	Eastbourne	H	W50-44	12+1 (5)	9+2 (4)	5+1 (4)	10+1 (5)	8 (4)	2 (3)		4+2 (5)	–			
3	25/3	Eastbourne	A	W46-44*	8+1 (5)	10+1 (6)	R/R	11 (5)	6 (4)	3+1 (4)	8+3 (6)	–	–	–	–	–
4	1/4	Coventry	A	L43-47	5+3 (4)	7 (4)	8+2 (5)	7 (4)	12 (5)	3+1 (5)	–	1 (3)	–	–	–	–
5	4/4	Belle Vue	A	L37-55	4+1 (4)	9 (5)	1 (4)	4 (4)	10+2 (5)	5 (4)	–	4+2 (5)	–	–	–	–
6	6/4	Arena-Essex	H	W55-40	8+3 (4)	13 (5)	9+2 (4)	10+1 (4)	11+2 (5)	2 (4)	–	2+1 (4)	–	–	–	–
7	8/4	Peterborough	A	W50-40	10+2 (5)	10+2 (5)	8+1 (4)	7+1 (4)	7 (4)	2 (3)	–	6+1 (5)	–	–	–	–
8	11/4	Wolverhampton	A	L38-56	10+1 (5)	8 (4)	2 (4)	8 (5)	6+1 (4)	2+1 (4)	–	2+2 (4)	–	–	–	–
9	13/4	Belle Vue	H	W53-41	10+3 (5)	12+1 (5)	11 (4)	6+2 (4)	9 (4)	1+1 (3)	–	4 (5)	–	–	–	–
10	14/4	Ipswich	A	W49-44	7 (4)	5+1 (4)	5+1 (4)	10+1 (5)	10+1 (5)	7+2 (4)	5+2 (4)	–	–	–	–	–
11	27/4	Wolverhampton	H	W46-44	9+2 (5)	10 (4)	8 (4)	10+2 (5)	8 (4)	–			1 (5)			0 (3)
12	2/5	Swindon	H	W54-40	6+3 (4)	11 (5)	6 (4)	8 (4)	14 (5)	–		5+1 (4)	–			4+1 (4)
13	11/5	Coventry	H	W57-36*	9+2 (4)	15 (5)	9+2 (4)	6+1 (4)	13+1 (5)	–		5+1 (5)	–	0 (3)		–
14	12/5	Oxford	A	L41-49	10 (5)	12+1 (5)	0 (3)	7+2 (4)	6 (4)	–	6+1 (6)	–		0 (4)		–
15	18/5	Peterborough	H	W52-41*	9+1 (4)	9 (4)	5 (4)	10+3 (5)	12+1 (5)	–		4 (4)	–	3+1 (4)		–
16	1/6	Oxford	H	W54-41*	11+3 (5)	13 (5)	7 (4)	8 (4)	6+2 (4)	–		6+3 (5)	–	3 (3)		–
17	2/6	Swindon	A	D45-45*	9 (5)	7 (4)	5+3 (4)	6+3 (4)	10 (5)	–	5+1 (4)	–		3+1 (4)		–
18	4/6	Eastbourne	A	L40-46	14 (5)	5 (4)	(R/R)	6 (5)	7+1 (4)	–		4+2 (5)	–	4 (4)		–
19	6/6	Ipswich	H	W47-43*	9+1 (6)	14 (6)	10+1 (5)	7 (5)	R/R	–	6+1 (5)	–		1 (3)		–
20	20/6	Coventry	A	L44-49	7+1 (4)	8+1 (5)	8+1 (4)	4 (4)	8 (5)	–		8+1 (5)	–	1 (3)		–

No	DATE	OPPONENTS	H/A	RESULT	Pedersen	Kasprzak	Ferjan	Lindback	Sullivan	Morton	Kennett	Ashworth	Svab	Johansson	Suchanek	Others
21	22/6	Eastbourne	H	W50-40*	14 (5)	10 (5)	6+1 (4)	7+1 (4)	9+2 (4)	–	–	3 (4)	–	1 (4)	–	–
22	29/6	Oxford	H	W46-44	12+1 (5)	–	4+1 (4)	9+3 (5)	8 (4)	–	9+1 (6)	–	–	3+1 (3)	–	1+1 (3)
23	4/7	Belle Vue	A	L42-53	14 (5)	–	2 (4)	11+2 (6)	7 (4)	–	–	2 (3)	–	1+1 (4)	–	5 (4)
24	6/7	Wolverhampton	H	W52-43	11+1 (5)	12 (5)	9+1 (4)	4+1 (3)	8 (4)	–	–	8+1 (6)	–	0 (3)	–	–
25	13/7	Swindon	H	W50-40	12+1 (5)	9 (4)	12+1 (5)	7+1 (4)	8+2 (4)	–	–	2 (5)	–	0 (3)	–	–
26	20/7	Arena-Essex	H	W52-38	18 (6)	5+1 (4)	6+1 (5)	R/R	11+1 (5)	–	8+3 (5)	–	–	–	–	4 (5)
27	22/7	Arena-Essex	A	L44-51*	22+1 (7)	10 (5)	3 (4)	R/R	2 (4)	–	6 (7)	–	–	–	–	1 (3)
28	10/8	Belle Vue	H	W53-41*	14+1 (5)	8 (4)	8 (4)	6+1 (4)	9 (5)	–	7+2 (5)	–	–	–	1 (3)	–
29	11/8	Ipswich	A	L45-51	14+1 (5)	8 (5)	4 (4)	3 (4)	12 (4)	–	–	–	–	–	0 (3)	4+2 (5)
30	15/8	Peterborough	H	L44-46	9+2 (5)	–	4+1 (4)	14 (5)	3+1 (4)	–	5+1 (5)	–	–	–	2 (3)	7 (4)
31	18/8	Oxford	A	L44-46*	R/R	9+1 (6)	2+2 (4)	4+1 (5)	13 (6)	–	14 (6)	–	–	–	2 (3)	–
32	29/8	Wolverhampton	A	L42-54	12+1 (5)	3 (4)	4+2 (4)	10+1 (6)	1 (3)	–	11 (5)	–	–	–	1+1 (3)	–
33	31/8	Coventry	H	L46-47	18 (6)	9 (4)	7+1 (5)	11+1 (6)	R/R	–	–	0 (3)	–	–	1 (6)	–
34	2/9	Peterborough	A	L42-48	11 (5)	12+1 (6)	8+1 (5)	8 (5)	R/R	–	3 (6)	–	–	–	0 (3)	–
35	7/9	Ipswich	H	L44-46	10+2 (5)	5 (4)	7 (4)	11 (5)	–	–	5 (4)	–	–	–	–	6+1 (8)
36	8/9	Swindon	A	L39-53	8 (5)	9 (5)	0 (3)	10 (4)	–	–	1 (3)	–	–	–	–	11+4 (10)

NOTE: Match No. 18 originally ended in a 46-44 defeat, but was amended following a protest over the Pirates' use of rider replacement for Matej Ferjan. The points and rides have been amended accordingly.

DETAILS OF OTHER RIDERS:

Match No. 11: Kristian Lund 0 (3); Match No. 12: Richard Hall 4+1 (4); Match No. 22: Glen Phillips 1+1 (3); Match No. 23: Mark Loram 5 (4); Match No. 26: Zdenek Simota 4 (5); Match No. 27: Zdenek Simota 1 (3); Match No. 29: Shaun Tacey 4+2 (5); Match No. 30: Leigh Adams 7 (4); Match No. 35: Robert Kosciecha 5+1 (5); Jason Doyle 1 (3); Match No. 36: Robert Kosciecha 11+4 (7); Jason Doyle 0 (3).

TACTICAL SUBSTITUTE AND TACTICAL RIDES, AS INCLUDED IN THE SCORES GRID:

Match No. 1: Kasprzak 2 points (TR); Lindback 0 points (TR); Match No. 5: Sullivan 2 points (TR); Lindback 2 points (TR); Match No. 8: Kasprzak 6 points (TR); Lindback 2 points (TR); Match No. 20: Ferjan 6 points (TR); Match No. 23: Pedersen 6 points (TR); Sullivan 2 points (TR); Lindback 2 points (TS); Match No. 27: Kasprzak 6 points (TR); Pedersen 4 points (TS); Kennett 0 points (TR); Match No. 29: Pedersen 6 points (TR); Sullivan 6 points (TR); Match No. 32: Pedersen 6 points (TR); Kennett 4 points (TR); Lindback 2 points (TS); Match No. 33: Pedersen 6 points (TR); Match No. 36: Lindback 4 points (TR).

ELITE LEAGUE AVERAGES

Rider	Mts	Rds	Pts	Bon	Tot	Avge	Max
Bjarne Pedersen	35	172	362	39	401	9.33	1 full; 2 paid
Krzysztof Kasprzak	33	155	296	14	310	8.00	1 full
Ryan Sullivan	31	136	252	17	269	7.91	–
Antonio Lindback	34	154	257	29	286	7.43	–
Robert Kosciecha	2	12	16	5	21	7.00	–
Matej Ferjan	34	140	193	26	219	6.26	–
Edward Kennett	16	81	98	16	114	5.63	–
Ricky Ashworth	18	80	70	17	87	4.35	–

Ray Morton	10	38	30	6	36	3.79 –
Tobias Johansson	13	45	20	4	24	2.13 –
Tomas Suchanek	7	24	7	1	8	1.33 –
Toni Svab	1	5	1	0	1	0.80 –
Guests	10	37	27	4	31	3.35 –

(Leigh Adams [1]; Jason Doyle [2]; Richard Hall [1]; Mark Loram [1]; Kristian Lund [1]; Glen Phillips [1]; Zdenek Simota [2]; Shaun Tacey [1]).

KNOCK-OUT CUP

No	DATE	OPPONENTS	H/A	RESULT	Pedersen	Kasprzak	Ferjan	Lindback	Sullivan	Morton	Kennett	Svab
1	20/4	Swindon	H	W51-41	10+1 (5)	14+1 (5)	8+1 (4)	5 (4)	8+1 (4)	0 (1)	6 (7)	–
2	21/4	Swindon	A	L36-60	13 (5)	R/R	1+1 (3)	10 (4)	7 (6)	–	4 (6)	1 (6)

TACTICAL SUBSTITUTE AND TACTICAL RIDES, AS INCLUDED IN THE SCORES GRID:

Match No. 2: Pedersen 6 points (TR); Lindback 4 points (TR); Sullivan 2 points (TS).

OTHER MEETINGS

17 March: Air-Tek Trophy (first leg)

Swindon 53 Poole 41 (Antonio Lindback 15; Krzysztof Kasprzak 8+1; Matej Ferjan 5+1; Bjarne Pedersen 4; Ryan Sullivan 3+1; Ray Morton 3; Edward Kennett 3).

20 March: Air-Tek Trophy (second leg)

Poole 46 (Krzysztof Kasprzak 12+1; Antonio Lindback 10; Bjarne Pedersen 7+2; Matej Ferjan 7; Ryan Sullivan 6; Edward Kennett 3; Ray Morton 1) Swindon 44 – Swindon won 97-87 on aggregate.

30 March: Magnus Zetterstrom Testimonial

DJN Associates Kangaroos 40 (Leigh Adams 12; Ryan Sullivan 12; Shane Parker 6; Craig Boyce 5; Steve Johnston 5), Poole Bay Freight Euros 35 (Bjarne Pedersen 10; Piotr Protasiewicz 10; Matej Ferjan 8; Jesper B. Jensen 4; Brent Werner 3), Farson Transport Vikings 32 (Antonio Lindback 10; Magnus Zetterstrom 7; Fredrik Lindgren 7; Erik Andersson 4; Sebastian Alden 4), Travis Perkins Bulldogs 18 (David Howe 11; Chris Neath 3; Glenn Cunningham 2; Lee Richardson 1; Daniel King 1; Ben Barker 0). Zorro's Individual Challenge: FIRST SEMI-FINAL: 1st Sullivan; 2nd Lindback; 3rd Neath; 4th Protasiewicz. SECOND SEMI-FINAL: 1st Adams; 2nd Pedersen; 3rd Lindgren; 4th Howe. FINAL: 1st Sullivan; 2nd Pedersen; 3rd Adams; 4th Lindback.

15 June: International

Team Great Britain 41 (Scott Nicholls 11+1; Edward Kennett 9+1; Lee Richardson 8+1; Chris Harris 5; Simon Stead 4; David Norris 2; Ricky Ashworth 2) Australia 49 (Jason Crump 13; Leigh Adams 9+2; Davey Watt 9+2; Steve Johnston 8+2; Adam Shields 4; Jason Lyons 4; Travis McGowan 2).

21 September: Craven Shield (first leg)

Poole 58 (Bjarne Pedersen 13; Krzysztof Kasprzak 12+2; Antonio Lindback 9+1; Robert Kosciecha 8+2; Matej Ferjan 6+3; Edward Kennett 5+1; Grzegorz Walasek 5) Ipswich 33.

22 September: Craven Shield (second leg)

Ipswich 47 Poole 50 (Bjarne Pedersen 11; Edward Kennett 9+3; Robert Kosciecha 7; Matej Ferjan 6+2; Antonio Lindback 6+1; Krzysztof Kasprzak 6; Grzegorz Walasek 5+1) – Poole won 108-80 on aggregate.

POOLE: From left to right, back row: Bjarne Pedersen, Edward Kennett, Ricky Ashworth, Neil Middleditch (Team Manager), Krzysztof Kasprzak, Toni Svab, Antonio Lindback. Front, kneeling: Matej Ferjan, Ray Morton. On bike: Ryan Sullivan.

24 September: South Coast Trophy

Eastbourne (52) 2 Poole (40) 1 (Antonio Lindback 10; Billy Janniro 10; Craig Boyce 7+1; Mark Lemon 6+1; Robert Kosciecha 4+1; David Howe 2; Ricky Ashworth 1). NOTE: The meeting was split into three sections for the football-style result.

27 September: Craven Shield (first leg)

Arena-Essex 52 Poole 41 (Leigh Adams 14; Antonio Lindback 13; Krzysztof Kasprzak 7; Matej Ferjan 5+1; Ricky Ashworth 2+1; Grzegorz Walasek 0; Robert Kosciecha 0).

28 September: Craven Shield (second leg)

Poole 22 (Leigh Adams 6; Antonio Lindback 4+1; Ricky Ashworth 4+1; Grzegorz Walasek 3; Robert Kosciecha 2+1; Krzysztof Kasprzak 2; Matej Ferjan 1) Arena-Essex 14 – meeting abandoned after heat six. No result counted towards the final table.

4 October: Craven Shield semi-final (first leg at Peterborough)

Peterborough 38 Coventry 36, Poole 34 (Bjarne Pedersen 10; Adam Shields 7; Robert Kosciecha 5+2; Grzegorz Walasek 5+1; Antonio Lindback 5; Matej Ferjan 2).

5 October: Craven Shield semi-final (second leg at Poole)

Poole 38 (Grzegorz Walasek 10+1; Bjarne Pedersen 10; Antonio Lindback 8+3; Adam Shields 8; Robert Kosciecha 2+1; Matej Ferjan 0), Peterborough 35, Coventry 34.

7 October: Craven Shield semi-final (third leg at Coventry)

Poole 40 (Bjarne Pedersen 9; Mark Loram 9; Grzegorz Walasek 8; Antonio Lindback 5+2; Robert Kosciecha 5+1; Edward Kennett 4+1), Coventry 34, Peterborough 34. Aggregate result: Poole 112, Peterborough 107, Coventry 104.

22 October: Craven Shield final (first leg at Eastbourne)

Eastbourne 41, Oxford 40, Poole 27 (Bjarne Pedersen 10; Joonas Kylmakorpi 8; Jason Lyons 5; Ricky Ashworth 2+1; Robert Kosciecha 2; Glen Phillips 0).

26 October: Craven Shield final (second leg at Poole)

Oxford 39, Poole 35 (Bjarne Pedersen 10; Sebastian Ulamek 8+1; Billy Janniro 7; Grzegorz Walasek 4+2; Robert Kosciecha 3; Ricky Ashworth 3), Eastbourne 34.

28 October: Craven Shield final (third leg at Oxford)

Eastbourne 39, Oxford 36, Poole 33 (Bjarne Pedersen 12; Sebastian Ulamek 10; Billy Janniro 9; Grzegorz Walasek 1+1; Glen Phillips 1; Robert Kosciecha 0). Aggregate result: Oxford 115, Eastbourne 114, Poole 95.

INDIVIDUAL MEETING

3 August: DJ Satellites & Aerials Young Guns Championship

QUALIFYING SCORES: Matej Zagar 12; Ricky Ashworth 9; Edward Kennett 8; Ritchie Hawkins 7; Zdenek Simota 6; James Wright 6; Krzysztof Stojanowski 5; Nikolai Klindt 5; Jamie Smith 5; Jason Doyle 4; Ben Wilson 3; Richard Hall 3. RACE-OFF: 1st Simota; 2nd Kennett; 3rd Hawkins; 4th Wright. FINAL: 1st Zagar; 2nd Simota; 3rd Kennett; 4th Ashworth.

SWINDON ROBINS IN ASSOCIATION WITH TEAM PARTNERS PEBLEY BEACH & EDGE LOGISTICS LTD

ADDRESS: Swindon Stadium, Blunsdon, nr Swindon, Wiltshire, SN25 4DN.
PROMOTERS: Terry Russell & Alun Rossiter.
TRACK LENGTH: 363 metres.
TRACK RECORD: 64.46 seconds – Leigh Adams (13 May 2004).
FIRST MEETING: 23 July 1949.
YEARS OF OPERATION: 1949 Open & National League Division Three; 1950–51 National League Division Three; 1952–53 Southern League; 1954–56 National League Division Two; 1957–64 National League; 1965–67 British League; 1968–74 British League Division One; 1975–90 British League; 1991–92 British League Division One; 1993–94 British League Division Two; 1995 Premier League; 1996 Premier League & Conference League; 1997 Elite League & Amateur League; 1998 Elite League; 1999–01 Premier League; 2002 Premier League & Conference Trophy; 2003 Premier League & Conference League; 2004 Elite League & Conference League; 2005 Elite League.
NOTE: In 1997, Swindon shared their Amateur League fixtures with Reading, under the banner of 'M4 Raven Sprockets'.

CLUB HONOURS

LEAGUE CHAMPIONS: 1956, 1957, 1967.
PAIRS CHAMPIONS: 1994, 2004, 2005.
KNOCK-OUT CUP WINNERS: 2000.
YOUNG SHIELD WINNERS: 2000.
FOUR-TEAM CHAMPIONS: 2003.

RIDER ROSTER 2005

Leigh ADAMS; Sebastian ALDEN; Olly ALLEN; Tommy ALLEN; Jonas DAVIDSSON; Charlie GJEDDE; Mads KORNELIUSSEN; Peter LJUNG; Ulrich OSTERGAARD; Lee RICHARDSON; Sebastien TRESARRIEU.

OTHER APPEARANCES/GUESTS (official matches only):
Henning BAGER; Luke BOWEN; Steve BOXALL; Michael COLES; Richard HALL; Trevor HARDING; Ritchie HAWKINS; Paul HURRY; Nathan IRWIN; Niels-Kristian IVERSEN; Fredrik LINDGREN; Kauko NIEMINEN; Shaun TACEY; Mathieu TRESARRIEU.

SKY BET ELITE LEAGUE

(*Denotes bonus-point victory)

No	DATE	OPPONENTS	H/A	RESULT	Adams	Alden	Davidsson	Gjedde	Richardson	Tresarrieu	Korneliussen	O. Allen	T. Allen	Ljung	Ostergaard	Others
1	21/3	Belle Vue†	A	L32-40	8 (3)	2 (4)	5 (3)	3 (3)	8 (3)	4+1 (5)	2+1 (3)	–	–	–	–	–
2	24/3	Oxford	H	W46-43	13+1 (5)	3 (4)	5 (4)	7+2 (4)	11+1 (5)	3 (4)	–	4+1 (4)	–	–	–	–
3	25/3	Oxford	A	W49-41*	15 (5)	0 (3)	1+1 (4)	11 (5)	9 (3)	10+1 (6)	3 (4)	–	–	–	–	–
4	31/3	Wolverhampton	H	W48-42	11+1 (5)	4 (4)	3+1 (4)	15 (5)	11 (4)	3 (4)	–	1 (4)	–	–	–	–
5	12/4	Belle Vue	H	W46-44	12 (5)	3 (4)	5 (4)	10+1 (4)	9+1 (5)	2+1 (4)	5+2 (4)	–	–	–	–	–
6	14/4	Coventry	H	W49-41	14+1 (5)	2 (4)	5+2 (4)	9 (4)	11 (5)	0 (3)	8+1 (5)	–	–	–	–	–
7	25/4	Wolverhampton	A	L33-57	13 (5)	2+1 (4)	3 (4)	5 (4)	6 (5)	4 (5)	–	–	0 (3)	–	–	–
8	28/4	Eastbourne	H	W48-44	12+1 (5)	2+1 (4)	7+3 (4)	11+1 (5)	10 (4)	6+1 (5)	–	–	0 (3)	–	–	–
9	2/5	Poole	A	L40-54	14 (5)	1 (4)	3+1 (4)	12+1 (5)	3+1 (4)	–	6 (5)	–	–	–	–	1 (3)
10	5/5	Ipswich	H	W49-44	14+1 (5)	6 (4)	4 (4)	8 (4)	12 (5)	1+1 (2)	4 (6)	–	–	–	–	–
11	7/5	Eastbourne	A	L40-56	16 (5)	2+1 (4)	1+1 (4)	8 (5)	10 (4)	–	–	–	–	–	–	3 (8)
12	9/5	Peterborough	H	W46-44	15 (5)	4 (4)	3+1 (4)	6 (4)	11+2 (5)	–	7+1 (5)	–	–	–	–	0 (3)
13	12/5	Ipswich	A	L40-55	18 (5)	2 (4)	2+1 (4)	11 (5)	3 (4)	–	1 (4)	–	3 (4)	–	–	–
14	19/5	Arena-Essex	A	W53-38	14+1 (5)	1 (4)	6 (5)	11 (5)	13+1 (5)	R/R	8+1 (6)	–	–	–	–	–
15	30/5	Coventry	A	L40-54	12+1 (5)	3+1 (5)	2 (5)	7 (4)	13 (6)	R/R	3+2 (5)	–	–	–	–	–
16	2/6	Poole	H	D45-45	12+2 (5)	5 (6)	2 (5)	10+1 (5)	15 (5)	R/R	–	–	1 (4)	–	–	–
17	16/6	Belle Vue	H	W53-39	14+1 (5)	7+1 (6)	9+1 (5)	16+1 (6)	5 (4)	R/R	–	2+2 (4)	–	–	–	–
18	20/6	Belle Vue	A	L41-52*	5 (4)	1 (3)	5 (4)	12 (5)	10 (5)	3+1 (4)	–	5+1 (5)	–	–	–	–
19	23/6	Wolverhampton	H	W48-42	8+3 (5)	5 (4)	6 (4)	14 (5)	10 (4)	4 (4)	1 (4)	–	–	–	–	–
20	30/6	Ipswich	H	W52-41	12+1 (5)	2+1 (4)	2 (4)	10+1 (4)	14+1 (5)	6+2 (4)	–	6 (4)	–	–	–	–
21	6/7	Arena-Essex	A	L42-53*	15 (5)	5+1 (5)	1 (3)	7+1 (5)	8 (4)	2 (4)	4 (4)	–	–	–	–	–
22	7/7	Oxford	H	W54-38	10+1 (4)	9 (6)	5+3 (4)	11 (5)	15 (5)	1+1 (3)	–	3+2 (4)	–	–	–	–
23	11/7	Coventry	A	L45-51	3 (2)	6+1 (6)	2+1 (4)	15+1 (5)	14 (5)	4+1 (4)	–	1 (4)	–	–	–	–
24	13/7	Poole	A	L40-50	–	8+1 (5)	10+3 (5)	8 (5)	9+1 (5)	0 (3)	1 (3)	–	–	–	–	4 (4)
25	14/7	Arena-Essex	H	W58-35	13+1 (5)	5 (4)	10+1 (4)	12+1 (5)	7+1 (4)	6 (4)	5 (4)	–	–	–	–	–
26	18/7	Ipswich♦	A	D42-42*	9+1 (4)	9+2 (6)	4+3 (5)	6 (4)	10 (4)	4+3 (5)	R/R	–	–	–	–	–
27	21/7	Eastbourne	H	L44-46	13+1 (5)	3 (5)	6 (5)	10 (4)	11 (5)	–	–	–	1 (3)	0 (3)	–	–
28	30/7	Eastbourne	A	L39-55	15 (5)	4 (6)	0 (4)	11 (6)	7 (3)	–	–	–	R/R	–	–	2+2 (5)
29	8/8	Wolverhampton	A	L40-53	14 (5)	2 (5)	5+1 (4)	7+1 (4)	9+1 (5)	–	–	–	0 (3)	3 (4)	–	–
30	11/8	Peterborough	H	W47-43	13+2 (5)	5+1 (4)	3 (4)	9+1 (4)	10 (5)	–	2+1 (4)	–	–	5 (4)	–	–
31	17/8	Peterborough	A	L41-55	14 (5)	4+1 (5)	0 (4)	8 (4)	14 (5)	–	–	–	0 (4)	1 (3)	–	–
32	31/8	Arena-Essex	A	L42-52*	18 (5)	–	5+1 (5)	–	13+1 (5)	–	2 (4)	–	–	R/R	–	4 (11)
33	4/9	Coventry	H	W47-43	–	–	11+3 (5)	R/R	13 (6)	–	3+1 (4)	–	–	7 (5)	4+1 (5)	9+3 (5)
34	5/9	Peterborough	A	L43-53	18 (5)	–	1 (5)	R/R	16+2 (6)	–	0 (3)	–	–	4 (5)	4 (6)	–
35	8/9	Poole	H	W53-39*	12+1 (5)	–	8 (5)	R/R	14+1 (6)	–	7 (5)	–	–	5+1 (4)	7 (5)	–
36	20/10	Oxford	A	L42-51*	14 (5)	–	0 (4)	R/R	10+3 (6)	–	6 (4)	–	4+3 (6)	–	–	8 (5)

†Meeting abandoned after heat twelve, with the result permitted to stand.   ♦Meeting abandoned after heat fourteen, with the result permitted to stand.

DETAILS OF OTHER RIDERS:

Match No. 9: Trevor Harding 1 (3); Match No. 11: Mathieu Tresarrieu 3 (5); Nathan Irwin 0 (3); Match No. 12: Michael Coles 0 (3); Match No. 24: Niels-Kristian Iversen 4 (4); Match No. 28: Ritchie Hawkins 2+2 (6); Match No. 32: Steve Boxall 3 (6); Luke Bowen 1 (5); Match No. 33: Fredrik Lindgren 9+3 (5); Match No. 36: Paul Hurry 8 (5).

TACTICAL RIDES, AS INCLUDED IN THE SCORES GRID:

Match No. 7: Adams 2 points (TR); Richardson 0 points (TR); Match No. 9: Adams 4 points (TR); Gjedde 4 points (TR); Match No. 11: Richardson 6 points (TR); Adams 6 points (TR); Match No. 13: Adams 6 points (TR); Gjedde 4 points (TR); Match No. 15: Adams 4 points (TR); Richardson 4 points (TR); Match No. 18: Gjedde 6 points (TR); Adams 0 points (TR); Match No. 21: Adams 6 points (TR); Richardson 4 points (TR); Match No. 23: Richardson 6 points (TR); Gjedde 6 points (TR); Match No. 28: Gjedde 4 points (TR); Adams 4 points (TR); Match No. 29: Adams 4 points (TR); Gjedde 2 points (TR); Match No. 31: Richardson 6 points (TR); Adams 6 points (TR); Match No. 32: Adams 6 points (TR); Richardson 2 points (TR); Match No. 34: Richardson 6 points (TR); Adams 6 points (TR); Match No. 36: Adams 6 points (TR).

ELITE LEAGUE AVERAGES

Rider	Mts	Rds	Pts	Bon	Tot	Avge	Max
Leigh Adams	34	162	403	21	424	10.47	5 full; 5 paid
Lee Richardson	36	169	357	17	374	8.85	2 full; 1 paid
Charlie Gjedde	31	142	287	13	300	8.45	1 full
Jonas Davidsson	36	153	150	28	178	4.65	–
Sebastien Tresarrieu	18	73	63	13	76	4.16	–
Mads Korneliussen	19	82	76	9	85	4.15	–
Ulrich Ostergaard	3	16	15	1	16	4.00	–
Olly Allen	8	33	24	7	31	3.76	–
Peter Ljung	7	28	25	1	26	3.71	–
Sebastian Alden	31	140	117	13	130	3.71	–
Tommy Allen	8	30	9	3	12	1.60	–
Guests	10	45	31	5	36	3.20	–

(Luke Bowen [1]; Steve Boxall [1]; Michael Coles [1]; Trevor Harding [1]; Ritchie Hawkins [1]; Paul Hurry [1]; Nathan Irwin [1]; Niels-Kristian Iversen [1]; Fredrik Lindgren [1]; Mathieu Tresarrieu [1]).

KNOCK-OUT CUP

(*Denotes aggregate victory)

No	DATE	OPPONENTS	H/A	RESULT	Adams	Alden	Davidsson	Gjedde	Richardson	Korneliussen	Tresarrieu	O. Allen	Ljung	T. Allen	Others
1	20/4	Poole	A	L41-51	9+1 (5)	0 (3)	3+1 (4)	6 (4)	9 (5)	11+1 (6)	3+2 (4)	–	–	–	–
2	21/4	Poole	H	W60-36*	15 (5)	7+1 (4)	6+1 (4)	10+1 (4)	12+2 (5)	8+1 (4)	2+1 (4)	–	–	–	–
3	20/5	Coventry	A	L41-51	11 (5)	–	–	7 (4)	16+1 (6)	–	R/R	–	–	–	7+2 (15)
4	12/6	Coventry	H	W55-39*	14+1 (5)	11+2 (6)	7+1 (4)	9+1 (4)	11+2 (5)	1 (4)	2 (3)	–	–	–	–
5	27/7	Belle Vue	A	L32-61	14 (5)	0 (4)	2 (5)	9+1 (5)	4 (4)	–	–	–	2+1 (4)	1+1 (3)	–
6	18/8	Belle Vue†	H	W37-35	8 (3)	8 (4)	1+1 (4)	7+1 (3)	8 (3)	–	–	–	5+1 (4)	0 (3)	–

†Meeting abandoned after heat twelve, with the result permitted to stand.

DETAILS OF OTHER RIDERS:

Match No. 3: Mathieu Tresarrieu 4+2 (7); Shaun Tacey 3 (5); Richard Hall 0 (3).

TACTICAL RIDES, AS INCLUDED IN THE SCORES GRID:

Match No. 1: Korneliussen 4 points (TR); Match No. 3: Richardson 4 points (TR); Match No. 5: Adams 4 points (TR); Richardson 2 points (TR).

OTHER MEETINGS

17 March: Air-Tek Trophy (first leg)

Swindon 53 (Leigh Adams 11+1; Charlie Gjedde 9; Jonas Davidsson 8+3; Lee Richardson 8; Olly Allen 7+3; Sebastian Alden 7+1; Sebastien Tresarrieu 3) Poole 41.

20 March: Air-Tek Trophy (second leg)

Poole 46 Swindon 44 (Leigh Adams 11; Lee Richardson 9+1; Sebastien Tresarrieu 7+2; Charlie Gjedde 6+1; Jonas Davidsson 5; Olly Allen 4+1; Sebastian Alden 2) – Swindon won 97-87 on aggregate.

4 April: Elite League

Peterborough 10 Swindon 8 (Leigh Adams 3; Sebastien Tresarrieu 3; Charlie Gjedde 1; Olly Allen 1; Sebastian Alden 0; Jonas Davidsson 0; Lee Richardson DNR – meeting abandoned after heat three.

12 September: Craven Shield (first leg)

Wolverhampton 58 Swindon 36 (Leigh Adams 15; Lee Richardson 11+3; Ulrich Ostergaard 5; Kauko Nieminen 4; Mads Korneliussen 1; Jonas Davidsson 0; Charlie Gjedde R/R).

15 September: Craven Shield (first leg)

Oxford 41 Swindon 34 (Leigh Adams 11; Lee Richardson 9; Ulrich Ostergaard 8+1; Mads Korneliussen 4; Peter Ljung 2; Henning Bager 0; Charlie Gjedde R/R) – meeting abandoned after heat twelve, with the result permitted to stand.

22 September: Craven Shield (second leg)

Swindon 54 (Jonas Davidsson 13+2; Leigh Adams 12+2; Lee Richardson 10+1; Peter Ljung 9; Mads Korneliussen 8; Ulrich Ostergaard 2; Charlie Gjedde R/R) Wolverhampton 40 – Wolverhampton won 98-90 on aggregate.

29 September: Craven Shield (second leg)

Swindon 44 (Lee Richardson 14+1; Leigh Adams 13+1; Ulrich Ostergaard 7+2; Jonas Davidsson 6+1; Henning Bager 3; Mads Korneliussen 1; Charlie Gjedde R/R) Oxford 46 – Oxford won 87-78 on aggregate.

INDIVIDUAL MEETING

9 October: The Wellie (Malcolm Holloway) Farewell

THE FINAL RIDE: 1st Malcolm Holloway; 2nd Ashley Holloway; 3rd Richard Holloway; 4th Wayne Holloway.

RIDERS ELIMINATED FROM KNOCK-OUT EVENT: Ashley Holloway; Mikael Teurnberg; Chris Neath; Matt Bates; Billy Legg, Danny Warwick; Patrick Hougaard; Neil Collins; Shawn McConnell; Emil Kramer; Edward Kennett; Richard Hellsen; Joe Screen, Paul Fry; Simon Stead; Ronnie Correy.

FIRST SEMI-FINAL: 1st Niels-Kristian Iversen; 2nd Leigh Adams; 3rd Glenn Cunningham; 4th Mads Korneliussen; SECOND-SEMI-FINAL: 1st Brian Karger; 2nd Hans N. Andersen; 3rd Steve Johnston; 4th Chris Harris. FINAL: 1st Adams; 2nd Andersen; 3rd Karger; 4th Iversen.

SWINDON: From left to right, back row: Alun Rossiter (Promoter/Team Manager), Tommy Allen, Sebastian Alden, Peter Ljung, Charlie Gjedde. Front, kneeling: Jonas Davidsson, Lee Richardson. On bike: Leigh Adams.

WOLVERHAMPTON PARRYS INTERNATIONAL WOLVES

ADDRESS: Ladbroke Stadium, Sutherland Avenue, Wolverhampton, West Midlands, WV2 2JJ.
PROMOTERS: Chris Van Straaten, John Woolridge & Peter Adams.
TRACK LENGTH: 264 metres.
TRACK RECORD: 55.49 seconds – Mikael Max (18 July 2005).
FIRST MEETING: 30 May 1928.
YEARS OF OPERATION: 1928-30 Open; 1950 Open; 1951 National League Division
Three; 1952 Southern League; 1953-54 National League Division Two; 1961-64
Provincial League; 1965-67 British League; 1968-74 British League Division One;
1975-80 British League; 1981 National League; 1984-90 British League; 1991-94 British
League Division One; 1995-96 Premier League; 1997 Elite League & Amateur League;
1998-2001 Elite League; 2002 Elite League & Conference Trophy; 2003 Elite League &
Conference League; 2004-05 Elite League.

NOTE: In 1997, Wolverhampton shared their Amateur League fixtures with Long Eaton, under the banner of 'Shuttle Cubs'.

CLUB HONOURS

LEAGUE CHAMPIONS: 1963, 1991, 1996, 2002.
PREMIERSHIP WINNERS: 1992, 1997.
GOLD CUP WINNERS: 1992.
KNOCK-OUT CUP WINNERS: 1996.

RIDER ROSTER 2005

Ronnie CORREY; James GRIEVES; David HOWE; Steve JOHNSTON; Magnus KARLSSON;
Fredrik LINDGREN; Mikael MAX; Krzysztof PECYNA; Adam SKORNICKI.

OTHER APPEARANCES/GUESTS (official matches only):
Tony ATKIN; Jason CRUMP; Sam ERMOLENKO; Charlie GJEDDE; Greg HANCOCK; Jack
HARGREAVES; Peter KARLSSON; Mark LORAM; Scott NICHOLLS; Lee RICHARDSON;
George STANCL; Simon STEAD; Sebastian ULAMEK.

SKY BET ELITE LEAGUE

(*Denotes bonus-point victory)

No	DATE	OPPONENTS	H/A	RESULT	Max	Correy	Lindgren	Johnston	Howe	Karlsson	Pecyna	Skornicki	Grieves	Others
1	25/3	Belle Vue	A	L42-53	12 (5)	4+1 (4)	4 (4)	9+1 (4)	8 (5)	2+1 (4)	3+1 (4)	–	–	–
2	28/3	Belle Vue	H	L40-50	9 (5)	4+4 (4)	7+1 (5)	6 (4)	5 (4)	5+1 (4)	4 (4)	–	–	–
3	31/3	Swindon	A	L42-48	10 (5)	4+3 (4)	5 (4)	5 (4)	3+1 (3)	9+3 (6)	6+1 (4)	–	–	–
4	11/4	Poole	H	W56-38	11+2 (5)	9+2 (4)	6+1 (4)	12 (5)	7 (4)	8+2 (4)	3 (4)	–	–	–
5	13/4	Arena-Essex	A	L41-52	7+1 (4)	2 (4)	9+1 (5)	9 (5)	10 (4)	4 (5)	0 (3)	–	–	–

No	DATE	OPPONENTS	H/A	RESULT	Max	Correy	Lindgren	Johnston	Howe	Karlsson	Pecyna	Skornicki	Grieves	Others
6	18/4	Arena-Essex	H	W49-47	13 (5)	6+1 (4)	8+1 (5)	8 (4)	6 (4)	3+1 (4)	5+2 (4)	–	–	–
7	23/4	Eastbourne	A	D45-45	9 (5)	5+1 (4)	11 (5)	4+3 (4)	4+1 (4)	10 (5)	2+1 (3)	–	–	–
8	25/4	Swindon	H	W57-33*	12 (5)	7+2 (4)	11+1 (4)	9+4 (5)	4+1 (4)	7+1 (4)	7 (4)	–	–	–
9	27/4	Poole	A	L44-46*	9+2 (5)	5+2 (4)	9+1 (5)	2+1 (4)	4+1 (3)	5+1 (4)	10 (5)	–	–	–
10	2/5	Eastbourne	H	L46-47	–	9 (4)	15+3 (6)	8+2 (4)	10+1 (5)	–	3 (6)	–	–	1 (5)
11	9/5	Coventry	H	W48-45	12 (5)	8+2 (4)	9+2 (5)	9 (4)	6 (4)	4+1 (5)	0 (3)	–	–	–
12	23/5	Peterborough	H	W55-40	10+1 (5)	6+2 (3)	12 (5)	7+2 (4)	9 (4)	6 (5)	5+1 (4)	–	–	–
13	27/5	Peterborough	A	L43-47*	9 (5)	4+2 (4)	13+1 (5)	6 (4)	5 (4)	2 (4)	4+1 (4)	–	–	–
14	30/5	Arena-Essex	H	W63-31	15 (5)	9+3 (5)	11 (5)	10+4 (6)	R/R	12+3 (5)	6+1 (4)	–	–	–
15	2/6	Oxford	A	L45-50	5+1 (5)	4+1 (4)	14+1 (6)	3+1 (5)	R/R	7 (5)	12+1 (6)	–	–	–
16	6/6	Oxford	H	W55-38*	14 (5)	7+3 (5)	7+2 (5)	10+2 (5)	R/R	3+2 (4)	14 (6)	–	–	–
17	20/6	Peterborough	H	W55-41	11+1 (5)	4+1 (4)	5 (4)	5+2 (4)	–	7+1 (4)	11+1 (4)	12+1 (5)	–	–
18	23/6	Swindon	A	L42-48	R/R	0 (3)	9 (6)	7+3 (5)	–	10+1 (6)	2 (4)	14+1 (6)	–	–
19	27/6	Ipswich	H	W47-43	14 (5)	5+2 (4)	7 (5)	5+2 (4)	–	2+1 (3)	8+1 (5)	6+1 (4)	–	–
20	29/6	Arena-Essex	A	W60-36*	10 (4)	6+4 (4)	9+1 (5)	7+4 (4)	–	6+1 (4)	10+1 (4)	12+1 (5)	–	–
21	4/7	Coventry	H	L38-55	15 (5)	2+1 (4)	7 (5)	3 (4)	–	2 (3)	7+2 (5)	2+1 (4)	–	–
22	6/7	Poole	A	L43-52	13 (5)	2+2 (4)	6+2 (5)	2+1 (4)	–	6 (5)	5+1 (3)	9 (4)	–	–
23	18/7	Eastbourne	H	W49-41	12 (5)	2+2 (4)	7+2 (5)	4+1 (4)	10 (4)	6+2 (4)	8+1 (5)	–	–	–
24	20/7	Belle Vue	A	L38-58	–	2+1 (4)	10 (5)	2+1 (4)	13 (4)	–	1 (4)	–	0 (3)	10+1 (6)
25	22/7	Coventry	A	L39-55	–	0 (3)	4 (4)	7+1 (5)	3+1 (4)	–	1 (4)	–	8 (5)	16 (5)
26	25/7	Belle Vue	H	L39-51	–	4+2 (4)	6 (5)	6+3 (5)	8 (4)	–	5+1 (5)	–	4+2 (3)	6 (4)
27	8/8	Swindon	H	W53-40*	–	11+2 (5)	8 (4)	4+1 (4)	14 (5)	2 (3)	3+1 (4)	–	–	11 (5)
28	10/8	Peterborough	A	L39-51*	–	7+2 (7)	7 (5)	9 (5)	1+1 (1)	2+1 (4)	3+1 (4)	–	–	10 (4)
29	12/8	Eastbourne	A	L41-49*	–	6+2 (4)	6 (5)	5+1 (4)	5 (4)	2 (3)	4 (4)	–	–	13 (6)
30	15/8	Oxford	H	D45-45	–	11+1 (6)	5 (4)	3+1 (4)	12+1 (5)	5+1 (3)	3+2 (4)	–	–	6 (4)
31	18/8	Ipswich	A	L44-51	–	5+1 (4)	12+1 (5)	12 (5)	1 (4)	3 (4)	4+1 (4)	–	–	7+1 (4)
32	22/8	Ipswich	H	W59-34	–	6+1 (4)	11+1 (5)	9+2 (4)	14+1 (5)	4+1 (4)	4 (4)	–	–	11 (4)
33	29/8	Poole	H	W54-42*	–	9+2 (5)	12+1 (5)	5+1 (4)	10+1 (4)	6 (4)	0 (3)	–	–	12+2 (5)
34	2/9	Coventry	A	L41-48	–	0 (3)	15 (5)	3 (4)	6 (4)	1 (3)	4 (6)	–	–	12 (5)
35	3/9	Ipswich	A	L42-50*	–	5+1 (4)	13 (5)	4+1 (4)	7+1 (5)	3+1 (4)	–	–	–	10+4 (8)
36	28/10	Oxford	A	L43-47	–	1 (3)	R/R	–	–	5+2 (5)	10+1 (6)	–	–	–

DETAILS OF OTHER RIDERS:

Match No. 10: Tony Atkin 1 (3); Jack Hargreaves 0 (2); Match No. 24: Scott Nicholls 10+1 (6); Match No. 25: Lee Richardson 16 (5); Match No. 26: Charlie Gjedde 6 (4); Match No. 27: Scott Nicholls 11 (5); Match No. 28: Scott Nicholls 10 (4); Match No. 29: Peter Karlsson 13 (6); Match No. 30: Mark Loram 6 (4); Match No. 31: Mark Loram 7+1 (4); Match No. 32: Scott Nicholls 11 (4); Match No. 33: Greg Hancock 12+2 (5); Match No. 34: Jason Crump 12 (5); Match No. 35: Simon Stead 6 (4); George Stancl 4+4 (4); Match No. 36: Sebastian Ulamek 15 (6); Adam Skornicki 7+1 (5); Sam Ermolenko 5+1 (4).

TACTICAL SUBSTITUTE AND TACTICAL RIDES, AS INCLUDED IN THE SCORES GRID:

Match No. 1: Johnston 6 points (TR); Max 4 points (TR); Match No. 5: Howe 6 points (TR); Match No. 10: Lindgren 6 points (TR); Match No. 15: Lindgren 6 points (TR); Correy 4 points (TR); Match No. 21: Max 6 points (TR); Lindgren 0 points (TR); Match No. 22: Skornicki 6 points (TR); Max 4 points (TR); Match No. 24: Howe 6 points (TR); Lindgren 4 points (TR); Nicholls 2 points (TS); Match No. 25: Lindgren 4 points (TR); Richardson 4 points (TR); Match No. 29: P. Karlsson 0 points (TS); Match No. 31: Lindgren 6 points (TR); Johnston 4 points (TR); Match No. 35: Lindgren 4 points (TR).

ELITE LEAGUE AVERAGES

Rider	Mts	Rds	Pts	Bon	Tot	Avge	Max
Mikael Max	21	103	225	8	233	9.05	1 full
Adam Skornicki	6	28	52	5	57	8.14	–
Fredrik Lindgren	35	170	295	23	318	7.48	1 full; 1 paid
David Howe	26	105	179	11	190	7.24	1 paid
Steve Johnston	35	152	214	45	259	6.82	–
Ronnie Correy	36	148	179	56	235	6.35	–
Magnus Karlsson	32	134	159	28	187	5.58	1 paid
Krzysztof Pecyna	35	150	177	23	200	5.33	1 paid
James Grieves	3	11	12	2	14	5.09	–
Guests	18	80	149	10	159	7.95	–

(Tony Atkin [1]; Jason Crump [1]; Sam Erm olenko [1]; Charlie Gjedde [1]; Greg Hancock [1]; Jack Hargreaves [1]; Peter Karlsson [1]; Mark Loram [2]; Scott Nicholls [4]; Lee Richardson [1]; Adam Skornicki [1]; George Stancl [1]; Simon Stead [1]; Sebastian Ulamek [1]).

KNOCK-OUT CUP

No	DATE	OPPONENTS	H/A	RESULT	Max	Correy	Lindgren	Johnston	Howe	Karlsson	Pecyna
1	4/4	Ipswich	H	L37-53	8+1 (5)	7+2 (4)	9 (5)	3+1 (4)	5 (4)	4 (5)	1+1 (3)
2	7/4	Ipswich	A	L40-55	8 (4)	3+1 (4)	11 (5)	3 (4)	4 (5)	10+1 (5)	1+1 (3)

TACTICAL RIDES, AS INCLUDED IN THE SCORES GRID:

Match No. 2: Max 6 points (TR); Lindgren 6 points (TR).

OTHER MEETINGS

17 March: Air-Tek Trophy (first leg)

Oxford 47 Wolverhampton 41 (Mikael Max 8; David Howe 8; Steve Johnston 7; Fredrik Lindgren 6+2; Magnus Karlsson 6+2; Ronnie Correy 4+2; Krzysztof Pecyna 2).

21 March: Air-Tek Trophy (second leg)

Wolverhampton 55 (Mikael Max 11; Fredrik Lindgren 10+1; David Howe 8+1; Ronnie Correy 7+3; Steve Johnston 7+2; Krzysztof Pecyna 6+1; Magnus Karlsson 6) Oxford 38 – Wolverhampton won 96-85 on aggregate.

12 September: Craven Shield (first leg)

Wolverhampton 58 (David Howe 11+1; Fredrik Lindgren 10+1; Ronnie Correy 9+2; Steve Johnston 8+1; Adam Skornicki 7+1; Magnus Karlsson 7+1; James Grieves 6+2) Swindon 36.

19 September: Craven Shield (first leg)

Oxford 48 Wolverhampton 42 (Peter Karlsson 11+1; David Howe 8; Fredrik Lindgren 7; Steve Johnston 5+2; Magnus Karlsson 5; Ronnie Correy 3+1; Krzysztof Pecyna 3).

22 September: Craven Shield (second leg)

Swindon 54 Wolverhampton 40 (Fredrik Lindgren 9; David Howe 8+1; Peter Karlsson 8; Magnus

WOLVERHAMPTON: From left to right: Ronnie Correy, David Howe, Krzysztof Pecyna, Steve Johnston (on bike), Mikael Max, Fredrik Lindgren, Magnus Karlsson.

Karlsson 5+1; Ronnie Correy 4+2; Steve Johnston 3+1; Krzysztof Pecyna 3) – Wolverhampton won 98-90 on aggregate.

26 September: Craven Shield (second leg)

Wolverhampton 51 (Peter Karlsson 12; Ronnie Correy 10+1; David Howe 9; Steve Johnston 7; Magnus Karlsson 5; Fredrik Lindgren 5; Krzysztof Pecyna 3+1) Oxford 45 – Aggregate score 93-93, with Oxford winning the bonus point run-off.

14 October: Midland Cup (first leg)

Coventry 66 Wolverhampton 33 (Billy Hamill 15; David Howe 6; Krzysztof Pecyna 4; Fredrik Lindgren 2; Ronnie Correy 2; Steve Johnston 2; Magnus Karlsson 2).

17 October: Midland Cup (second leg)

Wolverhampton 45 (Leigh Adams 13+1; Fredrik Lindgren 10+1; Krzysztof Pecyna 10+1; Steve Johnston 6+1; Ronnie Correy 5; Magnus Karlsson 1; David Howe 0) Coventry 51 – Coventry won 117-78 on aggregate.

INDIVIDUAL MEETINGS

13 June: Midland Open Championship

QUALIFYING SCORES: Mikael Max 11; Billy Hamill 11; Charlie Gjedde 10; Fredrik Lindgren 10; Billy Janniro 9; Steve Johnston 8; Daniel Nermark 7; James Grieves 7; Ronnie Correy 5; Magnus Karlsson 4; Theo Pijper 4; Magnus Zetterstrom 3; Adam Skornicki 3; Chris Neath 2; Robbie Kessler 1; Eric Andersson 1; Jack Hargreaves (Res) 0. SEMI-FINAL: 1st Gjedde; 2nd Lindgren; 3rd Johnston; 4th Janniro. FINAL (6 laps): 1st Gjedde; 2nd Max; 3rd Lindgren; 4th Hamill.

5 September: British Under-18 Championship

1st William Lawson 15; 2nd Lewis Bridger 14; 3rd Jack Hargreaves 12; Adam Roynon 10; Chris Johnson 9; Sean Stoddart 9; Simon Lambert 8; Ben Taylor 8; Lee Smart 8; Barry Burchatt 5; Josh Auty 5; Charles Wright 3; Kriss Irving 3; James Purchase (Res) 3; Danny Betson 2; Jamie Courtney 2; Shane Waldron 1; Gary Cottham (Res) 1.

10 October: Banks's Olympique

1st Fredrik Lindgren (after run-off) 12; 2nd Hans N. Andersen 12; 3rd Travis McGowan (after run-off) 11; Scott Nicholls 11; David Howe 10; Adam Skornicki 9; Krzysztof Pecyna 7; Christian Hefenbrock 7; Peter Karlsson 6; Ronnie Correy 6; Daniel Nermark 6; Sam Ermolenko 6; Magnus Karlsson 6; Patrick Hougaard 4; Steve Johnston 3; Luke Priest 2; Jack Hargreaves (Res) 1.

PREMIER LEAGUE 2005

PREMIER LEAGUE TABLE

	Mts	Won	Drn	Lst	For	Agn	Pts	Bon	Tot
Rye House	28	20	1	7	1,448	1,133	41	12	53
Berwick	28	19	0	9	1,371	1,208	38	11	49
Sheffield	28	16	0	12	1,361	1,249	32	11	43
King's Lynn	27	17	0	10	1,305	1,185	34	7	41
Edinburgh	28	15	1	12	1,323	1,263	31	10	41
Isle of Wight	28	15	1	12	1,363	1,237	31	8	39
Workington	28	14	2	12	1,282	1,287	30	7	37
Newcastle	28	14	2	12	1,251	1,338	30	5	35
Exeter	28	13	0	15	1,262.5	1,342.5	26	6	32
Reading	28	12	0	16	1,281	1,310	24	4	28
Somerset	28	11	0	17	1,250	1,317	22	6	28
Glasgow	27	11	0	16	1,243	1,241	22	5	27
Hull	26	11	0	15	1,129.5	1,257.5	22	5	27
Stoke	28	11	0	17	1,230	1,347	22	4	26
Newport	28	5	1	22	1,097	1,482	11	2	13

Two matches were not ridden: Hull *v.* Glasgow; Hull *v.* King's Lynn.

YOUNG SHIELD

QUARTER-FINALS

Rye House	62	Isle of Wight	30	
Isle of Wight	54	Rye House	41	(Rye House won 103-84 on aggregate)
Berwick	60	Newcastle	35	
Newcastle	48	Berwick	42	(Berwick won 102-83 on aggregate)
Sheffield	57	Edinburgh	37	
Edinburgh	54	Sheffield	38	(Sheffield won 95-91 on aggregate)
Workington	50	King's Lynn	42	
King's Lynn	52	Workington	42	(King's Lynn won 94-92 on aggregate)

SEMI-FINALS

Berwick	49	King's Lynn	48	
King's Lynn	57	Berwick	35	(King's Lynn won 105-84 on aggregate)
Sheffield	59	Rye House	36	
Rye House	62	Sheffield	30	(Rye House won 98-89 on aggregate)

FINAL

King's Lynn	59	Rye House	34	
Rye House	51	King's Lynn	42	(King's Lynn won 101-85 on aggregate)

PREMIER TROPHY

PREMIER TROPHY (SOUTH) TABLE

	Mts	Won	Drn	Lst	For	Agn	Pts	Bon	Tot
Rye House	12	10	0	2	610	494	20	6	26
Exeter	12	6	0	6	566	541	12	4	16
King's Lynn	12	7	0	5	549	570	14	2	16
Isle of Wight	12	6	0	6	537	561	12	2	14
Newport	12	5	0	7	540	558	10	3	13
Somerset	12	4	0	8	536	575	8	2	10
Reading	12	4	0	8	532	571	8	2	10

PREMIER TROPHY (NORTH) TABLE

	Mts	Won	Drn	Lst	For	Agn	Pts	Bon	Tot
Workington	14	9	0	5	680	611	18	5	23
Sheffield	14	7	0	7	687	623	14	6	20
Edinburgh	14	7	1	6	664	633	15	5	20
Hull	14	8	0	6	645	661	16	3	19
Stoke	14	6	1	7	634	661	13	3	16
Berwick	14	6	2	6	636	669	14	1	15
Newcastle	14	6	0	8	616	676	12	2	14
Glasgow	14	3	4	7	629	657	10	3	13

SEMI-FINALS

Rye House	66	Sheffield	26	
Sheffield	50	Rye House	39	(Rye House won 105-76 on aggregate)

Workington	60	Exeter	31	
Exeter	56	Workington	40	(Workington won 100-87 on aggregate)

FINAL

Workington	44	Rye House	46	
Rye House	61	Workington	32	(Rye House won 107-76 on aggregate)

KNOCK-OUT CUP

ROUND ONE

Sheffield	51	Isle of Wight	39	
Isle of Wight	55	Sheffield	34	(Isle of Wight won 94-85 on aggregate)

Glasgow	56	Hull	34	
Hull	44	Glasgow	46	(Glasgow won 102-78 on aggregate)
Edinburgh	47	Rye House	43	
Rye House	57	Edinburgh	33	(Rye House won 100-80 on aggregate)
Somerset	44	Workington	46	
Workington	47	Somerset	43	(Workington won 93-87 on aggregate)
Newcastle	53	King's Lynn	36	
King's Lynn	58	Newcastle	32	(King's Lynn won 94-85 on aggregate)
Reading	54	Newport	36	
Newport	39	Reading	51	(Reading won 105-75 on aggregate)
Stoke	42	Berwick	48	
Berwick	56	Stoke	34	(Berwick won 104-76 on aggregate)

QUARTER-FINALS

Berwick	49	Workington	41	
Workington	42	Berwick	48	(Berwick won 97-83 on aggregate)
Rye House	48	Glasgow	42	
Glasgow	33	Rye House	57	(Rye House won 105-75 on aggregate)
Exeter	45	King's Lynn	45	
King's Lynn	63	Exeter	27	(King's Lynn won 108-72 on aggregate)
Isle of Wight	46	Reading	44	
Reading	51	Isle of Wight	33	(Reading won 95-79 on aggregate)

SEMI-FINALS

Berwick	45	King's Lynn	44	
King's Lynn	56	Berwick	34	(King's Lynn won 100-79 on aggregate)
Reading	43	Rye House	47	
Rye House	65	Reading	25	(Rye House won 112-68 on aggregate)

FINAL

King's Lynn	63	Rye House	27	
Rye House	56	King's Lynn	34	(King's Lynn won 97-83 on aggregate)

BERWICK KIRKLAND CARPETS BANDITS

ADDRESS: Shielfield Park, Tweedmouth, Berwick-upon-Tweed, Northumberland, TD15 2EF.
PROMOTER: Peter Waite.
TRACK LENGTH: 368 metres.
TRACK RECORD: 64.2 seconds – Sean Wilson (21 August 1999).
FIRST MEETING: 18 May 1968.
YEARS OF OPERATION: 1968-74 British League Division Two; 1975-80 National League;
1995 Demonstration; 1996 Conference League; 1997 Premier League & Amateur League;
1998-2005 Premier League.

PREVIOUS VENUE: Berrington Lough Stadium, nr Ancroft, Northumberland.
YEARS OF OPERATION: 1982-90 National League; 1991 British League Division One;
1992 British League Division Two; 1993 Open; 1994 British League Division Three; 1995
Academy League.

CLUB HONOURS

KNOCK-OUT CUP WINNERS: 1980, 1989, 1995.
GOLD CUP WINNERS: 1991.
LEAGUE CHAMPIONS: 1994, 1995.
FOUR-TEAM CHAMPIONS: 2002.

RIDER ROSTER 2005

Simon CARTWRIGHT; Piotr DYM; Joachim KUGELMANN; Tom P. MADSEN; Michal
MAKOVSKY; Adam PIETRASZKO; Adrian RYMEL; Chris SCHRAMM; Scott SMITH; Carl
WILKINSON.

OTHER APPEARANCES/GUESTS (official matches only):
Tony ATKIN; Tom BROWN; Richard HALL; Claus KRISTENSEN; Trent LEVERINGTON; Chris
MILLS; Andrew MOORE; Luke PRIEST; Jamie ROBERTSON; Scott ROBSON; Paul THORP.

PREMIER LEAGUE

(*Denotes bonus-point victory)

No	DATE	OPPONENTS	H/A	RESULT	Rymel	Pietraszko	Schramm	Madsen	Makovsky	Smith	Kugelmann	Wilkinson	Others
1	21/5	King's Lynn	H	W49-41	12+1 (5)	6 (5)	R/R	7+3 (4)	6+3 (5)	17+1 (7)	1 (4)	–	–
2	22/5	Glasgow	A	W48-46	10+1 (5)	–	R/R	8 (4)	10 (5)	12+1 (7)	3+1 (4)	–	5+2 (5)
3	28/5	Isle of Wight	H	W50-40	10+2 (5)	0 (2)	6+1 (4)	8+1 (4)	13 (5)	10+1 (6)	–	–	3+2 (4)
4	10/6	Somerset	A	L42-48	3+2 (4)	11 (5)	0 (3)	9 (4)	1+1 (3)	10+2 (7)	–	8+2 (5)	–
5	18/6	Newport	H	W61-32	13+1 (5)	10+2 (5)	R/R	8+1 (5)	11+1 (5)	10+1 (5)	–	9+2 (5)	–

BERWICK: From left to right, back row: Chris Schramm, Carl Wilkinson, Peter Waite (Promoter/Team Manager), Adam Pietraszko, Scott Smith. Front, kneeling: Adrian Rymel, Tom P. Madsen. On bike: Michal Makovsky.

No	DATE	OPPONENTS	H/A	RESULT	Rymel	Pietraszko	Schramm	Madsen	Makovsky	Smith	Kugelmann	Wilkinson	Others
6	20/6	Reading	A	W49-44	12 (5)	7 (4)	7+2 (4)	4+1 (4)	10+2 (5)	5 (4)	–	4+2 (4)	–
7	21/6	Isle of Wight	A	L46-50*	13+2 (5)	7 (4)	3 (4)	0 (3)	14+1 (5)	6 (5)	–	3+2 (4)	–
8	22/6	King's Lynn	A	L44-45*	R/R	12+1 (6)	5+2 (4)	11+1 (6)	5 (5)	0 (3)	–	11+1 (6)	–
9	25/6	Hull	H	W61-32	15 (5)	9+2 (4)	4 (4)	7+1 (4)	10+3 (5)	10 (4)	–	6+2 (4)	–
10	2/7	Glasgow	H	W54-40*	10 (5)	9+2 (5)	7+2 (4)	2+1 (3)	10+1 (5)	9+1 (4)	–	7+2 (4)	–
11	9/7	Sheffield	H	W55-37	12+1 (5)	5+2 (5)	3+1 (4)	7+3 (4)	10 (5)	9+1 (4)	–	9+1 (4)	–
12	10/7	Newport	A	L41-49*	5 (5)	10+1 (6)	7+1 (4)	5 (2)	3+1 (4)	0 (3)	–	11 (6)	–
13	11/7	Exeter	A	W52-38	R/R	13+1 (6)	3+2 (4)	2+1 (3)	13+1 (6)	10+1 (5)	–	11+4 (6)	–
14	15/7	Edinburgh	A	L34-59	R/R	2 (2)	4 (6)	15 (6)	4+2 (5)	–	–	8+1 (7)	1+1 (4)
15	23/7	Edinburgh	H	W54-41	7 (5)	–	7+1 (5)	R/R	11+2 (5)	–	–	15 (7)	14+4 (8)
16	29/7	Rye House	A	L25-65	1 (4)	4+1 (6)	1 (4)	7 (4)	4 (5)	R/R	–	8+2 (7)	–
17	30/7	Rye House	H	W57-35	17+1 (6)	11+1 (6)	7+2 (5)	R/R	11+1 (5)	0 (2)	–	11+3 (6)	–
18	31/7	Newcastle	A	L43-47	R/R	16 (7)	1 (4)	–	8+2 (5)	–	–	7+2 (4)	11+1 (10)
19	6/8	Newcastle	H	W55-40*	14+1 (5)	10+1 (5)	2+1 (4)	6+1 (4)	10 (5)	R/R	–	13+5 (7)	–
20	10/8	Hull	A	W46-44*	3 (4)	12+1 (6)	3+1 (5)	7+2 (4)	7+1 (5)	R/R	–	14 (7)	–
21	13/8	Somerset	H	W58-36*	12 (5)	14+1 (5)	8+3 (5)	9+1 (4)	9+1 (5)	R/R	–	6+3 (6)	–
22	17/8	Stoke	H	W51-39	12+2 (5)	10 (5)	9+2 (6)	2+1 (3)	11 (5)	R/R	–	7+3 (6)	–
23	21/8	Stoke	A	W49-46*	10+1 (5)	9+1 (6)	7+1 (5)	10+1 (4)	4+2 (4)	R/R	–	9+1 (6)	–
24	27/8	Workington	H	W56-38	12 (5)	12 (5)	13+3 (6)	1 (3)	10 (5)	R/R	–	8+2 (6)	–
25	29/8	Workington	A	L33-59	12 (5)	1+1 (4)	7+2 (5)	R/R	7 (6)	–	–	2 (5)	4+2 (5)
26	10/9	Reading	H	W60-32*	11+2 (5)	14+1 (5)	7 (4)	8+1 (4)	8+1 (5)	5+3 (4)	–	7+2 (4)	–
27	17/9	Exeter	H	W57-37*	9+1 (4)	11 (5)	6+3 (4)	5+3 (4)	13 (5)	9+1 (4)	–	4+2 (4)	–
28	22/9	Sheffield†	A	L41-48*	–	10 (4)	2+1 (4)	1 (2)	3 (4)	14+2 (6)	–	1+1 (4)	10 (4)

†Meeting abandoned after heat fourteen, with the result permitted to stand.

DETAILS OF OTHER RIDERS:

Match No. 2: Chris Mills 5+2 (5); Match No. 3: Tom Brown 3+2 (4); Match No. 14: Trent Leverington 1+1 (4); Match No. 15: Claus Kristensen 10+2 (5); Trent Leverington 4+2 (3); Match No. 18: Scott Robson 7 (6); Andrew Moore 4+1 (4); Match No. 25: Tony Atkin 4+2 (5); Match No. 28: Paul Thorp 10 (4).

TACTICAL RIDES, AS INCLUDED IN THE SCORES GRID:

Match No. 7: Makovsky 6 points (TR); Rymel 6 points (TR); Match No. 14: Madsen 4 points (TR); Makovsky 2 points (TR); Match No. 16: Pietraszko 0 points (TR); Rymel 0 points (TR); Match No. 25: Rymel 4 points (TR); Wilkinson 0 points (TR); Match No. 28: Pietraszko 6 points (TR); Smith 4 points (TR).

PREMIER LEAGUE AVERAGES

Rider	Mts	Rds	Pts	Bon	Tot	Avge	Max
Adrian Rymel	23	112	230	18	248	8.86	1 full; 2 paid
Adam Pietraszko	26	128	232	19	251	7.84	2 paid
Michal Makovsky	28	136	232	26	258	7.59	–
Scott Smith	17	80	134	15	149	7.45	–
Tom P. Madsen	24	92	147	23	170	7.39	–

Carl Wilkinson	25	134	199	45	244	7.28	–
Chris Schramm	25	111	129	31	160	5.77	–
Joachim Kugelmann	2	8	4	1	5	2.50	–
Guests	9	40	48	12	60	6.00	–

(Tony Atkin [1]; Tom Brown [1]; Claus Kristensen [1]; Trent Leverington [2]; Chris Mills [1]; Andrew Moore [1]; Scott Robson [1]; Paul Thorp [1]).

PREMIER TROPHY

(*Denotes bonus-point victory)

No	DATE	OPPONENTS	H/A	RESULT	Rymel	Pietraszko	Cartwright	Makovsky	Dym	Schramm	Kugelmann	Smith	Madsen	Others
1	5/3	Sheffield	H	W55-40	8+1 (3)	R/R	5+2 (5)	13+2 (6)	6+1 (5)	14+2 (7)	9 (4)	–	–	–
2	19/3	Newcastle	H	W55-39	14+1 (5)	8+2 (4)	2+2 (3)	12+1 (5)	8+1 (4)	10+1 (6)	1+1 (3)	–	–	–
3	20/3	Glasgow	A	D45-45	9 (5)	5+1 (4)	9+1 (4)	8+2 (5)	4 (4)	9+1 (5)	1 (3)	–	–	–
4	25/3	Workington	A	L40-54	8 (5)	2 (4)	0 (3)	15 (5)	7 (4)	3+3 (4)	5+1 (6)	–	–	–
5	26/3	Workington	H	W53-39	10 (5)	5+1 (4)	7+1 (4)	8+2 (4)	11+1 (5)	6+3 (4)	6+1 (4)	–	–	–
6	2/4	Stoke	A	L40-53	4+1 (5)	10 (6)	1 (3)	9 (6)	R/R	4 (4)	12+1 (6)	–	–	–
7	8/4	Edinburgh	A	L29-62	5 (4)	4 (4)	4 (4)	7+1 (5)	5 (5)	1+1 (4)	3+2 (4)	–	–	–
8	9/4	Glasgow	H	D45-45	5 (4)	10+2 (5)	1+1 (3)	8 (4)	8+1 (5)	9+2 (5)	4+1 (4)	–	–	–
9	13/4	Hull	A	L42-54	4+1 (4)	5+1 (5)	R/R	12 (5)	11 (5)	8+1 (7)	2+1 (4)	–	–	–
10	16/4	Edinburgh	H	W53-43	12+1 (5)	6 (5)	R/R	10+1 (4)	12+1 (5)	8+2 (6)	5+3 (5)	–	–	–
11	23/4	Hull	H	W57-37*	14+1 (6)	14+2 (6)	–	9+3 (5)	R/R	6+2 (5)	7+1 (4)	7 (4)	–	–
12	12/5	Sheffield	A	L35-59	4+1 (4)	9 (5)	–	7+1 (5)	3 (4)	6+3 (7)	–	6 (4)	–	–
13	14/5	Stoke	H	W52-41	14 (5)	6+1 (4)	–	12 (5)	6 (4)	5+3 (4)	8+1 (4)	1 (4)	–	–
14	30/5	Newcastle	A	L35-58	8 (5)	4 (4)	–	7 (5)	–	7 (5)	–	4+1 (4)	4+1 (4)	1+1 (3)

DETAILS OF OTHER RIDER:

Match No. 14: Luke Priest 1+1 (3).

TACTICAL SUBSTITUTE AND TACTICAL RIDES, AS INCLUDED IN THE SCORES GRID:

Match No. 4: Makovsky 6 points (TR); Rymel 2 points (TR); Match No. 6: Pietraszko 4 points (TR); Kugelmann 2 points (TR); Match No. 7: Cartwright 2 points (TR); Rymel 0 points (TR); Match No. 9: Dym 6 points (TR); Makovsky 6 points (TR); Match No. 12: Pietraszko 4 points (TR); Smith 4 points (TR); Match No. 14: Pietraszko 4 points (TR); Makovsky 2 points (TR); Schramm 0 points (TS).

PREMIER TROPHY AVERAGES

Rider	Mts	Rds	Pts	Bon	Tot	Avge	Max
Michal Makovsky	14	69	130	13	143	8.29	–
Adrian Rymel	14	65	118	7	125	7.69	1 paid
Piotr Dym	11	50	78	5	83	6.64	–
Chris Schramm	14	73	96	24	120	6.58	–
Adam Pietraszko	13	60	82	10	92	6.13	–
Joachim Kugelmann	12	51	62	13	75	5.88	–

Tom P. Madsen	1	4	4	1	5	5.00	–
Simon Cartwright	8	29	28	7	35	4.83	–
Scott Smith	4	16	16	1	17	4.25	–
Guest	1	3	1	1	2	2.67	–

(Luke Priest [1]).

KNOCK-OUT CUP

(*Denotes aggregate victory)

No	DATE	OPPONENTS	H/A	RESULT	Rymel	Pietraszko	Schramm	Madsen	Makovsky	Smith	Wilkinson	Others
1	12/6	Stoke	A	W48-42	9+2 (5)	4+1 (4)	R/R	2+2 (3)	8+1 (5)	13+1 (7)	12+2 (7)	–
2	29/6	Stoke	H	W56-34*	10+1 (5)	8 (4)	5+1 (4)	3 (4)	13+1 (5)	10+1 (4)	7+1 (4)	–
3	16/7	Workington	H	W49-41	6 (4)	–	3+1 (4)	3+1 (2)	9+3 (5)	8+3 (5)	14+1 (6)	6+1 (4)
4	17/7	Workington	A	W48-42*	11+1 (5)	–	7+3 (6)	R/R	10 (5)	3 (2)	12+1 (7)	5+2 (5)
5	3/9	King's Lynn	H	W45-44	14 (5)	10+1 (4)	4+1 (5)	7+1 (4)	6+1 (5)	–	3 (4)	1 (3)
6	7/9	King's Lynn	A	L34-56	6 (4)	5+1 (5)	2 (3)	6 (5)	5+1 (4)	–	4+1 (4)	6+2 (6)

DETAILS OF OTHER RIDERS:

Match No. 3: Jamie Robertson 6+1 (4); Match No. 4: Jamie Robertson 5+2 (5); Match No. 5: Claus Kristensen 1 (3); Match No. 6: Richard Hall 6+2 (6).

YOUNG SHIELD

(*Denotes aggregate victory)

No	DATE	OPPONENTS	H/A	RESULT	Rymel	Wilkinson	Madsen	Pietraszko	Makovsky	Schramm	Smith	Others
1	24/9	Newcastle	H	W60-35	–	2 (4)	R/R	15 (6)	12+2 (5)	5+1 (4)	14+3 (7)	12 (4)
2	25/9	Newcastle	A	L42-48*	–	5 (5)	R/R	10 (6)	3+1 (4)	12+2 (7)	2+1 (3)	10 (5)
3	8/10	King's Lynn	H	W49-48	7 (4)	9+1 (6)	R/R	10 (5)	11 (5)	5+4 (5)	7+3 (5)	–
4	14/10	King's Lynn	A	L35-57	7 (5)	7+2 (5)	R/R	11 (6)	6 (4)	4+1 (6)	0 (4)	–

DETAILS OF OTHER RIDER:

Match No. 1: Paul Thorp 12 (4); Match No. 2: Paul Thorp 10 (5).

TACTICAL RIDES, AS INCLUDED IN THE SCORES GRID:

Match No. 4: Wilkinson 4 points (TR); Makovsky 2 points (TR).

OTHER MEETING

12 March: Challenge

Berwick 47 (Michal Makovsky 12+2; Adrian Rymel 12; Piotr Dym 7; Simon Cartwright 6+1; Chris Schramm 5+1; Freddie Eriksson 5; John Branney 0) Hull 43.

INDIVIDUAL MEETINGS

1 October: Anderson's Quality Butchers Bordernapolis
> QUALIFYING SCORES: Chris Harris 10; Adrian Rymel 9; Adam Pietraszko 9; Henning Bager 8; Michal Makovsky 8; Piotr Dym 7; Adam Skornicki 7; George Stancl 5; Scott Smith 3; Theo Pijper 3; Carl Wilkinson 2; Mariusz Frankow 1. FINAL: 1st Rymel; 2nd Harris; 3rd Pietraszko; 4th Bager.

22 October: Northumbrian Open
> QUALIFYING SCORES: Hans N. Andersen 12; Mark Lemon 11; Sean Wilson 9; Michal Makovsky 8; Adrian Rymel 8; Theo Pijper 8; James Wright 4; Chris Schramm 4; David Meldrum 3; Scott Smith 3; Artur Boginczuk 2; Carl Wilkinson 0. FINAL: 1st Andersen; 2nd Makovsky; 3rd Wilson; 4th Lemon.

EDINBURGH FULFILMENT FACTORY MONARCHS

NOTE: The information below relates only to the main Edinburgh team. For details of the second side, please refer to the Conference League section.

ADDRESS: Armadale Stadium, 2 Bathgate Road, Armadale, West Lothian, EH48 2PD.
PROMOTERS: John Campbell & Alex Harkess.
TRACK LENGTH: 260 metres.
TRACK RECORD: 55.4 seconds – Charlie Gjedde (24 September 2004).
FIRST MEETING: 4 April 1997.
YEARS OF OPERATION: 1997-2005 Premier League.

PREVIOUS VENUES AS 'MONARCHS':
(1) Old Meadowbank Stadium, Clockmill Road, Edinburgh.
YEARS OF OPERATION: 1948-54 National League Division Two; 1957 Training; 1959 Open; 1960-64 Provincial League; 1965-67 British League; 1998 Demonstration.
(2) Cliftonhill Stadium, Main Street, Coatbridge, Lanarkshire.
YEARS OF OPERATION: 1968-69 British League Division One (Team rode as 'Coatbridge Monarchs').
(3) Powderhall Stadium, Beaverhall Road, Edinburgh.
YEARS OF OPERATION: 1977-90 National League; 1991-94 British League Division Two; 1995 Premier League.
(4) Shawfield Stadium, Glasgow Road, Rutherglen, Glasgow.
YEARS OF OPERATION: 1996 Premier League (Team rode as 'Scottish Monarchs').

CLUB HONOURS

QUEEN'S CUP WINNERS: 1953.
FOUR-TEAM CHAMPIONS: 1981, 1993.
KNOCK-OUT CUP WINNERS: 1981, 1997, 1999.
PAIRS CHAMPIONS: 1986.
PREMIERSHIP WINNERS: 1998.
LEAGUE CHAMPIONS: 2003.

EDINBURGH: From left to right: Robert Ksiezak, Ross Brady, Rusty Harrison, Theo Pijper (on bike), William Lawson, Daniel Nermark, Cameron Woodward.

RIDER ROSTER 2005

Ross BRADY; Rusty HARRISON; Robert KSIEZAK; William LAWSON; Kristian LUND; David McALLAN; Daniel NERMARK; Theo PIJPER; Matthew WETHERS; Cameron WOODWARD.

OTHER APPEARANCES/GUESTS (official matches only):

Adam ALLOTT; Andre COMPTON; Jamie COURTNEY; Josef FRANC; Ashley JONES; Joachim KUGELMANN; Michal MAKOVSKY; Chris MILLS; Blair SCOTT; Zdenek SIMOTA; Andrew TULLY; Brent WERNER.

PREMIER LEAGUE

(*Denotes bonus-point victory)

No	DATE	OPPONENTS	H/A	RESULT	Nemark	Brady	Woodward	Pijper	Harrison	Lawson	McAllan	Lund	Ksiezak	Wethers	Others
1	20/5	King's Lynn	H	W57-38	9+4 (5)	10 (4)	7+2 (4)	13 (5)	7+1 (4)	8+2 (4)	3+2 (4)	–	–	–	–
2	22/5	Newport	A	L46-47	6 (4)	7 (4)	6+2 (4)	8 (5)	12 (5)	4 (4)	3+1 (4)	–	–	–	–
3	27/5	Isle of Wight	H	W63-30	8+2 (4)	11+1 (5)	9+3 (4)	15 (5)	9+1 (4)	3+1 (4)	8+3 (4)	–	–	–	–
4	15/6	Hull	A	W53-38	5+3 (4)	14 (5)	14+2 (6)	8 (4)	8+2 (5)	1 (3)	3+1 (3)	–	–	–	–
5	17/6	Newport	H	W60-35*	9+4 (5)	15 (5)	8+1 (4)	8+2 (4)	8 (4)	7 (4)	5 (4)	–	–	–	–
6	18/6	Workington	A	W48-42	6+1 (4)	7 (4)	9+2 (6)	9+2 (5)	12 (5)	3 (3)	2+1 (3)	–	–	–	–
7	20/6	Newcastle	A	L47-49	9+1 (5)	9 (4)	3 (3)	9 (5)	5+1 (4)	5+2 (4)	7+2 (5)	–	–	–	–
8	24/6	Stoke	H	W53-42	8+3 (5)	13+1 (4)	8+1 (4)	7+1 (4)	5+1 (4)	5+1 (4)	7+2 (4)	–	–	–	–
9	1/7	Sheffield	H	W45-43	13 (6)	R/R	6+2 (5)	11 (5)	7 (4)	7+5 (6)	–	–	–	–	1+1 (4)
10	6/7	Somerset	A	L32-60	7+3 (5)	–	8 (4)	2 (4)	3 (4)	0 (3)	–	9 (6)	–	–	3 (5)
11	7/7	Sheffield	A	L36-57	7+3 (5)	–	7+1 (4)	10 (5)	6 (4)	2 (4)	–	0 (3)	–	–	4+2 (5)
12	8/7	Rye House	H	L40-52	9 (4)	–	3+1 (4)	7 (5)	10 (5)	7+2 (5)	3+1 (4)	1+1 (3)	–	–	–
13	11/7	Reading	A	W47-46	7+1 (4)	–	6+1 (4)	–	8+2 (5)	6 (5)	–	7+2 (4)	0 (3)	–	13 (5)
14	12/7	Isle of Wight	A	L34-61*	3+1 (4)	–	9 (5)	–	8 (5)	5 (5)	–	0 (3)	0 (3)	–	9 (5)
15	15/7	Berwick	H	W59-34	8+1 (4)	–	13 (5)	–	14+1 (5)	10+3 (5)	–	8+2 (4)	1 (3)	–	5 (4)
16	23/7	Berwick	A	L41-54*	4 (4)	–	6 (4)	–	11+1 (5)	3 (5)	–	1 (3)	1 (4)	–	15 (5)
17	3/8	King's Lynn	A	L41-55*	8 (4)	–	5+1 (5)	–	10 (5)	4+1 (4)	–	1+1 (3)	1 (4)	–	12+1 (5)
18	8/8	Exeter	A	L42-53	16 (6)	–	R/R	8 (4)	12 (5)	1 (4)	–	1 (4)	4+2 (7)	–	–
19	12/8	Somerset	H	W55-39	7+2 (4)	1+1 (1)	–	11+3 (5)	14+1 (5)	8 (4)	–	–	3 (5)	11+2 (6)	–
20	14/8	Glasgow	A	L39-51	6+2 (5)	R/R	–	8+1 (6)	13 (6)	5+2 (4)	–	–	1 (3)	6+2 (7)	–
21	21/8	Rye House	A	L37-58	5 (5)	R/R	–	–	16 (6)	0 (3)	–	–	0 (4)	8+2 (6)	8 (6)
22	26/8	Workington†	H	D36-36*	9+1 (4)	3 (2)	–	7 (3)	4+1 (3)	5+1 (4)	–	–	4 (3)	4+2 (5)	–
23	28/8	Stoke	A	L42-47*	11+1 (5)	6 (4)	–	6 (4)	8+2 (5)	6+1 (4)	–	–	2 (3)	3+2 (5)	–
24	2/9	Hull	H	W60-35*	14+1 (6)	9 (4)	–	R/R	15 (5)	9+1 (5)	–	–	2+1 (4)	11+4 (6)	–
25	10/9	Reading	H	W46-43*	7+1 (4)	4+2 (4)	–	4+2 (4)	10+2 (5)	8 (4)	–	–	2+1 (3)	11 (6)	–
26	16/9	Exeter	H	W60-35*	9+3 (5)	12 (4)	–	12 (5)	6+2 (4)	7+2 (4)	–	–	5 (4)	9+2 (4)	–
27	23/9	Glasgow	H	W51-43	7+3 (4)	6+1 (4)	–	11+1 (5)	9 (5)	6+2 (4)	–	–	0 (3)	12+3 (6)	–
28	7/10	Newcastle	H	W53-40*	7+2 (5)	R/R	–	12+1 (6)	14 (5)	10+1 (6)	–	–	4+2 (4)	6+2 (4)	–

†Meeting abandoned after heat twelve, with the result permitted to stand.

DETAILS OF OTHER RIDERS:

Match No. 9: Blair Scott 1+1 (4); Match No. 10: Chris Mills 3 (5); Match No. 11: Chris Mills 4+2 (5); Match No. 13: Brent

Werner 13 (5); Match No. 14: Michal Makovsky 9 (5); Match No. 15: Andre Compton 5 (4); Match No. 16: Josef Franc 15 (5); Match No. 17: Adam Allott 12+1 (5); Match No. 21: Zdenek Simota 8 (6).

TACTICAL SUBSTITUTE AND TACTICAL RIDES, AS INCLUDED IN THE SCORES GRID:

Match No. 10: Woodward 4 points (TR); Pijper 0 points (TR); Lund 0 points (TS); Match No. 11: Woodward 4 points (TR); Harrison 2 points (TR); Match No. 12: Nermark 4 points (TR); Match No. 14: Makovsky 4 points (TR); Woodward 4 points (TS); Harrison 2 points (TR); Match No. 16: Franc 6 points (TR); Harrison 4 points (TR); Match No. 17: Allott 6 points (TR); Harrison 4 points (TR); Woodward 2 points (TS); Match No. 18: Nermark 6 points (TR); Pijper 4 points (TR); Match No. 21: Harrison 6 points (TR); Simota 4 points (TR).

PREMIER LEAGUE AVERAGES

Rider	Mts	Rds	Pts	Bon	Tot	Avge	Max
Ross Brady	15	59	127	6	133	9.02	2 full
Rusty Harrison	28	131	255	18	273	8.34	1 full; 2 paid
Daniel Nermark	28	129	219	43	262	8.12	–
Theo Pijper	21	98	184	13	197	8.04	1 full
Matthew Wethers	10	55	81	21	102	7.42	–
Cameron Woodward	17	75	120	19	139	7.41	1 paid
David McAllan	9	35	41	13	54	6.17	–
William Lawson	28	118	145	27	172	5.83	–
Kristian Lund	9	33	28	6	34	4.12	–
Robert Ksiezak	16	60	30	6	36	2.40	–
Guests	9	44	60	4	64	5.82	–

(Adam Allott [1]; Andre Compton [1]; Josef Franc [1]; Michal Makovsky [1]; Chris Mills [2]; Blair Scott [1]; Zdenek Simota [1]; Brent Werner [1]).

PREMIER TROPHY

(*Denotes bonus-point victory)

No	DATE	OPPONENTS	H/A	RESULT	Nermark	Pijper	Harrison	Woodward	Brady	Lawson	Ksiezak	McAllan	Others
1	19/3	Workington	A	L34-60	5 (5)	4 (4)	14 (5)	1 (4)	6 (4)	0 (4)	4+1 (4)	–	–
2	25/3	Newcastle	H	W53-43	11+2 (5)	10+2 (4)	12+1 (5)	5+1 (4)	8+1 (4)	4 (4)	3+2 (4)	–	–
3	30/3	Hull	A	L42-53	12 (5)	4+1 (4)	9 (4)	3+2 (4)	6 (4)	3+1 (4)	5 (5)	–	–
4	31/3	Sheffield	A	L40-50	3+1 (4)	7+1 (4)	10 (5)	2+1 (4)	9 (5)	3 (3)	6+2 (5)	–	–
5	8/4	Berwick	H	W62-29	12+3 (5)	13+2 (5)	10+1 (4)	5 (4)	12 (4)	5 (4)	5+2 (4)	–	–
6	15/4	Sheffield	H	W60-34*	7+3 (5)	14 (5)	9 (4)	8+1 (4)	11 (4)	4+2 (4)	7+2 (4)	–	–
7	16/4	Berwick	A	L43-53*	10 (5)	3+1 (3)	12 (5)	10 (4)	5 (4)	0 (5)	3 (5)	–	–
8	17/4	Newcastle	A	L41-48*	8+1 (5)	R/R	15 (6)	4+2 (5)	4 (4)	10+1 (7)	0 (1)	–	0 (1)
9	22/4	Stoke	H	W53-43	10+2 (5)	13+1 (5)	9 (4)	3+2 (4)	5+1 (4)	6+1 (4)	–	–	7+2 (4)
10	24/4	Glasgow	A	D46-46	7+2 (4)	9+1 (5)	11 (5)	4+1 (4)	7+1 (4)	6+2 (5)	–	–	2+1 (3)
11	29/4	Hull	H	L42-49	8+2 (5)	9+1 (4)	5+2 (4)	6 (4)	7 (4)	5 (5)	–	–	2+2 (4)
12	6/5	Glasgow	H	W53-40*	10 (5)	10+1 (4)	8+1 (5)	6+1 (4)	6+1 (4)	12 (6)	–	–	1 (3)
13	13/5	Workington	H	W49-41	12+2 (5)	5 (4)	9+2 (5)	0 (3)	6 (4)	10 (5)	–	7+2 (4)	–
14	5/6	Stoke	A	W46-44*	2+1 (3)	9 (5)	10+1 (5)	6+1 (5)	9 (4)	1 (3)	–	9+2 (5)	–

DETAILS OF OTHER RIDERS:

Match No. 8: Andrew Tully 0 (1); Match No. 9: Joachim Kugelmann 7+2 (4); Match No. 10: Joachim Kugelmann 2+1 (3); Match No. 11: Ashley Jones 2+2 (4); Match No. 12: Jamie Courtney 1 (3).

TACTICAL RIDES, AS INCLUDED IN THE SCORES GRID:

Match No. 1: Harrison 6 points (TR); Brady 2 points (TR); Match No. 3: Nermark 6 points (TR); Harrison 4 points (TR); Match No. 7: Harrison 6 points (TR); Woodward 6 points (TR); Match No. 11: Woodward 2 points (TR).

PREMIER TROPHY AVERAGES

Rider	Mts	Rds	Pts	Bon	Tot	Avge	Max
David McAllan	2	9	16	4	20	8.89	–
Rusty Harrison	14	66	135	8	143	8.67	–
Theo Pijper	13	56	110	11	121	8.64	2 paid
Daniel Nermark	14	66	114	19	133	8.06	1 paid
Ross Brady	14	57	100	4	104	7.30	1 full
Robert Ksiezak	8	32	33	9	42	5.25	–
Cameron Woodward	14	57	59	12	71	4.98	–
William Lawson	14	63	69	7	76	4.83	–
Guests	5	15	12	5	17	4.53	–

(Jamie Courtney [1]; Ashley Jones [1]; Joachim Kugelmann [2]; Andrew Tully [1]).

KNOCK-OUT CUP

No	DATE	OPPONENTS	H/A RESULT	Pijper	Lawson	Brady	Nermark	Harrison	Woodward	McAllan
1	3/6	Rye House	H W47-43	9 (5)	5 (4)	12+1 (5)	6+2 (4)	6 (4)	7+1 (5)	2+1 (3)
2	4/6	Rye House	A L33-57	9 (5)	3 (4)	6+1 (5)	6+1 (4)	4 (4)	4+1 (5)	1+1 (3)

YOUNG SHIELD

No	DATE	OPPONENTS	H/A RESULT	Brady	Nermark	Pijper	Lawson	Harrison	Wethers	Ksiezak
1	29/9	Sheffield	A L37-57	2 (2)	9+1 (4)	10 (6)	2+2 (3)	9 (5)	5+1 (6)	0 (4)
2	30/9	Sheffield	H W54-38	R/R	8+1 (5)	12 (6)	5+2 (4)	15+1 (6)	13+3 (7)	1+1 (2)

TACTICAL SUBSTITUTE AND TACTICAL RIDES, AS INCLUDED IN THE SCORES GRID:

Match No. 1: Nermark 4 points (TR); Harrison 2 points (TR); Pijper 2 points (TS).

OTHER MEETINGS

13 March: Spring Trophy (first leg)

Glasgow 49 Edinburgh 43 (Rusty Harrison 14+2; William Lawson 9+2; Cameron Woodward 8+2; Theo Pijper 6; Ross Brady 4; Daniel Nermark 1+1; Robert Ksiezak 1).

1 April: Spring Trophy (second leg)

Edinburgh 54 (Rusty Harrison 12+1; Daniel Nermark 11+2; Theo Pijper 9; Ross Brady 8; William Lawson 7; Robert Ksiezak 4+2; Cameron Woodward 3+1) Glasgow 42 – Edinburgh won 97-91 on aggregate.

9 April: Premier Trophy

Stoke 31 Edinburgh 28 (Theo Pijper 7; Cameron Woodward 7; Rusty Harrison 6+1; Ross Brady 5; Robert Ksiezak 2+1; William Lawson 1; Daniel Nermark 0) – meeting abandoned after heat ten.

22 July: Scottish Cup (first leg)

Edinburgh 41 (Daniel Nermark 12; Rusty Harrison 9; Kristian Lund 6; Brent Werner 5+3; Cameron Woodward 4+1; William Lawson 4; Robert Ksiezak 1) Glasgow 48.

19 August: Premier League

Edinburgh 24 (Theo Pijper 8; Rusty Harrison 5+2; Daniel Nermark 5; Matthew Wethers 4; William Lawson 1+1; Robert Ksiezak 1; Ross Brady R/R) Newcastle 18 – meeting abandoned after heat seven.

25 September: Scottish Cup (second leg)

Glasgow 53 Edinburgh 37 (Theo Pijper 9+1; Rusty Harrison 7; Matthew Wethers 7; Ross Brady 4+1; William Lawson 4+1; Daniel Nermark 4; Robert Ksiezak 2+1) – Glasgow won 101-78 on aggregate.

INDIVIDUAL MEETING

5 August: Keyline Scottish Open Championship

QUALIFYING SCORES: David Howe 13; Theo Pijper 11; Shane Parker 11; Mark Lemon 11; Jason Lyons 10; George Stancl 9; Daniel Nermark 9; Rusty Harrison 9; Nicolai Klindt 7; Ronnie Correy 7; James Wright 7; David McAllan 7; William Lawson 4; Cameron Woodward 2; Anders Nielsen 2; Adam McKinna (Res) 1; Rafal Kowalski 0. SEMI-FINAL: 1st Stancl; 2nd Parker; 3rd Lemon; 4th Lyons. FINAL: 1st Howe; 2nd Pijper; 3rd Stancl; 4th Parker.

EXETER FALCONS

ADDRESS: County Ground Stadium, Cowick Street, St Thomas, Exeter, Devon, EX2 9BQ.
PROMOTERS: Terry Russell & David Short.
TRACK LENGTH: 396 metres.
TRACK RECORD: 64.3 seconds – Mark Loram (29 April 1996).
FIRST MEETING: 9 March 1929.
YEARS OF OPERATION: 1929-31 Open; 1934 Open; 1947-51 National League Division Three; 1952-53 Southern League; 1954-55 National League Division Two; 1957-58 Open; 1960 Open; 1961-64 Provincial League; 1965-67 British League; 1968-74 British League Division One; 1975-79 British League; 1980-83 National League; 1984 British League; 1985-90 National League; 1991-94 British League Division Two; 1995-2005 Premier League.

NOTE: Exeter also ran a second team in the 1995 Academy League, the 1996 Conference League and the 1997 Amateur

League. The team of 1995-96 rode as 'Devon Demons' whereas in 1997 the fixtures were shared with Newport, under the banner of 'Welsh Western Warriors'.

CLUB HONOURS

LEAGUE CHAMPIONS: 1948, 1974, 2000.
NATIONAL TROPHY (DIVISION THREE) WINNERS: 1951.
KNOCK-OUT CUP WINNERS: 1962, 1983.
YOUNG SHIELD WINNERS: 1997.
PREMIER TROPHY WINNERS: 2004.

RIDER ROSTER 2005

Ben BARKER; Jernej KOLENKO; Mark LEMON; Ray MORTON; Pavel ONDRASIK; Nick SIMMONS; Lee SMETHILLS; Seemond STEPHENS; Toni SVAB; Sebastien TRESARRIEU.

OTHER APPEARANCES/GUESTS (official matches only):
Sebastian ALDEN; Matt BATES; Danny BETSON; Craig BRANNEY; John BRANNEY; Kevin DOOLAN; Daniel GIFFARD; Sam HURST; Kriss IRVING; Ben POWELL; Scott SMITH; Shaun TACEY; Mark THOMPSON; Mathieu TRESARRIEU; Danny WARWICK.

PREMIER LEAGUE

(*Denotes bonus-point victory)

No	DATE	OPPONENTS	H/A	RESULT	Lemon	Smethills	Kolenko	Svab	Stephens	Simmons	Ondrasik	Morton	Barker	Tresarrieu	Others
1	8/5	Glasgow	A	L38-55	11 (5)	5+2 (5)	R/R	9 (5)	3 (5)	0 (3)	10+1 (7)	–			
2	22/5	Newcastle	A	L40-54	16+1 (5)	–	–	12+1 (6)	7 (5)	1 (4)	2 (5)	R/R	–	–	2+1 (5)
3	23/5	Stoke	H	W46-44	9+1 (5)	–	–	7+1 (5)	10+1 (6)	1 (3)	11+2 (6)	R/R			8 (5)
4	30/5	Somerset	H	W54-40	12+1 (5)	8+1 (7)	–	8+2 (4)	10+1 (5)	–	5+2 (4)	10+1 (4)	1 (1)	–	–
5	6/6	Sheffield	H	W56-39	13 (5)	10+1 (5)	–	7+2 (4)	10+1 (5)	–	5+1 (4)	10+1 (4)	1+1 (3)	–	–
6	8/6	Hull	A	L46.5-49.5	15.5(5)	10 (5)	–	4+1 (5)	5 (4)	–	3+2 (4)	8 (4)	1 (3)	–	–
7	13/6	Workington	H	W61-32	10 (4)	12+1 (5)	–	10+1 (4)	15 (5)	–	3+1 (4)	8+3 (4)	3+1 (4)	–	–
8	17/6	Somerset	A	L42-53*	14 (5)	5 (6)	–	15 (6)	3 (4)	–	1+1 (4)	R/R	4+1 (5)	–	–
9	20/6	Hull	H	W49-41*	9+1 (5)	10+2 (5)	–	R/R	12 (6)	–	3+1 (5)	11 (5)	4+1 (4)	–	–
10	27/6	Isle of Wight	H	W50-45	11 (4)	12 (5)	–	10+2 (5)	5+2 (4)	–	3+1 (4)	9 (5)	0 (3)	–	–
11	4/7	Newcastle	H	W60-35*	8+1 (4)	10+2 (4)	–	13 (5)	12 (5)	–	8+2 (4)	8+2 (4)	1 (4)	–	–
12	11/7	Berwick	H	L38-52	7 (4)	8 (5)	–	1 (3)	10+1 (5)	–	2 (5)	5+1 (4)	5 (4)	–	–
13	14/7	Sheffield	A	L37-56	12+1 (5)	7+1 (4)	–	0 (4)	2+1 (4)	–	4+1 (4)	7 (4)	5+1 (5)	–	–
14	16/7	Stoke	A	L40-50	10 (5)	2 (4)	–	5+1 (4)	8+1 (5)	–	3+1 (5)	10+1 (4)	2 (3)	–	–
15	25/7	Glasgow	H	W57-37*	11+1 (5)	13+2 (5)	–	–	12 (5)	–	12+3 (6)	R/R	9+2 (6)	–	0 (3)
16	1/8	Newport	H	W65-28	11+2 (5)	10+3 (5)	–	–	12+1 (5)	–	14+3 (6)	R/R	7+2 (5)	11+1 (4)	–
17	8/8	Edinburgh	H	W53-42	10+2 (5)	9 (4)	–	–	9 (5)	–	11+2 (5)	8+1 (4)	–	2+1 (3)	4+1 (4)
18	15/8	King's Lynn	H	W55-40	13+2 (5)	8+1 (4)	–	–	9 (4)	–	4 (3)	7+1 (4)	–	13+1 (5)	1+1 (5)
19	21/8	Newport	A	W46-44*	12+1 (5)	3+1 (3)	–	R/R	–	–	–	–	6 (5)		25+1 (15)

No	DATE	OPPONENTS	H/A	RESULT	Lemon	Smethills	Kolenko	Svab	Stephens	Simmons	Ondrasik	Morton	Barker	Tresarrieau	Others
20	29/8	Reading	A	L32-61	8+1 (5)	2 (5)	–	–	R/R	–	4+1 (6)	–	–	10 (6)	8 (8)
21	29/8	Reading	H	W54-39	12 (5)	7+2 (5)	–	–	R/R	–	10+2 (6)	–	–	11 (5)	14+4 (9)
22	4/9	Rye House	A	L26-66	10 (6)	1 (5)	–	–	–	–	4+1 (4)	R/R	–	–	11+2 (15)
23	6/9	Isle of Wight	A	L33-60	17 (6)	1 (4)	–	–	–	–	3 (5)	R/R	–	7+1 (6)	5+1 (9)
24	10/9	Workington	A	L40-54*	17 (6)	5+2 (5)	–	–	7+1 (6)	–	5+1 (6)	R/R	–	5 (3)	1 (4)
25	12/9	Rye House	H	L37-53	8 (6)	5+1 (5)	–	–	7+1 (5)	–	9+1 (6)	R/R	–	6 (5)	2+1 (3)
26	14/9	King's Lynn	A	L35-56	5+1 (6)	6+1 (5)	–	–	5+2 (5)	–	6 (4)	R/R	–	–	13+2 (10)
27	16/9	Edinburgh	A	L35-60	6 (6)	2 (4)	–	–	4 (5)	–	2 (5)	R/R	–	11+1 (6)	0 (4)
28	17/9	Berwick	A	L37-57	1 (5)	3 (4)	–	–	6 (6)	–	15+1 (7)	R/R	–	12+1 (5)	0 (3)

DETAILS OF OTHER RIDERS:

Match No. 2: Craig Branney 2+1 (5); Match No. 3: Scott Smith 8 (5); Match No. 15: Sam Hurst 0 (3); Match No. 17: Daniel Giffard 4+1 (4); Match No. 18: Ben Powell 1+1 (5); Match No. 19: Sebastian Alden 17+1 (6); Ben Powell 5 (7); Daniel Giffard 3 (2); Match No. 20: Kevin Doolan 8 (5); Mark Thompson 0 (3); Match No. 21: Kevin Doolan 11+2 (6); Mark Thompson 3+2 (3); Match No. 22: Shaun Tacey 7 (6); John Branney 2+1 (4); Danny Betson 2+1 (5); Match No. 23: Shaun Tacey 4 (5); Ben Powell 1+1 (4); Match No. 24: Kriss Irving 1 (4); Match No. 25: Danny Warwick 2+1 (3); Match No. 26: Mathieu Tresarrieu 9+1 (6); Mark Thompson 4+1 (4); Match No. 27: Matt Bates 0 (4); Match No. 28: Matt Bates 0 (3).

TACTICAL SUBSTITUTE AND TACTICAL RIDES, AS INCLUDED IN THE SCORES GRID:

Match No. 1: Lemon 4 points (TR); Ondrasik 2 points (TR); Match No. 2: Lemon 6 points (TR); Stephens 2 points (TR); Match No. 6: Lemon 6 points (TR); Morton 6 points (TR); Match No. 8: Svab 6 points (TR); Lemon 4 points (TR); Match No. 13: Lemon 4 points (TR); Morton 2 points (TR); Match No. 20: Lemon 4 points (TR); S. Tresarrieu 2 points (TR); Match No. 22: Lemon 4 points (TR); Tacey 0 points (TR); Smethills 0 points (TS); Match No. 23: Lemon 6 points (TR); S. Tresarrieu 2 points (TR); Match No. 24: Lemon 6 points (TR); Ondrasik 2 points (TR); Match No. 25: S. Tresarrieu 0 points (TR); Match No. 26: Lemon 2 points (TR); Smethills 0 points (TR); Match No. 27: Lemon 6 points (TR); S. Tresarrieu 4 points (TR); Match No. 28: Ondrasik 6 points (TR); S. Tresarrieu 4 points (TR).

PREMIER LEAGUE AVERAGES

Rider	Mts	Rds	Pts	Bon	Tot	Avge	Max
Ray Morton	12	50	97	11	108	8.64	–
Mark Lemon	28	142	282.5	16	298.5	8.41	1 paid
Toni Svab	13	60	98	11	109	7.27	–
Sebastien Tresarrieu	11	53	88	6	94	7.09	1 paid
Seemond Stephens	23	114	182	13	195	6.84	1 full
Lee Smethills	26	123	174	23	197	6.41	2 paid
Pavel Ondrasik	27	134	157	31	188	5.61	–
Ben Barker	13	50	43	9	52	4.16	–
Nick Simmons	3	10	2	0	2	0.80	–
Guests	23	102	94	14	108	4.24	1 paid

(Sebastian Alden [1]; Matt Bates [2]; Danny Betson [1]; Craig Branney [1]; John Branney [1]; Kevin Doolan [2]; Daniel Giffard [2]; Sam Hurst [1]; Kriss Irving [1]; Ben Powell [3]; Scott Smith [1]; Shaun Tacey [2]; Mark Thompson [3]; Mathieu Tresarrieu [1]; Danny Warwick [1]).

EXETER: From left to right: Graeme Gordon (Team Manager), Nick Simmons, Pavel Ondrasik, Seemond Stephens (on bike), Mark Lemon, Toni Svab, Lee Smethills.

PREMIER TROPHY

(*Denotes bonus-point victory)

No	DATE	OPPONENTS	H/A	RESULT	Lemon	Smethills	Kolenko	Svab	Stephens	Simmons	Ondrasik	Barker	Morton
1	25/3	Somerset	A	L41-52	13 (5)	3+1 (5)	R/R	10 (6)	8+1 (5)	2+1 (4)	5 (5)	–	–
2	28/3	Somerset	H	W51-43	11 (5)	10+2 (5)	R/R	7+1 (5)	14 (6)	4+1 (4)	5 (5)	–	–
3	30/3	King's Lynn	A	L37-56	14 (5)	1 (4)	R/R	9+1 (6)	7 (5)	4+1 (6)	2+1 (4)	–	–
4	3/4	Newport	A	W49-41	13+1 (5)	5 (5)	R/R	11+1 (6)	8+1 (5)	0 (3)	12+2 (6)	–	–
5	4/4	Isle of Wight	H	W53-39	11+3 (5)	6 (4)	3+1 (4)	5 (4)	15 (5)	2 (3)	11+1 (5)	–	–
6	9/4	Rye House	A	L33-59	12 (5)	4+2 (5)	R/R	9 (6)	3 (5)	1+1 (4)	4 (5)	–	–
7	11/4	Rye House	H	W54-41	12+3 (5)	7+2 (4)	3 (4)	5 (4)	15 (5)	1 (3)	11 (5)	–	–
8	18/4	Reading	H	W55-40	11 (4)	8+1 (5)	R/R	13+1 (5)	13+1 (6)	7+2 (6)	3+2 (5)	–	–
9	2/5	King's Lynn	H	W64-29*	11+2 (5)	14+1 (5)	R/R	15+3 (6)	11 (5)	4+2 (4)	9+2 (5)	–	–
10	16/5	Newport	H	L43-47*	13+1 (5)	0 (3)	–	7 (4)	11+1 (5)	4+3 (5)	8 (5)	0 (3)	–
11	17/5	Isle of Wight	A	L42-48*	11+1 (5)	R/R	–	6+1 (5)	9+1 (5)	3+2 (6)	10+1 (7)	–	3 (2)
12	10/6	Reading	A	L44-46*	9 (5)	4 (4)	–	14 (5)	7 (4)	–	4 (4)	1 (4)	5+1 (4)
13	2/7	Workington	A	L31-60	4 (4)	5+1 (5)	–	4+2 (5)	R/R	–	9 (6)	4+1 (5)	5+1 (5)
14	8/7	Workington	H	W56-40	9+1 (5)	9 (4)	–	4+1 (4)	13+1 (5)	–	10+1 (5)	3+1 (3)	8+2 (4)

TACTICAL RIDES, AS INCLUDED IN THE SCORES GRID:

Match No. 1: Lemon 4 points (TR); Stephens 2 points (TR); Match No. 3: Lemon 4 points (TR); Stephens 4 points (TR); Match No. 6: Lemon 4 points (TR); Svab 0 points (TR); Match No. 13: Morton 2 points (TR); Lemon 0 points (TR).

PREMIER TROPHY AVERAGES

Rider	Mts	Rds	Pts	Bon	Tot	Avge	Max
Mark Lemon	14	68	148	12	160	9.41	1 paid
Seemond Stephens	13	66	131	6	137	8.30	2 full
Toni Svab	14	71	119	11	130	7.32	1 paid
Ray Morton	4	15	20	4	24	6.40	–
Pavel Ondrasik	14	72	103	10	113	6.28	–
Lee Smethills	13	58	76	10	86	5.93	1 paid
Nick Simmons	11	48	32	13	45	3.75	–
Jernej Kolenko	2	8	6	1	7	3.50	–
Ben Barker	4	15	8	2	10	2.67	–

KNOCK-OUT CUP

No	DATE	OPPONENTS	H/A	RESULT	Lemon	Smethills	Stephens	Morton	Svab	Barker	Ondrasik	Others
1	18/7	King's Lynn	H	D45-45	–	5 (4)	6 (4)	8+3 (5)	5 (4)	3+1 (3)	6+3 (5)	12 (5)
2	20/7	King's Lynn	A	L27-63	–	2+2 (4)	1+1 (5)	4 (2)	2 (4)	7 (7)	0 (4)	11 (5)

DETAILS OF OTHER RIDER:

Match No. 1: Shaun Tacey 12 (5); Match No. 2: Shaun Tacey 11 (5).

OTHER MEETINGS

23 September: West Country Championship Challenge (first leg)

Somerset 59 Exeter 36 (Lee Smethills 12+2; Mark Lemon 8; Emiliano Sanchez 7; Seemond Stephens 5; Artur Boginczuk 3+1; Luke Priest 1; Sebastien Tresarrieu R/R).

26 September: West Country Championship Challenge (second leg)

Exeter 55 (Lee Smethills 13; Seemond Stephens 11+3; Pavel Ondrasik 9+2; Mark Lemon 8+3; Ben Powell 7+1; Michael Coles 7; Ray Morton R/R) Somerset 39 – Somerset won 98-91 on aggregate.

INDIVIDUAL MEETINGS

22 August: Junior Westernapolis

1st Artur Boginczuk 15; 2nd Simon Walker 14; 3rd Danny Warwick 13; Karlis Ezergailis 10; Tom Brown 9; Lewis Bridger 8; Tyron Proctor 8; Matt Bates 8; Luke Priest 6; Paul Candy 6; Ben Powell 5; Billy Legg 3; Andy Carfield 3; Chris Ferguson 3; Sam Hurst 3; Daniel Giffard 2; Ray Dickson (Res) 2.

19 September: Colin Hill Westernapolis

1st Brent Werner 13; 2nd Shaun Tacey 12; 3rd Mads Korneliussen (on countback) 11; Olly Allen 11; Paul Fry 11; Pavel Ondrasik 10; Michael Coles 9; Lee Smethills 8; Mark Lemon 8; Seemond Stephens 7; Ben Powell 7; Danny Warwick 5; Glenn Cunningham 3; Daniel Giffard 3; Karlis Ezergailis 2; Matt Bates 0; Tyron Proctor (Res) 0.

10 October: End of an Era

QUALIFYING SCORES: Lee Richardson 13; Leigh Adams 12; Adam Shields 11; Simon Stead 11; Bjarne Pedersen 11; Magnus Zetterstrom 11; Chris Harris 10; Mark Lemon 8; Seemond Stephens 7; Billy Janniro 7; Craig Boyce 6; Jason Doyle 5; Roman Povazhny 4; Danny Warwick 3; Davey Watt 1; Shawn McConnell 0. SEMI-FINAL: 1st Zetterstrom; 2nd Shields; 3rd Stead; 4th Pedersen. FINAL: 1st Adams; 2nd Shields; 3rd Richardson; 4th Zetterstrom.

GLASGOW PREMIER TRAVEL INN TIGERS

ADDRESS: Ashfield Stadium, Saracen Park, 404 Hawthorn Street, Possilpark, Glasgow, G22 6RU.
PROMOTERS: Alan C. Dick, Stewart Dickson & Gordon Pairman.
TRACK LENGTH: 302 metres.
TRACK RECORD: 57.6 seconds – Shane Parker (18 May 2004).
FIRST MEETING: 19 April 1949.
YEARS OF OPERATION: 1949–52 National League Division Two; 1953 Open; 1999–2005 Premier League.

NOTE: (1) Between 1949-53, the track was home to 'Ashfield Giants'; (2) Ashfield Stadium also played host to a second team in the 2000 Conference League, under the banner of 'Lightning Ashfield Giants'.

PREVIOUS VENUES:

(1) White City Stadium, Paisley Road West, Ibrox, Glasgow.

YEARS OF OPERATION: 1928-29 Open; 1930-31 Northern League; 1939 Union Cup; 1940 Open; 1945 Open; 1946 Northern League; 1947-53 National League Division Two; 1954 Northern Shield; 1956 Open; 1964 Provincial League; 1965-67 British League; 1968 British League Division One.

NOTE: Glasgow first acquired the 'Tigers' moniker in 1946.

(2) Hampden Park, Mount Florida, Glasgow.

YEARS OF OPERATION: 1969-72 British League Division One.

(3) Cliftonhill Stadium, Main Street, Coatbridge, Lanarkshire.

YEARS OF OPERATION: 1973 British League Division One; 1974 British League Division Two; 1975-77 National League (Team rode as 'Coatbridge Tigers' throughout their stay at the venue).

(4) Blantyre Sports Stadium, Glasgow Road, Blantyre, nr Glasgow.

YEARS OF OPERATION: 1977-81 National League (Coatbridge moved to Blantyre midway through the 1977 season, reverting back to the name of 'Glasgow Tigers').

(5) Craighead Park, Forrest Street, Blantyre, nr Glasgow.

YEARS OF OPERATION: 1982-86 National League.

(6) Derwent Park, Workington, Cumbria.

YEAR OF OPERATION: 1987 National League (Began year as 'Glasgow Tigers', before becoming 'Workington Tigers').

(7) Shawfield Stadium, Glasgow Road, Rutherglen, Glasgow.

YEARS OF OPERATION: 1988-90 National League; 1991-94 British League Division Two; 1995 Premier League; 1997-98 Premier League.

NOTE: In 1996, Shawfield Stadium was used by the 'Scottish Monarchs', who participated in the Premier League.

CLUB HONOURS

NATIONAL SERIES WINNERS: 1990.
LEAGUE CHAMPIONS: 1993, 1994.
KNOCK-OUT CUP WINNERS: 1993, 1994.
PAIRS CHAMPIONS: 2005.

RIDER ROSTER 2005

Paul BENTLEY; James BIRKINSHAW; James COCKLE; Stefan EKBERG; Claus KRISTENSEN; Trent LEVERINGTON; Shane PARKER; Adam ROYNON; George STANCL; Matthew WETHERS.

OTHER APPEARANCES/GUESTS (official matches only):
Jonathon BETHELL; James GRIEVES; Danny NORTON; Luke PRIEST; Adrian RYMEL; Sean STODDART; Mark THOMPSON; Matthew WRIGHT.

PREMIER LEAGUE

(*Denotes bonus-point victory)

No	DATE	OPPONENTS	H/A	RESULT	Stancl	Wethers	Birkinshaw	Bentley	Parker	Cockle	Leverington	Kristensen	Ekberg	Roynon	Others
1	8/5	Exeter	H	W55-38	12+2 (5)	6+2 (4)	3+2 (3)	8 (4)	15 (5)	5+2 (5)	6 (4)	–			
2	13/5	Somerset	A	L39-56	12+1 (5)	2+1 (4)	1 (3)	–	10 (5)	1+1 (3)	10+1 (6)	3 (4)	–	–	–
3	14/5	Rye House	A	L40-55	14 (5)	3 (4)	3+2 (4)	–	11 (5)	3 (5)	1+1 (3)	5 (4)	–	–	–
4	15/5	Reading	H	W52-42	9 (4)	6+1 (4)	3+1 (4)	–	12+1 (5)	7+1 (4)	4+2 (4)	11 (5)	–	–	–
5	22/5	Berwick	H	L46-48	5+1 (5)	4 (5)	3+2 (4)	–	19 (6)	4 (5)	11 (5)	R/R	–	–	–
6	30/5	Workington	A	L39-57	13 (5)	5+2 (4)	6+1 (5)	–	9+1 (5)	3 (5)	2 (3)	1 (3)	–	–	–
7	5/6	Workington	H	L42-51	7+1 (5)	4 (4)	3+1 (5)	–	20 (6)	2+1 (5)	6 (5)	R/R	–	–	–
8	9/6	Sheffield	A	L44-51	6+1 (5)	3 (4)	17 (7)	–	14 (5)	1 (3)	2 (3)	1+1 (3)	–	–	–
9	10/6	Newport	A	L44-51	16+1 (5)	4+1 (5)	7+1 (6)	–	0 (1)	2 (4)	5 (4)	10 (5)	–	–	–
10	16/6	Newport	H	W48-42	15 (5)	1 (4)	5+1 (4)	–	–	3 (4)	5+1 (4)	7+1 (4)	–	–	12+2 (5)
11	2/7	Berwick	A	L40-54	11 (7)	–		–	18 (5)	3+1 (4)	–	4 (5)	R/R	4 (6)	
12	3/7	Isle of Wight	H	W46-44	8+1 (5)	–		–	14 (5)	3+2 (4)	–	5+3 (4)	7 (4)	5 (4)	4 (4)
13	9/7	Stoke	A	W46-44	9 (4)	–		–	13 (5)	2+1 (4)	6+1 (4)	2 (4)	11 (5)	3 (4)	
14	10/7	Somerset	H	W54-41	12+1 (5)	–		–	13+1 (5)	5+2 (5)	7+2 (4)	7+1 (4)	10+1 (4)	0 (3)	
15	25/7	Exeter	A	L37-57	11 (6)	–		–	2 (4)	1 (4)	3+2 (4)	9 (4)	9+3 (5)	2 (3)	
16	31/7	Rye House	H	L43-47	6 (4)	–		–	13 (5)	1+1 (3)	6+2 (4)	4+2 (4)	7+1 (5)	6+1 (5)	
17	7/8	Hull	H	W64-29	10+2 (5)	–		–	15 (5)	10 (4)	9+3 (4)	10+1 (4)	7+2 (4)	3+1 (4)	
18	14/8	Edinburgh	H	W51-39	14+1 (5)	–		–	13+2 (5)	10+1 (5)	4 (4)	4 (4)	6 (4)	0 (3)	
19	17/8	King's Lynn	A	L44-45	7 (5)	–		–	13 (5)	9+2 (5)	3+2 (4)	5+1 (4)	6+1 (4)	1 (3)	
20	21/8	King's Lynn†	H	L35-36	4+2 (3)	–		–	8 (3)	5+1 (4)	6 (4)	7 (4)	5+2 (3)	0 (3)	
21	28/8	Newcastle	H	W59-34	12+1 (5)	–		–	15 (5)	6+1 (4)	5+1 (4)	11 (4)	7+3 (4)	3+1 (4)	
22	29/8	Newcastle	A	L43-47*	9+1 (4)	–		–	10 (5)	3+1 (5)	6+2 (4)	5+1 (4)	8 (5)	2 (4)	
23	4/9	Stoke	H	W53-40*	5+2 (4)	–		–	12 (4)	8 (5)	7+2 (4)	6+1 (4)	15 (5)	0 (4)	
24	11/9	Sheffield	H	W51-41*	12 (5)	–		–	10+3 (5)	13+3 (7)	2 (4)	5+2 (4)	9 (4)	0 (0)	
25	13/9	Isle of Wight	A	L39-54	14+1 (5)	–		–	13 (5)	2 (5)	3+1 (4)	5 (4)	–	–	2+1 (7)
26	23/9	Edinburgh	A	L43-51*	14+1 (5)	–		–	14 (5)	7 (6)	1 (4)	1 (4)	5+1 (4)	–	1+1 (3)
27	26/9	Reading	A	L46-47*	15+1 (5)	–		–	8+2 (5)	8+1 (5)	3 (4)	6 (4)	6+1 (4)	–	0 (3)

NOTE: One match was not ridden, v. Hull (away).

†Meeting abandoned after heat twelve, with the result permitted to stand.

DETAILS OF OTHER RIDERS:

Match No. 10: James Grieves 12+2 (5); Match No. 12: Sean Stoddart 4 (4); Match No. 25: Matthew Wright 2+1 (4); Luke Priest 0 (3); Match No. 26: Jonathon Bethell 1+1 (3); Match No. 27: Matthew Wright 0 (3).

TACTICAL SUBSTITUTE AND TACTICAL RIDES, AS INCLUDED IN THE SCORES GRID:

Match No. 2: Stancl 6 points (TR); Parker 6 points (TR); Match No. 3: Stancl 6 points (TR); Parker 4 points (TR); Match No. 5: Leverington 6 points (TR); Parker 4 points (TS); Stancl 0 points (TR); Match No. 6: Stancl 6 points (TR); Parker 4 points (TR); Birkinshaw 2 points (TS); Match No. 7: Parker 6 points (TS); Match No. 8: Parker 6 points (TR); Birkinshaw 4 points (TR); Match No. 9: Stancl 6 points (TR); Kristensen 2 points (TR); Wethers 2 points (TS); Match No. 11: Parker 6 points (TR); Kristensen 2 points (TR); Stancl 0 points (TS); Match No. 15: Kristensen 4 points (TR); Ekberg 2 points (TR); Stancl 2 points (TS); Match No. 25: Stancl 6 points (TR); Parker 2 points (TR); Match No. 26: Stancl 6 points (TR); Parker 2 points (TR); Match No. 27: Stancl 6 points (TR).

GLASGOW: From left to right: James Birkinshaw, George Stancl, James Cockle, Stewart Dickson (Co-Promoter/Team Manager), Shane Parker (on bike), Matthew Wethers, Trent Leverington, Alan C. Dick (Co-Promoter), Claus Kristensen.

PREMIER LEAGUE AVERAGES

Rider	Mts	Rds	Pts	Bon	Tot	Avge	Max
Shane Parker	26	124	294	10	304	9.81	5 full; 1 paid
George Stancl	27	131	260	21	281	8.58	1 full; 1 paid
Stefan Ekberg	15	64	117	15	132	8.25	1 full
Paul Bentley	1	4	8	0	8	8.00	–
Claus Kristensen	24	97	130	14	144	5.94	–
Trent Leverington	25	101	120	23	143	5.66	1 paid
James Birkinshaw	10	45	48	11	59	5.24	–
James Cockle	27	122	127	22	149	4.89	–
Matthew Wethers	10	42	37	7	44	4.19	–
Adam Roynon	14	50	29	3	32	2.56	–
Guests	6	22	19	4	23	4.18	–

(Jonathon Bethell [1]; James Grieves [1]; Luke Priest [1]; Sean Stoddart [1]; Matthew Wright [2]).

PREMIER TROPHY

(*Denotes bonus-point victory)

No	DATE	OPPONENTS	H/A	RESULT	Stancl	Wethers	Birkinshaw	Bentley	Parker	Leverington	Cockle	Kristensen	Ekberg	Others
1	12/3	Workington	A	L43-47	8+1 (4)	3+2 (4)	6+3 (4)	9 (5)	13 (5)	3 (5)	–	–	–	1 (3)
2	20/3	Berwick	H	D45-45	13+2 (5)	3+1 (4)	1 (4)	4 (4)	15 (5)	9+1 (7)	–	–	–	0 (0)
3	27/3	Workington	H	L44-46	8+2 (5)	5 (4)	4+1 (4)	7 (4)	12 (5)	8+2 (6)	0 (2)	–	–	–
4	3/4	Hull	H	W52-40	12+2 (5)	3+2 (4)	4+2 (4)	7+1 (4)	15 (5)	11+2 (5)	–	–	–	0 (3)
5	6/4	Hull	A	L41-52*	14 (5)	1 (3)	3 (4)	4 (4)	9+1 (6)	8+1 (5)	–	–	–	2+1 (3)
6	7/4	Sheffield	A	L36-61	7 (4)	2+2 (4)	13 (6)	0 (3)	12 (5)	2 (4)	–	–	–	0 (4)
7	9/4	Berwick	A	D45-45*	11+1 (5)	4+2 (4)	0 (3)	6 (4)	14+1 (5)	8 (6)	–	–	–	2 (3)
8	10/4	Sheffield	H	W52-43	15 (5)	3+1 (4)	5 (4)	5+1 (4)	12+1 (5)	8+1 (4)	4+1 (4)	–	–	–
9	23/4	Stoke	A	D45-45	8+2 (5)	8 (4)	3+1 (4)	6 (4)	10 (5)	0 (3)	10+1 (5)	–	–	–
10	24/4	Edinburgh	H	D46-46	12 (5)	2+1 (3)	0 (1)	4+1 (4)	18+2 (6)	9 (6)	1 (5)	–	–	–
11	2/5	Newcastle	A	L42-48	7 (4)	5 (4)	1 (3)	5 (4)	13 (5)	6+1 (4)	5+2 (6)	–	–	–
12	6/5	Edinburgh	A	L40-53	12+1 (6)	3 (5)	1 (3)	R/R	14 (6)	5+1 (5)	5+1 (5)	–	–	–
13	24/5	Newcastle	H	W54-40*	12+2 (5)	7+1 (5)	6+2 (4)	–	14 (5)	10+2 (5)	5+3 (5)	R/R	–	–
14	19/6	Stoke	H	L44-46	8 (5)	6+1 (4)	–	–	5+1 (4)	3+1 (4)	5+2 (4)	–	9+1 (5)	8 (4)

DETAILS OF OTHER RIDERS:

Match No. 1: Gary Beaton 1 (3); Match No. 2: Gary Beaton 0 (0); Match No. 4: Gary Beaton 0 (3); Match No. 5: Danny Norton 2+1 (3); Match No. 6: Mark Thompson 0 (4); Match No. 7: Mark Thompson 2 (3); Match No. 14: Adrian Rymel 8 (4).

TACTICAL SUBSTITUTE AND TACTICAL RIDES, AS INCLUDED IN THE SCORES GRID:

Match No. 5: Stancl 6 points (TR); Parker 2 points (TS); Match No. 6: Parker 6 points (TR); Stancl 4 points (TR); Birkinshaw 4 points (TS); Match No. 10: Parker 4 points (TS); Match No. 12: Stancl 4 points (TR); Parker 2 points (TS); Wethers 0 points (TR).

PREMIER TROPHY AVERAGES

Rider	Mts	Rds	Pts	Bon	Tot	Avge	Max
Shane Parker	13	68	164	5	169	9.94	2 full; 1 paid
George Stancl	14	68	140	13	153	9.00	1 full; 1 paid
Stefan Ekberg	1	5	9	1	10	8.00	–
Claus Kristensen	1	4	5	2	7	7.00	–
Trent Leverington	14	69	92	12	104	6.03	–
Paul Bentley	11	44	57	3	60	5.45	–
Matthew Wethers	14	56	55	13	68	4.86	–
James Cockle	8	36	33	9	42	4.67	–
James Birkinshaw	13	48	45	9	54	4.50	–
Guests	7	20	13	1	14	2.80	–

(Gary Beaton [3]; Danny Norton [1]; Adrian Rymel [1]; Mark Thompson [2]).

KNOCK-OUT CUP

(*Denotes aggregate victory)

No	DATE	OPPONENTS	H/A RESULT	Stancl	Wethers	Leverington	Kristensen	Parker	Cockle	Birkinshaw	Ekberg	Roynon
1	29/5	Hull	H W56-34	13+2 (5)	5+1 (4)	10+1 (4)	6+1 (4)	14 (5)	3+1 (4)	5+2 (4)	–	–
2	13/7	Hull	A W46-44*	7 (4)	–	6+1 (4)	5+1 (4)	10 (5)	4 (4)	–	12+1 (5)	2 (4)
3	16/7	Rye House	A L42-48	12 (5)	–	2 (4)	5 (4)	6 (4)	2 (3)	–	10 (5)	5+3 (5)
4	24/7	Rye House	H L33-57	2 (4)	–	3+1 (4)	2+2 (4)	11 (5)	5+1 (5)	–	5 (3)	5 (5)

OTHER MEETINGS

13 March: Spring Trophy (first leg)

Glasgow 49 (George Stancl 10+1; Shane Parker 10; Matthew Wethers 8+3; Paul Bentley 8+1; Trent Leverington 7; James Birkinshaw 5+1; Gary Beaton 1) Edinburgh 43.

1 April: Spring Trophy (second leg)

Edinburgh 54 Glasgow 42 (Shane Parker 17+1; George Stancl 9; Matthew Wethers 7+1; Trent Leverington 6+2; Paul Bentley 2; Gary Beaton 1; James Birkinshaw 0) – Edinburgh won 97-91 on aggregate.

22 July: Scottish Cup (first leg)

Edinburgh 41 Glasgow 48 (Shane Parker 15; George Stancl 8; Stefan Ekberg 7+1; Adam Roynon 6; Claus Kristensen 5+1; James Cockle 4+1; Trent Leverington 3).

14 September: Premier League

Hull 11 Glasgow 7 (George Stancl 2; Stefen Ekberg 2; Luke Priest 2; Trent Leverington 1+1; Claus Kristensen 0; James Cockle 0; Shane Parker DNR) – meeting abandoned after heat three.

25 September: Scottish Cup (second leg)

Glasgow 53 (Shane Parker 15; George Stancl 13+2; Stefan Ekberg 8; James Cockle 7; Trent Leverington 5+1; Claus Kristensen 5; Luke Priest 0) Edinburgh 37 – Glasgow won 101-78 on aggregate.

INDIVIDUAL MEETINGS

17 July: Party With Parks – Shane Parker Testimonial

    1st Sam Ermolenko 14; 2nd Steve Johnston 13; 3rd Gary Havelock (on race wins) 11; Simon Stead 11; Shane Parker 11; Jason Lyons 10; Chris Harris 10; George Stancl 8; Stefan Ekberg 7; Rusty Harrison 7; Joe Screen 5; Trent Leverington 5; Chris Louis 3; James Grieves 2; Paul Thorp 2; Craig Boyce 1; Adam Roynon (Res) 0.

2 October: City of Glasgow Ashfield Classic

    QUALIFYING SCORES: George Stancl 14; Adam Skornicki 12; Adrian Rymel 11; Mariusz Frankow 11; Shane Parker 10; James Grieves 10; Henning Bager 9; David Howe 7; Adam Pietraszko 7; James Wright 6; William Lawson 6; Piotr Dym 5; Trent Leverington 4; Mark Lemon 3; Theo Pijper 2; Claus Kristensen 1. SEMI-FINAL: 1st Rymel; 2nd Grieves; 3rd Frankow; 4th Parker. FINAL: 1st Stancl; 2nd Grieves; 3rd Skornicki; 4th Rymel.

16 October: Heathersfield Golden Helmet

    1st Gary Flint 14; 2nd Sean Stoddart 13; 3rd Adam McKinna (on countback) 12; Gary Beaton 12; Karl Langley 12; Andrew Tully 11; Cal McDade 8; John Morrison 7; David Haigh 7; Keiran Morris 7; John MacPhail 6; Alan Ferrow 5; Rusty Hodgson 2; Keith Maben 2; Maurice Crang 1; Glyn Picken (Res) 1; Peter Gemmill 0: Adam Scott (Res) 0. SCOTTISH JUNIOR CHAMPIONSHIP: 1st McKinna; 2nd Stoddart; 3rd Beaton; 4th Tully.

HULL CPD VIKINGS

ADDRESS: Craven Park Stadium, Poorhouse Lane, Preston Road, Kingston Upon Hull, East Yorkshire, HU9 5HE.

PROMOTERS: Paul Hodder & Dave Peet.

TRACK LENGTH: 346 metres.

TRACK RECORD: 64.4 seconds – Magnus Karlsson (30 June 2004).

FIRST MEETING: 5 April 1995.

YEARS OF OPERATION: 1995–98 Premier League; 1999 Elite League; 2000–2005 Premier League.

PREVIOUS VENUE AS 'VIKINGS': The Boulevard Stadium, Airlie Street, Kingston Upon Hull, East Yorkshire.

YEARS OF OPERATION: 1971–73 British League Division Two; 1974 British League Division One; 1975–81 British League.

CLUB HONOURS

INTER-LEAGUE KNOCK-OUT CUP WINNERS: 1976.

PREMIER TROPHY WINNERS: 2000.

KNOCK-OUT CUP WINNERS: 2001, 2004.

PREMIERSHIP WINNERS: 2002.

LEAGUE CHAMPIONS: 2004.

YOUNG SHIELD WINNERS: 2004.

RIDER ROSTER 2005

Craig BRANNEY; Lee DICKEN; Daniel GIFFARD; Emil KRAMER; Joel PARSONS; Michael PICKERING; Emiliano SANCHEZ; Garry STEAD; Simone TERENZANI; Paul THORP.

OTHER APPEARANCES/GUESTS (official matches only):

Tommy ALLEN; Gary BEATON; John BRANNEY; James BRUNDLE; Benji COMPTON; Barrie EVANS; Daniel GIFFARD; Robbie KESSLER; Robert KSIEZAK; Michal MAKOVSKY; Chris MILLS; Daniel NERMARK; Danny NORTON; Glen PHILLIPS; Michael PICKERING; Luke PRIEST; Jamie ROBERTSON; Nick SIMMONS; Lubos TOMICEK; Ben WILSON.

PREMIER LEAGUE

(*Denotes bonus-point victory)

No	DATE	OPPONENTS	H/A	RESULT	Thorp	Sanchez	Dicken	Kramer	Stead	C. Branney	Parsons	Terenzani	Giffard	Others
1	2/5	Rye House	A	L44-50	11+3 (6)	14+1 (6)	R/R	3+2 (4)	6+1 (4)	8+1 (6)	2 (4)	–	–	–
2	11/5	Isle of Wight	H	W55-37	9+2 (4)	5+1 (4)	–	12 (5)	13 (5)	7+2 (4)	4+2 (4)	5+1 (4)	–	–
3	18/5	Newport	H	W52-38	R/R	17+1 (6)	–	13+1 (5)	11+1 (5)	2 (5)	2 (4)	7+2 (5)	–	–
4	21/5	Workington	A	L43-47	9+1 (5)	3+1 (4)	–	10 (4)	12 (5)	3+1 (4)	2+1 (3)	4+1 (5)	–	–
5	25/5	Reading	H	W47-43	12+1 (5)	9+2 (5)	–	7+1 (4)	5+1 (4)	4+2 (4)	2+1 (3)	8 (5)	–	–
6	28/5	Stoke	A	L43-51	3 (4)	10+3 (5)	–	8 (4)	13 (5)	0 (3)	5+2 (4)	4 (5)	–	–
7	8/6	Exeter	H	W49.5 -46.5	15 (6)	9½(5)	–	R/R	8 (4)	7+1 (5)	0 (3)	10+4 (7)	–	–
8	12/6	Newcastle	A	L42-48	10 (5)	–	–	14+1 (6)	8+1 (4)	R/R	5+1 (5)	–	–	5+1 (10)
9	15/6	Edinburgh	H	L38-53	5+1 (4)	9+1 (5)	–	6 (4)	11 (5)	0 (3)	4+1 (5)	3 (4)	–	–
10	19/6	Newport	A	W48-42*	11+1 (5)	11+1 (5)	–	6+1 (4)	7+1 (4)	4 (3)	7+1 (5)	2 (4)	–	–
11	20/6	Exeter	A	L41-49	11 (5)	2+1 (4)	–	11+1 (5)	6 (4)	6 (4)	4+2 (5)	1 (3)	–	–
12	22/6	Rye House	H	W57-33*	11 (5)	8+1 (4)	–	10+2 (5)	3 (2)	9+1 (4)	8+2 (5)	8+1 (5)	–	–
13	25/6	Berwick	A	L32-61	10 (5)	R/R	–	8+1 (5)	–	0 (3)	6+2 (7)	7 (6)	–	1 (4)
14	20/7	Sheffield	H	W50-45	12+1 (5)	5+2 (4)	–	11 (5)	–	0 (0)	–	11+2 (7)	–	11+2 (9)
15	21/7	Sheffield	A	L39-56	13 (5)	3+2 (6)	–	13 (6)	–	R/R	–	2 (3)	–	8 (9)
16	3/8	Newcastle	H	W51-43*	10+2 (5)	6 (4)	–	12+1 (5)	8+1 (4)	5+2 (4)	–	4+1 (4)	–	6+2 (4)
17	7/8	Glasgow	A	L29-64	8+1 (5)	R/R	–	6 (7)	9 (6)	4+1 (5)	–	0 (4)	–	2+1 (3)
18	10/8	Berwick	H	L44-46	15 (6)	R/R	–	10+1 (6)	7 (4)	7 (5)	–	2+1 (5)	–	3+1 (4)
19	14/8	King's Lynn	A	L29-64	5+2 (6)	R/R	–	8 (6)	11 (6)	2+1 (5)	–	3+1 (4)	–	0 (3)
20	15/8	Reading	A	L36-58	10 (6)	R/R	–	11 (6)	4 (5)	4+2 (4)	–	4+3 (5)	3 (4)	–
21	16/8	Isle of Wight	A	L36-59	12+1 (6)	R/R	–	5 (6)	12 (6)	3+1 (5)	–	1 (4)	3 (4)	–
22	17/8	Workington	H	W55-40*	8+2 (4)	13+1 (5)	–	6+1 (4)	11 (5)	8+1 (4)	–	6+1 (4)	3+2 (4)	–
23	24/8	Stoke	H	W56-36*	11 (4)	8+4 (5)	–	10+1 (4)	11 (5)	5+1 (4)	–	10+2 (5)	–	1 (3)
24	31/8	Somerset†	H	W40-32	9+1 (4)	6+2 (3)	–	5+1 (3)	9 (3)	5 (4)	–	5+1 (4)	–	1+1 (3)
25	2/9	Edinburgh	A	L35-60	9+1 (4)	10+3 (5)	–	4+1 (4)	6 (5)	4 (4)	–	2 (5)	–	0 (3)
26	9/9	Somerset	A	L38-56	8 (4)	2+2 (5)	–	13 (5)	9 (5)	0 (3)	–	–	3+1 (4)	3 (4)

NOTE: Two matches were not ridden, v. Glasgow (home) and v. King's Lynn (home).

†Meeting abandoned after heat twelve, with the result permitted to stand.

HULL: From left to right, back row: Paul Hodder (Promoter), Garry Stead, Emil Kramer, Lee Dicken, Joel Parsons, Dave Peet (Co-Promoter/Team Manager). Front, kneeling: Emiliano Sanchez, Craig Branney. On bike: Paul Thorp.

DETAILS OF OTHER RIDERS:

Match No. 8: Chris Mills 5+1 (7); Luke Priest 0 (3); Match No. 13: Daniel Nermark 1 (4); Match No. 14: Robbie Kessler 6+1 (4); Danny Norton 5+1 (5); Match No. 15: Robbie Kessler 8 (4); Danny Norton 0 (5); Match No. 16: Daniel Giffard 6+2 (4); Match No. 17: Luke Priest 2+1 (3); Match No. 18: Benji Compton 3+1 (4); Match No. 19: John Branney 0 (3); Match No. 23: Michael Pickering 1 (3); Match No. 24: John Branney 1+1 (3); Match No. 25: Gary Beaton 0 (3); Match No. 26: Glen Phillips 3 (4).

TACTICAL SUBSTITUTE AND TACTICAL RIDES, AS INCLUDED IN THE SCORES GRID:

Match No. 1: Sanchez 4 points (TR); Thorp 4 points (TR); Match No. 6: Sanchez 4 points (TR); Stead 4 points (TR); Match No. 9: Kramer 2 points (TR); Stead 0 points (TR); Match No. 13: Kramer 4 points (TR); Terenzani 2 points (TS); Thorp 0 points (TR); Match No. 15: Thorp 6 points (TR); Kessler 4 points (TR); Sanchez 0 points (TS); Match No. 17: Thorp 4 points (TR); Stead 2 points (TR); Kramer 2 points (TS); Match No. 19: Stead 4 points (TR); Kramer 2 points (TS); Thorp 0 points (TR); Match No. 20: Kramer 4 points (TR); Thorp 4 points (TR); Match No. 21: Thorp 6 points (TR); Stead 4 points (TR); Kramer 0 points (TS); Match No. 25: Sanchez 6 points (TR); Thorp 4 points (TR); Match No. 26: Kramer 4 points (TR); Thorp 4 points (TR); Sanchez 0 points (TS).

PREMIER LEAGUE AVERAGES

Rider	Mts	Rds	Pts	Bon	Tot	Avge	Max
Paul Thorp	25	123	231	20	251	8.16	–
Emiliano Sanchez	19	90	143.5	29	172.5	7.67	1 paid
Garry Stead	23	105	193	6	199	7.58	–
Emil Kramer	25	122	213	16	229	7.51	–
Simone Terenzani	23	107	108	21	129	4.82	–
Craig Branney	24	95	97	17	114	4.80	–
Joel Parsons	13	57	51	15	66	4.63	–
Daniel Giffard	4	16	12	3	15	3.75	–
Michael Pickering	1	3	1	0	1	1.33	–
Guests	14	56	38	8	46	3.29	–

(Gary Beaton [1]; John Branney [2]; Benji Compton [1]; Daniel Giffard [1]; Robbie Kessler [2]; Chris Mills [1]; Daniel Nermark [1]; Danny Norton [2]; Glen Phillips [1]; Luke Priest [2]).

PREMIER TROPHY

(*Denotes bonus-point victory)

No	DATE	OPPONENTS	H/A	RESULT	Thorp	Sanchez	Dicken	Kramer	Stead	Parsons	C. Branney	Terenzani	Others
1	16/3	Stoke	H	W53-42	8+1 (4)	9+2 (5)	8 (4)	5+1 (4)	14 (5)	3+1 (2)	6+2 (6)	–	–
2	19/3	Stoke	A	L44-52*	0 (4)	15 (5)	2 (4)	5 (4)	15+1 (5)	–	5+2 (5)	–	2 (3)
3	23/3	Newcastle	H	W59-36	10+2 (5)	9+1 (4)	7+2 (4)	8+1 (4)	15 (5)	–	6+3 (4)	–	4 (4)
4	30/3	Edinburgh	H	W53-42	12+1 (5)	12+3 (5)	3 (4)	11 (4)	10 (4)	–	4 (5)	–	1+1 (3)
5	3/4	Glasgow	A	L40-52	7 (4)	5+2 (4)	1+1 (4)	13 (5)	9 (5)	–	3+1 (5)	–	2 (3)
6	6/4	Glasgow	H	W52-41	15 (5)	7+2 (4)	5+2 (4)	10 (4)	10+1 (5)	–	4+3 (5)	–	1 (3)
7	9/4	Workington	A	L36-56	12 (5)	3 (4)	2+2 (3)	5 (5)	5+1 (4)	–	8 (6)	–	1+1 (3)
8	13/4	Berwick	H	W54-42	11+2 (5)	9+1 (4)	1 (1)	5+2 (4)	15 (5)	–	11+1 (6)	–	2 (5)
9	20/4	Workington	H	W51-39	12+2 (5)	12+2 (5)	3+2 (4)	5+1 (4)	9 (4)	–	9+1 (5)	–	1+1 (3)
10	23/4	Berwick	A	L37-57	3 (5)	2 (4)	1 (3)	11+1 (4)	11 (5)	–	1 (3)	–	8+1 (6)

No	DATE	OPPONENTS	H/A	RESULT	Thorp	Sanchez	Dicken	Kramer	Stead	Parsons	C. Branney	Terenzani	Others
11	24/4	Newcastle	A	L42-51*	5+2 (5)	16 (5)	3 (3)	3 (4)	3 (4)	–	9+1 (6)	–	3+1 (3)
12	27/4	Sheffield	H	W47-45	9 (4)	11+3 (5)	4+1 (3)	6+1 (4)	12+1 (5)	–	2+1 (4)	–	3 (5)
13	29/4	Edinburgh	A	W49-42*	9+2 (5)	11 (5)	R/R	9 (4)	11+1 (5)	1 (4)	8+1 (7)	–	–
14	5/5	Sheffield	A	L28-64	8 (5)	3+1 (4)	–	7 (5)	6 (4)	0 (3)	4+1 (5)	0 (4)	–

DETAILS OF OTHER RIDERS:

Match No. 2: Nick Simmons 2 (3); Match No. 3: Ben Wilson 4 (4); Match No. 4: Barrie Evans 1+1 (3); Match No. 5: Robert Ksiezak 2 (3); Match No. 6: Ben Wilson 1 (3); Match No. 7: James Brundle 1+1 (3); Match No. 8: Jamie Robertson 2 (5); Match No. 9: Tommy Allen 1+1 (3); Match No. 10: Jamie Robertson 8+1 (6); Match No. 11: Ben Wilson 3+1 (3); Match No. 12: Lubos Tomicek 3 (5).

TACTICAL SUBSTITUTE AND TACTICAL RIDES, AS INCLUDED IN THE SCORES GRID:

Match No. 2: Stead 6 points (TR); Sanchez 6 points (TR); Match No. 5: Kramer 6 points (TR); Match No. 7: Thorp 2 points (TR); C. Branney 2 points (TS); Stead 0 points (TR); Match No. 10: Kramer 6 points (TR); Stead 2 points (TR); Thorp 0 points (TS); Match No. 11: Sanchez 6 points (TR); Match No. 14: Sanchez 2 points (TR); Thorp 2 points (TR).

PREMIER TROPHY AVERAGES

Rider	Mts	Rds	Pts	Bon	Tot	Avge	Max
Garry Stead	14	65	141	5	146	8.98	2 full
Emiliano Sanchez	14	63	117	17	134	8.51	1 paid
Paul Thorp	14	66	119	12	131	7.94	1 full
Emil Kramer	14	59	97	7	104	7.05	–
Craig Branney	14	72	79	17	96	5.33	–
Lee Dicken	12	41	40	10	50	4.88	–
Joel Parsons	3	9	4	1	5	2.22	–
Simone Terenzani	1	4	0	0	0	0.00	–
Guests	11	41	28	5	33	3.22	–

(Tommy Allen [1]; James Brundle [1]; Barrie Evans [1]; Robert Ksiezak [1]; Jamie Robertson [2]; Nick Simmons [1]; Lubos Tomicek [1]; Ben Wilson [3]).

KNOCK-OUT CUP

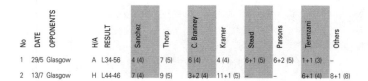

No	DATE	OPPONENTS	H/A	RESULT	Sanchez	Thorp	C. Branney	Kramer	Stead	Parsons	Terenzani	Others
1	29/5	Glasgow	A	L34-56	4 (4)	7 (5)	6 (4)	4 (4)	6+1 (5)	6+2 (5)	1+1 (3)	–
2	13/7	Glasgow	H	L44-46	7 (4)	9 (5)	3+2 (4)	11+1 (5)	–	–	6+1 (4)	8+1 (8)

DETAILS OF OTHER RIDERS:

Match No. 2: Daniel Giffard 5+1 (4); Michal Makovsky 3 (4).

OTHER MEETINGS

9 March: Yorkshire Cup (first leg)

Hull 53 (Emil Kramer <u>15</u>; Garry Stead 12+1; Paul Thorp 9; Craig Branney 7+2; Emiliano Sanchez 6+1; Lee Dicken 2+1; Joel Parsons 2) Sheffield 39.

12 March: Challenge

Berwick 47 Hull 43 (Garry Stead 12; Lee Dicken 7+1; Craig Branney 6+2; Emil Kramer 6; Paul Thorp 5; Emiliano Sanchez 4; Joel Parsons 3).

17 March: Yorkshire Cup (second leg)

Sheffield 55 Hull 36 (Jan Jaros 10; Paul Thorp 8; Emil Kramer 7; Emiliano Sanchez 4; Garry Stead 4; Lee Dicken 3+2; Craig Branney 0) – Sheffield won 94-89 on aggregate.

31 July: Conference Challenge

Scunthorpe 53 Hull 40 (James Birkinshaw <u>18</u>; Luke Priest 9; Daniel Hodgson 6; Neil Martin 4+1; Paul Burnett 2+1; Michael Pickering 1; David Baker 0).

14 September: Premier League

Hull 11 (Paul Thorp 3; Emil Kramer 3; Simone Terenzani 3; Craig Branney 1; Daniel Giffard 1; Emiliano Sanchez 0; Garry Stead DNR) Glasgow 7 – meeting abandoned after heat three.

INDIVIDUAL MEETING

4 May: CPD Yorkshire Classic

1st Paul Thorp 14; 2nd Ross Brady 13; 3rd Michal Makovsky 12; Steve Johnston 11; Emiliano Sanchez 10; Kauko Nieminen 10; Daniel Nermark 9; Ben Wilson 9; Richard Hall 7; James Birkinshaw 6; Jamie Robertson 4; Joel Parsons 4; Craig Branney 3; Garry Stead 3; Simone Terenzani 2; Ricky Ashworth 2; Neil Martin (Res) 0.

ISLE OF WIGHT WIGHTLINK ISLANDERS

ADDRESS: Smallbrook Stadium, Ashey Road, Ryde, Isle of Wight, PO33 4BH.
PROMOTERS: Dave Pavitt & Martin Newnham.
TRACK LENGTH: 385 metres.
TRACK RECORD: 67.7 seconds – Krister Marsh (28 July 2005) & Craig Boyce (28 July 2005 & 16 August 2005).
FIRST MEETING: 13 May 1996.
YEARS OF OPERATION: 1995 Demonstration; 1996 Conference League; 1997 Amateur League & Premier League; 1998–2005 Premier League.

CLUB HONOURS

YOUNG SHIELD WINNERS: 1998, 2001.
PAIRS CHAMPIONS: 2002.
KNOCK-OUT CUP WINNERS: 2003.

ISLE OF WIGHT: From left to right: Manuel Hauzinger, Krister Marsh, Jason Doyle, Craig Boyce (on bike), Ulrich Ostergaard, Steen Jensen, David Croucher (Team Manager).

RIDER ROSTER 2005

Craig BOYCE; Jason BUNYAN; Jason DOYLE; Manuel HAUZINGER; Steen JENSEN; Krister MARSH; Ulrich OSTERGAARD; Glen PHILLIPS; Krzysztof STOJANOWSKI; Tomas SUCHANEK.

OTHER APPEARANCES/GUESTS (official matches only):

Luke BOWEN; Tom BROWN; Edward KENNETT; Michael PICKERING; Nick SIMMONS; Danny WARWICK.

PREMIER LEAGUE

(*Denotes bonus-point victory)

No	DATE	OPPONENTS	H/A	RESULT	Boyce	Hauzinger	Marsh	Ostergaard	Bunyan	Doyle	Suchanek	Jensen	Phillips	Stojanowski	Others
1	11/5	Hull	A	L37-55	13 (6)	1 (3)	3+3 (3)	13 (6)	R/R	6 (7)	-	-	-	-	1 (4)
2	24/5	Stoke	H	W50-46	11 (5)	4 (4)	8+1 (4)	8 (4)	-	6+1 (4)	4+1 (4)	9+2 (5)	-	-	-
3	27/5	Edinburgh	A	L30-63	13 (5)	0 (3)	3 (4)	2 (4)	-	5 (5)	0 (3)	7+2 (6)	-	-	-
4	28/5	Berwick	A	L40-50	14 (5)	R/R	2+1 (4)	8 (5)	-	6+2 (6)	3 (4)	7+2 (6)	-	-	-
5	14/6	Workington	H	D45-45	13 (5)	-	6+2 (4)	9+1 (5)	-	3 (5)	9+1 (4)	3 (3)	2 (4)	-	-
6	21/6	Berwick	H	W50-46	15 (5)	-	6+2 (4)	9+1 (5)	-	5+1 (4)	4+1 (4)	8 (5)	3 (4)	-	-
7	27/6	Exeter	A	L45-50	17 (5)	-	6+1 (4)	11+2 (5)	-	-	1 (4)	4 (5)	2 (3)	-	4+2 (4)
8	30/6	Sheffield	A	L45-50	14 (5)	-	1+1 (3)	15 (5)	-	4 (4)	1 (4)	8+2 (5)	2 (4)	-	-
9	3/7	Glasgow	A	L44-46	13 (5)	-	4+1 (4)	8+1 (5)	-	10+1 (4)	4+1 (4)	0 (4)	5 (4)	-	-
10	12/7	Edinburgh	H	W61-34	15 (5)	-	7+1 (4)	14+1 (5)	-	5+1 (4)	9+2 (4)	6 (4)	5+1 (4)	-	-
11	19/7	Sheffield	H	W59-33*	11+1 (5)	-	9 (4)	9+3 (5)	-	12+1 (5)	8+2 (4)	6 (4)	4 (3)	-	-
12	23/7	Workington	A	L42-50	12 (5)	-	5+1 (4)	12 (5)	-	3 (4)	3 (4)	3+1 (4)	4+1 (4)	-	-
13	24/7	Newcastle	A	L36-56	12 (5)	-	6+1 (4)	8 (5)	-	6 (5)	1 (4)	3 (4)	0 (3)	-	-
14	4/8	Somerset	H	W56-37	-	-	9+2 (5)	13+1 (5)	-	9+2 (5)	-	6+2 (3)	3+1 (4)	7+2 (4)	9 (4)
15	9/8	King's Lynn	H	W56-40	15 (5)	-	6+1 (5)	R/R	-	11+1 (5)	-	9+2 (4)	4+3 (5)	11+2 (6)	-
16	14/8	Newport	A	W50-40	9 (4)	-	4 (4)	R/R	-	2 (5)	-	19 (7)	3+1 (4)	13+4 (6)	-
17	16/8	Hull	H	W59-36*	15 (5)	-	9 (4)	R/R	-	7+2 (5)	-	8+2 (5)	8+1 (5)	12+2 (6)	-
18	21/8	Rye House	A	L37-59	12 (5)	-	5+1 (4)	R/R	-	7+1 (6)	-	DNA	5+1 (6)	8+2 (6)	-
19	23/8	Rye House	H	W54-40	11 (5)	-	4+1 (4)	13 (5)	-	5 (4)	-	8+2 (4)	7+1 (4)	6+3 (4)	-
20	25/8	Newcastle	H	W71-23*	15 (5)	-	9+3 (4)	11+1 (4)	-	7+2 (4)	-	9+2 (4)	7+4 (4)	13+2 (5)	-
21	26/8	Somerset	A	W51-43*	11 (5)	-	6 (4)	11 (5)	-	8+2 (5)	-	4+1 (3)	4+2 (4)	7+1 (4)	-
22	31/8	King's Lynn	A	L37-57	11 (5)	-	7+2 (4)	9 (5)	-	4+2 (5)	-	0 (3)	2 (4)	4 (4)	-
23	1/9	Newport	H	W65-31*	13+2 (5)	-	10 (4)	9+3 (4)	-	11+1 (5)	-	4 (4)	8 (4)	10+2 (4)	-
24	6/9	Exeter	H	W60-33*	12 (4)	-	7+1 (4)	12+2 (5)	-	8+1 (4)	-	6+1 (4)	8+3 (4)	7+1 (5)	-
25	13/9	Glasgow	H	W54-39*	12 (5)	-	10+1 (6)	12+2 (5)	-	9+2 (5)	-	R/R	7+1 (5)	4+1 (4)	-
26	19/9	Reading	A	L45-50	13+1 (5)	-	6+3 (5)	10 (6)	-	9 (6)	-	R/R	2+1 (5)	5 (4)	-
27	20/9	Reading	H	W50-42*	10 (5)	-	6 (5)	8+3 (6)	-	13+1 (5)	-	R/R	10+1 (5)	3+2 (4)	-
28	2/10	Stoke†	A	L34-43	11 (3)	-	0 (2)	9 (3)	-	6+4 (7)	-	R/R	4+1 (6)	4 (3)	-

†Meeting abandoned after heat twelve, with the result permitted to stand.

DETAILS OF OTHER RIDERS:

Match No. 1: Michael Pickering 1 (4); Match No. 7: Nick Simmons 4+2 (4); Match No. 14: Edward Kennett 9 (4).

TACTICAL SUBSTITUTE AND TACTICAL RIDES, AS INCLUDED IN THE SCORES GRID:

Match No. 1: Ostergaard 4 points (TR); Marsh 0 points (TR; excluded for touching the tapes, then excluded for exceeding the two-minute time allowance); Match No. 3: Boyce 4 points (TR); Jensen 2 points (TR); Match No. 7: Boyce 6 points (TR); Ostergaard 4 points (TR); Match No. 8: Boyce 6 points (TR); Ostergaard 6 points (TR); Match No. 12: Boyce 4 points (TR); Match No. 13: Ostergaard 2 points (TR); Boyce 2 points (TR); Doyle 2 points (TS); Match No. 18: Boyce 6 points (TR); Stojanowski 4 points (TR); Phillips 2 points (TS); Match No. 22: Boyce 4 points (TR); Marsh 4 points (TR); Doyle 0 points (TS); Match No. 26: Ostergaard 4 points (TR); Boyce 4 points (TR); Doyle 2 points (TS); Match No. 28: Boyce 6 points (TR); Ostergaard 4 points (TR).

PREMIER LEAGUE AVERAGES

Rider	Mts	Rds	Pts	Bon	Tot	Avge	Max
Craig Boyce	27	132	322	4	326	9.88	6 full; 1 paid
Ulrich Ostergaard	24	117	231	21	252	8.62	3 paid
Krzysztof Stojanowski	15	69	112	24	136	7.88	2 paid
Krister Marsh	28	114	162	30	192	6.74	1 paid
Steen Jensen	22	96	136	21	157	6.54	–
Jason Doyle	27	133	185	28	213	6.41	–
Glen Phillips	24	102	108	23	131	5.14	–
Tomas Suchanek	12	47	47	8	55	4.68	–
Manuel Hauzinger	3	10	5	0	5	2.00	–
Guests	3	12	14	2	16	5.33	–

(Edward Kennett [1]; Michael Pickering [1]; Nick Simmons [1]).

PREMIER TROPHY

(*Denotes bonus-point victory)

No	DATE	OPPONENTS	H/A RESULT	Boyce	Hauzinger	Marsh	Ostergaard	Bunyan	Jensen	Doyle	Suchanek	Phillips	Others
1	27/3	Reading	A W47-46	13 (5)	4+1 (4)	9+1 (5)	6+2 (4)	5+1 (4)	6 (4)	4+2 (4)	–	–	–
2	28/3	Rye House	A L32-61	15 (6)	1 (4)	4+1 (4)	6+1 (5)	2 (4)	3+1 (4)	1 (3)	–	–	–
3	4/4	Exeter	A L39-53	8 (5)	2 (4)	5+2 (4)	10 (5)	5+1 (4)	5+1 (4)	4+2 (5)	–	–	–
4	5/4	King's Lynn	H W54-39	13 (5)	1 (4)	7 (4)	9+2 (4)	11+2 (5)	9+2 (4)	4+2 (4)	–	–	–
5	12/4	Somerset	H W50-40	18 (6)	1 (3)	6+2 (5)	8 (5)	R/R	15+2 (7)	2+1 (4)	–	–	–
6	15/4	Somerset	A L44-46*	17 (6)	3+1 (4)	8 (5)	8 (6)	R/R	7 (5)	1 (4)	–	–	–
7	19/4	Reading	H W51-39*	14+1 (6)	10+1 (5)	8+1 (6)	9+2 (5)	R/R	–	9+4 (5)	–	1 (3)	–
8	20/4	King's Lynn	A L36-57	20 (7)	1+1 (4)	6 (5)	7+1 (6)	R/R	–	0 (5)	–	2+1 (3)	–
9	10/5	Rye House	H L44-46	15 (6)	6 (5)	6+1 (5)	11 (6)	R/R	4 (4)	2+2 (4)	–	–	–
10	17/5	Exeter	H W48-42	13 (5)	6+1 (4)	8+2 (5)	8+2 (4)	–	4+1 (4)	6 (4)	3 (4)	–	–
11	31/5	Newport	H W52-42	15 (5)	–	7 (4)	8+1 (4)	–	4+1 (4)	5+1 (4)	9 (5)	4 (4)	–
12	1/6	Newport	A L40-50	12 (5)	–	4 (4)	9+1 (5)	–	3 (4)	7 (6)	–	4+2 (4)	1+1 (3)

DETAILS OF OTHER RIDERS:

Match No. 7: Danny Warwick 1 (3); Match No. 8: Luke Bowen 2+1 (3); Match No. 12: Tom Brown 1+1 (3).

TACTICAL SUBSTITUTE AND TACTICAL RIDES, AS INCLUDED IN THE SCORES GRID:

Match No. 2: Boyce 4 points (TS); Ostergaard 2 points (TR); Bunyan 0 points (TR); Match No. 3: Ostergaard 4 points (TR); Match No. 8: Boyce 4 points (TS); Marsh 2 points (TR); Ostergaard 0 points (TR); Match No. 12: Marsh 2 points (TR).

PREMIER TROPHY AVERAGES

Rider	Mts	Rds	Pts	Bon	Tot	Avge	Max
Craig Boyce	12	67	169	1	170	10.15	2 full
Ulrich Ostergaard	12	59	96	12	108	7.32	–
Jason Bunyan	4	17	23	4	27	6.35	–
Steen Jensen	10	44	60	8	68	6.18	–
Krister Marsh	12	56	76	10	86	6.14	–
Tomas Suchanek	2	9	12	0	12	5.33	–
Glen Phillips	2	8	8	2	10	5.00	–
Jason Doyle	12	52	45	14	59	4.54	–
Manuel Hauzinger	10	41	35	5	40	3.90	–
Guests	3	9	4	2	6	2.67	–

(Luke Bowen [1]; Tom Brown [1]; Danny Warwick [1]).

KNOCK-OUT CUP

(*Denotes aggregate victory)

No	DATE	OPPONENTS	H/A RESULT	Boyce	Hauzinger	Marsh	Ostergaard	Suchanek	Doyle	Jensen	Phillips	Stojanowski
1	26/5	Sheffield	A L39-51	12+1 (5)	1 (3)	5+1 (4)	9+1 (5)	1 (3)	5 (5)	6+1 (5)	–	
2	7/6	Sheffield	H W55-34*	13 (5)	–	7+2 (4)	15 (5)	3 (3)	6+2 (4)	5 (4)	6+2 (4)	–
3	28/7	Reading	H W46-44	12 (5)	–	9 (4)	2+1 (4)	7+2 (5)	7 (4)	3+2 (4)	6+1 (4)	–
4	8/8	Reading†	A L33-51	5+1 (4)	–	4+1 (4)	5+2 (4)	–	4 (4)	4+1 (4)	4 (4)	7 (4)

†Meeting abandoned after heat fourteen, with the result permitted to stand.

YOUNG SHIELD

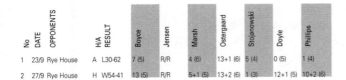

No	DATE	OPPONENTS	H/A RESULT	Boyce	Jensen	Marsh	Ostergaard	Stojanowski	Doyle	Phillips
1	23/9	Rye House	A L30-62	7 (5)	R/R	4 (6)	13+1 (6)	5 (4)	0 (5)	1 (4)
2	27/9	Rye House	H W54-41	13 (5)	R/R	5+1 (5)	13+2 (6)	1 (3)	12+1 (5)	10+2 (6)

TACTICAL SUBSTITUTE AND TACTICAL RIDES, AS INCLUDED IN THE SCORES GRID:

Match No. 1: Ostergaard 4 points (TR); Boyce 2 points (TR); Marsh 0 points (TS).

OTHER MEETING

2 August: Ray Morton Testimonial

Ripper's Rebels 46 (Mark Lemon 15+1; Jason Doyle 11; Krister Marsh 7; Glen Phillips 5+3; Ronnie Correy 5; Steve Boxall 2+1; Olly Allen 1) Thorpy's Tape Touchers 47 (Edward Kennett 12+2; Paul Thorp 9; Andrew Appleton 6+1; Dean Barker 6+1; Paul Hurry 6; Ricky Ashworth 5; Steen Jensen 3).

PAIRS MEETING

22 March: JT Commercials Solent Pairs Championship

1st (after run-off) Steen Jensen (15+2) & Ulrich Ostergaard (11+1) = 26; 2nd Sebastien Tresarrieu (19) & Mathieu Tresarrieu (7+1) = 26; 3rd Craig Boyce (17+1) & Jason Doyle (7) = 24; Jason Bunyan (19) & Chris Johnson (4) = 23; Manuel Hauzinger (12+1) & Krister Marsh (9+1) = 21; Glen Phillips (13) & Gary Phelps (2) = 15.

KING'S LYNN MONEY CENTRE STARS

ADDRESS: Norfolk Arena, Saddlebow Road, King's Lynn, Norfolk, PE34 3AG.
PROMOTER: Keith 'Buster' Chapman & Jonathan Chapman.
TRACK LENGTH: 342 metres.
TRACK RECORD: 57.6 seconds – Nicki Pedersen (11 September 2002).
FIRST MEETING: 23 May 1965.
YEARS OF OPERATION: 1965 Open; 1966–67 British League; 1968 British League Division One; 1969–70 British League Division One & Division Two; 1971–74 British League Division One; 1975–90 British League; 1991–94 British League Division One; 1995 Premier League; 1996 Training; 1997 Elite League & Amateur League; 1998–99 Elite League & Conference League; 2000–01 Elite League; 2002 Elite League & Conference League; 2003 Premier League; 2004 Premier League & Conference Trophy; 2005 Premier League.

NOTE: (1) In 1997, King's Lynn shared their Amateur League fixtures with Ipswich, under the banner of 'Anglian Angels'; (2) The track has also been occupied by Boston for their Conference League operation from 2000-05.

CLUB HONOURS

KNOCK-OUT CUP WINNERS: 1977, 2000, 2005.
INTER-LEAGUE KNOCK-OUT CUP WINNERS: 1978, 1980.
PREMIERSHIP WINNERS: 2001.
YOUNG SHIELD WINNERS: 2005.

RIDER ROSTER 2005

Olly ALLEN; Adam ALLOTT; Troy BATCHELOR; James BRUNDLE; Kevin DOOLAN; Jan JAROS; Ashley JONES; Paul LEE; Thomas STANGE; Tomas TOPINKA; Matthew WETHERS.

OTHER APPEARANCES/GUESTS (official matches only):
James BIRKINSHAW; Michael COLES; Benji COMPTON; Lee DERBYSHIRE; Barrie EVANS; Daniel GIFFARD; James GRIEVES; Trevor HARDING; Claus KRISTENSEN; Simon LAMBERT; Tom P. MADSEN; Darren MALLETT; Chris NEATH; Luke PRIEST; Adam ROYNON; Blair SCOTT; George STANCL; Shaun TACEY; Davey WATT.

PREMIER LEAGUE

(*Denotes aggregate victory)

No	DATE	OPPONENTS	H/A	RESULT	Topinka	Lee	Allott	Brundle	Allen	Jones	Jaros	Stange	Batchelor	Wethers	Doolan	Others
1	11/5	Stoke	H	W61-34	14 (5)	8+3 (5)	11 (4)	7+2 (4)	–	7+2 (4)	4+1 (4)	–	–	–	–	10 (4)
2	18/5	Somerset	H	W62-32	15 (5)	8+2 (5)	12 (4)	R/R	–	10+2 (7)	4 (4)	–	–	–	–	13+2 (5)
3	20/5	Edinburgh	A	L38-57	17 (5)	9 (6)	1+1 (4)	0 (2)	–	5+1 (6)	0 (3)	–	–	–	–	6 (4)
4	21/5	Berwick	A	L41-49	14 (5)	8+1 (6)	3 (4)	R/R	–	4 (5)	7+3 (7)	–	–	–	–	5+1 (3)
5	25/5	Workington	H	W53-43	10+1 (5)	5+1 (4)	13+1 (5)	–	9 (4)	4+1 (4)	11+3 (5)	1 (3)	–	–	–	–
6	30/5	Reading	A	L41-51	15+1 (5)	6 (5)	7 (4)	–	4 (4)	3+1 (4)	3+2 (4)	3 (4)	–	–	–	–
7	8/6	Reading	H	W53-39*	14 (5)	5+1 (4)	13+1 (5)	–	10+1 (4)	2 (4)	4 (4)	5+2 (4)	–	–	–	–
8	15/6	Sheffield	H	W52-39	13 (5)	5+1 (4)	11 (5)	–	10+1 (4)	6+2 (4)	3 (4)	–	4+1 (4)	–	–	–
9	18/6	Stoke	A	L39-55*	9 (4)	10 (5)	3+1 (4)	–	–	7+2 (5)	7 (6)	–	0 (3)	–	–	3+1 (3)
10	22/6	Berwick	H	W45-44	15 (5)	2 (2)	7 (4)	–	10+1 (5)	2+1 (4)	4 (5)	–	5+1 (5)	–	–	–
11	25/6	Workington	A	L38-55	12 (5)	–	–	–	6+1 (5)	2 (4)	–	–	1+1 (3)	9+2 (5)	5+1 (4)	3+1 (4)
12	3/7	Newcastle	A	L38-58	11 (5)	–	–	–	12 (4)	2+1 (4)	4+1 (4)	–	3 (6)	0 (2)	6+1 (5)	–
13	9/7	Rye House	A	L34-61	15 (5)	–	–	–	6+1 (5)	0 (3)	4 (4)	–	2 (3)	–	1 (4)	6+1 (6)
14	13/7	Rye House	H	W53-38	14 (5)	–	–	–	8+2 (5)	5+3 (4)	5+1 (4)	–	5 (4)	–	9 (4)	7+3 (4)
15	15/7	Somerset	A	W47-43*	12 (5)	–	–	–	4+1 (4)	3+2 (4)	1+1 (3)	–	14+1 (6)	–	7+1 (4)	6+1 (5)
16	3/8	Edinburgh	H	W55-41	–	–	–	–	2+1 (1)	6+1 (4)	3 (4)	–	16+1 (7)	8+3 (5)	7+1 (4)	13 (5)
17	7/8	Newport	A	W58-35	15 (5)	–	–	–	3 (1)	5+2 (4)	0 (4)	4+1 (4)	19+1 (7)	–	12+1 (5)	–
18	9/8	Isle of Wight	A	L40-56	12+1 (6)	–	–	–	R/R	4+1 (5)	0 (3)	1 (4)	17+1 (7)	–	6 (5)	–
19	10/8	Newport	H	W67-26*	12 (4)	–	–	–	8+4 (4)	2+1 (2)	9+2 (5)	5 (4)	18 (6)	–	13+2 (5)	–
20	14/8	Hull	H	W64-29	9 (4)	–	–	–	15 (5)	7+3 (4)	7+2 (4)	4 (4)	8+2 (4)	–	14+1 (5)	–
21	15/8	Exeter	A	L40-55	8 (5)	–	–	–	8 (5)	3+1 (4)	6 (5)	2+2 (3)	8+2 (4)	–	5 (4)	–
22	17/8	Glasgow	H	W45-44	12+1 (5)	–	–	–	10+1 (4)	3+1 (4)	5+1 (5)	4+1 (3)	5+1 (4)	–	6 (4)	–
23	21/8	Glasgow†	A	W36-35*	8 (3)	–	–	–	9 (3)	5+1 (3)	2 (3)	2 (5)	5 (4)	–	5 (3)	–
24	31/8	Isle of Wight	H	W57-37*	14+1 (5)	–	–	–	12+2 (5)	5+1 (4)	–	5 (4)	9+2 (4)	–	8 (4)	4+1 (4)
25	9/9	Newcastle	H	W52-38	15 (5)	–	–	–	11+1 (4)	4+1 (5)	6+2 (7)	2 (3)	R/R	–	14+1 (6)	–
26	14/9	Exeter	H	W56-35*	15 (5)	–	–	–	13+1 (5)	8+3 (5)	11+1 (6)	–	R/R	–	6 (5)	3+1 (4)
27	6/10	Sheffield	A	L40-56	14 (5)	–	–	–	5 (4)	1+1 (4)	5 (5)	–	4 (4)	–	10+1 (5)	1+1 (3)

NOTE: One match was not ridden, v. Hull (away).

†Meeting abandoned after heat twelve, with the result permitted to stand.

DETAILS OF OTHER RIDERS:

Match No. 1: Chris Neath 10 (4); Match No. 2: Davey Watt 13+2 (5); Match No. 3: James Grieves 6 (4); Match No. 4: Claus Kristensen 5+1 (3); Match No. 9: Luke Priest 3+1 (3); Match No. 11: Lee Derbyshire 3+1 (4); Match No. 13: Trevor Harding 6+1 (6); Match No. 14: Trevor Harding 7+3 (4); Match No. 15: Trevor Harding 6+1 (5); Match No. 16: Shaun Tacey 13 (5); Match No. 24: Darren Mallett 4+1 (4); Match No. 26: Simon Lambert 3+1 (4); Match No. 27: Darren Mallett 1+1 (3).

TACTICAL SUBSTITUTE AND TACTICAL RIDES, AS INCLUDED IN THE SCORES GRID:

Match No. 3: Topinka 6 points (TR); Grieves 2 points (TR); Lee 2 points (TS); Match No. 6: Topinka 6 points (TR); Match No. 9: Topinka 4 points (TR); Lee 4 points (TR); Match No. 11: Wethers 4 points (TR); Topinka 2 points (TR); Allen 0 points (TS); Match No. 12: Topinka 6 points (TR); Allen 6 points (TR); Match No. 13: Topinka 6 points (TR); Allen 4 points (TR); Match No. 18: Topinka 6 points (TR); Batchelor 6 points (TR); Match No. 21: Batchelor 6 points (TR); Topinka 4 points (TR); Match No. 27: Topinka 6 points (TR); Doolan 6 points (TR).

KING'S LYNN: From left to right, back row: Ashley Jones, Rob Lyon (Team Manager), Tomas Topinka (on bike), Troy Batchelor, Darren Mallett, Thomas Stange. Front, kneeling: Olly Allen, Kevin Doolan.

PREMIER LEAGUE AVERAGES

Rider	Mts	Rds	Pts	Bon	Tot	Avge	Max
Tomas Topinka	26	126	311	5	316	10.03	6 full; 1 paid
Olly Allen	21	86	170	18	188	8.74	1 full; 2 paid
Adam Allott	10	43	81	4	85	7.91	1 full
Kevin Doolan	17	76	131	10	141	7.42	2 paid
Troy Batchelor	18	85	137	14	151	7.11	1 full
Matthew Wethers	3	12	15	5	20	6.67	–
Paul Lee	10	46	63	9	72	6.26	–
James Brundle	2	6	7	2	9	6.00	–
Ashley Jones	27	113	115	35	150	5.31	–
Jan Jaros	25	112	115	20	135	4.82	–
Thomas Stange	12	45	38	6	44	3.91	–
Guests	13	54	79	13	92	6.81	1 paid

(Lee Derbyshire [1]; James Grieves [1]; Trevor Harding [3]; Claus Kristensen [1]; Simon Lambert [1]; Darren Mallett [2]; Chris Neath [1]; Luke Priest [1]; Shaun Tacey [1]; Davey Watt [1]).

PREMIER TROPHY

(*Denotes bonus-point victory)

No	DATE	OPPONENTS	H/A	RESULT	Topinka	Brundle	Doolan	Allott	Allen	Jaros	Batchelor	Jones	Lee	Others
1	23/3	Somerset	H	W51-44	12 (5)	3+2 (4)	8+1 (5)	8 (4)	9 (4)	3+1 (4)	8 (4)	–	–	–
2	30/3	Exeter	H	W56-37	14 (5)	6 (4)	5+2 (4)	12 (5)	9+1 (4)	3+1 (4)	7+2 (4)	–	–	–
3	5/4	Isle of Wight	A	L39-54	14 (5)	3 (4)	7 (4)	1+1 (4)	7 (5)	6+2 (5)	–	1+1 (3)	–	–
4	6/4	Reading	H	W49-44	14 (5)	5 (4)	7+2 (5)	10+1 (4)	2 (1)	3 (2)	–	8+1 (7)	–	–
5	8/4	Somerset	A	L43-54	13+1 (5)	6+1 (5)	5+1 (4)	1+1 (3)	–	–	–	6 (5)	–	12+1 (8)
6	11/4	Reading	A	L39-52	9+2 (5)	3 (4)	4+1 (4)	5 (4)	–	–	–	2 (1)	–	16 (12)
7	20/4	Isle of Wight	H	W57-36*	11 (4)	7+2 (4)	7+3 (5)	12 (5)	–	–	–	7+2 (4)	–	13+1 (8)
8	23/4	Rye House	A	L34-59	10 (5)	0 (4)	10 (6)	1+1 (4)	–	–	–	7+1 (5)	–	6+2 (7)
9	27/4	Rye House	H	W52-41	14+1 (5)	9+1 (5)	7+2 (4)	9+1 (4)	–	1+1 (3)	–	3 (5)	–	9 (4)
10	2/5	Exeter	A	L29-64	11+1 (5)	1 (4)	5 (4)	1+1 (4)	–	6 (5)	–	0 (3)	–	5 (5)
11	4/5	Newport	H	W53-39	12 (5)	5+1 (4)	9+2 (5)	10+1 (4)	–	2 (3)	–	6+4 (5)	–	9+1 (4)
12	15/5	Newport	A	W47-46*	12 (5)	0 (1)	–	3 (4)	–	4+1 (4)	–	9+2 (7)	10+1 (5)	9 (4)

DETAILS OF OTHER RIDERS:

Match No. 5: Davey Watt 12+1 (5); Adam Roynon 0 (3); Match No. 6: Davey Watt 15 (6); Darren Mallett 1 (6); Match No. 7: George Stancl 8 (4); Darren Mallett 5+1 (4); Match No. 8: Daniel Giffard 3+2 (5); Tom P. Madsen 3 (2); Match No. 9: Davey Watt 9 (4); Match No. 10: Michael Coles 5 (5); Match No. 11: Shaun Tacey 9+1 (4); Match No. 12: Chris Neath 9 (4).

TACTICAL SUBSTITUTE AND TACTICAL RIDES, AS INCLUDED IN THE SCORES GRID:

Match No. 3: Topinka 6 points (TR); Match No. 5: Topinka 6 points (TR); Watt 6 points (TR); Brundle 2 points (TS); Match No. 6: Watt 2 points (TS); Match No. 8: Topinka 4 points (TR); Madsen 2 points (TR); Doolan 2 points (TS); Match No. 10: Topinka 4 points (TR); Jaros 2 points (TS); Coles 0 points (TR).

PREMIER TROPHY AVERAGES

Rider	Mts	Rds	Pts	Bon	Tot	Avge	Max
Tomas Topinka	12	59	136	5	141	9.56	1 paid
Paul Lee	1	5	10	1	11	8.80	–
Troy Batchelor	2	8	15	2	17	8.50	–
Olly Allen	4	14	27	1	28	8.00	–
Kevin Doolan	11	50	73	14	87	6.96	–
Adam Allott	12	49	73	7	80	6.53	–
Ashley Jones	10	45	49	11	60	5.33	–
James Brundle	12	47	47	7	54	4.60	–
Jan Jaros	8	30	27	6	33	4.40	–
Guests	12	52	74	5	79	6.08	–

(Michael Coles [1]; Daniel Giffard [1]; Tom P. Madsen [1]; Darren Mallett [2]; Chris Neath [1]; Adam Roynon [1]; George Stancl [1]; Shaun Tacey [1]; Davey Watt [3]).

KNOCK-OUT CUP

(*Denotes aggregate victory)

No	DATE	OPPONENTS	H/A	RESULT	Topinka	Jones	Lee	Allott	Allen	Jaros	Wethers	Doolan	Batchelor	Stange	Others
1	5/6	Newcastle	A	L36-53	11 (5)	2+2 (4)	7 (5)	4 (4)	5 (4)	6 (4)	–	–	–	–	1 (5)
2	29/6	Newcastle	H	W58-32*	12+2 (5)	7+3 (4)	–	–	12 (4)	2 (3)	6+3 (4)	10 (4)	9+2 (6)	–	–
3	18/7	Exeter	A	D45-45	14 (5)	3 (4)	–	–	7 (4)	6+1 (4)	–	5 (4)	9+1 (5)	–	1 (4)
4	20/7	Exeter	H	W63-27*	13+1 (5)	6+1 (4)	–	–	9+1 (4)	4+2 (4)	–	15 (5)	6+3 (4)	–	10+2 (4)
5	3/9	Berwick	A	L44-45	12+1 (5)	2+1 (5)	–	–	11 (6)	7+2 (6)	–	8 (5)	R/R	4 (3)	–
6	7/9	Berwick	H	W56-34*	15 (5)	4+1 (5)	–	–	15+3 (6)	6+1 (5)	–	14 (5)	R/R	2 (4)	–
7	21/10	Rye House	H	W63-27	15 (5)	8+3 (4)	–	–	12+1 (5)	5+3 (5)	–	10+2 (4)	10+1 (4)	–	3 (3)
8	22/10	Rye House	A	L34-56*	6 (4)	3+1 (4)	–	–	11 (5)	4 (4)	–	3 (4)	7+1 (5)	–	0 (4)

DETAILS OF OTHER RIDERS:

Match No. 1: Blair Scott 1 (5); Match No. 3: Barrie Evans 1 (4); Match No. 4: Trevor Harding 10+2 (4); Match No. 7: Simon Lambert 3 (3); Match No. 8: Benji Compton 0 (4).

YOUNG SHIELD

(*Denotes aggregate victory)

No	DATE	OPPONENTS	H/A	RESULT	Allen	Jones	Batchelor	Doolan	Topinka	Jaros	Mallett	Others
1	1/10	Workington	A	L42-50	13+2 (6)	7 (5)	R/R	7+2 (5)	9+1 (5)	4+2 (6)	–	2 (3)
2	5/10	Workington	H	W52-42*	13+1 (5)	3 (4)	7 (4)	8+1 (4)	14+1 (4)	4+2 (5)	3 (3)	–
3	8/10	Berwick	A	L48-49	13+1 (5)	1 (4)	5 (4)	14+1 (6)	8 (4)	7+1 (4)	0 (3)	–
4	14/10	Berwick	H	W57-35*	15 (5)	6+1 (4)	10+3 (5)	9+1 (4)	9+1 (4)	4+1 (4)	4+3 (4)	–
5	26/10	Rye House	H	W59-34	9+1 (4)	6+2 (4)	11+2 (5)	11+1 (4)	15 (5)	7+1 (5)	–	0 (3)
6	29/10	Rye House	A	L42-51*	9 (4)	2 (4)	5+2 (5)	15 (5)	9+1 (4)	2+1 (5)	–	0 (3)

DETAILS OF OTHER RIDERS:

Match No. 1: James Birkinshaw 2 (3); Match No. 5: Simon Lambert 0 (3); Match No. 6: Benji Compton 0 (3).

TACTICAL SUBSTITUTE AND TACTICAL RIDES, AS INCLUDED IN THE SCORES GRID:

Match No. 1: Doolan 4 points (TR); Match No. 3: Allen 6 points (TR); Topinka 6 points (TR); Doolan 2 points (TS); Match No. 6: Doolan 4 points (TR); Topinka 2 points (TR).

OTHER MEETINGS

9 March: Maurice Littlechild Memorial Trophy

King's Lynn Stars 37 (Davey Watt 9; Tomas Topinka 7; Adam Allott 6+1; Olly Allen 5+1; Jason Crump 5; Kevin Doolan 3+1; James Brundle 2+1) King's Lynn Knights 52 (Nicki Pedersen 15; Freddie Eriksson 12+1; Adam Shields 10; Craig Boyce 6+4; Shane Parker 5+2; Steve Masters 3+1; Robbie Kessler 1).

16 March: A10 Trophy

King's Lynn 46 (Tomas Topinka 13; Adam Allott 10; Olly Allen 9; Kevin Doolan 6+1; Troy Batchelor 5+1; James Brundle 2; Jan Jaros 1+1) Rye House 44.

INDIVIDUAL MEETINGS

27 July: Premier League Champions' Chase

ELIMINATED IN ROUND TWO: Emil Kramer; Cameron Woodward; Ricky Ashworth; Neil Collins; Brent Werner; Seemond Stephens; Kauko Nieminen; Tony Atkin; Michal Makovsky; George Stancl; Olly Allen; Adrian Rymel; Paul Fry; Craig Boyce; Phil Morris; Matej Zagar. ELIMINATED IN ROUND THREE: Rusty Harrison; Ulrich Ostergaard; Andrew Appleton; Josef Franc; Mark Lemon; Shaun Tacey; Alan Mogridge; Paul Thorp. FIRST SEMI-FINAL: 1st Shane Parker; 2nd Tomas Topinka; 3rd Adam Allott; 4th Robbie Kessler. SECOND SEMI-FINAL: 1st Magnus Zetterstrom; 2nd Chris Neath; 3rd Stuart Robson; 4th Andre Compton. FINAL: 1st Zetterstrom; 2nd Neath; 3rd Topinka; 4th Parker.

28 September: Pride of the East

David Howe 6; Tomas Topinka 5; Freddie Eriksson 4; Shaun Tacey 4; Billy Janniro 3; Adam Shields 3; Olly Allen 3; Emil Kramer 3; Henning Bager 3; Simon Stead 3; Chris Louis 2; Kim Jansson 2; Kevin Doolan 2; Matej Zagar 2; Andrew Moore 2; Ashley Jones (Res) 1; Jan Jaros 0; Matthew Wethers 0; Artur Boginczuk 0; Jurica Pavlic 0; Davey Watt 0 – meeting abandoned after heat eight.

NEWCASTLE DIAMONDS POWERED BY 'THE GATE'

ADDRESS: Brough Park Stadium, Fossway, Byker, Newcastle-upon-Tyne, Tyne & Wear, NE6 2XJ.

PROMOTERS: George English, Darryl Illingworth & Barry Wallace.

TRACK LENGTH: 300 metres.

TRACK RECORD: 62.1 seconds – Kenneth Bjerre (20 July 2003).

FIRST MEETING: 17 May 1929.

YEARS OF OPERATION: 1929 English Dirt-track League; 1930 Open; 1938-39 National

League Division Two; 1945 Open; 1946 Northern League; 1947–51 National League Division Two; 1961–64 Provincial League; 1965–67 British League; 1968–70 British League Division One; 1975–83 National League; 1984 British League; 1986–87 National League; 1989–90 National League; 1991–94 British League Division Two; 1997–2001 Premier League; 2002–04 Premier League & Conference League; 2005 Premier League.

NOTE: Although Newcastle have predominantly used 'Diamonds' as a nickname, there were three seasons when they ran with an alternative, namely 'Brough' in 1946, 'Magpies' in 1949 and 'Federation Specials' in 1986.

CLUB HONOURS

LEAGUE CHAMPIONS: 1964, 1976, 1982, 1983, 2001.
PAIRS CHAMPIONS: 1975.
FOUR-TEAM CHAMPIONS: 1976, 1982, 1983.
KNOCK-OUT CUP WINNERS: 1976, 1982.
SUPERNATIONAL WINNERS: 1982, 1983.
GOLD CUP WINNERS: 1991, 1992.

RIDER ROSTER 2005

James BIRKINSHAW; Josef FRANC; James GRIEVES; Christian HENRY; Richard JUUL; Claus KRISTENSEN; Kristian LUND; Phil MORRIS; Jamie ROBERTSON; Lubos TOMICEK.

OTHER APPEARANCES/GUESTS (official matches only):
Byron BEKKER; Craig BRANNEY; Richie DENNIS; Karlis EZERGAILIS; Trevor HARDING; Robbie KESSLER; David McALLAN; Adam McKINNA; Chris MILLS; Scott ROBSON; George STANCL; Paul THORP; Sean WILSON.

PREMIER LEAGUE

(*Denotes bonus-point victory)

No	DATE	OPPONENTS	H/A	RESULT	Morris	Henry	Juul	Franc	Grieves	Tomicek	Robertson	Lund	Birkinshaw	Others
1	15/5	Workington	H	W58–36	11+3 (5)	7 (4)	5+1 (4)	9 (4)	15 (5)	6+1 (5)	5 (4)	–	–	–
2	16/5	Reading	A	W47–45	6+1 (5)	7 (4)	7+3 (4)	7+1 (4)	5+1 (4)	12+1 (6)	3+1 (3)	–	–	–
3	22/5	Exeter	H	W54–40	9 (4)	5+1 (4)	4+1 (4)	11 (5)	11+1 (5)	8+1 (4)	6+3 (4)	–	–	–
4	29/5	Newport	A	D45–45	7+1 (5)	6+1 (4)	7+2 (4)	8+2 (4)	9 (5)	5+1 (5)	3+1 (3)	–	–	–
5	12/6	Hull	H	W48–42	2+1 (4)	6 (4)	8 (4)	5+2 (4)	15 (5)	9 (5)	3+1 (4)	–	–	–
6	20/6	Edinburgh	H	W49–47	7+1 (4)	4 (4)	3 (4)	14+1 (5)	16 (5)	4+1 (4)	1 (4)	–	–	–
7	24/6	Somerset	A	L34–58	8 (5)	0 (3)	6+1 (5)	4+1 (4)	4+1 (4)	4+1 (4)	8 (5)	–	–	–
8	25/6	Rye House	A	L41–54	6 (4)	5 (6)	6+2 (5)	12+1 (5)	7 (5)	R/R	5+2 (5)	–	–	–
9	27/6	Rye House	H	D45–45	0 (4)	9+1 (4)	3+2 (4)	10 (5)	13+2 (5)	5 (4)	5+2 (4)	–	–	–
10	3/7	King's Lynn	H	W58–38	13 (5)	3 (3)	7+3 (4)	5+2 (4)	9 (4)	9 (4)	12+4 (6)	–	–	–
11	4/7	Exeter	A	L35–60	7 (4)	–	3+1 (4)	9+1 (5)	10 (5)	2 (4)	1+1 (4)	–	3 (5)	–
12	11/7	Newport	H	W55–36*	7+2 (4)	–	6+3 (4)	11+2 (5)	15 (5)	4 (4)	1 (3)	–	–	11 (5)
13	24/7	Isle of Wight	H	W56–36	8 (4)	9+3 (4)	3+1 (4)	10+1 (5)	13+1 (5)	5+1 (4)	8+2 (4)	–	–	–

No	DATE	OPPONENTS	H/A	RESULT	Morris	Henry	Juul	Franc	Grieves	Tomicek	Robertson	Lund	Birkinshaw	Others
14	31/7	Berwick	H	W47–43	R/R	7+1 (6)	5+2 (4)	16+1 (6)	–	4+1 (5)	3 (4)	–	–	12+1 (5)
15	3/8	Hull	A	L43–51	R/R	8 (6)	5+2 (5)	15 (6)	–	1+1 (4)	3 (4)	–	–	11+1 (5)
16	6/8	Berwick	A	L40–55	R/R	6+2 (6)	0 (2)	12+1 (6)	–	–	5 (6)	–	–	17+1 (10)
17	7/8	Stoke	H	W48–41	R/R	12 (7)	3+1 (4)	16 (6)	5+1 (4)	–	5+1 (4)	–	–	7 (5)
18	13/8	Workington	A	L36–58	R/R	–	–	15 (6)	8 (5)	0 (5)	11+1 (7)	2 (5)	–	0 (3)
19	14/8	Somerset	H	W60–36*	R/R	8+1 (3)	–	18 (6)	12+3 (5)	3+1 (5)	10+2 (6)	9+1 (5)	–	–
20	18/8	Sheffield	A	L29–63	R/R	–	–	10 (6)	0 (4)	0 (3)	4 (6)	1 (4)	14+1 (7)	–
21	21/8	Sheffield	H	W49–41	R/R	–	–	11+2 (6)	12 (5)	6+1 (5)	15+1 (7)	4+2 (4)	1 (3)	–
22	25/8	Isle of Wight	A	L23–71	R/R	–	–	6 (6)	0 (3)	0 (3)	10 (7)	2+1 (5)	5 (6)	–
23	28/8	Glasgow	A	L34–59	11 (5)	–	–	3 (5)	9 (5)	R/R	1 (2)	2+1 (5)	8+3 (7)	–
24	29/8	Glasgow	H	W47–43	5+1 (3)	–	–	9+1 (5)	15 (5)	6 (4)	–	6+1 (4)	3 (5)	3+1 (4)
25	3/9	Stoke	A	L42–48*	4+1 (4)	–	–	5+2 (5)	15 (5)	5+1 (4)	6+1 (5)	7 (4)	0 (3)	–
26	9/9	King's Lynn	A	L38–52*	R/R	–	–	5 (5)	8 (5)	9+1 (6)	7+2 (6)	3 (4)	6+2 (4)	–
27	11/9	Reading	H	W50–42*	7 (4)	–	–	12 (5)	9 (4)	3+1 (4)	12+1 (6)	6 (4)	1 (3)	–
28	7/10	Edinburgh	A	L40–53	6+1 (4)	–	–	12 (5)	12+1 (5)	2 (4)	2+1 (4)	5 (4)	–	1 (4)

DETAILS OF OTHER RIDERS:

Match No. 11: Karlis Ezergailis 3 (5); Match No. 12: Trevor Harding 11 (5); Match No. 14: Paul Thorp 12+1 (5); Match No. 15: Sean Wilson 11+1 (5); Match No. 16: George Stancl 14 (5); David McAllan 3+1 (5); Match No. 17: Kristian Lund 7 (5); Match No. 18: Byron Bekker 0 (3); Match No. 24: Adam McKinna 3+1 (4); Match No. 28: Byron Bekker 1 (4).

TACTICAL SUBSTITUTE AND TACTICAL RIDES, AS INCLUDED IN THE SCORES GRID:

Match No. 6: Franc 6 points (TR); Grieves 6 points (TR); Match No. 7: Morris 4 points (TR); Robertson 0 points (TR); Match No. 8: Franc 6 points (TR); Morris 4 points (TR); Match No. 11: Franc 6 points (TR); Morris 4 points (TR); Match No. 15: Wilson 4 points (TR); Franc 4 points (TR); Match No. 16: Stancl 6 points (TR); Franc 4 points (TR); Match No. 18: Franc 4 points (TR); Robertson 4 points (TR); Match No. 20: Franc 2 points (TR); Birkinshaw 2 points (TR); Match No. 22: Franc 4 points (TR); Robertson 2 points (TR); Birkinshaw 2 points (TS); Match No. 23: Morris 4 points (TR); Grieves 2 points (TR); Match No. 28: Franc 4 points (TR); Grieves 2 points (TR).

PREMIER LEAGUE AVERAGES

Rider	Mts	Rds	Pts	Bon	Tot	Avge	Max
James Grieves	25	117	242	11	253	8.65	5 full; 2 paid
Josef Franc	28	143	260	21	281	7.86	1 full
Phil Morris	18	77	116	12	128	6.65	–
Christian Henry	16	72	102	10	112	6.22	1 paid
Richard Juul	17	69	81	25	106	6.14	–
Jamie Robertson	27	127	152	27	179	5.64	–
Lubos Tomicek	24	105	112	14	126	4.80	–
James Birkinshaw	8	38	36	6	42	4.42	–
Kristian Lund	11	48	47	6	53	4.42	–
Guests	10	46	60	4	64	5.57	–

(Byron Bekker [2]; Karlis Ezergailis [1]; Trevor Harding [1]; Kristian Lund [1]; David McAllan [1]; Adam McKinna [1]; George Stancl [1]; Paul Thorp [1]; Sean Wilson [1]).

PREMIER TROPHY

(*Denotes bonus-point victory)

No	DATE	OPPONENTS	H/A	RESULT	Morris	Henry	Kristensen	Franc	Grieves	Tomicek	Robertson	Juul	Others
1	19/3	Berwick	A	L39-55	1 (3)	0 (2)	12 (5)	8+1 (4)	8 (5)	7 (6)	3+1 (5)	–	–
2	20/3	Sheffield	H	W48-41	14 (5)	0 (3)	10+1 (4)	8+1 (4)	10+1 (5)	0 (4)	6 (5)	–	–
3	23/3	Hull	A	L36-59	11 (5)	0 (4)	8+1 (5)	6+1 (5)	8 (4)	0 (1)	3 (6)	–	–
4	25/3	Edinburgh	A	L43-53	7 (4)	3+1 (4)	3 (4)	12 (5)	14 (6)	3 (4)	1+1 (3)	–	–
5	2/4	Workington	A	L30-64	12 (5)	5 (4)	6 (5)	1 (4)	5 (4)	1 (4)	0 (4)	–	–
6	3/4	Workington	H	L42-48	0 (1)	3 (4)	2 (4)	11 (5)	14 (5)	3 (4)	9+1 (7)	–	–
7	10/4	Stoke	H	W51-39	7+2 (5)	2 (3)	7+1 (4)	4+1 (4)	15 (5)	6 (4)	–	–	10+3 (5)
8	16/4	Stoke	A	L44-45*	3 (3)	3 (3)	3 (4)	12+2 (5)	15 (5)	7 (6)	1 (4)	–	–
9	17/4	Edinburgh	H	W48-41	–	R/R	2+1 (4)	15 (6)	15 (5)	8+1 (6)	3+1 (5)	–	5 (4)
10	21/4	Sheffield	A	L38-58	–	0 (4)	2 (4)	9 (5)	4+1 (4)	–	6 (5)	–	17+1 (9)
11	24/4	Hull	H	W51-42	9+1 (4)	5 (4)	5+1 (4)	13+1 (5)	13 (5)	5+2 (4)	1 (4)	–	–
12	2/5	Glasgow	H	W48-42	6+1 (4)	4+1 (4)	4 (3)	5+1 (4)	14 (5)	10+2 (6)	5+2 (4)	–	–
13	24/5	Glasgow	A	L40-54	4+2 (4)	5+1 (4)	–	12 (5)	9 (5)	3+1 (4)	4 (4)	3 (4)	–
14	30/5	Berwick	H	W58-35*	12+2 (5)	4+1 (4)	–	14 (5)	12 (4)	4+2 (4)	7 (4)	5+2 (4)	–

DETAILS OF OTHER RIDERS:

Match No. 7: Craig Branney 10+3 (5); Match No. 9: Scott Robson 5 (4); Match No. 10: Robbie Kessler 15 (5); Richie Dennis 2+1 (4).

TACTICAL SUBSTITUTE AND TACTICAL RIDES, AS INCLUDED IN THE SCORES GRID:

Match No. 1: Kristensen 6 points (TR); Franc 4 points (TR); Match No. 3: Morris 6 points (TR); Grieves 6 points (TR); Franc 0 points (TS); Match No. 4: Franc 6 points (TR); Morris 4 points (TR); Grieves 2 points (TS); Match No. 5: Morris 6 points (TR); Grieves 2 points (TR); Match No. 10: Kessler 6 points (TR); Franc 6 points (TR); Match No. 13: Franc 6 points (TR); Grieves 2 points (TR).

PREMIER TROPHY AVERAGES

Rider	Mts	Rds	Pts	Bon	Tot	Avge	Max
James Grieves	14	67	150	2	152	9.07	4 full
Josef Franc	14	66	119	8	127	7.70	–
Phil Morris	12	48	78	8	86	7.17	–
Claus Kristensen	12	50	61	5	66	5.28	–
Richard Juul	2	8	8	2	10	5.00	–
Lubos Tomicek	13	57	57	8	65	4.56	–
Jamie Robertson	13	60	49	6	55	3.67	–
Christian Henry	13	47	34	4	38	3.23	–
Guests	4	18	29	4	33	7.33	–

(Craig Branney [1]; Richie Dennis [1]; Robbie Kessler [1]; Scott Robson [1]).

NEWCASTLE: From left to right, back row: James Grieves, Phil Morris (on bike), Christian Henry, Jamie Robertson. Front, kneeling: Claus Kristensen, Josef Franc, Lubos Tomicek.

KNOCK-OUT CUP

No	DATE	OPPONENTS	H/A	RESULT	Morris	Juul	Tomicek	Franc	Grieves	Henry	Robertson
1	5/6	King's Lynn	H	W53-36	7+1 (5)	6 (4)	4+2 (4)	9+1 (4)	13+1 (5)	8+1 (4)	6+1 (4)
2	29/6	King's Lynn	A	L32-58	0 (3)	2 (4)	9 (5)	10+1 (5)	5 (4)	4 (5)	2+1 (5)

YOUNG SHIELD

No	DATE	OPPONENTS	H/A	RESULT	Franc	Lund	Tomicek	Morris	Grieves	Birkinshaw	Robertson	Others
1	24/9	Berwick	A	L35-60	R/R	0 (3)	–	4 (3)	12 (6)	7+1 (6)	3 (5)	9+1 (6)
2	25/9	Berwick	H	W48-42	12+2 (5)	3 (4)	8+1 (4)	6+2 (4)	14 (5)	1 (3)	4+1 (5)	–

DETAILS OF OTHER RIDER:

Match No. 1: Chris Mills 9+1 (6)

TACTICAL SUBSTITUTE AND TACTICAL RIDES, AS INCLUDED IN THE SCORES GRID:

Match No. 1: Mills 4 points (TR); Grieves 4 points (TR); Birkinshaw 2 points (TS)

OTHER MEETINGS

12 March: Trent/Tyne Trophy (first leg)

Stoke 43 Newcastle 51 (Phil Morris 13+1; James Grieves 12; Josef Franc 10+1; Christian Henry 6+1; Lubos Tomicek 6; Claus Kristensen 3; Jamie Robertson 1).

13 March: Trent/Tyne Trophy (second leg)

Newcastle 60 (Claus Kristensen 11+1; James Grieves 11+1; Phil Morris 9; Lubos Tomicek 8+2; Jamie Robertson 8+2; Josef Franc 8+1; Christian Henry 5+1) Stoke 30 – Newcastle won 111-73 on aggregate.

19 August: Premier League

Edinburgh 24 Newcastle 18 (Josef Franc 6; James Grieves 5; Jamie Robertson 3+1; Kristian Lund 2; Craig Branney 2; David McAllan 0; Phil Morris R/R) – meeting abandoned after heat seven.

INDIVIDUAL MEETINGS

19 June: Championship of Great Britain Qualifying Round

Chris Harris 5; Andrew Moore 5; David McAllan 5; James Grieves 4; Glenn Cunningham 4; Ross Brady 3; Ricky Ashworth 3; Phil Morris 3; Jamie Robertson 3; Adam Allott 3; Ben Wilson 3; Ritchie Hawkins 2; Shaun Tacey 2; Scott Robson 1; Lee Smethills 1; Scott Courtney (Res) 1; Andre Compton 0 – meeting abandoned after heat eight.

4 September: George English Memorial Trophy

    QUALIFYING SCORES: Jason Lyons 9; Sean Wilson 8; James Wright 8; Josef Franc 7; James Grieves 6; Lubos Tomicek 5; Adrian Rymel 4; Richard Hall 1. FINAL: 1st Lyons; 2nd Wilson; 3rd Franc; 4th Wright.

4 September: Chris Prime Memorial Trophy

    QUALIFYING SCORES: Jamie Robertson 9; Kristian Lund 8; Derek Sneddon 7; Adam McKinna 5; James Birkinshaw 4; Karl Langley 3; David Haigh 0; John Morrison 0. FINAL: 1st Sneddon; 2nd Robertson; 3rd Lund; 4th McKinna.

NEWPORT WASPS

NOTE: The information below relates only to the main Newport team. For details of the second side, please refer to the Conference League section.

ADDRESS: Hayley Stadium, Plover Close, Longditch Road, Queensway Meadows, Newport, South Wales, NS19 4SU.
PROMOTER: Tim Stone.
TRACK LENGTH: 285 metres.
TRACK RECORD: 58.38 seconds – Craig Watson (3 August 2003).
FIRST MEETING: 4 May 1997.
YEARS OF OPERATION: 1997–2005 Premier League.

PREVIOUS VENUE: Somerton Park, Newport, South Wales.
YEARS OF OPERATION: 1964 Provincial League; 1965–67 British League; 1968–74 British League Division One; 1975–76 British League; 1977 National League.

NOTE: Newport did not use a nickname from 1973-76 inclusive, and in 1977 they were known as 'Dragons'.

CLUB HONOURS

PREMIER NATIONAL TROPHY WINNERS: 1999

RIDER ROSTER 2005

Tony ATKIN; Michael COLES; Neil COLLINS; Lee DICKEN; Karlis EZERGAILIS; Jason KING; Mads KORNELIUSSEN; Kristian LUND; Karl MASON; Henrik VEDEL; Craig WATSON.

OTHER APPEARANCES/GUESTS (official matches only):
Jason DOYLE; James GRIEVES; Chris HARRIS; Magnus KARLSSON; Kyle LEGAULT; Trent LEVERINGTON; Travis McGOWAN; Chris NEATH; Theo PIJPER; Stuart ROBSON; Seemond STEPHENS; Carl STONEHEWER; Simone TERENZANI; Carl WILKINSON.

NEWPORT: From left to right: Neil Collins, Karlis Ezergailis, Kristian Lund, Neil Street (Team Manager), Tony Atkin (on bike), Mads Korneliussen, Craig Watson, Michael Coles.

PREMIER LEAGUE

(*Denotes bonus-point victory)

No	DATE	OPPONENTS	H/A	RESULT	Coles	Lund	Korneliussen	Collins	Watson	Atkin	Ezergailis	Dicken	Vedel	King	Mason	Others
1	7/5	Workington	A	W49-43	5+1 (4)	5+1 (4)	8+1 (4)	11+2 (5)	11 (5)	8+3 (5)	1 (3)	–	–	–	–	–
2	8/5	Stoke	H	L46-48	6+1 (4)	3 (1)	7+1 (5)	12+1 (5)	9 (4)	7+1 (6)	2+1 (5)	–	–	–	–	–
3	18/5	Hull	A	L38-52	3 (4)	7+1 (5)	6+1 (5)	6+1 (4)	–	7+2 (5)	1 (3)	–	–	–	–	8 (4)
4	22/5	Edinburgh	H	W47-46	R/R	3 (4)	7+1 (6)	6+1 (5)	–	13 (6)	0 (3)	–	–	–	–	18+1 (6)
5	23/5	Reading	A	L41-49	R/R	4+1 (4)	12+1 (6)	8+2 (5)	–	7+1 (6)	0 (3)	–	–	–	–	10 (6)
6	29/5	Newcastle	H	D45-45	R/R	1 (5)	11 (5)	7 (5)	–	12+2 (7)	1 (3)	–	–	–	–	13+1 (5)
7	2/6	Sheffield	A	L41-53	R/R	0 (4)	8+1 (4)	11+1 (6)	–	9+1 (7)	1+1 (4)	–	–	–	–	12+1 (5)
8	10/6	Glasgow	H	W51-44	R/R	8+2 (5)	13 (5)	11+1 (6)	–	10+3 (7)	3 (5)	–	–	–	–	6 (2)
9	16/6	Glasgow	A	L42-48*	R/R	7+2 (5)	8+1 (5)	12 (6)	–	8 (7)	2+1 (3)	–	–	–	–	5+1 (4)
10	17/6	Edinburgh	A	L35-60	R/R	5 (5)	11 (5)	12 (6)	–	7+1 (7)	0 (6)	–	–	–	–	0 (1)
11	18/6	Berwick	A	L32-61	R/R	6+1 (5)	10 (5)	8 (6)	–	1 (5)	1 (5)	–	–	–	–	6 (4)
12	19/6	Hull	H	L42-48	R/R	1 (5)	7 (5)	12 (5)	–	10+4 (7)	1+1 (3)	–	–	–	–	11 (5)
13	2/7	Stoke	A	L38-55	R/R	–	13 (5)	4 (4)	–	7+2 (6)	3 (4)	5+2 (7)	–	–	–	6 (4)
14	3/7	Workington	H	W48-42*	R/R	–	11+1 (5)	8 (4)	–	8+2 (5)	2+2 (4)	8+2 (7)	–	–	–	11+1 (5)
15	10/7	Berwick	H	W49-41	R/R	–	14 (5)	9 (4)	–	5+3 (5)	1+1 (4)	8+1 (7)	–	–	–	12+1 (5)
16	11/7	Newcastle	A	L36-55	R/R	–	3+1 (4)	11 (5)	–	7 (6)	2 (4)	5+3 (7)	–	–	–	8 (4)
17	29/7	Somerset	A	L30-64	R/R	–	–	12 (5)	–	8+1 (6)	5 (5)	1 (6)	3+2 (4)	–	–	1 (4)
18	31/7	Sheffield	H	L38-53	R/R	–	3 (2)	11+1 (5)	–	8 (6)	3 (7)	7+1 (6)	6+2 (4)	–	–	–
19	1/8	Exeter	A	L28-65	–	–	R/R	3 (5)	–	12 (6)	2 (5)	3+1 (5)	0 (6)	–	–	8 (3)
20	7/8	King's Lynn	H	L35-58	–	–	R/R	15 (6)	–	9 (6)	1+1 (4)	5+2 (5)	4+1 (5)	1+1 (4)	–	–
21	10/8	King's Lynn	A	L26-67	–	–	R/R	9 (6)	–	6+1 (5)	0 (6)	4 (6)	7+1 (6)	0 (1)	–	–
22	14/8	Isle of Wight	H	L40-50	–	–	R/R	11+2 (6)	–	8 (5)	–	4 (3)	2 (5)	–	5+3 (5)	10 (6)
23	21/8	Exeter	H	L44-46	–	–	R/R	13 (6)	–	11 (6)	–	2 (3)	7+2 (5)	–	7+3 (5)	4 (5)
24	28/8	Somerset	H	L41-49	–	–	R/R	13+1 (6)	–	11 (5)	–	1 (3)	4+1 (5)	–	4+1 (5)	8+1 (6)
25	1/9	Isle of Wight	A	L31-65	–	–	6 (4)	7+1 (4)	–	9+1 (6)	–	1+1 (4)	7 (6)	R/R	1 (6)	–
26	4/9	Reading	H	L42-53	–	–	6 (4)	15 (5)	–	8+4 (6)	–	7 (5)	4 (4)	R/R	2+2 (6)	–
27	11/9	Rye House	H	L34-58	–	–	12 (5)	7 (4)	–	5 (6)	–	5+1 (4)	3 (5)	R/R	2+1 (6)	–
28	17/9	Rye House	A	L28-64	–	–	6+1 (4)	10 (5)	–	2+1 (5)	1 (6)	2 (5)	7 (5)	R/R	–	–

DETAILS OF OTHER RIDERS:

Match No. 3: Magnus Karlsson 8 (4); Match No. 4: Chris Harris 18+1 (6); Match No. 5: Chris Neath 10 (6); Match No. 6: Stuart Robson 13+1 (5); Match No. 7: Chris Harris 12+1 (5); Match No. 8: Stuart Robson 6 (2); Match No. 9: Theo Pijper 5+1 (4); Match No. 10: Carl Stonehewer 0 (1); Match No. 11: Trent Leverington 6 (4); Match No. 12: Stuart Robson 11 (5); Match No. 13: James Grieves 6 (4); Match No. 14: Stuart Robson 11+1 (5); Match No. 15: Travis McGowan 12+1 (5); Match No. 16: Stuart Robson 8 (4); Match No. 17: Seemond Stephens 1 (4); Match No. 19: Jason Doyle 8 (3); Match No. 22: Carl Wilkinson 10 (6); Match No. 23: Simone Terenzani 4 (5); Match No. 24: Kyle Legault 8+1 (6).

TACTICAL SUBSTITUTE AND TACTICAL RIDES, AS INCLUDED IN THE SCORES GRID:

Match No. 4: Harris 6 points (TR); Match No. 7: Harris 4 points (TR); Korneliussen 4 points (TR); Match No. 10: Korneliussen 6 points (TR); Collins 4 points (TR); Match No. 11: Korneliussen 4 points (TR); Leverington 2 points (TR); Match No. 13: Korneliussen 4 points (TR); Atkin 2 points (TR); Match No. 16: Collins 2 points (TR); Match No. 17: Collins 6 points (TR); Atkin 2 points (TR); Match No. 18: Dicken 2 points (TR); Match No. 19: Doyle 4 points (TR); Atkin 2 points (TR); Match No. 20: Collins

4 points (TR); Atkin 2 points (TR); Match No. 21: Collins 4 points (TR); Vedel 2 points (TR); Match No. 25: Atkin 4 points (TR); Vedel 4 points (TS); Collins 4 points (TR); Match No. 26: Collins 6 points (TR); Dicken 4 points (TR); Match No. 27: Korneliussen 6 points (TR); Collins 0 points (TR); Vedel 0 points (TS); Match No. 28: Collins 2 points (TR); Korneliussen 2 points (TR).

PREMIER LEAGUE AVERAGES

Rider	Mts	Rds	Pts	Bon	Tot	Avge	Max
Craig Watson	2	9	20	0	20	8.89	–
Neil Collins	28	144	258	14	272	7.56	–
Mads Korneliussen	21	98	169	10	179	7.31	–
Tony Atkin	28	165	217	33	250	6.06	–
Michael Coles	3	12	14	2	16	5.33	–
Kristian Lund	12	52	50	8	58	4.46	–
Henrik Vedel	12	60	51	9	60	4.00	–
Lee Dicken	16	83	65	14	79	3.81	–
Karl Mason	6	33	21	10	31	3.76	–
Karlis Ezergailis	22	95	33	8	41	1.73	–
Jason King	2	5	1	1	2	1.60	–
Guests	19	84	149	7	156	7.43	–

(Jason Doyle [1]; James Grieves [1]; Chris Harris [2]; Magnus Karlsson [1]; Kyle Legault [1]; Trent Leverington [1]; Travis McGowan [1]; Chris Neath [1]; Theo Pijper [1]; Stuart Robson [5]; Seemond Stephens [1]; Carl Stonehewer [1]; Simone Terenzani [1]; Carl Wilkinson [1]).

PREMIER TROPHY

(*Denotes bonus-point victory)

No	DATE	OPPONENTS	H/A	RESULT	Coles	Lund	Korneliussen	Collins	Watson	Atkin	Ezergailis	Others
1	19/3	Rye House	A	L40-50	8+1 (5)	6+1 (4)	7+1 (4)	4+1 (4)	8 (5)	5 (5)	2 (3)	–
2	20/3	Reading	H	W49-44	7+1 (5)	8+2 (4)	6 (4)	7+1 (4)	12 (5)	6+1 (4)	3+1 (4)	–
3	27/3	Rye House	H	L38-52	9 (5)	1+1 (4)	10+1 (5)	5 (4)	3 (4)	6 (5)	4+1 (4)	–
4	3/4	Exeter	H	L41-49	4+2 (4)	6 (4)	7+1 (5)	8 (4)	12 (5)	3 (4)	1+1 (4)	–
5	4/4	Reading	A	L44-48*	6+1 (4)	5 (4)	10+2 (5)	5 (4)	14+1 (5)	4 (4)	0 (4)	–
6	24/4	Somerset	H	W55-36	6+1 (4)	7+1 (4)	11 (4)	7+3 (4)	11 (5)	6+2 (4)	7+3 (5)	–
7	4/5	King's Lynn	A	L39-53	6 (4)	1 (3)	10 (5)	6 (4)	11 (5)	5+2 (6)	0 (3)	–
8	15/5	King's Lynn	H	L46-47	3 (4)	4+1 (4)	9+3 (5)	9 (4)	–	5+1 (5)	1+1 (3)	15+1 (5)
9	16/5	Exeter	A	W47-43	7 (4)	6+1 (4)	6+2 (5)	12 (5)	–	9+2 (5)	1 (3)	6+1 (4)
10	20/5	Somerset	A	W49-44*	1+1 (3)	8 (4)	10+1 (5)	7+2 (4)	–	12+1 (6)	2+1 (3)	9+1 (5)
11	31/5	Isle of Wight	A	L42-52	R/R	2+2 (5)	12 (5)	7 (5)	–	13+1 (7)	1+1 (3)	7+1 (5)
12	1/6	Isle of Wight	H	W50-40*	R/R	2+1 (4)	14 (5)	10 (5)	–	13+3 (7)	3+1 (4)	8+2 (5)

DETAILS OF OTHER RIDERS:

Match No. 8: Stuart Robson 15+1 (5); Match No. 9: Chris Neath 6+1 (4); Match No. 10: Chris Neath 9+1 (5); Match No. 11: Chris Neath 7+1 (5); Match No. 12: Chris Neath 8+2 (5).

TACTICAL RIDES, AS INCLUDED IN THE SCORES GRID:

Match No. 3: Collins 0 points (TR); Match No. 5: Watson 4 points (TR); Match No. 7: Collins 4 points (TR); Watson 0 points (TR); Match No. 8: Robson 6 points (TR); Match No. 11: Korneliussen 6 points (TR); Atkin 2 points (TR).

PREMIER TROPHY AVERAGES

Rider	Mts	Rds	Pts	Bon	Tot	Avge	Max
Mads Korneliussen	12	57	109	11	120	8.42	–
Craig Watson	7	34	69	1	70	8.24	–
Neil Collins	12	51	85	7	92	7.22	–
Tony Atkin	12	62	86	13	99	6.39	–
Michael Coles	10	42	57	7	64	6.10	–
Kristian Lund	12	48	56	10	66	5.50	–
Karlis Ezergailis	12	43	25	10	35	3.26	–
Guests	5	24	42	6	48	8.00	–

(Chris Neath [4]; Stuart Robson [1]).

KNOCK-OUT CUP

No	DATE	OPPONENTS	H/A	RESULT	Korneliussen	Lund	Coles	Collins	Atkin	Ezergailis	Dicken	Others
1	6/6	Reading	A	L36-54	9+1 (5)	0 (4)	R/R	5 (5)	11+1 (7)	2+2 (4)	–	9+1 (5)
2	17/7	Reading	H	L39-51	3 (1)	–	R/R	12+1 (5)	8+1 (5)	0 (7)	3 (7)	13 (5)

DETAILS OF OTHER RIDERS:

Match No. 1: Chris Harris 9+1 (5); Match No. 2: Stuart Robson 13 (5).

OTHER MEETINGS

13 March: M4 Trophy (first leg)

Newport 50 (Craig Watson 15; Mads Korneliussen 12+2; Neil Collins 6+1; Michael Coles 6; Kristian Lund 5+2; Karlis Ezergailis 4; Tony Atkin 2+1) Somerset 46.

18 March: M4 Trophy (second leg)

Somerset 17 Newport 32 (Kristian Lund 8+1; Craig Watson 6; Mads Korneliussen 5+1; Neil Collins 5+1; Michael Coles 4; Tony Atkin 4; Karlis Ezergailis 0) – meeting abandoned after heat eight.

10 April: M4 Trophy (first leg)

Newport 57 (Craig Watson 15; Mads Korneliussen 9; Kristian Lund 8+1; Neil Collins 7+3; Karlis Ezergailis 7+2; Tony Atkin 7+1; Michael Coles 4+2) Somerset 38.

3 September: M4 Trophy (second leg)

Somerset 61 Newport 34 (Neil Collins 11; Mads Korneliussen 11; Henrik Vedel 5; Tony Atkin 4+1; Karl Mason 2; Lee Dicken 1; Jason King R/R) – Somerset won 99-91 on aggregate.

INDIVIDUAL MEETINGS

2 January: New Year Classic

QUALIFYING SCORES: Chris Harris 12; Niels-Kristian Iversen 11; David Howe 10; Stuart Robson 10; Mads Korneliussen 9; Brent Werner 8; Michael Coles 8; Neil Collins 7; Robbie Kessler 4; Karl Mason 4; Josh Larsen 3; Jamie Westacott (Res) 3; Kristian Lund 1. FINAL: 1st Harris; 2nd Iversen; 3rd Robson; 4th Howe.

6 March: Prince of Wales Trophy

QUALIFYING SCORES: David Howe 14; Niels-Kristian Iversen 11; Michael Coles 9; Chris Neath 8; Tony Atkin 7; Chris Harris 7; Jan Staechmann 7; Craig Watson 6; Kristian Lund 6; Mads Korneliussen 5; Magnus Zetterstrom 4; Neil Collins 3; Karlis Ezergailis (Res) 3. FINAL: 1st Howe; 2nd Iversen; 3rd Coles; 4th Neath.

12 June: Welsh Open Championship

QUALIFYING SCORES: Niels-Kristian Iversen 15; Magnus Zetterstrom 14; Adam Shields 12; Davey Watt 10; Ronnie Correy 10; Adam Skornicki 10; Henning Bager 8; Leigh Lanham 8; Andy Smith 7; George Stancl 7; Mads Korneliussen 6; Henrik Gustafsson 4; Mark Lemon 3; Kristian Lund 2; Karlis Ezergailis (Res) 2; Miroslav Fencl 1; Patrick Linhart 0. FINAL: 1st Iversen; 2nd Shields; 3rd Zetterstrom; 4th Watt.

READING IDEAL VIDEO RACERS

ADDRESS: Smallmead Stadium, A33 Relief Road, Smallmead, Reading, Berkshire, RG2 0JL.
PROMOTERS: Pat Bliss & Chris Shears.
TRACK LENGTH: 307 metres.
TRACK RECORD: 58.1 seconds – Per Jonsson (12 October 1987).
FIRST MEETING: 28 April 1975.
YEARS OF OPERATION: 1975–90 British League; 1991–94 British League Division One; 1995–2005 Premier League.

NOTE: Reading also ran a second team in the 1996 Conference League and the 1997 Amateur League. The 1996 side ran as 'Reading Ravens', whereas in 1997 the fixtures were shared with Swindon, under the banner of 'M4 Raven Sprockets'.

PREVIOUS VENUE: Reading Greyhound Stadium, Oxford Road, Tilehurst, Reading, Berkshire.
YEARS OF OPERATION: 1968–70 British League Division Two; 1971–73 British League Division One.

CLUB HONOURS

LEAGUE CHAMPIONS: 1980, 1990, 1992, 1997.
KNOCK-OUT CUP WINNERS: 1990, 1998.
PREMIERSHIP WINNERS: 1991, 1993.
BSPA CUP WINNERS: 1992.
FOUR-TEAM CHAMPIONS: 1993.
PAIRS CHAMPIONS: 2004.

READING: From left to right, back row: Richard Wolff, Matej Zagar, Chris Johnson, Chris Mills, Mathieu Tresarrieu, Andrew Appleton, Ivan Shears (Team Manager). Front, on bike: Danny Bird.

RIDER ROSTER 2005

Andrew APPLETON; Danny BIRD; Chris JOHNSON; Steve MASTERS; Chris MILLS; Zdenek SIMOTA; Mathieu TRESARRIEU; Richard WOLFF; Matej ZAGAR.

OTHER APPEARANCES/GUESTS (official matches only):

Ben BARKER; Steve BOXALL; Tom BROWN; Peter COLLYER; Richie DENNIS; Kevin DOOLAN; Daniel GIFFARD; Jan JAROS; Steen JENSEN; Ashley JONES; Daniel KING; Simon LAMBERT; Leigh LANHAM; Travis McGOWAN; Danny NORTON; Luke PRIEST; Lee SMART; Simon STEAD; Tomas SUCHANEK; Simone TERENZANI; Mark THOMPSON; Paul THORP; Danny WARWICK; Jamie WESTACOTT; Cameron WOODWARD.

PREMIER LEAGUE

(*Denotes bonus-point victory)

No	DATE	OPPONENTS	H/A	RESULT	Appleton	Masters	Wolff	Simota	Zagar	Johnson	Tresarrieu	Bird	Others
1	14/5	Workington	A	L38-56	3 (4)	2 (4)	3 (4)	9+1 (6)	–	–	2 (4)	–	19+1 (8)
2	15/5	Glasgow	A	L42-52	7 (5)	3+1 (4)	5 (4)	2+1 (3)	–	–	7 (5)	–	18 (9)
3	16/5	Newcastle	H	L45-47	14+1 (5)	3 (4)	2 (4)	0 (2)	20+1 (6)	–	5+1 (5)	–	1 (4)
4	19/5	Sheffield	A	L35-60	4 (4)	1 (3)	4 (5)	2 (4)	13+1 (5)	–	10+1 (6)	–	1 (3)
5	23/5	Newport	H	W49-41	10+2 (5)	2 (4)	6+1 (4)	6 (4)	15 (5)	1+1 (2)	9 (6)	–	–
6	25/5	Hull	A	L43-47	7+1 (5)	0 (2)	8+1 (4)	6 (4)	14 (5)	–	6+1 (6)	–	2 (4)
7	30/5	King's Lynn	H	W51-41	12+2 (6)	R/R	6 (4)	7+1 (4)	14 (5)	–	12+1 (7)	–	0 (4)
8	8/6	King's Lynn	A	L39-53	12 (6)	R/R	3+2 (5)	5 (4)	10 (5)	1 (4)	–	–	8+2 (7)
9	20/6	Berwick	H	L44-49	11 (6)	R/R	7+1 (5)	3 (5)	14 (5)	1 (3)	8+3 (6)	–	–
10	27/6	Sheffield	H	W56-37	11 (5)	R/R	12+1 (6)	7+3 (5)	12 (5)	2 (3)	12+5 (7)	–	–
11	2/7	Rye House	A	L36-57	6+2 (5)	R/R	6 (6)	7 (6)	–	2+1 (3)	11+1 (6)	–	4+1 (4)
12	4/7	Workington	H	W49-44	8 (5)	R/R	16+2 (7)	8+3 (5)	11 (5)	3+2 (3)	3+1 (5)	–	–
13	11/7	Edinburgh	H	L46-47	6+1 (4)	–	9+1 (7)	10 (5)	15 (5)	1+1 (3)	5 (2)	–	0 (3)
14	18/7	Somerset	H	W46-44	7+1 (4)	4+2 (4)	3 (5)	9+2 (5)	15 (5)	1 (3)	7 (4)	–	–
15	25/7	Rye House	H	L44-46	4+1 (4)	1+1 (4)	6 (5)	10+1 (5)	15 (5)	3+1 (3)	5 (4)	–	–
16	15/8	Hull	H	W58-36*	14+1 (5)	–	3 (4)	7+2 (4)	14+1 (5)	–	7+1 (5)	12 (4)	1 (3)
17	19/8	Somerset	A	L43-47	3 (4)	–	2+1 (4)	3+2 (4)	13+1 (5)	–	–	7 (4)	15+1 (9)
18	29/8	Exeter	H	W61-32	14+1 (5)	–	4+1 (4)	8 (4)	14+1 (5)	–	11+1 (5)	8+1 (4)	2 (3)
19	29/8	Exeter	A	L39-54*	12 (5)	–	1 (3)	1+1 (3)	13 (5)	–	8+1 (7)	4 (3)	0 (4)
20	4/9	Newport	A	W53-42*	–	–	7+1 (4)	11+1 (6)	15 (6)	5+1 (4)	–	R/R	15 (10)
21	10/9	Edinburgh	A	L43-46	10 (6)	–	5 (5)	8 (5)	–	2+1 (4)	0 (4)	R/R	18 (6)
22	10/9	Berwick	A	L32-60	5 (5)	–	3 (5)	2 (5)	–	1 (3)	7 (6)	R/R	14 (6)
23	11/9	Newcastle	A	L42-50	11 (6)	–	2 (4)	5+2 (5)	–	0 (3)	5+2 (5)	R/R	19 (7)
24	12/9	Stoke	H	W58-39	15+2 (6)	–	8+1 (5)	14+1 (6)	12 (5)	3+1 (4)	6+1 (4)	R/R	–
25	17/9	Stoke	A	W50-42*	11 (5)	–	5+1 (5)	14+2 (6)	14+1 (6)	1+1 (3)	5 (5)	R/R	–
26	19/9	Isle of Wight	H	W50-45	13+2 (6)	–	7 (5)	9+1 (5)	14+1 (6)	1 (3)	6+1 (5)	R/R	–
27	20/9	Isle of Wight	A	L42-50	4+1 (5)	–	–	5+1 (6)	20 (7)	0 (3)	7+1 (5)	R/R	6 (4)
28	26/9	Glasgow	H	W47-46	8 (5)	–	–	8+1 (6)	14 (6)	5+1 (4)	7+1 (5)	R/R	5+1 (4)

DETAILS OF OTHER RIDERS:

Match No. 1: Simon Stead 18 (5); Luke Priest 1+1 (3); Match No. 2: Simon Stead 18 (6); Luke Priest 0 (3); Match No. 3: Tom Brown 1 (4); Match No. 4: Richie Dennis 1 (3); Match No. 6: Danny Norton 2 (4); Match No. 7: Mark Thompson 0 (4); Match No. 8: Simon Lambert 8+2 (7); Match No. 11: Paul Thorp 4+1 (4); Match No. 13: Jamie Westacott 0 (3); Match No. 16: Peter Collyer 1 (3); Match No. 17: Tomas Suchanek 14+1 (6); Lee Smart 1 (3); Match No. 18: Lee Smart 2 (3); Match No. 19: Lee Smart 0 (4); Match No. 20: Steen Jensen 10 (5); Simone Terenzani 5 (5); Match No. 21: Travis McGowan 18 (6); Match No. 22: Travis McGowan 14 (6); Match No. 23: Travis McGowan 19 (7); Match No. 27: Ashley Jones 6 (4); Match No. 28: Ashley Jones 5+1 (4).

TACTICAL SUBSTITUTE AND TACTICAL RIDES, AS INCLUDED IN THE SCORES GRID:

Match No. 1: Stead 6 points (TR); Simota 2 points (TS); Match No. 2: Stead 4 points (TS); Appleton 4 points (TR); Match No. 3: Zagar 6 points (TS); Match No. 4: Zagar 6 points (TR); Appleton 4 points (TR); Match No. 8: Appleton 4 points (TR); Zagar 0 points (TR); Match No. 9: Zagar 6 points (TR); Wolff 0 points (TR); Match No. 11: Tresarrieu 6 points (TR); Appleton 2 points (TR); Match No. 13: Zagar 6 points (TR); Match No. 19: Zagar 6 points (TR); Match No. 22: McGowan 4 points (TR); Simota 0 points (TR); Match No. 23: McGowan 4 points (TS); Match No. 27: Zagar 4 points (TS).

PREMIER LEAGUE AVERAGES

Rider	Mts	Rds	Pts	Bon	Tot	Avge	Max
Matej Zagar	22	117	294	7	301	10.29	3 full; 3 paid
Danny Bird	4	15	31	1	32	8.53	1 full
Andrew Appleton	27	136	235	18	253	7.44	3 paid
Zdenek Simota	28	132	185	26	211	6.39	–
Mathieu Tresarrieu	25	129	168	23	191	5.92	–
Richard Wolff	26	123	143	14	157	5.11	–
Chris Johnson	18	58	33	11	44	3.03	–
Steve Masters	8	29	16	4	20	2.76	–
Guests	23	102	139	6	145	5.69	2 full

(Tom Brown [1]; Peter Collyer [1]; Richie Dennis [1]; Steen Jensen [1]; Ashley Jones [2]; Simon Lambert [1]; Travis McGowan [3]; Danny Norton [1]; Luke Priest [2]; Lee Smart [3]; Simon Stead [2]; Tomas Suchanek [1]; Simone Terenzani [1]; Mark Thompson [1]; Paul Thorp [1]; Jamie Westacott [1]).

PREMIER TROPHY

(*Denotes bonus-point/aggregate victory)

No	DATE	OPPONENTS	H/A	RESULT	Bird	Mills	Appleton	Zagar	Johnson	Tresarrieu	Wolff	Simota	Masters	Others
1	20/3	Newport	A	L44-49	12+2 (5)	7+1 (4)	4 (4)	12+1 (5)	4 (4)	3+2 (4)	–	–	–	2+1 (4)
2	27/3	Isle of Wight	H	L46-47	5 (2)	3+1 (4)	8+1 (5)	20 (6)	2+1 (4)	6 (5)	2+1 (4)			–
3	1/4	Somerset	A	L45-48	R/R	0 (2)	12+1 (6)	–	2 (5)	4 (6)	6 (5)			21 (6)
4	2/4	Rye House	A	L40-55	R/R	–	3+1 (5)		3 (4)	10+1 (7)	4 (5)			20 (9)
5	4/4	Newport	H	W48-44	R/R	–	9+1 (6)	16 (6)	4+2 (4)	6+2 (4)	8 (5)			5+1 (5)
6	6/4	King's Lynn	A	L44-49	R/R	–	11 (6)	18+1 (6)	2+1 (4)	4+1 (4)	1 (5)			8+2 (5)
7	11/4	King's Lynn	H	W52-39*	R/R	4+3 (5)	8 (5)	17 (6)	2 (3)	11+2 (5)	10+2 (6)			–
8	18/4	Exeter	A	L40-55	–	2+1 (4)	9 (5)	17 (5)	1 (5)	3 (3)	4 (4)		4+1 (4)	–

No	DATE	OPPONENTS	H/A	RESULT	Bird	Mills	Appleton	Zagar	Johnson	Tresarrieu	Wolff	Simota	Masters	Others
9	19/4	Isle of Wight	A	L39-51	–	4+1 (4)	11 (5)	11+1 (5)	4+1 (6)	–	8 (4)	–	–	1+1 (6)
10	2/5	Somerset	H	W48-42*	–	8+2 (4)	5 (4)	14 (5)	–	3+1 (5)	6+2 (4)	12+1 (5)	–	0 (3)
11	9/5	Rye House	H	L40-48	–	6 (4)	5+1 (4)	12 (5)	–	–	8+1 (5)	5+1 (4)	–	4+1 (7)
12	10/6	Exeter	H	W46-44	–	–	11+1 (6)	13 (5)	1 (3)	7+1 (7)	8+1 (5)	6 (4)	R/R	–

DETAILS OF OTHER RIDERS:

Match No. 1: Jamie Westacott 2+1 (4); Match No. 3: Simon Stead 21 (6); Match No. 4: Leigh Lanham 20 (6); Daniel Giffard 0 (3); Match No. 5: Steve Boxall 5+1 (5); Match No. 6: Daniel King 8+2 (5); Match No. 9: Daniel Giffard 1+1 (3); Tom Brown 0 (3); Match No. 10: Jamie Westacott 0 (3); Match No. 11: Ben Barker 4+1 (5); Daniel Giffard 0 (2).

TACTICAL RIDES, AS INCLUDED IN THE SCORES GRID:

Match No. 1: Mills 4 points (TR); Bird 4 points (TR); Match No. 2: Zagar 6 points (TR); Match No. 3: Stead 6 points (TR); Match No. 4: Lanham 6 points (TR); Tresarrieu 4 points (TR); Match No. 6: Zagar 6 points (TR); Match No. 8: Zagar 6 points (TR); Appleton 4 points (TR).

PREMIER TROPHY AVERAGES

Rider	Mts	Rds	Pts	Bon	Tot	Avge	Max
Matej Zagar	10	54	141	3	144	10.67	–
Danny Bird	2	7	15	2	17	9.71	–
Zdenek Simota	4	17	27	3	30	7.06	–
Andrew Appleton	12	61	94	6	100	6.56	–
Richard Wolff	11	52	65	7	72	5.54	–
Chris Mills	8	31	32	9	41	5.29	–
Mathieu Tresarrieu	10	50	55	10	65	5.20	–
Chris Johnson	10	42	25	5	30	2.86	–
Guests	11	45	55	6	61	5.42	1 full

(Ben Barker [1]; Steve Boxall [1]; Tom Brown [1]; Daniel Giffard [3]; Daniel King [1]; Leigh Lanham [1]; Simon Stead [1]; Jamie Westacott [2]).

KNOCK-OUT CUP

(*Denotes aggregate victory)

No	DATE	OPPONENTS	H/A	RESULT	Simota	Masters	Appleton	Wolff	Zagar	Johnson	Tresarrieu	Bird	Others
1	6/6	Newport	H	W54-36	6 (4)	R/R	12+1 (6)	11+3 (5)	15 (5)	1 (3)	–	–	9+3 (7)
2	17/7	Newport	A	W51-39*	7 (4)	8 (4)	5+2 (4)	11+3 (7)	14 (5)	6+2 (5)	0 (2)	–	–
3	28/7	Isle of Wight	A	L44-46	5 (5)	R/R	12+2 (6)	10+2 (7)	9+2 (5)	1+1 (3)	7+1 (4)	–	–
4	8/8	Isle of Wight†	H	W51-33*	6+1 (4)	–	11 (4)	4+2 (4)	12 (4)	2 (4)	5 (4)	11+1 (4)	–
5	5/9	Rye House	H	L43-47	8 (5)	–	12+1 (6)	4+1 (5)	14 (6)	–	5+1 (5)	R/R	0 (3)
6	24/9	Rye House	A	L25-65	–	–	7+1 (6)	–	–	1 (4)	4+1 (6)	R/R	13+1 (15)

†Meeting abandoned after heat fourteen, with the result permitted to stand.

DETAILS OF OTHER RIDERS:

Match No. 1: Cameron Woodward 9+3 (7); Match No. 5: Danny Warwick 0 (3); Match No. 6: Kevin Doolan 6 (5); Ashley Jones 4 (5); Jan Jaros 3+1 (5).

OTHER MEETING

21 March: Challenge

Reading 61 (Danny Bird 14+1; Matej Zagar 12; Andrew Appleton 11; Mathieu Tresarrieu 9+1; Chris Johnson 6+2; Richard Wolff 6+1; Chris Mills 3) Racers Past 34 (Phil Morris 11; Glenn Cunningham 10+1; Ray Morton 8; Shane Colvin 2; Danny Warwick 1+1; Glen Phillips 1; Jamie Westacott 1).

RYE HOUSE SILVER SKI ROCKETS

NOTE: The information below relates only to the main Rye House team. For details of the second side, please refer to the Conference League section.

ADDRESS: Rye House Stadium, Rye Road, Hoddesdon, Hertfordshire, EN11 0EH.
PROMOTERS: Len Silver & Hazal Naylor.
TRACK LENGTH: 271 metres.
TRACK RECORD: 55.8 seconds – Chris Harris (19 June 2004).
FIRST MEETING: 3 August 1958.
YEARS OF OPERATION: 1958 Open; 1959 Southern Area League; 1960-66 Open & Training; 1967 Training; 1969-73 Open & Training; 1974 British League Division Two; 1975-90 National League; 1991-93 British League Division Two; 1999-2001; Conference League; 2002-05 Premier League.

NOTE: In 1999, Rye House staged their home matches at Eastbourne, King's Lynn and Mildenhall.

PREVIOUS VENUE: Hoddesdon Stadium, Rye Road, Hoddesdon, Hertfordshire.
YEARS OF OPERATION: 1935 Open & Training; 1936-37 Open; 1938 Sunday Dirt-track League; 1939-43 Open; 1945-53 Open; 1954-57 Southern Area League.

NOTE: Rye House first acquired the 'Rockets' moniker in 1974, having previously been known as 'Roosters' in 1955 and 'Red Devils' from 1960-73.

CLUB HONOURS

KNOCK-OUT CUP WINNERS: 1979.
LEAGUE CHAMPIONS: 1980, 2005.
PREMIER TROPHY WINNERS: 2005.

RIDER ROSTER 2005

Tommy ALLEN; Steve BOXALL; Edward KENNETT; Daniel KING; Chris NEATH; Stuart ROBSON; Brent WERNER.

OTHER APPEARANCES/GUESTS (official matches only):

Olly ALLEN; Luke BOWEN; Barry BURCHATT; Harland COOK; Karlis EZERGAILIS; Shaun TACEY; Mathieu TRESARRIEU.

PREMIER LEAGUE

(*Denotes bonus-point victory)

No	DATE	OPPONENTS	H/A	RESULT	St. Robson	Kennett	Neath	T. Allen	Werner	Boxall	King	Others
1	2/5	Hull	H	W50-44	9+2 (5)	7 (4)	15 (5)	0 (3)	8+1 (4)	–	9+1 (7)	2 (4)
2	7/5	Sheffield	H	W61-32	8+2 (4)	12 (5)	8+2 (4)	11+1 (4)	11 (5)	–	8+1 (4)	3+1 (4)
3	14/5	Glasgow	H	W55-40	11+1 (5)	9+2 (4)	7+1 (4)	5+2 (4)	10+1 (5)	–	13+1 (5)	0 (3)
4	28/5	Workington	H	W57-36	11+1 (5)	8 (4)	8 (4)	9+1 (5)	10+2 (5)	6+3 (4)	5+1 (4)	–
5	22/6	Hull	A	L33-57	4+1 (4)	8 (4)	6 (4)	0 (0)	10 (5)	0 (1)	5+1 (4)	–
6	25/6	Newcastle	H	W54-41	12+1 (5)	8 (4)	14+1 (5)	4 (5)	14 (5)	–	R/R	2+1 (6)
7	27/6	Newcastle	A	D45-45*	9+1 (5)	5+1 (4)	11+1 (5)	10+2 (7)	9 (5)	–	R/R	1+1 (3)
8	2/7	Reading	H	W57-36	7+2 (4)	11+1 (5)	12+1 (5)	13+2 (7)	12+1 (5)	2+1 (4)	R/R	–
9	8/7	Edinburgh	A	W52-40	10+1 (5)	7 (4)	13+1 (5)	3+1 (4)	8+1 (4)	6+1 (4)	5 (4)	–
10	9/7	King's Lynn	H	W61-34	10+4 (5)	10 (4)	8 (4)	9+1 (4)	11+2 (5)	6+1 (4)	7+1 (4)	–
11	13/7	King's Lynn	A	L38-53*	11 (5)	5+1 (5)	6 (4)	4 (4)	4+1 (4)	3 (5)	5+1 (3)	–
12	25/7	Reading	A	W46-44*	7+2 (4)	5+2 (4)	11+1 (5)	9+2 (5)	10 (5)	1 (3)	3+1 (4)	–
13	29/7	Berwick	H	W65-25	9+3 (5)	11+1 (4)	15 (5)	8+1 (4)	8+3 (4)	3+1 (4)	11+1 (4)	–
14	30/7	Berwick	A	L35-57*	10+1 (5)	6 (4)	6 (5)	1 (4)	3+1 (4)	2 (5)	7+1 (4)	–
15	31/7	Glasgow	A	W47-43*	6 (4)	12+2 (5)	9 (4)	2 (3)	2 (4)	9 (6)	7 (4)	–
16	5/8	Somerset	A	L42-48	6+1 (4)	5 (4)	11 (5)	8+2 (7)	2 (3)	4+1 (3)	6+1 (4)	–
17	11/8	Sheffield	A	L30-64	11+1 (6)	4+2 (4)	1 (3)	5 (5)	1+1 (4)	0 (3)	8 (5)	–
18	21/8	Isle of Wight	H	W59-37	15 (5)	6+2 (4)	6 (4)	6 (4)	11+1 (5)	7+2 (4)	8+1 (4)	–
19	21/8	Edinburgh	H	W58-37*	9+3 (5)	10+1 (4)	15 (5)	5 (4)	5+2 (4)	3 (4)	11 (4)	–
20	23/8	Isle of Wight	A	L40-54*	16 (5)	0 (4)	4 (4)	4 (6)	11+1 (5)	5+2 (6)	R/R	–
21	27/8	Stoke	A	W56-36	7+1 (5)	6 (4)	15 (5)	7+3 (4)	10+1 (4)	–	8+1 (4)	3 (4)
22	29/8	Stoke	H	W63-27*	11+4 (5)	12 (4)	10+1 (4)	6+4 (4)	14 (5)	6 (4)	4+2 (4)	–
23	3/9	Workington	A	L43-47*	10+1 (5)	9+1 (4)	4 (4)	2+2 (6)	6+2 (4)	3 (3)	9 (5)	–
24	4/9	Exeter	H	W66-26	10+2 (4)	13+2 (5)	10 (4)	8+2 (4)	15 (5)	–	6+1 (4)	4+2 (4)
25	11/9	Newport	A	W58-34	7+1 (4)	12+1 (5)	–	9+2 (5)	13+1 (5)	–	5 (4)	12+1 (7)
26	12/9	Exeter	A	W53-37*	13+2 (5)	8+1 (4)	–	6+1 (5)	4+1 (4)	–	9+1 (4)	13+1 (8)
27	17/9	Newport	H	W64-28*	14+1 (6)	R/R	–	13+2 (5)	16 (6)	10+2 (5)	–	11+3 (8)
28	1/10	Somerset	H	W60-31*	R/R	14+3 (6)	16+1 (6)	5+2 (4)	12+1 (5)	2+1 (4)	11+1 (5)	–

DETAILS OF OTHER RIDERS:

Match No. 1: Karlis Ezergailis 2 (4); Match No. 2: Harland Cook 3+1 (4); Match No. 3: Harland Cook 0 (3); Match No. 6: Barry Burchatt 2+1 (6); Match No. 7: Barry Burchatt 1+1 (3); Match No. 21: Luke Bowen 3 (4); Match No. 24: Luke Bowen 4+2 (4); Match No. 25: Olly Allen 11+1 (4); Luke Bowen 1 (3); Match No. 26: Shaun Tacey 13+1 (5); Luke Bowen 0 (3); Match No. 27: Olly Allen 6+1 (4); Luke Bowen 5+2 (4).

TACTICAL SUBSTITUTE AND TACTICAL RIDES, AS INCLUDED IN THE SCORES GRID:

Match No. 5: Kennett 4 points (TR); Stuart Robson 0 points (TR; excluded 2 minutes); Werner 0 points (TS); Match No. 11:

T. Allen 4 points (TR); Stuart Robson 0 points (TR); Match No. 14: Stuart Robson 2 points (TR); King 2 points (TR); Match No. 17: King 4 points (TR); Stuart Robson 4 points (TS); Kennett 0 points (TR); Match No. 20: Stuart Robson 6 points (TR); Werner 2 points (TR).

PREMIER LEAGUE AVERAGES

Rider	Mts	Rds	Pts	Bon	Tot	Avge	Max
Stuart Robson	27	129	257	39	296	9.18	1 full; 3 paid
Chris Neath	25	112	241	10	251	8.96	4 full; 1 paid
Brent Werner	28	128	249	24	273	8.53	1 full
Edward Kennett	27	116	221	23	244	8.41	1 full; 2 paid
Daniel King	23	98	167	18	185	7.55	1 paid
Tommy Allen	28	126	170	33	203	6.44	2 paid
Steve Boxall	19	76	78	15	93	4.89	–
Guests	13	51	51	10	61	4.78	1 paid

(Olly Allen [2]; Luke Bowen [5]; Barry Burchatt [2]; Harland Cook [2]; Karlis Ezergailis [1]; Shaun Tacey [1]).

PREMIER TROPHY

(*Denotes bonus-point/aggregate victory)

No	DATE	OPPONENTS	H/A	RESULT	St. Robson	Kennett	Neath	T. Allen	Werner	Boxall	King	Others
1	12/3	Somerset	H	W50-43	11+2 (5)	5 (4)	8+1 (5)	R/R	12+1 (5)	1+1 (5)	13+1 (6)	–
2	19/3	Newport	H	W50-40	13+1 (5)	4+1 (4)	16+1 (6)	R/R	6+2 (4)	0 (4)	11+1 (7)	–
3	27/3	Newport	A	W52-38*	10+3 (5)	8 (4)	10+2 (5)	R/R	12 (5)	3 (4)	9+2 (7)	–
4	28/3	Isle of Wight	H	W61-32	8+3 (4)	12+1 (5)	15 (5)	R/R	8+3 (5)	9+2 (6)	9+1 (5)	–
5	2/4	Reading	H	W55-40	7+1 (4)	12+1 (5)	11+2 (5)	R/R	10+2 (5)	7+2 (5)	8+1 (6)	–
6	9/4	Exeter	H	W59-33	6+2 (4)	15 (5)	14 (5)	R/R	13 (5)	4+1 (6)	7+1 (5)	–
7	11/4	Exeter	A	L41-54*	5 (5)	2 (4)	9 (4)	6+1 (4)	1 (4)	2+1 (3)	16+1 (7)	–
8	23/4	King's Lynn	H	W59-34	13+2 (5)	13+2 (5)	9 (4)	3+1 (4)	7+2 (4)	6 (4)	8+1 (4)	–
9	27/4	King's Lynn	A	L41-52*	6+1 (5)	2 (3)	11 (5)	0 (3)	1 (3)	–	12+1 (6)	9 (5)
10	29/4	Somerset	A	W48-44*	6 (4)	4+1 (4)	11 (5)	6+3 (4)	6 (4)	–	11+2 (7)	4+1 (3)
11	9/5	Reading	A	W48-40*	8+1 (4)	9+3 (5)	13 (5)	4 (4)	7 (4)	–	7 (5)	0 (1)
12	10/5	Isle of Wight	A	W46-44*	11+1 (5)	5 (4)	12 (5)	4+2 (4)	5+1 (4)	–	9+1 (5)	0 (3)
13	12/6	Sheffield	H	W66-26	R/R	11+2 (5)	13+2 (6)	8+1 (4)	17+1 (6)	5+1 (4)	12+3 (5)	–
14	16/6	Sheffield	A	L39-50*	14 (5)	7+2 (5)	1 (3)	4+1 (4)	4+2 (4)	6 (6)	3 (3)	–
15	6/8	Workington	A	W46-44	11+1 (5)	0 (1)	5 (4)	3 (4)	12+1 (5)	11+2 (7)	4+3 (4)	–
16	7/8	Workington	H	W61-32*	7 (4)	10+2 (4)	13+1 (5)	10+2 (5)	13+1 (5)	4+1 (4)	4+2 (4)	–

DETAILS OF OTHER RIDERS:

Match No. 9: Mathieu Tresarrieu 9 (5); Match No. 10: Mathieu Tresarrieu 4+1 (3); Match No. 11: Harland Cook 0 (1); Match No. 12: Barry Burchatt 0 (3).

TACTICAL RIDES, AS INCLUDED IN THE SCORES GRID:

Match No. 7: King 6 points (TR); Neath 6 points (TR); Match No. 9: King 6 points (TR).

RYE HOUSE: From left to right, back row: John Sampford (Team Manager), Edward Kennett, Daniel King, Brent Werner (on bike), Stuart Robson, Tommy Allen, Steve Boxall, Len Silver (Promoter). Front, kneeling: Charlie Martin (Mascot), Chris Neath.

PREMIER TROPHY AVERAGES

Rider	Mts	Rds	Pts	Bon	Tot	Avge	Max
Chris Neath	16	77	168	9	177	9.19	1 full
Stuart Robson	15	69	136	18	154	8.93	1 paid
Brent Werner	16	72	134	16	150	8.33	1 paid
Edward Kennett	16	67	119	15	134	8.00	1 full; 2 paid
Daniel King	16	86	137	21	158	7.35	1 paid
Tommy Allen	10	39	48	11	59	6.05	1 paid
Steve Boxall	12	58	58	11	69	4.76	–
Guests	4	12	13	1	14	4.67	–

(Barry Burchatt [1]; Harland Cook [1]; Mathieu Tresarrieu [2]).

KNOCK-OUT CUP

(*Denotes aggregate victory)

No	DATE	OPPONENTS	H/A	RESULT	St. Robson	Kennett	Werner	King	Neath	Boxall	T. Allen	Bowen
1	3/6	Edinburgh	A	L43-47	12+1 (5)	6+1 (4)	3 (4)	7+1 (4)	8+2 (5)	1 (3)	6+1 (5)	–
2	4/6	Edinburgh	H	W57-33*	9+3 (5)	14+1 (5)	R/R	10 (5)	14 (5)	5+1 (5)	5+2 (5)	–
3	16/7	Glasgow	H	W48-42	10+2 (5)	11+1 (5)	5+2 (4)	4 (4)	7 (4)	2+1 (3)	9+1 (5)	–
4	24/7	Glasgow	A	W57-33*	12+2 (5)	12+2 (5)	9+2 (4)	9 (4)	10+1 (4)	0 (4)	5+2 (4)	–
5	5/9	Reading	A	W47-43	3+1 (4)	8+1 (4)	4 (4)	13 (5)	13+1 (5)	–	3+1 (5)	3 (3)
6	24/9	Reading	H	W65-25*	R/R	6+2 (5)	17+1 (6)	15+3 (6)	15 (5)	3+1 (4)	9+1 (4)	–
7	21/10	King's Lynn	A	L27-63	R/R	4 (5)	9 (6)	2+1 (5)	4 (6)	1 (1)	7 (7)	–
8	22/10	King's Lynn	H	W56-34	R/R	8+1 (5)	14+3 (6)	9+1 (5)	11+1 (6)	5 (3)	9+2 (5)	–

YOUNG SHIELD

(*Denotes aggregate victory)

No	DATE	OPPONENTS	H/A	RESULT	St. Robson	Kennett	Werner	King	Neath	Boxall	T. Allen	Bowen
1	23/9	Isle of Wight	H	W62-30	3 (2)	11 (5)	10 (4)	7+2 (4)	15 (5)	7+2 (5)	9+2 (5)	–
2	27/9	Isle of Wight	A	L41-54*	R/R	8 (5)	15 (6)	4+2 (5)	10+1 (6)	0 (3)	4+1 (5)	–
3	13/10	Sheffield	A	L36-59	R/R	9+1 (6)	1+1 (4)	9 (5)	6 (6)	2+1 (3)	7+1 (5)	2 (1)
4	15/10	Sheffield	H	W62-30*	R/R	11 (5)	13+2 (6)	10+2 (5)	12+1 (6)	8+3 (4)	8+2 (4)	–
5	26/10	King's Lynn	A	L34-59	R/R	4+1 (5)	2 (4)	13+1 (6)	9 (6)	2+2 (4)	4 (5)	–
6	29/10	King's Lynn	H	W51-42	R/R	8+1 (5)	9+2 (5)	12+1 (6)	13 (6)	4+3 (4)	5 (4)	–

TACTICAL SUBSTITUTE AND TACTICAL RIDES, AS INCLUDED IN THE SCORES GRID:

Match No. 2: Werner 6 points (TR); Kennett 4 points (TR); Match No. 3: Kennett 6 points (TR); Bowen 2 points (TS); King 2 points (TR); Match No. 5: King 4 points (TR); Neath 2 points (TR).

OTHER MEETINGS

16 March: A10 Trophy

King's Lynn 46 Rye House 44 (Daniel King 19+1; Chris Neath 8+2; Stuart Robson 8; Edward Kennett 4+1; Brent Werner 4+1; Steve Boxall 1; Tommy Allen R/R).

30 May: Inter-League Challenge

Rye House 48 (Brent Werner 10; Stuart Robson 9+2; Tommy Allen 8+1; Edward Kennett 7+1; Chris Neath 5+1; Daniel King 5; Steve Boxall 4+1) Belle Vue Select 47.

INDIVIDUAL MEETINGS

23 July: Vic Harding Memorial Trophy

QUALIFYING SCORES: Edward Kennett 13; Steve Masters 12; Tommy Allen 12; David Howe 11; Stuart Robson 9; Chris Neath 8; Brent Werner 8; Olly Allen 5; Mathieu Tresarrieu 5; Steve Boxall 4; Zdenek Simota 2; Luke Bowen 1. FIRST SEMI-FINAL: 1st Kennett; 2nd T. Allen; 3rd Robson; 4th Werner; SECOND SEMI-FINAL: 1st Neath; 2nd Howe; 3rd O. Allen; 4th Masters; FINAL: 1st T. Allen; 2nd Neath; 3rd Kennett; 4th Howe.

8 October: Brent Werner Testimonial

QUALIFYING SCORES: Hans N. Andersen 12; Morten Risager 11; Sam Ermolenko 10; Brent Werner 9; Edward Kennett 9; Steve Boxall 9; Billy Janniro 9; Ronnie Correy 8; Leigh Lanham 8; Daniel King 8; Chris Neath 7; Chris Harris 7; Steve Johnston 6; Tommy Allen 4; Shawn McConnell 2; Patrick Hougaard 1. FINAL: 1st Risager; 2nd Andersen; 3rd Ermolenko; 4th Werner.

SHEFFIELD PIRTEK TIGERS

ADDRESS: Owlerton Sports Stadium, Penistone Road, Owlerton, Sheffield, South Yorkshire, S6 2DE.
PROMOTERS: Neil Machin & Malcolm Wright.
TRACK LENGTH: 361 metres.
TRACK RECORD: 59.5 seconds – Simon Stead (8 August 2004).
FIRST MEETING: 30 March 1929.
YEARS OF OPERATION: 1929 English Dirt-track League; 1930–31 Northern League; 1932 Speedway National Association Trophy; 1933 National League; 1938–39 National League Division Two; 1945 Open; 1946 Northern League; 1947–50 National League Division Two; 1951–52 Open; 1960–64 Provincial League; 1965–67 British League; 1968–74 British League Division One; 1975–88 British League; 1991–94 British League Division Two; 1995 Premier League; 1996 Premier League & Conference League; 1997–99 Premier League; 2000–03 Premier League & Conference League; 2004 Premier League & Conference Trophy; 2005 Premier League.

CLUB HONOURS

BRITISH SPEEDWAY CUP (DIVISION TWO) WINNERS: 1947.
KNOCK-OUT CUP WINNERS: 1974, 2002.
FOUR-TEAM CHAMPIONS: 1999, 2000.
LEAGUE CHAMPIONS: 1999, 2002.
YOUNG SHIELD WINNERS: 1999, 2002.
PREMIERSHIP WINNERS: 2000.

RIDER ROSTER 2005

Ricky ASHWORTH; Andre COMPTON; Benji COMPTON; Paul COOPER; Richard HALL; Trevor HARDING; Kyle LEGAULT; Ben WILSON; Sean WILSON.

OTHER APPEARANCES/GUESTS (official matches only):
James COCKLE; Josef FRANC; Jan JAROS; Robbie KESSLER; Emil KRAMER; David McALLAN; Chris MILLS; Andrew MOORE; Ray MORTON; Scott SMITH; George STANCL; Shaun TACEY; Mark THOMPSON; Brent WERNER.

PREMIER LEAGUE

(*Denotes bonus-point victory)

No	DATE	OPPONENTS	H/A	RESULT	S. Wilson	B. Wilson	Hall	Ashworth	A. Compton	Cooper	Harding	Legault	Others
1	7/5	Rye House	A	L32-61	9 (5)	1+1 (4)	4+1 (4)	5 (4)	10+1 (5)	1 (4)	2+1 (4)	–	–
2	19/5	Reading	H	W60-35	14+1 (5)	9+1 (4)	5+1 (4)	7+1 (4)	11 (5)	9+1 (4)	5+1 (4)	–	–
3	27/5	Somerset	A	W46-44	–	7+1 (4)	–	9+1 (5)	10 (5)	5+1 (4)	7+2 (5)	–	8+2 (7)
4	2/6	Newport	H	W53-41	R/R	17+3 (7)	0 (1)	11 (6)	15 (6)	6+1 (5)	4 (5)	–	–
5	6/6	Exeter	A	L39-56	–	6+1 (6)	R/R	8 (5)	10 (5)	0 (5)	2+1 (4)	–	13+1 (5)
6	9/6	Glasgow	H	W51-44	–	13+2 (7)	R/R	13 (6)	12 (5)	2 (4)	8+3 (5)	–	3 (3)
7	15/6	King's Lynn	A	L39-52	–	6+4 (6)	–	R/R	10+2 (6)	1+1 (4)	4 (4)	–	18 (10)
8	27/6	Reading	A	L37-56*	–	4+2 (6)	R/R	1 (4)	13+1 (5)	0 (4)	–	7 (7)	12 (4)
9	30/6	Isle of Wight	H	W50-45	–	8+1 (6)	R/R	12+2 (6)	13 (5)	6+3 (5)	–	3+1 (4)	8+1 (4)
10	1/7	Edinburgh	A	L43-45	–	0 (5)	R/R	10 (5)	10 (5)	3 (5)	–	5+1 (5)	15 (5)
11	7/7	Edinburgh	H	W57-36*	–	12 (5)	R/R	15 (5)	14 (5)	3+1 (5)	–	7+1 (6)	6+3 (4)
12	9/7	Berwick	A	L37-55	–	7 (6)	R/R	4 (5)	8 (4)	1+1 (5)	–	3 (6)	14+1 (5)
13	14/7	Exeter	H	W56-37*	12+1 (5)	6+1 (4)	6+1 (4)	12 (4)	12+2 (5)	1 (3)	–	7+2 (5)	–
14	19/7	Isle of Wight	A	L33-59	9 (5)	3 (4)	3 (4)	3+1 (4)	8+2 (5)	6 (4)	–	1+1 (4)	–
15	20/7	Hull	A	L45-50	17 (5)	3+1 (4)	0 (0)	6 (4)	9 (4)	8+1 (6)	–	2+1 (6)	–
16	21/7	Hull	H	W56-39*	11+1 (5)	6+2 (5)	R/R	12+1 (5)	11+1 (5)	7+2 (5)	–	9+1 (5)	–
17	31/7	Newport	A	W53-38*	11+1 (5)	6+2 (4)	5+1 (4)	10+1 (4)	12+1 (5)	3+1 (4)	–	6+2 (4)	–
18	4/8	Stoke	H	W56-40	10+2 (5)	7+1 (4)	4+2 (4)	11 (4)	10+1 (5)	6 (4)	–	8+2 (4)	–
19	6/8	Stoke	A	L41-55*	9 (4)	3 (4)	0 (4)	11 (5)	12 (5)	1 (4)	–	5+2 (4)	–
20	11/8	Rye House	H	W64-30*	9+3 (5)	11+1 (4)	4 (4)	12 (4)	15 (5)	3+1 (3)	–	10+3 (5)	–
21	18/8	Newcastle	H	W63-29	7+1 (4)	8+1 (4)	7+2 (4)	14+1 (5)	15 (5)	3+1 (4)	–	9+2 (4)	–

No	DATE	OPPONENTS	H/A	RESULT	S. Wilson	B. Wilson	Hall	Ashworth	A. Compton	Cooper	Harding	Legault	Others
22	21/8	Newcastle	A	L41-49*	11 (5)	5+1 (4)	4+1 (4)	11 (5)	5+2 (4)	2 (4)	–	3+1 (5)	–
23	25/8	Workington	H	W59-36	10+4 (5)	8 (4)	6+2 (4)	11 (4)	15 (5)	3 (4)	–	6+3 (4)	–
24	1/9	Somerset	H	W65-30*	14+1 (5)	5+2 (4)	9+3 (4)	9 (4)	13+2 (5)	4+1 (4)	–	11 (4)	–
25	11/9	Glasgow	A	L41-51	4+1 (4)	10 (6)	4+1 (5)	R/R	20 (6)	0 (1)	–	3 (7)	–
26	22/9	Berwick†	H	W48-41	8 (4)	8 (4)	6+3 (4)	11 (4)	10+1 (4)	–	–	5 (4)	0 (1)
27	6/10	King's Lynn	H	W56-40*	12 (5)	8+3 (4)	4 (4)	10+1 (4)	14+1 (5)	–	–	8 (5)	0 (3)
28	8/10	Workington	A	L40-55*	13+1 (5)	2+1 (4)	8 (5)	4+1 (4)	6 (4)	–	–	7 (4)	0 (4)

†Meeting abandoned after heat fourteen, with the result permitted to stand.

NOTE: Guest Emil Kramer is not credited with a full maximum from the away match at Reading, as he missed a programmed ride (heat eleven) through a two minute exclusion.

DETAILS OF OTHER RIDERS:

Match No. 3: Brent Werner 5 (4); Chris Mills 3+2 (3); Match No. 5: Scott Smith 13+1 (5); Match No. 6: Scott Smith 3 (3); Match No. 7: Shaun Tacey 10 (5); Andrew Moore 8 (5); Match No. 8: Emil Kramer 12 (4); Match No. 9: Robbie Kessler 8+1 (4); Match No. 10: George Stancl 15 (5); Match No. 11: George Stancl 6+3 (4); Match No. 12: Josef Franc 14+1 (5); Match No. 26: Benji Compton 0 (1); Match No. 27: Benji Compton 0 (3); Match No. 28: David McAllan 0 (4).

TACTICAL RIDES, AS INCLUDED IN THE SCORES GRID:

Match No. 1: S. Wilson 4 points (TR); A. Compton 2 points (TR); Match No. 5: Smith 6 points (TR); A. Compton 4 points (TR); Match No. 7: Moore 2 points (TR); Tacey 0 points (TR); Match No. 8: A. Compton 6 points (TR); Kramer 0 points (TR; excluded two-minutes); Match No. 12: Franc 4 points (TR); A. Compton 0 points (TR); Match No. 14: A. Compton 2 points (TR); S. Wilson 2 points (TR); Match No. 15: S. Wilson 6 points (TR); A. Compton 4 points (TR); Match No. 19: S. Wilson 6 points (TR); Ashworth 6 points (TR); Match No. 25: A. Compton 6 points (TR); Match No. 28: S. Wilson 6 points (TR); A. Compton 4 points (TR).

PREMIER LEAGUE AVERAGES

Rider	Mts	Rds	Pts	Bon	Tot	Avge	Max
Andre Compton	28	138	309	17	326	9.45	3 full; 2 paid
Sean Wilson	18	86	178	17	195	9.07	2 paid
Ricky Ashworth	26	119	239	10	249	8.37	3 full; 1 paid
Ben Wilson	28	133	189	32	221	6.65	1 paid
Kyle Legault	21	102	125	23	148	5.80	–
Richard Hall	18	67	79	18	97	5.79	1 paid
Trevor Harding	7	31	32	8	40	5.16	–
Paul Cooper	25	104	84	16	100	3.85	–
Guests	14	55	91	8	99	7.20	1 full

(Benji Compton [2]; Josef Franc [1]; Robbie Kessler [1]; Emil Kramer [1]; David McAllan [1]; Chris Mills [1]; Andrew Moore [1]; Scott Smith [2]; George Stancl [2]; Shaun Tacey [1]; Brent Werner [1]).

PREMIER TROPHY

(*Denotes bonus-point victory)

No	DATE	OPPONENTS	H/A	RESULT	S. Wilson	B. Wilson	Hall	Ashworth	A. Compton	Cooper	Legault	Harding	Others
1	5/3	Berwick	A	L40-55	10 (5)	3 (4)	1+1 (4)	6 (4)	11 (5)	6+2 (4)	3 (4)	-	-
2	20/3	Newcastle	A	L41-48	13+1 (6)	6+1 (5)	9+1 (6)	4 (4)	R/R	-	4 (5)	-	5+2 (4)
3	24/3	Stoke	H	W60-35	13 (5)	6 (4)	8+1 (4)	8+2 (4)	13+1 (5)	7+1 (4)	5+1 (4)	-	-
4	26/3	Stoke	A	L37-55*	11 (5)	5+2 (4)	8+1 (5)	3 (4)	5 (4)	4+1 (4)	1+1 (4)	-	-
5	31/3	Edinburgh	H	W50-40	12+2 (5)	3+1 (4)	3+2 (4)	9+1 (4)	15 (5)	6 (4)	2+1 (4)	-	-
6	7/4	Glasgow	H	W61-36	15 (5)	7+1 (4)	4+1 (4)	11 (4)	12+1 (5)	6+1 (4)	6+3 (4)	-	-
7	10/4	Glasgow	A	L43-52*	4+2 (4)	9 (4)	12+1 (5)	6+1 (4)	6+1 (5)	4 (4)	2 (4)	-	-
8	15/4	Edinburgh	A	L34-60	9 (5)	3 (5)	R/R	5 (5)	12 (5)	0 (3)	5 (7)	-	-
9	21/4	Newcastle	H	W58-38*	14+1 (5)	8 (4)	10+2 (5)	7+1 (4)	5+1 (4)	5 (4)	9+1 (4)	-	-
10	23/4	Workington	A	L42-55	9 (5)	4 (4)	5+2 (4)	13 (5)	3+1 (4)	3 (4)	5+1 (4)	-	-
11	27/4	Hull	A	L45-47	9 (5)	4+1 (4)	10+1 (5)	4+1 (4)	6+1 (4)	11+1 (5)	-	-	1+1 (3)
12	28/4	Workington	H	W53-39*	11+1 (5)	5+1 (4)	8+1 (4)	9+1 (4)	12+1 (5)	6+2 (5)	-	-	2 (3)
13	5/5	Hull	H	W64-28*	12+2 (5)	7+2 (4)	6+1 (4)	9 (4)	15 (5)	8+2 (4)	-	7+1 (4)	-
14	12/5	Berwick	H	W59-35*	13+2 (5)	6 (4)	6+3 (4)	12 (4)	15 (5)	4+1 (4)	-	3 (4)	-
15	12/6	Rye House	A	L26-66	-	1+1 (5)	R/R	8+1 (6)	9 (5)	0 (4)	5+2 (6)	-	3 (4)
16	16/6	Rye House	H	W50-39	-	8+3 (7)	R/R	15 (5)	10 (5)	7+2 (5)	-	3 (4)	7+2 (4)

DETAILS OF OTHER RIDERS:

Match No. 2: Benji Compton 5+2 (4); Match No. 11: James Cockle 1+1 (3); Match No. 12: Jan Jaros 2 (3); Match No. 15: Andrew Moore 3 (4); Match No. 16: Robbie Kessler 7+2 (4).

TACTICAL RIDES, AS INCLUDED IN THE SCORES GRID:

Match No. 1: A. Compton 6 points (TR); S. Wilson 4 points (TR); Match No. 4: S. Wilson 4 points (TR); A. Compton 0 points (TR); Match No. 7: Hall 6 points (TR); B. Wilson 4 points (TR); Match No. 8: S. Wilson 6 points (TR); A. Compton 4 points (TR); Match No. 10: Ashworth 6 points (TR); Hall 2 points (TR); Match No. 11: Hall 4 points (TR); Match No. 15: A. Compton 2 points (TR); Ashworth 2 points (TR).

PREMIER TROPHY AVERAGES

Rider	Mts	Rds	Pts	Bon	Tot	Avge	Max
Sean Wilson	14	70	148	11	159	9.09	1 full; 2 paid
Andre Compton	15	71	143	7	150	8.45	3 full
Ricky Ashworth	16	69	125	8	133	7.71	2 full
Richard Hall	13	58	84	18	102	7.03	-
Benji Compton	1	4	5	2	7	7.00	-
Paul Cooper	15	62	77	13	90	5.81	-
Ben Wilson	16	70	83	13	96	5.49	-
Trevor Harding	4	18	18	3	21	4.67	-
Kyle Legault	10	44	42	8	50	4.55	-
Guests	4	14	13	3	16	4.57	-

(James Cockle [1]; Jan Jaros [1]; Robbie Kessler [1]; Andrew Moore [1]).

SHEFFIELD: From left to right, back row: Ricky Ashworth, Kyle Legault, Richard Hall, Ben Wilson, Paul Cooper, Andre Compton. Front, on bike: Sean Wilson.

KNOCK-OUT CUP

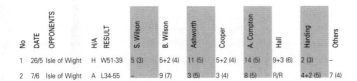

No	DATE	OPPONENTS	H/A	RESULT	S. Wilson	B. Wilson	Ashworth	Cooper	A. Compton	Hall	Harding	Others
1	26/5	Isle of Wight	H	W51-39	5 (3)	5+2 (4)	11 (5)	5+2 (4)	14 (5)	9+3 (6)	2 (3)	–
2	7/6	Isle of Wight	A	L34-55	–	9 (7)	3 (5)	3 (4)	8 (5)	R/R	4+2 (5)	7 (4)

DETAILS OF OTHER RIDER:

Match No. 2: Ray Morton 7 (4).

YOUNG SHIELD

(*Denotes aggregate victory)

No	DATE	OPPONENTS	H/A	RESULT	S. Wilson	B. Wilson	Ashworth	Hall	A. Compton	Legault	Others
1	29/9	Edinburgh	H	W57-37	15 (5)	2 (4)	12 (4)	5+2 (4)	13+2 (5)	8+1 (5)	2 (3)
2	30/9	Edinburgh	A	L38-54*	12 (5)	0 (3)	6+1 (4)	2 (4)	11+1 (5)	2 (3)	5 (6)
3	13/10	Rye House	H	W59-36	13+2 (5)	7+2 (4)	12+1 (5)	4+2 (4)	9 (4)	12+1 (5)	2 (3)
4	15/10	Rye House	A	L30-62	13 (5)	1 (4)	1 (4)	4+1 (4)	5+1 (4)	6 (6)	0 (3)

DETAILS OF OTHER RIDERS:

Match No. 1: Mark Thompson 2 (3); Match No. 2: David McAllan 5 (6); Match No. 3: David McAllan 2 (3); Match No. 4: David McAllan 0 (3).

TACTICAL RIDES, AS INCLUDED IN THE SCORES GRID:

Match No. 2: S. Wilson 2 points (TR); A. Compton 2 points (TR); Match No. 4: S. Wilson 2 points (TR); A. Compton 2 points (TR).

OTHER MEETINGS

9 March: Yorkshire Cup (first leg)

> Hull 53 Sheffield 39 (Andre Compton 10+1; Sean Wilson 8; Ricky Ashworth 7+1; Richard Hall 6+1; Paul Cooper 4+1; Ben Wilson 2+2; Kyle Legault 2).

17 March: Yorkshire Cup (second leg)

> Sheffield 55 (Sean Wilson 14; Richard Hall 12+1; Ben Wilson 8+2; Ricky Ashworth 7+1; Andre Compton 6+1; Paul Cooper 6; Kyle Legault 2) Hull 36 – Sheffield won 94-89 on aggregate.

23 June: Inter-League Challenge

> Sheffield 47 (Ricky Ashworth 15; Andre Compton 13+1; Matej Zagar 10; Paul Cooper 3+1; Adam Allott 3; Trevor Harding 2+1; Ben Wilson 1) Belle Vue 49.

17 September: Premier League

> Workington 3 Sheffield 3 (Sean Wilson 2; Ben Wilson 1+1; Kyle Legault 0; Ricky Ashworth DNR; Richard Hall DNR; Andre Compton DNR; Benji Compton DNR) – meeting abandoned after heat one.

23 October: Conference Challenge

> Scunthorpe 47 Sheffield 43 (Richard Hall 15; Luke Priest 10; Grant Hayes 8+1; Ben Wilson 4; Rusty Hodgson 3+1; David Speight 2+2; Michael Mitchell 1).

INDIVIDUAL MEETINGS

22 September: British Under-15 Championship (Round Six)

   1st Joe Haines 15; 2nd Ben Taylor 14; 3rd Ben Hopwood 13; Adam Wrathall 12; George Piper 10; Kye Norton 9; Brendan Johnson 8; Daniel Greenwood 8; Jamie Pickard 7; Richard Franklin 7; Ben Reade 4; Scott Meakins 3; Ben Thompson 3; Jack Butler (Res) 3; Rickylee Beecroft 2; Tom Davies 1; Dan Kirkman 0; Ben Johnson (Res) 0.

20 October: Northern Riders' Classic

   QUALIFYING SCORES: Andre Compton 15; Sean Wilson 13; Simon Stead 12; Magnus Karlsson 11; Mark Lemon 9; Ben Wilson 9; Robbie Kessler 9; Richard Hall 6; Adam Skornicki 6; Sam Ermolenko 5; Kyle Legault 5; Rusty Harrison 4; Adrian Rymel 4; Scott Smith 4; Luke Priest (Res) 3; James Birkinshaw 2; Ricky Ashworth 1; Benji Compton (Res) 1. SEMI-FINAL: 1st Stead; 2nd Karlsson; 3rd Lemon; 4th B. Wilson. FINAL: 1st Stead; 2nd Karlsson; 3rd S. Wilson; 4th A. Compton.

SOMERSET MIKE MANNING AUDIO REBELS

ADDRESS: Oak Tree Arena, Edithmead, nr Highbridge, Somerset.
PROMOTERS: Peter Toogood & Jo Lawson.
TRACK LENGTH: 300 metres.
TRACK RECORD: 56.40 seconds – Kenneth Bjerre (20 June 2003).
FIRST MEETING: 2 June 2000.
YEARS OF OPERATION: 2000–01 Conference League; 2002–05 Premier League.

CLUB HONOURS

CONFERENCE TROPHY WINNERS: 2001.
KNOCK-OUT CUP WINNERS: 2001.
FOUR-TEAM CHAMPIONS: 2005.

RIDER ROSTER 2005

Glenn CUNNINGHAM; Paul FRY; Trevor HARDING; Ritchie HAWKINS; Jason KING; Chris MILLS; Lee SMART; Jamie SMITH; Simon WALKER; Magnus ZETTERSTROM.

OTHER APPEARANCES/GUESTS (official matches only):
Ben BARKER; Benji COMPTON; Rob GRANT; Daniel KING; David MELDRUM; Sean STODDART.

PREMIER LEAGUE

(*Denotes bonus-point victory)

No	DATE	OPPONENTS	H/A	RESULT	Zetterstrom	Smith	Hawkins	Fry	Cunningham	Smart	J. King	Mills	Harding	Walker	Others
1	6/5	Workington†	H	L39-45	8 (4)	3 (4)	3 (2)	10+1 (4)	9 (4)	3 (6)	3+1 (4)	–	–	–	–
2	7/5	Stoke	A	L42-48	10+1 (5)	R/R	4+2 (5)	5 (4)	13 (5)	3 (4)	7+2 (7)	–	–	–	–
3	13/5	Glasgow	H	W56-39	10+1 (5)	7+2 (4)	6+1 (4)	7+1 (4)	12 (5)	4+1 (3)	10+2 (5)	–	–	–	–
4	18/5	King's Lynn	A	L32-62	6 (4)	3+2 (4)	8+1 (5)	3 (4)	8 (5)	2 (4)	2+1 (4)	–	–	–	–
5	27/5	Sheffield	H	L44-46	12 (5)	0 (4)	6+4 (4)	11 (5)	10+1 (4)	2 (3)	3 (5)	–	–	–	–
6	30/5	Exeter	A	L40-54	14 (5)	R/R	5 (5)	6 (4)	9 (5)	0 (4)	6+2 (7)	–	–	–	–
7	10/6	Berwick	H	W48-42	9+2 (5)	3 (4)	9 (4)	4 (4)	14+1 (5)	1 (3)	8 (5)	–	–	–	–
8	17/6	Exeter	H	W53-42	13 (5)	6+2 (4)	8+1 (4)	11+2 (5)	9+1 (4)	0 (3)	6+1 (5)	–	–	–	–
9	24/6	Newcastle	H	W58-34	14+1 (5)	8+2 (5)	14+1 (5)	R/R	15+1 (6)	2+1 (4)	5 (5)	–	–	–	–
10	6/7	Edinburgh	H	W60-32	15 (5)	6+1 (4)	11+1 (5)	7 (4)	11+1 (4)	4+1 (4)	6+1 (4)	–	–	–	–
11	9/7	Workington	A	L46-47	14 (5)	3 (4)	7+1 (4)	10 (4)	8 (5)	1 (4)	3 (4)	–	–	–	–
12	10/7	Glasgow	A	L41-54*	10 (5)	4+1 (4)	2+1 (4)	13 (5)	5 (4)	3 (4)	4+2 (4)	–	–	–	–
13	15/7	King's Lynn	H	L43-47	12+1 (5)	4+1 (4)	9 (4)	3 (2)	11 (5)	2 (5)	2 (5)	–	–	–	–
14	18/7	Reading	A	L44-46	12 (5)	4+2 (5)	10+1 (5)	R/R	9 (6)	0 (3)	–	–	–	–	9+2 (6)
15	22/7	Stoke	H	W56-40*	14 (5)	2+1 (4)	8+3 (4)	10 (5)	11+1 (4)	–	–	5 (4)	6+2 (4)	–	–
16	29/7	Newport	H	W64-30	14+1 (5)	5+1 (4)	8+3 (4)	14+1 (5)	12 (4)	–	–	5+2 (4)	6+1 (4)	–	–
17	4/8	Isle of Wight	A	L37-56	12 (5)	2 (4)	4 (4)	10 (5)	8 (4)	–	–	0 (4)	–	–	1 (4)
18	5/8	Rye House	H	W48-42	13 (5)	5 (4)	9 (4)	9+2 (4)	11+1 (5)	–	–	1 (5)	–	–	0 (3)
19	12/8	Edinburgh	A	L39-55*	9+1 (4)	3+2 (4)	4+1 (4)	8 (5)	11 (5)	–	–	–	–	–	4 (8)
20	13/8	Berwick	A	L36-58	15 (5)	3 (4)	8 (5)	4 (4)	4 (4)	–	–	–	–	–	2+1 (8)
21	14/8	Newcastle	A	L36-60	7 (3)	5+1 (4)	10+1 (5)	6 (5)	6 (4)	–	–	–	–	–	2 (8)
22	19/8	Reading	H	W47-43*	8 (4)	5+1 (4)	8+2 (5)	10+1 (5)	7 (4)	–	–	6+2 (5)	–	–	3 (3)
23	26/8	Isle of Wight	H	L43-51	14 (5)	4 (4)	1+1 (2)	11 (5)	8+1 (4)	–	–	4+1 (5)	–	1 (5)	–
24	28/8	Newport	A	W49-41*	14 (5)	–	R/R	11 (5)	11 (5)	–	–	2+1 (4)	–	6+2 (6)	5 (5)
25	31/8	Hull♦	A	L32-40	7+1 (3)	4+1 (5)	R/R	9 (4)	5 (3)	–	–	6+1 (5)	–	1+1 (4)	–
26	1/9	Sheffield	A	L30-65	8 (4)	0 (4)	R/R	6+2 (6)	5 (5)	–	–	10 (7)	–	1 (4)	–
27	9/9	Hull	H	W56-38*	13 (5)	7+1 (4)	6+1 (4)	10 (4)	12 (5)	–	–	6+2 (4)	–	2+1 (4)	–
28	1/10	Rye House	A	L31-60	R/R	3+1 (5)	1 (5)	13 (6)	9 (6)	–	–	3 (5)	–	2+1 (3)	–

†Meeting abandoned after heat fourteen, with the result permitted to stand.

♦Meeting abandoned after heat twelve, with the result permitted to stand.

DETAILS OF OTHER RIDERS:

Match No. 14: Chris Mills 9+2 (6); Match No. 17: Simon Walker 1 (4); Match No. 18: Simon Walker 0 (3); Match No. 19: Rob Grant 3 (4); Benji Compton 1 (4); Match No. 20: Rob Grant 2+1 (6); Benji Compton 0 (2); Match No. 21: Sean Stoddart 1 (4); Rob Grant 1 (4); Match No. 22: Simon Walker 3 (3); Match No. 24: David Meldrum 5 (5).

TACTICAL RIDES, AS INCLUDED IN THE SCORES GRID:

Match No. 4: Zetterstrom 4 points (TR); Cunningham 4 points (TR); Match No. 6: Zetterstrom 6 points (TR); Cunningham 2 points (TR); Match No. 11: Hawkins 6 points (TR); Match No. 12: Fry 6 points (TR); Zetterstrom 4 points (TR); Match No. 17: Cunningham 4 points (TR); Zetterstrom 2 points (TR); Match No. 19: Zetterstrom 4 points (TR); Cunningham 4 points (TR); Match No. 20: Zetterstrom 4 points (TR); Hawkins 4 points (TR); Match No. 21: Zetterstrom 6 points (TR); Hawkins 6 points (TR); Match No. 23: Fry 6 points (TR); Zetterstrom 4 points (TR); Match No. 26: Mills 6 points (TR); Zetterstrom 4 points (TR); Match No. 28: Cunningham 2 points (TR); Fry 2 points (TR).

PREMIER LEAGUE AVERAGES

Rider	Mts	Rds	Pts	Bon	Tot	Avge	Max
Magnus Zetterstrom	27	126	288	9	297	9.43	1 full; 2 paid
Glenn Cunningham	28	129	255	8	263	8.16	1 full; 3 paid
Paul Fry	26	117	214	10	224	7.66	1 paid
Trevor Harding	2	8	12	3	15	7.50	–
Ritchie Hawkins	25	106	161	26	187	7.06	1 paid
Jason King	13	64	65	12	77	4.81	–
Jamie Smith	25	104	99	22	121	4.65	–
Chris Mills	11	52	45	9	54	4.15	–
Simon Walker	6	26	13	5	18	2.77	–
Lee Smart	14	54	27	3	30	2.22	–
Guests	11	45	26	3	29	2.58	–

(Benji Compton [2]; Rob Grant [3]; David Meldrum [1]; Chris Mills [1]; Sean Stoddart [1]; Simon Walker [3]).

PREMIER TROPHY

(*Denotes bonus-point victory)

No	DATE	OPPONENTS	H/A	RESULT	Zetterstrom	Smith	Hawkins	Fry	Cunningham	Smart	J. King	Others
1	12/3	Rye House	A	L43-50	14 (5)	5+2 (4)	2+1 (4)	10 (5)	6 (4)	2 (3)	4+1 (5)	–
2	23/3	King's Lynn	A	L44-51	17 (5)	2 (4)	5+2 (4)	7 (4)	8 (5)	1+1 (4)	4 (4)	–
3	25/3	Exeter	H	W52-41	13+1 (5)	6 (4)	6+1 (4)	11 (4)	11 (5)	0 (4)	5+1 (4)	–
4	28/3	Exeter	A	L43-51*	7 (5)	2+1 (4)	3+1 (4)	9 (5)	13 (5)	1+1 (3)	8+2 (4)	–
5	1/4	Reading	H	W48-45	10+1 (5)	7+2 (4)	6+2 (4)	10 (5)	8 (4)	1 (3)	6+2 (5)	–
6	8/4	King's Lynn	H	W54-43*	13+1 (5)	9+2 (4)	8+2 (4)	10+1 (5)	5 (4)	3 (4)	6+1 (4)	–
7	12/4	Isle of Wight	A	L40-50	9+2 (5)	8+1 (5)	–	R/R	13+1 (6)	4+2 (5)	6+1 (5)	0 (4)
8	15/4	Isle of Wight	H	W46-44	5+1 (4)	7+2 (4)	3 (4)	12+1 (5)	11 (5)	1+1 (3)	7+2 (5)	–
9	24/4	Newport	A	L36-55	14 (5)	1 (3)	5 (4)	4 (4)	8+1 (5)	0 (4)	4 (5)	–
10	29/4	Rye House	H	L44-48	14+2 (5)	R/R	8 (5)	4+1 (4)	8 (5)	2 (3)	8 (6)	0 (2)
11	2/5	Reading	A	L42-48	13 (5)	R/R	8 (5)	4+1 (4)	8+1 (5)	4+1 (4)	3+2 (5)	2+1 (2)
12	20/5	Newport	H	L44-49	10 (5)	3+1 (4)	4+2 (4)	9 (4)	13 (5)	1+1 (4)	4 (4)	–

DETAILS OF OTHER RIDERS:

Match No. 7: Daniel King 0 (4); Match No. 10: Ben Barker 0 (2); Match No. 11: Ben Barker 2+1 (2).

TACTICAL SUBSTITUTE AND TACTICAL RIDES, AS INCLUDED IN THE SCORES GRID:

Match No. 1: Zetterstrom 6 points (TR); Match No. 2: Zetterstrom 6 points (TR); Cunningham 4 points (TR); Match No. 4: J. King 4 points (TR); Cunningham 4 points (TR); Zetterstrom 0 points (TS); Match No. 9: Cunningham 2 points (TR); Smith 0 points (TR); Match No. 10: Zetterstrom 4 points (TR); Match No. 12: Cunningham 6 points (TR).

SOMERSET: From left to right, back row: Paul Fry, Glenn Cunningham, Lee Smart, Jamie Smith, Mick Bell (Team Manager). Front, kneeling: Jason King, Ritchie Hawkins. On bike: Magnus Zetterstrom.

PREMIER TROPHY AVERAGES

Rider	Mts	Rds	Pts	Bon	Tot	Avge	Max
Magnus Zetterstrom	12	59	131	8	139	9.42	–
Paul Fry	11	49	90	4	94	7.67	–
Glenn Cunningham	12	58	104	3	107	7.38	–
Jamie Smith	10	40	50	11	61	6.10	–
Ritchie Hawkins	11	46	58	11	69	6.00	–
Jason King	12	56	63	12	75	5.36	–
Lee Smart	12	44	20	7	27	2.45	–
Guests	3	8	2	1	3	1.50	–

(Ben Barker [2]; Daniel King [1]).

KNOCK-OUT CUP

No	DATE	OPPONENTS	H/A RESULT	0.2	Smith	Hawkins	Fry	Cunningham	Smart	King
1	3/6	Workington	H L44-46	7+1 (4)	4 (3)	6+1 (4)	8+3 (5)	13 (5)	0 (3)	6+1 (6)
2	4/6	Workington	A L43-47	10+1 (5)	4 (4)	9+3 (5)	7 (4)	7 (4)	1 (3)	5+1 (5)

OTHER MEETINGS

13 March: M4 Trophy (first leg)

Newport 50 Somerset 46 (Magnus Zetterstrom 13+1; Paul Fry 11+1; Jason King 8; Glenn Cunningham 7; Ritchie Hawkins 4+3; Jason Smith 3+1; Lee Smart 0).

18 March: M4 Trophy (second leg)

Somerset 17 (Jason King 4+1; Glenn Cunningham 4; Jamie Smith 3; Paul Fry 3; Magnus Zetterstrom 2; Lee Smart 1; Ritchie Hawkins 0) Newport 32 – meeting abandoned after heat eight.

10 April: M4 Trophy (first leg)

Newport 57 Somerset 38 (Chris Neath 14; Jamie Smith 7+1; Glenn Cunningham 5; Lee Smart 4; Jason King 4; Ritchie Hawkins 2+1; Paul Fry 2).

3 September: M4 Trophy (second leg)

Somerset 61 (Paul Fry 14+1; Magnus Zetterstrom 12+2; Jamie Smith 12+1; Chris Mills 10+2; Glenn Cunningham 10; Simon Walker 3; Ritchie Hawkins R/R) Newport 34 – Somerset won 99-91 on aggregate.

23 September: West Country Championship Challenge (first leg)

Somerset 59 (Magnus Zetterstrom 14+1; Glenn Cunningham 12; Paul Fry 11; Jamie Smith 7+2; Lee Smart 5+2; Chris Mills 5+1; Ritchie Hawkins 5) Exeter 36.

26 September: West Country Championship Challenge (second leg)

Exeter 55 Somerset 39 (Magnus Zetterstrom 15; Paul Fry 10; Glenn Cunningham 9; Ritchie Hawkins 2; Lee Smart 1+1; Jamie Smith 1; Simon Walker 1) – Somerset won 98-91 on aggregate.

INDIVIDUAL MEETING

16 September: Junior Individual Challenge

    1st Lee Dicken (after run-off) 14; 2nd Simon Walker 14; 3rd Steve Bishop (after run-off) 13; Lee Smart 13; Jonathon Bethell 8; Lee Derbyshire 8; Danny Warwick 7; Billy Legg 6; Carl Belfield 6; Karlis Ezergailis 5; Tyron Proctor 5; Andrew Bargh 5; Paul Candy 4; Shane Colvin 4; Jessica Lamb 3; Sam Hurst 2; Andy Carfield (Res) 0; Tim Webster (Res) 0.

STOKE EASY-RIDER POTTERS

NOTE: The information below relates only to the main Stoke team. For details of the second side, please refer to the Conference League section.

ADDRESS: Chesterton Stadium, Loomer Road, Chesterton, Newcastle-under-Lyme, Staffordshire, ST5 7LB.
PROMOTER: David Tattum.
TRACK LENGTH: 312 metres.
TRACK RECORD: 61.0 seconds – Billy Hamill (11 September 1996).
FIRST MEETING: 12 April 1973.
YEARS OF OPERATION: 1972 Training; 1973–74 British League Division Two; 1975–90 National League; 1991–92 British League Division Two; 1994 British League Division Three; 1995 Academy League; 1996–2005 Premier League.

NOTE: (1) The team rode under the name of 'Chesterton' in 1973; (2) The team rode under the name of 'Cradley Heath & Stoke' in 1996.

PREVIOUS VENUE: Hanley Stadium, Sun Street, Hanley, Staffordshire.
YEARS OF OPERATION: 1929 English Dirt-track League & Open; 1939 National League Division Two; 1947–49 National League Division Three; 1950–53 National League Division Two; 1960–63 Provincial League.

CLUB HONOURS

LEAGUE CHAMPIONS: 1949.
PAIRS CHAMPIONS: 1984, 1988, 1989.
FOUR-TEAM CHAMPIONS: 1990.

RIDER ROSTER 2005

Adam ALLOTT; Peter CARR; Paul CLEWS; Barrie EVANS; Rob GRANT; Jack HARGREAVES; Robbie KESSLER; David MELDRUM; Alan MOGRIDGE; Paul PICKERING; Luke PRIEST; Jan STAECHMANN.

OTHER APPEARANCES/GUESTS (official matches only):

Ricky ASHWORTH; Glenn CUNNINGHAM; Paul FRY; James GRIEVES; Rusty HARRISON; Magnus KARLSSON; Phil MORRIS; Glen PHILLIPS; Theo PIJPER; Stuart ROBSON; George STANCL; Garry STEAD; Sean STODDART; Paul THORP; James WRIGHT.

PREMIER LEAGUE

(*Denotes bonus-point victory)

No	DATE	OPPONENTS	H/A	RESULT	Mogridge	Clews	Carr	Kessler	Grant	Evans	Hargreaves	Priest	Allott	Meldrum	Others
1	7/5	Somerset	H	W48-42	7+2 (5)	8+2 (4)	9+1 (4)	5+2 (4)	1 (3)	7+2 (5)	–	–			11 (5)
2	8/5	Newport	A	W48-46	8+2 (6)	7 (4)	7+2 (4)	7+2 (4)	1 (3)	3+1 (4)	–	–			15 (5)
3	11/5	King's Lynn	A	L34-61	0 (5)	5 (5)	R/R	14 (6)	0 (4)	3 (5)	–	–			12+1 (5)
4	23/5	Exeter	A	L44-46	11 (5)	3+1 (4)	5 (4)	9 (4)	–	6+2 (5)	0 (3)	–			10 (5)
5	24/5	Isle of Wight	A	L46-50	14+1 (5)	5 (4)	4+1 (4)	5 (3)	–	6+1 (6)	1 (3)	–			11 (5)
6	28/5	Hull	H	W51-43	8 (5)	5 (4)	8+1 (4)	7 (4)	–	7 (4)	4+1 (4)	–			12 (5)
7	18/6	King's Lynn	H	W55-39	12+1 (6)	9+3 (5)	R/R	15+2 (6)	–	4+1 (4)	6 (4)	–			9 (5)
8	24/6	Edinburgh	A	L42-53	11 (6)	3 (5)	R/R	9+1 (5)	–	1 (5)	–	0 (3)			18 (6)
9	2/7	Newport	H	W55-38*	18 (6)	8+3 (5)	R/R	10+3 (6)	–	6+1 (4)	–	2 (4)			11 (5)
10	9/7	Glasgow	H	L44-46	8+2 (5)	7+2 (4)	6 (4)	7+1 (4)	–	1 (3)	7+2 (5)	–			8+1 (5)
11	16/7	Exeter	H	W50-40*	13+1 (5)	6+2 (4)	5 (4)	6+1 (4)	–	9 (5)	1 (3)	–			10+2 (5)
12	22/7	Somerset	A	L40-56	5 (4)	4 (4)	4+1 (4)	12+1 (5)	–	2 (4)	1 (4)	–			12+1 (5)
13	29/7	Workington	A	L44-45	12 (5)	3 (4)	–	8 (4)	–	5+2 (5)	4+1 (3)	–	3 (4)		9+1 (5)
14	30/7	Workington	H	W50-43*	14+1 (5)	8 (4)	–	9+1 (5)	–	5 (4)	4 (5)	–	4+1 (4)		6+1 (3)
15	4/8	Sheffield	A	L40-56	5 (4)	2 (4)	–	12 (5)	–	3 (5)	0 (3)	–	4 (4)		14 (5)
16	6/8	Sheffield	H	W55-41	10+1 (5)	9+1 (4)	–	11+2 (5)	–	10+1 (5)	1 (3)	–	9+1 (4)		5+1 (4)
17	7/8	Newcastle	A	L41-48	9 (5)	2 (4)	–	6+1 (4)	–	6+2 (5)	2 (3)	–	5+3 (4)		11 (5)
18	17/8	Berwick	A	L39-51	6 (5)	7 (4)	–	9+1 (4)	–	2 (5)	1 (3)	–	3 (4)		11 (5)
19	21/8	Berwick	H	L46-49	13+2 (5)	3 (4)	–	5 (4)	–	5 (4)	–	3 (4)	3 (4)		14 (5)
20	24/8	Hull	A	L36-56	0 (4)	3 (4)	–	3+1 (4)	–	7 (5)	–	4+1 (4)	4 (4)		15 (5)
21	27/8	Rye House	H	L36-56	4+1 (3)	3 (4)	–	11+2 (5)	2+2 (4)	–	–	1 (5)	6+1 (4)		9 (5)
22	28/8	Edinburgh	H	W47-42	R/R	7+1 (5)	–	14+1 (6)	–	7+1 (7)	–	8+1 (6)	0 (0)		11 (6)
23	29/8	Rye House	A	L27-63	R/R	3+1 (6)	–	5 (5)	–	5 (5)	–	2 (4)	–		12+2 (10)
24	3/9	Newcastle	H	W48-42	11+1 (5)	3+2 (4)	–	12 (5)	–	2+1 (3)	–	10+1 (5)	–	3+1 (4)	7+1 (4)
25	4/9	Glasgow	A	L40-53	8 (4)	6+2 (5)	–	13+1 (5)	–	3+2 (5)	–	–	2+1 (4)		8 (7)
26	12/9	Reading	A	L39-58	12 (6)	12 (5)	–	1+1 (2)	–	4+2 (6)	–	0 (3)	2+1 (4)		8 (4)
27	17/9	Reading	H	L42-50	11 (5)	4 (4)	–	9+1 (4)	–	8+4 (6)	–	1 (3)	–	1 (3)	8 (5)
28	2/10	Isle of Wight†	H	W43-34*	9 (3)	14 (5)	–	3+2 (3)	–	6+2 (3)	0 (3)	6+2 (4)	–	R/R	5 (3)

†Meeting abandoned after heat twelve, with the result permitted to stand.

DETAILS OF OTHER RIDERS:

Match No. 1: Rusty Harrison 11 (5); Match No. 2: Rusty Harrison 15 (5); Match No. 3: Stuart Robson 12+1 (5); Match No. 4: Stuart Robson 10 (5); Match No. 5: Stuart Robson 11 (5); Match No. 6: Magnus Karlsson 12 (5); Match No. 7: Stuart Robson 9 (5); Match No. 8: Stuart Robson 18 (6); Match No. 9: Glenn Cunningham 11 (5); Match No. 10: Phil Morris 8+1 (5); Match No. 11: Glenn Cunningham 10+2 (5); Match No. 12: Stuart Robson 12+1 (5); Match No. 13: Ricky Ashworth 9+1 (5); Match No. 14: Phil Morris 6+1 (3); Match No. 15: Paul Thorp 14 (5); Match No. 16: Glenn Cunningham 5+1 (4); Match No. 17: Rusty

Harrison 11 (5); Match No. 18: Theo Pijper 11 (5); Match No. 19: James Wright 14 (5); Match No. 20: Stuart Robson 15 (5); Match No. 21: Glenn Cunningham 9 (5); Match No. 22: Garry Stead 11 (6); Match No. 23: Rusty Harrison 7+1 (5); Glen Phillips 5+1 (5); Match No. 24: Paul Thorp 7+1 (4); Match No. 25: Rusty Harrison 5 (3); Sean Stoddart 3 (4); Match No. 26: Paul Fry 8 (4); Match No. 27: Garry Stead 8 (5); Match No. 28: Garry Stead 5 (3).

TACTICAL SUBSTITUTE AND TACTICAL RIDES, AS INCLUDED IN THE SCORES GRID:

Match No. 2: Harrison 6 points (TR); Mogridge 2 points (TR); Match No. 3: Kessler 6 points (TR); Robson 4 points (TR); Match No. 5: Mogridge 6 points (TR); Robson 6 points (TR); Match No. 8: Robson 6 points (TR); Kessler 4 points (TR); Match No. 12: Robson 6 points (TR); Kessler 6 points (TR); Match No. 15: Thorp 6 points (TR); Kessler 6 points (TR); Match No. 19: Wright 6 points (TR); Mogridge 4 points (TR); Match No. 20: Robson 6 points (TR); Clews 0 points (TR); Match No. 21: Kessler 4 points (TR); Mogridge 0 points (TR); Match No. 23: Harrison 2 points (TR); Kessler 0 points (TR); Match No. 25: Kessler 6 points (TR); Match No. 26: Fry 6 points (TR); Clews 4 points (TR); Mogridge 4 points (TS); Match No. 27: Kessler 4 points (TR).

PREMIER LEAGUE AVERAGES

Rider	Mts	Rds	Pts	Bon	Tot	Avge	Max
Robbie Kessler	28	125	219	27	246	7.87	–
Alan Mogridge	26	127	231	15	246	7.75	1 full; 1 paid
Peter Carr	8	32	48	6	54	6.75	–
Paul Clews	28	122	157	20	177	5.80	–
Adam Allott	10	36	41	6	47	5.22	–
Barrie Evans	27	127	133	25	158	4.98	–
Luke Priest	11	45	37	5	42	3.73	–
Jack Hargreaves	14	49	32	4	36	2.94	–
David Meldrum	4	15	8	3	11	2.93	–
Rob Grant	4	14	4	2	6	1.71	–
Guests	30	142	265	11	276	7.77	–

(Ricky Ashworth [1]; Glenn Cunningham [4]; Paul Fry [1]; Rusty Harrison [5]; Magnus Karlsson [1]; Phil Morris [2]; Glen Phillips [1]; Theo Pijper [1]; Stuart Robson [7]; Garry Stead [3]; Sean Stoddart [1]; Paul Thorp [2]; James Wright [1]).

PREMIER TROPHY

(*Denotes bonus-point victory)

No	DATE	OPPONENTS	H/A RESULT	Pickering	Clews	Kessler	Mogridge	Staechmann	Grant	Evans	Carr	Hargreaves	Others
1	16/3	Hull	A L42-53	4 (3)	4 (4)	4 (4)	12 (5)	12+1 (5)	3+1 (5)	3 (4)	–		
2	19/3	Hull	H W52-44	R/R	10+2 (5)	11+1 (5)	13+1 (6)	10+3 (6)	2+1 (4)	6+1 (4)	–		
3	24/3	Sheffield	A L35-60	R/R	3 (5)	9 (5)	12 (6)	10 (6)	1 (4)	0 (4)	–		
4	26/3	Sheffield	H W55-37	R/R	5+1 (5)	12+2 (5)	14+1 (6)	14 (5)	4 (4)	6+2 (5)	–		
5	2/4	Berwick	H W53-40	R/R	6+2 (5)	15 (6)	11+2 (6)	–	5+1 (4)	3 (4)			13 (5)
6	10/4	Newcastle	A L39-51	R/R	5+1 (5)	10+1 (6)	12+1 (6)		2 (4)	1+1 (4)	–		9 (5)
7	16/4	Newcastle	H W45-44	–	4+1 (4)	10+1 (5)	6+1 (5)		6 (4)	5+3 (4)	5 (4)		9 (4)
8	22/4	Edinburgh	A L43-53	–	4 (4)	14 (5)	5+1 (4)		1 (4)	0 (4)	5+1 (4)	–	14 (5)
9	23/4	Glasgow	H D45-45	–	5+2 (4)	5+1 (4)	14 (5)		5 (4)	3+1 (4)	4+1 (4)	–	9+2 (5)

No	DATE	OPPONENTS	H/A	RESULT	Pickering	Clews	Kessler	Mogridge	Staechmann	Grant	Evans	Carr	Hargreaves	Others
10	30/4	Workington	H	W52-42	–	5+1 (4)	10+2 (5)	12 (5)	10+1 (4)	7 (4)	4 (4)	4+1 (4)	–	–
11	2/5	Workington	A	L42-50*		0 (1)	6 (5)	17 (6)	6 (4)	3+1 (5)	6+4 (5)	4+1 (4)	–	–
12	14/5	Berwick	A	L41-52*		4+1 (4)	7 (4)	12 (5)	–	2 (4)	3+1 (4)	1+1 (4)	–	12 (5)
13	5/6	Edinburgh	H	L44-46		4 (5)	12 (6)	6+3 (5)	–	0 (3)	4 (5)	R/R	–	18 (6)
14	19/6	Glasgow	A	W46-44*		3+1 (5)	14+1 (6)	16+2 (6)	–	–	1+1 (4)	R/R	2 (4)	10+1 (5)

DETAILS OF OTHER RIDERS:

Match No. 5: George Stancl 13 (5); Match No. 6: Garry Stead 9 (5); Match No. 7: Stuart Robson 9 (4); Match No. 8: James Grieves 14 (5); Match No. 9: Rusty Harrison 9+2 (5); Match No. 12: Rusty Harrison 12 (5); Match No. 13: Stuart Robson 18 (6); Match No. 14: Rusty Harrison 10+1 (5).

TACTICAL RIDES, AS INCLUDED IN THE SCORES GRID:

Match No. 1: Staechmann 6 points (TR); Mogridge 4 points (TR); Match No. 3: Mogridge 6 points (TR); Kessler 4 points (TR); Match No. 8: Grieves 6 points (TR); Kessler 6 points (TR); Match No. 11: Mogridge 4 points (TR); Match No. 12: Mogridge 6 points (TR).

PREMIER TROPHY AVERAGES

Rider	Mts	Rds	Pts	Bon	Tot	Avge	Max
Alan Mogridge	14	76	152	12	164	8.63	1 paid
Jan Staechmann	6	30	59	5	64	8.53	–
Robbie Kessler	14	71	134	9	143	8.06	–
Paul Pickering	1	3	4	0	4	5.33	–
Paul Clews	14	60	62	12	74	4.93	–
Peter Carr	6	24	23	5	28	4.67	–
Barrie Evans	14	59	45	14	59	4.00	–
Rob Grant	13	53	41	4	45	3.40	–
Jack Hargreaves	1	4	2	0	2	2.00	–
Guests	8	40	91	3	94	9.40	1 full

(James Grieves [1]; Rusty Harrison [3]; Stuart Robson [2]; George Stancl [1]; Garry Stead [1]).

KNOCK-OUT CUP

No	DATE	OPPONENTS	H/A	RESULT	Carr	Clews	Kessler	Mogridge	Evans	Hargreaves	Priest	Others
1	12/6	Berwick	H	L42–48	R/R	1+1 (5)	7+2 (5)	12+2 (6)	2 (4)	2 (4)	–	18 (6)
2	29/6	Berwick	A	L34–56	R/R	5+1 (5)	5 (4)	8+1 (6)	4 (6)	–	1+1 (3)	11 (6)

DETAILS OF OTHER RIDERS:

Match No. 1: Magnus Karlsson 18 (6); Match No. 2: Theo Pijper 11 (6).

STOKE: From left to right, back row: Paul Clews, John Adams (Team Manager), Barrie Evans, Jack Hargreaves. Front, kneeling: Peter Carr, Alan Mogridge, Robbie Kessler.

OTHER MEETINGS

12 March: Trent/Tyne Trophy (first leg)

Stoke 43 (Alan Mogridge 10+1; Robbie Kessler 8+1; Paul Clews 7+2; Barrie Evans 6+4; Paul Pickering 6; Jan Staechmann 6; Rob Grant 0) Newcastle 51.

13 March: Trent/Tyne Trophy (second leg)

Newcastle 60 Stoke 30 (Jan Staechmann 12; Alan Mogridge 8+2; Paul Clews 4; Robbie Kessler 4; Rob Grant 1; Barrie Evans 1; Paul Pickering 0) – Newcastle won 111-73 on aggregate.

9 April: Premier Trophy

Stoke 31 (Alan Mogridge 9; Robbie Kessler 7+3; Paul Clews 5; Barrie Evans 4+2; Andre Compton 3; Rob Grant 3; Paul Pickering R/R) Edinburgh 28 – meeting abandoned after heat ten.

23 July: Moggo Mania! – Alan Mogridge Testimonial

Moggo's Maniacs 47 (Alan Mogridge 11; Shane Parker 10+1; Robbie Kessler 8+1; David McAllan 7; Barrie Evans 6+1; Paul Clews 4+1; Adam Allott 1+1; Arlo Bugeja 0) Super Seven Select 43 (Glenn Cunningham 12; James Grieves 10; Ritchie Hawkins 6; Paul Fry 5+1; Tony Atkin 5+1; David Meldrum 4; Peter Carr 1).

WORKINGTON THOMAS ARMSTRONG COMETS

ADDRESS: Derwent Park Stadium, Workington, Cumbria, CA14 2HG.
PROMOTERS: Graham Drury & Tony Mole.
TRACK LENGTH: 364 metres.
TRACK RECORD: 64.1 seconds – Simon Stead (17 July 2004).
FIRST MEETING: 3 April 1970.
YEARS OF OPERATION: 1970-74 British League Division Two; 1975–81 National League; 1985 Open; 1987 National League; 1994 Demonstration; 1999–2005 Premier League.

NOTE: In 1987 the track was occupied by 'Glasgow Tigers', who later that year became known as 'Workington Tigers'.

CLUB HONOURS

PAIRS CHAMPIONS: 1999, 2000, 2001, 2003.
FOUR-TEAM CHAMPIONS: 2001, 2004.

RIDER ROSTER 2005

Adam ALLOTT; Jonathon BETHELL; Aidan COLLINS; Jamie COURTNEY; Scott COURTNEY; Tony DART; Lee DERBYSHIRE; Scott JAMES; Kevin LITTLE; Kauko NIEMINEN; Tomasz PISZCZ; Scott ROBSON; Carl STONEHEWER; Shaun TACEY; James WRIGHT.

OTHER APPEARANCES/GUESTS (official matches only):
Tony ATKIN; James BIRKINSHAW; Craig BRANNEY; John BRANNEY; Tom BROWN; Barry BURCHATT; Benji COMPTON; Richie DENNIS; Josef FRANC; James GRIEVES;

Rusty HARRISON; Ritchie HAWKINS; Jason KING; Simon LAMBERT; William LAWSON; Trent LEVERINGTON; Chris MILLS; Danny NORTON; Pavel ONDRASIK; Stuart ROBSON; Adam ROYNON; George STANCL; Garry STEAD; Paul THORP; Sean WILSON; Magnus ZETTERSTROM.

PREMIER LEAGUE

(*Denotes bonus-point victory)

No	DATE	OPPONENTS	H/A	RESULT	Stonehewer	Collins	Sc. Robson	Nieminen	Tacey	Little	Bethell	James	Wright	J. Courtney	Piszcz	Others
1	6/5	Somerset†	A	W45-39	7+2 (4)	R/R	7+2 (4)	8+1 (5)	9+1 (4)	10+2 (7)	4+3 (4)	–	–	–	–	–
2	7/5	Newport	H	L43-49	19 (6)	R/R	2 (2)	4+1 (5)	6 (5)	9+2 (7)	1 (3)	2 (2)	–	–	–	–
3	14/5	Reading	H	W56-38	8+2 (5)	–	R/R	11+1 (5)	13 (5)	14+3 (7)	–	1+1 (5)	–	–	–	9+3 (5)
4	14/5	Newcastle	A	L36-58	7 (5)	–	R/R	5 (5)	12 (5)	8+1 (7)	–	–	–	–	–	4 (8)
5	21/5	Hull	H	W47-43	13+1 (5)	–	R/R	12 (5)	7+1 (5)	8+1 (7)	–	0 (3)	–	–	–	7+3 (5)
6	25/5	King's Lynn	A	L43-53	6 (4)	–	R/R	12 (5)	18 (6)	5+1 (7)	–	–	2+1 (5)	–	–	0 (3)
7	28/5	Rye House	A	L36-57	18 (6)	–	10 (6)	R/R	4 (5)	3 (5)	0 (3)	–	1+1 (5)	–	–	–
8	30/5	Glasgow	H	W57-39	15+2 (6)	–	9 (5)	R/R	9+3 (5)	10+2 (5)	1 (3)	–	13 (6)	–	–	–
9	5/6	Glasgow	A	W51-42*	15 (6)	–	7+1 (4)	R/R	10+2 (5)	6+1 (4)	–	–	13+2 (7)	–	–	0 (4)
10	13/6	Exeter	A	L32-61	11+1 (6)	–	6 (5)	R/R	2+2 (6)	3+1 (5)	–	–	9 (5)	–	–	1 (3)
11	14/6	Isle of Wight	A	D45-45	15+1 (6)	–	2+1 (4)	R/R	7+1 (4)	6+1 (6)	–	–	15+1 (7)	–	–	0 (3)
12	18/6	Edinburgh	H	L42-48	–	–	3 (4)	R/R	10 (5)	8+1 (6)	–	–	–	–	–	21+1 (15)
13	25/6	King's Lynn	H	W55-38*	16+1 (6)	–	4 (4)	R/R	9 (5)	–	–	0 (4)	17+1 (6)	–	–	9+3 (5)
14	3/7	Newport	A	L42-48	14 (6)	–	10 (5)	R/R	4 (5)	–	–	–	9+2 (6)	–	–	5 (8)
15	4/7	Reading	A	L44-49*	18+1 (6)	–	6+2 (5)	R/R	10+2 (6)	–	–	–	6 (5)	–	–	4 (9)
16	9/7	Somerset	H	W47-46*	12 (5)	8+3 (6)	5 (4)	–	8+1 (4)	–	–	–	8 (4)	–	–	6 (7)
17	23/7	Isle of Wight	H	W50-42*	11+2 (5)	4 (7)	5+2 (4)	11 (4)	7+1 (4)	–	–	–	12 (5)	0 (0)	–	–
18	29/7	Stoke	H	W45-44	–	4 (3)	4 (4)	11 (5)	5+2 (4)	–	–	–	11+2 (5)	5 (4)	–	5 (4)
19	30/7	Stoke	A	L43-50	–	6 (4)	R/R	11 (6)	–	–	–	10+1 (6)	0 (3)	–	16+3 (11)
20	13/8	Newcastle	H	W58-36*	–	4+1 (4)	8+1 (4)	8+1 (4)	8+3 (4)	–	–	–	11 (5)	8 (4)	–	11+1 (5)
21	17/8	Hull	A	L40-55	–	3 (4)	9+1 (4)	4+1 (4)	0 (3)	–	–	3+1 (5)	9 (5)	–	–	12 (5)
22	25/8	Sheffield	A	L36-59	–	–	R/R	6+1 (5)	11 (5)	–	–	–	3 (4)	–	4+1 (7)	12 (9)
23	26/8	Edinburgh♦	A	D36-36	–	–	6 (4)	3+1 (3)	5+1 (4)	–	–	1 (2)	5 (3)	–	8+2 (4)	8+1 (3)
24	27/8	Berwick	A	L38-56	–	–	2 (3)	3 (4)	9+1 (4)	–	–	2 (3)	9 (4)	–	5+1 (7)	8+1 (5)
25	29/8	Berwick	H	W59-33*	–	–	7 (4)	13+2 (5)	3 (3)	–	–	1 (3)	11 (4)	–	12+2 (6)	12+2 (5)
26	3/9	Rye House	H	W47-43	–	–	3 (3)	6 (4)	4+1 (4)	–	–	–	10 (5)	–	11+3 (6)	13+1 (8)
27	10/9	Exeter	H	W54-40	–	–	R/R	7+2 (4)	10 (6)	–	–	–	14 (5)	–	13+1 (7)	10+1 (8)
28	8/10	Sheffield	H	W55-40	–	–	R/R	4+1 (4)	13 (5)	–	–	2+1 (4)	7+3 (5)	–	15+1 (7)	14 (5)

†Meeting abandoned after heat fourteen, with the result permitted to stand.

♦Meeting abandoned after heat twelve, with the result permitted to stand.

DETAILS OF OTHER RIDERS:

Match No. 3: Pavel Ondrasik 9+3 (5); Match No. 4: William Lawson 3 (5); John Branney 1 (3); Match No. 5: Tony Atkin 7+3 (5); Match No. 6: Simon Lambert 0 (3); Match No. 9: Adam Roynon 0 (4); Match No. 10: Tom Brown 1 (3); Match No. 11: Tom Brown 0 (3); Match No. 12: Garry Stead 16 (6); James Birkinshaw 4+1 (5); Tom Brown 1 (4); Match No. 13: Ritchie Hawkins 9+3 (5); Match No. 14: Pavel Ondrasik 4 (5); Barry Burchatt 1 (3); Match No. 15: Chris Mills 4 (6); Barry Burchatt 0 (3); Match

No. 16: Adam Allott 5 (4); Lee Derbyshire 1 (3); Match No. 18: Sean Wilson 5 (4); Match No. 19: James Grieves 9+1 (4); Trent Leverington 7+2 (7); Match No. 20: Paul Thorp 11+1 (5); Match No. 21: Sean Wilson 12 (5); Match No. 22: Stuart Robson 11 (5); Benji Compton 1 (4); Match No. 23: Stuart Robson 8+1 (3); Match No. 24: George Stancl 8+1 (5); Match No. 25: Magnus Zetterstrom 12+2 (5); Match No. 26: Rusty Harrison 12+1 (5); John Branney 1 (3); Match No. 27: Josef Franc 6 (4); John Branney 4+1 (4); Match No. 28: Magnus Zetterstrom 14 (5).

TACTICAL SUBSTITUTE AND TACTICAL RIDES, AS INCLUDED IN THE SCORES GRID:

Match No. 2: Stonehewer 4 points (TS); Match No. 4: Tacey 6 points (TR); Stonehewer 2 points (TR); Match No. 6: Tacey 6 points (TR); Nieminen 6 points (TR); Match No. 7: Stonehewer 6 points (TR); Scott Robson 0 points (TR); Match No. 10: Wright 4 points (TR); Stonehewer 2 points (TR); Match No. 15: Stonehewer 6 points (TR); Match No. 19: Grieves 6 points (TR); Match No. 21: Scott Robson 6 points (TR); Wilson 4 points (TR); Match No. 22: Tacey 6 points (TR); Stuart Robson 4 points (TR); Match No. 24: Wright 6 points (TR); Piszcz 2 points (TR).

PREMIER LEAGUE AVERAGES

Rider	Mts	Rds	Pts	Bon	Tot	Avge	Max
Carl Stonehewer	16	87	195	13	208	9.56	–
James Wright	22	112	200	14	214	7.64	1 paid
Kauko Nieminen	17	76	125	12	137	7.21	1 paid
Shaun Tacey	28	132	215	22	237	7.18	–
Tomasz Piszcz	7	44	67	11	78	7.09	–
Scott Robson	21	86	118	10	128	5.95	–
Kevin Little	12	73	90	16	106	5.81	–
Adam Allott	1	4	5	0	5	5.00	–
Jamie Courtney	4	11	13	0	13	4.73	–
Aidan Collins	5	24	23	4	27	4.50	–
Scott James	8	27	12	3	15	2.22	–
Jonathon Bethell	5	17	6	3	9	2.12	–
Lee Derbyshire	1	3	1	0	1	1.33	–
Guests	31	136	174	20	194	5.71	–

(Tony Atkin [1]; James Birkinshaw [1]; John Branney [3]; Tom Brown [3]; Barry Burchatt [2]; Benji Compton [1]; Josef Franc [1]; James Grieves [1]; Rusty Harrison [1]; Ritchie Hawkins [1]; Simon Lambert [1]; William Lawson [1]; Trent Leverington [1]; Chris Mills [1]; Pavel Ondrasik [2]; Stuart Robson [2]; Adam Roynon [1]; George Stancl [1]; Garry Stead [1]; Paul Thorp [1]; Sean Wilson [2]; Magnus Zetterstrom [2]).

PREMIER TROPHY

(*Denotes bonus-point/aggregate victory)

No	DATE	OPPONENTS	H/A	RESULT	Stonehewer	Little	Sc. Robson	Nieminen	Tacey	Dart	Wright	S. Courtney	Bethell	Collins	Derbyshire	Others
1	12/3	Glasgow	H	W47-43	12 (5)	4+2 (4)	4 (4)	5+1 (4)	0 (1)	3 (5)	19 (7)	–	–	–	–	–
2	19/3	Edinburgh	H	W60-34	9+2 (4)	7+1 (4)	13+2 (5)	12+1 (5)	5+1 (4)	5+2 (4)	9 (4)	–	–	–	–	–
3	25/3	Berwick	H	W54-40	14+1 (5)	7 (4)	4+2 (4)	10+1 (5)	6+2 (4)	0 (3)	13 (5)	–	–	–	–	–
4	26/3	Berwick	A	L39-53*	4+1 (4)	2 (3)	4+1 (4)	10 (5)	12 (5)	0 (3)	7 (6)	–	–	–	–	–

No	DATE	OPPONENTS	H/A	RESULT	Stonehewer	Little	Sc. Robson	Nieminen	Tacey	Dart	Wright	S. Courtney	Bethell	Collins	Derbyshire	Others
5	27/3	Glasgow	A	W46-44*	14 (5)	3+2 (4)	9+2 (5)	7 (4)	4+1 (4)	1+1 (3)	8+1 (6)	–	–	–	–	–
6	2/4	Newcastle	H	W64-30	14 (5)	3 (3)	9+3 (4)	11+2 (5)	8+2 (4)	7 (4)	12+1 (5)	–	–	–	–	–
7	3/4	Newcastle	A	W48-42*	12+1 (5)	6+1 (4)	10+1 (5)	5+2 (4)	3+1 (3)	0 (2)	12+1 (6)	–	–	–	–	–
8	9/4	Hull	H	W56-36	13+1 (5)	4 (3)	6+1 (4)	11+1 (5)	8+1 (4)	–	14+2 (6)	0 (3)	–	–	–	–
9	20/4	Hull	A	L39-51*	9 (5)	4+1 (4)	6 (4)	11+1 (5)	5 (4)	–	3+1 (5)	1 (3)	–	–	–	–
10	23/4	Sheffield	H	W55-42	17 (5)	6+3 (4)	5+1 (4)	8 (4)	12+1 (5)	–	–	–	0 (3)	–	–	7+1 (5)
11	28/4	Sheffield	A	L39-53	11 (5)	0 (3)	2 (3)	1 (4)	7 (5)	–	–	–	–	–	–	18 (10)
12	30/4	Stoke	A	L42-52	15 (5)	2+1 (4)	2+1 (4)	4+1 (4)	6 (4)	–	–	–	0 (3)	–	–	13 (6)
13	2/5	Stoke	H	W50-42	10+1 (5)	13+2 (7)	5+1 (4)	13 (5)	8 (4)	–	–	–	1 (5)	0 (0)	–	–
14	13/5	Edinburgh	A	L41-49*	11 (5)	14+2 (7)	R/R	6+2 (4)	7 (5)	–	–	–	0 (4)	–	–	3+1 (5)
15	2/7	Exeter	H	W60-31	17+1 (6)	–	7+3 (5)	R/R	8+1 (5)	–	18 (6)	–	–	–	1 (3)	9+2 (5)
16	8/7	Exeter	A	L40-56*	14 (5)	–	2 (4)	R/R	18 (6)	–	3 (6)	–	–	–	–	3+1 (9)
17	6/8	Rye House	H	L44-46	–	–	2 (3)	7 (5)	4 (4)	–	8 (4)	–	–	3+1 (4)	–	20+2 (10)
18	7/8	Rye House	A	L32-61	–	–	8 (4)	4+1 (4)	2+1 (4)	–	5+1 (5)	–	–	3+1 (5)	–	10 (9)

DETAILS OF OTHER RIDERS:

Match No. 10: Tony Atkin 7+1 (5); Match No. 11: James Birkinshaw 17 (7); Danny Norton 1 (3); Match No. 12: Tony Atkin 13 (6); Match No. 14: Craig Branney 3+1 (5); Match No. 15: Craig Branney 9+2 (5); Match No. 16: Jason King 3+1 (6); Jamie Courtney 0 (3); Match No. 17: Magnus Zetterstrom 14 (5); Jamie Courtney 6+2 (5); Match No. 18: Magnus Zetterstrom 8 (5); Jamie Courtney 2 (4).

TACTICAL RIDES, AS INCLUDED IN THE SCORES GRID:

Match No. 4: Nieminen 4 points (TR); Scott Robson 0 points (TR); Match No. 10: Stonehewer 6 points (TR); Match No. 11: Birkinshaw 4 points (TR); Stonehewer 0 points (TR); Match No. 12: Stonehewer 4 points (TR); Atkin 4 points (TR); Match No. 16: Tacey 6 points (TR); Stonehewer 6 points (TR); Match No. 18: Scott Robson 4 points (TR); Wright 2 points (TR).

PREMIER TROPHY AVERAGES

Rider	Mts	Rds	Pts	Bon	Tot	Avge	Max
Carl Stonehewer	16	79	188	8	196	9.92	2 paid
James Wright	13	71	130	7	137	7.72	1 full
Kauko Nieminen	16	72	123	13	136	7.56	–
Shaun Tacey	18	75	120	11	131	6.99	–
Scott Robson	17	70	96	18	114	6.51	2 paid
Kevin Little	14	58	75	15	90	6.21	–
Aidan Collins	3	9	6	2	8	3.56	–
Jamie Courtney	3	12	8	2	10	3.33	–
Tony Dart	7	24	16	3	19	3.17	–
Lee Derbyshire	1	3	1	0	1	1.33	–
Scott Courtney	4	14	2	0	2	0.57	–
Jonathon Bethell	2	7	0	0	0	0.00	–
Guests	9	47	71	5	76	6.47	–

(Tony Atkin [2]; James Birkinshaw [1]; Craig Branney [2]; Jason King [1]; Danny Norton [1]; Magnus Zetterstrom [2]).

WORKINGTON: From left to right, back row: Scott Courtney, Scott Robson, Shaun Tacey, James Wright. Front, kneeling: Kauko Nieminen, Carl Stonehewer, Kevin Little.

KNOCK-OUT CUP

(*Denotes aggregate victory)

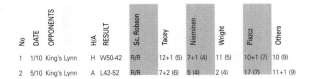

No	DATE	OPPONENTS	H/A	RESULT	Stonehewer	Little	Tacey	Sc. Robson	Nieminen	Wright	Allott	Collins	J. Courtney	Others
1	3/6	Somerset	A	W46-44	16 (6)	5+1 (5)	11 (6)	2+1 (3)	R/R	10+1 (7)	–	–	2+1 (3)	–
2	4/6	Somerset	H	W47-43*	17 (6)	4+2 (5)	8 (5)	6 (4)	R/R	10+2 (7)	–	–	–	2 (3)
3	16/7	Berwick	A	L41-49	13 (5)	–	1 (4)	9 (4)	–	7+1 (5)	0 (3)	6+1 (4)	5+1 (5)	–
4	17/7	Berwick	H	L42-48	15 (5)	–	9 (5)	2 (4)	–	3 (1)	1 (3)	3 (6)	9+1 (6)	–

DETAILS OF OTHER RIDER:

Match No. 2: Adam Roynon 2 (3).

YOUNG SHIELD

No	DATE	OPPONENTS	H/A	RESULT	Sc. Robson	Tacey	Nieminen	Wright	Piszcz	Others
1	1/10	King's Lynn	H	W50-42	R/R	12+1 (5)	7+1 (4)	11 (5)	10+1 (7)	10 (9)
2	5/10	King's Lynn	A	L42-52	R/R	7+2 (6)	5 (4)	2 (4)	17 (7)	11+1 (9)

DETAILS OF OTHER RIDERS:

Match No. 1: Garry Stead 9 (5); John Branney 1 (4); Match No. 2: Magnus Zetterstrom 10 (5); Richie Dennis 1+1 (4).

TACTICAL RIDES, AS INCLUDED IN THE SCORES GRID:

Match No. 2: Piszcz 6 points (TR); Zetterstrom 2 points (TR).

OTHER MEETING

17 September: Premier League

Workington 3 (Magnus Zetterstrom 3; Matthew Wethers 0; Shaun Tacey DNR; Kauko Nieminen DNR; John Branney DNR; Tomasz Piszcz DNR; James Wright R/R) Sheffield 3 – meeting abandoned after heat one.

INDIVIDUAL MEETINGS

24 September: Carl's Big Special (Carl Stonehewer Testimonial)

1st Simon Stead (after run-off) 12; 2nd Leigh Adams 12; 3rd Sam Ermolenko 11; Billy Hamill 11; George Stancl 10; Shane Parker 9; Rusty Harrison 9; Joe Screen 9; James Wright 8; Jason Lyons 6; Chris Harris 6; Gary Havelock 4; Steve Johnston 4; Kauko Nieminen 4; Sean Wilson 3; Charles Wright (Res) 2; Neil Collins 0.

15 October: Cumberland Classic

1st Simon Stead 14; 2nd James Wright 13; 3rd Rusty Harrison 12 (on countback); Shaun Tacey 12; Mark Lemon 10; Jason Lyons 10; Kauko Nieminen 10; Henning Bager 9; Ronnie Correy 6; Garry Stead 5; Craig Branney 5; Ritchie Hawkins 5; Norbert Magosi 4; Andreas Lekander 3; Scott James (Res) 1; Artur Boginczuk 0; Charles Wright (Res) 0.

CONFERENCE LEAGUE 2005

CONFERENCE LEAGUE TABLE

	Mts	Won	Drn	Lst	For	Agn	Pts	Bon	Tot
Oxford	22	15	3	4	1,091	909	33	9	42
Wimbledon	22	15	0	7	1,106	932	30	11	41
Weymouth	22	13	0	9	1,075	956	26	7	33
Mildenhall	22	12	1	9	1,067	968	25	8	33
Armadale	22	12	0	10	1,025	986	24	7	31
Rye House	22	12	0	10	1,046.5	987.5	24	5	29
Stoke	22	12	0	10	1,031	982	24	5	29
Scunthorpe	22	11	0	11	1,012	1,000	22	5	27
Boston	22	11	0	11	982.5	1,055.5	22	4	26
Newport	22	9	0	13	968	1,051	18	3	21
Buxton	22	6	1	15	890	1,112	13	1	14
Sittingbourne	22	1	1	20	823	1,178	3	1	4

CONFERENCE TROPHY

CONFERENCE TROPHY (SOUTH) TABLE

	Mts	Won	Drn	Lst	For	Agn	Pts	Bon	Tot
Weymouth	6	5	0	1	303	247	10	3	13
Boston	6	3	0	3	269	282	6	1	7
Wimbledon	6	2	0	4	270	282	4	2	6
Mildenhall	6	2	0	4	260	291	4	0	4

CONFERENCE TROPHY (NORTH) TABLE

	Mts	Won	Drn	Lst	For	Agn	Pts	Bon	Tot
Armadale	6	3	1	2	306	260	7	3	10
Stoke	6	3	0	3	284	281	6	2	8
Scunthorpe	6	2	1	3	272	286	5	1	6
Buxton	6	3	0	3	259	294	6	0	6

SEMI-FINALS

Weymouth	44	Stoke	46	
Stoke	52	Weymouth	41	(Stoke won 98-85 on aggregate)

Armadale	53	Boston	43	
Boston	42	Armadale	48	(Armadale won 101-85 on aggregate)

FINAL

Armadale	49	Stoke	41	
Stoke	43	Armadale	50	(Armadale won 99-84 on aggregate)

KNOCK-OUT CUP

ROUND ONE

Boston	53	Scunthorpe	41	
Scunthorpe	40	Boston	49	(Boston won 102-81 on aggregate)
Oxford	60	Wimbledon	33	
Wimbledon	46	Oxford	44	(Oxford won 104-79 on aggregate)

QUARTER-FINALS

Newport	56	Rye House	38	
Rye House	50	Newport	40	(Newport won 96-88 on aggregate)
Buxton	51	Weymouth	43	
Weymouth	55	Buxton	40	(Weymouth won 98-91 on aggregate)
Boston	59	Stoke	35	
Stoke	54	Boston	39	(Boston won 98-89 on aggregate)
Mildenhall	54	Oxford	40	
Oxford	53	Mildenhall	42	(Mildenhall won 96-93 on aggregate)

SEMI-FINALS

Weymouth	51	Newport	43	
Newport	41	Weymouth	50	(Weymouth won 101-84 on aggregate)
Boston	41	Mildenhall	51	
Mildenhall	60	Boston	33	(Mildenhall won 111-74 on aggregate)

FINAL

Weymouth	54	Mildenhall	40	
Mildenhall	51	Weymouth	45	(Weymouth won 99-91 on aggregate)

ARMADALE AWG DALE DEVILS

NOTE: The information below relates only to the second Edinburgh team. For details of the main side, please refer to the Premier League section.

ADDRESS: Armadale Stadium, 2 Bathgate Road, Armadale, West Lothian, EH48 2PD.
CLUB CHAIRMAN: John Campbell.
TRACK LENGTH: 260 metres.
CL TRACK RECORD: 57.3 seconds – William Lawson (14 October 2005).
FIRST MEETING: 31 May 2003.
YEARS OF OPERATION: 2003 Conference Trophy; 2004–05 Conference League.

CLUB HONOURS

CONFERENCE TROPHY WINNERS: 2005.

RIDER ROSTER 2005

Gary BEATON; Karl LANGLEY; William LAWSON; John MacPHAIL; James McBAIN; Cal McDADE; Colin McDONALD; Adam McKINNA; Keiran MORRIS; Michael PICKERING; Blair SCOTT; Derek SNEDDON; Sean STODDART; Andrew TULLY.

OTHER APPEARANCES/GUESTS (official matches only):
Marc ANDREWS; Jessica LAMB; Niall STRUDWICK; Karl WHITE.

CONFERENCE LEAGUE

(*Denotes bonus-point victory)

No	DATE	OPPONENTS	H/A	RESULT	Scott	Tully	Stoddart	Beaton	Lawson	McBain	McKinna	Sneddon	McDade	Langley	Pickering	Others
1	26/3	Buxton	H	W54-41	11 (4)	2 (4)	12 (5)	5+2 (4)	14+1 (5)	1 (3)	9 (5)	–	–	–	–	–
2	23/4	Boston	H	W52-41	14 (5)	4 (4)	6 (4)	8+3 (4)	–	–	7+2 (5)	12+2 (5)	1+1 (3)	–	–	–
3	1/5	Mildenhall	A	L44-51	16 (6)	3 (4)	3 (4)	6+2 (4)	–	–	3+1 (4)	12 (5)	1 (3)	–	–	–
4	7/5	Sittingbourne	H	W47-45	6 (5)	6+3 (4)	7 (4)	7+2 (4)	–	0 (3)	11+2 (5)	10+1 (5)	–	–	–	–
5	14/5	Oxford	H	L41-53	9 (5)	0 (4)	14 (5)	3+1 (3)	–	–	7+1 (5)	7 (5)	1 (3)	–	–	–
6	22/5	Newport	A	L43-45	12+1 (5)	11 (4)	1 (4)	2+1 (3)	–	3+1 (4)	3 (5)	11 (5)	–	–	–	–
7	12/6	Rye House	A	L41-51	16 (5)	4+2 (4)	–	–	12 (5)	–	–	6 (5)	0 (3)	–	–	3 (8)
8	22/6	Stoke	A	L44-46	15 (6)	9+2 (6)	5+2 (5)	R/R	–	–	8+2 (4)	7+1 (5)	0 (4)	–	–	–
9	9/7	Wimbledon	H	W57-36	12+1 (5)	13+2 (6)	5+1 (5)	R/R	–	–	5 (6)	18 (6)	4 (5)	–	–	–
10	13/7	Wimbledon	A	L34-56	–	R/R	10+1 (6)	–	–	–	2 (3)	14 (6)	5+1 (7)	–	–	3 (8)
11	30/7	Rye House	H	W46-43	10 (4)	–	7+1 (5)	6+3 (4)	–	–	3+2 (4)	12 (5)	2 (4)	6 (4)	–	–
12	6/8	Stoke	H	W54-39*	8+3 (4)	–	13+1 (5)	9+1 (4)	–	–	4 (4)	15 (5)	3+2 (4)	–	2+1 (4)	–
13	7/8	Buxton	A	W45-44*	15 (5)	–	6 (4)	3 (4)	–	–	3 (5)	12 (5)	6+1 (5)	–	0 (2)	–

No	DATE	OPPONENTS	H/A	RESULT	Scott	Tully	Stoddart	Beaton	Lawson	McBain	McKinna	Sneddon	McDade	Langley	Pickering	Others
14	13/8	Weymouth	H	W50-39	14 (5)	–	8+1 (4)	5+1 (4)	–	–	9+3 (5)	11 (5)	2+1 (4)	–	–	1+1 (3)
15	19/8	Weymouth	A	L43-54	14 (5)	–	8 (5)	4+1 (4)	–	–	3+1 (4)	13 (5)	1+1 (4)	–	–	–
16	21/8	Scunthorpe	A	L44-50	13 (5)	–	9 (5)	2 (3)	–	–	8+1 (5)	9+1 (5)	1 (4)	–	2+1 (3)	–
17	3/9	Scunthorpe	H	W58-38*	9 (4)	–	9 (5)	8+1 (4)	–	–	7+2 (4)	15 (5)	3+1 (4)	7+1 (4)	–	–
18	10/9	Mildenhall	H	W58-37*	–	–	6+1 (4)	10+2 (4)	11+1 (4)	–	10 (5)	15 (5)	4+1 (4)	2 (4)	–	–
19	25/9	Sittingbourne	A	W47-43*	R/R	–	12 (6)	4+1 (5)	–	–	11+1 (6)	15 (6)	1 (3)	–	4+1 (4)	–
20	26/9	Oxford†	A	L18-55	R/R	–	2 (4)	4 (4)	–	–	4+1 (6)	7 (3)	1 (3)	–	0 (4)	–
21	1/10	Newport	H	W61-34*	–	–	9 (4)	6+1 (4)	15 (5)	–	8+3 (4)	14+1 (5)	3+2 (4)	6+1 (4)	–	–
22	30/10	Boston	A	L44-45*	–	8+1 (5)	9+1 (6)	7+2 (5)	R/R	–	4 (4)	14+1 (6)	2+1 (4)	–	–	–

†Meeting abandoned after heat twelve, with the result permitted to stand.

DETAILS OF OTHER RIDERS:

Match No. 7: Karl White 2 (4); Colin McDonald 1 (4); Match No. 10: Marc Andrews 2 (4); Niall Strudwick 1 (3); Jessica Lamb 0 (1); Match No. 14: John MacPhail 1+1 (3).

TACTICAL SUBSTITUTE AND TACTICAL RIDES, AS INCLUDED IN THE SCORES GRID:

Match No. 3: Scott 4 points (TS), Sneddon 4 points (TR); Beaton 4 points (TR); Match No. 5: Stoddart 6 points (TR); Sneddon 2 points (TS); Tully 0 points (TR); Match No. 7: Scott 4 points (TS); Match No. 15: Sneddon 6 points (TR); Stoddart 4 points (TS); Scott 4 points (TR); Match No. 16: Scott 6 points (TR); Stoddart 4 points (TS); Match No. 20: Sneddon 4 points (TR); Pickering 0 points (TS); Stoddart 0 points (TR).

CONFERENCE LEAGUE AVERAGES

Rider	Mts	Rds	Pts	Bon	Tot	Avge	Max
William Lawson	4	19	52	2	54	11.37	1 full; 2 paid
Blair Scott	16	78	185	5	190	9.74	1 full
Derek Sneddon	21	107	241	7	248	9.27	4 full; 1 paid
Gary Beaton	18	71	97	24	121	6.82	1 paid
Sean Stoddart	21	96	154	9	163	6.79	–
Andrew Tully	10	45	60	10	70	6.22	–
Adam McKinna	21	98	129	22	151	6.16	–
Karl Langley	4	16	21	2	23	5.75	–
Cal McDade	19	75	41	12	53	2.83	–
John MacPhail	1	3	1	1	2	2.67	–
Michael Pickering	5	17	8	3	11	2.59	–
James McBain	3	10	4	1	5	2.00	–
Niall Strudwick	1	3	1	0	1	1.33	–
Colin McDonald	1	4	1	0	1	1.00	–
Jessica Lamb	1	1	0	0	0	0.00	–
Guests	2	8	4	0	4	2.00	–

(Marc Andrews [1]; Karl White [1]).

ARMADALE: From left to right, back row: Derek Sneddon, Sean Stoddart, Andrew Tully, Adam McKinna, James McBain, Gary Beaton. Front, on bike: Blair Scott.

CONFERENCE TROPHY

(*Denotes bonus-point/aggregate victory)

No	DATE	OPPONENTS	H/A	RESULT	Scott	Beaton	Stoddart	Tully	Sneddon	McDade	McKinna	Lawson	McBain	Morris	Langley
1	15/5	Scunthorpe	A	D46-46	13 (5)	5 (4)	11 (4)	4 (3)	7 (5)	0 (3)	6+3 (6)	–	–	–	–
2	10/6	Stoke	H	W54-44	15 (5)	–	–	9 (4)	9+1 (4)	1 (4)	5+1 (5)	13+2 (5)	2+1 (2)	–	–
3	2/7	Buxton	H	W64-29	13+2 (5)	R/R	12+1 (5)	13+2 (5)	15 (5)	4+2 (4)	7 (6)	–			
4	10/7	Buxton	A	L43-49*	0 (1)	R/R	14 (6)	1 (1)	15 (6)	6+3 (7)	7+1 (7)	–			
5	16/7	Scunthorpe	H	W53-42*	R/R	–	9 (6)	–	15 (5)	3+2 (4)	8 (6)	16+1 (6)	–	2+1 (3)	–
6	10/8	Stoke	A	L46-50*	15 (5)	3 (4)	5+1 (4)	–	15 (5)	3+1 (5)	5+1 (4)	–	–	0 (3)	–
7	17/9	Boston	H	W53-43	12+1 (5)	5+1 (4)	8+1 (4)	–	13 (5)	4+2 (3)	10+4 (6)	–	–		1 (3)
8	9/10	Boston	A	W48-42*	–	1 (3)	1+1 (3)	4 (4)	15 (5)	1 (3)	12+1 (7)	14+1 (5)			
9	14/10	Stoke	H	W49-41	–	4+1 (4)	8 (4)	0 (3)	14+1 (5)	1 (3)	7+1 (6)	15 (5)			
10	29/10	Stoke	A	W50-43*	–	2 (4)	7 (4)	5+3 (4)	14 (5)	2+1 (4)	7 (4)	13 (5)			

TACTICAL RIDES, AS INCLUDED IN THE SCORES GRID:

Match No. 1: Stoddart 6 points (TR); Match No. 4: Stoddart 6 points (TR); Match No. 6: Sneddon 6 points (TR); Scott 6 points (TR); Match No. 10: Sneddon 6 points (TR).

CONFERENCE TROPHY AVERAGES

Rider	Mts	Rds	Pts	Bon	Tot	Avge	Max
William Lawson	5	26	71	4	75	11.54	1 full; 2 paid
Blair Scott	6	26	65	3	68	10.46	1 full; 1 paid
Derek Sneddon	10	50	126	2	128	10.24	3 full; 1 paid
Sean Stoddart	9	40	69	4	73	7.30	–
Andrew Tully	7	24	36	5	41	6.83	1 paid
Adam McKinna	10	57	74	12	86	6.04	–
James McBain	1	2	2	1	3	6.00	–
Gary Beaton	6	23	20	2	22	3.83	–
Cal McDade	10	40	25	11	36	3.60	–
Keiran Morris	2	6	2	1	3	2.00	–
Karl Langley	1	3	1	0	1	1.33	–

OTHER MEETINGS

11 March: Conference League International

Scotland 37 (David McAllan 12; William Lawson 8; Blair Scott 8; Gary Beaton 3+2; Adam McKinna 2+1; Sean Stoddart 2; Andrew Tully 2) Great Britain Under-21 57 (James Wright 15; Jamie Robertson 13+2; John Branney 9+1; Ben Wilson 7; Adam Roynon 5+1; Benji Compton 5; Karl Mason 3+2).

2 April: Challenge

Scotland 60 (Blair Scott 12; David McAllan 11+1; William Lawson 11+1; Derek Sneddon 8+1; Andrew Tully 6+1; Sean Stoddart 5+1; Gary Beaton 4+1; Adam McKinna 3+1) USA Dream Team 34 (T.J. Fowler 12; Chris Kerr 9+1; Shaun Harmatiuk 5; Dario Galvin 4+1; Tim Gomez 2+1; Dale Facchini 2; Neil Facchini 0; Brian Starr 0).

INDIVIDUAL MEETING

28 May: British Under-15 Championship (Round Two)

1st Josh Auty <u>15</u>; 2nd Ben Taylor 14; 3rd Adam Wrathall 13; George Jarvis 10; George Piper 10; Daniel Greenwood 9; Ben Thompson 7; Rickylee Beecroft 6; Brendan Johnson 6; Ben Hopwood 6; Ben Johnson 4; Scott Meakins 4; Joe Haines 3; Tom Davies 2; Dan Kirkman 2.

BOSTON N.C. WILLIAMS & SON INSURANCE BARRACUDA-BRAVES

ADDRESS: Norfolk Arena, Saddlebow Road, King's Lynn, Norfolk, PE34 3AG.
CLUB CHAIRMEN: Stephen Lambert, Malcolm Vasey & Mick Smith.
TRACK LENGTH: 342 metres.
CL TRACK RECORD: 60.0 seconds – Trevor Harding (15 June 2003).
FIRST MEETING: 1 April 2000.
YEARS OF OPERATION: 2000–05 Conference League.

PREVIOUS VENUE: Boston Sports Stadium, New Hammond Beck Road, Boston, Lincolnshire.
YEARS OF OPERATION: 1970–74 British League Division Two; 1975–84 National League; 1986–87 National League.

CLUB HONOURS

LEAGUE CHAMPIONS: 1973.
KNOCK-OUT CUP WINNERS: 1973, 2000.
PAIRS CHAMPIONS: 1977.
CONFERENCE TROPHY WINNERS: 2003.

RIDER ROSTER 2005

Scott CAMPOS; James COCKLE; Wayne DUNWORTH; Ben HANNON; Trevor HARDING; Robert HOLLINGWORTH; James HORTON; Nathan IRWIN; Simon LAMBERT; Adam LOWE; David McALLAN; Darren MALLETT; Jeremy PESTELL; Michael PICKERING; Phil PICKERING; Ben POWELL; Mark RICHARDSON; Adam ROYNON; Simon WALKER; Karl WHITE; Carl WILKINSON.

OTHER APPEARANCES (official matches only):
Dean WILSON.

Super action from the first semi-final of the Slovenian Grand Prix at Krsko on 28 May as Matej Zagar and Leigh Adams battle for supremacy ahead of Nicki Pedersen and Ryan Sullivan.

Racing at close quarters from the league encounter between Somerset and Stoke at the Oak Tree Arena on 22 July, with Potters' guest Stuart Robson (5) just edging ahead of the hidden Magnus Zetterstrom, Jamie Smith (2) and Barrie Evans (6).

3 Andreas Jonsson caught in full flight at the Scandinavian Grand Prix in Malilla, Sweden on 13 August.

4 Action from heat ten of the Czech Republic Grand Prix at Prague on 9 July as Scott Nicholls narrowly leads Andreas Jonsson, with Leigh Adams and Jason Crump close behind.

5 On a tension-packed evening, 26 September, the second leg of the Elite League Play-Off final between Belle Vue and Coventry was played out before a packed Kirkmanshulme Lane audience

6 Antonio Lindback (14) and Andreas Jonsson (7) tussle for pole position ahead of Jaroslaw Hampel (8) and Hans N. Andersen (9) in heat sixteen of the Czech Republic Grand Prix.

7 2004 World Champion Jason Crump powers ahead of Tony Rickardsson in the second semi-final of the Scandinavian Grand Prix.

Tony Rickardsson (2) heads Tomasz Gollob (6), Nicki Pedersen (5) and Antonio Lindback (14) in heat two of the Swedish Grand Prix at Eskilstuna on 14 May.

Peterborough ace Ales Dryml crashes heavily in heat eleven of the Czech Republic Grand Prix.

10 Greg Hancock races away from Bjarne Pedersen and Piotr Protasiewicz in heat twelve of the Polish Grand Prix at Bydgoszcz on 27 August.

11 British Under-15 Champion Josh Auty shows his style during practice for the British Grand Prix at Cardiff's Millennium Stadium on 10 June.

12 Wonderful wheelies from Brent Werner and Tommy Allen during the Press and Practice Day at Rye House on 21 February.

13 Jason Crump (1) squeezes ahead of the partially hidden Tomasz Gollob, Hans N. Andersen (9) and Lee Richardson (11) in heat two of the Czech Republic Grand Prix.

14 A super shot from heat eight of Reading's Premier League fixture against Berwick at Smallmead on 20 June as Chris Schramm holds sway from Mathieu Tresarrieu, Carl Wilkinson and Zdenek Simota.

15 Oxford Silver Machine Academy celebrate clinching the Conference League Championship after defeating Newport Mavericks in the second part of a double-header at Sandy Lane on 6 October.

16 Swindon lynchpin Leigh Adams leads Tomasz Chrzanowski (15), Jason Crump and Tony Rickardsson in heat seventeen of the Polish Grand Prix.

17 Lukas Dryml (3) and Ronnie Correy (5) have a coming-together in heat five of Oxford's encounter with Wolverhampton in the Air-Tek Trophy at Cowley on 17 March.

18 Bjarne Pedersen (10) and Scott Nicholls tangle in heat nineteen of the Italian Grand Prix at Lonigo on 10 September.

19 Kyle Legault leads Jamie Robertson (7), Richie Dennis (6) and back marker Paul Cooper during heat two of Sheffield's Premier Trophy clash with Newcastle at Owlerton on 21 April.

20 Popular Poole racer Antonio Lindback heads Scott Nicholls in heat fifteen of the Polish Grand Prix.

21 Billy Hamill rushes inside Piotr Protasiewicz during heat four of Oxford's Elite League engagement with Ipswich at Sandy Lane on 14 July.

22 Tony Rickardsson sweeps around Lee Richardson in heat fifteen of the Polish Grand Prix at the fabulous Bydgoszcz raceway.

23 Tony Atkin and Mads Korneliussen head for a 5-1 during Newport's narrow 47-46 victory against Edinburgh in the Premier League at Queensway Meadows on 22 May.

24 Tony Rickardsson (9) and Hans N. Andersen (2) blast from the gate during Ipswich's Elite League match against Arena-Essex at Foxhall Heath on 25 March.

25 Andrew Appleton jets clear from Stuart Robson, Matej Zagar and Brent Werner in heat thirteen of the Premier Trophy fixture between Reading and Rye House at Smallmead on 9 May.

26 Jason Crump leads from the home duo of Henrik Gustafsson (11) and Stefan Andersson (10) during heat four of Oxford's Knock-Out Cup quarter-final encounter against Belle Vue at Cowley on 19 May.

27 The Coventry riders and supporters celebrate their Elite League Championship success following victory in the second leg of the Play-Off final at Belle Vue.

28 Daniel King and Brent Werner indulge in a spot of team riding during heat four of Rye House's Premier Trophy match at Reading.

29 Superb heat four activity shows Martin Smolinski inside Jason Crump, with Andy Smith chasing during the second leg of the Play-Off final between Belle Vue and Coventry.

30 Nicki Pedersen (5) and Jaroslaw Hampel (8) clash ahead of the hidden Tony Rickardsson during heat five of the Czech Republic Grand Prix.

31 Tony Rickardsson spectacularly leads Karol Baran during Arena-Essex's Good Friday visit to Ipswich.

CONFERENCE LEAGUE

(*Denotes bonus-point victory)

No	DATE	OPPONENTS	H/A	RESULT	Walker	Pickering	Mallett	Irwin	Wilkinson	Richardson	Lambert	Powell	Lowe	Hollingworth	McAllan	Others
1	28/3	Rye House	A	L37.5-54.5	2 (4)	0 (2)	3+2 (4)	7½(5)	11+1 (5)	0 (3)	14+2 (7)	–	–	–	–	–
2	17/4	Weymouth	H	W48-45	10+1 (5)	3+1 (4)	–	2 (4)	18 (5)	–	9+2 (5)	6 (4)	0 (3)	–	–	–
3	23/4	Armadale	A	L41-52	9 (4)	0 (3)	–	4+1 (4)	11 (5)	–	11+2 (7)	6+1 (4)	0 (3)	–	–	–
4	24/4	Stoke	H	W56-39	9 (5)	4+3 (4)	–	10+1 (5)	12 (4)	–	9+3 (5)	7 (4)	5+1 (3)	–	–	–
5	1/5	Sittingbourne	H	W62-31	8 (4)	7+3 (4)	13+1 (5)	8+1 (4)	13+1 (5)	–	9+3 (4)	–	4+1 (4)	–	–	–
6	8/5	Buxton	A	W46-44	6 (5)	2+1 (3)	4+1 (4)	1 (2)	15 (5)	–	14+1 (7)	–	4+1 (4)	–	–	–
7	12/5	Weymouth	A	L33-60	2 (2)	0 (4)	10 (5)	–	11+1 (5)	–	10 (7)	–	0 (4)	–	–	0 (3)
8	15/5	Buxton	H	W57-35*	10+1 (4)	–	3 (1)	–	12 (4)	5+2 (5)	19+2 (7)	–	3 (5)	–	–	5+1 (4)
9	18/5	Stoke	A	L41-53*	3+1 (4)	0 (3)	–	–	15 (4)	0 (4)	15 (7)	–	3+1 (4)	5+1 (4)	–	–
10	3/7	Newport	A	W48-44	10+2 (5)	2+1 (3)	–	–	–	–	8 (4)	–	2+2 (3)	6+1 (4)	–	20+2 (11)
11	22/7	Mildenhall	H	L44-49	11+1 (5)	2 (3)	10+1 (4)	–	–	–	–	–	0 (3)	–	18 (6)	3 (9)
12	24/7	Scunthorpe	A	L31-61	12 (6)	3+1 (4)	10 (6)	–	–	0 (2)	–	–	1 (3)	–	R/R	5+1 (9)
13	31/7	Oxford	H	L45-53	19 (6)	–	12 (6)	–	–	3 (4)	R/R	–	0 (4)	10+2 (6)	–	1+1 (4)
14	7/8	Wimbledon	H	W55-42	15 (5)	–	9+1 (4)	–	6 (5)	–	10 (4)	–	–	–	13+2 (5)	2 (7)
15	21/8	Mildenhall	A	L39-57	12 (5)	–	9 (4)	–	–	2+1 (3)	3+1 (4)	–	3 (4)	–	8 (6)	2 (4)
16	28/8	Rye House	H	L40-49	–	–	16 (6)	–	–	0 (3)	–	–	3+1 (4)	–	11+1 (5)	10 (12)
17	7/9	Wimbledon	A	L39-55	–	–	2+1 (6)	–	–	–	R/R	–	0 (3)	–	14 (5)	23+1 (16)
18	11/9	Scunthorpe	H	W48-42	12 (4)	–	7+1 (4)	–	–	–	9 (5)	–	2 (3)	–	14+1 (5)	4+1 (9)
19	18/9	Newport	H	W52-38*	15 (5)	–	9+2 (4)	–	–	–	12+2 (5)	–	3 (4)	9 (4)	–	4+1 (8)
20	25/9	Sittingbourne	A	W48-42*	–	–	10+1 (5)	–	–	–	9 (6)	–	2+1 (4)	–	18 (6)	9+1 (9)
21	26/9	Oxford	A	L27-66	–	–	13 (6)	3 (6)	–	–	5 (3)	–	1 (4)	3 (5)	–	2 (6)
22	30/10	Armadale	H	W45-44	–	–	–	7 (5)	–	1+1 (4)	12+1 (6)	–	–	–	R/R	25+1 (15)

DETAILS OF OTHER RIDERS:

Match No. 7: Phil Pickering 0 (3); Match No. 8: James Horton 5+1 (4); Match No. 10: Trevor Harding 11+1 (5); Karl White 9+1 (6); Match No. 11: Karl White 3 (6); Ben Hannon 0 (3); Match No. 12: Karl White 4+1 (5); Ben Hannon 1 (4); Match 13: Wayne Dunworth 1+1 (4); Match No. 14: Wayne Dunworth 1 (4); Ben Hannon 1 (3); Match No. 15: Wayne Dunworth 2 (4); Match No. 16: Scott Campos 7 (7); Wayne Dunworth 3 (4); Ben Hannon 0 (1); James Cockle R/R; Match No. 17: James Cockle 13+1 (6); Scott Campos 8 (6); Jeremy Pestell 2 (4); Match No. 18: Scott Campos 4+1 (6); Jeremy Pestell 0 (3); Match No. 19: Jeremy Pestell 4+1 (4); Scott Campos 0 (4); Match No. 20: Jeremy Pestell 5+1 (5); Scott Campos 4 (4); James Cockle R/R; Match No. 21: Scott Campos 2 (6); James Cockle R/R; Match No. 22: James Cockle 15 (6); Scott Campos 8+1 (6); Wayne Dunworth 2 (3).

TACTICAL SUBSTITUTE AND TACTICAL RIDES, AS INCLUDED IN THE SCORES GRID:

Match No. 1: Wilkinson 4 points (TR); Lambert 2 points (TR); Match No. 2: Wilkinson 6 points (TR); Match No. 3: Walker 6 points (TR); Match No. 7: Lambert 4 points (TR); Wilkinson 2 points (TR); Match No. 9: Wilkinson 6 points (TR); Lambert 4 points (TR); Match No. 10: Walker 4 points (TS); Match No. 11: McAllan 6 points (TR); Match No. 12: Walker 6 points (TR); Mallett 4 points (TR); Match No. 13: Walker 6 points (TR); Mallett 6 points (TR); Hollingworth 4 points (TS); Match No. 15: Mallett 6 points (TR); Walker 6 points (TR); McAllan 0 points (TS); Match No. 17: Cockle 6 points (TR); McAllan 4 points (TR); Mallett 0 points (TS); Match No. 21: Mallett 4 points (TR); Lambert 2 points (TR).

CONFERENCE LEAGUE AVERAGES

Rider	Mts	Rds	Pts	Bon	Tot	Avge	Max
Carl Wilkinson	9	42	109	3	112	10.67	5 full
David McAllan	7	38	91	4	95	10.00	1 full; 2 paid
Trevor Harding	1	5	11	1	12	9.60	–
James Cockle	2	12	25	1	26	8.67	–
Simon Lambert	17	93	172	19	191	8.22	1 paid
Simon Walker	17	78	151	6	157	8.05	3 full
Darren Mallett	16	74	130	11	141	7.62	–
Ben Powell	3	12	19	1	20	6.67	–
Robert Hollingworth	5	23	31	4	35	6.09	–
James Horton	1	4	5	1	6	6.00	–
Nathan Irwin	8	35	42.5	3	45.5	5.20	–
Karl White	3	17	16	2	18	4.24	–
Scott Campos	7	39	33	2	35	3.59	–
Michael Pickering	11	37	23	10	33	3.57	–
Jeremy Pestell	4	16	11	2	13	3.25	–
Adam Lowe	19	69	36	8	44	2.55	–
Mark Richardson	9	33	17	4	21	2.55	–
Wayne Dunworth	5	19	9	1	10	2.11	–
Ben Hannon	4	11	2	0	2	0.73	–
Phil Pickering	1	3	0	0	0	0.00	–

CONFERENCE TROPHY

(*Denotes bonus-point victory)

No	DATE	OPPONENTS	H/A	RESULT	Wilkinson	Lambert	Harding	Walker	Lowe	Richardson	Irwin	Roynon	Hollingworth	Cockle	White	Others
1	1/6	Wimbledon	A	L31-61	14 (6)	11 (6)	R/R	0 (2)	3 (6)	3 (5)	–	–	–	–	–	0 (4)
2	5/6	Mildenhall	H	W51-41	15 (6)	11+2 (5)	R/R	13 (6)	0 (3)	5+1 (5)	7+4 (5)	–	–	–	–	–
3	19/6	Wimbledon	H	W54-40	–	11+2 (5)	–	15 (5)	2 (7)	0 (0)	7+2 (4)	11+1 (4)	8 (4)	–	–	–
4	26/6	Mildenhall	A	W49-42*	–	5+1 (4)	10 (4)	8+1 (4)	1+1 (3)	–	–	6+2 (5)	–	16 (5)	3+1 (5)	–
5	8/7	Weymouth	A	L42-48	–	7+1 (4)	10+2 (5)	6 (4)	2 (4)	–	–	5+1 (4)	–	8 (5)	4+1 (4)	–
6	10/7	Weymouth	H	L42-50	–	14 (6)	–	17+1 (6)	2 (4)	–	–	–	5+1 (5)	R/R	1 (4)	3+1 (5)
7	17/9	Armadale	A	L43-53	–	R/R	–	8 (5)	0 (4)	–	–	–	–	15+1 (6)	–	20+1 (15)
8	9/10	Armadale	H	L42-48	–	10+1 (6)	–	–	1+1 (3)	–	4+4 (5)	–	–	R/R	–	27+3 (16)

DETAILS OF OTHER RIDERS:

Match No. 1: Dean Wilson 0 (4); Match No. 6: Michael Pickering 2+1 (4); Ben Hannon 1 (1); Match No. 7: David McAllan 17 (6); Scott Campos 2 (5); Jeremy Pestell 1+1 (4); Match No. 8: David McAllan 13 (6); Darren Mallett 8+2 (5); Scott Campos 6+1 (5).

TACTICAL SUBSTITUTE AND TACTICAL RIDES, AS INCLUDED IN THE SCORES GRID:

Match No. 1: Lambert 4 points (TR); Wilkinson 0 points (TS); Walker 0 points (TR); Match No. 4: Cockle 6 points (TR); Match No. 6: Walker 6 points (TR); Match No. 7: McAllan 6 points (TR); Cockle 6 points (TR).

BOSTON: From left to right, back row: Stephen Lambert (Co-Promoter), Adam Lowe, Carl Wilkinson, Nathan Irwin, Darren Mallett, Mick Smith (Co-Promoter). Front: Simon Lambert, Michael Pickering, Simon Walker.

CONFERENCE TROPHY AVERAGES

Rider	Mts	Rds	Pts	Bon	Tot	Avge	Max
Trevor Harding	2	9	20	2	22	9.78	–
Carl Wilkinson	2	12	29	0	29	9.67	–
David McAllan	2	12	27	0	27	9.00	–
James Cockle	3	16	33	1	34	8.50	–
Simon Walker	7	32	64	2	66	8.25	1 full
Simon Lambert	7	36	67	7	74	8.22	–
Nathan Irwin	3	14	18	10	28	8.00	–
Darren Mallett	1	5	8	2	10	8.00	–
Adam Roynon	3	13	22	4	26	8.00	1 paid
Robert Hollingworth	2	9	13	1	14	6.22	–
Ben Hannon	1	1	1	0	1	4.00	–
Scott Campos	2	10	8	1	9	3.60	–
Mark Richardson	3	10	8	1	9	3.60	–
Karl White	3	13	8	2	10	3.08	–
Michael Pickering	1	4	2	1	3	3.00	–
Jeremy Pestell	1	4	1	1	2	2.00	–
Adam Lowe	8	34	11	2	13	1.53	–
Dean Wilson	1	4	0	0	0	0.00	–

KNOCK-OUT CUP

(*Denotes aggregate victory)

No	DATE	OPPONENTS	H/A	RESULT	Wilkinson	Pickering	Richardson	Harding	Walker	Lowe	Lambert	Cockle	Dunworth	Mallett	Irwin	Others
1	29/5	Scunthorpe	H	W53–41	9 (4)	3+1 (3)	0 (3)	10+1 (5)	14 (5)	2 (3)	15+2 (7)	–	–	–	–	–
2	30/5	Scunthorpe	A	W49–40*	14 (5)	3+1 (3)	0 (3)	8+1 (4)	8+1 (5)	2+1 (4)	14+1 (6)	–	–	–	–	–
3	12/8	Stoke	H	W59–35	–	–	–	–	11 (5)	5+2 (3)	11+2 (5)	8 (4)	2+1 (3)	7+2 (4)	–	15+3 (6)
4	14/8	Stoke	A	L39–54*					10 (4)	0 (4)	10+1 (5)	–	0 (3)	5 (5)	–	14+1 (9)
5	7/10	Mildenhall	H	L41–51			3 (5)				7+1 (5)	R/R	–	15 (6)	6 (5)	10+1 (10)
6	9/10	Mildenhall	A	L33–60			1 (4)			3+1 (4)			2 (4)	16 (5)	4+2 (5)	7 (8)

DETAILS OF OTHER RIDERS:

Match No. 3: Adam Roynon 15+3 (6); Match No. 4: David McAllan 9 (4); Scott Campos 5+1 (5); Match No. 5: David McAllan 10+1 (6); Jeremy Pestell 0 (4); Match No. 6: David McAllan 4 (4); Scott Campos 3 (4).

TACTICAL RIDES, AS INCLUDED IN THE SCORES GRID:

Match No. 4: McAllan 4 points (TR); Lambert 4 points (TR); Match No. 5: Mallett 6 points (TR); Match No. 6: Mallett 6 points (TR); McAllan 0 points (TR).

OTHER MEETINGS

18 March: Challenge

Boston 52 (Carl Wilkinson 13; Simon Walker 10+2; Darren Mallett 9; Nathan Irwin 8+2; Simon Lambert 5+2; Mark Richardson 5+1; Michael Pickering 2+1) Mildenhall 44.

3 April: Spring Challenge Cup (first leg)

Boston 49 (Carl Wilkinson 14+1; Simon Lambert 11; Simon Walker 10; Nathan Irwin 9+1; Michael Pickering 3+1; Mark Richardson 2; Ben Powell 0) Wimbledon 43.

10 April: Challenge

Mildenhall 46 Boston 42 (Carl Wilkinson 10+1; Nathan Irwin 9+1; Darren Mallett 8+1; Simon Walker 7; Michael Pickering 5+3; Mark Richardson 2; Adam Lowe 1).

13 April: Spring Challenge Cup (second leg)

Wimbledon 48 Boston 40 (Simon Lambert 12+2; Ben Powell 11+1; Robert Hollingworth 8; Carl Wilkinson 6; Nathan Irwin 2+1; Adam Lowe 1; Michael Pickering 0) – Wimbledon won 91-89 on aggregate.

16 October: Lincolnshire Trophy (first leg)

Scunthorpe 53 Boston 41 (James Cockle 15; Simon Lambert 10; Darren Mallett 6+2; Robert Hollingworth 3; Scott Campos 3; Adam Lowe 2+2; Nathan Irwin 2).

16 October: Lincolnshire Trophy (second leg)

Boston 45 (James Cockle 19; Simon Lambert 11+1; Darren Mallett 6+1; Robert Hollingworth 3; Nathan Irwin 2; Mark Richardson 2; Scott Campos 2) Scunthorpe 47 – Scunthorpe won 100-86 on aggregate.

INDIVIDUAL MEETINGS

3 September: Lincolnshire Trophy

1st James Cockle 15; 2nd Simon Lambert 14; 3rd Mark Thompson 12; Simon Walker 11; Darren Mallett 10; Robert Hollingworth 10; Adam Roynon 9; Ricky Scarboro 9; Adam Lowe 7; Mark Richardson 6; Jeremy Pestell 5; Scott Campos 4; Wayne Dunworth 4; Ben Hannon 1; Scott Richardson 0; Karl White 0; James Fear (Res) 0.

21 September: David Nix Memorial Trophy

QUALIFYING SCORES: Darren Mallett 14; Jamie Robertson 13; Simon Walker 11; James Cockle 10; Lee Derbyshire 10; Barry Burchatt 9; Karlis Ezergailis 8; Simon Lambert 8; Carl Belfield 7; Artur Boginczuk 6; Ricky Scarboro 6; Jonathon Bethell 5; Tom Brown 4; Mark Richardson 3; Tyron Proctor (Res) 3; Jessica Lamb 2; Wayne Dunworth (Res) 1; Mark Thompson 0. SEMI-FINAL: 1st Walker; 2nd Burchatt; 3rd Cockle; 4th Derbyshire. FINAL: lst Mallett; 2nd Walker; 3rd Robertson; 4th Burchatt.

BUXTON HITMEN

ADDRESS: Buxton Raceway, Dale Head Lane, Axe Edge, nr Buxton, Derbyshire.
CLUB CHAIRMEN: Richard Moss & Jayne Moss.
TRACK LENGTH: 240 metres.
TRACK RECORD: 52.9 seconds – James Wright (27 June 2004).
FIRST MEETING: 19 May 1996.
YEARS OF OPERATION: 1996 Conference League; 1997 Amateur League; 1998–2005 Conference League.

PREVIOUS VENUE: Buxton Stadium, off A53 Leek-to-Buxton Road, Buxton, Derbyshire.
YEARS OF OPERATION: 1994 British League Division Three; 1995 Academy League.

CLUB HONOURS

KNOCK-OUT CUP WINNERS: 2002.

RIDER ROSTER 2005

Carl BELFIELD; Jonathon BETHELL; James BIRKINSHAW; Scott CHESTER; Lee DERBYSHIRE; David FARLEY; Dean FELTON; John MacPHAIL; Ross PARKER; Joe REYNOLDS; Paul SHARPLES; Charles WRIGHT.

OTHER APPEARANCES/GUESTS (official matches only):
Russell BARNETT; Wayne BUCKLAND; Ben THOMPSON.

CONFERENCE LEAGUE

(*Denotes bonus-point victory)

No	DATE	OPPONENTS	H/A	RESULT	Bethell	Belfield	Derbyshire	Wright	Felton	Reynolds	Parker	Farley	Sharples	MacPhail	Chester	Others
1	26/3	Armadale	A	L41-54	1+1 (4)	12+1 (5)	10 (5)	3 (3)	9 (4)	1+1 (4)	5+2 (5)	–				
2	3/4	Oxford	H	D45-45	10+1 (5)	7+1 (4)	10 (5)	7+1 (4)	9 (4)	0 (3)	–	2 (5)				
3	13/4	Stoke†	A	L30-46	6+1 (3)	3 (4)	–	3 (3)	4+1 (3)	1 (3)	9 (4)	–	4+2 (4)			
4	17/4	Rye House	H	W47-44	13+1 (5)	8+1 (5)	8 (4)	6+1 (4)	4 (4)	1 (3)	7+3 (5)	–				
5	24/4	Weymouth	H	L40-49	13 (5)	0 (4)	11 (5)	6+1 (4)	3 (4)	–	5 (5)	–		2+2 (3)		
6	28/4	Oxford	A	L31-63	13 (5)	3+2 (4)	7 (5)	1+1 (4)	3 (4)	–	2+1 (4)	–		2 (4)		
7	8/5	Boston	H	L44-46	14+1 (6)	4 (4)	14+2 (6)	8+2 (5)	–	–	4+1 (7)	0 (1)		0 (1)		R/R
8	15/5	Boston	A	L35-57	0 (2)	5+3 (4)	13 (5)	7+1 (5)	4 (4)	–	4+1 (6)	2 (4)				
9	29/5	Sittingbourne	H	W56-36	9 (5)	9+2 (4)	14+1 (5)	3+1 (4)	10+1 (4)	–	8+1 (4)	3 (4)				
10	12/6	Sittingbourne	A	W55-39*	8+2 (4)	8+2 (4)	13 (5)	7+2 (5)	9+1 (4)	–	7 (4)	–			3+1 (4)	
11	26/6	Newport	H	W48-41	15 (5)	7+1 (4)	5 (4)	4+2 (4)	11+2 (5)	–	4+1 (5)	2 (3)				
12	31/7	Mildenhall	H	L39-51	7+1 (5)	5 (4)	9 (5)	8+1 (4)	6+2 (4)	–	–	1 (4)			3 (4)	
13	7/8	Armadale	H	L44-45	R/R	6 (5)	12+2 (6)	11+3 (6)	9+1 (5)	–	–	3 (4)			3+1 (4)	
14	10/8	Wimbledon	A	L32-58	–		7 (5)	4+1 (4)	6+1 (4)	–	–	4 (4)	2+2 (4)		2+1 (4)	7 (4)
15	20/8	Rye House	A	L30-64	R/R	5+2 (6)	4 (5)	5 (5)	13+1 (6)	–	–	0 (4)			3 (4)	
16	26/8	Weymouth	A	L33-58	7 (4)	5+3 (5)	9 (5)	7 (4)	0 (4)	–	–				4 (6)	1+1 (2)
17	28/8	Scunthorpe	H	W54-38	6+1 (4)	7+1 (4)	12 (5)	12+2 (5)	7+3 (4)	2 (3)	–				8+2 (5)	
18	4/9	Stoke	H	W47-43	5 (4)	9+1 (5)	13+1 (5)	7 (4)	10+1 (4)	1+1 (3)	–				2 (5)	
19	18/9	Mildenhall	A	L36-59	7 (4)	5+1 (4)	10 (5)	11 (6)	2+2 (4)	–	–				1 (6)	
20	25/9	Wimbledon	H	L38-53	13+1 (5)	2 (4)	9+1 (5)	5 (4)	6 (5)	–	0 (0)				3 (6)	
21	16/10	Newport	A	L28-63	1 (4)	1 (3)	5+1 (5)	–	5 (5)	–	9 (3)				6+1 (6)	1+1 (4)
22	31/10	Scunthorpe	A	L37-60	11 (5)	2 (4)	7 (5)	12 (5)	3+2 (4)	–	–				2+1 (4)	0 (3)

†Meeting abandoned after heat twelve, with the result permitted to stand.

DETAILS OF OTHER RIDERS:

Match No. 7: Scott Courtney R/R; Match No. 14: James Birkinshaw 7 (4); Match No. 16: Wayne Buckland 1+1 (2); Match No. 21: Russell Barnett 1+1 (4); Match No. 22: Ben Thompson 0 (3).

TACTICAL SUBSTITUTE AND TACTICAL RIDES, AS INCLUDED IN THE SCORES GRID:

Match No. 1: Belfield 6 points (TR); Felton 4 points (TR); Match No. 3: Parker 4 points (TR); Bethell 4 points (TR); Match No. 6: Derbyshire 4 points (TR); Bethell 4 points (TR); Match No. 8: Derbyshire 4 points (TR); Wright 0 points (TR); Match No. 14: Derbyshire 2 points (TR); Birkinshaw 2 points (TR); Match No. 15: Felton 6 points (TR); Belfield 2 points (TR); Match No. 16: Derbyshire 4 points (TR); Felton 0 points (TR); Match No. 19: Bethell 4 points (TR); Wright 4 points (TS); Derbyshire 2 points (TR); Match No. 20: Bethell 4 points (TR); Derbyshire 0 points (TR); Felton 0 points (TS); Match No. 21: Parker 4 points (TR); Bethell 0 points (TR); Match No. 22: Bethell 6 points (TR); Wright 4 points (TR); Derbyshire 4 points (TS).

CONFERENCE LEAGUE AVERAGES

Rider	Mts	Rds	Pts	Bon	Tot	Avge	Max
Lee Derbyshire	21	105	192	8	200	7.62	1 paid
Jonathon Bethell	19	84	148	10	158	7.52	1 full
Charles Wright	21	92	133	19	152	6.61	–
Dean Felton	21	89	128	18	146	6.56	–
James Birkinshaw	1	4	6	0	6	6.00	–
Carl Belfield	21	90	109	21	130	5.78	–
Ross Parker	12	52	60	10	70	5.38	–
Paul Sharples	2	8	6	4	10	5.00	–
Wayne Buckland	1	2	1	1	2	4.00	–
Scott Chester	12	58	40	7	47	3.24	–
John MacPhail	3	8	4	2	6	3.00	–
David Farley	9	33	17	0	17	2.06	–
Joe Reynolds	6	19	6	2	8	1.68	–
Ben Thompson	1	3	0	0	0	0.00	–
Guest	1	4	1	1	2	2.00	–

(Russell Barnett [1]).

CONFERENCE TROPHY

No	DATE	OPPONENTS	H/A	RESULT	Bethell	Sharples	Derbyshire	Wright	Belfield	MacPhail	Parker	Felton	Farley	Chester
1	1/5	Scunthorpe	H	W46-43	15 (5)	1+1 (4)	12+1 (5)	5+2 (4)	4 (4)	2+1 (4)	7 (4)	–	–	–
2	2/5	Scunthorpe	A	L44-51	14 (5)	3 (4)	4+3 (5)	8 (4)	7+1 (4)	3 (4)	5+2 (4)	–	–	–
3	15/6	Stoke	A	L39-51	R/R	–	10 (6)	5+3 (5)	6+1 (5)	–	10+1 (6)	5+3 (5)	3 (3)	–
4	19/6	Stoke	H	W52-42	5+2 (4)	–	11+1 (5)	8 (4)	7+2 (4)	–	9+2 (5)	11+1 (5)	1 (3)	–
5	2/7	Armadale	A	L29-64	8 (4)	–	6 (5)	3+1 (4)	4+2 (5)	–	–	6 (4)	1 (4)	1 (4)
6	10/7	Armadale	H	W49-43	9+1 (4)	–	9+1 (4)	9+2 (5)	13 (5)	–	–	4+1 (4)	3+1 (4)	2+1 (4)

TACTICAL RIDES, AS INCLUDED IN THE SCORES GRID:

Match No. 2: Bethell 6 points (TR); Wright 4 points (TR); Match No. 5: Bethell 4 points (TR); Derbyshire 2 points (TR).

BUXTON: From left to right, back row: Lee Derbyshire, David Farley, Jonathon Bethell (on bike), Ross Parker, Jack Lee (Team Manager), Dean Felton, Carl Belfield. Front, kneeling: Charles Wright, Joshua Moss (Mascot), Scott Chester.

CONFERENCE TROPHY AVERAGES

Rider	Mts	Rds	Pts	Bon	Tot	Avge	Max
Jonathon Bethell	5	22	46	3	49	8.91	1 full
Lee Derbyshire	6	30	51	6	57	7.60	–
Ross Parker	4	19	31	5	36	7.58	–
Carl Belfield	6	27	41	6	47	6.96	–
Dean Felton	4	18	26	5	31	6.89	–
Charles Wright	6	26	36	8	44	6.77	–
John MacPhail	2	8	5	1	6	3.00	–
David Farley	4	14	8	1	9	2.57	–
Paul Sharples	2	8	4	1	5	2.50	–
Scott Chester	2	8	3	1	4	2.00	–

KNOCK-OUT CUP

No	DATE	OPPONENTS	H/A	RESULT	Bethell	Wright	Felton	Belfield	Derbyshire	Farley	Chester	Reynolds
1	3/7	Weymouth	H	W51-43	12 (5)	8 (4)	8+1 (4)	8 (4)	8+1 (5)	5+1 (5)	2 (3)	–
2	22/7	Weymouth	A	L40-55	13 (6)	5+1 (4)	11+2 (6)	9 (6)	R/R	–	2 (5)	0 (3)

TACTICAL SUBSTITUTE AND TACTICAL RIDES, AS INCLUDED IN THE SCORES GRID:

Match No. 2: Felton 4 points (TR); Bethell 4 points (TR); Belfield 2 points (TS).

OTHER MEETINGS

12 June: Challenge

Mildenhall 51 Buxton 42 (Jonathon Bethell 13+1; Ross Parker 12+1; Lee Derbyshire 8+2; Charles Wright 4+1; Dean Felton 4+1; Scott Chester 1+1; Carl Belfield 0).

24 July: Conference League

Buxton 37 (Jonathon Bethell 9; Carl Belfield 7+1; Charles Wright 6+1; Scott Chester 6; Lee Derbyshire 5+1; Dean Felton 4; Joe Reynolds 0) Wimbledon 23 – meeting abandoned after heat ten.

21 August: Challenge

Buxton 55 (Charles Wright 14; Carl Belfield 9; Lee Derbyshire 9; Scott Chester 8; Dean Felton 7+4; Jonathon Bethell 6+2; David Farley 2) Clwb Caerfyrddin 42 (Wayne Broadhurst 13; Darren Pugh 10; Daniel Hodgson 9; Paul Candy 6+1; Jessica Lamb 3+1; Darren Hatton 1+1; Tim Webster 0).

8 October: Conference League

Scunthorpe 20 Buxton 16 (Jonathon Bethell 5; Lee Derbyshire 5; Charles Wright 2; Ross Parker 2; Dean Felton 1+1; Scott Chester 1+1; Carl Belfield 0) – meeting abandoned after heat six.

9 October: Challenge

Buxton 63 (Charles Wright 12+1; Dean Felton 10+3; Lee Derbyshire 10; Carl Belfield 9+1; Jonathon Bethell 8+1; Ross Parker 7+3; Scott Chester 7+1); Belle Vue Colts 30 (Wayne Broadhurst 13; Daniel Hodgson 7; Paul Sharples 3+1; Paul Burnett 3; Byron Bekker 2; David Farley 1; Ashley Johnson 1).

23 October: Challenge

> Buxton 42 (Charles Wright 10; Lee Derbyshire 9; Jonathon Bethell 7; Dean Felton 6+2; Carl Belfield 6; Scott Chester 4+1; Ross Parker 0) GB Under-18s 53 (Lee Smart 12+3; Lewis Bridger 12; Barry Burchatt 10; Chris Johnson 8+1; Ben Taylor 5+3; Shane Waldron 4+1; Sam Hurst 2)

INDIVIDUAL MEETING

1 May: British Under-15 Championship (Round One)

> 1st Josh Auty 15; 2nd Ben Taylor 14; 3rd Joe Haines 13; Adam Wrathall 11; Ben Hopwood 11; George Piper 10; Dan Kirkman 8; Ben Thompson 8; Ryan Goodger (Res) 7; George Jarvis 6; Daniel Greenwood 5; Scott Meakins 4; Kye Norton 0; Chris Widman 0; Rickylee Beecroft 0; Jack Butler 0; Brendan Johnson 0.

MILDENHALL UK FIRE FEN TIGERS

ADDRESS: Mildenhall Stadium, Hayland Drove, West Row Fen, Mildenhall, Suffolk, IP28 8QU.

CLUB CHAIRMEN: Mick Horton, Neil Watson & Trevor Swales, with the latter standing down from the role at the end of May 2005. Neil Watson stood down shortly afterwards, leaving Mick Horton in sole control.

TRACK LENGTH: 260 metres.

TRACK RECORD: 50.25 seconds – Paul Lee (16 May 2004).

FIRST MEETING: 18 May 1975.

YEARS OF OPERATION: 1973 Training; 1974 Open & Training; 1975–89 National League; 1990–91 Training; 1992 British League Division Two; 1994 British League Division Three; 1995 Academy League; 1996 Conference League; 1997 Amateur League; 1998–2005 Conference League.

CLUB HONOURS

LEAGUE CHAMPIONS: 1979, 2003, 2004.
FOUR-TEAM CHAMPIONS: 1984, 1987, 2004.
PAIRS CHAMPIONS: 1987.
LEAGUE CUP WINNERS: 2000.
CONFERENCE TROPHY WINNERS: 2002, 2004.
KNOCK-OUT CUP WINNERS: 2003, 2004.

RIDER ROSTER 2005

Jon ARMSTRONG; Andrew BARGH; Matt BATES; Paul BURNETT; Scott CAMPOS; Aidan COLLINS; Chris GEER; Trevor HEATH; Gareth HICKMOTT; James HORTON; Chris JOHNSON; Joel PARSONS; James PURCHASE; Adam ROYNON; Lee SMART; Mark THOMPSON.

OTHER APPEARANCES/GUESTS (official matches only):

Tim WEBSTER; Karl WHITE.

CONFERENCE LEAGUE

(*Denotes bonus-point victory)

No	DATE	OPPONENTS	H/A	RESULT	Armstrong	Roynon	Thompson	Campos	Purchase	Collins	Horton	Smart	Heath	Johnson	Bargh	Others
1	16/4	Rye House	A	L42-47	14 (5)	10 (5)	2 (2)	3 (4)	8+3 (7)	–	–	–	–	–	–	5+3 (7)
2	17/4	Newport	H	W54-37	12+1 (5)	9+1 (4)	11+1 (4)	4+1 (4)	6 (5)	12 (4)	–	–	–	–	–	0 (4)
3	24/4	Wimbledon	H	L42-48	14 (5)	11+1 (5)	7 (4)	6+1 (4)	2+1 (4)	–	1+1 (4)	–	–	–	–	1 (4)
4	1/5	Armadale	H	W51-44	14 (5)	7+1 (4)	6 (4)	6+2 (5)	7 (4)	9+1 (5)	–	–	–	–	–	2+1 (3)
5	25/5	Wimbledon	A	L46-50	19 (6)	–	5+2 (5)	0 (3)	3+1 (6)	R/R	–	19 (7)	0 (3)	–	–	–
6	29/5	Stoke	H	W54-42	15 (5)	5 (4)	10+1 (5)	4+1 (4)	9+2 (5)	–	–	9+1 (4)	2+2 (3)	–	–	–
7	18/6	Scunthorpe	A	L43-50	8 (6)	–	R/R	1 (3)	–	–	–	13+2 (6)	–	7+1 (5)	11 (7)	14 (10)
8	3/7	Oxford	H	D46-46	12+1 (5)	–	7+1 (4)	–	5+1 (5)	–	–	1 (3)	7+1 (5)	10+1 (6)	4 (2)
9	10/7	Sittingbourne	H	W63-30	14+3 (6)	–	15 (6)	3+1 (4)	4+1 (3)	–	–	–	–	13+2 (5)	14+3 (6)	R/R
10	22/7	Boston	A	W49-44	14 (6)	–	9+3 (6)	–	9+1 (4)	–	–	–	5+2 (4)	7 (5)	5+3 (5)	R/R
11	29/7	Weymouth	A	L40-51	10+1 (6)	–	8 (4)	–	4 (3)	–	–	5+1 (5)	1+1 (3)	4+2 (4)	8+2 (5)	–
12	31/7	Buxton	A	W51-39	13+1 (5)	–	2 (3)	–	9+1 (5)	–	–	13+1 (5)	2+1 (4)	8+1 (4)	4 (4)	–
13	7/8	Weymouth	H	W56-39*	10+1 (4)	–	13 (5)	–	4 (5)	–	–	11 (4)	4+2 (4)	8+2 (4)	6+1 (4)	–
14	13/8	Sittingbourne	A	W47-43*	7+2 (4)	–	5 (4)	–	8 (5)	–	8 (4)	11 (5)	2+2 (3)	–	6 (5)	–
15	14/8	Rye House	H	W51-39*	14+1 (5)	–	8 (4)	–	7 (4)	–	6+1 (4)	7 (5)	5 (4)	–	4 (4)	–
16	21/8	Boston	H	W57-39*	14 (5)	–	13 (5)	–	6+2 (5)	–	5+1 (4)	10+1 (4)	3+1 (3)	–	6+1 (4)	–
17	4/9	Newport	A	L43-48*	9 (5)	–	1 (3)	–	6 (4)	–	–	10+1 (5)	1 (4)	–	4+3 (4)	12 (5)
18	10/9	Armadale	A	L37-58	12+1 (6)	–	6+1 (4)	–	4+1 (4)	–	–	7+1 (5)	1+1 (4)	–	5 (4)	2 (3)
19	12/9	Oxford†	A	L38-49	15 (5)	–	R/R	–	5 (7)	–	0 (1)	12+1 (5)	2+1 (5)	–	4+1 (5)	–
20	18/9	Buxton	H	W59-36*	5 (4)	–	8+1 (4)	–	6 (4)	–	–	13+1 (5)	3+1 (4)	11+1 (4)	13 (5)	–
21	25/9	Scunthorpe	H	W57-37*	12+1 (5)	–	–	–	6+2 (4)	–	–	12 (5)	5+2 (4)	11 (4)	6+2 (4)	5+2 (4)
22	15/10	Stoke	A	L41-52*	6+1 (5)	–	4+1 (4)	–	8+2 (5)	–	–	6 (4)	1 (3)	10 (4)	6+1 (5)	–

†Meeting abandoned after heat fourteen, with the result permitted to stand.

DETAILS OF OTHER RIDERS:

Match No. 1: Karl White 4+3 (4); Gareth Hickmott 1 (3); Match No. 2: Chris Geer 0 (4); Match No. 3: Gareth Hickmott 1 (4); Match No. 4: Chris Geer 2+1 (3); Match No. 7: Tim Webster 3 (3); Match No. 8: Joel Parsons 4 (2); Match No. 9: Joel Parsons R/R; Match No. 10: Joel Parsons R/R; Match No. 17: Paul Burnett 12 (5); Match No. 18: Paul Burnett 2 (3); Match No. 21: Paul Burnett 5+2 (4).

TACTICAL SUBSTITUTE AND TACTICAL RIDES, AS INCLUDED IN THE SCORES GRID:

Match No. 5: Armstrong 6 points (TR); Smart 6 points (TS); Match No. 7: Smart 6 points (TR); Bargh 6 points (TR); Match No. 11: Armstrong 2 points (TS); Match No. 17: Armstrong 2 points (TS); Match No. 18: Bargh 4 points (TR); Armstrong 4 points (TS); Smart 2 points (TR); Match No. 19: Armstrong 6 points (TR); Match No. 22: Johnson 6 points (TR).

MILDENHALL: From left to right, back row: Chris Johnson, Andrew Bargh, James Purchase, Lee Smart. Front, kneeling: Jon Armstrong, Mark Thompson, Trevor Heath.

CONFERENCE LEAGUE AVERAGES

Rider	Mts	Rds	Pts	Bon	Tot	Avge	Max
Aidan Collins	2	9	21	1	22	9.78	1 full
Jon Armstrong	22	113	253	14	267	9.45	1 full; 1 paid
Lee Smart	15	74	151	10	161	8.70	–
Chris Johnson	10	44	83	10	93	8.45	2 paid
Adam Roynon	5	22	42	3	45	8.18	–
Joel Parsons	1	2	4	0	4	8.00	–
Mark Thompson	19	80	140	11	151	7.55	1 paid
Paul Burnett	3	12	19	2	21	7.00	–
Andrew Bargh	16	77	107	18	125	6.49	–
James Purchase	21	98	126	18	144	5.88	–
James Horton	5	17	20	3	23	5.41	–
Scott Campos	8	31	27	6	33	4.26	–
Trevor Heath	16	58	38	16	54	3.72	–
Chris Geer	2	7	2	1	3	1.71	–
Gareth Hickmott	2	7	2	0	2	1.14	–
Guests	2	7	7	3	10	5.71	–

(Karl White [1]; Tim Webster [1]).

CONFERENCE TROPHY

No	DATE	OPPONENTS	H/A	RESULT	Armstrong	Bates	Roynon	Smart	Thompson	Campos	Purchase	Heath	Collins	Johnson	Bargh
1	22/5	Wimbledon	H	W51-42	14 (5)	1 (2)	9+2 (4)	8 (4)	11+2 (5)	0 (1)	8+1 (7)	–	–		
2	5/6	Boston	A	L41-51	19 (7)	–	–	4+2 (5)	7 (6)	1 (3)	8+1 (6)	2+1 (3)	R/R	–	–
3	19/6	Weymouth	H	W49-43	16 (6)	–	–	10+1 (6)	R/R	1 (3)	–	3+2 (4)	–	8+1 (5)	11 (6)
4	26/6	Boston	H	L42-49	6 (2)	–	–	–	11+2 (5)	0 (3)	–	6+1 (5)	7 (5)	5 (4)	7+3 (6)
5	1/7	Weymouth	A	L37-56	14 (6)	–	–	–	8 (6)	–	3 (4)	0 (3)	R/R	5+2 (5)	7+2 (6)
6	6/7	Wimbledon	A	L40-50	11 (4)	–	–	–	8 (4)	2+1 (5)	5+2 (4)	4 (5)	–	5+1 (4)	5+2 (4)

TACTICAL SUBSTITUTE RIDES, AS INCLUDED IN THE SCORES GRID:

Match No. 2: Armstrong 4 points (TS); Match No. 5: Armstrong 4 points (TR); Bargh 2 points (TR).

CONFERENCE TROPHY AVERAGES

Rider	Mts	Rds	Pts	Bon	Tot	Avge	Max
Adam Roynon	1	4	9	2	11	11.00	–
Jon Armstrong	6	30	76	0	76	10.13	–
Mark Thompson	5	26	45	4	49	7.54	–
Lee Smart	3	15	22	3	25	6.67	–
Andrew Bargh	4	22	29	7	36	6.55	–
Chris Johnson	4	18	23	4	27	6.00	–

Aidan Collins	1	5	7	0	7	5.60	–
James Purchase	4	21	24	4	28	5.33	–
Trevor Heath	5	20	15	4	19	3.80	–
Matt Bates	1	2	1	0	1	2.00	–
Scott Campos	5	15	4	1	5	1.33	–

KNOCK-OUT CUP

(*Denotes aggregate victory)

No	DATE	OPPONENTS	H/A	RESULT	Armstrong	Bargh	Thompson	Horton	Smart	Purchase	Heath	Johnson
1	28/8	Oxford	H	W54-40	14 (5)	5+1 (4)	11+1 (5)	6+1 (4)	7 (4)	4+2 (4)	7+2 (4)	–
2	12/9	Oxford	A	L42-53*	8+1 (5)	3+1 (4)	13 (4)	1 (4)	10+1 (5)	6+1 (5)	1 (3)	–
3	7/10	Boston	A	W51-41	10+2 (5)	5+1 (4)	15 (5)	–	6+2 (4)	6+2 (5)	3+1 (3)	6 (4)
4	9/10	Boston	H	W60-33*	10+1 (4)	9+2 (5)	11 (4)	–	11+1 (4)	13+2 (6)	6+3 (6)	0 (1)
5	14/10	Weymouth	A	L40-54	11 (5)	5+1 (4)	3+1 (4)	–	5 (4)	3+2 (5)	1 (3)	12 (5)
6	16/10	Weymouth	H	W51-45	12+1 (5)	8+1 (4)	11+1 (5)	–	5 (4)	5+1 (5)	1 (3)	9+2 (4)

TACTICAL RIDES, AS INCLUDED IN THE SCORES GRID:

Match No. 2: Thompson 6 points (TR); Smart 4 points (TR); Match No. 5: Armstrong 4 points (TR); Johnson 4 points (TR).

OTHER MEETINGS

18 March: Challenge

Boston 52 Mildenhall 44 (Jon Armstrong 20; Adam Roynon 11; James Horton 5+2; James Purchase 4+2; Mark Thompson 3; Scott Campos 1; Gareth Hickmott 0).

27 March: Challenge

Mildenhall 49 (Jon Armstrong 12; Adam Roynon 10+1; James Purchase 9+2; Mark Thompson 9; James Horton 8+1; Scott Campos 1+1; Gareth Hickmott 0; Bevan Gilbert-Jarrett 0) USA Dream Team 41 (Chris Kerr 14; T.J. Fowler 8; Neil Facchini 7+1; Tim Gomez 6+2; Dario Galvin 2+1; Dale Facchini 2; Brian Starr 2; Shaun Harmatiuk R/R).

10 April: Challenge

Mildenhall 46 (Jon Armstrong 15; Adam Roynon 7+1; Mark Thompson 6+1; Chris Geer 6+1; Scott Campos 6; James Horton 3; James Purchase 3) Boston 42.

12 June: Challenge

Mildenhall 51 (Jon Armstrong 15; Lee Smart 10; Chris Johnson 8+1; Mark Thompson 8; Scott Campos 6+1; Trevor Heath 4; James Purchase 0) Buxton 42.

30 October: The Big Bang! (30th Anniversary Meeting)

Team 'C' 27 (Ritchie Hawkins 9; Daniel King 8; Jon Armstrong 7; Lee Smart 3), Team 'B' 26 (James Brundle 10; Jason King 8; Daniel Giffard 5; James Purchase 3), Team 'D' 26 (Sean Wilson 10; Lewis Bridger 8; Chris Johnson 5; Mark Thompson 3), Team 'A' 17 (Shaun Tacey 11; Olly Allen 5; Trevor Heath 1; Chris Schramm 0).

INDIVIDUAL MEETINGS

3 April: British Under-21 Championship qualifying round

1st Ben Wilson <u>15</u>; 2nd Steve Boxall 14; 3rd James Brundle 12; Jason King 11; Barrie Evans 10; Adam Roynon 9; Luke Bowen 9; Darren Mallett 7; Lee Smart 7; Matthew Wright 6; Barry Burchatt 5; Harland Cook 5; James Theobald 4; Ross Parker 3; Scott Campos 2; Gary Cottham 1.

2 October: Europress Bronze Helmet

QUALIFYING SCORES: Jon Armstrong <u>15</u>; Lewis Bridger 12; Jamie Courtney 12; Mark Burrows 11; Lee Derbyshire 10; Darren Mallett 10; Chris Mills 8; Wayne Carter 7; Matthew Wright 7; Andre Cross 6; Billy Legg 5; Sean Stoddart 5; Mark Baseby (Res) 5; Karlis Ezergailis 4; James Purchase (Res) 1; Luke Bowen 0; Steve Boxall 0; Lee Smart 0. FIRST SEMI-FINAL: 1st Courtney; 2nd Armstrong; 3rd Mills; 4th Derbyshire. SECOND SEMI-FINAL: 1st Bridger; 2nd Burrows; 3rd Mallett; 4th Carter; FINAL: 1st Bridger; 2nd Courtney.

2 October: British Under-15 Championship (Round Seven)

1st Josh Auty <u>15</u>; 2nd Ben Taylor 14; 3rd Joe Haines 13; Brendan Johnson 11; Ben Hopwood 11; Kye Norton 10; George Piper 8; Adam Wrathall 7; Daniel Greenwood 6; Richard Franklin 6; Rickylee Beecroft 5; Jamie Pickard 4; Ben Reade 4; Scott Meakins 3; Ben Thompson 1; Aaron Baseby (Res) 1; Dan Kirkman 0; Tom Davies (Res) 0; Jack Butler (Res) 0. OVERALL SERIES POINTS: 1st Auty 68; 2nd Taylor 60; 3rd Haines 59; Hopwood 53; Piper 50; Wrathall 49; Brendan Johnson 46; Greenwood 41; George Jarvis 38; Norton 37; Thompson 32; Franklin 29; Kirkman 24; Reade 24; Meakins 23; Beecroft 23; Pickard 21; Davies 16, Butler 16, Ryan Goodger 16; Chris Widman 15; Baseby 8; Ben Johnson 6.

PAIRS MEETING

9 October: Steve Heath Memorial Pairs

1st Daniel King (20) & Andrew Bargh (9+1) = 29; 2nd Jon Armstrong (14+2) & Norbert Magosi (9+1) = 23; 3rd Jason King (14) & Artur Boginczuk (8+2) = 22; Mark Thompson (12+1) & Lee Smart (9+1) = 21; James Brundle (17) & James Purchase (2+1) = 19; Shaun Tacey (19) & Trevor Heath (0) = 19.

NEWPORT GMB MAVERICKS

NOTE: The information below relates only to the second Newport team. For details of the main side, please refer to the Premier League section.

ADDRESS: Hayley Stadium, Plover Close, Longditch Road, Queensway Meadows, Newport, South Wales, NS19 4SU.
CLUB CHAIRMAN: Tim Stone.
TRACK LENGTH: 285 metres.
CL TRACK RECORD: 60.27 Scott Pegler (9 September 2000).
FIRST MEETING: 30 May 1997.
YEARS OF OPERATION: 1997 Amateur League; 1998–2005 Conference League.

NOTE: In 1997 Newport shared their Amateur League fixtures with Exeter under the banner of 'Welsh Western Warriors'.

NEWPORT: From left to right, back row: Lee Dicken, Jamie Westacott, Karlis Ezergailis, Danny Warwick, Sam Hurst, Billy Legg. Front, on bike: Karl Mason.

CLUB HONOURS

LEAGUE CHAMPIONS: 1999.

RIDER ROSTER 2005

Russell BARNETT; Lewis DALLAWAY; Lee DICKEN; Karlis EZERGAILIS; Sam HURST; Billy LEGG; Karl MASON; Scott PEGLER; Matt TUTTON; Carl WARWICK; Danny WARWICK; Jamie WESTACOTT.

OTHER APPEARANCES/GUESTS (official matches only):
Paul BURNETT.

CONFERENCE LEAGUE

(*Denotes bonus-point victory)

No	DATE	OPPONENTS	H/A	RESULT	Pegler	Dallaway	Westacott	D. Warwick	Mason	Legg	Hurst	Ezergailis	Barnett	C. Warwick	Dicken	Others
1	17/4	Mildenhall	A	L37-54	7 (4)	3+1 (3)	8+1 (5)	5+1 (4)	8 (5)	4+1 (4)	2+2 (5)	–	–	–	–	–
2	27/4	Stoke	A	L35-57	R/R	–	7+3 (5)	5 (5)	10+1 (6)	4+1 (3)	7+2 (6)	2 (5)	–	–	–	–
3	8/5	Stoke	H	W45-41	R/R	–	12 (6)	2+2 (4)	9+1 (6)	7+2 (6)	3+1 (3)	12+1 (5)	–	–	–	–
4	18/5	Wimbledon	A	L27-64	R/R	1 (4)	11 (6)	1 (5)	4 (5)	8 (5)	2+1 (5)	–	–	–	–	–
5	22/5	Armadale	H	W45-43	R/R	–	8+1 (6)	5+1 (5)	6 (4)	4+1 (4)	6+2 (5)	16 (6)	–	–	–	–
6	19/6	Scunthorpe	H	L42-47	R/R	0 (2)	7+1 (5)	6+1 (4)	12 (6)	4 (4)	2+1 (4)	11+1 (5)	–	–	–	–
7	26/6	Buxton	A	L41-48	R/R	–	9+1 (6)	8+1 (5)	7+1 (6)	3 (4)	5+2 (4)	9 (5)	–	–	–	–
8	3/7	Boston	H	L44-48	R/R	–	–	9+1 (5)	10+1 (6)	5 (5)	4+2 (5)	16 (6)	0 (3)	–	–	–
9	5/8	Weymouth	A	L37-53	–	–	R/R	9 (4)	7+1 (6)	4+1 (5)	7+3 (5)	8 (6)	–	2 (4)	–	–
10	7/8	Oxford	H	W67-26	–	–	8 (4)	11+1 (4)	13+2 (5)	7+2 (4)	13+2 (5)	11+1 (4)	–	–	–	4+1 (4)
11	13/8	Sittingbourne	A	W46-45	–	–	R/R	11 (5)	11+3 (6)	6+2 (7)	4+1 (3)	13 (6)	–	–	–	1+1 (3)
12	21/8	Wimbledon	H	W49-46	–	–	R/R	9+1 (5)	11+1 (5)	3+1 (5)	13+2 (5)	11+2 (6)	–	2+1 (4)	–	–
13	28/8	Sittingbourne	H	L46-47	–	–	R/R	12+1 (6)	11 (4)	7+3 (7)	3 (3)	10 (6)	3 (4)	–	–	–
14	29/8	Scunthorpe	A	L35-57	–	–	R/R	13+1 (6)	–	5+2 (6)	–	7+2 (6)	1 (3)	–	–	9+1 (9)
15	3/9	Rye House	A	L40-56	–	–	R/R	9+1 (5)	10+1 (6)	3 (5)	4 (4)	11+1 (6)	–	3 (4)	–	–
16	4/9	Mildenhall	H	W48-43	–	–	R/R	12 (5)	11+1 (5)	2+1 (4)	6+2 (6)	13 (6)	–	4 (4)	–	–
17	11/9	Rye House	H	W58-38*	–	–	R/R	7+2 (5)	DNR	9+4 (6)	12+2 (7)	14 (6)	–	–	16+1 (6)	–
18	18/9	Boston	A	L38-52	–	–	–	6+1 (5)	R/R	6+1 (6)	6+2 (5)	10+1 (6)	0 (3)	–	10 (5)	–
19	1/10	Armadale	A	L34-61	–	–	–	3 (5)	R/R	6+1 (5)	2 (4)	9 (6)	0 (4)	–	14 (6)	–
20	6/10	Oxford	A	L39-54*	–	–	3+1 (5)	6+1 (4)	R/R	7+3 (6)	5+2 (6)	4 (4)	–	–	14 (5)	–
21	9/10	Weymouth	H	W52-43	–	–	7+1 (3)	7 (4)	9+1 (4)	8+3 (5)	4+2 (4)	8+2 (5)	–	–	9+1 (5)	–
22	16/10	Buxton	H	W63-28*	–	–	9+3 (4)	14+1 (5)	12+1 (5)	0 (4)	6+2 (4)	10+2 (4)	–	–	12 (4)	–

DETAILS OF OTHER RIDERS:

Match No. 10: Matt Tutton 4+1 (4); Match No. 11: Matt Tutton 1+1 (3); Match No. 14: Paul Burnett 8 (5); Matt Tutton 1+1 (4).

TACTICAL SUBSTITUTE AND TACTICAL RIDES, AS INCLUDED IN THE SCORES GRID:

Match No. 1: Pegler 4 points (TR); Mason 0 points (TR); Match No. 2: Mason 4 points (TS); Westacott 2 points (TR); Ezergailis 0 points (TR); Match No. 4: Westacott 4 points (TR); Mason 0 points (TR); Match No. 14: D. Warwick 4 points (TR); Tutton 0 points (TR); Match No. 15: D. Warwick 6 points (TR); Mason 4 points (TS); Hurst 2 points (TR); Match No. 19: Ezergailis 6 points (TR); Dicken 4 points (TR); Match No. 20: Dicken 6 points (TR).

CONFERENCE LEAGUE AVERAGES

Rider	Mts	Rds	Pts	Bon	Tot	Avge	Max
Lee Dicken	6	31	70	2	72	9.29	1 full
Karlis Ezergailis	20	109	202	13	215	7.89	2 paid
Karl Mason	17	90	157	15	172	7.64	1 paid
Jamie Westacott	11	55	86	12	98	7.13	1 paid
Danny Warwick	22	105	165	17	182	6.93	2 paid
Sam Hurst	21	98	115	33	148	6.04	2 paid
Billy Legg	22	110	112	29	141	5.13	–
Scott Pegler	1	4	5	0	5	5.00	–
Matt Tutton	3	11	6	3	9	3.27	–
Carl Warwick	4	16	11	1	12	3.00	–
Lewis Dallaway	2	9	4	1	5	2.22	–
Russell Barnett	5	17	4	0	4	0.94	–
Guest	1	5	8	0	8	6.40	–

(Paul Burnett [1]).

KNOCK-OUT CUP

(*Denotes aggregate victory)

No	DATE	OPPONENTS	H/A	RESULT	Pegler	Ezergailis	Westacott	D. Warwick	Mason	Legg	Hurst	C. Warwick	Dicken
1	27/3	Rye House	H	W56-38	8+2 (4)	6+1 (4)	13 (5)	5+1 (4)	9+2 (4)	5+1 (4)	10+3 (5)	–	–
2	2/5	Rye House	A	L40-50*	1+1 (3)	6 (4)	12 (4)	7+2 (5)	8 (5)	0 (1)	6+2 (6)	–	–
3	23/9	Weymouth	A	L43-51	–	8 (4)	–	5+1 (6)	R/R	7+3 (6)	15+3 (6)	0 (3)	8+1 (5)
4	9/10	Weymouth	H	L41-50	–	7 (5)	7 (5)	2+1 (4)	6+1 (4)	5+3 (4)	6+1 (4)	–	8 (4)

TACTICAL RIDES, AS INCLUDED IN THE SCORES GRID:

Match No. 2: Westacott 6 points (TR); Match No. 3: Hurst 6 points (TR); Ezergailis 4 points (TR).

OTHER MEETINGS

28 March: Challenge

Young Wales 47 (Tom Brown 17+2; Jamie Westacott 15; Darren Hatton 7; Matt Tutton 4+1; Russell Barnett 4; David Tutton 0; Tony Atkin R/R) USA Dream Team 48 (Chris Kerr 16; Dario Galvin 8; Tim Gomez 7+1; Neil Facchini 6+2; T.J. Fowler 5; Brian Starr 4+1; Dale Facchini 2; Shaun Harmatiuk R/R).

31 July: Conference League

Newport 19 (Danny Warwick 6; Karlis Ezergailis 5; Billy Legg 3+2; Sam Hurst 3; Karl Mason 2+1; Russell Barnett 0; Scott Pegler R/R) Weymouth 17 – meeting abandoned after heat six.

INDIVIDUAL MEETING

14 August: British Under-15 Championship (Round Five)

1st Josh Auty 15; 2nd Ben Taylor 14; 3rd Joe Haines 13; Brendan Johnson 12; George Piper 11; Daniel Greenwood 10; Ben Thompson 8; Richard Franklin 7; Jamie Pickard 6; Ben Reade 6; Tom Davies 4; Jack Butler 4; Scott Meakins 2; Ben Hopwood 1; Dan Kirkman 0; Chris Widman 0.

OXFORD SILVER MACHINE ACADEMY

NOTE: The information below relates only to the second Oxford team. For details of the main side, please refer to the Elite League section.

ADDRESS: Oxford Stadium, Sandy Lane, Cowley, Oxford, OX4 6LJ.
CLUB CHAIRMAN: Nigel Wagstaff.
TRACK LENGTH: 297 metres.
CL TRACK RECORD: 60.89 seconds – Andy Smith (6 June 2003) & Daniel Giffard (6 October 2005).
FIRST MEETING: 25 May 1997.
YEARS OF OPERATION: 1997 Amateur League; 2003–05 Conference League.

CLUB HONOURS

LEAGUE CHAMPIONS: 2005.

RIDER ROSTER 2005

Marc ANDREWS; Ben BARKER; Craig BRANNEY; John BRANNEY; Jamie COURTNEY; Scott COURTNEY; Kyle HUGHES; Sam MARTIN; Chris MILLS; Jason NEWITT; Jamie ROBERTSON; Ricky SCARBORO.

OTHER APPEARANCES/GUESTS (official matches only):
Russell BARNETT.

OXFORD: From left to right, back row: Marc Andrews, Sam Martin, Jamie Courtney, Ben Barker, Scott Courtney, Kyle Hughes, Bryn Williams (Team Manager). Front, kneeling: Jason Newitt, Craig Branney, Chris Mills, Christopher Bint (Mascot).

CONFERENCE LEAGUE

(*Denotes bonus-point victory)

No	DATE	OPPONENTS	H/A	RESULT	C. Branney	Barker	J. Branney	J. Courtney	Martin	Hughes	Mills	Robertson	Newitt	Others
1	3/4	Buxton	A	D45-45	R/R	11+2 (6)	7+2 (5)	13 (6)	5+2 (4)	3+1 (4)	–			6+1 (5)
2	17/4	Scunthorpe	A	W49-44	14 (5)	10+3 (6)	6+2 (5)	10 (6)	4+1 (4)	5+1 (4)	R/R			
3	24/4	Sittingbourne	A	D45-45	R/R	7+2 (5)	4+1 (5)	16 (6)	4+1 (3)	6 (5)	8+3 (6)			
4	28/4	Buxton	H	W63-31*	12 (4)	9 (4)	9+4 (5)	13 (5)	2+1 (4)	9+3 (4)	9+3 (4)			
5	28/4	Sittingbourne	H	W53-37*	8 (4)	9+2 (5)	5+1 (4)	11 (4)	4+1 (4)	6+1 (4)	10+2 (5)			
6	14/5	Armadale	A	W53-41	9+2 (4)	13+1 (5)	4+1 (4)	10 (5)	5+1 (4)	3+2 (4)	9+2 (4)			
7	30/5	Weymouth	A	L44-45	13+1 (5)	13+1 (5)	0 (3)	4 (3)	1+1 (5)	7+1 (5)	6+2 (4)			
8	3/7	Mildenhall	A	D46-46	11+1 (5)	4+2 (4)	2 (4)	16 (5)	1 (3)	9+1 (5)	3+1 (4)			
9	31/7	Boston	A	W53-45	9 (4)	10+2 (4)	5+1 (4)	12+1 (5)	2 (4)	8+2 (5)	7 (4)			
10	3/8	Stoke	A	L43-50	R/R	2+2 (2)	11+1 (5)	11+2 (7)	4+1 (5)	2+1 (5)	13 (6)			
11	4/8	Rye House	H	W58-35	12+2 (5)	–	5+2 (4)	15 (5)	7 (5)	7+2 (4)	–	11 (4)	1 (3)	
12	4/8	Scunthorpe†	H	W50-30*	12 (4)	–	7+1 (3)	9+2 (4)	2+1 (4)	8+1 (4)	–	10+1 (4)	2+1 (3)	
13	7/8	Newport	A	L26-67	R/R	–	14 (6)	–	7 (7)	0 (1)	2 (2)	–	3 (7)	0 (5)
14	4/9	Rye House	A	W46-44*	16 (6)	R/R	9 (5)	–	4+1 (7)	–	16+2 (6)	–	1 (3)	0 (3)
15	8/9	Wimbledon	H	W46-44	14+2 (6)	R/R	4+2 (5)	10 (5)	1 (3)	5 (4)	12+1 (7)	–		
16	12/9	Mildenhall♦	H	W49-38*	–	R/R	4+2 (5)	12+1 (5)	7+3 (4)	6 (4)	13 (5)	–		7 (5)
17	21/9	Wimbledon	A	L43-50	16+2 (6)	R/R	8+1 (5)	6+1 (5)	2 (4)	1 (4)	10+1 (6)	–		
18	22/9	Stoke	H	W53-43*	15 (6)	R/R	5+3 (5)	10 (5)	3 (3)	8+1 (5)	12+3 (6)	–		
19	26/9	Armadale♣	H	W55-18*	11+1 (4)	R/R	9+3 (4)	14+1 (5)	5 (3)	8+2 (4)	8+1 (4)	–		
20	26/9	Boston	H	W66-27*	13+2 (5)	R/R	9+2 (6)	11+3 (5)	7+2 (4)	11+3 (5)	15 (5)	–		
21	6/10	Weymouth	H	W51-45*	13+1 (5)	R/R	–	14 (5)	6 (5)	9+1 (5)	7+1 (5)	–	2 (4)	0 (1)
22	6/10	Newport	H	W54-39	15 (5)	–	–	9+1 (4)	8+1 (6)	DNR	13+2 (5)	–	–	9+1 (7)

NOTE: Craig Branney is not credited with a paid maximum in the home match v. Armadale, as the meeting was abandoned prior to the completion of his programmed rides. Similarly, John Branney is not credited with a paid maximum in the home encounter against Armadale.

†Meeting abandoned after heat thirteen, with the result permitted to stand.

♦Meeting abandoned after heat fourteen, with the result permitted to stand.

♣Meeting abandoned after heat twelve, with the result permitted to stand.

DETAILS OF OTHER RIDERS:

Match No. 1: Ricky Scarboro 6+1 (5); Match No. 13: Russell Barnett 0 (5); Match No. 14: Marc Andrews 0 (3); Match No. 16: Scott Courtney 7 (5); Match No. 21: Marc Andrews 0 (1); Match No. 22: Scott Courtney 8+1 (4); Marc Andrews 1 (3).

TACTICAL SUBSTITUTE AND TACTICAL RIDES, AS INCLUDED IN THE SCORES GRID:

Match No. 8: J. Courtney 6 points (TR); Match No. 10: J. Branney 6 points (TR): J. Courtney 0 points (TS); Match No. 13: J. Branney 6 points (TR); Newitt 2 points (TS); Mills 0 points (TR); Match No. 15: Mills 2 points (TS); Match No. 17: C. Branney 6 points (TR).

CONFERENCE LEAGUE AVERAGES

Rider	Mts	Rds	Pts	Bon	Tot	Avge	Max
Jamie Robertson	2	8	21	1	22	11.00	–
Craig Branney	17	83	210	14	224	10.80	3 full; 1 paid

Jamie Courtney	20	100	223	12	235	9.40	1 full; 1 paid
Ben Barker	10	46	88	17	105	9.13	1 paid
Chris Mills	18	88	172	24	196	8.91	1 full; 3 paid
Scott Courtney	2	9	15	1	16	7.11	–
Kyle Hughes	20	85	121	23	144	6.78	1 paid
John Branney	20	92	121	29	150	6.52	–
Ricky Scarboro	1	5	6	1	7	5.60	–
Sam Martin	22	95	91	17	108	4.55	–
Jason Newitt	5	20	8	1	9	1.80	–
Marc Andrews	3	7	1	0	1	0.57	–
Guest	1	5	0	0	0	0.00	–

(Russell Barnett [1]).

KNOCK-OUT CUP

(*Denotes aggregate victory)

No	DATE	OPPONENTS	H/A	RESULT	Mills	Barker	J. Courtney	J. Branney	C. Branney	Martin	Hughes	S. Courtney	Newitt	Andrews
1	26/5	Wimbledon	H	W60-33	6+3 (4)	12+1 (5)	15 (5)	8+2 (4)	12 (4)	0 (3)	7+2 (5)	–	–	–
2	26/6	Wimbledon	A	L44-46*	12 (6)	8 (5)	12+1 (6)	6+3 (5)	R/R	3 (4)	3+3 (4)	–	–	–
3	28/8	Mildenhall	A	L40-54	–	–	R/R	12+2 (6)	18 (6)	0 (1)	–	7 (6)	2+1 (5)	1 (6)
4	12/9	Mildenhall	H	W53-42	7+1 (5)	R/R	18 (6)	6+2 (5)	13 (6)	3+1 (3)	6+1 (5)	–	–	–

TACTICAL SUBSTITUTE AND TACTICAL RIDES, AS INCLUDED IN THE SCORES GRID:

Match No. 3: J. Branney 4 points (TR); C. Branney 4 points (TR); S. Courtney 0 points (TS).

RYE HOUSE ELMSIDE RAIDERS

NOTE: The information below relates only to the second Rye House team. For details of the main side, please refer to the Premier League section.

ADDRESS: Rye House Stadium, Rye Road, Hoddesdon, Hertfordshire, EN11 0EH.
CLUB CHAIRMEN: Len Silver & Hazal Naylor.
TRACK LENGTH: 271 metres.
FIRST MEETING: 1 April 2002
CL TRACK RECORD: 57.0 seconds – Edward Kennett (21 April 2003).
YEARS OF OPERATION: 2002-05 Conference League.

CLUB HONOURS

FOUR-TEAM CHAMPIONS: 2003.

RIDER ROSTER 2005

Luke BOWEN; Steve BOXALL; Barry BURCHATT; Harland COOK; Gary COTTHAM; Daniel HALSEY; Trevor HARDING; Chris JOHNSON; Robert MEAR; Ben POWELL; Shane WALDRON; Karl WHITE.

OTHER APPEARANCES/GUESTS (official matches only):
Scott RICHARDSON.

CONFERENCE LEAGUE

(*Denotes bonus-point victory)

No	DATE	OPPONENTS	H/A	RESULT	Boxall	Johnson	Cook	Burchatt	Bowen	Mear	Cottham	White	Halsey	Powell	Waldron	Other
1	28/3	Boston	H	W54.5-37.5	10 (4)	R/R	12+2 (5)	13+2 (5)	10½(5)	5+3 (5)	4 (4)	0 (2)	-	-	-	-
2	16/4	Mildenhall	H	W47-42	R/R	13 (6)	5+2 (5)	10+2 (6)	6+1 (4)	0 (3)	13+3 (6)	-	-	-	-	-
3	17/4	Buxton	A	L44-47	-	R/R	13 (5)	10+2 (6)	13 (6)	0 (3)	3 (5)	-	5+1 (5)	-	-	-
4	24/4	Scunthorpe	A	L38-55	R/R	1+1 (1)	15+1 (6)	6 (5)	-	-	7 (7)	3+1 (4)	6+1 (6)	-	-	0 (1)
5	8/5	Wimbledon	A	L40-52	-	-	17 (6)	6 (5)	R/R	-	5 (4)	2 (3)	2+1 (7)	8+1 (6)	-	-
6	30/5	Wimbledon	H	W52-43	12+2 (5)	-	10+1 (4)	7+2 (4)	12 (5)	-	3 (4)	-	0 (4)	8 (4)	-	-
7	12/6	Armadale	H	W51-41	13 (5)	-	5+1 (4)	9 (5)	6+1 (4)	-	6+4 (4)	-	5+1 (4)	7 (4)	-	-
8	18/6	Sittingbourne	H	W59-36	14+1 (5)	-	10+2 (4)	14+1 (5)	7+1 (4)	-	6+1 (4)	1 (4)	7+1 (4)	R/R	-	-
9	30/7	Armadale	A	L43-46*	R/R	-	-	13 (6)	13 (6)	-	11+1 (7)	0 (1)	4+1 (6)	2 (4)	-	-
10	4/8	Oxford	A	L35-58	R/R	-	-	3 (3)	14 (6)	-	8+2 (7)	2+1 (4)	4 (5)	4+1 (5)	-	-
11	6/8	Scunthorpe	H	W53-42	R/R	-	12 (5)	-	14 (6)	-	3 (3)	5+2 (4)	8+3 (6)	11+3 (6)	-	-
12	14/8	Mildenhall	A	L39-51	11+1 (5)	-	5 (4)	-	6+2 (4)	-	9 (5)	1+1 (4)	0 (3)	7+3 (5)	-	-
13	20/8	Buxton	H	W64-30*	14+1 (5)	-	7+1 (4)	13+2 (5)	11 (4)	-	7+4 (4)	-	7+2 (5)	5+1 (3)	-	-
14	28/8	Boston	A	W49-40*	R/R	-	2+1 (4)	10+1 (6)	7 (5)	-	10+2 (5)	-	6+2 (4)	14+1 (6)	-	-
15	29/8	Stoke	H	W60-34	10+1 (4)	-	6+1 (4)	10 (4)	13+1 (5)	-	11+2 (5)	-	7+2 (5)	3+1 (3)	-	-
16	3/9	Newport	H	W56-40	R/R	-	7+3 (4)	13 (5)	13+1 (5)	-	9 (4)	-	4+1 (4)	7 (4)	3 (4)	-
17	4/9	Oxford	H	L44-46	R/R	-	6+1 (5)	12 (6)	5 (5)	-	9+1 (5)	-	4+1 (3)	5+3 (4)	3+1 (2)	-
18	7/9	Stoke	A	L40-50*	R/R	-	-	5+1 (5)	11 (6)	-	7+1 (7)	1 (3)	-	15 (6)	1+1 (3)	-
19	11/9	Newport	A	L38-58	R/R	-	-	16+1 (6)	4 (5)	-	1 (5)	2 (4)	-	14 (6)	1 (4)	-
20	16/9	Weymouth	A	L40-53	-	-	R/R	9 (5)	6 (4)	-	2+1 (3)	3+2 (4)	7+1 (6)	11 (5)	2+1 (3)	-
21	17/9	Weymouth	H	W51-45	11+1 (4)	-	-	4+2 (5)	15 (5)	-	8 (4)	1 (3)	6+3 (5)	6 (4)	-	-
22	1/10	Sittingbourne	A	W49-41*	-	-	R/R	16 (6)	15+1 (6)	-	6+2 (6)	1 (4)	1+1 (3)	10+2 (5)	-	-

DETAILS OF OTHER RIDER:

Match No. 4: Scott Richardson 0 (1).

TACTICAL RIDES, AS INCLUDED IN THE SCORES GRID:

Match No. 3: Cook 6 points (TR); Match No. 4: Cook 6 points (TR); Match No. 5: Cook 6 points (TR); Powell 0 points (TR); Match No. 10: Bowen 4 points (TR); Cottham 2 points (TR); Match No. 19: Powell 6 points (TR); Burchatt 6 points (TR); Match No. 20: Powell 6 points (TR).

RYE HOUSE: From left to right, back row: Harland Cook, Shane Waldron, Barry Burchatt, John Sampford (Team Manager), Steve Boxall (on bike), Luke Bowen, Gary Cottham, Len Silver (Promoter). Front, kneeling: Chris Johnson, Robert Mear, Charlie Martin (Mascot), Karl White.

CONFERENCE LEAGUE AVERAGES

Rider	Mts	Rds	Pts	Bon	Tot	Avge	Max
Steve Boxall	8	37	95	7	102	11.03	3 paid
Chris Johnson	2	7	14	1	15	8.57	–
Luke Bowen	20	100	199.5	8	207.5	8.30	1 full
Barry Burchatt	20	103	196	16	212	8.23	3 paid
Harland Cook	15	69	123	16	139	8.06	1 paid
Ben Powell	17	80	131	16	147	7.35	–
Gary Cottham	22	108	147	24	171	6.33	–
Daniel Halsey	18	85	83	22	105	4.94	–
Shane Waldron	5	16	10	3	13	3.25	–
Robert Mear	3	11	5	3	8	2.91	–
Karl White	13	44	22	7	29	2.64	–
Guest	1	1	0	0	0	0.00	–

(Scott Richardson [1]).

KNOCK-OUT CUP

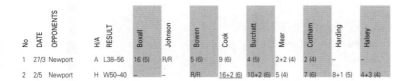

No	DATE	OPPONENTS	H/A	RESULT	Boxall	Johnson	Bowen	Cook	Burchatt	Mear	Cottham	Harding	Halsey
1	27/3	Newport	A	L38–56	16 (5)	R/R	5 (6)	9 (6)	4 (5)	2+2 (4)	2 (4)	–	–
2	2/5	Newport	H	W50–40	–	–	R/R	16+2 (6)	10+2 (6)	5 (4)	7 (6)	8+1 (5)	4+3 (4)

TACTICAL RIDES, AS INCLUDED IN THE SCORES GRID:

Match No. 1: Boxall 6 points (TR); Cook 2 points (TR).

SCUNTHORPE SCORPIONS

ADDRESS: Normanby Road, Scunthorpe, North Lincolnshire DN15 8QZ.
CLUB CHAIRMEN: Norman Beeney & Robert Godfrey.
TRACK LENGTH: 285 metres.
TRACK RECORD: 59.0 – Richard Hall (23 October 2005).
FIRST MEETING: 27 March 2005.
YEARS OF OPERATION: 2005 Conference League.

CLUB HONOURS

NONE.

RIDER ROSTER 2005

Josh AUTY; David BAKER; Byron BEKKER; Paul BURNETT; Wayne CARTER; Benji COMPTON; Richie DENNIS; Michael GODFREY; Grant HAYES; Ashley JOHNSON; Danny NORTON; Scott RICHARDSON; Ricky SCARBORO; David SPEIGHT; Tim WEBSTER; Chris WIDMAN.

OTHER APPEARANCES/GUESTS (official matches only):

Peter GEMMILL; Jessica LAMB; Keiran MORRIS.

CONFERENCE LEAGUE

(*Denotes bonus-point victory)

No	DATE	OPPONENTS	H/A	RESULT	Norton	Dennis	Compton	Carter	Hayes	Burnett	Johnson	Bekker	Richardson	Scarboro	Others
1	17/4	Oxford	H	L44-49	11 (5)	16+2 (6)	5+2 (4)	7 (4)	2 (3)	–	–	–	–	–	3+2 (8)
2	24/4	Rye House	H	W55-38	9 (4)	13+2 (5)	9+1 (4)	14 (5)	–	4+1 (4)	5+1 (4)	–	–	–	1 (4)
3	20/5	Weymouth	A	L42-54	3 (4)	16 (5)	4+2 (5)	11 (5)	1 (3)	4 (4)	3 (4)	–	–	–	
4	12/6	Sittingbourne†	A	W42-34	R/R	8+1 (4)	5+1 (4)	12 (4)	2 (4)	–	4+1 (4)	11+1 (4)	–	–	
5	18/6	Mildenhall	H	W50-43	7+3 (4)	10+1 (4)	9+1 (5)	12+1 (5)	1+1 (4)	–	3 (4)	8 (4)	–	–	
6	19/6	Newport	A	W47-42	8 (5)	11 (5)	5+3 (4)	10+1 (4)	3+1 (3)	–	5 (5)	5 (4)	–	–	
7	10/7	Wimbledon	H	W54-40	9 (4)	15 (5)	7+2 (4)	10 (5)	1 (4)	–	–	9+1 (4)	3 (4)	–	
8	24/7	Boston	H	W61-31	9 (4)	13+1 (5)	12+3 (5)	10+1 (4)	–	–	8+1 (5)	9+2 (4)	–	–	0 (3)
9	4/8	Oxford♦	A	L30-50	R/R	6 (4)	3+1 (4)	12+1 (5)	3+1 (5)	–	4+1 (4)	2+1 (4)	–	–	
10	6/8	Rye House	A	L42-53*	8 (5)	R/R	12+2 (6)	17+1 (6)	0 (4)	–	3+2 (5)	2 (3)	–	–	
11	7/8	Sittingbourne	H	W64-29*	12 (5)	R/R	13+2 (5)	14+1 (5)	10+3 (5)	–	8+2 (5)	7+1 (5)	–	–	0 (0)
12	21/8	Armadale	H	W50-44	9 (5)	R/R	11 (5)	16+1 (6)	6+1 (7)	–	4+1 (2)	4+1 (5)	–	–	
13	28/8	Buxton	A	L38-54	3 (5)	R/R	2+1 (4)	19 (6)	2 (4)	–	–	7 (6)	5 (5)	–	
14	29/8	Newport	H	W57-35*	12 (5)	R/R	14+1 (5)	14+1 (5)	9+2 (5)	–	–	3+1 (5)	5 (5)	–	
15	31/8	Stoke	A	W45-44	6+2 (5)	R/R	10 (6)	13+1 (6)	1 (4)	–	–	8+3 (5)	7+2 (4)	–	
16	3/9	Armadale	A	L38-58	–	R/R	–	16+1 (6)	6 (6)	–	6 (6)	9 (6)	–	–	1+1 (6)
17	4/9	Weymouth	H	L42-48	5 (5)	R/R	13+1 (6)	13+1 (6)	1+1 (3)	–	5 (5)	5+1 (5)	–	–	
18	11/9	Boston	A	L42-48*	7+1 (4)	R/R	11+1 (6)	9+2 (6)	–	–	2+2 (5)	5+3 (5)	–	–	8 (4)
19	14/9	Wimbledon	A	L31-63	–	R/R	4 (4)	16 (5)	1+1 (4)	–	2 (4)	1 (6)	–	6 (6)	1 (1)
20	18/9	Stoke	H	L41-49	–	5+2 (4)	6+1 (4)	11 (5)	3 (4)	–	2+2 (4)	9 (5)	–	5+2 (4)	
21	25/9	Mildenhall	A	L37-57	–	R/R	–	19 (6)	1 (4)	–	0 (2)	2+2 (5)	5 (7)	10 (6)	
22	31/10	Buxton	H	W60-37*	–	15 (5)	8 (4)	10+1 (4)	3+1 (4)	–	–	8+3 (4)	–	4+1 (4)	12+1 (5)

†Meeting abandoned after heat twelve, with the result permitted to stand.

♦Meeting abandoned after heat thirteen, with the result permitted to stand.

DETAILS OF OTHER RIDERS:

Match No. 1: David Speight 2+1 (4); David Baker 1+1 (4); Match No. 2: Chris Widman 1 (4); Match No. 8: Tim Webster 0 (3); Match No. 11: Michael Godfrey 0 (0); Match No. 16: Peter Gemmill 1+1 (3); Keiran Morris 0 (3); Match No. 18: Josh Auty 8 (4); Match No. 19: Jessica Lamb 1 (1); Match No. 22: Josh Auty 12+1 (5).

TACTICAL SUBSTITUTE AND TACTICAL RIDES, AS INCLUDED IN THE SCORES GRID:

Match No. 1: Dennis 6 points (TS); Match No. 3: Dennis 6 points (TR); Carter 4 points (TR); Compton 2 points (TS); Match

SCUNTHORPE: From left to right, back row: Kenny Smith (Team Manager), Ashley Johnson, Wayne Carter (on bike), Ricky Scarboro, Grant Hayes. Front, kneeling: Scott Richardson, Byron Bekker.

No. 9: Carter 4 points (TS); Bekker 0 points (TR); Match No. 10: Carter 6 points (TR); Compton 4 points (TR); Norton 4 points (TS); Match No. 13: Carter 6 points (TR); Richardson 2 points (TS); Bekker 0 points (TR); Match No. 16: Carter 6 points (TR); Bekker 4 points (TR); Johnson 4 points (TS); Match No. 19: Carter 6 points (TR); Scarboro 2 points (TR); Bekker 0 points (TS); Match No. 21: Carter 6 points (TR); Scarboro 4 points (TR).

CONFERENCE LEAGUE AVERAGES

Rider	Mts	Rds	Pts	Bon	Tot	Avge	Max
Richie Dennis	11	52	122	9	131	10.08	2 full; 1 paid
Wayne Carter	22	113	266	14	280	9.91	1 full; 2 paid
Josh Auty	2	9	20	1	21	9.33	–
Benji Compton	20	94	160	25	185	7.87	3 paid
Danny Norton	15	69	116	6	122	7.07	–
Byron Bekker	19	89	112	20	132	5.93	1 paid
Ricky Scarboro	4	20	22	3	25	5.00	–
Paul Burnett	2	8	8	1	9	4.50	–
Ashley Johnson	16	68	62	13	75	4.41	–
Scott Richardson	5	25	24	2	26	4.16	–
Jessica Lamb	1	1	1	0	1	4.00	–
Grant Hayes	19	80	56	12	68	3.40	–
David Speight	1	4	2	1	3	3.00	–
David Baker	1	4	1	1	2	2.00	–
Chris Widman	1	4	1	0	1	1.00	–
Tim Webster	1	3	0	0	0	0.00	–
Michael Godfrey	1	0	0	0	0	0.00	–
Guests	2	6	1	1	2	1.33	–

(Peter Gemmill [1]; Keiran Morris [1]).

CONFERENCE TROPHY

(*Denotes bonus-point victory)

No	DATE	OPPONENTS	H/A	RESULT	Norton	Burnett	Dennis	Compton	Carter	Johnson	Widman	Richardson	Bekker	Hayes
1	1/5	Buxton	A	L43–46	4+1 (4)	11+1 (5)	7+1 (4)	2+1 (4)	10 (5)	8 (5)	1 (3)	–	–	–
2	2/5	Buxton	H	W51–44*	13 (5)	5 (4)	13+2 (5)	9+1 (4)	6 (4)	5 (4)	0 (4)	–	–	–
3	15/5	Armadale	H	D46–46	11 (5)	4 (4)	13 (5)	6+1 (4)	5 (4)	4+1 (4)	–	3 (4)	–	–
4	26/6	Stoke	H	W55–39	R/R	–	15 (6)	7+1 (5)	13+1 (5)	6+3 (5)	–	–	10+2 (5)	4 (4)
5	13/7	Stoke	A	L35–58	9 (5)	–	6 (4)	6+1 (4)	9+1 (6)	1 (4)	–	–	4+1 (4)	0 (3)
6	16/7	Armadale	A	L42–53	4 (5)	–	R/R	13 (6)	13 (6)	4 (4)	–	–	6+1 (5)	2+2 (4)

TACTICAL SUBSTITUTE AND TACTICAL RIDES, AS INCLUDED IN THE SCORES GRID:

Match No. 5: Carter 2 points (TS); Dennis 2 points (TR); Norton 2 points (TR); Match No. 6: Carter 6 points (TR); Compton 6 points (TR); Norton 0 points (TS).

CONFERENCE TROPHY AVERAGES

Rider	Mts	Rds	Pts	Bon	Tot	Avge	Max
Richie Dennis	5	24	53	3	56	9.33	1 paid
Wayne Carter	6	30	52	2	54	7.20	–
Byron Bekker	3	14	20	4	24	6.86	–
Danny Norton	5	24	40	1	41	6.83	–
Benji Compton	6	27	40	5	45	6.67	–
Paul Burnett	3	13	20	1	21	6.46	–
Ashley Johnson	6	26	28	4	32	4.92	–
Scott Richardson	1	4	3	0	3	3.00	–
Grant Hayes	3	11	6	2	8	2.91	–
Chris Widman	2	7	1	0	1	0.57	–

KNOCK-OUT CUP

No	DATE	OPPONENTS	H/A	RESULT	Norton	Compton	Dennis	Burnett	Carter	Johnson	Richardson
1	29/5	Boston	A	L41-53	9+1 (5)	10+1 (6)	12 (6)	R/R	7+1 (6)	0 (3)	3 (4)
2	30/5	Boston	H	L40-49	5 (4)	0 (2)	14+1 (6)	4+1 (4)	11 (5)	6+1 (5)	0 (4)

TACTICAL SUBSTITUTE AND TACTICAL RIDES, AS INCLUDED IN THE SCORES GRID:

Match No. 1: Norton 6 points (TR); Carter 2 points (TS); Dennis 0 points (TR); Match No. 2: Dennis 2 points (TS).

OTHER MEETINGS

3 April: Challenge

Scunthorpe 42 (Richie Dennis 11+1; Wayne Carter 11; Benji Compton 8+1; Danny Norton 7; David Speight 3+1; Dean Wilson 2; Grant Hayes 0) Middlesbrough 49 (Paul Cooper 15; Luke Priest 11; Derek Sneddon 7; Adam McKinna 6+2; Gary Flint 4+1; Paul Burnett 4+1; Kriss Irving 2).

8 May: Conference League

Scunthorpe 25 (Richie Dennis 6; Wayne Carter 6; Paul Burnett 5+1; Danny Norton 5; Benji Compton 2+1; Ashley Johnson 1; Scott Richardson 0) Sittingbourne 23 – meeting abandoned after heat eight.

22 May: Challenge

Scunthorpe Select 45 (Andre Compton 13; Richie Dennis 9; Simon Lambert 7+1; Danny Norton 7; Benji Compton 6+2; Ashley Johnson 2+1; Paul Burnett 1+1) Halifax Select 45 (Garry Stead 13; Ben Wilson 12+1; Wayne Carter 8; Ross Parker 5+1; David Speight 4; Luke Priest 3; Michael Mitchell 0).

31 July: Challenge

Scunthorpe 53 (Richie Dennis 12+1; Danny Norton 11+1; Byron Bekker 9+2; Wayne Carter 8+2; Benji Compton 5+2; Grant Hayes 5+1; Ashley Johnson 3+1) Hull 40.

14 August: Conference League

Scunthorpe 35 (Wayne Carter 10; Danny Norton 9+1; Ashley Johnson 6+1; Byron Bekker 5+2; Paul Burnett 3+1; Grant Hayes 2+1; Richie Dennis R/R) Weymouth 31 – meeting abandoned after heat eleven.

8 October: Conference League

Scunthorpe 20 (Wayne Carter 6; Byron Bekker 4+1; Josh Auty 4+1; Ricky Scarboro 2; Benji Compton 2; Richie Dennis 2; Ashley Johnson 0) Buxton 16 – meeting abandoned after heat six.

16 October: Lincolnshire Trophy (first leg)

Scunthorpe 53 (Wayne Carter 13; Richie Dennis 9; Benji Compton 8+1; Byron Bekker 8+1; Ricky Scarboro 6+2; Scott Richardson 5+1; Josh Auty 4) Boston 41.

16 October: Lincolnshire Trophy (second leg)

Boston 45 Scunthorpe 47 (Josh Auty 11+3; Benji Compton 9+1; Richie Dennis 9; Wayne Carter 7+2; Ricky Scarboro 7+1; Byron Bekker 3; Scott Richardson 1 – Scunthorpe won 100-86 on aggregate.

23 October: Challenge

Scunthorpe 47 (Benji Compton 12; Wayne Carter 10+1; Richie Dennis 9+1; Josh Auty 8+1; Ricky Scarboro 4+3; Byron Bekker 4+1; Scott Richardson 0) Sheffield 43.

INDIVIDUAL MEETINGS

27 March: Scunthorpe Telegraph Trophy

QUALIFYING SCORES: Carl Wilkinson 15; Danny Norton 13; Paul Cooper 11; Jonathon Bethell 11; Wayne Carter 11; Darren Mallett 7; Lee Derbyshire 7; Charles Wright 7; Richie Dennis 7; Simon Lambert 7; Robert Hollingworth 7; Ricky Scarboro 7; Benji Compton 6; David Speight 2; Michael Pickering 1; Gary Flint 0. SEMI-FINAL: 1st Bethell; 2nd Carter; 3rd Cooper; 4th Derbyshire; FINAL: 1st Norton; 2nd Bethell; 3rd Carter; 4th Wilkinson.

10 April: British Under-21 Championship Qualifying Round

1st Jamie Robertson (after run-off) 12; 2nd Tommy Allen 12; 3rd William Lawson 12; Danny Norton 12; Simon Lambert 11; Karl Mason 10; Jack Hargreaves 9; Richie Dennis 7; Charles Wright 7; Andrew Tully 5; Benji Compton 5; Sam Hurst 5; Sean Stoddart 4; John Branney 4; Gary Beaton 2; Adam McKinna 2.

3 July: British Under-15 Championship (Round Four)

1st Josh Auty 15; 2nd Ben Taylor 14; 3rd George Jarvis 13; Ben Hopwood 10; George Piper 10; Kye Norton 9; Dan Kirkman 8; Daniel Greenwood 7; Ben Thompson 6; Ryan Goodger 6; Brendan Johnson 4; Tom Davies 4; Richard Franklin (Res) 3; Chris Widman 2; Scott Meakins 2; Joe Haines 2; Jack Butler (Res) 1.

PAIRS MEETING

3 July: Best Pairs

QUALIFYING SCORES: Benji Compton (12) & Paul Burnett (10+1) = 22; Danny Norton (16) & Scott Richardson (6) = 22; Richie Dennis (12+1) & Grant Hayes (5) = 17; Ashley Johnson (8) & Byron Bekker (7+1) = 15; Wayne Carter (14) & Chris Widman (0) = 14. FIRST SEMI-FINAL: 1st Norton; 2nd Johnson; 3rd Bekker; 4th Richardson; SECOND SEMI-FINAL: 1st Compton; 2nd Burnett; 3rd Dennis; 4th Hayes. FINAL: 1st Compton; 2nd Burnett; 3rd Johnson; 4th Bekker.

SITTINGBOURNE A.C. ASSOCIATES CRUSADERS

ADDRESS: The Old Gun Site, Old Ferry Road, Iwade, Sittingbourne, Kent, ME9 8SP.
CLUB CHAIRMAN: Graham Arnold.
TRACK LENGTH: 251 metres.
TRACK RECORD: 58.4 seconds – Edward Kennett (4 July 2004).
FIRST MEETING: 5 November 1972.
YEARS OF OPERATION: 1971 Training; 1972-93 Open & Training; 1994 British League Division Three; 1995 Academy League; 1996 Conference League; 1997-2003 Open & Training; 2004 Conference League Knock-Out Cup, Open & Training; 2005 Conference League.

CLUB HONOURS

NONE.

RIDER ROSTER 2005

Darren ANDREWS; Trevor BANKS; Aaron BASEBY; Mark BASEBY; Daniel BLAKE; Paul CANDY; James COCKLE; Peter COLLYER; Shane COLVIN; Andre CROSS; Stefan DE GROOT; Lee DICKEN; Carl DOWNS; Jordan FRAMPTON; Dean GARROD; Chris HUNT; David McALLAN; David MELDRUM; Wayne PARKER; Gary PHELPS; Karl RUSHEN; Ricky SCARBORO; Nick SIMMONS; James THEOBALD; Keith YORKE.

CONFERENCE LEAGUE

(*Denotes bonus-point victory)

No	DATE	OPPONENTS	H/A	RESULT	McAllan	Hunt	Cross	Frampton	M. Baseby	Cockle	Blake	Scarboro	Andrews	Theobald	Collyer	Others
1	24/4	Oxford	H	D45-45	15 (5)	5+1 (4)	9+1 (5)	7+2 (4)	4+1 (5)	–	–	–	–	–	–	5+1 (7)
2	28/4	Oxford	A	L37-53	15 (6)	–	2+1 (3)	6 (6)	4+1 (5)	10 (6)	–	–	–	–	–	0 (4)
3	1/5	Boston	A	L31-62	17 (6)	5 (5)	–	2 (5)	5 (6)	R/R	2 (4)	–	–	–	–	0 (4)
4	7/5	Armadale	A	L45-47	18 (6)	6 (5)	–	4+1 (5)	3+1 (5)	14+1 (6)	0 (3)	–	–	–	–	–
5	15/5	Wimbledon	H	L36-57	–	5 (4)	3+1 (4)	13+1 (6)	2 (5)	–	0 (3)	–	–	–	–	13+1 (8)
6	22/5	Weymouth	H	L39-55	–	11 (5)	3+1 (4)	7 (5)	2+2 (4)	–	1 (4)	–	–	–	–	15+1 (9)
7	29/5	Buxton	A	L36-56	–	7 (5)	–	2 (2)	5+2 (7)	R/R	0 (4)	14 (6)	8+2 (6)	–	–	–
8	10/6	Weymouth	A	L20-66	–	6+1 (5)	–	–	–	–	DNA	10 (5)	–	4 (5)	–	0 (5)
9	12/6	Buxton	H	L39-55	–	11 (4)	–	–	0 (2)	–	4 (6)	12 (5)	7 (4)	4+1 (5)	–	1 (4)
10	12/6	Scunthorpe†	H	L34-42	–	4 (2)	4+2 (4)	–	–	–	8 (4)	5 (3)	3+2 (3)	8+1 (4)	–	2+1 (4)
11	18/6	Rye House	A	L36-59	–	–	10 (5)	–	6+1 (5)	–	0 (3)	12 (5)	3+1 (4)	3+1 (4)	–	2 (4)
12	22/6	Wimbledon	A	L34-60	–	–	6 (4)	–	2 (5)	–	1+1 (3)	7 (5)	–	–	–	18+1 (13)
13	10/7	Mildenhall	A	L30-63	–	–	9 (5)	–	11+1 (7)	–	0 (3)	–	2+1 (3)	3 (4)	–	5+1 (7)
14	7/8	Scunthorpe	A	L29-64	–	–	3+1 (4)	3 (5)	8 (6)	–	–	–	–	2 (4)	–	13 (12)
15	13/8	Newport	H	L45-46	–	3 (4)	–	–	11+1 (6)	–	3+1 (3)	–	–	–	6+1 (4)	22+1 (13)

No	DATE	OPPONENTS	H/A	RESULT	McAllan	Hunt	Cross	Frampton	M. Baseby	Cockle	Blake	Scarboro	Andrews	Theobald	Collyer	Others
16	13/8	Mildenhall	H	L43-47	–	–	–	–	8 (5)	–	1+1 (3)	–	–	5+1 (4)	6+2 (4)	23+1 (14)
17	17/8	Stoke	A	L29-63	–	2 (2)	–	3 (5)	6 (6)	–	–	–	–	3+1 (4)	3 (4)	12+2 (9)
18	28/8	Newport	A	W47-46*	–	2+2 (2)	–	–	8+2 (5)	–	1 (5)	–	–	3 (4)	14+1 (5)	19+1 (9)
19	17/9	Stoke	H	L42-48	–	8+1 (4)	–	8+1 (4)	6 (5)	–	–	–	–	3+1 (4)	7+1 (4)	10+4 (9)
20	25/9	Armadale	H	L43-47	–	2 (2)	2+1 (4)	13+1 (7)	12+1 (6)	–	–	–	–	5+2 (4)	9+1 (6)	0 (1)
21	25/9	Boston	H	L42-48	–	–	5+1 (5)	5 (5)	7+2 (6)	–	2+1 (3)	–	–	12+1 (6)	11 (6)	R/R
22	1/10	Rye House	H	L41-49	–	4 (3)	5 (4)	–	15 (7)	–	0 (4)	–	–	7+1 (6)	10+2 (6)	0 (1)

†Meeting abandoned after heat twelve, with the result permitted to stand.

DETAILS OF OTHER RIDERS:

Match No. 1: Karl Rushen 1+1 (3); Dean Garrod 4 (4); Match No. 2: Stefan De Groot 0 (4); Tony Dart R/R; Match No. 3: Dean Garrod 0 (3); Keith Yorke 0 (1); Match No. 4: Tony Dart R/R; Match No. 5: Shane Colvin 13+1 (5); Carl Downs 0 (3); Match No. 6: Trevor Banks 10 (5); Wayne Parker 5+1 (4); Match No. 8: Wayne Parker 0 (3); Nick Simmons 0 (2); James Humby DNA; Match No. 9: Carl Downs 1 (4); Match No. 10: Stefan De Groot 2+1 (4); Match No. 11: Wayne Parker 2 (4); Match No. 12: Lee Dicken 14+1 (6); Carl Downs 3 (4); Stefan De Groot 1 (3); Match No. 13: Gary Phelps 3+1 (4); Carl Downs 2 (3); Match No. 14: Shane Colvin 9 (6); Keith Yorke 2 (3); Gary Phelps 2 (3); Match No. 15: Shane Colvin 11 (5); David Meldrum 10 (5); Karl Rushen 1+1 (3); Match No. 16: Shane Colvin 10+1 (5); David Meldrum 10 (5); Karl Rushen 3 (4); Match No. 17: Shane Colvin 11+1 (5); Paul Candy 1+1 (4); Match No. 18: David Meldrum 13+1 (5); Paul Candy 6 (4); Match No. 19: Shane Colvin 7+2 (5); Paul Candy 3+2 (4); Match No. 20: Aaron Baseby 0 (1); Shane Colvin R/R; Match No. 21: Shane Colvin R/R; Match No. 22: Aaron Baseby 0 (1); Shane Colvin R/R.

TACTICAL SUBSTITUTE AND TACTICAL RIDES, AS INCLUDED IN THE SCORES GRID:

Match No. 3: McAllan 6 points (TR); Hunt 2 points (TR); Match No. 4: Cockle 6 points (TR); Match No. 5: Colvin 4 points (TR); Frampton 2 points (TR); Match No. 6: Hunt 4 points (TR); Banks 4 points (TR); Match No. 7: Scarboro 4 points (TR); Andrews 2 points (TR); Match No. 8: Scarboro 4 points (TS); Simmons 0 points (TR); Theobald 0 points (TR); Match No. 9: Scarboro 6 points (TR); Andrews 2 points (TR); Match No. 10: Theobald 4 points (TS); Blake 4 points (TR); Match No. 11: Cross 6 points (TR); Scarboro 6 points (TR); Match No. 12: Scarboro 4 points (TR); Cross 2 points (TR); Dicken 2 points (TS); Match No. 13: Cross 4 points (TR); M. Baseby 2 points (TR); Match No. 14: M. Baseby 0 and 4 points (TR twice); Colvin 2 points (TS); Match No. 15: Colvin 4 points (TR); Match No. 17: Colvin 4 points (TR); Frampton 0 points (TR; ex 2 mins); Match No. 18: Collyer 6 points (TR).

CONFERENCE LEAGUE AVERAGES

Rider	Mts	Rds	Pts	Bon	Tot	Avge	Max
David McAllan	4	23	62	0	62	10.78	2 full
Lee Dicken	1	6	13	1	14	9.33	–
David Meldrum	3	15	33	1	34	9.07	–
Shane Colvin	6	31	54	5	59	7.61	–
James Cockle	2	12	21	1	22	7.33	–
Peter Collyer	8	39	63	8	71	7.28	–
Ricky Scarboro	6	29	48	0	48	6.62	–
Trevor Banks	1	5	8	0	8	6.40	–
Chris Hunt	15	56	78	5	83	5.93	–

SITTINGBOURNE: From left to right, back row: Jordan Frampton, Darren Andrews, Chris Hunt, Ricky Scarboro. Front, kneeling: Keith Yorke, Daniel Blake, Mark Baseby.

Darren Andrews	5	20	21	6	27	5.40	–
Jordan Frampton	12	59	72	6	78	5.29	–
Mark Baseby	20	108	122	15	137	5.07	–
Andre Cross	12	51	55	9	64	5.02	–
James Theobald	13	58	60	10	70	4.83	–
Paul Candy	3	12	10	3	13	4.33	–
Gary Phelps	2	7	5	1	6	3.43	–
Wayne Parker	3	11	7	1	8	2.91	–
Karl Rushen	3	10	5	2	7	2.80	–
Dean Garrod	2	7	4	0	4	2.29	–
Keith Yorke	2	4	2	0	2	2.00	–
Daniel Blake	15	55	21	4	25	1.82	–
Carl Downs	4	14	6	0	6	1.71	–
Stefan De Groot	3	11	3	1	4	1.45	–
Aaron Baseby	2	2	0	0	0	0.00	–
Nick Simmons	1	2	0	0	0	0.00	–

OTHER MEETINGS

26 March: Challenge

Sittingbourne 42 (Mark Baseby 11+2; Dean Garrod 9; Trevor Banks 8; James Theobald 6+2; Andre Cross 5+2; Daniel Blake 3+1; Chris Hunt 0) USA Dream Team 46 (Chris Kerr 15; Tim Gomez 8+1; Brian Starr 6; T.J. Fowler 5+1; Shaun Harmatiuk 5; Dale Facchini 4+1; Dario Galvin 3).

14 April: Challenge

Weymouth 64 Sittingbourne 30 (James Cockle 13; Andre Cross 5; Jordan Frampton 5; Chris Hunt 4+1; Dean Garrod 2; James Theobald 1; Mark Baseby 0).

8 May: Conference League

Scunthorpe 25 Sittingbourne 23 (Mark Baseby 8+1; David McAllan 5; Chris Hunt 4; Daniel Blake 2+2; Dean Garrod 2+1; Jordan Frampton 2+1; James Cockle R/R) – meeting abandoned after heat eight.

STOKE SAS SPITFIRES

NOTE: The information below relates only to the second Stoke team. For details of the main side, please refer to the Premier League section.

ADDRESS: Chesterton Stadium, Loomer Road, Chesterton, Newcastle-under-Lyme, Staffordshire, ST5 7LB.

CLUB CHAIRMAN: David Tattum.

TRACK LENGTH: 312 metres.

CL TRACK RECORD: 63.0 seconds – Barrie Evans (22 June 2005).

FIRST MEETING: 13 April 2003.

YEARS OF OPERATION: 2003 Conference Trophy; 2004–05 Conference League.

CLUB HONOURS

NONE.

RIDER ROSTER 2005

Marc ANDREWS; Andrew BLACKBURN; Mark BRADLEY; Wayne BROADHURST; Justin ELKINS; Barrie EVANS; Gary FLINT; Rob GRANT; Jack HARGREAVES; James HUMBY; Kriss IRVING; Gareth ISHERWOOD; Michael MITCHELL; Luke PRIEST; Joe REYNOLDS.

OTHER APPEARANCES/GUESTS (official matches only):
Martin ELLIOTT; David SPEIGHT; Keith YORKE.

CONFERENCE LEAGUE

(*Denotes bonus-point victory)

No	DATE	OPPONENTS	H/A	RESULT	Elkins	Flint	Priest	Hargreaves	Grant	Isherwood	Irving	Evans	Blackburn	Humby	Reynolds	Others
1	13/4	Buxton†	H	W46-30	9 (3)	6+1 (4)	11+1 (4)	7+2 (3)	9 (3)	4 (6)	0 (1)	–	–	–	–	–
2	24/4	Boston	A	L39-56	3 (3)	3 (4)	12+1 (5)	9+3 (5)	–	0 (5)	–	11 (4)	1 (4)	–	–	–
3	27/4	Newport	H	W57-35	12 (4)	5+1 (4)	8+2 (4)	15 (5)	–	3+1 (4)	–	13+2 (5)	1 (4)	–	–	–
4	8/5	Newport	A	L41-45*	–	3+1 (4)	11+1 (5)	–	6 (4)	–	–	15 (5)	–	3+1 (7)	3 (4)	0 (0)
5	18/5	Boston	H	W53-41	9+1 (4)	6+4 (4)	13+1 (5)	11+3 (5)	10 (4)	–	–	–	–	1 (3)	3 (5)	–
6	29/5	Mildenhall	A	L42-54	6+1 (4)	5 (4)	6+2 (4)	11 (5)	–	1 (5)	–	13 (5)	–	–	0 (3)	–
7	22/6	Armadale	H	W46-44	–	1 (4)	7+1 (4)	11 (5)	8+1 (4)	3+1 (5)	2+2 (3)	14 (5)	–	–	–	–
8	20/7	Wimbledon	H	W54-39	6 (4)	2+1 (3)	6+3 (5)	11 (4)	–	2+1 (3)	12+1 (6)	15 (5)	–	–	–	–
9	3/8	Oxford	H	W50-43	9 (5)	2+1 (4)	9 (4)	6 (4)	–	1+1 (3)	8+3 (5)	15 (5)	–	–	–	–
10	6/8	Armadale	A	L39-54	5 (4)	4+1 (5)	11+2 (6)	R/R	–	2 (4)	16+1 (6)	–	–	–	–	1 (5)
11	11/8	Weymouth	A	L40-53	2 (2)	4 (4)	9+1 (5)	10+1 (5)	–	1+1 (6)	0 (1)	14 (5)	–	–	–	–
12	17/8	Sittingbourne	H	W63-29	–	7+2 (5)	17 (6)	R/R	16 (6)	5+2 (4)	7+2 (4)	–	–	–	–	11+2 (5)
13	29/8	Rye House	A	L34-60	–	2 (4)	9 (6)	R/R	8 (5)	1 (3)	2 (6)	12 (6)	–	–	–	–
14	31/8	Scunthorpe	H	L44-45	–	0 (3)	12+1 (5)	8+1 (4)	4 (4)	1 (4)	5 (5)	14+1 (5)	–	–	–	–
15	4/9	Buxton	A	L43-47*	–	1 (4)	10+2 (6)	9 (6)	8+1 (5)	5+1 (4)	10+1 (5)	R/R	–	–	–	–
16	7/9	Rye House	H	W50-40	–	1 (4)	8+1 (4)	3+1 (2)	13+1 (5)	3+1 (4)	9 (6)	13+1 (5)	–	–	–	–
17	17/9	Sittingbourne	A	W48-42*	–	7+1 (5)	18 (6)	R/R	–	2 (4)	4+1 (6)	16+2 (6)	–	–	–	1 (3)
18	18/9	Scunthorpe	A	W49-41*	–	0 (3)	13 (6)	R/R	5 (5)	2 (4)	11+2 (6)	18 (6)	–	–	–	–
19	22/9	Oxford	A	L43-53	–	0 (2)	13+2 (5)	11+1 (5)	3 (4)	0 (4)	5+1 (5)	11 (5)	–	–	–	–
20	28/9	Wimbledon	A	L35-58	–	4 (5)	–	R/R	8 (7)	0 (4)	5 (5)	17 (6)	–	–	–	1+1 (3)
21	15/10	Mildenhall	H	W52-41	–	5 (4)	10+2 (5)	11+1 (4)	6+2 (4)	1+1 (4)	–	15 (5)	–	–	4+1 (4)	–
22	22/10	Weymouth	H	W63-32*	–	6+1 (4)	13+2 (5)	13+2 (5)	6 (4)	5+2 (4)	8+2 (4)	12 (4)	–	–	–	–

†Meeting abandoned after heat twelve, with the result permitted to stand.

DETAILS OF OTHER RIDERS:

Match No. 4: Michael Mitchell 0 (0); Match No. 10: David Speight 1 (5); Match No. 12: Wayne Broadhurst 11+2 (5); Match No. 17: Keith Yorke 1 (3); Match No. 20: Martin Elliott 1+1 (3).

TACTICAL SUBSTITUTE AND TACTICAL RIDES, AS INCLUDED IN THE SCORES GRID:

Match No. 2: Evans 6 points (TR); Priest 4 points (TR); Match No. 6: Evans 6 points (TR); Hargreaves 6 points (TR); Match No. 10: Irving 6 points (TR); Elkins 0 points (TR); Match No. 11: Hargreaves 4 points (TR); Evans 4 points (TR); Priest 2 points (TS); Match No. 13: Evans 6 points (TR); Grant 2 points (TR); Match No. 19: Priest 6 points (TR); Hargreaves 4 points (TR); Evans 2 points (TS); Match No. 20: Evans 6 points (TR); Grant 2 points (TS); Irving 0 points (TR).

CONFERENCE LEAGUE AVERAGES

Rider	Mts	Rds	Pts	Bon	Tot	Avge	Max
Barrie Evans	17	87	223	6	229	10.53	6 full; 3 paid
Wayne Broadhurst	1	5	11	2	13	10.40	–
Luke Priest	21	105	220	25	245	9.33	1 full; 2 paid
Jack Hargreaves	15	67	139	15	154	9.19	1 full; 2 paid
Justin Elkins	9	33	61	2	63	7.64	1 full
Rob Grant	14	64	108	5	113	7.06	–
Kriss Irving	16	74	101	16	117	6.32	–
Gary Flint	22	87	74	14	88	4.05	–
Joe Reynolds	4	16	10	1	11	2.75	–
Gareth Isherwood	20	84	42	12	54	2.57	–
James Humby	2	10	4	1	5	2.00	–
Keith Yorke	1	3	1	0	1	1.33	–
Andrew Blackburn	2	8	2	0	2	1.00	–
David Speight	1	5	1	0	1	0.80	–
Michael Mitchell	1	0	0	0	0	0.00	–
Guest	1	3	1	1	2	2.67	–

(Martin Elliott [1]).

CONFERENCE TROPHY

(*Denotes bonus-point/aggregate victory)

No	DATE	OPPONENTS	H/A	RESULT	Elkins	Flint	Priest	Hargreaves	Grant	Bradley	Isherwood	Mitchell	Reynolds	Evans	Irving
1	10/6	Armadale	A	L44-54	10 (3)	5+3 (4)	7+1 (5)	12+1 (5)	6 (4)	2+1 (4)	2+1 (5)	–	–	–	–
2	15/6	Buxton	H	W51-39	11 (4)	1 (4)	14+1 (5)	10+2 (4)	13+2 (5)	0 (3)	2 (5)	–	–	–	–
3	19/6	Buxton	A	L42-52	6 (4)	2 (4)	12 (5)		14 (5)		2 (5)	5+2 (4)	1+1 (3)	–	–
4	26/6	Scunthorpe	A	L39-55	10 (4)	3 (4)	10+1 (5)	–	10 (5)		1 (4)	4+1 (4)	1 (4)	–	–
5	13/7	Scunthorpe	H	W58-35*	11 (4)	1 (4)	12+2 (5)	9+2 (4)	–		3 (3)	–	–	12+1 (5)	10+2 (5)
6	10/8	Armadale	H	W50-46	11+1 (5)	5+2 (4)	9 (4)	10+1 (5)	7 (4)		1 (3)	–	–	–	7+3 (4)
7	9/9	Weymouth	A	W46-44		2+2 (4)	14 (6)	R/R	7 (5)		0 (3)	–	–	15+2 (6)	8+2 (6)
8	24/9	Weymouth	H	W52-41*		2+2 (4)	12+2 (5)	10+2 (4)	6 (4)		0 (1)	–	–	15 (5)	7+1 (7)
9	14/10	Armadale	A	L41-49		4+1 (4)	8+1 (5)	5+2 (4)	5+1 (4)		6+1 (7)	–	–	10 (5)	3 (1)
10	29/10	Armadale	H	L43-50		3+2 (4)	5+3 (4)	11 (5)	4 (4)		1 (3)	–	–	12 (5)	7 (5)

TACTICAL SUBSTITUTE AND TACTICAL RIDES, AS INCLUDED IN THE SCORES GRID:

Match No. 1: Elkins 6 points (TS); Hargreaves 6 points (TR); Priest 4 points (TR); Match No. 3: Priest 6 points (TR); Grant 4 points (TR); Match No. 4: Elkins 4 points (TR); Priest 4 points (TR).

STOKE: From left to right, back row: Jack Hargreaves, Rob Grant, Gary Flint, Barrie Evans, David Tattum (Promoter/Team Manager). Front, kneeling: Gareth Isherwood, Kriss Irving. On bike: Luke Priest.

CONFERENCE TROPHY AVERAGES

Rider	Mts	Rds	Pts	Bon	Tot	Avge	Max
Barrie Evans	5	26	64	3	67	10.31	1 full
Jack Hargreaves	7	31	64	10	74	9.55	2 paid
Justin Elkins	6	24	54	1	55	9.17	–
Luke Priest	10	49	96	11	107	8.73	1 paid
Rob Grant	9	40	70	3	73	7.30	1 paid
Kriss Irving	6	28	42	8	50	7.14	–
Michael Mitchell	2	8	9	3	12	6.00	–
Gary Flint	10	40	28	12	40	4.00	–
Gareth Isherwood	10	39	18	2	20	2.05	–
Mark Bradley	2	7	2	1	3	1.71	–
Joe Reynolds	2	7	2	1	3	1.71	–

KNOCK-OUT CUP

No	DATE	OPPONENTS	H/A	RESULT	Evans	Flint	Elkins	Hargreaves	Priest	Isherwood	Andrews	Irving
1	12/8	Boston	A	L35-59	11 (5)	1 (4)	2 (4)	13 (5)	7+1 (5)	1 (4)	0 (3)	–
2	14/8	Boston	H	W54-39	8 (5)	5+1 (4)	R/R	15+1 (6)	13+2 (6)	3 (4)	–	10+2 (5)

TACTICAL RIDES, AS INCLUDED IN THE SCORES GRID:

Match No. 1: Hargreaves 6 points (TR); Evans 2 points (TR).

OTHER MEETING

23 March: Challenge

Stoke 66 (Barrie Evans 15; Kriss Irving 14+2; Jack Hargreaves 12+1; Luke Priest 8+3; Gary Flint 6+3; Justin Elkins 6; Gareth Isherwood 5+2) USA Dream Team 24 (T.J. Fowler 13+1; Tim Gomez 6; Dario Galvin 2; Shaun Harmatiuk 1; Chris Kerr 1; Brian Starr 1; Dale Facchini 0; Neil Facchini 0).

WEYMOUTH CARPETS GALORE WILDCATS

ADDRESS: Wessex Stadium (2), Radipole Lane, Weymouth, Dorset, DT4 9XJ.
CLUB CHAIRMEN: Brian White & Phil Bartlett.
TRACK LENGTH: 223 metres.
TRACK RECORD: 53.3 seconds – Lewis Bridger (5 August 2005).
FIRST MEETING: 15 August 2003.
YEARS OF OPERATION: 2003 Open; 2004–05 Conference League.

PREVIOUS VENUE: Wessex Stadium (1), Radipole Lane, Weymouth, Dorset.
YEARS OF OPERATION: 1954 Open; 1955 National League Division Two; 1962-63 Open; 1964 Metropolitan League; 1965 Open; 1966-67 Training; 1968 British League Division Two; 1969-70 Training; 1971-73 Open & Training; 1974 British League Division Two; 1975-84 National League; 1985 Open & Training.

CLUB HONOURS

PAIRS CHAMPIONS: 1982, 1983.
FOUR-TEAM CHAMPIONS: 2005.
KNOCK-OUT CUP WINNERS: 2005.

RIDER ROSTER 2005

Marc ANDREWS; Matt BATES; Lewis BRIDGER; Tom BROWN; Paul CANDY; James CLEMENT; Lewis DALLAWAY; Adam FILMER; Daniel GIFFARD; Jack GLEDHILL; Danny HUGHES; Dan KIRKMAN; David MASON; Lee SMART; Shane WALDRON.

OTHER APPEARANCES/GUESTS (official matches only):
Joe Reynolds; Tim Webster.

CONFERENCE LEAGUE

(*Denotes bonus-point victory)

No	DATE	OPPONENTS	H/A	RESULT	Mason	Gledhill	Brown	Smart	Giffard	Bridger	Candy	Bates	Filmer	Dallaway	Clement	Others
1	17/4	Boston	A	L45–48	10 (5)	6+2 (4)	9 (5)	5+3 (4)	8 (4)	6 (5)	–	–	–	–	–	1 (3)
2	24/4	Buxton	A	W49–40	8+1 (4)	1+1 (4)	8+1 (4)	–	13+1 (5)	15 (6)	2+2 (4)	2+1 (4)	–	–	–	–
3	12/5	Boston	H	W60–33*	10 (4)	8+1 (5)	9+2 (4)	10+2 (4)	10+1 (4)	10+1 (5)	–	3+2 (4)	–	–	–	–
4	20/5	Scunthorpe	H	W54–42	11+1 (5)	5+1 (4)	11+2 (5)	–	10+1 (4)	10 (4)	4 (4)	–	3+1 (4)	–	–	–
5	22/5	Sittingbourne	A	W55–39	14+1 (5)	5 (5)	15+1 (6)	–	R/R	17+1 (6)	3 (4)	–	1 (4)	–	–	–
6	30/5	Oxford	H	W45–44	6 (4)	4+2 (4)	10+1 (5)	–	10 (5)	12+1 (6)	3+1 (3)	–	0 (3)	–	–	–
7	10/6	Sittingbourne	H	W66–20*	14+1 (5)	14+1 (5)	6+1 (4)	–	12 (4)	9+3 (4)	7+1 (4)	–	4+1 (4)	–	–	–
8	29/7	Mildenhall	H	W51–40	13+2 (5)	6+1 (5)	7+1 (4)	–	15 (5)	8 (4)	–	–	–	0 (4)	–	2 (4)
9	5/8	Newport	H	W53–37	9+2 (4)	3+1 (4)	10+1 (4)	–	14+1 (5)	11+1 (5)	4 (4)	–	–	2 (5)	–	–
10	7/8	Mildenhall	A	L39–56	12 (5)	3 (6)	13+1 (6)	–	0 (1)	7 (4)	–	–	–	2 (4)	2+2 (4)	–
11	11/8	Stoke	H	W53–40	9 (4)	5 (4)	12+1 (5)	–	9 (4)	9+2 (5)	–	–	–	5+3 (4)	4 (4)	–
12	13/8	Armadale	A	L39–50	9+1 (5)	–	5+1 (4)	–	8 (4)	10 (5)	–	–	–	0 (3)	7+1 (6)	DNA
13	19/8	Armadale	H	W54–43*	9+1 (4)	6+1 (4)	6+1 (4)	–	12+1 (5)	14 (5)	–	–	–	1 (3)	6+1 (5)	–
14	26/8	Buxton	H	W58–33*	18 (6)	5 (4)	12 (5)	–	R/R	15+3 (6)	–	3 (3)	–	–	5 (5)	–
15	29/8	Wimbledon	H	L44–46	12+1 (5)	2+1 (4)	11 (6)	–	R/R	12+1 (6)	–	1+1 (3)	–	–	6+2 (6)	–
16	31/8	Wimbledon	A	L44–46	10+1 (6)	4+1 (4)	8+1 (5)	–	R/R	14 (6)	–	–	–	2+1 (3)	6+3 (6)	–
17	4/9	Scunthorpe	A	W48–42*	4+1 (4)	5+2 (4)	7 (4)	–	13 (5)	12 (5)	–	5+1 (5)	–	–	2 (3)	–
18	16/9	Rye House	H	W53–40	7 (4)	–	10+2 (4)	–	15 (5)	12+1 (5)	–	–	–	3 (5)	6+1 (4)	0 (3)

No	DATE	OPPONENTS	H/A	RESULT	Mason	Gledhill	Brown	Smart	Giffard	Bridger	Candy	Bates	Filmer	Dallaway	Clement	Others
19	17/9	Rye House	A	L45–51*	7 (4)	–	4+3 (4)	–	13 (5)	17+1 (6)	–	–	–	1 (4)	–	3+1 (7)
20	6/10	Oxford	A	L45–51	6+2 (4)	–	12+2 (5)	–	9 (4)	13 (6)	–	–	–	–	1 (4)	4 (4)
21	9/10	Newport	A	L43–52*	13 (4)	–	1 (5)	–	10+1 (5)	15 (5)	–	–	–	–	DNA	4+1 (8)
22	22/10	Stoke	A	L32–63	R/R	–	11 (6)	–	11 (6)	–	–	–	–	–	2 (4)	8+2 (14)

DETAILS OF OTHER RIDERS:

Match No. 1: Marc Andrews 1 (3); Match No. 8: Danny Hughes 2 (4); Match No. 12: Danny Hughes DNA; Match No. 18: Dan Kirkman 0 (3); Match No. 19: Shane Waldron 3+1 (4); Dan Kirkman 0 (3); Match No. 20: Shane Waldron 4 (4); Match No. 21: Shane Waldron 4+1 (5); Danny Hughes 0 (3); Match No. 22: Danny Hughes 5+1 (5); Shane Waldron 2+1 (5); Joe Reynolds 1 (4).

TACTICAL SUBSTITUTE AND TACTICAL RIDES, AS INCLUDED IN THE SCORES GRID:

Match No. 10: Bridger 6 points (TR); Brown 4 points (TS); Mason 4 points (TR); Match No. 19: Giffard 6 points (TR); Bridger 6 points (TS); Match No. 20: Bridger 4 points (TS); Brown 4 points (TR); Giffard 4 points (TR); Match No. 21: Bridger 6 points (TR); Mason 4 points (TR); Brown 0 points (TS); Match No. 22: Giffard 6 points (TR); Brown 4 points (TR).

CONFERENCE LEAGUE AVERAGES

Rider	Mts	Rds	Pts	Bon	Tot	Avge	Max
Lee Smart	2	8	15	5	20	10.00	1 paid
Daniel Giffard	18	80	184	6	190	9.50	3 full; 1 paid
David Mason	21	96	207	15	222	9.25	1 full; 3 paid
Lewis Bridger	21	109	237	15	252	9.25	3 paid
Tom Brown	22	104	191	22	213	8.19	1 paid
Jack Gledhill	16	69	82	15	97	5.62	1 paid
Paul Candy	6	23	23	4	27	4.70	–
James Clement	11	51	47	10	57	4.47	–
Matt Bates	5	19	14	5	19	4.00	–
Shane Waldron	4	18	13	3	16	3.56	–
Adam Filmer	4	15	8	2	10	2.67	–
Danny Hughes	3	12	7	1	8	2.67	–
Lewis Dallaway	9	35	16	4	20	2.29	–
Marc Andrews	1	3	1	0	1	1.33	–
Joe Reynolds	1	4	1	0	1	1.00	–
Dan Kirkman	2	6	0	0	0	0.00	–

CONFERENCE TROPHY

(*Denotes bonus-point victory)

No	DATE	OPPONENTS	H/A	RESULT	Mason	Gledhill	Brown	Candy	Giffard	Bridger	Bates	Filmer	Dallaway	Hughes	Clement	Waldron
1	2/5	Wimbledon	H	W58-35	10 (4)	5+1 (4)	14+1 (4)	3 (4)	14+1 (5)	8 (4)	4+1 (4)	–	–	–	–	–
2	12/6	Wimbledon	A	W48-42*	8+2 (4)	4+2 (4)	8 (4)	0 (3)	13+1 (5)	14 (7)	–	1 (3)	–	–	–	–

WEYMOUTH: From left to right, back row: Brian White (Promoter/Team Manager), Tom Brown, David Mason, Shane Waldron, Lewis Bridger. Front, kneeling: James Clement, Daniel Giffard.

No	DATE	OPPONENTS	H/A	RESULT	Mason	Gledhill	Brown	Candy	Giffard	Bridger	Bates	Filmer	Dallaway	Hughes	Clement	Waldron
3	19/6	Mildenhall	A	L43-49	10 (5)	4+1 (3)	8+2 (5)	0 (3)	11 (5)	10 (6)	–	0 (3)	–	–	–	
4	1/7	Mildenhall	H	W56-37*	10+1 (4)	7+1 (6)	8 (5)	3+1 (3)	12 (4)	14+1 (5)	–		2 (3)	–	–	
5	8/7	Boston	H	W48-42	R/R	2+2 (6)	9 (5)	4 (4)	15 (6)	14+2 (6)	–		4+1 (3)	–	–	
6	10/7	Boston	A	W50-42*	14 (5)	8+2 (5)	7+2 (4)	–	6 (4)	9 (5)	–		3+1 (3)	3+2 (4)	–	
7	9/9	Stoke	H	L44-46	9 (5)	3 (3)	9+1 (6)	–	R/R	13 (6)	2+1 (3)	–	–	–	8+2 (7)	
8	24/9	Stoke	A	L41-52	8 (5)	–	6+2 (4)	–	6 (4)	15 (6)	–		1+1 (3)	2+1 (3)	–	3+1 (5)

TACTICAL SUBSTITUTE RIDES, AS INCLUDED IN THE SCORES GRID:

Match No. 3: Giffard 4 points (TS); Match No. 8: Bridger 6 points (TS).

CONFERENCE TROPHY AVERAGES

Rider	Mts	Rds	Pts	Bon	Tot	Avge	Max
Daniel Giffard	7	33	75	2	77	9.33	1 full; 1 paid
David Mason	7	32	69	3	72	9.00	–
Lewis Bridger	8	45	94	3	97	8.62	1 paid
Tom Brown	8	38	69	8	77	8.11	1 paid
James Clement	1	7	8	2	10	5.71	–
Jack Gledhill	7	31	33	9	42	5.42	–
Matt Bates	2	7	6	2	8	4.57	–
Danny Hughes	2	7	5	3	8	4.57	–
Lewis Dallaway	4	12	10	3	13	4.33	–
Shane Waldron	1	5	3	1	4	3.20	–
Paul Candy	5	17	10	1	11	2.59	–
Adam Filmer	2	6	1	0	1	0.67	–

KNOCK-OUT CUP

(*Denotes aggregate victory)

No	DATE	OPPONENTS	H/A	RESULT	Mason	Candy	Brown	Bridger	Giffard	Webster	Dallaway	Hughes	Gledhill	Clement	Waldron
1	3/7	Buxton	A	L43-51	11 (4)	4+1 (4)	5 (5)	11+1 (5)	10 (5)	0 (4)	2 (3)	–	–	–	
2	22/7	Buxton	H	W55-40*	10+1 (4)	4 (4)	–	14+1 (5)	15 (5)	–	4+1 (4)	4+1 (3)	4 (5)	–	
3	23/9	Newport	H	W51-43	10+1 (5)	–	10+2 (4)	15 (5)	8+1 (4)	–	1 (4)	–	–	3+1 (3)	4+2 (5)
4	9/10	Newport	A	W50-41*	14+1 (5)	–	5 (4)	15 (5)	10 (5)	–	–	1+1 (3)	–	DNA	5+1 (5)
5	14/10	Mildenhall	H	W54-40	11 (4)	–	7+2 (4)	13+1 (5)	13 (5)	–	–	1 (3)	–	5 (5)	4+1 (4)
6	16/10	Mildenhall	A	L45-51*	11 (4)	–	6+1 (5)	11+1 (5)	11 (4)	–	–	0 (3)	–	2 (3)	4+1 (6)

TACTICAL SUBSTITUTE AND TACTICAL RIDES, AS INCLUDED IN THE SCORES GRID:

Match No. 1: Mason 6 points (TR); Brown 2 points (TS); Match No. 4: Giffard 2 points (TR); Match No. 6: Mason 6 points (TR); Giffard 4 points (TR); Brown 2 points (TS).

OTHER MEETINGS

25 March: Challenge

Weymouth 56 (David Mason 13; Lewis Bridger 12+3; Tom Brown 10; Daniel Giffard 10; Paul Candy 5+3; Jack Gledhill 3+2; Matt Bates 3) USA Dream Team 37 (Chris Kerr 16; Tim Gomez 12; Brian Starr 4+1; Neil Facchini 3; Dale Facchini 2+1; Shaun Harmatiuk 0; T.J. Fowler 0; Dario Galvin 0).

14 April: Challenge

Weymouth 64 (Lee Smart 15; David Mason 11; Tom Brown 10+3; Jack Gledhill 8+2; Daniel Giffard 8+2; Lewis Bridger 8+1; Matt Bates 4+1) Sittingbourne 30.

20 April: Trevor Hedge Racing Challenge Cup (first leg)

Wimbledon 38 Weymouth 55 (Daniel Giffard 13; Lee Smart 12; Lewis Bridger 11+1; David Mason 8; Tom Brown 6+2; Jack Gledhill 5+2; Marc Andrews 0).

21 April: Trevor Hedge Racing Challenge Cup (second leg)

Weymouth 57 (Tom Brown 13+2; Lewis Bridger 12+3; Daniel Giffard 11; David Mason 9+1; Lee Smart 8+1; Jack Gledhill 3; Marc Andrews 1) Wimbledon 36 – Weymouth won 112-74 on aggregate.

15 July: Challenge

Weymouth 51 (Daniel Giffard 15; Lewis Bridger 14+1; David Mason 10+1; Tom Brown 7+2; Danny Hughes 3+1; Lewis Dallaway 2; Marc Andrews 0) Travis Perkins' Select 41 (Paul Candy 10+2; James Purchase 8+4; Danny Betson 6+1; Luke Priest 6; James Clement 5+1; Gary Phelps 5; Adam Filmer 1).

31 July: Conference League

Newport 19 Weymouth 17 (Daniel Giffard 6; David Mason 3; Tom Brown 3; Lewis Bridger 2+1; Jack Gledhill 2; Danny Hughes 1+1; Lewis Dallaway 0) – meeting abandoned after heat six.

14 August: Conference League

Scunthorpe 35 Weymouth 31 (David Mason 9; Lewis Bridger 9; Daniel Giffard 6; Tom Brown 4+1; James Clement 3; Jack Gledhill 0; Lewis Dallaway 0) – meeting abandoned after heat eleven.

7 October: Challenge

Weymouth 60 (Lewis Bridger 15; David Mason 14+1; Daniel Giffard 10+1; Shane Waldron 6+2; Tom Brown 6+1; James Clement 5+1; Jordan Frampton 4) Club Caerfyrddin 33 (Tyron Proctor 11+1; Ben Powell 9; Dean Felton 7; Darren Hatton 3+1; Rob Smith 2+2; Jessica Lamb 1; Tim Webster 0; Wayne Broadhurst R/R).

INDIVIDUAL MEETINGS

28 March: British Under-21 Championship Qualifying Round

1st Daniel Giffard 15; 2nd Chris Schramm 13; 3rd Tom Brown 12; Chris Johnson 11; Luke Priest 11; Jamie Courtney 10; Ben Barker 9; Jack Gledhill 8; Lewis Bridger 7; James Clement 6; Matt Bates 5; James Purchase 4; Kyle Hughes 3; Steve Braidford 2; Michael Mitchell 2; Marc Andrews 0.

30 May: British Under-15 Championship (Round Three)

1st Josh Auty 15; 2nd Ben Taylor 14; 3rd George Piper 13; Ben Hopwood 12; George Jarvis 11; Daniel Greenwood 10; Brendan Johnson 8; Scott Meakins 8; Chris Widman 7; Ben Thompson 5; Aaron Baseby 5; Ben Reade 4; Rickylee Beecroft 3; Jack Butler 3; Richard Franklin 1; Dan Kirkman 0.

17 June: Wessex Rosebowl

1st Trevor Harding (after run-off) 15; 2nd Daniel Giffard 15; 3rd Tom Brown 10; David Mason 9; Sam Hurst 9; Lewis Bridger 8; Jack Gledhill 7; Paul Candy 6; Kyle Hughes 5; Chris Ferguson 3; Gary Cottham 2; Adam Filmer 0.

28 October: King of the Wessex

QUALIFYING SCORES: Lewis Bridger <u>15</u>; David Mason 13; Daniel Giffard 12; Chris Johnson 11; Tom Brown 8; Billy Legg 8; Dean Felton 7; Rob Smith 6; Jordan Frampton 6; James Clement 2; Shane Waldron 2. FINAL: 1st Bridger; 2nd Mason; 3rd Johnson; 4th Giffard.

PAIRS MEETING

2 September: Wessex Pairs Championship

1st David Mason (<u>20</u>) & Jack Gledhill (11+3) = 31; 2nd Tom Brown (16+2) & James Clement (10+1) = 26; 3rd Lewis Bridger (13+1) & Rob Smith (10) = 23; Danny Warwick (13+1) & James Purchase (8+2) = 21; Tyron Proctor (11) & Karlis Ezergailis (7+1) = 18; Andrew Bargh (12) & Paul Candy (2) = 14.

WIMBLEDON ROBERT HEATH HEATING DONS

ADDRESS: Wimbledon Stadium, Plough Lane, London, SW17 0BL.
CLUB CHAIRMEN: Ian Perkin & Dingle Brown.
TRACK LENGTH: 250 metres.
TRACK RECORD: 59.5 seconds – Wayne Barrett (18 July 2002).
FIRST MEETING: 28 May 1928.
YEARS OF OPERATION: 1928 Open; 1929-31 Southern League; 1932-33 National League; 1934 National League & Reserve League; 1935-36 National League; 1937-39 National League Division One; 1946 National League; 1947-56 National League Division One; 1957-64 National League; 1965-67 British League; 1968-74 British League Division One; 1975-84 British League; 1985-90 National League; 1991 British League Division One; 2002-05 Conference League.

CLUB HONOURS

NATIONAL TROPHY WINNERS: 1938, 1950, 1951, 1953, 1956, 1959, 1960, 1962.
RAC CUP WINNERS: 1954.
LEAGUE CHAMPIONS: 1954, 1955, 1956, 1958, 1959, 1960, 1961.
BRITANNIA SHIELD WINNERS: 1959.
KNOCK-OUT CUP WINNERS: 1962, 1968, 1969, 1970.
PAIRS CHAMPIONS: 2004, 2005.

RIDER ROSTER 2005

Andrew BARGH; Danny BETSON; Mark BURROWS; James CLEMENT; Peter COLLYER; Scott JAMES; Grant MacDONALD; Rob SMITH; Lee STRUDWICK; Karl WHITE; Matthew WRIGHT.

CONFERENCE LEAGUE

(*Denotes bonus-point victory)

No	DATE	OPPONENTS	H/A	RESULT	James	Clement	Wright	Collyer	Burrows	Bargh	Betson	Strudwick	Smith	MacDonald	White
1	24/4	Mildenhall	A	W48-42	6+1 (3)	7+1 (4)	8+1 (5)	4+2 (4)	11 (5)	5+1 (5)	7+2 (4)	–	–	–	–
2	8/5	Rye House	H	W52-40	7+2 (4)	11+1 (5)	7+1 (4)	5+3 (4)	12 (5)	6 (4)	4+2 (4)	–			
3	15/5	Sittingbourne	A	W57-36	8 (4)	4+1 (4)	8 (5)	5+3 (4)	13+2 (5)	11+1 (4)	8+1 (4)	–			
4	18/5	Newport	H	W64-27	10+2 (4)	7+1 (5)	11+1 (4)	10+3 (5)	12 (4)	–	11+1 (4)	3+1 (4)			
5	25/5	Mildenhall	H	W50-46*	8 (4)	6+2 (4)	7+1 (4)	4+3 (4)	11 (5)	–	12+2 (6)	2+1 (3)			
6	30/5	Rye House	A	L43-52*	4+2 (4)	0 (3)	5+1 (4)	3+1 (4)	14+1 (5)	–	15 (7)	2 (3)			
7	22/6	Sittingbourne	H	W60-34*	12+2 (5)	11+1 (5)	13+1 (5)	R/R	10+1 (5)	–	8+2 (4)	3+2 (4)	3+1 (2)		
8	9/7	Armadale	A	L36-57	2 (4)	4+2 (4)	6 (4)	–	10 (5)	–	7+1 (5)	2+2 (4)	5+1 (4)		
9	10/7	Scunthorpe	A	L40-54	12 (5)	5+3 (4)	7 (5)	–	5+1 (4)	–	4+1 (4)	4 (4)	3+2 (4)		
10	13/7	Armadale	H	W56-34*	10+2 (5)	7+1 (4)	6 (4)	–	14 (5)	–	9+2 (4)	7+2 (4)	3+1 (4)		
11	20/7	Stoke	A	L39-54	15+2 (6)	6+2 (5)	4 (5)	–	12+1 (6)	–	R/R	1+1 (4)	1 (4)		
12	7/8	Boston	A	L42-55	6 (4)	–	3+1 (4)	–	11 (6)	–	9+2 (5)	6+1 (4)	0 (3)	7+2 (4)	
13	10/8	Buxton	H	W58-32	7 (4)	–	13+2 (5)	–	12 (4)	–	7 (4)	7+2 (5)	0 (3)	12+3 (5)	
14	21/8	Newport	A	L46-49*	9 (5)	–	3 (4)	–	10+1 (5)	–	2+1 (4)	4+1 (4)	–	18 (5)	0 (3)
15	29/8	Weymouth	A	W46-44	R/R	–	6+1 (5)	–	14+1 (6)	–	5 (5)	9+3 (5)	–	12+1 (6)	0 (3)
16	31/8	Weymouth	H	W46-44*	4+1 (4)	–	7+1 (4)	–	13 (5)	–	8 (4)	1+1 (5)	–	12+2 (5)	1 (3)
17	7/9	Boston	H	W55-39*	R/R	–	15+1 (6)	–	12 (6)	–	6+1 (5)	7+2 (5)	4+1 (3)	11+1 (5)	–
18	8/9	Oxford	A	L44-46	R/R	–	5+1 (5)	–	11 (6)	–	7 (5)	4+2 (4)	5+2 (5)	12 (6)	
19	14/9	Scunthorpe	H	W63-31*	9 (4)	–	11+3 (5)	–	12 (4)	–	5+3 (4)	5+1 (4)	10+3 (5)	11 (4)	
20	21/9	Oxford	H	W50-43*	4+1 (4)	–	11+1 (5)	–	11 (5)	–	5 (4)	9+2 (5)	2+1 (3)	8 (4)	
21	25/9	Buxton	A	W53-38*	8 (6)	–	10+1 (6)	–	13 (5)	–	R/R	9+2 (7)	0 (0)	13+1 (5)	
22	28/9	Stoke	H	W58-35*	8 (4)	–	13+1 (5)	–	12+1 (5)	–	6+4 (4)	9+2 (5)	2 (3)	8+3 (4)	

TACTICAL SUBSTITUTE AND TACTICAL RIDES, AS INCLUDED IN THE SCORES GRID:

Match No. 6: Burrows 6 points (TR); Betson 4 points (TR); Match No. 8: Burrows 4 points (TR); Wright 4 points (TR); Match No. 9: James 4 points (TR); Wright 4 points (TR); Match No. 11: James 4 points (TR); Wright 2 points (TR); Match No. 12: Betson 6 points (TR); MacDonald 4 points (TR); Burrows 4 points (TS); Match No. 14: MacDonald 6 points (TR); Burrows 2 points (TR); James 2 points (TS).

CONFERENCE LEAGUE AVERAGES

Rider	Mts	Rds	Pts	Bon	Tot	Avge	Max
Grant MacDonald	11	53	119	13	132	9.96	1 full; 1 paid
Mark Burrows	22	111	247	9	256	9.23	3 full; 1 paid
Scott James	19	83	144	15	159	7.66	1 paid
Matthew Wright	22	103	174	19	193	7.50	2 paid
Andrew Bargh	3	13	22	2	24	7.38	1 paid
Peter Collyer	6	25	31	15	46	7.36	–
Danny Betson	20	90	140	25	165	7.33	1 paid
James Clement	11	47	68	15	83	7.06	–
Lee Strudwick	19	83	94	28	122	5.88	–

WIMBLEDON: From left to right, back row: Andrew Bargh, Mark Burrows (on bike), Danny Betson, James Clement, Scott James, Jon Stevens. Front, kneeling: Martin Elliott, Matthew Wright.

| Rob Smith | 13 | 43 | 38 | 12 | 50 | 4.65 | – |
| Karl White | 3 | 9 | 1 | 0 | 1 | 0.44 | – |

CONFERENCE TROPHY

(*Denotes bonus-point victory)

No	DATE	OPPONENTS	H/A	RESULT	James	Clement	Wright	Collyer	Burrows	Bargh	Betson	Strudwick	Smith
1	2/5	Weymouth	A	L35-58	7 (4)	3 (4)	12+1 (5)	1+1 (3)	4 (4)	4 (6)	4 (4)	–	–
2	22/5	Mildenhall	A	L42-51	4+1 (4)	1 (3)	3 (3)	3+1 (4)	9+1 (5)	–	18 (7)	4+1 (4)	–
3	1/6	Boston	H	W61-31	9+2 (5)	10+1 (4)	8 (5)	6+2 (4)	12 (4)	–	9+3 (4)	7+1 (4)	–
4	12/6	Weymouth	H	L42-48	6+1 (4)	3 (3)	7 (5)	0 (3)	12 (5)	–	12+4 (7)	2+2 (3)	–
5	19/6	Boston	A	L40-54*	12 (6)	2+2 (3)	8+1 (5)	–	3+1 (4)	–	9+2 (6)	3+1 (2)	3 (4)
6	6/7	Mildenhall	H	W50-40*	11+1 (5)	6+2 (4)	8+2 (4)	–	14 (5)	–	8 (4)	3+1 (5)	0 (3)

TACTICAL SUBSTITUTE AND TACTICAL RIDES, AS INCLUDED IN THE SCORES GRID:

Match No. 1: Wright 6 points (TR); Burrows 0 points (TR); Match No. 2: Betson 6 points (TR); Match No. 5: James 4 points (TS), Wright 2 points (TR); Burrows 2 points (TR).

CONFERENCE TROPHY AVERAGES

Rider	Mts	Rds	Pts	Bon	Tot	Avge	Max
Danny Betson	6	32	57	9	66	8.25	1 paid
Mark Burrows	6	27	53	2	55	8.15	1 full
Scott James	6	28	47	5	52	7.43	–
Matthew Wright	6	27	42	4	46	6.81	–
James Clement	6	21	25	5	30	5.71	–
Lee Strudwick	5	18	19	6	25	5.56	–
Peter Collyer	4	14	10	4	14	4.00	–
Andrew Bargh	1	6	4	0	4	2.67	–
Rob Smith	2	7	3	0	3	1.71	–

KNOCK-OUT CUP

No	DATE	OPPONENTS	H/A	RESULT	James	Clement	Wright	Collyer	Burrows	Strudwick	Betson	Smith
1	26/5	Oxford	A	L33-60	9 (5)	1+1 (3)	3 (4)	2+1 (4)	3 (2)	–	12+1 (7)	3+1 (4)
2	26/6	Oxford	H	W46-44	8+1 (5)	–	13+1 (6)	R/R	17 (6)	1+1 (4)	7 (7)	0 (2)

TACTICAL RIDES, AS INCLUDED IN THE SCORES GRID:

Match No. 1: James 4 points (TR); Burrows 2 points (TR).

OTHER MEETINGS

3 April: Spring Challenge Cup (first leg)

    Boston 49 Wimbledon 43 (Mark Burrows 13; Andre Cross 9; Andrew Bargh 8; Scott James 6; Peter Collyer 4+3; Danny Betson 2+1; James Clement 1+1).

13 April: Spring Challenge Cup (second leg)

    Wimbledon 48 (Mark Burrows 12; James Clement 9+1; Scott James 7+1; Matthew Wright 7+1; Peter Collyer 7+1; Andrew Bargh 4+1; Danny Betson 2+1) Boston 40 – Wimbledon won 91-89 on aggregate.

20 April: Trevor Hedge Racing Challenge Cup (first leg)

    Wimbledon 38 (Mark Burrows 14+1; Scott James 9; Andrew Bargh 6; Matthew Wright 4; Peter Collyer 2+1; Lee Strudwick 2+1; James Clement 1) Weymouth 55.

21 April: Trevor Hedge Racing Challenge Cup (second leg)

    Weymouth 57 Wimbledon 36 (Mark Burrows 12; Scott James 5; Matthew Wright 5; Lee Strudwick 4+3; Peter Collyer 4+1; James Clement 4; Andrew Bargh 2) – Weymouth won 112-74 on aggregate.

4 May: Challenge

    Wimbledon 48 (Mark Burrows 15; Danny Betson 10+1; James Clement 7+1; Matthew Wright 5+1; Andrew Bargh 5; Scott James 3+1; Peter Collyer 3+1) Ex-Dons Select 42 (Barrie Evans 12; Daniel Giffard 9+1; Ben Powell 7+1; Robert Hollingworth 7+1; Chris Hunt 5+2; Lee Strudwick 2; Martin Elliott 0).

24 July: Conference League

    Buxton 37 Wimbledon 23 (Scott James 7; Matthew Wright 6; Mark Burrows 5; Lee Strudwick 3; Rob Smith 2; Danny Betson R/R; James Clement DNA) – meeting abandoned after heat ten.

3 August: Summer Fours

    Scott's Speedsters 28 (Scott James 10; Grant MacDonald 10; James Clement 7; Rob Smith 1; Niall Strudwick 0), Buzz's Stingers 24 Mark Burrows 10; Billy Legg 5; Lee Strudwick 5; Dean Felton 4), Wright's Knights 22 (Matthew Wright 11; David Mason 6; Andre Cross 4; Keith Yorke 1; Chris Hunt 0), Betson's Jetsons 21 (Peter Collyer 9; Robert Hollingworth 6; Danny Betson 5; James Purchase 1).

17 August: 75th Anniversary International Challenge

    Lions Select 49 (Mark Burrows 14; Grant MacDonald 12+1; Danny Betson 8; David Mason 7+1; Jon Armstrong 5+1; Lee Strudwick 3+1; Matthew Wright 0) World Select 41 (Tom Brown 9; Ben Powell 9; Byron Bekker 9; Jamie Courtney 6+2; Karlis Ezergailis 5; Andrew Bargh 2; Robert Hollingworth 1+1).

INDIVIDUAL MEETINGS

5 June: Paul Strank Roofing Open Championship

    1st Lewis Bridger 14; 2nd Mark Burrows (after run-off) 13; 3rd Matthew Wright 13; David Mason 12; Robert Hollingworth 10; Scott James 10; Karl Mason 9; Luke Priest 8; James Clement 7; Luke Bowen 7; Billy Legg 5; Danny Betson 4; Lee Strudwick 3; Harland Cook 2; Peter Collyer (Res) 2; Paul Candy 1; Rob Smith 0; Martin Elliott (Res) 0.

5 October: The Laurels

    1st Mark Burrows 15; 2nd Barrie Evans 14; 3rd Daniel Giffard 12; Ben Powell 11; Lewis Bridger 10; Scott James 8; Byron Bekker 8; Grant MacDonald 8; Tom Brown 7; Wayne Broadhurst 7; Matthew Wright 7; Peter Collyer 5; Karlis Ezergailis 4; David Mason 3; Chris Hunt 1; Lee Strudwick 0; Rob Smith (Res) 0; Martin Elliott (Res) 0.

ACADEMY LEAGUE

ACADEMY LEAGUE TABLE

	Mts	Won	Drn	Lst	For	Agn	Pts
Buffalo	4	4	0	0	92	54	8
Cobras	4	2	0	2	82	61	4
Dinosaurs	4	2	0	2	88	90	4
Rhinos	4	2	0	2	70	82	4
Bulls	4	0	0	4	68	113	0

SUMMARY OF LEAGUE SCORERS

BUFFALO: Lewis Bridger 26; Brendan Johnson 23; Joe Reynolds 15; George Piper 10; Ben Reade 6; Matt Bates 6; Jamie Pickard 5; Ben Thompson 1; George Jarvis 0.

BULLS: Chris Widman 10; Ben Taylor 9; Joe Haines 8; Brendan Johnson 7; Joe Reynolds 7; James Sealey 6; Scott Meakins 5; Andy Braithwaite 4; Billy Legg 4; Daniel Greenwood 3; Ben Thompson 3; Jamie Pickard 2; James Humby 0; Sam Hurst 0.

COBRAS: Ben Taylor 25; Ben Hopwood 16; Gary Irving 12; Adam Wrathall 6; Andy Braithwaite 6; Joe Haines 5; George Jarvis 4; Ben Thompson 2; Tom Davies 2; Ben Johnson 2; Ben Hannon 1; Sean Paterson 1.

DINOSAURS: Josh Auty 35; Joe Haines 15; Daniel Greenwood 12; Brendan Johnson 10; Richard Franklin 5; Gary Irving 5; Ben Thompson 3; Jack Butler 2; Kye Norton 1; George Jarvis 0; Tom Davies 0.

RHINOS: Matt Bates 17; Tim Webster 15; Daniel Greenwood 12; Shane Waldron 11; Josh Auty 6; Rickylee Beecroft 3; Andy Braithwaite 3; Gary Irving 2; Joe Haines 1; Sam Hurst 0; Dan Kirkman 0; Rusty Dougan 0; Jamie Pickard 0.

PLAY-OFFS

QUARTER-FINAL

Dinosaurs	30	Rhinos	16
Cobras	27	Bulls	21

SEMI-FINAL

Cobras	21	Dinosaurs	20

FINAL

Buffalo	24	Cobras	22

ANGLO-POLISH AGENCY KNOCK-OUT CUP

QUARTER-FINAL

Buffalo	26	Cobras	21

SEMI-FINALS

Buffalo	23	Rhinos	22
Bulls	25	Dinosaurs	22

FINAL

Buffalo	32	Bulls	15

SOUTHERN TRACK RIDERS' MEETINGS 2005

2 May: Newport

Open: Sam Martin 13; Trevor Heath 13; Karl Rushen 12; Adam Lowe 11; Lewis Dallaway 9; Jason Newitt 9; Thomas Rowlett 9; Lee Strudwick 8; Glyn Edwards 6; Scott Chester 6; Mark Richardson 6; Paul Quarterman 5; Harvey Bell 4; Gordon Walker 4; Steve Cook 1.

Support: Stefan De Groot 9; Jason Taylor 9; Steve Oakey 9; Sid Higgins 9; David Tutton 7; Phil Hindley 6; Ted Ede 5; Shawn Taylor 5; Paul Evans 4; Richard Earl 3; Steve Lockyer 3; Pete Shakespeare 2.

Novice: Lee Coley 12; Stuart Madle 9; Dennis Cairns 8; Alec Jones 8; Barry Byles 5; Sam Howett 4.

15 May: King's Lynn

Open: Barry Burchatt 15; Wayne Dunworth 13; Lewis Dallaway 12; Daniel Halsey 11; Karl Rushen 10; Michael Holding 9; Andrew Blackburn 9; Karl White 7; Wes Sheasby 7; Paul Quarterman 6; Steve Cook 6; Barry Young 4; Sid Higgins 4; Thomas Rowlett 3; Terry Durdin 1.

Novice: Steve Oakey 15; David Tutton 12; Jason Taylor 12; Matthew Jarman 12; Gary Emeny 11; Gary Henriksen 9; Shawn Taylor 9; James Fear 9; Lee Coley 7; Paul Evans 5; Bill Smith 5; Stuart Madle 4; Sam Howett 4.

Over 40s: Adrian Townsend 11; Hakan Hartzelius 10; Derek Jones 10; Kevin Garwood 7; Pete Shakespeare 6; Barry Byles 2; Alec Jones 2.

5 June: King's Lynn

Open: Dean Garrod 14; Carl Downs 13; Lewis Dallaway 11; Sam Martin 11; Karl Rushen 10; Wayne Dunworth 9; Michael Holding 8; Rod Woodhouse 8; Karl White 7; Wes Sheasby 6; Glyn Edwards 5; Terry Durdin 4; Gordon Walker 4; Steve Oakey 3; Dave Lidgett 3; Andrew Blackburn 2.

Novice: Phil Hindley 15; Pete Shakespeare 13; Matthew Jarman 12; Kevin Garwood 12; James Fear 10; Bill Smith 9; Adrian Townsend 9; Lee Coley 8; Robin Couzins 8; Tony Venables 7; Richard Walsh 5; Alec Jones 5; Andy Holiday 3; Mark Consadine 2; Barry Byles 1; Sam Howett 1.

Support: Tim Webster 11; Steve Cook 11; Jason Taylor 9; Stefan De Groot 8; Harvey Bell 5; Sid Higgins 3; Gary Henriksen 1; Shawn Taylor 0.

26 June: Newport

Open: Daniel Halsey 15; Dean Garrod 13; Gordon Meakins 12; Lewis Dallaway 12; Karl Rushen 11; Matt Tutton 10; Jason Newitt 9; Jessica Lamb 9; Scott Chester 7; Jason Taylor 6; Sid Higgins 4; Harvey Bell 4; Gordon Walker 4; Terry Durdin 2; Steve Cook 1.

Novice: David Tutton 15; Gary Emeny 13; Gary Henriksen 12; Bill Smith 12; Shawn Taylor 11; Greg Walsh 10; Lee Coley 10; Pete Shakespeare 9; Jamie Pickard 7; Phil Hindley 7; Jim Luckman 6; Tony Venables 6; Steve Oakey 5; Stuart Madle 5; Barry Byles 5; Alec Jones 5; Sam Howett 5; Richard Walsh 4; Norman Hornblow 3.

7 August: Sittingbourne

Over 40s Championship: Terry Durdin 15; Harvey Bell 13; Sid Higgins 12; Steve Cook 11; Ted Ede 11; Bill Haynes 10; Steve Lockyer 10; Adrian Townsend 8; Pete Shakespeare 7; Phil Hindley 6; Tony Venables 5; Mark Consadine 4; Norman Hornblow 3; Barry Byles 2.

Support: Shawn Taylor 12; Jamie Pickard 11; Gary Emeny 10; Andrew Holiday 10; Paul Chester 9;

Matthew Jarman 8; Lee Coley 7; Stuart Madle 5; Robin Couzins 4; Bill Smith 3. Final: 1st Pickard; 2nd Taylor; 3rd Emeny; 4th Holiday.

Mini Open: Karl Rushen 15; Jason Taylor 13; Gary Fawdrey 12; Steve Oakey 13; Jim Luckman 6.

28 August: King's Lynn

Open: Adam Lowe 12; Lewis Dallaway 11; Paul Quarterman 10; Michael Holding 9; Steve Cook 9; Rod Woodhouse 9; Jason Taylor 8; Ben Hannon 7; Gary Fawdrey 6; Sid Higgins 3; Ian Leverington 3; Matt Tutton 2; Harvey Bell 2; Pete Shakespeare 2; Andrew Blackburn 2; Tony Venables 1.

Novice: Paul Chester 12; Shawn Taylor 11; Matt Jarman 11; Michael Faulkner 9; Haken Hartzelius 9; Andrew Holiday 7; Greg Walsh 7; Phil Hindley 6; Adi Burdsill 4; Robin Couzins 4; Sam Howett 3; Bill Smith 3; Nigel Knott 3; Adrian Townsend 2; Alec Jones 2; Richard Walsh 2.

Support: David Tutton 10; Jamie Pickard 9; Paul Evans 7; Lee Coley 7; Steve Lockyer 6; James Fear 4; Kevin Garwood 4; Gary Emeny 1.

18 September: King's Lynn

Open: Lewis Dallaway 15; Adam Lowe 14; Wayne Dunworth 13; Michael Holding 11; Karl Rushen 11; Karl White 10; Steve Cook 8; Andrew Blackburn 8; Gary Fawdrey 5; Rod Woodhouse 5; Sid Higgins 5; Paul Quarterman 4; Harvey Bell 4.

Novice: Stefan De Groot 15; Jason Taylor 15; Kevin Garwood 14; Gary Henriksen 12; Gary Emeny 12; Andrew Holiday 11; Shawn Taylor 11; Matt Jarman 10; Paul Evans 8; Stuart Madle 8; Lee Coley 8; Tony Venables 6; Bill Smith 5; Alec Jones 4; Sam Howett 3; Steve Oakey 0. Final: 1st De Groot; 2nd Garwood; 3rd J. Taylor; 4th Henriksen.

25 September: Newport

Open: Kevin Howse 12; Glyn Edwards 11; Jason Taylor 9; Harvey Bell 9; Sid Higgins 8; Stefan De Groot 7; Jason Newitt 4; Andrew Blackburn 4; David Tutton 3. Final: 1st Howse; 2nd Taylor; 3rd Bell; 4th Edwards.

Support: Kyle Barlow 15; Shawn Taylor 14; Gary Emeny 12; Pete Shakespeare 11; Bill Smith 10; Sam Howett 9; Phil Hindley 7; Paul Evans 6; Frank Whitby 5; Richard Earl 5; Lee Coley 5; Norman Hornblow 5; Alistair Turner 4; Matt Jarman 4; Ken Turner 1.

16 October: King's Lynn

Open: Matt Tutton 14; Daniel Halsey 13; Dean Garrod 13; Wayne Dunworth 12; Mark Baseby 12; Michael Holding 11; Karl Rushen 9; Jason Taylor 8; Paul Evans 6; Gordon Walker 6; Sid Higgins 2.

Novice: Adi Burdsill 14; Lee Coley 14; Shawn Taylor 14; Andrew Holiday 12; Tony Venables 9; Bill Smith 9; Barry Byles 8; Phil Hindley 8; Andy Garner 7; Richard Sar-Butt 7; Robin Couzins 6; Sam Howett 5; Alistair Turner 3; Alec Jones 3; Ken Turner 0.

Support: Aaron Baseby 11; Gary Henriksen 11; Michael Faulkner 10; Kevin Garwood 9; Steve Lockyer 6; Lee Lingham 5; Gary Emeny 4; Jamie Pickard 2; Pete Shakespeare 2; Frank Whitby 0. Final: 1st Baseby; 2nd Faulkner; 3rd Garwood; 4th Henriksen.

30 October: Newport

Open: Dean Garrod 10; James Humby 9; Matt Tutton 8; Karl White 8; Gary Fawdrey 7; Pete Shakespeare 6; David Tutton 6; Harvey Bell 3. Final: 1st Humby; 2nd Garrod; 3rd D. Tutton; 4th Fawdrey.

Novice: Gary Henriksen 15; Richard Earl 13; Gary Emeny 12; Sam Howett 12; Richard Sar-Butt 11; Bill Smith 10; Paul Evans 9; Martin Hartwell 7; Vince Hurst 7; Phil Hindley 7; Norman Hornblow 4; Andy Garner 4; Alec Jones 3.

MAJOR BRITISH MEETINGS 2005

ELITE LEAGUE PAIRS CHAMPIONSHIP 2005
27 MARCH, PETERBOROUGH

1st SWINDON
2nd BELLE VUE
3rd ARENA-ESSEX
4th WOLVERHAMPTON

GROUP A	QUALIFYING SCORES				TOTALS
ARENA-ESSEX 26					
Tony Rickardsson	4	4	3*	4	15 (1)
Gary Havelock	2	2	4	3*	11 (1)
WOLVERHAMPTON 19					
Mikael Max	3	4	2*	2*	11 (2)
David Howe	0	2	3	3	8
EASTBOURNE 18					
David Norris	3*	0	0	0	3 (1)
Nicki Pedersen	4	3	4	4	15
OXFORD 10					
Greg Hancock	2	2	2	4	10
Travis McGowan	0	0	0	0	0
POOLE 17					
Ryan Sullivan	0	3*	3	2	8 (1)
Bjarne Pedersen	3	4	2*	0	9 (1)

GROUP B	QUALIFYING SCORES				TOTALS
IPSWICH 16					
Piotr Protasiewicz	4	0	3	0	7
Hans N. Andersen	3*	2	2*	2	9 (2)
PETERBOROUGH 14					
Peter Karlsson	0	3	3	4	10
Sam Ermolenko	2	X	0	2	4
SWINDON 27					
Leigh Adams	3*	3*	4	4	14 (2)
Lee Richardson	4	4	2	3*	13 (1)

COVENTRY 15

Andreas Jonsson	0	2	0	R	2
Scott Nicholls	2	4	4	3	13

BELLE VUE 18

Jason Crump	2	3	0	4	9
Joe Screen	4	0	2	3*	9 (1)

RACE DETAILS

HEAT ONE:	Tony Rickardsson, Mikael Max, Gary Havelock, David Howe.
HEAT TWO:	Piotr Protasiewicz, Hans N. Andersen, Sam Ermolenko, Peter Karlsson.
HEAT THREE:	Nicki Pedersen, David Norris, Greg Hancock, Travis McGowan.
HEAT FOUR:	Lee Richardson, Leigh Adams, Scott Nicholls, Andreas Jonsson.
HEAT FIVE:	(Rerun) Mikael Max, Bjarne Pedersen, David Howe, Ryan Sullivan.
HEAT SIX:	(Rerun twice) Joe Screen, Peter Karlsson, Jason Crump, Sam Ermolenko (f, ex).
HEAT SEVEN:	Tony Rickardsson, Nicki Pedersen, Gary Havelock, David Norris.
HEAT EIGHT:	Lee Richardson, Leigh Adams, Hans N. Andersen, Piotr Protasiewicz.
HEAT NINE:	Bjarne Pedersen, Ryan Sullivan, Greg Hancock, Travis McGowan.
HEAT TEN:	Scott Nicholls, Jason Crump, Andreas Jonsson, Joe Screen.
HEAT ELEVEN:	Nicki Pedersen, David Howe, Mikael Max, David Norris.
HEAT TWELVE:	Leigh Adams, Peter Karlsson, Lee Richardson, Sam Ermolenko.
HEAT THIRTEEN:	Gary Havelock, Tony Rickardsson, Greg Hancock, Travis McGowan.
HEAT FOURTEEN:	Scott Nicholls, Piotr Protasiewicz, Hans N. Andersen, Andreas Jonsson.
HEAT FIFTEEN:	Nicki Pedersen, Ryan Sullivan, Bjarne Pedersen, David Norris.
HEAT SIXTEEN:	Leigh Adams, Lee Richardson, Joe Screen, Jason Crump.
HEAT SEVENTEEN:	Greg Hancock, David Howe, Mikael Max, Travis McGowan.
HEAT EIGHTEEN:	Peter Karlsson, Scott Nicholls, Sam Ermolenko, Andreas Jonsson (ret).
HEAT NINETEEN:	Tony Rickardsson, Gary Havelock, Ryan Sullivan, Bjarne Pedersen.
HEAT TWENTY:	Jason Crump, Joe Screen, Hans N. Andersen, Piotr Protasiewicz.
FIRST SEMI-FINAL:	Tony Rickardsson, Joe Screen, Jason Crump, Gary Havelock.
SECOND SEMI-FINAL:	Leigh Adams, Lee Richardson, Mikael Max, David Howe.
CONSOLATION FINAL:	Tony Rickardsson, Gary Havelock, Mikael Max, David Howe (f, rem).
GRAND FINAL:	Leigh Adams, Jason Crump, Lee Richardson, Joe Screen.

ROLL OF HONOUR

NOTE: Known as the British League Pairs Championship from 1976-78 and the British Open Pairs Championship from 1984-87.

YEAR	FIRST	SECOND
1976	Ipswich (John Louis & Billy Sanders)	Coventry (Ole Olsen & Mitch Shirra)
1977	Ipswich (Billy Sanders & John Louis)	King's Lynn (Michael Lee & David Gagen)
1978	Cradley Heath (Steve Bastable & Bruce Penhall) & Coventry (Ole Olsen & Mitch Shirra) [shared]	
1979-83	Not staged	
1984	Belle Vue (Peter Collins & Chris Morton)	Reading (Mitch Shirra & Tim Hunt)
1985	Oxford (Hans Nielsen & Simon Wigg)	Reading (John Davis & Mitch Shirra)
1986	Oxford (Simon Wigg & Hans Nielsen)	Coventry (Kelvin Tatum & John Jorgensen)
1987	Oxford (Hans Nielsen & Andy Grahame)	Swindon (Mitch Shirra & Jimmy Nilsen)

1988-2003 Not staged

2004   Swindon (Leigh Adams & Charlie Gjedde)   Belle Vue (Jason Crump & Joe Screen)

2005   Swindon (Leigh Adams & Lee Richardson)   Belle Vue (Jason Crump & Joe Screen)

BRITISH UNDER-21 CHAMPIONSHIP FINAL 2005
30 APRIL, RYE HOUSE

1st EDWARD KENNETT

2nd CHRIS SCHRAMM

3rd RICHARD HALL

4th DANIEL KING

RIDER	QUALIFYING SCORES					TOTAL
Edward Kennett	3	3	1	3	3	13
Chris Schramm	2	1	3	3	2	11
Steve Boxall	3	3	2	2	1	11
Richard Hall	2	3	1	1	3	10
Daniel King	3	2	X	2	3	10
Daniel Giffard	3	3	1	0	3	10
James Brundle	2	1	3	2	2	10
Tommy Allen	2	2	2	3	X	9
Ben Wilson	0	2	3	3	0	8
Adam Roynon	1	0	2	1	2	6
Jason King	0	2	1	F	2	5
Jamie Robertson	1	1	2	1	R	5
William Lawson	R	0	3	R	R	3
Tom Brown	1	1	X	0	1	3
Danny Norton	0	0	0	2	T	2
Luke Priest (Res)	1	–	–	–	–	1
Chris Johnson	F	0	0	–	–	0
Simon Lambert (Res)	X	0	–	–	–	0

RACE DETAILS

QUALIFYING RACE: Adam Roynon, Simon Lambert, Luke Priest.

HEAT ONE: Steve Boxall, Richard Hall, Adam Roynon, Jason King.

HEAT TWO: Daniel Giffard, James Brundle, Jamie Robertson, Ben Wilson (f, rem).

HEAT THREE: Daniel King, Chris Schramm, Tom Brown, Danny Norton.

HEAT FOUR: Edward Kennett, Tommy Allen, William Lawson (ret), Chris Johnson (fell).

HEAT FIVE: Daniel Giffard, Tommy Allen, Chris Schramm, Adam Roynon.

HEAT SIX: Steve Boxall, Daniel King, James Brundle, Chris Johnson.

HEAT SEVEN: Richard Hall, Ben Wilson, Tom Brown, William Lawson.

HEAT EIGHT: Edward Kennett, Jason King, Jamie Robertson, Danny Norton.

HEAT NINE: (Rerun) James Brundle, Adam Roynon, Edward Kennett, Tom Brown (f, ex).

HEAT TEN: (Rerun) William Lawson, Steve Boxall, Daniel Giffard, Danny Norton.

HEAT ELEVEN: Chris Schramm, Jamie Robertson, Richard Hall, Chris Johnson.

HEAT TWELVE:	(Rerun) Ben Wilson, Tommy Allen, Jason King, Daniel King (f, ex).
HEAT THIRTEEN:	(Rerun) Ben Wilson, Danny Norton, Adam Roynon, Simon Lambert (ex, foul riding).
HEAT FOURTEEN:	Tommy Allen, Steve Boxall, Jamie Robertson, Tom Brown.
HEAT FIFTEEN:	Edward Kennett, Daniel King, Richard Hall, Daniel Giffard.
HEAT SIXTEEN:	Chris Schramm, James Brundle, Jason King (fell), William Lawson (ret).
HEAT SEVENTEEN:	Daniel King, Adam Roynon, Jamie Robertson (ret), William Lawson (ret).
HEAT EIGHTEEN:	Edward Kennett, Chris Schramm, Steve Boxall, Ben Wilson.
HEAT NINETEEN:	(Rerun) Richard Hall, James Brundle, Luke Priest, Tommy Allen (f, ex), Danny Norton (ex, 2 mins).
HEAT TWENTY:	Daniel Giffard, Jason King, Tom Brown, Simon Lambert.
SEMI-FINAL:	Daniel King, Richard Hall, Daniel Giffard, Steve Boxall.
FINAL:	(Rerun) Edward Kennett, Chris Schramm, Richard Hall, Daniel King (f, ex).

ROLL OF HONOUR

NOTE: Became known as the British Under-21 Championship in 1987, having previously been called the Junior Championship of Great Britain.

YEAR	FIRST	SECOND	THIRD
1969	Graham Plant	Geoff Ambrose	Mick Bell
1970	Barry Thomas	Dave Jessup	Mick Bell
1971	Ian Turner	Dave Jessup	Peter Ingram
1972	Allen Emmett	Gordon Kennett	Tony Davey
1973	Peter Collins	Barney Kennett	David Gagen
1974	Chris Morton	Steve Bastable	Neil Middleditch
1975	Neil Middleditch	Steve Weatherley	Joe Owen
1976	Michael Lee	Steve Weatherley	Colin Richardson
1977	Les Collins	Phil Collins	Colin Richardson
1978	Phil Collins	Ian Gledhill	Bob Garrad
1979	Kenny Carter	Nigel Flatman	Mel Taylor
1980	Mark Courtney	Kevin Smith	John Barker
1981	Rob Lightfoot	Peter Carr	Neil Evitts
1982	Peter Carr	Martin Hagon	Simon Cross
1983	Keith Millard	Simon Cross	Kenny McKinna
1984	Marvyn Cox	Simon Cross	Andy Smith
1985	Carl Blackbird	David Mullett	Andy Smith
1986	Gary Havelock	Andrew Silver	Daz Sumner
1987	Daz Sumner	David Biles	Mark Loram
1988	Mark Loram	Andy Phillips	Martin Dugard
1989	Martin Dugard	Chris Louis	Dean Barker
1990	Joe Screen	Mark Loram	Chris Louis
1991	Not staged		
1992	Scott Smith	Mark Loram	Joe Screen
1993	Joe Screen	Carl Stonehewer	David Norris
1994	Paul Hurry	Ben Howe	James Grieves
1995	Ben Howe	Paul Hurry	Savalas Clouting
1996	Savalas Clouting	Scott Nicholls	Paul Hurry
1997	Leigh Lanham	Lee Richardson	Scott Nicholls

1998	Scott Nicholls	Lee Richardson	Paul Lee
1999	Scott Nicholls	Lee Richardson	David Howe
2000	David Howe	Lee Richardson	Paul Lee
2001	Simon Stead	David Howe	Paul Lee
2002	Simon Stead	Ross Brady	Olly Allen
2003	Simon Stead	Olly Allen	Edward Kennett
2004	Ritchie Hawkins	Steve Boxall	Edward Kennett
2005	Edward Kennett	Chris Schramm	Richard Hall

CORBETT BOOKMAKERS CONFERENCE LEAGUE FOUR-TEAM CHAMPIONSHIP 2005

25 JUNE, STOKE

1st WEYMOUTH
2nd OXFORD
3rd ARMADALE
4th BOSTON

FIRST SEMI-FINAL	QUALIFYING SCORES		TOTAL
BOSTON 16			
Simon Walker	3	2	5
Adam Roynon	1	2	3
Nathan Irwin	0	3	3
Simon Lambert	2	3	5
ARMADALE 14			
Blair Scott	3	1	4
Derek Sneddon	3	2	5
Sean Stoddart	0	1	1
Andrew Tully	1	3	4
STOKE 12			
Barrie Evans	2	3	5
Luke Priest	3	F	3
Rob Grant	2	2	4
Michael Mitchell	0	0	0
WIMBLEDON 5			
Scott James	1	0	1
Matthew Wright	R	1	1
Danny Betson	2	0	2
Mark Burrows	1	R	1

RACE DETAILS

HEAT ONE:	Blair Scott, Danny Betson, Adam Roynon, Michael Mitchell.
HEAT TWO:	Derek Sneddon, Barrie Evans, Mark Burrows, Nathan Irwin.
HEAT THREE:	(Rerun) Luke Priest, Simon Lambert, Scott James, Sean Stoddart.
HEAT FOUR:	Simon Walker, Rob Grant, Andrew Tully, Matthew Wright (ret).
HEAT FIVE:	Barrie Evans, Simon Walker, Blair Scott, Scott James.
HEAT SIX:	Andrew Tully, Adam Roynon, Mark Burrows (ret), Luke Priest (fell).
HEAT SEVEN:	(Rerun) Nathan Irwin, Rob Grant, Sean Stoddart, Danny Betson.
HEAT EIGHT:	(Rerun) Simon Lambert, Derek Sneddon, Matthew Wright, Michael Mitchell.

SECOND SEMI-FINAL	QUALIFYING SCORES		TOTAL
OXFORD 14			
Chris Mills	2	1	3
Ben Barker	0	3	3
Jamie Courtney	1	2	3
John Branney	2	3	5
WEYMOUTH 13			
David Mason	1	0	1
Daniel Giffard	3	2	5
Lewis Bridger	3	1	4
Tom Brown	2	1	3
SCUNTHORPE 11			
Wayne Carter	2	3	5
Byron Bekker	R	1	1
Danny Norton	3	0	3
Benji Compton	0	2	2
MILDENHALL 10			
Jon Armstrong	3	2	5
Lee Smart	R	X	0
Aidan Collins	1	3	4
Andrew Bargh	1	0	1

RACE DETAILS

HEAT ONE:	Danny Norton, John Branney, David Mason, Lee Smart (ret).
HEAT TWO:	Daniel Giffard, Chris Mills, Aidan Collins, Benji Compton.
HEAT THREE:	Lewis Bridger, Wayne Carter, Andrew Bargh, Ben Barker.
HEAT FOUR:	Jon Armstrong, Tom Brown, Jamie Courtney, Byron Bekker (ret).
HEAT FIVE:	Wayne Carter, Jon Armstrong, Chris Mills, David Mason.
HEAT SIX:	(Rerun) Ben Barker, Benji Compton, Tom Brown, Lee Smart (f, ex).
HEAT SEVEN:	Aidan Collins, Jamie Courtney, Lewis Bridger, Danny Norton.
HEAT EIGHT:	John Branney, Daniel Giffard, Byron Bekker, Andrew Bargh.

FINAL	QUALIFYING SCORES		TOTAL
WEYMOUTH 16			
Daniel Giffard	3	2	5
David Mason	2	3	5
Lewis Bridger	2	2	4
Tom Brown	1	1	2
OXFORD 15			
Chris Mills	3	2	5
Ben Barker	3	3	6
Jamie Courtney	1	3	4
John Branney	0	0	0
ARMADALE 9			
Blair Scott	3	0	3
Derek Sneddon	2	3	5
Sean Stoddart	1	0	1
Andrew Tully	0	X	0
BOSTON 8			
Simon Walker	2	1	3
Adam Roynon	1	2	3
Nathan Irwin	0	1	1
Simon Lambert	0	1	1

RACE DETAILS

HEAT ONE:	Daniel Giffard, Simon Walker, Jamie Courtney, Andrew Tully.
HEAT TWO:	Blair Scott, Lewis Bridger, Adam Roynon, John Branney.
HEAT THREE:	Chris Mills, Derek Sneddon, Tom Brown, Nathan Irwin.
HEAT FOUR:	Ben Barker, David Mason, Sean Stoddart, Simon Lambert.
HEAT FIVE:	David Mason, Chris Mills, Simon Walker, Blair Scott.
HEAT SIX:	Derek Sneddon, Daniel Giffard, Simon Lambert, John Branney.
HEAT SEVEN:	(Rerun) Jamie Courtney, Lewis Bridger, Nathan Irwin, Sean Stoddart (15 met).
HEAT EIGHT:	(Rerun) Ben Barker, Adam Roynon, Tom Brown, Andrew Tully (f, ex).

ROLL OF HONOUR

YEAR	FIRST	SECOND	THIRD	FOURTH
2003	Rye House	Mildenhall	Peterborough	Boston
2004	Mildenhall	Newcastle & Wimbledon	–	Stoke
2005	Weymouth	Oxford	Armadale	Boston

PREMIER LEAGUE PAIRS CHAMPIONSHIP 2005

26 JUNE, GLASGOW

1st GLASGOW
2nd SOMERSET
3rd RYE HOUSE
4th EXETER

GROUP A	QUALIFYING SCORES				TOTAL
RYE HOUSE 20					
Chris Neath	0	2	2	0	4
Stuart Robson	4	4	4	4	16
EXETER 20					
Seemond Stephens	4	3	2	2*	11 (1)
Mark Lemon	2	R	4	3	9
EDINBURGH 18					
Rusty Harrison	2*	4	3	3	12 (1)
Ross Brady	3	3	X	–	6 (1)
NEWCASTLE 16					
James Grieves	3	2	3	4	12
Josef Franc	2*	0	2*	0	4 (2)
SHEFFIELD 16					
Andre Compton	X	4	3	4	11
Ricky Ashworth	3	0	0	2	5

GROUP B	QUALIFYING SCORES				TOTAL
SOMERSET 22					
Magnus Zetterstrom	4	4	4	3	15
Glenn Cunningham	3*	2	0	2*	7 (2)
GLASGOW 21					
Shane Parker	3	3	3*	4	13 (1)
George Stancl	2*	R	4	2	8 (1)
HULL 18					
Paul Thorp	4	4	3	3	14
Emil Kramer	0	0	2*	2*	4 (2)
KING'S LYNN 15					
Tomas Topinka	2	4	2	4	12
Olly Allen	R	3*	R	0	3 (1)

WORKINGTON 14

| Carl Stonehewer | 3 | 0 | 4 | 3 | 10 |
| James Wright | 2* | 2 | R | 0 | 4 (1) |

RACE DETAILS

HEAT ONE:	(Rerun twice) Seemond Stephens, Ricky Ashworth, Mark Lemon (15 met), Andre Compton (ex, foul riding).
HEAT TWO:	Paul Thorp, Shane Parker, George Stancl, Emil Kramer.
HEAT THREE:	Stuart Robson, Ross Brady, Rusty Harrison, Chris Neath.
HEAT FOUR:	Magnus Zetterstrom, Glenn Cunningham, Tomas Topinka, Olly Allen (ret).
HEAT FIVE:	Andre Compton, James Grieves, Josef Franc, Ricky Ashworth.
HEAT SIX:	Paul Thorp, Carl Stonehewer, James Wright, Emil Kramer.
HEAT SEVEN:	Stuart Robson, Seemond Stephens, Chris Neath, Mark Lemon (ret).
HEAT EIGHT:	Magnus Zetterstrom, Shane Parker, Glenn Cunningham, George Stancl (ret).
HEAT NINE:	Rusty Harrison, Ross Brady, James Grieves, Josef Franc.
HEAT TEN:	Tomas Topinka, Olly Allen, James Wright, Carl Stonehewer.
HEAT ELEVEN:	Stuart Robson, Andre Compton, Chris Neath, Ricky Ashworth.
HEAT TWELVE:	Magnus Zetterstrom, Paul Thorp, Emil Kramer, Glenn Cunningham.
HEAT THIRTEEN:	(Rerun) Mark Lemon, Rusty Harrison, Seemond Stephens, Ross Brady (f, ex).
HEAT FOURTEEN:	George Stancl, Shane Parker, Tomas Topinka, Olly Allen (ret).
HEAT FIFTEEN:	Stuart Robson, James Grieves, Josef Franc, Chris Neath.
HEAT SIXTEEN:	Carl Stonehewer, Magnus Zetterstrom, Glenn Cunningham, James Wright (ret).
HEAT SEVENTEEN:	Andre Compton, Rusty Harrison, Ricky Ashworth, Ross Brady (ns).
HEAT EIGHTEEN:	Tomas Topinka, Paul Thorp, Emil Kramer, Olly Allen.
HEAT NINETEEN:	James Grieves, Mark Lemon, Seemond Stephens, Josef Franc.
HEAT TWENTY:	(Rerun) Shane Parker, Carl Stonehewer (15 met), George Stancl, James Wright.
FIRST SEMI-FINAL:	George Stancl, Stuart Robson, Shane Parker, Chris Neath.
SECOND SEMI-FINAL:	Magnes Zetterstrom, Glenn Cunningham, Mark Lemon, Seemond Stephens.
CONSOLATION FINAL:	Mark Lemon, Chris Neath, Stuart Robson, Seemond Stephens.
GRAND FINAL:	Magnus Zetterstrom, George Stancl, Shane Parker, Glenn Cunningham.

ROLL OF HONOUR

NOTE: Became known as the Premier League Pairs Championship in 1997, having previously been known as the National League Pairs Championship (1975-90) and Division Two Pairs Championship (1994).

YEAR	FIRST	SECOND
1975	Newcastle (Tom Owen & Brian Havelock)	Ellesmere Port (John Jackson & Colin Goad)
1976	Ellesmere Port (John Jackson & Chris Turner)	Newcastle (Joe Owen & Tom Owen)
1977	Boston (Robert Hollingworth & Colin Cook)	Newport (Jim Brett & Brian Woodward)
1978	Ellesmere Port (John Jackson & Steve Finch)	Newcastle (Tom Owen & Robbie Blackadder)
1979	Milton Keynes (Andy Grahame & Bob Humphreys)	Ellesmere Port (John Jackson & Steve Finch)
1980	Middlesbrough (Mark Courtney & Steve Wilcock)	Boston (Robert Hollingworth & Gary Guglielmi)
1981	Canterbury (Mike Ferreira & Denzil Kent)	Berwick (Wayne Brown & Steve McDermott)
1982	Weymouth (Martin Yeates & Simon Wigg)	Long Eaton (Alan Molyneux & Dave Perks)

1983	Weymouth (Martin Yeates & Simon Cross)	Glasgow (Jim McMillan & Steve Lawson)
1984	Stoke (Nigel Crabtree & Tom Owen)	Berwick (Bruce Cribb & Steve McDermott)
1985	Ellesmere Port (Joe Owen & Louis Carr)	Poole (Martin Yeates & Stan Bear)
1986	Edinburgh (Les Collins & Doug Wyer)	Hackney (Barry Thomas & Andy Galvin)
1987	Mildenhall (Dave Jessup & Mel Taylor)	Peterborough (Ian Barney & Kevin Hawkins)
1988	Stoke (Graham Jones & Steve Bastable)	Poole (Steve Schofield & David Biles)
1989	Stoke (Nigel Crabtree & Eric Monaghan)	Mildenhall (Preben Eriksen & Peter Glanz)
1990	Hackney (Steve Schofield & Andy Galvin)	Exeter (Steve Regeling & Peter Jeffery)
1991-93	Not staged	
1994	Swindon (Tony Olsson & Tony Langdon)	Glasgow (Nigel Crabtree & David Walsh)
1995-96	Not staged	
1997	Long Eaton (Martin Dixon & Carl Stonehewer)	Reading (David Mullett & Lee Richardson)
1998	Peterborough (Glenn Cunningham & Brett Woodifield)	Exeter (Frank Smart & Michael Coles)
1999	Workington (Carl Stonehewer & Brent Werner)	Arena-Essex (Colin White & Leigh Lanham)
2000	Workington (Carl Stonehewer & Mick Powell)	Isle of Wight (Ray Morton & Danny Bird)
2001	Workington (Carl Stonehewer & Peter I.Karlsson)	Newcastle (Bjarne Pedersen & Jesper Olsen)
2002	Isle of Wight (Adam Shields & Danny Bird)	Newport (Frank Smart & Craig Watson)
2003	Workington (Carl Stonehewer & Simon Stead)	Newport (Frank Smart & Niels-Kristian Iversen)
2004	Reading (Danny Bird & Phil Morris)	Stoke (Paul Pickering & Alan Mogridge)
2005	Glasgow (Shane Parker & George Stancl)	Somerset (Magnus Zetterstrom & Glenn Cunningham)

BETFRED CHAMPIONSHIP OF GREAT BRITAIN FINAL 2005
10 JULY, OXFORD

1st SCOTT NICHOLLS
2nd CHRIS HARRIS
3rd JOE SCREEN
4th MARK LORAM

RIDER	QUALIFYING SCORES					TOTAL
Scott Nicholls	2	3	2	3	3	13
Mark Loram	3	0	3	3	2	11
Joe Screen	3	1	3	3	1	11
Chris Harris	3	1	3	2	2	11
Edward Kennett	3	3	1	1	2	10
Dean Barker	2	2	2	0	3	9
Simon Stead	F	3	3	X	1	7
Stuart Robson	2	3	1	0	1	7
Leigh Lanham	0	2	2	2	1	7
James Grieves	2	1	1	2	0	6
Gary Havelock	1	1	1	1	2	6
Chris Louis	0	0	2	0	3	5
David Howe	1	0	0	1	3	5

Andrew Moore	1	0	0	3	0	4
David McAllan	1	2	0	1	0	4
Lee Richardson	R	2	M	–	–	2
Jamie Courtney (Res)	2	–	–	–	–	2
Ben Barker (Res)	0	0	–	–	–	0

RACE DETAILS

HEAT ONE: Chris Harris, Scott Nicholls, Gary Havelock, Simon Stead (fell).

HEAT TWO: Joe Screen, Dean Barker, David McAllan, Chris Louis.

HEAT THREE: Mark Loram, James Grieves, David Howe, Lee Richardson (ret).

HEAT FOUR: Edward Kennett, Stuart Robson, Andrew Moore, Leigh Lanham.

HEAT FIVE: Simon Stead, Leigh Lanham, Joe Screen, Mark Loram (f, rem).

HEAT SIX: Scott Nicholls, Dean Barker, James Grieves, Andrew Moore.

HEAT SEVEN: Edward Kennett, David McAllan, Gary Havelock, David Howe.

HEAT EIGHT: Stuart Robson, Lee Richardson, Chris Harris, Chris Louis.

HEAT NINE: Simon Stead, Dean Barker, Stuart Robson, David Howe.

HEAT TEN: Joe Screen, Scott Nicholls, Edward Kennett, Ben Barker, Lee Richardson (ex, 2 mins).

HEAT ELEVEN: Mark Loram, Chris Louis, Gary Havelock, Andrew Moore.

HEAT TWELVE: Chris Harris, Leigh Lanham, James Grieves, David McAllan.

HEAT THIRTEEN: (Rerun) Andrew Moore, Jamie Courtney, David McAllan, Simon Stead (f, ex).

HEAT FOURTEEN: Scott Nicholls, Leigh Lanham, David Howe, Chris Louis.

HEAT FIFTEEN: Joe Screen, James Grieves, Gary Havelock, Stuart Robson (f, rem).

HEAT SIXTEEN: Mark Loram, Chris Harris, Edward Kennett, Dean Barker.

HEAT SEVENTEEN: Chris Louis, Edward Kennett, Simon Stead, James Grieves.

HEAT EIGHTEEN: Scott Nicholls, Mark Loram, Stuart Robson, David McAllan.

HEAT NINETEEN: Dean Barker, Gary Havelock, Leigh Lanham, Ben Barker.

HEAT TWENTY: David Howe, Chris Harris, Joe Screen, Andrew Moore.

FINAL: Scott Nicholls, Chris Harris, Joe Screen, Mark Loram (f, rem).

ROLL OF HONOUR

NOTE: Became known as the Championship of Great Britain in 2002, having previously been called the British Final.

YEAR	FIRST	SECOND	THIRD
1961	Barry Briggs	Peter Craven	Ronnie Moore
1962	Peter Craven	Barry Briggs	Ronnie Moore
1963	Peter Craven	Barry Briggs	Leo McAuliffe
1964	Barry Briggs	Ken McKinlay	Ron How
1965	Barry Briggs	Nigel Boocock	Ken McKinlay
1966	Barry Briggs	Ivan Mauger	Colin Pratt
1967	Barry Briggs	Ivan Mauger	Eric Boocock
1968	Ivan Mauger	Barry Briggs	Eric Boocock
1969	Barry Briggs	Nigel Boocock	Ronnie Moore
1970	Ivan Mauger	Ronnie Moore	Roy Trigg
1971	Ivan Mauger	Barry Briggs	Tony Lomas
1972	Ivan Mauger	Nigel Boocock	Barry Briggs

1973	Ray Wilson	Bob Valentine	Peter Collins
1974	Eric Boocock	Terry Betts	Dave Jessup
1975	John Louis	Peter Collins	Malcolm Simmons
1976	Malcolm Simmons	Chris Morton	Doug Wyer
1977	Michael Lee	Dave Jessup	Doug Wyer
1978	Michael Lee	Dave Jessup	Malcolm Simmons
1979	Peter Collins	Michael Lee	Dave Jessup
1980	Dave Jessup	Michael Lee	Phil Collins
1981	Steve Bastable	Kenny Carter	John Louis
1982	Andy Grahame	Alan Grahame	Kenny Carter
1983	Chris Morton	Michael Lee	Andy Grahame
1984	Kenny Carter	Andy Grahame	Dave Jessup
1985	Kenny Carter	John Davis	Kelvin Tatum
1986	Neil Evitts	Phil Collins	Jeremy Doncaster
1987	Kelvin Tatum	Neil Evitts	Simon Wigg
1988	Simon Wigg	Kelvin Tatum	Chris Morton
1989	Simon Wigg	Kelvin Tatum	Alan Grahame
1990	Kelvin Tatum	Simon Cross	Jeremy Doncaster
1991	Gary Havelock	Kelvin Tatum	Chris Louis
1992	Gary Havelock	Martin Dugard	Andy Smith
1993	Andy Smith	Joe Screen	Gary Havelock
1994	Andy Smith	Joe Screen	Steve Schofield
1995	Andy Smith	Joe Screen	Dean Barker
1996	Joe Screen	Chris Louis	Carl Stonehewer
1997	Mark Loram	Chris Louis	Sean Wilson
1998	Chris Louis	Joe Screen	Paul Hurry
1999	Mark Loram	Joe Screen	Chris Louis
2000	Chris Louis	Paul Hurry	Martin Dugard
2001	Mark Loram	Stuart Robson	Martin Dugard
2002	Scott Nicholls	Lee Richardson	David Howe
2003	Scott Nicholls	Dean Barker	David Norris
2004	Joe Screen	David Norris	Mark Loram
2005	Scott Nicholls	Chris Harris	Joe Screen

GRA CONFERENCE LEAGUE PAIRS CHAMPIONSHIP 2005

17 JULY, WIMBLEDON

1st WIMBLEDON
2nd OXFORD
3rd STOKE
4th SCUNTHORPE

GROUP A	QUALIFYING SCORES		TOTALS
WIMBLEDON 14			
Mark Burrows	4	4	8
Barrie Evans	3*	3*	6 (2)
SITTINGBOURNE 7			
Gary Phelps	2*	2	4 (1)
Andre Cross	3	0	3
NEWPORT 6			
Karl Mason	4	2	6
Billy Legg	X	0	0

GROUP B	QUALIFYING SCORES		TOTALS
STOKE 12			
Barrie Evans	4	4	8
Jack Hargreaves	2	2	4
MILDENHALL 8			
Jon Armstrong	3	0	3
Lee Smart	2*	3	5 (1)
WIMBLEDON 'B' 7			
Matthew Wright	4	3	7
Danny Betson	X	–	0
Niall Strudwick (Res)	0	–	0

GROUP C	QUALIFYING SCORES		TOTALS
SCUNTHORPE 11			
Wayne Carter	4	3	7
Benji Compton	2	2*	4 (1)
BOSTON 8			
Karl White	0	2*	2 (1)
Robert Hollingworth	3	3	6

WEYMOUTH 8

Lewis Bridger	R	F	0
Daniel Giffard	4	4	8

GROUP D	QUALIFYING SCORES		TOTALS
OXFORD 11			
Craig Branney	4	4	8
Chris Mills	3*	0	3 (1)

BUXTON 9

Jonathon Bethell	2	4	6
Carl Belfield	0	3*	3 (1)

RYE HOUSE 7

Luke Bowen	0	2*	2 (1)
Barry Burchatt	2	3	5

RACE DETAILS

HEAT ONE:	(Rerun) David Mason, Andre Cross, Gary Phelps, Billy Legg (f, ex).
HEAT TWO:	(Rerun) Matthew Wright, Jon Armstrong, Lee Smart (f, rem), Danny Betson (f, ex).
HEAT THREE:	Wayne Carter, Robert Hollingworth, Benji Compton, Karl White.
HEAT FOUR:	Craig Branney, Chris Mills, Jonathon Bethell, Carl Belfield.
HEAT FIVE:	Mark Burrows, Scott James, David Mason, Billy Legg.
HEAT SIX:	Barrie Evans, Matthew Wright, Jack Hargreaves, Niall Strudwick.
HEAT SEVEN:	Daniel Giffard, Robert Hollingworth, Karl White, Lewis Bridger (ret).
HEAT EIGHT:	(Rerun) Jonathon Bethell, Carl Belfield, Barry Burchatt, Luke Bowen.
HEAT NINE:	Mark Burrows, Scott James, Gary Phelps, Andre Cross (f, rem).
HEAT TEN:	Barrie Evans, Lee Smart, Jack Hargreaves, Jon Armstrong.
HEAT ELEVEN:	(Rerun) Daniel Giffard, Wayne Carter, Benji Compton, Lewis Bridger (15 met; fell).
HEAT TWELVE:	Craig Branney, Barry Burchatt, Luke Bowen, Chris Mills.

FINAL	QUALIFYING SCORES			TOTALS
WIMBLEDON 16				
Mark Burrows	3	4	4	11
Scott James	2*	0	3*	5 (2)

OXFORD 16

Craig Branney	4	3	3	10
Chris Mills	2	2*	2*	6 (2)

STOKE 14

Barrie Evans	4	4	4	12
Jack Hargreaves	0	2	0	2

SCUNTHORPE 8

| Wayne Carter | X | 3 | 2 | 5 |
| Benji Compton | 3 | 0 | X | 3 |

RACE DETAILS

HEAT ONE:	(Rerun) Barrie Evans, Mark Burrows, Scott James, Jack Hargreaves.
HEAT TWO:	(Rerun) Craig Branney, Benji Compton, Chris Mills (f, rem), Wayne Carter (f, ex).
HEAT THREE:	(Rerun) Mark Burrows, Craig Branney, Chris Mills, Scott James.
HEAT FOUR:	(Rerun) Barrie Evans, Wayne Carter, Jack Hargreaves, Benji Compton (f, rem).
HEAT FIVE:	(Rerun) Mark Burrows, Scott James, Wayne Carter, Benji Compton (f, ex).
HEAT SIX:	Barrie Evans, Craig Branney, Chris Mills, Jack Hargreaves.
TITLE RUN-OFF:	(Rerun) Scott James, Mark Burrows, Chris Mills, Craig Branney.

ROLL OF HONOUR

YEAR	FIRST	SECOND
2004	Wimbledon	Mildenhall
	(Mark Burrows & Barrie Evans)	(Ritchie Hawkins &
		Jon Armstrong)
2005	Wimbledon	Oxford
	(Scott James & Mark Burrows)	(Chris Mills & Craig Branney)

PREMIER LEAGUE FOUR-TEAM CHAMPIONSHIP 2005
20 AUGUST, WORKINGTON

1st SOMERSET
2nd WORKINGTON
3rd EXETER
4th RYE HOUSE

FIRST SEMI-FINAL	QUALIFYING SCORES		TOTALS
SOMERSET 15			
Magnus Zetterstrom	3	3	6
Glenn Cunningham	2	2	4
Paul Fry	2	2	4
Ritchie Hawkins	1	0	1
RYE HOUSE 14			
Chris Neath	3	1	4
Stuart Robson	0	3	3
Brent Werner	3	0	3
Edward Kennett	1	3	4
BERWICK 11			
Adrian Rymel	3	0	3

Michal Makovsky	2	1	3
Tom P. Madsen	0	–	0
Adam Pietraszko	0	–	0
Carl Wilkinson (Res)	3	2	5

GLASGOW 8

Shane Parker	R	2	2
George Stancl	2	1	3
Stefan Ekberg	1	1	2
Claus Kristensen	1	0	1

RACE DETAILS

HEAT ONE: Chris Neath, Glenn Cunningham, Stefan Ekberg, Adam Pietraszko.
HEAT TWO: Adrian Rymel, Paul Fry, Claus Kristensen, Stuart Robson (f, rem).
HEAT THREE: Brent Werner, Michal Makovsky, Ritchie Hawkins, Shane Parker (ret).
HEAT FOUR: Magnus Zetterstrom, George Stancl, Edward Kennett, Tom P. Madsen.
HEAT FIVE: Magnus Zetterstrom, Shane Parker, Chris Neath, Adrian Rymel.
HEAT SIX: Edward Kennett, Glenn Cunningham, Michal Makovsky, Claus Kristensen.
HEAT SEVEN: Carl Wilkinson, Paul Fry, Stefan Ekberg, Brent Werner.
HEAT EIGHT: Stuart Robson, Carl Wilkinson, George Stancl, Ritchie Hawkins.

SECOND SEMI-FINAL	QUALIFYING SCORES		TOTALS
WORKINGTON 18			
James Wright	3	3	6
Kauko Nieminen	2	3	5
Shaun Tacey	2	2	4
Tomasz Piszcz	0	3	3
EXETER 11			
Mark Lemon	3	2	5
Sebastien Tresarrieu	1	1	2
Seemond Stephens	2	X	2
Lee Smethills	0	2	2
SHEFFIELD 10			
Sean Wilson	2	0	2
Andre Compton	1	R	1
Ricky Ashworth	3	1	4
Richard Hall	1	2	3
EDINBURGH 9			
Matthew Wethers	1	1	2
William Lawson	0	1	1
Rusty Harrison	3	3	6
Daniel Nermark	0	0	0

RACE DETAILS

HEAT ONE: Rusty Harrison, Sean Wilson, Sebastien Tresarrieu, Tomasz Piszcz.

HEAT TWO: James Wright, Seemond Stephens, Andre Compton, Daniel Nermark.

HEAT THREE: Ricky Ashworth, Kauko Nieminen, Matthew Wethers, Lee Smethills.

HEAT FOUR: Mark Lemon, Shaun Tacey, Richard Hall, William Lawson.

HEAT FIVE: James Wright, Mark Lemon, Matthew Wethers, Sean Wilson.

HEAT SIX: Kauko Nieminen, Richard Hall, Sebastien Tresarrieu, Daniel Nermark.

HEAT SEVEN: (Rerun) Rusty Harrison, Shaun Tacey, Ricky Ashworth, Seemond Stephens (f, ex).

HEAT EIGHT: Tomasz Piszcz, Lee Smethills, William Lawson, Andre Compton (ret).

FINAL	QUALIFYING SCORES			TOTALS
SOMERSET 21				
Magnus Zetterstrom	2	3	3	8
Glenn Cunningham	1	3	0	4
Paul Fry	1	1	1	3
Ritchie Hawkins	1	3	2	6
WORKINGTON 20				
James Wright	2	2	2	6
Kauko Nieminen	3	2	1	6
Shaun Tacey	0	3	X	3
Tomasz Piszcz	2	R	3	5
EXETER 16				
Mark Lemon	3	0	3	6
Sebastien Tresarrieu	3	1	0	4
Seemond Stephens	–	–	–	–
Lee Smethills	0	1	3	4
Ray Morton (Res)	0	0	2	2
RYE HOUSE 14				
Chris Neath	M	1	R	1
Stuart Robson	3	2	2	7
Brent Werner	1	2	1	4
Edward Kennett	2	R	–	2
Tommy Allen (Res)	X	–	–	0

RACE DETAILS

HEAT ONE: Kauko Nieminen, Magnus Zetterstrom, Brent Werner, Lee Smethills.

HEAT TWO: Mark Lemon, Edward Kennett, Glenn Cunningham, Shaun Tacey.

HEAT THREE: (Rerun twice) Sebastien Tresarrieu, Tomasz Piszcz, Paul Fry (15 met), Chris Neath
                 (15 met; ex, 2 mins).

HEAT FOUR: Stuart Robson, James Wright, Ritchie Hawkins, Ray Morton.

HEAT FIVE: Magnus Zetterstrom, James Wright, Chris Neath, Mark Lemon.

HEAT SIX: Ritchie Hawkins, Kauko Nieminen, Sebasten Tresarrieu, Edward Kennett (ret).

HEAT SEVEN: Shaun Tacey, Brent Werner, Paul Fry, Ray Morton.

HEAT EIGHT: Glenn Cunningham, Stuart Robson, Lee Smethills, Tomasz Piszcz (ret).

HEAT NINE: Tomasz Piszcz, Ray Morton, Paul Fry (f, rem), Chris Neath (ret).

HEAT TEN: (Rerun) Lee Smethills, Ritchie Hawkins, Tommy Allen (f, ex), Shaun Tacey (ex, not under power).

HEAT ELEVEN: Mark Lemon, James Wright, Brent Werner, Glenn Cunningham.

HEAT TWELVE: Magnus Zetterstrom, Stuart Robson, Kauko Nieminen, Sebastien Tresarrieu.

ROLL OF HONOUR

NOTE: Became known as the Premier League Four Team Championship in 1997, having previously been known as the National League Four Team Championship (1976-90) and the Division Two Four Team Championship (1991-94).

YEAR	FIRST	SECOND	THIRD	FOURTH
1976	Newcastle	Eastbourne	Ellesmere Port	Workington
1977	Peterborough	Canterbury	Eastbourne	Stoke
1978	Peterborough	Stoke	Canterbury	Ellesmere Port
1979	Ellesmere Port	Mildenhall	Peterborough	Berwick
1980	Crayford	Rye House	Ellesmere Port	Stoke
1981	Edinburgh	Newcastle	Middlesbrough	Wolverhampton
1982	Newcastle	Mildenhall	Middlesbrough	Rye House
1983	Newcastle	Mildenhall	Milton Keynes	Long Eaton
1984	Mildenhall	Stoke	Milton Keynes	Boston
1985	Middlesbrough	Peterborough	Hackney	Stoke
1986	Middlesbrough	Arena-Essex	Hackney	Mildenhall
1987	Mildenhall	Arena-Essex	Eastbourne	Wimbledon
1988	Peterborough	Mildenhall	Eastbourne	Poole
1989	Peterborough	Stoke	Exeter	Eastbourne
1990	Stoke	Poole	Hackney	Ipswich
1991	Arena-Essex	Long Eaton	Edinburgh	Milton Keynes
1992	Peterborough	Edinburgh	Rye House	Glasgow
1993	Edinburgh	Swindon	Long Eaton	Rye House
1994	Oxford	Long Eaton	Peterborough	Edinburgh
1995-96	Not staged			
1997	Long Eaton	Edinburgh	Oxford	Berwick
1998	Peterborough	Edinburgh	Hull	Reading
1999	Sheffield	Newport	Isle of Wight	Arena-Essex
2000	Sheffield	Isle of Wight	Swindon	Berwick
2001	Workington	Newcastle	Sheffield	Isle of Wight
2002	Berwick	Arena-Essex	Newport	Hull
2003	Swindon	Trelawny	Newport	Glasgow
2004	Workington	Stoke	Glasgow	Rye House
2005	Somerset	Workington	Exeter	Rye House

ELITE LEAGUE RIDERS' CHAMPIONSHIP 2005
28 AUGUST, SWINDON

1st NICKI PEDERSEN
2nd SCOTT NICHOLLS
3rd PETER KARLSSON
4th BJARNE PEDERSEN

RIDER	QUALIFYING SCORES					TOTAL
Bjarne Pedersen	3	1	2	3	3	12
Nicki Pedersen	1	3	3	2	3	12
Charlie Gjedde	3	1	1	3	3	11
Lee Richardson	2	0	3	2	3	10
Scott Nicholls	F	3	3	2	2	10
Peter Karlsson	3	1	3	1	2	10
Greg Hancock	2	3	2	0	2	9
Jason Crump	2	2	R	2	2	8
Krzysztof Kasprzak	0	3	1	3	1	8
Billy Hamill	3	2	X	–	–	5
Mark Loram	2	2	0	1	0	5
Ales Dryml	0	1	0	3	0	4
David Howe	1	2	0	0	1	4
Davey Watt	1	0	2	1	0	4
Fredrik Lindgren	R	0	2	1	1	4
Simon Stead	1	0	1	0	1	3

RACE DETAILS

HEAT ONE: Peter Karlsson, Jason Crump, Davey Watt, Fredrik Lindgren (ret).

HEAT TWO: Bjarne Pedersen, Lee Richardson, Nicki Pedersen, Scott Nicholls (fell).

HEAT THREE: Billy Hamill, Mark Loram, Simon Stead, Ales Dryml.

HEAT FOUR: Charlie Gjedde, Greg Hancock, David Howe, Krzysztof Kasprzak.

HEAT FIVE: Krzysztof Kasprzak, Billy Hamill, Bjarne Pedersen, Fredrik Lindgren.

HEAT SIX: Greg Hancock, Mark Loram, Peter Karlsson, Lee Richardson.

HEAT SEVEN: Nicki Pedersen, Jason Crump, Charle Gjedde, Simon Stead.

HEAT EIGHT: Scott Nicholls, David Howe, Ales Dryml, Davey Watt.

HEAT NINE: Lee Richardson, Fredrik Lindgren, Simon Stead, David Howe.

HEAT TEN: Peter Karlsson, Bjarne Pedersen, Charlie Gjedde, Ales Dryml.

HEAT ELEVEN: (Awarded) Scott Nicholls, Greg Hancock, Billy Hamill (f, ex), Jason Crump (ret).

HEAT TWELVE: Nicki Pedersen, Davey Watt, Krzysztof Kasprzak, Mark Loram.

HEAT THIRTEEN: (Rerun) Ales Dryml, Nicki Pedersen, Fredrik Lindgren, Greg Hancock.

HEAT FOURTEEN: Krzysztof Kasprzak, Scott Nicholls, Peter Karlsson, Simon Stead.

HEAT FIFTEEN: Bjarne Pedersen, Jason Crump, Mark Loram, David Howe.

HEAT SIXTEEN: Charlie Gjedde, Lee Richardson, Davey Watt, Billy Hamill (ns), (3 riders only).

HEAT SEVENTEEN: Charlie Gjedde, Scott Nicholls, Fredrik Lindgren, Mark Loram.

HEAT EIGHTEEN: Nicki Pedersen, Peter Karlsson, David Howe, Billy Hamill (ns), (3 riders only).

HEAT NINETEEN: Lee Richardson, Jason Crump, Krzysztof Kasprzak, Ales Dryml.

HEAT TWENTY: Bjarne Pedersen, Greg Hancock, Simon Stead, Davey Watt.

SEMI-FINAL: Peter Karlsson, Scott Nicholls, Charlie Gjedde, Lee Richardson.

FINAL: Nicki Pedersen, Scott Nicholls, Peter Karlsson, Bjarne Pedersen.

ROLL OF HONOUR

NOTE: Became known as the Elite League Riders' Championship in 1997, having previously been known as British League Riders' Championship (1965-67 and 1975-90), Division One Riders' Championship (1968-74 and 1991-94) and Premier League Riders' Championship (1995-96).

YEAR	FIRST	SECOND	THIRD
1965	Barry Briggs	Jimmy Gooch	Cyril Maidment
1966	Barry Briggs	Olle Nygren	Norman Hunter
1967	Barry Briggs	Nigel Boocock	Ray Wilson
1968	Barry Briggs	Eric Boocock	Ivan Mauger
1969	Barry Briggs	Ivan Mauger	Jim Airey
1970	Barry Briggs	Anders Michanek	Eric Boocock
1971	Ivan Mauger	Barry Briggs	Jim McMillan
1972	Ole Olsen	Martin Ashby	Ronnie Moore
1973	Ivan Mauger	Ray Wilson	Anders Michanek
1974	Peter Collins	Ivan Mauger	Phil Crump
1975	Peter Collins	Phil Crump	Martin Ashby
1976	Ole Olsen	Peter Collins	John Louis
1977	Ole Olsen	Peter Collins	Michael Lee
1978	Ole Olsen	Peter Collins	Steve Bastable
1979	John Louis	Bruce Penhall	Michael Lee
1980	Les Collins	Bruce Penhall	Larry Ross
1981	Kenny Carter	Chris Morton	Shawn Moran
1982	Kenny Carter	Shawn Moran	Hans Nielsen
1983	Erik Gundersen	Michael Lee	Hans Nielsen
1984	Chris Morton	Hans Nielsen	Erik Gundersen
1985	Erik Gundersen	Peter Collins	Chris Morton
1986	Hans Nielsen	Erik Gundersen	Shawn Moran
1987	Hans Nielsen	Chris Morton	Kelly Moran
1988	Jan O. Pedersen	Erik Gundersen	Hans Nielsen
1989	Shawn Moran	Hans Nielsen	Brian Karger
1990	Hans Nielsen	Kelly Moran	Ronnie Correy
1991	Sam Ermolenko	Hans Nielsen	Joe Screen
1992	Joe Screen	Per Jonsson	Gary Havelock
1993	Per Jonsson	Henrik Gustafsson	Chris Louis
1994	Sam Ermolenko	Hans Nielsen	Martin Dugard
1995	Gary Havelock	Billy Hamill	Jason Crump
1996	Sam Ermolenko	Jason Crump	Leigh Adams
1997	Greg Hancock	Tony Rickardsson	Chris Louis
1998	Tony Rickardsson	Jason Crump	Joe Screen
1999	Jason Crump	Todd Wiltshire	Jason Lyons
2000	Ryan Sullivan	Greg Hancock	Nicki Pedersen
2001	Jason Crump	Scott Nicholls	Nicki Pedersen

2002	Tony Rickardsson	Nicki Pedersen	Jason Crump
2003	Lee Richardson	Andreas Jonsson	Scott Nicholls
2004	Bjarne Pedersen	Ryan Sullivan	Hans N. Andersen
2005	Nicki Pedersen	Scott Nicholls	Peter Karlsson

SILVER SKI CONFERENCE LEAGUE RIDERS' CHAMPIONSHIP 2005
27 AUGUST, RYE HOUSE

1st STEVE BOXALL
2nd BARRIE EVANS
3rd BLAIR SCOTT
4th DAVID MASON

RIDER	RACE SCORES					TOTAL
Steve Boxall	3	3	3	3	3	15
Barrie Evans	3	3	3	0	2	11
Blair Scott	2	2	2	3	2	11
David Mason	3	2	3	3	0	11
Lewis Bridger	X	3	3	1	3	10
Jon Armstrong	2	1	2	2	3	10
Wayne Carter	3	2	1	2	1	9
Mark Burrows	1	3	F	2	2	8
Adam Roynon	1	1	1	1	3	7
Craig Branney	2	2	2	1	–	7
Karlis Ezergailis	2	M	2	0	1	5
Jonathon Bethell	1	0	1	0	2	4
Danny Betson	0	1	0	2	1	4
Mark Baseby (Res)	3	X	–	–	–	3
Harland Cook	R	1	0	1	1	3
Chris Hunt	1	0	1	0	0	2
Simon Lambert	0	X	R	–	–	0
Lee Smart (Res)	0	0	–	–	–	0

RACE DETAILS

HEAT ONE: David Mason, Blair Scott, Mark Burrows, Danny Betson.

HEAT TWO: Steve Boxall, Jon Armstrong, Chris Hunt, Simon Lambert (f, rem).

HEAT THREE: Wayne Carter, Karlis Ezergailis, Jonathon Bethell, Harland Cook (ret).

HEAT FOUR: (Rerun) Barrie Evans, Craig Branney, Adam Roynon, Lewis Bridger (f, ex).

HEAT FIVE: Barrie Evans, Blair Scott, Jon Armstrong, Jonathon Bethell.

HEAT SIX: Steve Boxall, Craig Branney, Danny Betson, Lee Smart, Karlis Ezergailis (ex, 2 mins).

HEAT SEVEN: Lewis Bridger, David Mason, Harland Cook, Chris Hunt.

HEAT EIGHT: (Rerun) Mark Burrows, Wayne Carter, Adam Roynon, Simon Lambert (f, ex).

HEAT NINE: Steve Boxall, Blair Scott, Adam Roynon, Harland Cook.

HEAT TEN:	Lewis Bridger, Jon Armstrong, Wayne Carter, Danny Betson.
HEAT ELEVEN:	David Mason, Craig Branney, Jonathon Bethell, Simon Lambert (ret).
HEAT TWELVE:	(Rerun) Barrie Evans, Karlis Ezergailis, Chris Hunt, Mark Burrows (fell).
HEAT THIRTEEN:	Blair Scott, Wayne Carter, Craig Branney, Chris Hunt.
HEAT FOURTEEN:	Mark Baseby, Danny Betson, Harland Cook, Barrie Evans (f, rem).
HEAT FIFTEEN:	David Mason, Jon Armstrong, Adam Roynon, Karlis Ezergailis.
HEAT SIXTEEN:	(Rerun) Steve Boxall, Mark Burrows, Lewis Bridger, Jonathon Bethell.
HEAT SEVENTEEN:	Lewis Bridger, Blair Scott, Karlis Ezergailis, Lee Smart.
HEAT EIGHTEEN:	Adam Roynon, Jonathon Bethell, Danny Betson, Chris Hunt.
HEAT NINETEEN:	Steve Boxall, Barrie Evans, Wayne Carter, David Mason.
HEAT TWENTY:	(Rerun – awarded) Jon Armstrong, Mark Burrows, Harland Cook, Mark Baseby (f, ex).
SECOND PLACE RUN-OFF:	Barrie Evans, Blair Scott, David Mason.

ROLL OF HONOUR

NOTE: Previously known as Division Three Riders' Championship (1994), Academy League Riders' Championship (1995) and Amateur League Riders' Championship (1997).

YEAR	FIRST	SECOND	THIRD
1994	Andy Howe	Kevin Little	Colin Earl
1995	Kevin Little	Chris Cobby	Andre Compton
1996	Mike Hampson	Justin Elkins	Graeme Gordon
1997	Jon Armstrong	Bobby Eldridge	David Howe
1998	Steve Bishop	Andrew Appleton	Seemond Stephens
1999	Jonathan Swales	Steve Camden	Scott Courtney
2000	Scott Pegler	Steve Bishop	Adam Allott
2001	David Mason	Scott Pegler	Simon Wolstenholme
2002	James Birkinshaw	Edward Kennett	Jamie Robertson
2003	Barrie Evans	Jamie Robertson	Trevor Harding
2004	James Wright	Mark Burrows	Richard Hall
2005	Steve Boxall	Barrie Evans	Blair Scott

PREMIER LEAGUE RIDERS' CHAMPIONSHIP 2005
18 SEPTEMBER, SHEFFIELD

1st SEAN WILSON
2nd ALAN MOGRIDGE
3rd TOMAS TOPINKA
4th MARK LEMON

RIDER	QUALIFYING SCORES					TOTAL
Alan Mogridge	2	3	3	3	2	13
Sean Wilson	3	2	3	3	1	12
Tomas Topinka	R	3	2	3	3	11
Mark Lemon	1	2	3	2	2	10
Shane Parker	1	1	2	2	3	9
Stuart Robson	3	2	1	2	1	9

Andre Compton	F	3	3	X	2	8
Magnus Zetterstrom	3	R	0	3	2	8
James Wright	1	2	0	1	3	7
Rusty Harrison	3	1	2	1	0	7
Craig Boyce	2	1	2	2	0	7
Matej Zagar	2	R	0	1	3	6
Garry Stead	2	3	–	–	–	5
Adrian Rymel	1	R	1	1	1	4
Mads Korneliussen	0	1	0	0	1	2
James Grieves	0	0	1	0	0	1
Benji Compton (Res)	1	0	–	–	–	1
Luke Priest (Res)	0	–	–	–	–	0

RACE DETAILS

HEAT ONE: Rusty Harrison, Craig Boyce, Shane Parker, Mads Korneliussen.

HEAT TWO: Sean Wilson, Garry Stead, Adrian Rymel, Andre Compton (fell).

HEAT THREE: Stuart Robson, Alan Mogridge, Mark Lemon, Tomas Topinka (ret).

HEAT FOUR: Magnus Zetterstrom, Matej Zagar, James Wright, James Grieves.

HEAT FIVE: Tomas Topinka, James Wright, Rusty Harrison, Adrian Rymel (ret).

HEAT SIX: Garry Stead, Stuart Robson, Craig Boyce, James Grieves.

HEAT SEVEN: Alan Mogridge, Sean Wilson, Mads Korneliussen, Matej Zagar (ret).

HEAT EIGHT: Andre Compton, Mark Lemon, Shane Parker, Magnus Zetterstrom (ret).

HEAT NINE: Alan Mogridge, Rusty Harrison, Benji Compton, Magnus Zetterstrom.

HEAT TEN: Mark Lemon, Craig Boyce, Adrian Rymel, Matej Zagar.

HEAT ELEVEN: Andre Compton, Tomas Topinka, James Grieves, Mads Korneliussen.

HEAT TWELVE: Sean Wilson, Shane Parker, Stuart Robson, James Wright.

HEAT THIRTEEN: Sean Wilson, Mark Lemon, Rusty Harrison, James Grieves.

HEAT FOURTEEN: (Rerun) Alan Mogridge, Craig Boyce, James Wright, Andre Compton (ex, foul riding)

HEAT FIFTEEN: Magnus Zetterstrom, Stuart Robson, Adrian Rymel, Mads Korneliussen.

HEAT SIXTEEN: Tomas Topinka, Shane Parker, Matej Zagar, Luke Priest.

HEAT SEVENTEEN: Matej Zagar, Andre Compton, Stuart Robson, Rusty Harrison.

HEAT EIGHTEEN: Tomas Topinka, Magnus Zetterstrom, Sean Wilson, Craig Boyce.

HEAT NINETEEN: James Wright, Mark Lemon, Mads Korneliussen, Benji Compton.

HEAT TWENTY: Shane Parker, Alan Mogridge, Adrian Rymel, James Grieves.

SEMI-FINAL: Mark Lemon, Tomas Topinka, Shane Parker, Stuart Robson.

FINAL: Sean Wilson, Alan Mogridge, Tomas Topinka, Mark Lemon.

ROLL OF HONOUR

NOTE: Became known as the Premier League Riders' Championship in 1997, having previously been known as the Division Two Riders' Championship (1968-74 and 1991-94) and National League Riders' Championship (1975-90).

YEAR	FIRST	SECOND	THIRD
1968	Graham Plant	Ken Eyre	Graeme Smith
1969	Geoff Ambrose	Mick Bell	Ross Gilbertson
1970	Dave Jessup	Barry Crowson	Gary Peterson
1971	John Louis	Malcolm Shakespeare	Hugh Saunders
1972	Phil Crump	Arthur Price	Bob Coles

1973	Arthur Price	Bobby McNeil	Lou Sansom
1974	Carl Glover	Ted Hubbard	Phil Herne
1975	Laurie Etheridge	Brian Collins	Arthur Browning
1976	Joe Owen	John Jackson	Ted Hubbard
1977	Colin Richardson	Martin Yeates	Tom Owen
1978	Steve Koppe	John Jackson	Ted Hubbard
1979	Ian Gledhill	Steve Wilcock	Andy Grahame
1980	Wayne Brown	Martin Yeates	Steve Finch
1981	Mike Ferreira	Simon Wigg	Bruce Cribb
1982	Joe Owen	Steve Lomas	Bob Garrad
1983	Steve McDermott	Richard Knight	Martin Yeates
1984	Ian Barney	Dave Perks	Martin Yeates
1985	Neil Middleditch	Kevin Hawkins	Trevor Banks
1986	Paul Thorp	Steve Schofield	Les Collins
1987	Andrew Silver	Nigel Crabtree	David Blackburn
1988	Troy Butler	Mark Loram	Kenny McKinna
1989	Mark Loram	Kenny McKinna	David Blackburn
1990	Andy Grahame	Chris Louis	Craig Boyce
1991	Jan Staechmann	David Bargh	Troy Butler
1992	Robert Nagy	Mick Poole	Richard Green
1993	Gary Allan	Mick Poole	Tony Langdon
1994	Paul Bentley	Tony Olsson	Tony Langdon
1995-96	Not staged		
1997	Peter Carr	Glenn Cunningham	Robert Eriksson
1998	Glenn Cunningham	Carl Stonehewer	Peter Carr
1999	Sean Wilson	Jesper Olsen	Craig Watson
2000	Carl Stonehewer	Peter Carr	Paul Pickering
2001	Carl Stonehewer	Sean Wilson	Bjarne Pedersen
2002	Adam Shields	Craig Watson	Phil Morris
2003	Sean Wilson	Adam Shields	Carl Stonehewer
2004	Andre Compton	Mark Lemon	Simon Stead
2005	Sean Wilson	Alan Mogridge	Tomas Topinka

GRAND PRIX 2005

Rider	Europe	Sweden	Slovenia	Britain	Denmark	Czech Rep.	Scandinavia	Poland	Italy	Total
TONY RICKARDSSON	25	20	25	25	25	25	18	8	25	196
JASON CRUMP	18	25	16	4	12	16	25	18	20	154
LEIGH ADAMS	20	13	9	7	7	8	16	11	16	107
NICKI PEDERSEN	10	16	20	6	16	10	10	9	5	102
GREG HANCOCK	11	6	8	6	20	7	8	16	18	100
BJARNE PEDERSEN	4	18	3	18	3	20	7	7	10	90
TOMASZ GOLLOB	6	6	10	8	6	9	9	25	4	83
ANDREAS JONSSON	8	1	3	12	8	8	20	10	10	80
SCOTT NICHOLLS	6	7	8	9	4	14	10	8	6	72
ANTONIO LINDBACK	16	8	3	8	18	6	7	0	5	71
JAROSLAW HAMPEL	10	–	–	20	8	18	5	6	–	67
HANS N. ANDERSEN	2	8	9	16	8	3	5	5	8	64
LEE RICHARDSON	5	3	3	5	6	4	3	20	6	55
RYAN SULLIVAN	7	3	13	1	5	9	5	2	–	45
TOMASZ CHRZANOWSKI	4	4	2	7	2	1	1	1	6	28
MATEJ ZAGAR	–	–	18	–	–	–	–	–	5	18
KENNETH BJERRE	–	8	4	–	–	–	–	–	–	12
PIOTR PROTASIEWICZ	–	–	–	–	–	–	–	11	–	11
NIELS–KRISTIAN IVERSEN	–	–	–	–	7	–	–	–	–	7
RUNE HOLTA	–	6	–	–	–	–	–	–	–	6
STEFAN ANDERSSON	–	–	–	–	–	–	–	–	5	5
KRZYSZTOF KASPRZAK	4	–	–	–	–	–	–	–	–	4
DAVID NORRIS	–	–	–	4	–	–	–	–	–	4
JONAS DAVIDSSON	–	–	–	–	–	–	4	–	–	4
ROMAN POVAZHNY	–	–	–	–	–	–	–	–	4	4
ALES DRYML	–	–	–	–	–	3	–	–	–	3
EDWARD KENNETT	–	–	–	1	–	–	–	–	–	1
MIKAEL MAX	–	0	–	–	–	–	–	–	–	0
PETER NAHLIN	–	0	–	–	–	–	–	–	–	0
IZAK SANTEJ	–	–	0	–	–	–	–	–	–	0
SIMON STEAD	–	–	–	0	–	–	–	–	–	0
DANIELE TESSARI	–	–	–	–	–	–	–	–	0	0

A revamped format made the Grand Prix series all the more exciting in 2005, with sixteen riders contesting each round instead of the twenty-four of previous seasons since 1998. Under this format, likened to the old-style one-off World Finals, each rider met every other competitor in the qualifying heats. A distinctive yellow race jacket was also introduced, which 2004 World Champion Jason Crump wore in the opening round. Thereafter, whoever was the series leader sported the special bib in the next round. After the twenty qualifying heats, the top eight scorers were split into two semi-finals, with the first two in each progressing to the final. The winner of the grand showdown received 25 points, with the other three riders gaining 20, 18 and 16 points in descending order. Meanwhile, all the other competitors carried forward the number of race points they accumulated in the qualifying phase.

The series began with the European Grand Prix at the well-appointed Olympic Stadium, Wroclaw, Poland on 30 April and legendary Swede Tony Rickardsson was in scintillating form after a brief stint in the Elite League with Arena-Essex. The multi-World Champion proved the absolute master of the 387.4m raceway, winning all five of his heats in the qualifying section before racing to victory in the first semi-final and, subsequently, the final. There were murmerings that he might even have missed the meeting, having suffered a painful injury to his lower back just five days prior to the event while representing Masarna in an away league fixture against Vargarna at Norrkoping in his homeland. However, if he was in any discomfort on the night, it certainly didn't show. Meanwhile, after netting 9 points in the heats, Aussie Leigh Adams followed the Swede home in both the semi-final and the final, with Jason Crump occupying third place in the meeting's most important race, while the fast-rising Antonio Lindback finished fourth. So, first blood to 'Ricko', who extended his amazing record to 15 GP wins from 71 consecutive appearances since the inaugural round, coincidentally at Wroclaw on 20 May 1995.

Round two was staged at a new GP venue, namely the Eskilstuna home of Swedish Elite League side Smederna. Norwegian Rune Holta came into the meeting as the wild card entrant, with diminutive Dane Kenneth Bjerre called up to complete the line-up after Jaroslaw Hampel had injured a thumb the previous Tuesday, ironically in a Swedish league fixture. On the 335m circuit, likened by some to the Swindon raceway, it was the Robins' skipper Leigh Adams who certainly looked at home in storming to 13 points in the qualifying heats. Joining him on that mark were the unrelated Pedersens, Bjarne (who was actually placed first by virtue of defeating his namesake in heat five and Adams in heat fourteen) and Nicki, while Tony Rickardsson recovered from an unusual first-race blip to tally 11 points. Adams wasn't able to carry his good form into the second semi-final, however, and was eliminated along with Hans N. Andersen, as the duo followed Antonio Lindback and Bjerre into the changing room. Rickardsson looked to have the final in the bag ahead of Crump, until an audacious move saw Nicki Pedersen send Bjarne Pedersen clattering into the air safety barrier. With the 2003 World Champion excluded for foul riding, his successor, Crump, took advantage of his reprieve, bravely sweeping around Rickardsson on the first corner before completing his eleventh GP win. The result took Ricko to 45 points overall with Crump right on his tail, just 2 points behind. Adams, meanwhile, slipped to third spot on 33 points, while Nicki Pedersen occupied fourth position with a tally of 26.

Prior to the third round of the series in Slovenia, both Tony Rickardsson (again) and Nicki Pedersen survived scares to take their places in the starting line-up. The Swede suffered concussion while racing for Tarnow in the Polish Extra League at Czestochowa on 19 May, while the Dane took a knock during Eastbourne's Elite League match at Coventry four days later. Jaroslaw Hampel wasn't so fortunate though and was again replaced by Kenneth Bjerre, having failed to recover sufficiently from his thumb injury. Reading's Slovenian racer Matej Zagar was the nominated wild card and, in a largely uneventful meeting, run in high temperatures of up to 32°C, it was the Premier League's leading rider who caught the eye with a marvellous display that carried him all the way to the final. His safe passage came at the expense of many seasoned campaigners, with a number of more illustrious competitors caught out by a nasty rut on the exit of the fourth bend. The showdown race still had a quality look about it though, as Rickardsson, Nicki Pedersen and reigning World Champion Jason Crump joined him in the final. However, it was the remarkable Rickardsson who powered to yet another GP success, while Pedersen displaced Zagar in mid-race, with 2004 World Champion Jason Crump at the rear throughout. The result raised Rickardsson's total to 70 points and extended his lead in the championship, with Crump (59), Nicki Pedersen (46) and Leigh Adams (42) trailing in his wake, as he sought a record-equalling sixth title.

The series moved on to the speedway showpiece of the year at Cardiff's majestic Millennium Stadium on 11 June, when an enthusiastic audience of some 40,000 gathered for a fifth successive season. Although perhaps unthinkable, the atmosphere for the occasion seemed to go up a notch on previous years, as those in attendance witnessed incidents galore in a meeting that became littered with reruns and exclusions. Frankly though, many of referee Marek Wojaczek's decisions were hotly disputed and left folk simply scratching their heads in disbelief. All of that added to the drama of course and, having returned to the series from injury, it was Pole Jaroslaw Hampel who made the biggest impact, assuredly compiling 12 points and then taking victory in the second semi-final. Swede Andreas Jonsson also notched a dozen points before dipping out at the semi-final stage, but it was his remarkable compatriot Tony Rickardsson who again took the accolades courtesy of a blistering first corner, which saw him skirt the air safety barrier as he rounded the field to post the seventeenth victory of his glittering GP career ahead of Hampel, with Bjarne Pedersen and Hans N. Andersen filling third and fourth place respectively. Ricko's performance kept him well on course to equal Ivan Mauger's record of world titles, his overall tally having reached 95 points. With his nearest challengers enduring an unproductive time, the Swede greatly increased his advantage over the chasing group, with Jason Crump (63), Nicki Pedersen (52), Leigh Adams (49) and Bjarne Pedersen (43) all wondering just how they could possibly catch up. For Crump in particular the meeting was an absolute nightmare, as the Aussie suffered three exclusions on his way to just 4 points, as his deficit on Rickardsson increased alarmingly by 21 points at one fell swoop. Fellow Australian Ryan Sullivan also endured an evening to forget, scoring but a single point from three rides before pulling out of the meeting in some discomfort. This followed a frightening head-first crash while riding for Czestochowa at Tarnow in the Polish Extra League just six days previously, which resulted in heavy bruising to his back and a knee.

Tony Rickardsson continued to annihilate the field in the Danish Grand Prix at Parken in Copenhagen on 25 June, as he collected his third win on the bounce and made it four successes in five rounds. Things had looked to be slipping from his grasp when he ran an uncharacteristic last in heat nine to leave him sitting on 5 points from three rides. However, he hadn't won five World Championships for nothing and finished with two victories to comfortably make the semi-final stage. American Greg Hancock, the only other rider with a 100 per cent GP attendance record alongside Rickardsson, found his best form to card four straight wins after finishing at the rear in his first outing. Jason Crump, Nicki Pedersen and Antonio Lindback also finished the qualifying heats in double figures, while Hans N. Andersen, Jaroslaw Hampel and Andreas Jonsson completed the line-up for the last eight. Pedersen took the first semi-final, with Hancock scooping second place after Andersen had fallen on the fourth bend while holding the all-important position behind his Danish compatriot. Then, a fierce first turn in the second semi-final left Crump with too much to do at the back, as Lindback and Rickardsson sailed on to the big showdown. Rickardsson duly sped away to triumph from Hancock, with Lindback registering his best GP finish in third spot. The win took Ricko's overall tally to 120 points, as he surged further away from Crump (75), Nicki Pedersen (68), Leigh Adams (56), Lindback (53) and Hancock (51) in the standings.

Tony Rickardsson maintained his relentless charge to a sixth World Championship in the Czech Republic round at beautiful Prague on 9 July, brilliantly scorching to a fourth successive GP victory. Played out on the 353m Marketa Stadium raceway, his win was all the more remarkable after a fall on the first bend of heat five had left him with a buckled bike and a thumb injury. Of the other competitors left to pick up the scraps in the wake of the Swede's dominance, Scott Nicholls dropped just 1 point in the qualifying heats, only to finish third in the first semi-final having lost too much ground on the vital first corner. Meanwhile, Poole's Bjarne Pedersen finished a good second in the final, with Jaroslaw Hampel and Jason Crump filling the third and fourth positions respectively. Rickardsson's win extended his total for the series to an amazing 145 points from a possible 150. With a 54-point advantage over second-placed Crump, it meant the Aussie could still mathematically retain the title, although his chances looked decidely slim, with 'TR' requiring just 22 points to be absolutely sure of another crown. In summary, the leading scorers after six rounds were: Rickardsson 145; Crump 91; Nicki Pedersen 78; Bjarne Pedersen 66; Leigh Adams 64; Antonio Lindback 59.

Following a break of five weeks, the Grand Prix series resumed on 13 August, when the 310m Malilla Motorstadion raceway in Sweden became the twenty-fifth venue to be employed in the competition since its inception in 1995. Riding in his homeland, all eyes were understandably on Tony Rickardsson as he stood on the cusp of lifting a sixth World title. However, on a rain-soaked circuit it was compatriot Andreas Jonsson and 2004 Champion Jason Crump who dominated the qualifying heats, each totalling 13 points. Ricko wasn't far behind though and easily claimed a semi-final slot, having posted a couple of race wins on his way to a tally of 11. Eight quickly became four as Tomasz Gollob, Nicki Pedersen, Scott Nicholls and Greg Hancock failed to negotiate the semi-final hurdle for a slot in the showpiece race. Crump subsequently swooped around Jonsson for the twelfth GP victory of his glittering career, while Rickardsson occupied third place ahead of Leigh Adams. Although the result cut the Swede's overall advantage to 47 points, it left him needing just 4 points from the remaining two rounds to achieve his goal. His total after seven rounds had clicked onto 163 points, with his nearest rivals being Crump (116), Nicki Pedersen (88), Adams (80), Bjarne Pedersen (73), Hancock (66), Lindback (66), Jaroslaw Hampel (61) and Jonsson (60).

Set at the Slaski Stadium, Katowice in Poland on 2 September 1979, Ivan Mauger's sixth World Championship success was finally equalled by Tony Rickardsson at the Polonia Stadium, Bydgoszcz in the same country on 27 August 2005. It didn't take the mighty Swede long either. Requiring just 4 points to guarantee the title, he took the chequered flag in heat three and then finished third in heat six. With the job done, Rickardsson could be forgiven for not showing his usual level of consistency thereafter. Indeed, he failed to reach the semi-final stage for the first time in the entire series and, looking even further back, the last time he had failed to progress beyond the qualifying heats actually occurred at the Danish GP on 26 June 2004. Although somewhat overshadowed by the achievement of the Swedish master, the event was dominated by remarkable Pole Tomasz Gollob, who took victory in his home Grand Prix for the fourth year on the bounce and, with the inclusion of another success in 1998, for the fifth time in total at the fabulous Bydgoszcz raceway. For the record, Gollob also secured wins at Wroclaw in 1995 and 1999, increasing his tally of Polish GP successes to a remarkable total of seven. Perhaps not at his brilliant best during the previous seven rounds of the 2005 championship Gollob was right back in the groove, using a fast outside line to wonderful effect as he headed the leaderboard on 13 points and stormed into the semi-finals. Joining him was wild card entrant and fellow countryman Piotr Protasiewicz, along with Greg Hancock, Leigh Adams, Andreas Jonsson, Nicki Pedersen, Jason Crump and comeback king Lee Richardson, who looked down and out after his first two outings, having run lasts in each. The battling Brit yielded 5 points from his next two rides, however, and then reached the last eight by coolly defeating Gollob in heat twenty. Gollob made mincemeat of the opposition in the first semi-final, beating Crump at a canter. Then the rejuvenated Richardson continued his winning ways by taking the second semi-final from Hancock. The final subsequently saw Gollob charge away and, although briefly challenged by Richardson on lap three, there was no stopping him from collecting the tenth GP victory of his career. As a measure of the Pole's standing on the world stage, only Rickardsson (19) and Crump (12) had carded more wins since the inception of the series in 1995. One other record of note saw Hancock take his overall tally of GP points to exactly 1,000, although he remained some way adrift of the only other ever-present rider... the one and only Tony Rickardsson, whose total at the end of the night had reached 1,335 points from 78 rounds. Summing up the 2005 series, with one round to go, the Swede had amassed 171 points, while Crump was assured of second place on 134 points. Third position was still up for grabs though, with Nicki Pedersen (97), Adams (91), Hancock (82), Bjarne Pedersen (80) and Gollob (79) all in with a shout.

The series concluded at the flat, pacy 334m Lonigo circuit in Italy on 10 September and, despite having already wrapped up the title, Tony Rickardsson produced another blistering effort to win his sixth round of a wonderful GP campaign. The super Swede simply dominated proceedings, reeling off seven straight race victories, including a couple from behind in heats eleven and thirteen. His awesome performance took his tally for the nine rounds to 196 points as he created a new GP record, bettering his own previous high score of 181 points in 2002. Second place on the night went the way of Jason Crump, who had already sealed the overall runner-up spot, the outgoing World Champion becoming the third rider to top four-figures in the event's history as his total reached 1,012 points, putting him within touching distance of Greg Hancock (1,018), but still some way short of the remarkable Rickardsson (1,360). With the number one and two podium positions set, it left the contest for third place an intriguing one. The 2003 Champ Nicki Pedersen held the position prior to the off but missed out on a semi-final slot after a robust challenge had sent Slovenian wild card Matej Zagar flying in heat twenty, earning the Dane an exclusion. That left Hancock and Leigh Adams in with a shot for the bronze medal and, although the American beat the Aussie for third spot in the final, it was Adams' 16 points that earned him third place overall. It was no less than the Swindon rider deserved, having been the most consistent performer in British racing for over a decade, as he finally shook off the disappointing aura of being the world number four for the previous three years.

GRAND PRIX OF EUROPE (ROUND ONE)

30 APRIL, OLYMPIC STADIUM, WROCLAW, POLAND

1st TONY RICKARDSSON
2nd LEIGH ADAMS
3rd JASON CRUMP
4th ANTONIO LINDBACK

RIDER	QUALIFYING SCORES					TOTAL
Tony Rickardsson	3	3	3	3	3	15
Jason Crump	3	3	0	2	3	11
Greg Hancock	2	2	3	1	3	11
Jaroslaw Hampel	3	3	2	0	2	10
Nicki Pedersen	3	2	2	3	0	10
Leigh Adams	1	3	2	2	1	9
Andreas Jonsson	0	1	1	3	3	8
Antonio Lindback	2	2	3	0	1	8
Ryan Sullivan	2	1	1	1	2	7
Scott Nicholls	2	0	0	3	1	6
Tomasz Gollob	0	0	3	1	2	6
Lee Richardson	1	1	1	2	0	5
Bjarne Pedersen	1	0	2	1	0	4
Krzysztof Kasprzak	0	1	1	0	2	4
Tomasz Chrzanowski	1	2	0	0	1	4
Hans N. Andersen	0	0	0	2	R	2
Janusz Kolodziej (Res)	–	–	–	–	–	0
Adrian Miedzinski (Res)	–	–	–	–	–	0

RACE DETAILS

HEAT ONE:	Jaroslaw Hampel, Ryan Sullivan, Leigh Adams, Tomasz Gollob.
HEAT TWO:	Nicki Pedersen, Scott Nicholls, Bjarne Pedersen, Krzysztof Kasprzak.
HEAT THREE:	Jason Crump, Greg Hancock, Tomasz Chrzanowski, Andreas Jonsson.
HEAT FOUR:	Tony Rickardsson, Antonio Lindback, Lee Richardson, Hans N. Andersen.
HEAT FIVE:	Jason Crump, Antonio Lindback, Ryan Sullivan, Scott Nicholls.
HEAT SIX:	Leigh Adams, Tomasz Chrzanowski, Lee Richardson, Bjarne Pedersen.
HEAT SEVEN:	Tony Rickardsson, Greg Hancock, Krzysztof Kasprzak, Tomasz Gollob.
HEAT EIGHT:	Jaroslaw Hampel, Nicki Pedersen, Andreas Jonsson, Hans N. Andersen.
HEAT NINE:	Greg Hancock, Bjarne Pedersen, Ryan Sullivan, Hans N. Andersen.
HEAT TEN:	Tony Rickardsson, Leigh Adams, Andreas Jonsson, Scott Nicholls.
HEAT ELEVEN:	Tomasz Gollob, Nicki Pedersen, Lee Richardson, Jason Crump.
HEAT TWELVE:	Antonio Lindback, Jaroslaw Hampel, Krzysztof Kasprzak, Tomasz Chrzanowski.
HEAT THIRTEEN:	Andreas Jonsson, Lee Richardson, Ryan Sullivan, Krzysztof Kasprzak.
HEAT FOURTEEN:	Nicki Pedersen, Leigh Adams, Greg Hancock, Antonio Lindback.
HEAT FIFTEEN:	Scott Nicholls, Hans N. Andersen, Tomasz Gollob, Tomasz Chrzanowski.
HEAT SIXTEEN:	Tony Rickardsson, Jason Crump, Bjarne Pedersen, Jaroslaw Hampel.

HEAT SEVENTEEN:	Tony Rickardsson, Ryan Sullivan, Tomasz Chrzanowski, Nicki Pedersen.
HEAT EIGHTEEN:	Jason Crump, Krzysztof Kasprzak, Leigh Adams, Hans N. Andersen (ret).
HEAT NINETEEN:	Andreas Jonsson, Tomasz Gollob, Antonio Lindback, Bjarne Pedersen.
HEAT TWENTY:	Greg Hancock, Jaroslaw Hampel, Scott Nicholls, Lee Richardson.
FIRST SEMI-FINAL:	Tony Rickardsson, Leigh Adams, Jaroslaw Hampel, Andreas Jonsson.
SECOND SEMI-FINAL:	Jason Crump, Antonio Lindback, Nicki Pedersen, Greg Hancock.
FINAL:	Tony Rickardsson, Leigh Adams, Jason Crump, Antonio Lindback (ret).

GRAND PRIX OF SWEDEN (ROUND TWO)
14 MAY, SMED STADIUM, ESKILSTUNA

1st JASON CRUMP
2nd TONY RICKARDSSON
3rd BJARNE PEDERSEN
4th NICKI PEDERSEN

RIDER	QUALIFYING SCORES					TOTAL
Bjarne Pedersen	2	3	2	3	3	13
Leigh Adams	3	2	3	2	3	13
Nicki Pedersen	3	2	2	3	3	13
Tony Rickardsson	0	3	3	3	2	11
Jason Crump	2	3	3	0	2	10
Antonio Lindback	2	1	2	0	3	8
Kenneth Bjerre	3	2	0	2	1	8
Hans N. Andersen	2	3	2	1	X	8
Scott Nicholls	T	2	1	2	2	7
Tomasz Gollob	1	0	1	3	1	6
Greg Hancock	1	1	3	0	1	6
Rune Holta	1	1	0	2	2	6
Tomasz Chrzanowski	3	0	0	1	0	4
Ryan Sullivan	1	0	1	1	0	3
Lee Richardson	0	1	1	R	1	3
Andreas Jonsson	0	0	T	1	0	1
Mikael Max (Res)	0	–	–	–	–	0
Peter Nahlin (Res)	R	–	–	–	–	0

RACE DETAILS

HEAT ONE:	Leigh Adams, Jason Crump, Rune Holta, Lee Richardson.
HEAT TWO:	Nicki Pedersen, Antonio Lindback, Tomasz Gollob, Tony Rickardsson.
HEAT THREE:	Tomasz Chrzanowski, Hans N. Andersen, Ryan Sullivan, Andreas Jonsson.
HEAT FOUR:	(Rerun) Kenneth Bjerre, Bjarne Pedersen, Greg Hancock, Mikael Max, Scott Nicholls (ex, tapes).
HEAT FIVE:	Bjarne Pedersen, Nicki Pedersen, Rune Holta, Andreas Jonsson.
HEAT SIX:	Tony Rickardsson, Leigh Adams, Greg Hancock, Tomasz Chrzanowski.
HEAT SEVEN:	Hans N. Andersen, Kenneth Bjerre, Lee Richardson, Tomasz Gollob.

HEAT EIGHT:	Jason Crump, Scott Nicholls, Antonio Lindback, Ryan Sullivan.
HEAT NINE:	Tony Rickardsson, Hans N. Andersen, Scott Nicholls, Rune Holta.
HEAT TEN:	Leigh Adams, Nicki Pedersen, Ryan Sullivan, Kenneth Bjerre.
HEAT ELEVEN:	(Rerun) Greg Hancock, Antonio Lindback, Lee Richardson, Peter Nahlin (ret), Andreas Jonsson (ex, tapes).
HEAT TWELVE:	Jason Crump, Bjarne Pedersen, Tomasz Gollob, Tomasz Chrzanowski.
HEAT THIRTEEN:	Tomasz Gollob, Rune Holta, Ryan Sullivan, Greg Hancock.
HEAT FOURTEEN:	Bjarne Pedersen, Leigh Adams, Hans N. Andersen, Antonio Lindback.
HEAT FIFTEEN:	Nicki Pedersen, Scott Nicholls, Tomasz Chrzanowski, Lee Richardson (ret).
HEAT SIXTEEN:	Tony Rickardsson, Kenneth Bjerre, Andreas Jonsson, Jason Crump.
HEAT SEVENTEEN:	Antonio Lindback, Rune Holta, Kenneth Bjerre, Tomasz Chrzanowski.
HEAT EIGHTEEN:	Leigh Adams, Scott Nicholls, Tomasz Gollob, Andreas Jonsson.
HEAT NINETEEN:	Bjarne Pedersen, Tony Rickardsson, Lee Richardson, Ryan Sullivan.
HEAT TWENTY:	(Rerun) Nicki Pedersen, Jason Crump, Greg Hancock, Hans N. Andersen (f, ex).
FIRST SEMI-FINAL:	Tony Rickardsson, Bjarne Pedersen, Antonio Lindback, Kenneth Bjerre.
SECOND SEMI-FINAL:	Nicki Pedersen, Jason Crump, Hans N. Andersen, Leigh Adams.
FINAL:	(Rerun) Jason Crump, Tony Rickardsson, Bjarne Pedersen, Nicki Pedersen (ex, foul riding).

GRAND PRIX OF SLOVENIA (ROUND THREE)
28 MAY, MATIJE GUBCA STADIUM, KRSKO

1st TONY RICKARDSSON
2nd NICKI PEDERSEN
3rd MATEJ ZAGAR
4th JASON CRUMP

RIDER	QUALIFYING SCORES					TOTAL
Ryan Sullivan	2	3	2	3	3	13
Tony Rickardsson	2	3	3	3	2	13
Jason Crump	3	2	3	1	3	12
Nicki Pedersen	3	3	2	3	0	11
Tomasz Gollob	1	2	2	2	3	10
Leigh Adams	3	1	1	1	3	9
Matej Zagar	2	2	3	2	0	9
Hans N. Andersen	2	1	2	2	2	9
Scott Nicholls	1	0	3	3	1	8
Greg Hancock	1	3	1	2	1	8
Kenneth Bjerre	3	1	0	0	0	4
Andreas Jonsson	0	0	0	1	2	3
Lee Richardson	0	2	1	0	R	3
Antonio Lindback	1	T	X	0	2	3
Bjarne Pedersen	0	1	0	1	1	3
Tomasz Chrzanowski	0	0	1	0	1	2
Izak Santej (Res)	0	–	–	–	–	0
Denis Stojs (Res)	–	–	–	–	–	0

RACE DETAILS

HEAT ONE: Kenneth Bjerre, Hans N. Andersen, Scott Nicholls, Bjarne Pedersen.

HEAT TWO: Jason Crump, Matej Zagar, Tomasz Gollob, Lee Richardson.

HEAT THREE: Leigh Adams, Tony Rickardsson, Greg Hancock, Tomasz Chrzanowski.

HEAT FOUR: Nicki Pedersen, Ryan Sullivan, Antonio Lindback, Andreas Jonsson.

HEAT FIVE: (Rerun) Ryan Sullivan, Lee Richardson, Hans N. Andersen, Tomasz Chrzanowski.

HEAT SIX: (Rerun) Greg Hancock, Matej Zagar, Kenneth Bjerre, Izak Santej, Antonio Lindback (ex, tapes).

HEAT SEVEN: Nicki Pedersen, Jason Crump, Leigh Adams, Scott Nicholls.

HEAT EIGHT: Tony Rickardsson, Tomasz Gollob, Bjarne Pedersen, Andreas Jonsson.

HEAT NINE: (Rerun) Matej Zagar, Hans N. Andersen, Leigh Adams, Andreas Jonsson.

HEAT TEN: Tony Rickardsson, Nicki Pedersen, Lee Richardson, Kenneth Bjerre.

HEAT ELEVEN: (Rerun) Scott Nicholls, Tomasz Gollob, Tomasz Chrzanowski, Antonio Lindback (f, ex).

HEAT TWELVE: Jason Crump, Ryan Sullivan, Greg Hancock, Bjarne Pedersen.

HEAT THIRTEEN: Tony Rickardsson, Hans N. Andersen, Jason Crump, Antonio Lindback.

HEAT FOURTEEN: Ryan Sullivan, Tomasz Gollob, Leigh Adams, Kenneth Bjerre.

HEAT FIFTEEN: Scott Nicholls, Greg Hancock, Andreas Jonsson, Lee Richardson.

HEAT SIXTEEN: Nicki Pedersen, Matej Zagar, Bjarne Pedersen, Tomasz Chrzanowski.

HEAT SEVENTEEN: (Rerun) Tomasz Gollob, Hans N. Andersen, Greg Hancock, Nicki Pedersen.

HEAT EIGHTEEN: Jason Crump, Andreas Jonsson, Tomasz Chrzanowski, Kenneth Bjerre.

HEAT NINETEEN: Ryan Sullivan, Tony Rickardsson, Scott Nicholls, Matej Zagar.

HEAT TWENTY: Leigh Adams, Antonio Lindback, Bjarne Pedersen, Lee Richardson (ret).

FIRST SEMI-FINAL: Matej Zagar, Nicki Pedersen, Leigh Adams, Ryan Sullivan.

SECOND SEMI-FINAL: Jason Crump, Tony Rickardsson, Hans N. Andersen, Tomasz Gollob.

FINAL: Tony Rickardsson, Nicki Pedersen, Matej Zagar, Jason Crump.

GRAND PRIX OF BRITAIN (ROUND FOUR)

11 JUNE, MILLENNIUM STADIUM, CARDIFF

1st TONY RICKARDSSON
2nd JAROSLAW HAMPEL
3rd BJARNE PEDERSEN
4th HANS N. ANDERSEN

RIDER	QUALIFYING SCORES					TOTAL
Andreas Jonsson	3	2	3	1	3	12
Jaroslaw Hampel	3	1	3	3	2	12
Tony Rickardsson	3	3	2	2	2	12
Hans N. Andersen	2	3	1	3	1	10
Scott Nicholls	3	R	1	3	2	9
Antonio Lindback	T	3	1	1	3	8
Bjarne Pedersen	1	2	3	2	0	8
Tomasz Gollob	2	1	2	R	3	8
Tomasz Chrzanowski	0	2	0	2	3	7

Leigh Adams	1	1	2	1	2	7
Greg Hancock	2	T	3	1	0	6
Nicki Pedersen	1	3	1	X	1	6
Lee Richardson	0	2	2	0	1	5
David Norris	X	1	0	3	0	4
Jason Crump	2	X	X	2	X	4
Ryan Sullivan	1	0	0	–	–	1
Edward Kennett (Res)	0	1	–	–	–	1
Simon Stead (Res)	0	0	–	–	–	0

RACE DETAILS

HEAT ONE: (Rerun) Jaroslaw Hampel, Jason Crump, Bjarne Pedersen, Tomasz Chrzanowski.

HEAT TWO: (Rerun) Scott Nicholls, Hans N. Andersen, Ryan Sullivan, Simon Stead, Antonio Lindback (ex, tapes).

HEAT THREE: (Rerun) Tony Rickardsson, Tomasz Gollob, Nicki Pedersen, David Norris (ex, foul riding).

HEAT FOUR: Andreas Jonsson, Greg Hancock, Leigh Adams, Lee Richardson.

HEAT FIVE: Nicki Pedersen, Andreas Jonsson, Jaroslaw Hampel, Scott Nicholls (f, rem, ret).

HEAT SIX: (Rerun) Hans N. Andersen, Lee Richardson, Tomasz Gollob, Jason Crump (ex, foul riding).

HEAT SEVEN: (Rerun) Antonio Lindback, Bjarne Pedersen, David Norris, Edward Kennett, Greg Hancock (ex, tapes).

HEAT EIGHT: Tony Rickardsson, Tomasz Chrzanowski, Leigh Adams, Ryan Sullivan.

HEAT NINE: Jaroslaw Hampel, Leigh Adams, Hans N. Andersen, David Norris.

HEAT TEN: (Rerun) Greg Hancock, Tony Rickardsson, Scott Nicholls, Jason Crump (f, ex).

HEAT ELEVEN: (Rerun) Bjarne Pedersen, Lee Richardson, Nicki Pedersen, Ryan Sullivan.

HEAT TWELVE: Andreas Jonsson, Tomasz Gollob, Antonio Lindback, Tomasz Chrzanowski.

HEAT THIRTEEN: Jaroslaw Hampel, Tony Rickardsson, Antonio Lindback, Lee Richardson.

HEAT FOURTEEN: David Norris, Jason Crump, Andreas Jonsson, Simon Stead, Ryan Sullivan (ns).

HEAT FIFTEEN: Scott Nicholls, Bjarne Pedersen, Leigh Adams, Tomasz Gollob (ret).

HEAT SIXTEEN: (Rerun) Hans N. Andersen, Tomasz Chrzanowski, Greg Hancock, Nicki Pedersen (ex, foul riding).

HEAT SEVENTEEN: Tomasz Gollob, Jaroslaw Hampel, Edward Kennett, Greg Hancock, Ryan Sullivan (ns).

HEAT EIGHTEEN: (Rerun) Antonio Lindback, Leigh Adams, Nicki Pedersen, Jason Crump (f, ex).

HEAT NINETEEN: Andreas Jonsson, Tony Rickardsson, Hans N. Andersen, Bjarne Pedersen.

HEAT TWENTY: Tomasz Chrzanowski, Scott Nicholls, Lee Richardson, David Norris.

FIRST SEMI-FINAL: Bjarne Pedersen, Hans N. Andersen, Antonio Lindback, Andreas Jonsson.

SECOND SEMI-FINAL: (Rerun) Jaroslaw Hampel, Tony Rickardsson, Tomasz Gollob (ret), Scott Nicholls (f,ex).

FINAL: Tony Rickardsson, Jaroslaw Hampel, Bjarne Pedersen, Hans N. Andersen.

GRAND PRIX OF DENMARK (ROUND FIVE)
25 JUNE, PARKEN, COPENHAGEN

1st TONY RICKARDSSON
2nd GREG HANCOCK
3rd ANTONIO LINDBACK
4th NICKI PEDERSEN

RIDER	QUALIFYING SCORES					TOTAL
Greg Hancock	0	3	3	3	3	12
Jason Crump	3	1	3	3	2	12
Tony Rickardsson	3	2	0	3	3	11
Nicki Pedersen	3	2	3	0	3	11
Antonio Lindback	1	3	2	2	2	10
Andreas Jonsson	X	3	1	3	1	8
Hans N. Andersen	2	1	0	2	3	8
Jaroslaw Hampel	1	3	2	1	1	8
Leigh Adams	2	0	3	R	2	7
Niels-Kristian Iversen	2	1	X	2	2	7
Lee Richardson	3	0	1	2	0	6
Tomasz Gollob	2	0	2	1	1	6
Ryan Sullivan	0	2	1	1	1	5
Scott Nicholls	0	2	2	F	X	4
Bjarne Pedersen	1	0	1	1	0	3
Tomasz Chrzanowski	1	1	0	0	0	2
Charlie Gjedde (Res)	–	–	–	–	–	–
Mads Korneliussen (Res)	–	–	–	–	–	–

RACE DETAILS

HEAT ONE:	(Rerun) Lee Richardson, Leigh Adams, Bjarne Pedersen, Ryan Sullivan.
HEAT TWO:	Tony Rickardsson, Niels-Kristian Iversen, Antonio Lindback, Scott Nicholls.
HEAT THREE:	Jason Crump, Hans N. Andersen, Tomasz Chrzanowski, Greg Hancock.
HEAT FOUR:	(Rerun) Nicki Pedersen, Tomasz Gollob, Jaroslaw Hampel, Andreas Jonsson (f, ex).
HEAT FIVE:	Antonio Lindback, Ryan Sullivan, Hans N. Andersen, Tomasz Gollob.
HEAT SIX:	Andreas Jonsson, Tony Rickardsson, Jason Crump, Lee Richardson.
HEAT SEVEN:	(Rerun) Greg Hancock, Nicki Pedersen, Niels-Kristian Iversen, Leigh Adams.
HEAT EIGHT:	Jaroslaw Hampel, Scott Nicholls, Tomasz Chrzanowski, Bjarne Pedersen.
HEAT NINE:	Greg Hancock, Jaroslaw Hampel, Ryan Sullivan, Tony Rickardsson.
HEAT TEN:	Nicki Pedersen, Antonio Lindback, Lee Richardson, Tomasz Chrzanowski.
HEAT ELEVEN:	Leigh Adams, Scott Nicholls, Andreas Jonsson, Hans N. Andersen.
HEAT TWELVE:	(Rerun) Jason Crump, Tomasz Gollob, Bjarne Pedersen, Niels-Kristian Iversen (f, ex).
HEAT THIRTEEN:	Andreas Jonsson, Niels-Kristian Iversen, Ryan Sullivan, Tomasz Chrzanowski.
HEAT FOURTEEN:	(Rerun) Greg Hancock, Lee Richardson, Tomasz Gollob, Scott Nicholls (fell).
HEAT FIFTEEN:	Jason Crump, Antonio Lindback, Jaroslaw Hampel, Leigh Adams (ret).
HEAT SIXTEEN:	Tony Rickardsson, Hans N. Andersen, Bjarne Pedersen, Nicki Pedersen.

HEAT SEVENTEEN: (Rerun) Nicki Pedersen, Jason Crump, Ryan Sullivan, Scott Nicholls (f, ex).

HEAT EIGHTEEN: Hans N. Andersen, Niels-Kristian Iversen, Jaroslaw Hampel, Lee Richardson.

HEAT NINETEEN: Tony Rickardsson, Leigh Adams, Tomasz Gollob, Tomasz Chrzanowski.

HEAT TWENTY: Greg Hancock, Antonio Lindback, Andreas Jonsson, Bjarne Pedersen.

FIRST SEMI-FINAL: Nicki Pedersen, Greg Hancock, Andreas Jonsson, Hans N. Andersen (f, rem).

SECOND SEMI-FINAL: Antonio Lindback, Tony Rickardsson, Jaroslaw Hampel, Jason Crump.

FINAL: Tony Rickardsson, Greg Hancock, Antonio Lindback, Nicki Pedersen.

GRAND PRIX OF THE CZECH REPUBLIC (ROUND SIX)
9 JULY, MARKETA STADIUM, PRAGUE

1st TONY RICKARDSSON
2nd BJARNE PEDERSEN
3rd JAROSLAW HAMPEL
4th JASON CRUMP

RIDER	QUALIFYING SCORES					TOTAL
Scott Nicholls	2	3	3	3	3	14
Tony Rickardsson	3	2	3	1	3	12
Nicki Pedersen	3	1	2	2	2	10
Bjarne Pedersen	3	3	1	0	2	9
Tomasz Gollob	3	0	3	2	1	9
Jaroslaw Hampel	0	3	2	1	3	9
Ryan Sullivan	2	3	3	0	1	9
Jason Crump	2	0	1	2	3	8
Andreas Jonsson	1	2	2	2	1	8
Leigh Adams	1	2	0	3	2	8
Greg Hancock	1	1	0	3	2	7
Antonio Lindback	2	0	1	3	X	6
Lee Richardson	R	2	1	1	0	4
Hans N. Andersen	1	0	2	0	0	3
Ales Dryml	0	1	X	1	1	3
Tomasz Chrzanowski	0	1	0	0	0	1
Bohumil Brhel (Res)	–	–	–	–	–	–
Lukas Dryml (Res)	–	–	–	–	–	–

RACE DETAILS

HEAT ONE: Tony Rickardsson, Antonio Lindback, Leigh Adams, Ales Dryml.

HEAT TWO: Tomasz Gollob, Jason Crump, Hans N. Andersen, Lee Richardson (ret).

HEAT THREE: Bjarne Pedersen, Scott Nicholls, Greg Hancock, Jaroslaw Hampel.

HEAT FOUR: Nicki Pedersen, Ryan Sullivan, Andreas Jonsson, Tomasz Chrzanowski.

HEAT FIVE: (Rerun) Jaroslaw Hampel, Tony Rickardsson, Nicki Pedersen, Jason Crump.

HEAT SIX: (Rerun) Ryan Sullivan, Leigh Adams, Greg Hancock, Hans N. Andersen.

HEAT SEVEN: Bjarne Pedersen, Andreas Jonsson, Ales Dryml, Tomasz Gollob.

HEAT EIGHT: Scott Nicholls, Lee Richardson, Tomasz Chrzanowski, Antonio Lindback.

HEAT NINE:	Tony Rickardsson, Hans N. Andersen, Bjarne Pedersen, Tomasz Chrzanowski.
HEAT TEN:	Scott Nicholls, Andreas Jonsson, Jason Crump, Leigh Adams.
HEAT ELEVEN:	(Rerun) Ryan Sullivan, Jaroslaw Hampel, Lee Richardson, Ales Dryml (f, ex).
HEAT TWELVE:	(Rerun) Tomasz Gollob, Nicki Pedersen, Antonio Lindback, Greg Hancock.
HEAT THIRTEEN:	Scott Nicholls, Tomasz Gollob, Tony Rickardsson, Ryan Sullivan.
HEAT FOURTEEN:	Leigh Adams, Nicki Pedersen, Lee Richardson, Bjarne Pedersen.
HEAT FIFTEEN:	Greg Hancock, Jason Crump, Ales Dryml, Tomasz Chrzanowski.
HEAT SIXTEEN:	Antonio Lindback, Andreas Jonsson, Jaroslaw Hampel, Hans N. Andersen.
HEAT SEVENTEEN:	Tony Rickardsson, Greg Hancock, Andreas Jonsson, Lee Richardson.
HEAT EIGHTEEN:	Jaroslaw Hampel, Leigh Adams, Tomasz Gollob, Tomasz Chrzanowski.
HEAT NINETEEN:	Scott Nicholls, Nicki Pedersen, Ales Dryml, Hans N. Andersen.
HEAT TWENTY:	(Rerun) Jason Crump, Bjarne Pedersen, Ryan Sullivan, Antonio Lindback (ex, foul riding).
FIRST SEMI-FINAL:	Jaroslaw Hampel, Bjarne Pedersen, Scott Nicholls, Ryan Sullivan.
SECOND SEMI-FINAL:	Jason Crump, Tony Rickardsson, Tomasz Gollob, Nicki Pedersen.
FINAL:	Tony Rickardsson, Bjarne Pedersen, Jaroslaw Hampel, Jason Crump.

GRAND PRIX OF SCANDINAVIA (ROUND SEVEN)
13 AUGUST, MALILLA, SWEDEN

1st JASON CRUMP
2nd ANDREAS JONSSON
3rd TONY RICKARDSSON
4th LEIGH ADAMS

RIDER	QUALIFYING SCORES					TOTAL
Andreas Jonsson	1	3	3	3	3	13
Jason Crump	3	3	3	2	2	13
Tony Rickardsson	2	2	1	3	3	11
Nicki Pedersen	3	2	3	X	2	10
Scott Nicholls	1	3	2	3	1	10
Leigh Adams	0	1	3	3	2	9
Tomasz Gollob	2	2	2	2	1	9
Greg Hancock	2	2	1	0	3	8
Bjarne Pedersen	3	1	0	0	3	7
Antonio Lindback	2	1	1	2	1	7
Jaroslaw Hampel	0	3	0	2	0	5
Ryan Sullivan	1	0	2	1	1	5
Hans N. Andersen	1	0	1	1	2	5
Jonas Davidsson	0	1	2	1	0	4
Lee Richardson	3	0	0	0	0	3
Tomasz Chrzanowski	0	0	0	1	0	1
Peter Ljung (Res)	–	–	–	–	–	–
Fredrik Lindgren (Res)	–	–	–	–	–	–

RACE DETAILS

HEAT ONE:	Lee Richardson, Tomasz Gollob, Hans N. Andersen, Tomasz Chrzanowski.
HEAT TWO:	Jason Crump, Greg Hancock, Scott Nicholls, Leigh Adams.
HEAT THREE:	Nicki Pedersen, Antonio Lindback, Andreas Jonsson, Jaroslaw Hampel.
HEAT FOUR:	Bjarne Pedersen, Tony Rickardsson, Ryan Sullivan, Jonas Davidsson.
HEAT FIVE:	(Rerun) Jaroslaw Hampel, Greg Hancock, Jonas Davidsson, Lee Richardson.
HEAT SIX:	Scott Nicholls, Tomasz Gollob, Antonio Lindback, Ryan Sullivan.
HEAT SEVEN:	Jason Crump, Nicki Pedersen, Bjarne Pedersen, Hans N. Andersen.
HEAT EIGHT:	Andreas Jonsson, Tony Rickardsson, Leigh Adams, Tomasz Chrzanowski.
HEAT NINE:	Nicki Pedersen, Scott Nicholls, Tony Rickardsson, Lee Richardson.
HEAT TEN:	Andreas Jonsson, Tomasz Gollob, Greg Hancock, Bjarne Pedersen.
HEAT ELEVEN:	Leigh Adams, Ryan Sullivan, Hans N. Andersen, Jaroslaw Hampel.
HEAT TWELVE:	Jason Crump, Jonas Davidsson, Antonio Lindback, Tomasz Chrzanowski.
HEAT THIRTEEN:	Andreas Jonsson, Jason Crump, Ryan Sullivan, Lee Richardson.
HEAT FOURTEEN:	(Rerun) Leigh Adams, Tomasz Gollob, Jonas Davidsson, Nicki Pedersen (ex, foul riding).
HEAT FIFTEEN:	Tony Rickardsson, Antonio Lindback, Hans N. Andersen, Greg Hancock.
HEAT SIXTEEN:	Scott Nicholls, Jaroslaw Hampel, Tomasz Chrzanowski, Bjarne Pedersen (f, rem).
HEAT SEVENTEEN:	Bjarne Pedersen, Leigh Adams, Antonio Lindback, Lee Richardson.
HEAT EIGHTEEN:	(Rerun) Tony Rickardsson, Jason Crump, Tomasz Gollob, Jaroslaw Hampel.
HEAT NINETEEN:	Andreas Jonsson, Hans N. Andersen, Scott Nicholls, Jonas Davidsson.
HEAT TWENTY:	Greg Hancock, Nicki Pedersen, Ryan Sullivan, Tomasz Chrzanowski.
FIRST SEMI-FINAL:	Andreas Jonsson, Leigh Adams, Tomasz Gollob, Nicki Pedersen.
SECOND SEMI-FINAL:	Jason Crump, Tony Rickardsson, Scott Nicholls, Greg Hancock.
FINAL:	Jason Crump, Andreas Jonsson, Tony Rickardsson, Leigh Adams.

GRAND PRIX OF POLAND (ROUND EIGHT)
27 AUGUST, POLONIA STADIUM, BYDGOSZCZ

1st TOMASZ GOLLOB
2nd LEE RICHARDSON
3rd JASON CRUMP
4th GREG HANCOCK

RIDER	QUALIFYING SCORES					TOTAL
Tomasz Gollob	3	3	2	3	2	13
Greg Hancock	2	3	3	3	1	12
Leigh Adams	3	R	3	2	3	11
Piotr Protasiewicz	2	2	2	2	3	11
Andreas Jonsson	2	3	2	1	2	10
Nicki Pedersen	1	2	0	3	3	9
Jason Crump	3	2	2	0	2	9
Lee Richardson	0	0	3	2	3	8
Tony Rickardsson	3	1	0	3	1	8
Scott Nicholls	1	2	3	1	1	8
Bjarne Pedersen	2	1	1	2	1	7

Jaroslaw Hampel	1	1	1	1	2	6
Hans N. Andersen	0	3	1	1	0	5
Ryan Sullivan	1	0	1	0	0	2
Tomasz Chrzanowski	0	1	0	0	0	1
Antonio Lindback	0	0	0	0	0	0
Krzysztof Kasprzak (Res)	–	–	–	–	–	–
Karol Zabik (Res)	–	–	–	–	–	–

RACE DETAILS

HEAT ONE: Jason Crump, Bjarne Pedersen, Ryan Sullivan, Antonio Lindback.

HEAT TWO: Leigh Adams, Piotr Protasiewicz, Nicki Pedersen, Lee Richardson.

HEAT THREE: Tony Rickardsson, Andreas Jonsson, Jaroslaw Hampel, Hans N. Andersen.

HEAT FOUR: Tomasz Gollob, Greg Hancock, Scott Nicholls, Tomasz Chrzanowski.

HEAT FIVE: Greg Hancock, Jason Crump, Jaroslaw Hampel, Lee Richardson.

HEAT SIX: Tomasz Gollob, Nicki Pedersen, Tony Rickardsson, Ryan Sullivan.

HEAT SEVEN: Hans N. Andersen, Piotr Protasiewicz, Tomasz Chrzanowski, Antonio Lindback.

HEAT EIGHT: Andreas Jonsson, Scott Nicholls, Bjarne Pedersen, Leigh Adams (ret).

HEAT NINE: (Rerun) Scott Nicholls, Jason Crump, Hans N. Andersen, Nicki Pedersen.

HEAT TEN: Lee Richardson, Andreas Jonsson, Ryan Sullivan, Tomasz Chrzanowski.

HEAT ELEVEN: Leigh Adams, Tomasz Gollob, Jaroslaw Hampel, Antonio Lindback.

HEAT TWELVE: Greg Hancock, Piotr Protasiewicz, Bjarne Pedersen, Tony Rickardsson.

HEAT THIRTEEN: Tomasz Gollob, Piotr Protasiewicz, Andreas Jonsson, Jason Crump.

HEAT FOURTEEN: (Rerun) Greg Hancock, Leigh Adams, Hans N. Andersen, Ryan Sullivan.

HEAT FIFTEEN: Tony Rickardsson, Lee Richardson, Scott Nicholls, Antonio Lindback.

HEAT SIXTEEN: Nicki Pedersen, Bjarne Pedersen, Jaroslaw Hampel, Tomasz Chrzanowski.

HEAT SEVENTEEN: Leigh Adams, Jason Crump, Tony Rickardsson, Tomasz Chrzanowski.

HEAT EIGHTEEN: Piotr Protasiewicz, Jaroslaw Hampel, Scott Nicholls, Ryan Sullivan.

HEAT NINETEEN: Nicki Pedersen, Andreas Jonsson, Greg Hancock, Antonio Lindback.

HEAT TWENTY: Lee Richardson, Tomasz Gollob, Bjarne Pedersen, Hans N. Andersen.

FIRST SEMI-FINAL: Tomasz Gollob, Jason Crump, Nicki Pedersen, Piotr Protasiewicz.

SECOND SEMI-FINAL: Lee Richardson, Greg Hancock, Leigh Adams, Andreas Jonsson.

FINAL: Tomasz Gollob, Lee Richardson, Jason Crump, Greg Hancock.

GRAND PRIX OF ITALY (ROUND NINE)
10 SEPTEMBER, MOTORCLUB LONIGO, ITALY

1st TONY RICKARDSSON
2nd JASON CRUMP
3rd GREG HANCOCK
4th LEIGH ADAMS

RIDER	QUALIFYING SCORES					TOTAL
Tony Rickardsson	3	3	3	3	3	15
Jason Crump	2	3	3	1	3	12
Leigh Adams	1	2	2	3	3	11

Bjarne Pedersen	1	2	3	2	2	10
Andreas Jonsson	1	3	2	2	2	10
Greg Hancock	3	1	1	2	1	8
Hans N. Andersen	2	2	2	1	1	8
Scott Nicholls	R	X	3	3	R	6
Tomasz Chrzanowski	3	2	1	0	0	6
Lee Richardson	0	1	2	1	2	6
Nicki Pedersen	2	3	0	0	X	5
Antonio Lindback	1	R	1	3	T	5
Stefan Andersson	3	1	0	0	1	5
Matej Zagar	2	X	0	2	1	5
Roman Povazhny	0	1	0	0	3	4
Tomasz Gollob	0	0	1	1	2	4
Simone Terenzani (Res)	0	–	–	–	–	0
Daniele Tessari (Res)	–	–	–	–	–	–

RACE DETAILS

HEAT ONE: Stefan Andersson, Nicki Pedersen, Andreas Jonsson, Tomasz Gollob.

HEAT TWO: Tomasz Chrzanowski, Hans N. Andersen, Bjarne Pedersen, Lee Richardson.

HEAT THREE: Greg Hancock, Matej Zagar, Leigh Adams, Roman Povazhny.

HEAT FOUR: Tony Rickardsson, Jason Crump, Antonio Lindback, Scott Nicholls (ret).

HEAT FIVE: (Rerun) Andreas Jonsson, Leigh Adams, Lee Richardson, Scott Nicholls (f, ex).

HEAT SIX: Tony Rickardsson, Bjarne Pedersen, Greg Hancock, Tomasz Gollob.

HEAT SEVEN: (Rerun) Jason Crump, Hans N. Andersen, Stefan Andersson, Matej Zagar (f, ex).

HEAT EIGHT: Nicki Pedersen, Tomasz Chrzanowski, Roman Povazhny, Antonio Lindback (ret).

HEAT NINE: Bjarne Pedersen, Andreas Jonsson, Antonio Lindback, Matej Zagar.

HEAT TEN: Jason Crump, Lee Richardson, Tomasz Gollob, Roman Povazhny.

HEAT ELEVEN: Tony Rickardsson, Leigh Adams, Tomasz Chrzanowski, Stefan Andersson.

HEAT TWELVE: Scott Nicholls, Hans N. Andersen, Greg Hancock, Nicki Pedersen.

HEAT THIRTEEN: Tony Rickardsson, Andreas Jonsson, Hans N. Andersen, Roman Povazhny.

HEAT FOURTEEN: Scott Nicholls, Matej Zagar, Tomasz Gollob, Tomasz Chrzanowski.

HEAT FIFTEEN: Antonio Lindback, Greg Hancock, Lee Richardson, Stefan Andersson.

HEAT SIXTEEN: Leigh Adams, Bjarne Pedersen, Jason Crump, Nicki Pedersen.

HEAT SEVENTEEN: Jason Crump, Andreas Jonsson, Greg Hancock, Tomasz Chrzanowski.

HEAT EIGHTEEN: (Rerun) Leigh Adams, Tomasz Gollob, Hans N. Andersen, Simone Terenzani, Antonio Lindback (ex, tapes).

HEAT NINETEEN: (Rerun) Roman Povazhny, Bjarne Pedersen, Stefan Andersson, Scott Nicholls (ret).

HEAT TWENTY: (Rerun) Tony Rickardsson, Lee Richardson, Matej Zagar, Nicki Pedersen (ex, foul riding).

FIRST SEMI-FINAL: Tony Rickardsson, Greg Hancock, Hans N. Andersen, Bjarne Pedersen.

SECOND SEMI-FINAL: (Rerun) Jason Crump, Leigh Adams, Scott Nicholls, Andreas Jonsson (f, ex).

FINAL: Tony Rickardsson, Jason Crump, Greg Hancock, Leigh Adams.

WORLD CHAMPIONSHIP ROLL OF HONOUR

NOTE: Run as a one-off World Final from 1936-1994 and as the Grand Prix from 1995-2005.

YEAR	FIRST	SECOND	THIRD
1936	Lionel Van Praag	Eric Langton	Bluey Wilkinson
1937	Jack Milne	Wilbur Lamoreaux	Cordy Milne
1938	Bluey Wilkinson	Jack Milne	Wilbur Lamoreaux
1939-48	Not staged		
1949	Tommy Price	Jack Parker	Louis Lawson
1950	Freddie Williams	Wally Green	Graham Warren
1951	Jack Young	Split Waterman	Jack Biggs
1952	Jack Young	Freddie Williams	Bob Oakley
1953	Freddie Williams	Split Waterman	Geoff Mardon
1954	Ronnie Moore	Brian Crutcher	Olle Nygren
1955	Peter Craven	Ronnie Moore	Barry Briggs
1956	Ove Fundin	Ronnie Moore	Arthur Forrest
1957	Barry Briggs	Ove Fundin	Peter Craven
1958	Barry Briggs	Ove Fundin	Aub Lawson
1959	Ronnie Moore	Ove Fundin	Barry Briggs
1960	Ove Fundin	Ronnie Moore	Peter Craven
1961	Ove Fundin	Bjorn Knutsson	Gote Nordin
1962	Peter Craven	Barry Briggs	Ove Fundin
1963	Ove Fundin	Bjorn Knutsson	Barry Briggs
1964	Barry Briggs	Igor Plechanov	Ove Fundin
1965	Bjorn Knutsson	Igor Plechanov	Ove Fundin
1966	Barry Briggs	Sverre Harrfeldt	Antoni Woryna
1967	Ove Fundin	Bengt Jansson	Ivan Mauger
1968	Ivan Mauger	Barry Briggs	Edward Jancarz
1969	Ivan Mauger	Barry Briggs	Soren Sjosten
1970	Ivan Mauger	Pawel Waloszek	Antoni Woryna
1971	Ole Olsen	Ivan Mauger	Bengt Jansson
1972	Ivan Mauger	Bernt Persson	Ole Olsen
1973	Jerzy Szczakiel	Ivan Mauger	Zenon Plech
1974	Anders Michanek	Ivan Mauger	Soren Sjosten
1975	Ole Olsen	Anders Michanek	John Louis
1976	Peter Collins	Malcolm Simmons	Phil Crump
1977	Ivan Mauger	Peter Collins	Ole Olsen
1978	Ole Olsen	Gordon Kennett	Scott Autrey
1979	Ivan Mauger	Zenon Plech	Michael Lee
1980	Michael Lee	Dave Jessup	Billy Sanders
1981	Bruce Penhall	Ole Olsen	Tommy Knudsen
1982	Bruce Penhall	Les Collins	Dennis Sigalos
1983	Egon Muller	Billy Sanders	Michael Lee
1984	Erik Gundersen	Hans Nielsen	Lance King
1985	Erik Gundersen	Hans Nielsen	Sam Ermolenko
1986	Hans Nielsen	Jan O. Pedersen	Kelvin Tatum
1987	Hans Nielsen	Erik Gundersen	Sam Ermolenko
1988	Erik Gundersen	Hans Nielsen	Jan O. Pedersen

1989	Hans Nielsen	Simon Wigg	Jeremy Doncaster
1990	Per Jonsson	Shawn Moran	Todd Wiltshire
1991	Jan O. Pedersen	Tony Rickardsson	Hans Nielsen
1992	Gary Havelock	Per Jonsson	Gert Handberg
1993	Sam Ermolenko	Hans Nielsen	Chris Louis
1994	Tony Rickardsson	Hans Nielsen	Craig Boyce
1995	Hans Nielsen	Tony Rickardsson	Sam Ermolenko
1996	Billy Hamill	Hans Nielsen	Greg Hancock
1997	Greg Hancock	Billy Hamill	Tomasz Gollob
1998	Tony Rickardsson	Jimmy Nilsen	Tomasz Gollob
1999	Tony Rickardsson	Tomasz Gollob	Hans Nielsen
2000	Mark Loram	Billy Hamill	Tony Rickardsson
2001	Tony Rickardsson	Jason Crump	Tomasz Gollob
2002	Tony Rickardsson	Jason Crump	Ryan Sullivan
2003	Nicki Pedersen	Jason Crump	Tony Rickardsson
2004	Jason Crump	Tony Rickardsson	Greg Hancock
2005	Tony Rickardsson	Jason Crump	Leigh Adams

NOTE: In 1990, Shawn Moran was subsequently stripped of second place, having tested positive in a drugs test at the Overseas Final.

MAJOR INTERNATIONAL MEETINGS 2005

WORLD CUP

QUALIFYING ROUND ONE
4 JUNE, TERENZANO, ITALY
GERMANY 33 (Thomas Stange 8; Martin Smolinski 8; Rene Schafer 7; Christian Hefenbrock 7; Michael Hertrich 3).
SLOVENIA 23 (Matej Zagar 11; Jernej Kolenko 6; Izak Santej 3; Denis Stojs 2; Ales Kraljic 1).
HUNGARY 22 (Sandor Tihanyi 6; Attila Stefani 6; Laszlo Szatmari 4; Zsolt Bencze 4; Norbert Magosi 2).
ITALY 18 (Emiliano Sanchez 9; Simone Terenzani 5; Daniele Tessari 3; Mattia Carpanese 1; Christiano Miotello 0).
Meeting abandoned after heat sixteen, with the result permitted to stand.

QUALIFYING ROUND TWO
5 JUNE, DAUGAVPILS, LATVIA
RUSSIA 61 (Renat Gafurov 14; Oleg Kurguzkin 13; Sergey Darkin 12; Semen Vlasov 12; Denis Gizatullin 10).

USA 52 (Greg Hancock 15; Sam Ermolenko 13; Billy Janniro 10; Josh Larsen 7; Brent Werner 7).
LATVIA 31 (Leonid Paura 7; Kjastas Puodzhuks 7; Andrej Korolev 7; Nikolaj Kokin 6; Aleksandr
Ivanov 4).
FRANCE 6 (Mathieu Tresarrieu 2; Sebastien Tresarrieu 2; Christophe Dubernand 2; Stephane
Tresarrieu 0; Jerome Lespinasse 0).

Staged in three of the sport's major countries, the final stages of the 2005 Speedway World Cup
were a rip-roaring success, finally resulting in an emphatic victory for a power-packed Poland.
The action got underway with Event One at Swindon on 31 July and, with the box office doing
a roaring trade from 10 a.m. onwards, unprecedented scenes were witnessed at Blunsdon, with
the stadium packed to the rafters and the pits looking resplendent due to the debut appearance of
an electronic scoreboard. Those present witnessed an exciting and well-presented meeting and,
to make it all the more exciting, Great Britain rode with passion to come out on top. Leading
them to victory, home rider Lee Richardson scorched to a 15-point maximum despite feeling
far from 100 per cent after being taken ill while racing for Swindon in an Elite League fixture
the previous evening at Eastbourne. 'Rico' wasn't the only star for GB though, as Simon Stead,
Scott Nicholls and Chris Harris all hit a dozen points, while Joe Screen recorded two race wins
in his tally of 8. That gave the Brits a total of 59 points and a direct passage to the World Cup
Final, with Denmark (54) and the Czech Republic (26) being the two sides that moved on to
the Race-Off. Russia brought up the rear at the Abbey Stadium, a 17-point tally belying their
spirited efforts on the day, particularly those of Renat Gafurov and Sergey Darkin.

Event Two was held at Eskilstuna, Sweden on 2 August and featured a terrific three-way contest
between Australia, Poland and the host nation, while Germany were completely overshadowed.
Everything boiled down to a dramatic last heat, with Sweden going into the race on 51 points,
while Australia had 47 and Poland 45. The Poles nominated Tomasz Gollob as a tactical joker and,
with Swede Peter Karlsson surprisingly hemmed in at the back by Martin Smolinski of Germany,
all eyes focussed on a terrific scrap between Gollob and Aussie Leigh Adams. In a brilliant and
close finish, Adams, on the outside, just had the speed to pip the legendary Pole on the line. That
meant Sweden had won on the night with no addition to their tally of 51 points, while Australia
(50) and Poland (49) would have to do it all again in the Race-Off.

The dreaded Race-Off took place at the Olympic Stadium, Wroclaw, Poland on 4 August,
with the home nation making a change to their line-up by calling up Grzegorz Walasek in place
of Krzysztof Kasprzak. This was to prove a masterstroke by team manager Szczepan Bukowski,
as the incoming rider sped to a 15-point maximum and helped his side ease through to the
World Cup Final to be staged at the very same circuit. Indeed the Poles, who looked terrific
in matching race suits and bike covers, totalled 63 points and dominated the meeting, their
side completed by Tomasz Gollob, Piotr Protasiewicz, Jaroslaw Hampel and Norwegian Rune
Holta, who was eligible to ride for them because he races on a Polish licence. While the Poles
were romping to victory, second place was always likely to be between Australia and Denmark.
However, the Aussies were severely weakened when Jason Crump was forced to pull out of
the meeting through illness, his place being taken by Steve Johnston. It proved vital, as Hans N.
Andersen and Nicki Pedersen each hit double figures to see the Danes comfortably progress
with 48 points, with Australia on 30 and the Czech Republic languishing on 16.

The four qualifiers subsequently met up for the World Cup Final at Wroclaw on 6 August,
with a huge contingent of partisan Polish fans in place to support their team. When Grzegorz
Walasek ran a last place in heat one it looked as if the favourites might be overawed by the

occasion, but they recovered from that minor setback brilliantly, scoring points galore in all of the other twenty-four races that followed. Such was the potency of the quintet that they carded sixteen race wins and six second places as they simply overpowered the opposition. In fact, they clinched the Ove Fundin Trophy with five races to spare and, fittingly, it was the amazing Tomasz Gollob who sealed their success when taking the flag in heat twenty. Gollob went on to total 14 points, losing only to an inspired Lee Richardson in heat fifteen, while his teammates all notched double figures thus: Piotr Protasiewicz 13, Jaroslaw Hampel 13, Rune Holta 12, Grzegorz Walasek 10. Meanwhile, Andreas Jonsson's 12 points helped Sweden to take the runner-up position on 34 points, with Denmark tallying 31 in the bronze medal position. Great Britain brought up the rear on 27 points, with Richardson posting four excellent victories to head their scoring. Simon Stead and Scott Nicholls suffered all sorts of bad luck on their way to 6 points apiece and, on another evening, the British lads may even have scooped second place on the rostrum. Nontheless, it was a very brave effort and the likes of Stead and Chris Harris will have learnt much from the experience.

EVENT ONE

31 JULY, SWINDON

GREAT BRITAIN 59	RACE SCORES						TOTAL
Joe Screen	R	3	3	1	1	–	8
Simon Stead	3	2	3	2	2	–	12
Lee Richardson	3	3	3	3	3	–	15
Scott Nicholls	3	2	2	3	2	–	12
Chris Harris	2	3	2	2	3	–	12
DENMARK 54							
Nicki Pedersen	3	3	2	3	1	–	12
Bjarne Pedersen	2	2	3	3	2	–	12
Hans N. Andersen	X	1	3	6	3	–	13
Niels-Kristian Iversen	2	3	2	2	1	–	10
Charlie Gjedde	3	X	2	0	2	–	7
CZECH REPUBLIC 26							
Adrian Rymel	1	1	0	R	0	–	2
Ales Dryml	R	2	0	2	2	6	12
Lukas Dryml	1	1	0	X	0	–	2
Tomas Topinka	1	2	1	0	3	–	7
Tomas Suchanek	0	1	1	1	–	–	3
RUSSIA 17							
Sergey Darkin	2	X	1	0	R	2	5
Oleg Kurguzkin	1	0	0	1	0	–	2
Semen Vlasov	2	0	X	–	–	–	2
Denis Gizatullin	0	0	1	1	0	–	2
Renat Gafurov	1	F	1	1	2	1	6

RACE DETAILS

HEAT ONE: Nicki Pedersen, Sergey Darkin, Adrian Rymel, Joe Screen (ret).

HEAT TWO: Simon Stead, Bjarne Pedersen, Oleg Kurguzkin, Ales Dryml (ret).

HEAT THREE: (Rerun) Lee Richardson, Semen Vlasov, Lukas Dryml (f, rem), Hans N. Andersen (f, ex).

HEAT FOUR: Scott Nicholls, Niels-Kristian Iversen, Tomas Topinka, Denis Gizatullin.

HEAT FIVE: Charlie Gjedde, Chris Harris, Renat Gafarov, Tomas Suchanek.

HEAT SIX: (Rerun twice) Lee Richardson, Tomas Topinka, Sergey Darkin (f, ex), Charlie Gjedde (ex, foul riding).

HEAT SEVEN: Nicki Pedersen, Scott Nicholls, Tomas Suchanek, Oleg Kurguzkin.

HEAT EIGHT: Chris Harris, Bjarne Pedersen, Adrian Rymel, Semen Vlasov.

HEAT NINE: Joe Screen, Ales Dryml, Hans N. Andersen, Denis Gitatullin.

HEAT TEN: Niels-Kristian Iversen, Simon Stead, Lukas Dryml, Renat Gafarov (fell).

HEAT ELEVEN: Bjarne Pedersen, Scott Nicholls, Sergey Darkin, Lukas Dryml.

HEAT TWELVE: Hans N. Andersen, Chris Harris, Tomas Topinka, Oleg Kurguzkin.

HEAT THIRTEEN: (Rerun) Joe Screen, Niels-Kristian Iversen, Tomas Suchanek, Semen Vlasov (f, ex).

HEAT FOURTEEN: Simon Stead, Charlie Gjedde, Denis Gizatullin, Adrian Rymel.

HEAT FIFTEEN: Lee Richardson, Nicki Pedersen, Renat Gafarov, Ales Dryml.

HEAT SIXTEEN: Hans N. Andersen (tactical joker), Simon Stead, Tomas Suchanek, Sergey Darkin.

HEAT SEVENTEEN: Lee Richardson, Niels-Kristian Iversen, Oleg Kurguzkin, Adrian Rymel (ret).

HEAT EIGHTEEN: Scott Nicholls, Ales Dryml, Renat Gafarov, Charlie Gjedde.

HEAT NINETEEN: (Rerun) Nicki Pedersen, Chris Harris, Denis Gizatullin, Lukas Dryml (ex, foul riding).

HEAT TWENTY: Bjarne Pedersen, Renat Gafarov, Joe Screen, Tomas Topinka.

HEAT TWENTY-ONE: Chris Harris, Ales Dryml, Niels-Kristian Iversen, Sergey Darkin (ret).

HEAT TWENTY-TWO: Ales Dryml (tactical joker), Charlie Gjedde, Joe Screen, Denis Gizatullin.

HEAT TWENTY-THREE: Tomas Topinka, Simon Stead, Nicki Pedersen, Oleg Kurguzkin.

HEAT TWENTY-FOUR: Lee Richardson, Bjarne Pedersen, Sergey Darkin (tactical joker), Lukas Dryml.

HEAT TWENTY-FIVE: Hans N. Andersen, Scott Nicholls, Renat Gafarov, Adrian Rymel.

EVENT TWO

2 AUGUST, ESKILSTUNA, SWEDEN

	RACE SCORES						TOTAL
SWEDEN 51							
Antonio Lindback	1	2	2	2	2	–	9
Andreas Jonsson	2	3	1	3	3	–	12
Tony Rickardsson	2	3	2	3	3	–	13
Peter Karlsson	2	3	1	2	0	–	8
Fredrik Lindgren	2	2	2	1	2	–	9
AUSTRALIA 50							
Leigh Adams	3	3	3	1	3	–	13
Ryan Sullivan	1	0	1	3	3	–	8
Jason Crump	1	2	6	2	3	–	14
Adam Shields	1	2	3	1	2	–	9
Davey Watt	1	1	0	2	2	–	6

POLAND 49

Krzysztof Kasprzak	2	1	2	1	1	–	7
Piotr Protasiewicz	3	2	1	2	R	–	8
Rune Holta	3	1	3	X	1	–	8
Jaroslaw Hampel	3	3	2	3	1	–	12
Tomasz Gollob	3	1	3	3	4	–	14

GERMANY 5

Christian Hefenbrock	R	0	0	0	0	–	0
Rene Schafer	0	0	0	0	0	–	0
Martin Smolinski	0	1	0	0	1	–	2
Thomas Stange	0	0	1	0	0	–	1
Mathias Schultz	0	0	0	1	1	–	2

RACE DETAILS

HEAT ONE:	Leigh Adams, Krzysztof Kasprzak, Antonio Lindback, Christian Hefenbrock (ret).
HEAT TWO:	Piotr Protasiewicz, Andreas Jonsson, Ryan Sullivan, Rene Schafer.
HEAT THREE:	Rune Holta, Tony Rickardsson, Jason Crump, Martin Smolinski.
HEAT FOUR:	Jaroslaw Hampel, Peter Karlsson, Adam Shields, Thomas Stange.
HEAT FIVE:	Tomasz Gollob, Fredrik Lindgren, Davey Watt, Mathias Schultz.
HEAT SIX:	Tony Rickardsson, Adam Shields, Krzysztof Kasprzak, Mathias Schultz.
HEAT SEVEN:	Peter Karlsson, Piotr Protasiewicz, Davey Watt, Christian Hefenbrock.
HEAT EIGHT:	Leigh Adams, Fredrik Lindgren, Rune Holta, Rene Schafer.
HEAT NINE:	Jaroslaw Hampel, Antonio Lindback, Martin Smolinski, Ryan Sullivan.
HEAT TEN:	Andreas Jonsson, Jason Crump, Tomasz Gollob, Thomas Stange.
HEAT ELEVEN:	Jason Crump (tactical joker), Krzysztof Kasprzak, Peter Karlsson, Rene Schafer.
HEAT TWELVE:	Adam Shields, Fredrik Lindgren, Piotr Protasiewicz, Martin Smolinski.
HEAT THIRTEEN:	Rune Holta, Antonio Lindback, Thomas Stange, Davey Watt.
HEAT FOURTEEN:	Leigh Adams, Jaroslaw Hampel, Andreas Jonsson, Mathias Schultz.
HEAT FIFTEEN:	Tomasz Gollob, Tony Rickardsson, Ryan Sullivan, Christian Hefenbrock.
HEAT SIXTEEN:	Andreas Jonsson, Davey Watt, Krzysztof Kasprzak, Martin Smolinski.
HEAT SEVENTEEN:	Tony Rickardsson, Piotr Protasiewicz, Leigh Adams, Thomas Stange.
HEAT EIGHTEEN:	(Rerun) Ryan Sullivan, Peter Karlsson, Mathias Schultz, Rune Holta (f, ex).
HEAT NINETEEN:	Jaroslaw Hampel, Jason Crump, Fredrik Lindgren, Christian Hefenbrock.
HEAT TWENTY:	Tomasz Gollob, Antonio Lindback, Adam Shields, Rene Schafer.
HEAT TWENTY-ONE:	Ryan Sullivan, Fredrik Lindgren, Krzysztof Kasprzak, Thomas Stange.
HEAT TWENTY-TWO:	Jason Crump, Antonio Lindback, Mathias Schultz, Piotr Protasiewicz (ret).
HEAT TWENTY-THREE:	Andreas Jonsson, Adam Shields, Rune Holta, Christian Hefenbrock.
HEAT TWENTY-FOUR:	(Rerun) Tony Rickardsson, Davey Watt, Jaroslaw Hampel, Rene Schafer.
HEAT TWENTY-FIVE:	Leigh Adams, Tomasz Gollob (tactical joker), Martin Smolinski, Peter Karlsson.

RACE-OFF

4 AUGUST, WROCLAW, POLAND

	RACE SCORES						TOTAL
POLAND 63							
Jaroslaw Hampel	3	2	3	1	1	–	10
Rune Holta	3	2	2	2	3	–	12
Tomasz Gollob	3	3	3	2	3	–	14
Piotr Protasiewicz	1	3	2	3	3	–	12
Grzegorz Walasek	3	3	3	3	3	–	15
DENMARK 48							
Kenneth Bjerre	2	1	1	1	–	–	5
Niels-Kristian Iversen	2	3	0	2	2	–	9
Hans N. Andersen	1	3	1	1	6	3	15
Nicki Pedersen	3	2	1	3	3	2	14
Bjarne Pedersen	1	1	1	2	–	–	5
AUSTRALIA 30							
Davey Watt	0	1	0	–	–	–	1
Adam Shields	1	2	2	0	0	–	5
Ryan Sullivan	2	2	0	1	0	0	5
Leigh Adams	2	1	3	6	2	1	15
Steve Johnston	X	1	1	2	0	–	4
CZECH REPUBLIC 16							
Tomas Suchanek	1	0	0	0	X	–	1
Ales Dryml	R	0	2	0	2	–	4
Tomas Topinka	0	0	0	0	–	–	0
Lukas Dryml	0	R	2	1	2	2	7
Adrian Rymel	2	0	0	1	1	–	4

RACE DETAILS

HEAT ONE:	Jaroslaw Hampel, Kenneth Bjerre, Tomas Suchanek, Davey Watt.
HEAT TWO:	Rune Holta, Niels-Kristian Iversen, Adam Shields, Ales Dryml (ret).
HEAT THREE:	Tomasz Gollob, Ryan Sullivan, Hans N. Andersen, Tomas Topinka.
HEAT FOUR:	Nicki Pedersen, Leigh Adams, Piotr Protasiewicz, Lukas Dryml.
HEAT FIVE:	(Rerun) Grzegorz Walasek, Adrian Rymel, Bjarne Pedersen, Steve Johnston (f, ex).
HEAT SIX:	Grzegorz Walasek, Ryan Sullivan, Kenneth Bjerre, Lukas Dryml (ret).
HEAT SEVEN:	Niels-Kristian Iversen, Jaroslaw Hampel, Leigh Adams, Adrian Rymel.
HEAT EIGHT:	Hans N. Andersen, Rune Holta, Steve Johnston, Tomas Suchanek.
HEAT NINE:	Tomasz Gollob, Nicki Pedersen, Davey Watt, Ales Dryml.
HEAT TEN:	Piotr Protasiewicz, Adam Shields, Bjarne Pedersen, Tomas Topinka.
HEAT ELEVEN:	Leigh Adams, Rune Holta, Kenneth Bjerre, Tomas Topinka
HEAT TWELVE:	Tomasz Gollob, Lukas Dryml, Steve Johnston, Niels-Kristian Iversen.
HEAT THIRTEEN:	Leigh Adams (tactical joker), Piotr Protasiewicz, Hans N. Andersen, Adrian Rymel.
HEAT FOURTEEN:	Grzegorz Walasek, Adam Shields, Nicki Pedersen, Tomas Suchanek.

HEAT FIFTEEN: Jaroslaw Hampel, Ales Dryml, Bjarne Pedersen, Ryan Sullivan.

HEAT SIXTEEN: (Rerun) Nicki Pedersen, Tomasz Gollob, Adrian Rymel, Adam Shields.

HEAT SEVENTEEN: Piotr Protasiewicz, Niels-Kristian Iversen, Ryan Sullivan, Tomas Suchanek.

HEAT EIGHTEEN: Grzegorz Walasek, Leigh Adams, Hans N. Andersen, Ales Dryml.

HEAT NINETEEN: Nicki Pedersen, Steve Johnston, Jaroslaw Hampel, Tomas Topinka.

HEAT TWENTY: Hans N. Andersen (tactical joker), Rune Holta, Lukas Dryml, Ryan Sullivan.

HEAT TWENTY-ONE: Piotr Protasiewicz, Ales Dryml, Kenneth Bjerre, Steve Johnston.

HEAT TWENTY-TWO: Grzegorz Walasek, Niels-Kristian Iversen, Lukas Dryml (tactical joker), Davey Watt.

HEAT TWENTY-THREE: Hans N. Andersen, Lukas Dryml, Jaroslaw Hampel, Adam Shields.

HEAT TWENTY-FOUR: Rune Holta, Nicki Pedersen, Adrian Rymel, Ryan Sullivan.

HEAT TWENTY-FIVE: (Rerun) Tomasz Gollob, Bjarne Pedersen, Leigh Adams, Tomas Suchanek (f, ex).

FINAL
6 AUGUST, WROCLAW, POLAND

	RACE SCORES						TOTAL
POLAND 62							
Grzegorz Walasek	0	1	3	3	3	–	10
Rune Holta	3	1	3	2	3	–	12
Piotr Protasiewicz	2	2	3	3	3	–	13
Jaroslaw Hampel	3	2	3	3	2	–	13
Tomasz Gollob	3	3	2	3	3	–	14
SWEDEN 34							
Tony Rickardsson	3	2	0	0	2	0	7
Peter Karlsson	2	R	1	1	0	–	4
Andreas Jonsson	1	3	2	4	2	–	12
Antonio Lindback	2	0	2	1	2	–	7
Fredrik Lindgren	1	2	0	1	–	–	4
DENMARK 31							
Hans N. Andersen	2	3	4	0	0	–	9
Bjarne Pedersen	0	1	1	2	1	–	5
Kenneth Bjerre	3	2	2	0	0	–	7
Nicki Pedersen	0	R	1	2	2	1	6
Niels–Kristian Iversen	2	0	1	1	–	–	4
GREAT BRITAIN 27							
Joe Screen	1	0	0	–	–	–	1
Simon Stead	1	1	1	R	2	1	6
Lee Richardson	0	3	3	3	0	3	12
Scott Nicholls	1	3	0	R	1	1	6
Chris Harris	0	1	0	1	–	–	2

RACE DETAILS

HEAT ONE: Tony Rickardsson, Hans N. Andersen, Joe Screen, Grzegorz Walasek.

HEAT TWO: Rune Holta, Peter Karlsson, Simon Stead, Bjarne Pedersen.

HEAT THREE: Kenneth Bjerre, Piotr Protasiewicz, Andreas Jonsson, Lee Richardson.

HEAT FOUR: Jaroslaw Hampel, Antonio Lindback, Scott Nicholls, Nicki Pedersen.

HEAT FIVE: Tomasz Gollob, Niels-Kristian Iversen, Fredrik Lindgren, Chris Harris.

HEAT SIX: Lee Richardson, Fredrik Lindgren, Grzegorz Walasek, Nicki Pedersen (ret).

HEAT SEVEN: Scott Nicholls, Tony Rickardsson, Rune Holta, Niels-Kristian Iversen.

HEAT EIGHT: Hans N. Andersen, Piotr Protasiewicz, Chris Harris, Peter Karlsson (ret).

HEAT NINE: Andreas Jonsson, Jaroslaw Hampel, Bjarne Pedersen, Joe Screen.

HEAT TEN: Tomasz Gollob, Kenneth Bjerre, Simon Stead, Antonio Lindback.

HEAT ELEVEN: Grzegorz Walasek, Kenneth Bjerre, Peter Karlsson, Scott Nicholls.

HEAT TWELVE: Rune Holta, Andreas Jonsson, Nicki Pedersen, Chris Harris.

HEAT THIRTEEN: Piotr Protasiewicz, Antonio Lindback, Niels-Kristian Iversen, Scott Nicholls (tactical joker, ret).

HEAT FOURTEEN: Jaroslaw Hampel, Hans N. Andersen (tactical joker), Simon Stead, Fredrik Lindgren.

HEAT FIFTEEN: Lee Richardson, Tomasz Gollob, Bjarne Pedersen, Tony Rickardsson.

HEAT SIXTEEN: Grzegorz Walasek, Andreas Jonsson (tactical joker), Niels-Kristian Iversen, Simon Stead (ret).

HEAT SEVENTEEN: Lee Richardson, Rune Holta, Antonio Lindback, Hans N. Andersen.

HEAT EIGHTEEN: Piotr Protasiewicz, Bjarne Pedersen, Scott Nicholls, Tony Rickardsson.

HEAT NINETEEN: Jaroslaw Hampel, Tony Rickardsson, Chris Harris, Kenneth Bjerre.

HEAT TWENTY: Tomasz Gollob, Nicki Pedersen, Peter Karlsson, Joe Screen.

HEAT TWENTY-ONE: Grzegorz Walasek, Antonio Lindback, Bjarne Pedersen, Lee Richardson.

HEAT TWENTY-TWO: Rune Holta, Simon Stead, Fredrik Lindgren, Kenneth Bjerre.

HEAT TWENTY-THREE: Piotr Protasiewicz, Nicki Pedersen, Simon Stead, Tony Rickardsson.

HEAT TWENTY-FOUR: Lee Richardson, Jaroslaw Hampel, Nicki Pedersen, Peter Karlsson.

HEAT TWENTY-FIVE: Tomasz Gollob, Andreas Jonsson, Scott Nicholls, Hans N. Andersen.

ROLL OF HONOUR

NOTE: Formerly known as the World Team Cup (1960-2000).

YEAR	FIRST	SECOND	THIRD	FOURTH
1960	Sweden	Great Britain	Czechoslovakia	Poland
1961	Poland	Sweden	Great Britain	Czechoslovakia
1962	Sweden	Great Britain	Poland	Czechoslovakia
1963	Sweden	Czechoslovakia	Great Britain	Poland
1964	Sweden	Soviet Union	Great Britain	Poland
1965	Poland	Sweden	Great Britain	Soviet Union
1966	Poland	Soviet Union	Sweden	Great Britain
1967	Sweden	Poland	Great Britain & Soviet Union	–
1968	Great Britain	Sweden	Poland	Czechoslovakia
1969	Poland	Great Britain	Soviet Union	Sweden
1970	Sweden	Great Britain	Poland	Czechoslovakia
1971	Great Britain	Soviet Union	Poland	Sweden
1972	Great Britain	Soviet Union	Poland	Sweden

1973	Great Britain	Sweden	Soviet Union	Poland
1974	England	Sweden	Poland	Soviet Union
1975	England	Soviet Union	Sweden	Poland
1976	Australia	Poland	Sweden	Soviet Union
1977	England	Poland	Czechoslovakia	Sweden
1978	Denmark	England	Poland	Czechoslovakia
1979	New Zealand	Denmark	Czechoslovakia	Poland
1980	England	USA	Poland	Czechoslovakia
1981	Denmark	England	West Germany	Soviet Union
1982	USA	Denmark	West Germany	Czechoslovakia
1983	Denmark	England	USA	Czechoslovakia
1984	Denmark	England	USA	Poland
1985	Denmark	USA	England	Sweden
1986	Denmark	USA	England	Sweden
1987	Denmark	England	USA	Czechoslovakia
1988	Denmark	USA	Sweden	England
1989	England	Denmark	Sweden	USA
1990	USA	England	Denmark	Czechoslovakia
1991	Denmark	Sweden	USA	England
1992	USA	Sweden	England	Denmark
1993	USA	Denmark	Sweden	England
1994	Sweden	Poland	Denmark	Australia
1995	Denmark	England	USA	Sweden
1996	Poland	Russia	Denmark	Germany
1997	Denmark	Poland	Sweden	Germany
1998	USA	Sweden	Denmark	Poland
1999	Australia	Czech Republic	USA	England
2000	Sweden	England	USA	Australia
2001	Australia	Poland	Sweden	Denmark
2002	Australia	Denmark	Sweden	Poland
2003	Sweden	Australia	Denmark	Poland
2004	Sweden	Great Britain	Denmark	Poland
2005	Poland	Sweden	Denmark	Great Britain

WORLD UNDER-21 TEAM CUP

QUALIFYING ROUND ONE
16 MAY, ABENSBERG, GERMANY

SWEDEN 56 (Antonio Lindback 15; Eric Andersson 12; Fredrik Lindgren 11; Jonas Davidsson 11; Sebastian Alden 7).
GERMANY 33 (Martin Smolinski 8; Mathias Schultz 8; Thomas Stange 8; Christian Hefenbrock 6; Tobias Kroner 3).
GREAT BRITAIN 24 (Daniel King 9; Richard Hall 6; Edward Kennett 4; Chris Schramm 4; Tommy Allen 1).

HUNGARY & SLOVENIA 3 (Jozsef Tabaka 2; Maks Gregoric 1; Matic Voldrih 0; Mate Szegedi 0; Roland Kovacs 0).

QUALIFYING ROUND TWO
28 AUGUST, RYBNIK, POLAND

POLAND 'A' 52 (Pawel Hlib 12; Janusz Kolodziej 12; Marcin Rempala 12; Krystian Klecha 10; Karol Zabik 6).
POLAND 'B' 36 (Kamil Brzozowski 11; Adrian Gomolski 8; Patryk Pawlaszczyk 7; Sebastian Brucheiser 6; Marcin Jedrzejewski 4).
RUSSIA 25 (Maksim Karaychentsev 7; Danil Ivanov 7; Aleksey Kharchenko 6; Roman Ivanov 5).
FINLAND 7 (Rene Lehtinen 4; Tero Aarnio 2; Joni Keskinen 1; Jani Eerikainen 0; Petteri Koivunen 0).

QUALIFYING ROUND THREE
28 AUGUST, HOLSTED, DENMARK

DENMARK 'A' 57 (Kenneth Bjerre 15; Morten Risager 15; Henrik Moller 12; Patrick Hougaard 9; Nicolai Klindt 6).
DENMARK 'B' 28 (Claus Vissing 10; Jan Graversen 7; Claus Jacobsen 6; Jesper Kristiansen 3; Steven Andersen 2).
NORWAY 28 (Rune Sola 10; Mikke Bjerk 9; Carl J. Raugsted 6; Remi Ueland 2; Emil A. Omsland 1).
UKRAINE 6 (Andrey Karpov 3; Ivan Mironov 2; Sergey Senko 1; Ljubomir Vojtyk 0; Oleksandr Pyatnychko 0).
Denmark 'B' defeated Norway in a run-off for second place.

FINAL
1 OCTOBER, PARDUBICE, CZECH REPUBLIC

POLAND 41 (Janusz Kolodziej 14; Krzysztof Kasprzak 13; Marcin Rempala 8; Krystian Klecha 3; Karol Zabik 3).
SWEDEN 35 (Antonio Lindback 11; Fredrik Lindgren 9; Eric Andersson 8; Jonas Davidsson 7).
DENMARK 24 (Morten Risager 10; Henrik Moller 7; Nicolai Klindt 5; Patrick Hougaard 2; Kristian Lund 0).
CZECH REPUBLIC 20 (Tomas Suchanek 12; Zdenek Simota 5; Lubos Tomicek 2; Filip Sitera 1; Martin Malek 0).

ROLL OF HONOUR

YEAR	FIRST	SECOND	THIRD	FOURTH
2005	Poland	Sweden	Denmark	Czech Republic

WORLD UNDER-21 CHAMPIONSHIP

NOTE: Formerly known as the European Junior Championship (1977-87).

QUALIFYING ROUNDS

ROUND ONE; 21 MAY, ST JOHANN IM PONGAU, AUSTRIA

QUALIFYING SCORES: Adrian Miedzinski 15; Krystian Klecha 14; Thomas Stange 11; Tommy Allen 11; Chris Schramm 9; Klaus Jacobsen 9; Ales Kraljic 9; Raman Ivanov 9; Patrick Linhart 8; Michael Hertrich (Res) 7; Marko Vlah 6; Michael Diener 4; Maks Gregoric 3; Ewgeny Gomozov 3; Guglielmo Franchetti 2; Manuel Novotny 0; Fritz Wallner 0. FINAL: 1st Klecha; 2nd Miedzinski; 3rd Stange; 4th Allen.

ROUND TWO; 21 MAY, PARDUBICE, CZECH REPUBLIC

QUALIFYING SCORES: Christian Hefenbrock 14; Mateusz Szczepaniak 13; Karol Zabik 12; Chris Kerr 12; Mathias Schultz 11; Zdenek Simota 11; Maxim Kalimullin 10; Lubos Tomicek 9; Filip Sitera 6; Maxim Karajchencev 5; Rene Van Weele 5; Kjastas Puodzhuks 5; Justin Boyle 3; Antonin Galliani (Res) 3; Roland Kovacs 1; Mate Szegedi 0; Andrey Karpov 0. FINAL: 1st Zabik; 2nd Hefenbrock; 3rd Szczepaniak; 4th Kerr.

ROUND THREE; 21 MAY, ELGANE, NORWAY

QUALIFYING SCORES: Jonas Davidsson 14; Fredrik Lindgren 14; Antinio Lindback 12; Kenneth Bjerre 11; Morten Risager 11; Henrik Moller 10; Eric Andersson 9; Andreas Messing 9; Sebastian Alden 7; Rune Sola 6; Mikke Bjerk 5; Jesper Kristensen 5; Casper Wortmann 3; Tero Aarnio 2; Rene Lehtinen 2; Joni Keskinen 0. FINAL: 1st Lindback; 2nd Davidsson; 3rd Lindgren; 4th Bjerre.

ROUND FOUR; 22 MAY, BELLE VUE

QUALIFYING SCORES: Pawel Hlib 13; Krzysztof Kasprzak 12; Rory Schlein 12; Daniel King 11; James Wright 11; Chris Holder 10; Martin Smolinski 10; Richard Hall 10; Bryan Yarrow 9; Mathieu Tresarrieu 6; Jan Jaros 5; Andrew Bargh 4; Sergey Senko 2; Kaj De Jong 1; Gabriel Dubernard 1; Rene Schafer 1; Daniel Giffard (Res) 1; Ben Barker (Res) 0. FINAL: 1st Kasprzak; 2nd Hlib; 3rd Schlein; 4th King.

FIRST SEMI-FINAL; 18 JUNE, LONIGO, ITALY

QUALIFYING SCORES: Antonio Lindback 12; Adrian Miedzinski 12; Kenneth Bjerre 11; Christian Hefenbrock 11; Krzysztof Kasprzak 10; Martin Smolinski 10; James Wright 9; Edward Kennett 9; Andreas Messing 8; Mattia Carpanese 6; Tommy Allen 6; Eric Andersson 5; Bryan Yarrow 4; Chris Kerr 3; Mateusz Szczepaniak 2; Henrik Moller 1; Ales Kraljic (res) 0. FINAL: 1st Lindback; 2nd Miedzinski; 3rd Bjerre; 4th Hefenbrock.

SECOND SEMI-FINAL; 18 JUNE, TARNOW, POLAND

QUALIFYING SCORES: Pawel Hlib 14; Marcin Rempala 12; Daniel King 10; Krystian Klecha 9; Tomas Suchanek 9; Fredrik Lindgren 9; Jonas Davidsson 9; Thomas Stange 7; Mathias Schultz 7; Morten Risager 7; Chris Schramm 6; Zdenek Simota 6; Chris Holder 5; Maxim Kalimullin 5; Lubos Tomicek 3; Klaus Jakobsen 1; Filip Sitera (Res) 0. RUN-OFF: 1st Stange; 2nd Schultz. FINAL: 1st Rempala; 2nd Hlib; 3rd Klecha; 4th King.

WORLD UNDER-21 CHAMPIONSHIP FINAL
17 SEPTEMBER, WIENER NEUSTADT, AUSTRIA

1st KRZYSZTOF KASPRZAK
2nd TOMAS SUCHANEK
3rd FREDRIK LINDGREN
4th PAWEL HLIB

RIDER	QUALIFYING SCORES					TOTAL
Krzysztof Kasprzak	3	3	2	–	–	8
Tomas Suchanek	3	2	3	–	–	8
Fredrik Lindgren	1	3	3	–	–	7
Pawel Hlib	2	2	3	–	–	7
Marcin Rempala	2	3	1	–	–	6
Antonio Lindback	1	2	3	–	–	6
James Wright	2	1	2	–	–	5
Edward Kennett	2	1	1	–	–	4
Krystian Klecha	3	0	0	–	–	3
Daniel King	0	3	F	–	–	3
Jonas Davidsson	3	X	0	–	–	3
Thomas Stange	1	1	1	–	–	3
Christian Hefenbrock	1	1	1	–	–	3
Adrian Miedzinski	0	0	2	–	–	2
Morten Risager (Res)	2	–	–	–	–	2
Martin Smolinski	R	2	M	–	–	2
Mathias Schultz (Res)	0	–	–	–	–	0
Fritz Wallner	R	M	F	–	–	0

RACE DETAILS

HEAT ONE:	Krystian Klecha, Edward Kennett, Fredrik Lindgren, Daniel King.
HEAT TWO:	Krzysztof Kasprzak, James Wright, Thomas Stange, Fritz Wallner (ret).
HEAT THREE:	Jonas Davidsson, Marcin Rempala, Christian Hefenbrock, Adrian Miedzinski.
HEAT FOUR:	Tomas Suchanek, Pawel Hlib, Antonio Lindback, Martin Smolinski (ret).
HEAT FIVE:	Daniel King, Martin Smolinski, Thomas Stange, Jonas Davidsson (f, ex).
HEAT SIX:	Krzysztof Kasprzak, Antonio Lindback, Christian Hefenbrock, Krystian Klecha.
HEAT SEVEN:	Marcin Rempala, Tomas Suchanek, Edward Kennett, Mathias Schultz, Fritz Wallner (ex, 2 mins).
HEAT EIGHT:	Fredrik Lindgren, Pawel Hlib, James Wright, Adrian Miedzinski.
HEAT NINE:	Pawel Hlib, Krzysztof Kasprzak, Marcin Rempala, Daniel King (fell).
HEAT TEN:	Tomas Suchanek, Adrian Miedzinski, Thomas Stange, Krystian Klecha.
HEAT ELEVEN:	Antonio Lindback, James Wright, Edward Kennett, Jonas Davidsson.
HEAT TWELVE:	Fredrik Lindgren, Morten Risager, Christian Hefenbrock, Fritz Wallner (fell), Martin Smolinski (ex, 2 mins).

NOTE: Due to poor weather conditions the meeting was abandoned after heat twelve, with the title subsequently decided on the toss of a coin between Krzysztof Kasprzak and Tomas Suchanek.

ROLL OF HONOUR

YEAR	FIRST	SECOND	THIRD
1977	Alf Busk	Joe Owen	Les Collins
1978	Finn Jensen	Kevin Jolly	Neil Middleditch
1979	Ron Preston	Airat Faljzulin	Ari Koponen
1980	Tommy Knudsen	Tony Briggs	Dennis Sigalos
1981	Shawn Moran	Toni Kasper	Jiri Hnidak
1982	Toni Kasper	Mark Courtney	Peter Ravn
1983	Steve Baker	David Bargh	Marvyn Cox
1984	Marvyn Cox	Neil Evitts	Steve Lucero
1985	Per Jonsson	Jimmy Nilsen	Ole Hansen
1986	Igor Marko	Tony Olsson	Brian Karger
1987	Gary Havelock	Piotr Swist	Sean Wilson
1988	Peter Nahlin	Henrik Gustafsson	Brian Karger
1989	Gert Handberg	Chris Louis	Niklas Karlsson
1990	Chris Louis	Rene Aas	Tony Rickardsson
1991	Brian Andersen	Morten Andersen	Jason Lyons
1992	Leigh Adams	Mark Loram	Joe Screen
1993	Joe Screen	Mikael Karlsson	Rune Holta
1994	Mikael Karlsson	Rune Holta	Jason Crump
1995	Jason Crump	Dalle Anderson	Ryan Sullivan
1996	Piotr Protasiewicz	Ryan Sullivan	Jesper B. Jensen
1997	Jesper B. Jensen	Rafal Dobrucki	Scott Nicholls
1998	Robert Dados	Krzysztof Jablonski	Matej Ferjan
1999	Lee Richardson	Ales Dryml	Nigel Sadler
2000	Andreas Jonsson	Krzysztof Cegielski	Jaroslaw Hampel
2001	David Kujawa	Lukas Dryml	Rafal Okoniewski
2002	Lukas Dryml	Krzysztof Kasprzak	David Howe
2003	Jaroslaw Hampel	Chris Harris	Rafal Szombierski
2004	Robert Miskowiak	Kenneth Bjerre	Matej Zagar
2005	Krzysztof Kasprzak	Tomas Suchanek	Fredrik Lindgren

EUROPEAN CHAMPIONSHIP 2005

QUALIFYING ROUNDS

FIRST SEMI-FINAL; 2 JULY, STRALSUND, GERMANY

1st Matej Ferjan 15; 2nd Slawomir Drabik (after run-off) 12; 3rd Ales Dryml 12; Tomasz Gapinski 11; Bohumil Brhel (after run-off) 10; Renat Gafurov 10; Tomas Suchanek 9; Grzegorz Walasek 8; Denis Gizatullin 8; Jernej Kolenko 7; Norbert Magosi 6; Fritz Wallner 5; Christian Hefenbrock 3; Theo Pijper 3; Mathias Schultz 2; Mirko Wolter 1.

SECOND SEMI-FINAL; 2 JULY, MISZKOLC, HUNGARY

1st Michal Szczepaniak (after run-off) 12; 2nd Damian Balinski 12; 3rd Piotr Swiderski 12; Sergey Darkin (after run-off) 11; Laszlo Szatmari 11; Lukas Dryml 11; Robert Kosciecha 10;

Matej Zagar 8; Sandor Tihanyi 8; Emiliano Sanchez 7; Robert Haupt 5; Mario Jirout 5; Kjastas Puodzhuks 3; Simone Terenzani 3; Daniele Tessari 1; Igor Marko 0.

SCANDINAVIAN FINAL: 31 JULY, SEINAJOKI, FINLAND

1st Kaj Laukkanen 13; 2nd Jesper B. Jensen 12; 3rd David Ruud (after run-off) 11; Peter Ljung 11; Henrik Moller (after run-off) 10; Henning Bager 10; Kauko Nieminen 10; Niklas Klingberg 9; Erik Andersson 8; Steven Andersen 7; Morten Risager 6; Daniel Davidsson 5; Juha Hautamaki 3; Mikke Bjerk 3; Patrick Hougaard 3; Marius Rokeberg 1.

EUROPEAN CHAMPIONSHIP FINAL: 9 OCTOBER, LONIGO, ITALY

1st Jesper B. Jensen (after run-off) 14; 2nd Ales Dryml 14; 3rd Kaj Laukkanen 12; Lukas Dryml 10; Damian Balinski 10; Renat Gafurov 10; David Ruud 9; Matej Ferjan 9; Piotr Swiderski 7; Laszlo Szatmari 6; Tomasz Gapinski 5; Peter Ljung 4; Michal Szczepaniak 3; Henrik Moller 3; Daniele Tessari 2; Slawomir Drabik 1.

ROLL OF HONOUR

YEAR	FIRST	SECOND	THIRD
2001	Bohumil Brhel	Mariusz Staszewski	Krzysztof Cegielski
2002	Magnus Zetterstrom	Krzysztof Kasprzak	Rafal Szombierski
2003	Krzysztof Kasprzak	Slawomir Drabik	Magnus Zetterstrom
2004	Matej Zagar	Matej Ferjan	Hans N. Andersen
2005	Jesper B. Jensen	Ales Dryml	Kaj Laukkanen

EUROPEAN UNDER-19 CHAMPIONSHIP FINAL 2005
20 AUGUST, MSENO, CZECH REPUBLIC

1st Karol Zabik 14; 2nd Kjastas Puodzhuks 11; 3rd Robert Pettersson (on countback) 10; Pawel Hlib 10; Ricky Kling 10; Krzysztof Buczkowski 10; Fritz Wallner 9; Kevin Wolbert 9; Andreas Messing 8; Jurica Pavlic (Res) 5; Mathieu Tresarrieu 5; Lubos Tomicek 5; Patryk Pawlaszczyk 5; Jan Graversen 3; Robin Thornquist 2; Klaus Jakobsen 2; Maksim Bogdanov 1; Marcin Jedrzejewski (Res) 1.

ROLL OF HONOUR

YEAR	FIRST	SECOND	THIRD
1998	Rafal Okoniewski	Ales Dryml	Hans N. Andersen
1999	Rafal Okoniewski	Karol Malecha	Jaroslaw Hampel
2000	Lukas Dryml	Niels-Kristian Iversen	Zbigniew Czerwinski
2001	Lukasz Romanek	Daniel Davidsson	Rafal Kurmanski
2002	Matej Zagar	Kenneth Bjerre	Fredrik Lindgren
2003	Kenneth Bjerre	Janusz Kolodziej	Antonio Lindback
2004	Antonio Lindback	Karol Zabik	Morten Risager
2005	Karol Zabik	Kjastas Puodzhuks	Robert Pettersson

RIDER INDEX 2005

The following is an A-Z list of riders who appeared in British racing in 2005, and includes all official meetings at Elite League, Premier League and Conference League level.

ADAMS, Leigh   BORN: 28 April 1971, Mildura, Victoria, Australia.
BRITISH CAREER: (1989) Poole; (1990-92) Swindon; (1993-95) Arena-Essex; (1996) London; (1997-98) Swindon; (1999-2000) King's Lynn; (2001-02) Oxford; (2003) Poole; (2004-05) Swindon.

ALDEN, Sebastian   BORN: 7 November 1985, Vasteras, Sweden.
BRITISH CAREER: (2005) Swindon.

ALLEN, Olly   BORN: 27 May 1982, Norwich, Norfolk.
BRITISH CAREER: (1997) Peterborough (AL); (1998) Mildenhall, Norfolk, Peterborough, Arena-Essex; (1999-2001) Swindon; (2002) Swindon, Peterborough; (2003) Swindon, Wolverhampton; (2004) Swindon; (2005) King's Lynn, Swindon, Eastbourne.

ALLEN, Tommy   BORN: 4 September 1984, Norwich, Norfolk.
BRITISH CAREER: (2002) Mildenhall, Swindon (CT); (2003) Swindon (PL & CL); (2004) Rye House (PL & CL); (2005) Rye House (PL), Swindon.

ALLOTT, Adam   BORN: 19 March 1983, Stockport, Cheshire.
BRITISH CAREER: (1998) Norfolk, Buxton; (1999) Buxton, Sheffield; (2000) Sheffield, Owlerton; (2001) Sheffield; (2002) Sheffield (CL), Swindon, Somerset; (2003) Buxton (CT), King's Lynn; (2004) King's Lynn; (2005) King's Lynn, Eastbourne, Workington, Stoke.

ANDERSEN, Hans N.   BORN: 3 November 1980, Odense, Denmark.
BRITISH CAREER: (2001-02) Poole; (2003) Peterborough; (2004-05) Ipswich.

ANDERSSON, Stefan   BORN: 13 September 1971, Vastervik, Sweden.
BRITISH CAREER: (1994-98) Eastbourne; (1999) King's Lynn; (2000) Peterborough; (2001-02) Eastbourne; (2005) Oxford.

ANDREWS, Darren   BORN: 19 January 1977, Banbury, Oxfordshire.
BRITISH CAREER: (1993) Coventry, Oxford; (1994) Coventry, Oxford, Mildenhall; (1995) Sittingbourne; (1996) Reading (CL); (1997) Long Eaton, Hull, Berwick, Oxford (PL & AL), Isle of Wight; (2000) St Austell; (2001) Rye House; (2002) Mildenhall; (2003) Oxford (CL & BLC), Carmarthen (CT); (2004) Stoke (CL), Coventry (CT); (2005) Sittingbourne.

ANDREWS, Marc   BORN: 23 November 1986, Poole, Dorset.
BRITISH CAREER: (2004) Stoke (CL), Swindon (CL), King's Lynn (CT); (2005) Weymouth, Stoke (CLKOC), Oxford (CL).

APPLETON, Andrew   BORN: 18 June 1982, Reading, Berkshire.
BRITISH CAREER: (1997) Oxford (AL); (1998) Newport (CL & PL), Arena-Essex, Edinburgh; (1999) Newport (PL & CL); (2000) Newport; (2001) Oxford; (2002) Oxford, Reading; (2003) Reading; (2004) Reading, Peterborough; (2005) Reading.

ARMSTRONG, Jon   BORN: 1 August 1974, Manchester.
BRITISH CAREER: (1992-93) Belle Vue; (1994) Coventry; (1996) Buxton, Sheffield; (1997) Buxton, Belle Vue (AL), Swindon, Stoke; (1998) Newport (CL & PL); (1999) Belle Vue, Stoke; (2000) Newport (PL); (2001) Stoke; (2002) Buxton, Stoke; (2003) Stoke; (2004) Mildenhall, Belle Vue; (2005) Mildenhall, Peterborough.

ASHWORTH, Ricky   BORN: 17 August 1982, Salford, Greater Manchester.
BRITISH CAREER: (2001) Sheffield (CL); (2002) Sheffield (PL & CL); (2003) Sheffield (PL); (2004) Sheffield (PL), Peterborough; (2005) Sheffield, Poole.

ATKIN, Tony   BORN: 8 April 1966, Wrexham, North Wales.
BRITISH CAREER: (1986) Stoke; (1994) Wolverhampton; (1995) Bradford; (1996) Sheffield, Wolverhampton, Buxton; (1997) Stoke; (1999-2002) Stoke; (2003-05) Newport.

AUTY, Josh   BORN: 8 September 1990, Mirfield, West Yorkshire.
BRITISH CAREER: (2005) Scunthorpe.

BAGER, Henning   BORN: 18 February 1981, Esbjerg, Denmark.
BRITISH CAREER: (2001) Glasgow; (2002) Peterborough, Isle of Wight; (2003) Arena-Essex; (2004-05) Peterborough.

BAKER, David   BORN: 12 December 1980, Beverley, East Yorkshire.
BRITISH CAREER: (2001) Newcastle; (2002) Peterborough (CL); (2005) Scunthorpe.

BAJERSKI, Tomasz   BORN: 9 September 1975, Torun, Poland.
BRITISH CAREER: (2001) King's Lynn; (2005) Oxford.

BANKS, Trevor   BORN: 4 October 1955, Folkestone, Kent
BRITISH CAREER: (1982) Crayford, Wimbledon; (1983) Crayford; (1984) Hackney, Wolverhampton; (1985) Hackney; (1986) Milton Keynes; (1987) Milton Keynes, Hackney; (1988) Milton Keynes, Sheffield; (1989-90) Milton Keynes; (2005) Sittingbourne.

BARAN, Karol   BORN: 16 August 1981, Rzeszow, Poland.
BRITISH CAREER: (2005) Ipswich.

BARGH, Andrew   BORN: 15 April 1986, Napier, New Zealand.
BRITISH CAREER: (2005) Wimbledon, Mildenhall.

BARKER, Ben   BORN: 10 March 1988, Truro, Cornwall.
BRITISH CAREER: (2003) Oxford (CL), Trelawny (CT); (2004) Oxford (CL), Coventry (CT); (2005) Oxford (CL), Exeter.

BARKER, Dean   BORN: 2 August 1970, Isleworth, Middlesex.
BRITISH CAREER: (1986) Eastbourne; (1987-88) Eastbourne, Cradley Heath; (1989) Eastbourne; (1990-92) Oxford; (1993-95) Eastbourne; (1997) Eastbourne; (1999-2003) Eastbourne; (2004) Arena-Essex; (2005) Eastbourne.

BARNETT, Russell   BORN: 26 May 1987, Newport, South Wales.
BRITISH CAREER: (2003) Mildenhall (CT), Rye House (CL), Newport (CL), Oxford (CL); (2004-05) Newport (CL).

BASEBY, Aaron   BORN: 31 May 1990, Pembury, Kent.
BRITISH CAREER: (2005) Sittingbourne.

BASEBY, Mark   BORN: 28 February 1988, Pembury, Kent.
BRITISH CAREER: (2003) Stoke (CT), Swindon (CL); (2004) Rye House (CL), Sittingbourne (KOC); (2005) Sittingbourne.

BATCHELOR, Troy   BORN: 29 August 1987, Brisbane, Queensland, Australia.
BRITISH CAREER: (2005) King's Lynn, Eastbourne.

BATES, Matt   BORN: 26 July 1989, Exeter, Devon.
BRITISH CAREER: (2004) Weymouth, Coventry (CT); (2005) Weymouth, Mildenhall (CT).

BEATON, Gary   BORN: 20 August 1986, Glasgow, Scotland.
BRITISH CAREER: (2002) Newport (CL), Newcastle (CL); (2003) Newcastle (CL), Wolverhampton (CL), Armadale; (2004-05) Armadale.

BEKKER, Byron   BORN: 2 July 1987, Johannesburg, South Africa.
BRITISH CAREER: (2004) Newcastle (CL); (2005) Scunthorpe.

BELFIELD, Carl   BORN: 1 September 1977, Stockport, Cheshire.
BRITISH CAREER: (2002) Buxton; (2004-05) Buxton.

BENTLEY, Paul   BORN: 18 January 1968, Newcastle-upon-Tyne, Tyne & Wear.
BRITISH CAREER: (1987) Newcastle; (1988-91) Middlesbrough; (1992) Coventry; (1993) Bradford; (1994) Middlesbrough; (1995-96) Coventry; (1997) Newcastle; (1998) Hull; (1999) Glasgow; (2000) Berwick; (2001) Hull; (2002-03) Berwick; (2004-05) Glasgow.

BETHELL, Jonathon   BORN: 18 March 1973, Kendal, Cumbria.
BRITISH CAREER: (2003) Oxford (CL), Buxton; (2004) Buxton; (2005) Buxton, Workington.

BETSON, Danny   BORN: 11 January 1988, Eastbourne, East Sussex.
BRITISH CAREER: (2004) Mildenhall, Swindon (CL); (2005) Wimbledon.

BIRD, Danny   BORN: 16 November 1979, Guildford, Surrey.
BRITISH CAREER: (1998-2001) Isle of Wight; (2002-03) Isle of Wight, Ipswich; (2004) Reading, Ipswich; (2005) Reading.

BIRKINSHAW, James BORN: 6 March 1980, Sheffield, South Yorkshire.

BRITISH CAREER: (1996) Owlerton, Sheffield, Hull; (1997) Sheffield, Belle Vue (AL), Newcastle; (1998) Newcastle, St Austell; (1999) Workington, Edinburgh, Linlithgow, Stoke, Sheffield; (2000) Glasgow, Sheffield (PL & CL); (2001) Newcastle, Sheffield (CL); (2002) Sheffield (PL), Boston, Wolverhampton (CT); (2003) Sheffield (PL); (2004) Sheffield (PL), Buxton; (2005) Glasgow, Buxton, Newcastle.

BJERRE, Kenneth BORN: 24 May 1984, Esbjerg, Denmark.

BRITISH CAREER: (2002) Newcastle; (2003) Newcastle, Peterborough; (2004-05) Belle Vue.

BLACKBURN, Andrew BORN: 20 March 1985, Sheffield, South Yorkshire.

BRITISH CAREER: (2004) Stoke (CL), Weymouth; (2005) Stoke (CL).

BLAKE, Daniel BORN: 7 August 1988, Harlow, Essex.

BRITISH CAREER: (2004) Mildenhall; (2005) Sittingbourne.

BOWEN, Luke BORN: 26 January 1986, Harlow, Essex.

BRITISH CAREER: (2002) Rye House (CL), Carmarthen; (2003) Rye House (CL); (2004) Rye House (CL), King's Lynn (CLKOC); (2005) Rye House (CL).

BOXALL, Steve BORN: 16 May 1987, Canterbury, Kent.

BRITISH CAREER: (2002) Rye House (CL); (2003) Rye House (CL); (2004-05) Rye House (PL & CL).

BOYCE, Craig BORN: 2 August 1967, Sydney, New South Wales, Australia.

BRITISH CAREER: (1988-90) Poole; (1991) Oxford; (1992-94) Poole; (1995) Swindon; (1996-98) Poole; (1999) Oxford; (2000) King's Lynn; (2001-02) Ipswich; (2003) Oxford, Poole (BLC), Ipswich; (2004-05) Isle of Wight.

BRADLEY, Mark BORN: 6 July 1984, Wolverhampton, West Midlands.

BRITISH CAREER: (2005) Stoke (CT).

BRADY, Ross BORN: 17 February 1981, Winchburgh, Broxburn, Scotland.

BRITISH CAREER: (1997) Lathallan, Peterborough (AL); (1998) Mildenhall, Peterborough (PL), Berwick; (1999-2000) Edinburgh; (2001-02) Hull; (2003) Glasgow, Sheffield (CL & PL); (2004) Hull; (2005) Edinburgh.

BRANNEY, Craig BORN: 31 July 1982, Whitehaven, Cumbria.

BRITISH CAREER: (2000) Ashfield; (2001) Workington, Buxton; (2002) Newcastle (CL), Hull; (2003) Newcastle (PL & CL), Armadale (CT); (2004) Oxford (CL), King's Lynn (CT); (2005) Hull, Oxford (EL & CL).

BRANNEY, John BORN: 7 November 1985, Whitehaven, Cumbria.

BRITISH CAREER: (2002) Rye House (CL), Newcastle (CL); (2003) Newcastle (CL), Wimbledon (CT), Buxton (CT); (2004) Newcastle (CL), King's Lynn (CT); (2005) Oxford (CL).

BRIDGER, Lewis BORN: 4 November 1989, Hastings, Sussex.

BRITISH CAREER: (2005) Weymouth.

BROADHURST, Wayne BORN: 28 February 1967, Minsterley, Shropshire.

BRITISH CAREER: (1987) Coventry; (1988) Coventry, Stoke; (1989) Coventry; (1999) Stoke, Workington; (2000) Stoke; (2001) Wolverhampton, Stoke; (2002) Mildenhall; (2003) Mildenhall; (2004) Wimbledon; (2005) Stoke (CL).

BROWN, Tom BORN: 19 June 1984, Pontypool, Wales.

BRITISH CAREER: (2000) Peterborough (CL), Newport (CL); (2001) Newport (CL & PL); (2002) Workington, Newport (CL), Swindon (CT), Isle of Wight; (2003) Trelawny (PL & CT); (2004) Stoke (CL), Berwick; (2005) Weymouth.

BRUNDLE, James BORN: 15 December 1986, King's Lynn, Norfolk.

BRITISH CAREER: (2002) King's Lynn (CL), Mildenhall; (2003) King's Lynn (PL), Mildenhall; (2004) Mildenhall, King's Lynn; (2005) King's Lynn.

BUCKLAND, Wayne BORN: 4 June 1987.

BRITISH CAREER: (2005) Buxton.

BUNYAN, Jason BORN: 9 March 1979, Milton Keynes, Buckinghamshire.

BRITISH CAREER: (1995) Poole; (1996) Eastbourne (CL); (1997) Oxford, Isle of Wight, Peterborough (AL); (1998) Isle of Wight; (1999-2001) Ipswich; (2002) Reading; (2003) Coventry; (2004) Isle of Wight, Coventry; (2005) Isle of Wight (PT).

BURCHATT, Barry   BORN: 25 October 1987, Farnborough, Kent.

BRITISH CAREER: (2003) Newport (CL), Rye House (CL), Wimbledon; (2004-05) Rye House (CL).

BURNETT, Paul   BORN: 24 October 1981, Bradford, West Yorkshire.

BRITISH CAREER: (1997) Buxton, Belle Vue (AL), Western Warriors; (1998-2004) Buxton; (2005) Scunthorpe, Mildenhall.

BURROWS, Mark   BORN: 6 June 1964, Sheffield, South Yorkshire.

BRITISH CAREER: (1984) Scunthorpe; (1985) Edinburgh; (1986) Edinburgh; (1987) Middlesbrough; (1992) Glasgow, Middlesbrough; (1993) Middlesbrough; (1994) Buxton, Cleveland, Middlesbrough, Sheffield; Belle Vue, Coventry; (1995) Buxton, Long Eaton, Middlesbrough, Hull; (1996) Buxton; (1997-2001) Stoke; (2002) Stoke, Belle Vue; (2003) Stoke (CT), Wimbledon; (2004-05) Wimbledon.

CAMPOS, Scott   BORN: 1 May 1989, Ipswich, Suffolk.

BRITISH CAREER: (2004) Mildenhall, Rye House (CL); (2005) Mildenhall, Boston.

CANDY, Paul   BORN: 4 February 1980, Basingstoke, Hampshire.

BRITISH CAREER: (2003) Carmarthen; (2004) Weymouth, Newport (CL); (2005) Weymouth, Sittingbourne.

CARR, Peter   BORN: 22 January 1963, Preston, Lancashire.

BRITISH CAREER: (1979) Ellesmere Port, Hackney; (1980) Ellesmere Port, Belle Vue, Birmingham, Hull; (1981) Ellesmere Port, Belle Vue; (1982-84) Belle Vue; (1985-88) Sheffield; (1989-90) Newcastle; (1991-93) Sheffield; (1994-95) Belle Vue; (1997-2004) Edinburgh; (2005) Stoke.

CARTER, Wayne   BORN: 19 December 1970, Halifax, West Yorkshire.

BRITISH CAREER: (1989) Mildenhall, Wolverhampton; (1990) Wolverhampton; (1991) Wolverhampton, Middlesbrough; (1992) Wolverhampton; (1993) Middlesbrough; (1994-95) Wolverhampton; (1996) Middlesbrough, Belle Vue; (1997) Skegness, Isle of Wight, Peterborough, Belle Vue, Wolverhampton, Bradford; (1998-99) Isle of Wight; (2000) Wolverhampton; (2001) Belle Vue, Berwick; (2002) Coventry, Newcastle; (2003) Wolverhampton (BLC), Edinburgh; (2004) Sheffield (CT), Swindon (CL); (2005) Scunthorpe.

CARTWRIGHT, Simon BORN: 2 November 1978, Northallerton, North Yorkshire.

BRITISH CAREER: (1996) Owlerton; (1997) Belle Vue (AL); (1998) Hull, Norfolk; (1999-2000) Sheffield; (2001) Stoke, Glasgow; (2002) Berwick; (2003) Hull; (2004) Berwick; (2005) Berwick (PT).

CHESTER, Scott   BORN: 6 January 1982, Leicester, Leicestershire.

BRITISH CAREER: (2004) Buxton, Weymouth (CT), King's Lynn (CT); (2005) Buxton.

CLEMENT, James   BORN: 29 August 1985, Crawley, West Sussex.

BRITISH CAREER: (2003-04) Wimbledon; (2005) Wimbledon, Weymouth.

CLEWS, Paul   BORN: 19 July 1979, Coventry, Warwickshire.

BRITISH CAREER: (1995) Coventry; (1996) Peterborough (CL & PL), Coventry, Oxford, Anglian Angels; (1997) Skegness, Isle of Wight, Peterborough (AL), Coventry; (1998) Peterborough; (1999-2003) Reading; (2004-05) Stoke.

COCKLE, James   BORN: 26 May 1986, Enfield, Middlesex.

BRITISH CAREER: (2001-03) Rye House (CL); (2004) Boston, Sheffield (CT), Reading, Glasgow; (2005) Glasgow, Sittingbourne, Boston.

COLES, Michael   BORN: 11 August 1965, Exeter, Devon.

BRITISH CAREER: (1982-83) Exeter; (1984) Exeter, Weymouth; (1985-87) Exeter; (1988) Mildenhall; (1989-93) Edinburgh; (1994) Belle Vue; (1995) Oxford; (1996) Exeter; (1997) Exeter, King's Lynn; (1998-2004) Exeter; (2005) Newport.

COLLINS, Aidan   BORN: 21 April 1982, Stockport, Cheshire.

BRITISH CAREER: (1998) Newport (CL); (1999) Buxton, Edinburgh; (2000) Glasgow, Ashfield; (2001) Glasgow; (2002) Buxton, Edinburgh; (2003-04) Workington; (2005) Mildenhall, Workington.

COLLINS, Neil   BORN: 15 October 1961, Partington, Greater Manchester.

BRITISH CAREER: (1978) Ellesmere Port; (1979) Nottingham, Workington, Sheffield; (1980) Edinburgh, Sheffield; (1981) Edinburgh, Cradley Heath, Belle Vue; (1982-83) Leicester; (1984-88) Sheffield; (1989-90) Wolverhampton; (1991) Belle Vue; (1992) Glasgow; (1993-94) Long Eaton; (1995) Sheffield; (1996)

Belle Vue; (1997) Glasgow; (1998) Stoke; (1999-2000) Swindon; (2001) Belle Vue, Workington; (2002) Somerset; (2003) Hull, Peterborough (BLC), Belle Vue; (2004) Somerset; (2005) Newport.

COLLYER, Peter   BORN: 2 December 1981, Frimley Green, Camberley, Surrey.
BRITISH CAREER: (1999) Reading, Newcastle, Rye House, Glasgow; (2002) Carmarthen, Wimbledon; (2003) Wimbledon; (2004) Wimbledon; (2005) Wimbledon, Sittingbourne.

COLVIN, Shane   BORN: 4 February 1982, Hastings, East Sussex.
BRITISH CAREER: (1997) Oxford (AL), Ryde, M4 Raven Sprockets; (1998) Newport (CL); (1999) Reading, Mildenhall; (2000) Reading, Ashfield, Mildenhall; (2001) Reading, Newport (CL); (2002) Carmarthen, Wolverhampton (CLKOC), Workington; (2003) Reading; (2004) Carmarthen, Sittingbourne (KOC), Sheffield; (2005) Sittingbourne.

COMPTON, Andre   BORN: 15 May 1977, Dewsbury, West Yorkshire.
BRITISH CAREER: (1993) Bradford, Newcastle; (1994) Stoke, Newcastle, Buxton; (1995) Hull, Buxton, Reading, Coventry, Belle Vue; (1996) Buxton, Bradford, Belle Vue; (1997) Newcastle, Berwick; (1998-99) Sheffield; (2000) Peterborough, Newcastle; (2001) Newcastle; (2002) Newcastle, Poole; (2003) Sheffield, Poole; (2004) Sheffield, Poole, Belle Vue; (2005) Sheffield.

COMPTON, Benji   BORN: 17 September 1986, Tenerife, Spain.
BRITISH CAREER: (2002) Newcastle (CL); (2003) Sheffield (CL), Mildenhall (CT & KOC); (2004) Buxton; (2005) Sheffield (PT), Scunthorpe.

COOK, Harland   BORN: 6 August 1988, Watford, Hertfordshire.
BRITISH CAREER: (2003) Rye House (CL); (2004) Rye House (CL), Coventry (CT); (2005) Rye House (CL).

COOPER, Paul   BORN: 7 June 1982, York, North Yorkshire.
BRITISH CAREER: (2003) Sheffield (CL); (2004) Oxford (CL), Sheffield (CT); (2005) Sheffield.

CORREY, Ronnie   BORN: 8 November 1966, Bellflower, California, USA.
BRITISH CAREER: (1987-93) Wolverhampton; (1995) Long Eaton; (1996-97) Wolverhampton; (1998-99) Belle Vue; (2000) Wolverhampton; (2004) Belle Vue; (2005) Wolverhampton.

COTTHAM, Gary   BORN: 13 September 1989, Eastbourne, East Sussex.
BRITISH CAREER: (2004-05) Rye House (CL).

COURTNEY, Jamie   BORN: 22 April 1988, Ashington, Northumberland.
BRITISH CAREER: (2003) Rye House (CL), Trelawny (CT); (2004) Swindon (CL), Isle of Wight, Oxford (CL); (2005) Oxford (CL), Workington.

COURTNEY, Scott   BORN: 3 January 1983, Middlesbrough, Cleveland.
BRITISH CAREER: (1999) Glasgow, Linlithgow; (2000) Glasgow, Ashfield; (2001) Glasgow, Buxton, Mildenhall, Trelawny; (2002) Arena-Essex, Rye House (CL); (2003) Poole (BLC), Rye House (CL); (2005) Workington (PT), Oxford (CL).

CROSS, Andre   BORN: 12 June 1967, Norwich, Norfolk.
BRITISH CAREER: (2002-04) Wimbledon; (2005) Sittingbourne.

CRUMP, Jason   BORN: 6 August 1975, Bristol, Avon.
BRITISH CAREER: (1991) Poole; (1992) Peterborough; (1993) Swindon; (1994-95) Poole; (1996-97) Peterborough; (1998) Oxford; (1999) Peterborough; (2000-01) King's Lynn; (2002-05) Belle Vue.

CUNNINGHAM, Glenn BORN: 10 June 1975, Bristol, Avon.
BRITISH CAREER: (1991-92) Oxford; (1993-96) Swindon; (1997) Reading; (1998) Peterborough; (1999) Swindon; (2000) Peterborough, Belle Vue; (2001) Newport; (2002) Somerset; (2003) Somerset, Eastbourne; (2004) Somerset, Swindon; (2005) Somerset.

DALLAWAY, Lewis   BORN: 26 February 1986, Walsall, West Midlands.
BRITISH CAREER: (2004) King's Lynn (CT); (2005) Newport (CL), Weymouth.

DARKIN, Sergey   BORN: 18 June 1973, Fergana, Uzbekistan.
BRITISH CAREER: (2001) Eastbourne; (2004) Coventry; (2005) Arena-Essex.

DART, Tony   BORN: 2 September 1979, Ashford, Kent.
BRITISH CAREER: (2003-04) Mildenhall; (2005) Workington (PT).

DAVIDSSON, Daniel   BORN: 17 March 1983, Mariestad, Sweden.
BRITISH CAREER: (2003) Poole (BLC); (2004) Poole; (2005) Coventry, Peterborough.

DAVIDSSON, Jonas   BORN: 7 August 1984, Motala, Sweden.
BRITISH CAREER: (2003) Reading; (2004) Oxford; (2005) Swindon.

DE GROOT, Stefan   BORN: 31 July 1985, Watford, Hertfordshire.
BRITISH CAREER: (2005) Sittingbourne.

DENNIS, Richie   BORN: 16 April 1988, Boston, Lincolnshire.
BRITISH CAREER: (2003) Peterborough (CL); (2004) Boston, King's Lynn (CT); (2005) Scunthorpe.

DERBYSHIRE, Lee   BORN: 3 December 1981, Stockport, Cheshire.
BRITISH CAREER: (2002–04) Buxton; (2005) Buxton, Workington.

DICKEN, Lee   BORN: 25 August 1978, Hull, East Yorkshire.
BRITISH CAREER: (1994) Buxton; (1995) Hull, Stoke, Peterborough; (1996) Hull, Owlerton, Sheffield; (1997–98) Hull; (1999) Hull, Exeter; (2000) Hull; (2001) Hull, Arena-Essex; (2002) Newport, Wolverhampton; (2003) Hull, Newcastle; (2004) Newcastle (CL & PL), Glasgow; (2005) Hull (PT), Sittingbourne, Newport (PL & CL).

DOOLAN, Kevin   BORN: 30 November 1980, Shepparton, Victoria, Australia.
BRITISH CAREER: (1999–2000) Belle Vue; (2002) Berwick; (2003) Glasgow; (2004) King's Lynn; (2005) King's Lynn, Ipswich.

DOWNS, Carl   BORN: 13 November 1983, Coventry, Warwickshire.
BRITISH CAREER: (1999) King's Lynn (CL); (2000) Boston, Peterborough (CL); (2001) Sheffield (CL), Mildenhall, Newport (CL); (2002) King's Lynn (CL); (2003) Oxford (CL), Coventry (BLC), Stoke (CT); (2004) Oxford (CL), Newcastle (CL), Coventry (CT), Sittingbourne (KOC); (2005) Sittingbourne.

DOYLE, Jason   BORN: 6 October 1985, Newcastle, New South Wales, Australia.
BRITISH CAREER: (2005) Isle of Wight.

DRYML, Ales   BORN: 19 October 1979, Pardubice, Czech Republic.
BRITISH CAREER: (2000–02) Oxford; (2003) Belle Vue, Poole; (2004–05) Peterborough.

DRYML, Lukas   BORN: 16 April 1981, Pardubice, Czech Republic.
BRITISH CAREER: (2000–02) Oxford; (2003) Poole; (2004) Peterborough; (2005) Oxford, Peterborough.

DUNWORTH, Wayne   BORN: 20 January 1967, Nottingham, Nottinghamshire.
BRITISH CAREER: (1984) Boston; (1986) Mildenhall; (2002) Boston, Carmarthen; (2003) Trelawny (CT), Boston, Peterborough (CL), Armadale (CT); (2004) Boston, King's Lynn (CT); (2005) Boston.

DYM, Piotr   BORN: 31 August 1976, Leszno, Poland.
BRITISH CAREER: (2005) Berwick (PT).

EKBERG, Stefan   BORN: 21 January 1972, Motala, Sweden.
BRITISH CAREER: (1994) Oxford; (1995) Eastbourne; (2005) Glasgow.

ELKINS, Justin   BORN: 27 August 1974, Salisbury, Wiltshire.
BRITISH CAREER: (1990) Poole; (1991) Rye House, Exeter; (1992) Swindon; (1993) Poole; (1994) Poole, Reading, Coventry, Exeter; (1995) Peterborough, Poole; (1996) Ryde, Eastbourne (PL & CL); (1997) Long Eaton; (1998) Reading; (1999) Reading, Edinburgh; (2000) Poole, Arena-Essex; (2001) Hull, Workington, Exeter; (2002) Isle of Wight, Wimbledon; (2003) Poole (BLC); (2004) Weymouth, Stoke (CL); (2005) Stoke (CL).

ERIKSSON, Freddie   BORN: 23 April 1981, Stockholm, Sweden.
BRITISH CAREER: (2001–02) King's Lynn; (2003) Ipswich; (2005) Oxford.

ERMOLENKO, Sam   BORN: 23 November 1960, Maywood, California, USA.
BRITISH CAREER: (1983–84) Poole; (1986–95) Wolverhampton; (1996) Sheffield; (1997) Belle Vue; (1998) Wolverhampton; (1999) Hull; (2000–01) Wolverhampton; (2002) Belle Vue; (2003–04) Wolverhampton; (2005) Peterborough.

EVANS, Barrie   BORN: 16 April 1984, King's Lynn, Norfolk.
BRITISH CAREER: (1999) Mildenhall; (2000–01) Arena-Essex, Mildenhall; (2002) Newport, Rye House (CL); (2003) Hull, Rye House (CL); (2004) Wimbledon, Newport (PL); (2005) Stoke (PL & CL).

EZERGAILIS, Karlis   BORN: 8 April 1985, Melbourne, Victoria, Australia.
BRITISH CAREER: (2004) Newport (CL), Coventry (CT); (2005) Newport (PL & CL).

FARLEY, David   BORN: 13 April 1983, Ashton-under-Lyne, Cheshire.

BRITISH CAREER: (2005) Buxton.

FELTON, Dean   BORN: 18 August 1969, Wolverhampton, West Midlands.

BRITISH CAREER: (1994) Buxton, Oxford, Ipswich; (1995-96) Buxton; (1997) Buxton, Stoke, Edinburgh, Skegness, Long Eaton, Shuttle Cubs; (1998) Stoke; (1999) Berwick, Glasgow; (2000) Buxton, Berwick; (2001) Stoke, Buxton; (2002-03) Carmarthen; (2004) Carmarthen, King's Lynn (CT); (2005) Buxton.

FERJAN, Matej   BORN: 5 January 1977, Ljubljana, Slovenia.

BRITISH CAREER: (1998) Belle Vue; (1999) Poole; (2000) Ipswich; (2001) Peterborough, Belle Vue; (2002) Belle Vue; (2003) Oxford; (2004-05) Poole.

FILMER, Adam   BORN: 26 September 1986, Maidstone, Kent.

BRITISH CAREER: (2005) Weymouth.

FLINT, Gary   BORN: 5 May 1982, Ashington, Durham.

BRITISH CAREER: (1999) Berwick, Linlithgow, St Austell; (2000) Ashfield, Berwick; (2001) Buxton; (2002) Newcastle (CL); (2003) Buxton, Stoke (CT), Sheffield (CL); (2004) Sheffield (CT), Stoke (CL), Oxford (CL); (2005) Stoke (CL).

FRAMPTON, Jordan   BORN: 8 March 1985, Poole, Dorset.

BRITISH CAREER: (2004) Swindon (CL), King's Lynn (CT), Sheffield (CT); (2005) Sittingbourne.

FRANC, Josef   BORN: 18 January 1979, Kutna Hora, Czech Republic.

BRITISH CAREER: (2001) Berwick; (2003-04) Berwick; (2005) Newcastle.

FRY, Paul   BORN: 25 October 1964, Ledbury, Hereford & Worcestershire.

BRITISH CAREER: (1984) Newcastle, Cradley Heath, Arena-Essex; (1986-87) Cradley Heath; (1988) Stoke; (1989-90) Long Eaton; (1991) King's Lynn; (1992-96) Exeter; (1997-98) Newport; (1999) Stoke; (2000-02) Swindon; (2003) Swindon, Peterborough; (2004) Somerset, Belle Vue; (2005) Somerset.

GAFUROV, Renat   BORN: 8 October 1982, Oktyabrsky, Russia.

BRITISH CAREER: (2005) Oxford.

GARROD, Dean   BORN: 11 October 1975, Norwich, Norfolk.

BRITISH CAREER: (1993) Middlesbrough; (1994) Mildenhall; (1995-96) Mildenhall, Poole; (1997) Mildenhall, Newport; (1998) Mildenhall, Arena-Essex, Sheffield; (1999) Mildenhall, Buxton; (2000-03) Boston; (2004) Boston, King's Lynn (CT); Sittingbourne (KOC); (2005) Sittingbourne.

GEER, Chris   BORN: 19 February 1985, Eastbourne, East Sussex.

BRITISH CAREER: (2001) Mildenhall; (2002) Wimbledon; (2004) Sittingbourne (KOC); (2005) Mildenhall.

GIFFARD, Daniel   BORN: 10 November 1984, Eastbourne, East Sussex.

BRITISH CAREER: (2000) Rye House; (2001) Rye House; (2002) Isle of Wight, Rye House (CL & PL); (2003) Wimbledon, Eastbourne (BLC), Stoke; (2004) Stoke (PL & CL), Weymouth; (2005) Weymouth, Hull.

GJEDDE, Charlie   BORN: 28 December 1979, Holstebro, Denmark.

BRITISH CAREER: (1998) Swindon; (1999) Coventry, Wolverhampton; (2001) Reading; (2002) Swindon; (2003) Swindon, Oxford; (2004-05) Swindon.

GLEDHILL, Jack   BORN: 25 June 1986, Leamington Spa, Warwickshire.

BRITISH CAREER: (2002) Swindon (CT), Newport (CL); (2003) Swindon (CL); (2004-05) Weymouth.

GODFREY, Michael   BORN: 9 March 1988, Scunthorpe, Lincolnshire.

BRITISH CAREER: (2005) Scunthorpe.

GRANT, Rob   BORN: 10 June 1984, Newcastle-upon-Tyne, Tyne & Wear.

BRITISH CAREER: (1999) Linlithgow; (2000) Ashfield, Newcastle; (2001) Newcastle; (2002) Newcastle, Stoke; (2003) Berwick, Sheffield (CL), Stoke; (2004-05) Stoke (PL & CL).

GRIEVES, James   BORN: 28 September 1974, Paisley, Scotland.

BRITISH CAREER: (1991-95) Glasgow; (1996-97) Wolverhampton; (1998) Wolverhampton, Berwick; (1999) Edinburgh; (2000-02) Glasgow; (2003-04) Glasgow, Wolverhampton; (2005) Newcastle, Wolverhampton.

GUSTAFSSON, Henrik   BORN: 14 August 1970, Kumla, Sweden.

BRITISH CAREER: (1990-93) King's Lynn; (1994) Belle Vue; (2001) Belle Vue; (2002) Poole; (2005) Oxford.

HALL, Richard   BORN: 23 August 1984, Northallerton, North Yorkshire.

BRITISH CAREER: (2001) Newcastle; (2002) Newcastle (PL & CL); (2003) Sheffield (CL), Coventry (BLC), Boston (KOC & CT); (2004) Sheffield (PL & CT), Boston; (2005) Sheffield, Eastbourne.

HALSEY, Daniel   BORN: 15 September 1988, Aylesbury, Buckinghamshire.

BRITISH CAREER: (2005) Rye House (CL).

HAMILL, Billy   BORN: 23 May 1970, Arcadia, California, USA.

BRITISH CAREER: (1990–95) Cradley Heath; (1996) Cradley Heath & Stoke; (1997) Belle Vue; (1998–2003) Coventry; (2005) Oxford.

HANCOCK, Greg   BORN: 3 June 1970, Whittier, California, USA.

BRITISH CAREER: (1989–95) Cradley Heath; (1996) Cradley Heath & Stoke; (1997–2001) Coventry; (2003–05) Oxford.

HANNON, Ben   BORN: 2 June 1989, Olney, Buckinghamshire.

BRITISH CAREER: (2005) Boston.

HARDING, Trevor   BORN: 1 November 1986, Perth, Western Australia.

BRITISH CAREER: (2002) Sheffield (CL), Carmarthen; (2003) King's Lynn, Boston; (2004) King's Lynn (PL & CT), Ipswich, Swindon (CL); (2005) Rye House (CLKOC), Sheffield, Boston, Somerset, Eastbourne.

HARGREAVES, Jack   BORN: 28 May 1988, Shrewsbury, Shropshire.

BRITISH CAREER: (2003) Wolverhampton (CL); (2004) Stoke (CL); (2005) Stoke (CL & PL).

HARRIS, Chris   BORN: 28 November 1982, Truro, Cornwall.

BRITISH CAREER: (1998) St Austell; (1999–2000) Exeter; (2001) Trelawny; (2002–03) Trelawny, Peterborough; (2004–05) Coventry.

HARRISON, Rusty   BORN: 11 October 1981, Adelaide, South Australia, Australia.

BRITISH CAREER: (2000) Glasgow; (2001–04) Workington; (2005) Edinburgh, Belle Vue.

HAUZINGER, Manuel   BORN: 3 December 1982, Vienna, Austria.

BRITISH CAREER: (2005) Isle of Wight.

HAVELOCK, Gary   BORN: 4 November 1968, Eaglescliffe, Yarm, Cleveland.

BRITISH CAREER: (1985) Middlesbrough, King's Lynn, Wolverhampton; (1986) Middlesbrough, Bradford; (1987–88) Bradford; (1990–97) Bradford; (1998) Eastbourne, Poole; (1999–2002) Poole; (2003–04) Peterborough; (2005) Arena-Essex.

HAWKINS, Ritchie   BORN: 9 November 1983, Peterborough, Cambridgeshire.

BRITISH CAREER: (2000) Sheffield (CL); (2001) Swindon, Sheffield (CL); (2002) Swindon (PL & CT); (2003) Swindon (PL & CL), Peterborough (BLC); (2004) Mildenhall, Berwick; (2005) Somerset, Peterborough.

HAYES, Grant   BORN: 24 January 1989, Halifax, West Yorkshire.

BRITISH CAREER: (2004) Weymouth, Sheffield (CT); (2005) Scunthorpe.

HEATH, Trevor   BORN: 21 March 1989, Cuckfield, West Sussex.

BRITISH CAREER: (2004) Sheffield (CT); (2005) Mildenhall.

HENRY, Christian   BORN: 20 February 1981, Sydney, New South Wales, Australia.

BRITISH CAREER: (2000) Edinburgh, Ashfield; (2001–02) Edinburgh; (2003) Glasgow; (2005) Newcastle.

HICKMOTT, Gareth (formerly Gareth Roberts)   BORN: 28 May 1980, Pembury, Tunbridge Wells, Kent.

BRITISH CAREER: (2003) Wimbledon; (2005) Mildenhall.

HOLLINGWORTH, Robert   BORN: 31 December 1955, Boston, Lincolnshire.

BRITISH CAREER: (1973) Berwick; (1974) Boston; (1975) Boston, King's Lynn, Wolverhampton, Poole, Hull; (1976) Boston, Wolverhampton, White City; (1977) Boston, Wolverhampton; (1978) Edinburgh, Wolverhampton; (1979) Boston, King's Lynn; (1980–81) Boston, Coventry; (1982) Boston, King's Lynn; (1983) Scunthorpe; (1984) Boston; (1985) Mildenhall; (1986) Boston; (1999) King's Lynn (CL); (2000–05) Boston.

HORTON, James   BORN: 22 June 1985, Slough, Berkshire.

BRITISH CAREER: (2000–02) Peterborough (CL); (2003) Peterborough (CL & BLC), Boston (CT), Trelawny (CT); (2005) Mildenhall, Boston.

HOWE, David   BORN: 1 March 1982, Leicester, Leicestershire.

BRITISH CAREER: (1997) Peterborough (AL); (1998) Peterborough, Norfolk; (1999-2001) Peterborough; (2002-05) Wolverhampton.

HUGHES, Danny   BORN: 2 September 1983, Manchester.

BRITISH CAREER: (1999) Workington; (2000) Buxton, Belle Vue; (2001) Buxton, Newport (CL); (2002) Newport (CL); (2003) Newport (CL), Belle Vue (BLC), Stoke (CT); (2004) Newcastle (CL), Coventry (CT); (2005) Weymouth.

HUGHES, Kyle   BORN: 15 June 1989, Bath, Somerset.

BRITISH CAREER: (2004) Mildenhall; (2005) Oxford (CL).

HUMBY, James   BORN: 12 June 1989, Romsey, Hampshire.

BRITISH CAREER: (2004) Stoke (CL), Wimbledon, Oxford (CL); (2005) Stoke (CL).

HUNT, Chris   BORN: 15 February 1964, Wallingford, Oxfordshire.

BRITISH CAREER: (1980) Exeter; (1981) Swindon; (1982) Exeter, Milton Keynes; (1983) Milton Keynes, Glasgow; (1984) Milton Keynes; (2001) Newport (CL); (2002-03) Wimbledon; (2004) Carmarthen; (2005) Sittingbourne.

HURRY, Paul   BORN: 9 April 1975, Canterbury, Kent.

BRITISH CAREER: (1991) Arena-Essex; (1992-93) Peterborough; (1994-95) Arena-Essex; (1996) London; (1997) King's Lynn; (1998-99) Oxford; (2000) Eastbourne; (2001-02) Wolverhampton; (2003) Ipswich; (2004-05) Arena-Essex.

HURST, Sam   BORN: 28 April 1989, Southampton, Hampshire.

BRITISH CAREER: (2004) Newport (CL), King's Lynn (CT); (2005) Newport (CL).

IRVING, Kriss   BORN: 3 April 1987, Whitehaven, Cumbria.

BRITISH CAREER: (2003) Newcastle (CL); (2004) Newcastle (CL), Stoke (CL); (2005) Stoke (CL).

IRWIN, Nathan   BORN: 28 March 1983, Cuckfield, Sussex.

BRITISH CAREER: (1999) King's Lynn (CL); (2000) Peterborough (CL); (2002) Wimbledon; (2004) Weymouth, Swindon (CL); (2005) Boston.

ISHERWOOD, Gareth   BORN: 28 November 1988, Manchester.

BRITISH CAREER: (2005) Stoke (CL).

IVERSEN, Niels-Kristian   BORN: 20 June 1982, Esbjerg, Denmark.

BRITISH CAREER: (2001) King's Lynn; (2003) Newport, Oxford; (2004-05) Oxford.

JAMES, Scott   BORN: 25 May 1984, Adelaide, South Australia.

BRITISH CAREER: (2002) Workington, Mildenhall; (2003) Mildenhall, Coventry (BLC); (2005) Wimbledon, Workington.

JANNIRO, Billy   BORN: 30 July 1980, Vallejo, California, USA.

BRITISH CAREER: (2001-04) Coventry; (2005) Peterborough, Coventry.

JANSSON, Kim   BORN: 30 October 1981, Gothenburg, Sweden.

BRITISH CAREER: (2002-05) Ipswich.

JAROS, Jan   BORN: 11 November 1984, Prague, Czech Republic.

BRITISH CAREER: (2003) King's Lynn (BLC); (2004) Belle Vue; (2005) King's Lynn.

JENSEN, Jesper B.   BORN: 14 October 1977, Esbjerg, Denmark.

BRITISH CAREER: (1997-2003) Wolverhampton; (2004) Ipswich; (2005) Oxford, Peterborough.

JENSEN, Steen   BORN: 17 November 1984, Brovst, Denmark.

BRITISH CAREER: (2004) Eastbourne; (2005) Isle of Wight, Eastbourne.

JOHANSSON, Tobias   BORN: 15 September 1977, Vaxjo, Sweden.

BRITISH CAREER: (2004) Belle Vue, Edinburgh; (2005) Poole.

JOHNSON, Ashley   BORN: 29 September 1984, Middlesbrough, Cleveland.

BRITISH CAREER: (2004) Newcastle (CL); (2005) Scunthorpe.

JOHNSON, Chris   BORN: 13 October 1987, Chichester, Sussex.

BRITISH CAREER: (2002) Wimbledon; (2003) Oxford (CL), Trelawny (CT), Isle of Wight; (2004) Isle of Wight, Swindon (CL), King's Lynn (CT); (2005) Reading, Rye House (CL), Mildenhall.

JOHNSTON, Steve   BORN: 12 October 1971, Kalgoorlie, Western Australia.

BRITISH CAREER: (1992) Sheffield; (1993) Sheffield, Long Eaton; (1994-96) Long Eaton; (1997) Ipswich;

(1998-2002) Oxford; (2003) Belle Vue; (2004) Swindon; (2005) Wolverhampton.

JONES, Ashley   BORN: 19 November 1981, Albury-Wodonga, Victoria, Australia.
BRITISH CAREER: (2002) Newport; (2005) King's Lynn.

JONSSON, Andreas   BORN: 3 September 1980, Hallstavik, Sweden.
BRITISH CAREER: (1998-99) Coventry; (2001-05) Coventry.

JUUL, Richard   BORN: 30 October 1970, Copenhagen, Denmark.
BRITISH CAREER: (1991-94) Newcastle; (1995) Wolverhampton; (1997) Newcastle, Berwick; (1998) Stoke; (1999) Wolverhampton; (2000) Glasgow, Isle of Wight; (2001-05) Newcastle.

KARLSSON, Magnus   BORN: 28 December 1981, Gullspang, Sweden.
BRITISH CAREER: (2002) Edinburgh; (2003) Edinburgh, Wolverhampton; (2004) Hull, Wolverhampton; (2005) Wolverhampton.

KARLSSON, Peter   BORN: 17 December 1969, Gullspang, Sweden.
BRITISH CAREER: (1990) Wolverhampton; (1992-97) Wolverhampton; (1999) Wolverhampton; (2000) Peterborough; (2001) King's Lynn, Belle Vue; (2002-03) Wolverhampton; (2005) Peterborough.

KASPRZAK, Krzysztof BORN: 18 July 1984, Leszno, Poland.
BRITISH CAREER: (2003-05) Poole.

KENNETT, Edward   BORN: 28 August 1986, Hastings, Sussex.
BRITISH CAREER: (2001) Rye House, Mildenhall; (2002-03) Rye House (CL & PL), Eastbourne; (2004) Eastbourne; (2005) Rye House, Poole.

KESSLER, Robbie   BORN: 5 April 1973, Neuwied, Germany.
BRITISH CAREER: (1994) Sheffield; (1996-97) Sheffield; (1999) King's Lynn; (2000-01) Sheffield; (2002) Hull; (2003) Stoke; (2004) Stoke, Peterborough; (2005) Stoke.

KING, Daniel   BORN: 14 August 1986, Maidstone, Kent.
BRITISH CAREER: (2001) Peterborough (CL); (2002) Peterborough (CL), Swindon (CT); (2003) Peterborough (CL), Ipswich (BLC), Reading, Mildenhall, Arena-Essex; (2004) Ipswich, Mildenhall; (2005) Rye House, Ipswich.

KING, Jason   BORN: 13 April 1985, Maidstone, Kent.
BRITISH CAREER: (2000) Peterborough (CL); (2001) Peterborough (CL); (2002) Swindon (PL & CT), Peterborough (CL); (2003) Arena-Essex, Peterborough (CL); (2004) Mildenhall, Rye House; (2005) Somerset, Newport.

KIRKMAN, Dan   BORN: 26 July 1990, Plymouth, Devon.
BRITISH CAREER: (2005) Weymouth.

KOLENKO, Jernej   BORN: 20 November 1982, Ljubljana, Slovenia.
BRITISH CAREER: (2002) King's Lynn; (2003) Oxford; (2005) Exeter (PT).

KORNELIUSSEN, Mads   BORN: 15 June 1983, Aalborg, Denmark.
BRITISH CAREER: (2003-04) Newport; (2005) Newport, Swindon.

KOSCIECHA, Robert   BORN: 22 November 1977, Grudziadz, Poland.
BRITISH CAREER: (2005) Poole.

KRAMER, Emil   BORN: 14 November 1979, Mariestad, Sweden.
BRITISH CAREER: (2002) King's Lynn, Hull; (2003) Hull; (2004-05) Hull, Oxford.

KRISTENSEN, Claus   BORN: 11 June 1977, Holstebro, Denmark.
BRITISH CAREER: (1999) Berwick; (2000-01) Swindon; (2002-03) Berwick; (2004) Berwick, Swindon; (2005) Newcastle (PT), Glasgow.

KRONER, Tobias   BORN: 16 October 1985, Dohren, nr Bremen, Germany.
BRITISH CAREER: (2005) Oxford.

KSIEZAK, Robert   BORN: 15 January 1987, Adelaide, South Australia.
BRITISH CAREER: (2005) Edinburgh.

KUGELMANN, Joachim   BORN: 18 August 1971, Schongau, Germany.
BRITISH CAREER: (1999) Stoke; (2001) King's Lynn; (2002) Oxford; (2005) Berwick.

KYLMAKORPI, Joonas BORN: 14 February 1980, Stockholm, Sweden.
BRITISH CAREER: (2001) Eastbourne; (2002) Ipswich; (2003) Arena-Essex, Eastbourne; (2004) Eastbourne; (2005) Peterborough, Coventry.

LAMB, Jessica   BORN: 5 February 1977, Poole, Dorset.
BRITISH CAREER: (2001) Boston; (2003) Somerset (CT), Trelawny (CT); (2005) Armadale, Scunthorpe.

LAMBERT, Simon   BORN: 21 February 1989, Boston, Lincolnshire.
BRITISH CAREER: (2004) Boston, King's Lynn (CT); (2005) Boston.

LANGLEY, Karl   BORN: 2 June 1981, Whitehaven, Cumbria.
BRITISH CAREER: (2002) Workington; (2003) Newcastle (CL), Armadale (CLKOC), Mildenhall; (2004) Newcastle (CL), Sheffield (CT); (2005) Armadale.

LANHAM, Leigh   BORN: 15 August 1977, Ipswich, Suffolk.
BRITISH CAREER: (1993) Ipswich, Arena-Essex; (1994-96) Ipswich; (1997) Exeter, Bradford, King's Lynn; (1998-99) Arena-Essex; (2001) Arena-Essex; (2002-03) Arena-Essex, Ipswich; (2004-05) Arena-Essex.

LARSEN, Josh   BORN: 12 May 1972, Anaheim, California, USA.
BRITISH CAREER: (1992-93) Arena-Essex; (1995) Arena-Essex; (1996) London; (1997) Bradford; (1999) Eastbourne; (2003) Belle Vue; (2004-05) Arena-Essex.

LAWSON, William   BORN: 27 February 1987, Perth, Perthshire, Scotland.
BRITISH CAREER: (2002) Newcastle (CL); (2003) Newcastle (PL & CL); (2004) Newcastle (PL & CL); (2005) Edinburgh, Armadale.

LEE, Paul   BORN: 21 March 1981, Nottingham, Nottinghamshire.
BRITISH CAREER: (1996) Peterborough (CL); (1997) Long Eaton, Shuttle Cubs, Peterborough (EL), Coventry; (1998) Hull; (1999-2000) Sheffield; (2001) Coventry; (2002) Swindon; (2003) Mildenhall; (2004) Mildenhall, King's Lynn; (2005) Peterborough, King's Lynn.

LEGAULT, Kyle   BORN: 30 May 1985, St Catharines, Ontario, Canada.
BRITISH CAREER: (2005) Sheffield.

LEGG, Billy   BORN: 6 September 1988, Swindon, Wiltshire.
BRITISH CAREER: (2003) Swindon (CL); (2004) Newport (CL), Mildenhall, Weymouth; (2005) Newport (CL).

LEMON, Mark   BORN: 12 February 1973, Bairnsdale, Victoria, Australia.
BRITISH CAREER: (1990) Poole; (1991) Poole, Middlesbrough; (1992) Middlesbrough, Long Eaton; (1996) Oxford; (1997-98) Poole; (1999) Eastbourne, Hull; (2000) Oxford; (2002) Oxford; (2003) Somerset, Belle Vue; (2004) Exeter, Poole; (2005) Exeter.

LEVERINGTON, Trent BORN: 13 May 1980, Brisbane, Queensland, Australia.
BRITISH CAREER: (2003) Glasgow, Armadale, Wolverhampton (CL); (2004) Buxton, Stoke; (2005) Glasgow.

LINDBACK, Antonio   BORN: 5 May 1985, Rio De Janeiro, Brazil.
BRITISH CAREER: (2003-05) Poole.

LINDGREN, Fredrik   BORN: 15 September 1985, Orebro, Sweden.
BRITISH CAREER: (2003-05) Wolverhampton.

LITTLE, Kevin   BORN: 24 September 1972, Edinburgh, Scotland.
BRITISH CAREER: (1989) Glasgow, Berwick; (1990-91) Berwick; (1992) Bradford; (1993) Edinburgh; (1994) Edinburgh, Berwick; (1995) Berwick, Belle Vue, Edinburgh, Coventry; (1996) Coventry; (1997) Berwick; (1998-2000) Edinburgh; (2001-04) Newcastle; (2005) Workington.

LJUNG, Peter   BORN: 30 October 1982, Aseda, Sweden.
BRITISH CAREER: (2003) Eastbourne, Reading; (2004) Eastbourne, Swindon; (2005) Swindon.

LORAM, Mark   BORN: 12 January 1971, Mtarfa, Malta.
BRITISH CAREER: (1987) Hackney; (1988) Hackney, King's Lynn, Belle Vue, Reading, Swindon; (1989) Ipswich; (1990-94) King's Lynn; (1995-96) Exeter; (1997) Bradford; (1998) Wolverhampton; (1999-2000) Poole; (2001) Peterborough; (2002-03) Eastbourne; (2004-05) Arena-Essex.

LOUIS, Chris   BORN: 9 July 1969, Ipswich, Suffolk.
BRITISH CAREER: (1988) Hackney, Wolverhampton, King's Lynn, Ipswich; (1989-2002) Ipswich; (2004-05) Ipswich.

LOWE, Adam   BORN: 17 February 1989, Leicester, Leicestershire.
BRITISH CAREER: (2005) Boston.

LUND, Kristian   BORN: 8 August 1984, Outrup, Denmark.
BRITISH CAREER: (2003) Newcastle; (2004) Newcastle, Newport; (2005) Newport, Edinburgh, Newcastle.

LYONS, Jason   BORN: 15 June 1970, Mildura, Victoria, Australia.
BRITISH CAREER: (1990-91) Glasgow; (1992-2003) Belle Vue; (2004) Poole, Newcastle; (2005) Belle Vue.

MacDONALD, Grant   BORN: 7 December 1979, Barrow-in-Furness, Cumbria.
BRITISH CAREER: (1996) Linlithgow, Cradley Heath & Stoke, Sheffield, London, Poole; (1997) Glasgow, Lathallan; (1998) Glasgow; (1999) Workington; (2000) Newcastle; (2001) Peterborough, Stoke, Newcastle; (2002) Glasgow; (2005) Wimbledon.

MacPHAIL, John   BORN: 13 April 1988, Edinburgh, Scotland.
BRITISH CAREER: (2003) Stoke (CT); (2004) Armadale, Newcastle (CL), Stoke (CL); (2005) Buxton, Armadale.

McALLAN, David   BORN: 20 June 1980, Edinburgh, Scotland.
BRITISH CAREER: (1996) Berwick; (1997) Berwick (PL & AL), Sheffield; (1998) Berwick, Newcastle; (1999) Edinburgh, Linlithgow; (2000) Ashfield, Stoke; (2001) Berwick, Boston, Workington; (2002) Glasgow, Sheffield (CL); (2003-04) Glasgow, Boston; (2005) Sittingbourne, Edinburgh, Boston.

McBAIN, James   BORN: 14 December 1988, Glasgow, Scotland.
BRITISH CAREER: (2004-05) Armadale.

McDADE, Cal   BORN: 25 April 1987, Glasgow, Scotland.
BRITISH CAREER: (2004) Swindon (CL); (2005) Armadale.

McGOWAN, Travis   BORN: 13 January 1981, Mildura, Victoria, Australia.
BRITISH CAREER: (1999-2000) King's Lynn; (2002) King's Lynn; (2003-05) Oxford.

McKINNA, Adam   BORN: 17 August 1986, Crewe, Cheshire.
BRITISH CAREER: (2004-05) Armadale.

MADSEN, Tom   BORN: 24 November 1977, Esbjerg, Denmark.
BRITISH CAREER: (1999) Berwick; (2000-02) King's Lynn; (2003) Ipswich, King's Lynn; (2004) King's Lynn, Oxford, Berwick; (2005) Oxford, Berwick.

MAKOVSKY, Michal   BORN: 6 April 1976, Hradec Kralove, Czech Republic.
BRITISH CAREER: (2001-04) Berwick; (2005) Berwick, Oxford.

MALLETT, Darren   BORN: 25 May 1986, Boston, Lincolnshire.
BRITISH CAREER: (2001) Somerset, Boston; (2002) Boston; (2003) Boston, King's Lynn; (2004) King's Lynn (PL & CT), Boston; (2005) Boston.

MARSH, Krister   BORN: 23 March 1976, Hereford, Hereford & Worcestershire.
BRITISH CAREER: (1995) Devon; (1996) Swindon (CL & PL), Sheffield, London; (1997) Oxford (AL & PL), Reading; (1998) Reading; (1999) Swindon; (2000) Reading, Newcastle; (2001) Newport, Swindon, Exeter; (2002-03) Exeter; (2004) Isle of Wight; (2005) Isle of Wight, Belle Vue.

MARTIN, Sam   BORN: 8 February 1989, Adelaide, South Australia.
BRITISH CAREER: (2004-05) Oxford (CL).

MASON, David   BORN: 20 December 1976, Crawley, West Sussex.
BRITISH CAREER: (1995) Sittingbourne, Reading, Arena-Essex, Swindon, Poole, Oxford; (1996) Sittingbourne, London, Reading; (1997) Arena-Essex; (1998) Newport, Stoke, Arena-Essex, Mildenhall (KOC); (1999) Swindon, Rye House; (2000) Rye House, Arena-Essex, Poole; (2001-03) Rye House; (2004-05) Weymouth.

MASON, Karl   BORN: 4 March 1986, Hillingdon, London.
BRITISH CAREER: (2001) Buxton, Mildenhall, Somerset; (2002) Newport (CL); (2003) Newport (CL & PL); (2004) Newport (PL & CL), Coventry (CT); (2005) Newport (CL & PL).

MASTERS, Steve   BORN: 6 December 1970, Eastbourne, East Sussex.
BRITISH CAREER: (1989-91) Eastbourne; (1992-93) Swindon; (1994) Swindon (KOC), Cradley Heath, Reading, Poole; (1995) Poole; (1996-97) Swindon; (1998) Swindon, Isle of Wight; (1999) Swindon; (2000) King's Lynn; (2001) Newport; (2002) Trelawny; (2003) Trelawny, Oxford; (2004) Rye House, Swindon; (2005) Belle Vue, Reading.

MAX, Mikael (formerly Mikael Karlsson)   BORN: 21 August 1973, Gullspang, Sweden.
BRITISH CAREER: (1993-94) Wolverhampton; (1996-99) Wolverhampton; (2001-05) Wolverhampton.

MEAR, Robert   BORN: 12 January 1989, Welwyn Garden City, Hertfordshire.
BRITISH CAREER: (2004-05) Rye House (CL).

MELDRUM, David   BORN: 6 October 1977, Berwick-upon-Tweed, Northumberland.
BRITISH CAREER: (1994-95) Berwick; (1996) Berwick, Eastbourne (CL); (1997) Berwick (PL & AL);
(1998) Berwick, Buxton; (1999-2001) Berwick; (2002) Somerset, Wimbledon; (2003) Berwick; (2004)
Berwick, Newcastle (PL & CL); (2005) Sittingbourne, Stoke.

MILLS, Chris   BORN: 29 March 1983, Chelmsford, Essex.
BRITISH CAREER: (2001) Arena-Essex; (2002) King's Lynn (CL), Wimbledon (CT); (2003) Isle of Wight,
Oxford (CL); (2004) Reading, Oxford (CL); (2005) Reading (PT), Oxford (EL & CL), Somerset.

MISKOWIAK, Robert   BORN: 21 November 1983, Rawicz, Poland.
BRITISH CAREER: (2005) Ipswich.

MITCHELL, Michael   BORN: 21 April 1984, Halifax, West Yorkshire.
BRITISH CAREER: (2000) Peterborough (CL), Newport (CL); (2001) Sheffield (CL), Newport (CL);
(2002) Sheffield (CL), Buxton, Boston; (2003) Sheffield (CL), Stoke (CT), Carmarthen, Rye House
(CL); (2004) Stoke (CL), Sheffield (CT); (2005) Stoke (CL).

MOGRIDGE, Alan   BORN: 6 November 1963, Westminster, London.
BRITISH CAREER: (1981) Wimbledon; (1982-83) Crayford, Wimbledon; (1984) Canterbury,
Wolverhampton; (1985) Hackney; (1986) Canterbury, Rye House, Ipswich, Hackney; (1987) Hackney;
(1988) Hackney, Sheffield, Bradford; (1989-90) Ipswich; (1991-92) Arena-Essex; (1993) Peterborough;
(1994) Middlesbrough, Sheffield; (1995) Arena-Essex; (1996) London, Eastbourne; (1997) Eastbourne;
(1999-2000) Berwick; (2001) Swindon; (2002-05) Stoke.

MOORE, Andrew   BORN: 6 October 1982, Lincoln, Lincolnshire.
BRITISH CAREER: (1998) Skegness, Norfolk; (1999) Mildenhall, Sheffield (PL); (2000) Sheffield (CL &
PL), Berwick; (2001) Sheffield (CL & PL); (2002-03) Sheffield (PL); (2004) Sheffield (PL), Swindon,
Eastbourne; (2005) Eastbourne.

MORRIS, Keiran   BORN: 10 October 1988, Glasgow, Scotland.
BRITISH CAREER: (2005) Armadale.

MORRIS, Phil   BORN: 10 September 1975, Newport, Gwent, Wales.
BRITISH CAREER: (1991-96) Reading; (1997) Stoke; (1998-2003) Reading; (2004) Reading, Poole;
(2005) Newcastle, Arena-Essex.

MORTON, Ray   BORN: 19 June 1968, Peckham, London.
BRITISH CAREER: (1985-87) King's Lynn; (1988) Wimbledon, King's Lynn; (1989-90) Wimbledon;
(1991-92) Reading; (1993) Poole; (1994-95) Reading; (1996) Reading, Hull; (1998) Isle of Wight; (1999)
Hull; (2000-03) Isle of Wight; (2004) Isle of Wight, Arena-Essex; (2005) Poole, Exeter.

NEATH, Chris   BORN: 29 January 1982, Worcester, Hereford & Worcestershire.
BRITISH CAREER: (1998-99) Newport (CL & PL); (2000-01) Newport; (2002-03) Swindon,
Wolverhampton; (2004) Rye House, Wolverhampton; (2005) Rye House.

NERMARK, Daniel   BORN: 30 July 1977, Karlstad, Sweden.
BRITISH CAREER: (2001-02) Wolverhampton; (2003) Ipswich; (2004) Wolverhampton; (2005) Edinburgh.

NEWITT, Jason   BORN: 13 January 1978, Oxford, Oxfordshire.
BRITISH CAREER: (1996) Peterborough (CL); (1997) Peterborough (AL), Oxford (AL & PL); (2000)
Somerset; (2003) Oxford (CL), Mildenhall; (2004-05) Oxford (CL).

NICHOLLS, Scott   BORN: 16 May 1978, Ipswich, Suffolk.
BRITISH CAREER: (1994) Peterborough; (1995-98) Ipswich; (1999-2000) Poole; (2001-04) Ipswich;
(2005) Coventry.

NIEMINEN, Kauko   BORN: 29 August 1979, Seinajoki, Finland.
BRITISH CAREER: (2002-05) Workington.

NORRIS, David   BORN: 20 August 1972, Eastbourne, East Sussex.
BRITISH CAREER: (1988-89) Eastbourne; (1990-92) Ipswich; (1993) Ipswich, Eastbourne; (1994)
Eastbourne; (1995) Reading; (1996-2005) Eastbourne.

NORTON, Danny   BORN: 27 August 1986, Boston, Lincolnshire.

BRITISH CAREER: (2001–02) Peterborough (CL); (2003) Peterborough (CL & BLC), Armadale (CT), Reading, Mildenhall (KOC & CT); (2004) Oxford (CL), Reading; (2005) Scunthorpe.

ONDRASIK, Pavel   BORN: 10 December 1975, Prague, Czech Republic.

BRITISH CAREER: (2001–03) Trelawny; (2004) Newport; (2005) Exeter.

OSTERGAARD, Ulrich BORN: 19 April 1981, Odense, Denmark.

BRITISH CAREER: (2003) Eastbourne (BLC); (2004) Eastbourne, Isle of Wight; (2005) Isle of Wight, Eastbourne, Swindon.

PARKER, Ross   BORN: 11 December 1988, Wythenshawe, Greater Manchester.

BRITISH CAREER: (2004–05) Buxton.

PARKER, Shane   BORN: 29 April 1970, Adelaide, South Australia, Australia.

BRITISH CAREER: (1990–94) Ipswich; (1995–96) Middlesbrough; (1997–98) King's Lynn; (1999) Hull; (2000) King's Lynn, Belle Vue; (2001–02) Peterborough; (2003) King's Lynn, Peterborough; (2004–05) Glasgow.

PARKER, Wayne   BORN: 26 March 1971, Swindon, Wiltshire.

BRITISH CAREER: (1993) Oxford; (2004) Weymouth; (2005) Sittingbourne.

PARSONS, Joel   BORN: 24 July 1985, Broken Hill, New South Wales, Australia.

BRITISH CAREER: (2003) Rye House (CL), Wimbledon (CT); (2004) Rye House (CL), Hull, King's Lynn (CT); (2005) Hull, Mildenhall.

PECYNA, Krzysztof   BORN: 14 September 1978, Pila, Poland.

BRITISH CAREER: (2005) Wolverhampton.

PEDERSEN, Bjarne   BORN: 12 July 1978, Ryde, Denmark.

BRITISH CAREER: (2000–01) Newcastle; (2002) Poole; (2003) Poole, Newcastle; (2004–05) Poole.

PEDERSEN, Nicki   BORN: 2 April 1977, Odense, Denmark.

BRITISH CAREER: (1998) Newcastle; (1999–2000) Wolverhampton; (2001–02) King's Lynn; (2003) Oxford, Eastbourne; (2004–05) Eastbourne.

PEGLER, Scott   BORN: 3 August 1973, Exeter, Devon.

BRITISH CAREER: (1989–90) Exeter; (1992–94) Exeter; (1995) Exeter, Devon; (1996) Swindon (PL & CL); (1997) Newport (PL); (1998) Newport (PL & CL); (1999) Newport (PL); (2000–05) Newport (CL).

PESTELL, Jeremy   BORN: 18 October 1984, Northampton, Northamptonshire.

BRITISH CAREER: (2001) Rye House; (2002) Rye House (CL), Wimbledon; (2003) Wolverhampton (CL); (2004) Coventry (CT); (2005) Boston.

PHELPS, Gary   BORN: 30 March 1977, Swindon, Wiltshire.

BRITISH CAREER: (1996) Swindon (CL); (1997) M4 Raven Sprockets, Swindon; (1998) Norfolk, Isle of Wight; (1999) Workington, Berwick, King's Lynn (CL), St Austell, Edinburgh, Isle of Wight, Newcastle; (2000) Arena-Essex, St Austell, Isle of Wight, Workington; (2001) Trelawny, Somerset; (2002) Somerset, Isle of Wight; (2003) Isle of Wight; (2004) Edinburgh, Armadale, Mildenhall; (2005) Sittingbourne.

PHILLIPS, Glen   BORN: 22 November 1982, Farnborough, Kent.

BRITISH CAREER: (1999) Exeter, Isle of Wight, King's Lynn (CL); (2000) Isle of Wight, Somerset; (2001) Isle of Wight; (2002) Wimbledon, Reading; (2003–05) Isle of Wight.

PICKERING, Michael   BORN: 28 October 1982, Hull, East Yorkshire.

BRITISH CAREER: (1998) Buxton; (2000) Somerset (LC); (2002) Newport (CL); (2003) Hull, Newcastle (CL); (2004) Newcastle (CL), King's Lynn (CLKOC); (2005) Boston, Armadale.

PICKERING, Paul   BORN: 15 February 1966, Hartlepool, Cleveland.

BRITISH CAREER: (1992) Middlesbrough; (1993) Middlesbrough, Bradford; (1994–96) Bradford; (1997) Reading; (1998–2003) Stoke; (2004) Stoke, Ipswich; (2005) Stoke (PT).

PICKERING, Phil   BORN: 25 October 1963, Hull, East Yorkshire.

BRITISH CAREER: (1996) Peterborough (CL), Sheffield (CL), Oxford; (1998) Buxton, Berwick; (1999) Berwick, Buxton; (2000) Buxton, Berwick, Newcastle, Hull; (2001) Berwick, Boston; (2003) Buxton; (2004) Newcastle (CL); (2005) Boston.

PIETRASZKO, Adam   BORN: 18 August 1982, Czestochowa, Poland.

BRITISH CAREER: (2004) Berwick, Peterborough; (2005) Berwick.

PIJPER, Theo BORN: 11 February 1980, Dokkum, Holland.
BRITISH CAREER: (2002-05) Edinburgh.

PISZCZ, Tomasz BORN: 8 June 1977, Gdansk, Poland.
BRITISH CAREER: (2004) Peterborough, Coventry; (2005) Workington.

POVAZHNY, Roman BORN: 23 October 1976, Togliatti, Russia.
BRITISH CAREER: (1999) Eastbourne; (2000) Oxford, Wolverhampton; (2001) Eastbourne; (2002) King's Lynn; (2004) Eastbourne, Arena-Essex; (2005) Arena-Essex.

POWELL, Ben BORN: 29 November 1984, Helensvale, Queensland, Australia.
BRITISH CAREER: (2002) Sheffield (CL); (2003) Carmarthen; (2004) Carmarthen, Coventry (CT), Boston; (2005) Boston, Rye House (CL).

PRIEST, Luke BORN: 18 June 1985, Birmingham, West Midlands.
BRITISH CAREER: (2000) Ashfield, Owlerton; (2001) Sheffield (CL), Boston; (2002) Sheffield (CL); (2003) Sheffield (CL), Stoke (CT); (2004) Newport (PL), Stoke (CL), Sheffield (CT); (2005) Stoke (CL).

PROTASIEWICZ, Piotr BORN: 25 January 1975, Zielona Gora, Poland.
BRITISH CAREER: (1998) King's Lynn; (2002-03) Peterborough; (2005) Ipswich.

PUODZHUKS, Kjastas BORN: 23 August 1986, Daugavpils, Latvia.
BRITISH CAREER: (2005) Oxford.

PURCHASE, James BORN: 21 October 1987, Southampton, Hampshire.
BRITISH CAREER: (2003) Oxford (CL), Peterborough (CL); (2004) Swindon (CL), King's Lynn (CT); (2005) Mildenhall.

PUSZAKOWSKI, Mariusz BORN: 25 May 1978, Golub-Dodrzyn, Poland.
BRITISH CAREER: (2005) Ipswich.

REYNOLDS, Joe BORN: 20 March 1989, Wordsley, West Midlands.
BRITISH CAREER: (2004) Buxton; (2005) Buxton, Stoke (CL), Weymouth.

RICHARDSON, Lee BORN: 25 April 1979, Hastings, Sussex.
BRITISH CAREER: (1995) Reading; (1996) Reading (CL), Poole; (1997) Reading, Peterborough, King's Lynn; (1998) Reading; (1999) Poole; (2000-03) Coventry; (2004) Peterborough; (2005) Swindon.

RICHARDSON, Mark BORN: 21 June 1988, Boston, Lincolnshire.
BRITISH CAREER: (2004) Boston, Sheffield (CT); (2005) Boston.

RICHARDSON, Scott BORN: 16 September 1988, Mirfield, Yorkshire.
BRITISH CAREER: (2005) Scunthorpe.

RICKARDSSON, Tony BORN: 17 August 1970, Grytas, Sweden.
BRITISH CAREER: (1991-94) Ipswich; (1997-98) Ipswich; (1999) King's Lynn; (2001-04) Poole; (2005) Arena-Essex.

RISAGER, Morten BORN: 30 September 1987, Arhus, Denmark.
BRITISH CAREER: (2004-05) Coventry.

ROBERTSON, Jamie BORN: 8 October 1986, Berwick-upon-Tweed, Northumberland.
BRITISH CAREER: (2002) Newcastle (CL); (2003) Newcastle (PL & CL); (2004) Newcastle (PL & CL); (2005) Newcastle (PL), Oxford (CL).

ROBSON, Scott BORN: 15 August 1971, Sunderland, Tyne & Wear.
BRITISH CAREER: (1987-92) Berwick; (1993-94) Newcastle; (1995-96) Middlesbrough; (1997) Hull; (1998) Eastbourne, Berwick; (1999-2000) Coventry; (2001) Berwick; (2002) Rye House; (2003) Rye House, Eastbourne; (2004) Rye House, Belle Vue; (2005) Workington.

ROBSON, Stuart BORN: 8 November 1976, Sunderland, Tyne & Wear.
BRITISH CAREER: (1993-94) Newcastle, Edinburgh; (1995) Coventry; (1996) Coventry, Middlesbrough; (1997) Hull; (1998-2002) Coventry; (2003) Coventry, Newcastle; (2004) Coventry; (2005) Rye House.

ROYNON, Adam BORN: 30 August 1988, Barrow-in-Furness, Cumbria.
BRITISH CAREER: (2003) Swindon (CL), Armadale (CT); (2004) Newcastle (CL), Mildenhall; (2005) Mildenhall, Boston (CT & KOC), Glasgow.

RUSHEN, Karl BORN: 26 January 1979, Chelmsford, Essex.
BRITISH CAREER: (2005) Sittingbourne.

RYMEL, Adrian   BORN: 30 October 1975, Koprivnice, Czech Republic.
BRITISH CAREER: (2001-03) Berwick; (2004) Berwick, Peterborough; (2005) Berwick, Coventry.

SANCHEZ, Emiliano   BORN: 9 December 1977, Buenos Aires, Argentina.
BRITISH CAREER: (1999-2001) Glasgow; (2002-03) Trelawny; (2004) Hull, Peterborough; (2005) Hull.

SCARBORO, Ricky   BORN: 31 July 1966, Gunby, Lincolnshire.
BRITISH CAREER: (1999) Mildenhall, King's Lynn (CL); (2000-01) Boston; (2002) Boston, King's Lynn (CL); (2003) Oxford (CL & BLC), Mildenhall (CT), Stoke (CT); (2004) Oxford (CL), Coventry (CT); (2005) Oxford (CL), Sittingbourne, Scunthorpe.

SCHLEIN, Rory   BORN: 1 September 1984, Darwin, Northern Territory, Australia.
BRITISH CAREER: (2001-02) Edinburgh, Sheffield (CL); (2003-04) Edinburgh, Belle Vue; (2005) Coventry.

SCHRAMM, Chris   BORN: 30 May 1984, Maldon, Essex.
BRITISH CAREER: (2000) Peterborough (CL), Berwick, Arena-Essex; (2001-02) Peterborough (CL), Reading; (2003) Newport (PL), Wimbledon (CT), Peterborough (CL), Oxford (CL); (2004) Reading, Oxford (CL); (2005) Berwick, Peterborough.

SCOTT, Blair   BORN: 14 May 1980, Edinburgh, Scotland.
BRITISH CAREER: (1996) Linlithgow, Scottish Monarchs; (1997) Edinburgh, Lathallan; (1998-2001) Edinburgh; (2002) Edinburgh, Belle Vue, Workington; (2003) Workington; (2004) Armadale, Berwick; (2005) Armadale.

SCREEN, Joe   BORN: 27 November 1972, Chesterfield, Derbyshire.
BRITISH CAREER: (1989-93) Belle Vue; (1994-97) Bradford; (1998) Belle Vue; (1999) Hull; (2000-02) Eastbourne; (2003) Eastbourne, Belle Vue; (2004-05) Belle Vue.

SHARPLES, Paul   BORN: 25 April 1974, Manchester.
BRITISH CAREER: (2002) Belle Vue; (2003) Buxton; (2004) Buxton, Newcastle (CL); (2005) Buxton.

SHIELDS, Adam   BORN: 8 February 1977, Kurri-Kurri, New South Wales, Australia.
BRITISH CAREER: (2000-02) Isle of Wight; (2003) Isle of Wight, Eastbourne; (2004-05) Eastbourne.

SIMMONS, Nick   BORN: 24 July 1981, Leamington Spa, Warwickshire.
BRITISH CAREER: (1997) Shuttle Cubs, Ryde; (1998) Newport (CL & PL), Isle of Wight, Exeter; (1999) Isle of Wight, Stoke, Newport (CL); (2000) Arena-Essex; (2001) Newport (PL & CL), Somerset; (2002) Isle of Wight; (2003) Stoke, Mildenhall; (2004) Exeter, Weymouth; (2005) Exeter, Sittingbourne.

SIMOTA, Zdenek   BORN: 4 May 1985, Prachatice, Czech Republic.
BRITISH CAREER: (2005) Reading.

SKORNICKI, Adam   BORN: 22 October 1976, Wolsztyn, Poland.
BRITISH CAREER: (2000-04) Wolverhampton; (2005) Wolverhampton, Arena-Essex.

SMART, Lee   BORN: 5 April 1988, Swindon, Wiltshire.
BRITISH CAREER: (2003) Swindon (CL), Stoke (CT); (2004) Mildenhall; (2005) Somerset, Weymouth, Mildenhall.

SMETHILLS, Lee   BORN: 30 March 1982, Bolton, Lancashire.
BRITISH CAREER: (1998) Mildenhall; (1999) Workington, Buxton, Rye House, Belle Vue, Newcastle; (2000) Workington, Buxton; (2001) Workington; (2002) Hull, Belle Vue; (2003) Exeter; (2004) Newcastle, Berwick; (2005) Exeter.

SMITH, Andy   BORN: 25 May 1966, York, North Yorkshire.
BRITISH CAREER: (1982-88) Belle Vue; (1989-90) Bradford; (1991) Swindon; (1992-95) Coventry; (1996) Bradford; (1997) Coventry; (1998) Belle Vue, Swindon; (1999-2001) Belle Vue; (2003) Oxford (EL & CL); (2004) Swindon; (2005) Belle Vue.

SMITH, Jamie   BORN: 20 July 1983, Peterborough, Cambridgeshire.
BRITISH CAREER: (1998) Norfolk; (1999) Eastbourne, Glasgow; (2000) Newcastle, Peterborough (CL), Hull, Somerset; (2001) Hull, Somerset; (2002) Hull; (2003) Swindon; (2004) Somerset, Coventry; (2005) Somerset.

SMITH, Rob   BORN: 18 February 1988, Eastbourne, East Sussex.
BRITISH CAREER: (2004) Mildenhall; (2005) Wimbledon.

SMITH, Scott A.   BORN: 29 September 1973, Sheffield, South Yorkshire.
BRITISH CAREER: (1990–95) Cradley Heath; (1996–99) Sheffield; (2000) Berwick; (2001–02) Sheffield; (2003) Sheffield, Exeter; (2005) Berwick.

SMOLINSKI, Martin   BORN: 6 December 1984, Graefelfing, nr Munich, Germany.
BRITISH CAREER: (2004–05) Coventry.

SNEDDON, Derek   BORN: 27 July 1982, Falkirk, Scotland.
BRITISH CAREER: (1998) Hull; (1999) Linlithgow, Isle of Wight; (2000) Ashfield, Edinburgh; (2001) Edinburgh, Glasgow; (2002) Newcastle; (2003) Edinburgh; (2004–05) Armadale.

SPEIGHT, David   BORN: 21 March 1980, Bradford, West Yorkshire.
BRITISH CAREER: (2000) Owlerton; (2001) Sheffield (CL); (2002) Hull, Sheffield (CL), Wolverhampton (CT); (2003) Sheffield (CL); (2004) Newcastle (CL), Sheffield (CT), Stoke (CL); (2005) Scunthorpe, Stoke (CL).

STAECHMANN, Jan   BORN: 5 June 1966, Kolding, Denmark.
BRITISH CAREER: (1985–90) Wolverhampton; (1991–94) Long Eaton; (1995–96) Hull; (1997) Peterborough; (1998–99) Oxford; (2000) Oxford, Belle Vue; (2001–02) Stoke; (2003) Stoke, Oxford; (2004) Stoke; (2005) Stoke (PT).

STANCL, George   BORN: 19 August 1975, Prague, Czech Republic.
BRITISH CAREER: (1994–95) Sheffield; (1996–99) Wolverhampton; (2000) Coventry; (2002–04) Glasgow; (2005) Glasgow, Ipswich.

STANGE, Thomas   BORN: 15 February 1985, Gegenbach, Germany.
BRITISH CAREER: (2005) King's Lynn.

STASZEK, Pawel   BORN: 20 May 1976, Lublin, Poland.
BRITISH CAREER: (2005) Oxford.

STEAD, Garry   BORN: 5 January 1972, Holmfirth, West Yorkshire.
BRITISH CAREER: (1990–92) Stoke; (1993) Newcastle; (1994) Newcastle, Bradford; (1995) Bradford; (1996) Sheffield; (1997) Bradford; (1998) Wolverhampton; (1999–2002) Hull; (2003) Hull, Eastbourne; (2004–05) Hull.

STEAD, Simon   BORN: 25 April 1982, Sheffield, South Yorkshire.
BRITISH CAREER: (1997) Peterborough (AL); (1998) Peterborough (PL), Buxton; (1999–2001) Sheffield; (2002) Sheffield, Peterborough; (2003–04) Workington, Wolverhampton; (2005) Belle Vue.

STEPHENS, Seemond   BORN: 9 August 1967, St Austell, Cornwall.
BRITISH CAREER: (1998) St Austell, Exeter, Sheffield, Swindon; (1999) Eastbourne, Swindon, St Austell; (2000–01) Exeter; (2002) Trelawny, Exeter; (2003) Exeter, Eastbourne; (2004–05) Exeter.

STODDART, Sean   BORN: 20 January 1987, Edinburgh, Scotland.
BRITISH CAREER: (2003) Armadale, Trelawny (CT), Carmarthen (CT), Newcastle (CL); (2004) Armadale, Edinburgh; (2005) Armadale.

STOJANOWSKI, Krzysztof   BORN: 5 January 1979, Zielona Gora, Poland.
BRITISH CAREER: (2005) Isle of Wight.

STONEHEWER, Carl   BORN: 16 May 1972, Manchester.
BRITISH CAREER: (1988–89) Belle Vue; (1990) Wolverhampton; (1991–93) Belle Vue; (1994) Peterborough; (1995–96) Long Eaton; (1997) Long Eaton, King's Lynn, Peterborough, Coventry, Eastbourne; (1998) Sheffield; (1999–2002) Workington; (2003) Workington, Belle Vue; (2004–05) Workington.

STRUDWICK, Lee   BORN: 23 July 1988, Pembury, Kent.
BRITISH CAREER: (2005) Wimbledon.

STRUDWICK, Niall   BORN: 29 May 1990, Pembury, Kent.
BRITISH CAREER: (2005) Armadale.

SUCHANEK, Tomas   BORN: 7 April 1984, Pardubice, Czech Republic.
BRITISH CAREER: (2003) King's Lynn (BLC); (2005) Isle of Wight, Poole.

SULLIVAN, Ryan   BORN: 20 January 1975, Melbourne, Victoria, Australia.
BRITISH CAREER: (1994–97) Peterborough; (1998) Poole; (1999–2003) Peterborough; (2004–05) Poole.

SVAB, Toni   BORN: 9 June 1974, Vlasim, Czech Republic.

BRITISH CAREER: (1994-95) Exeter; (1996) Middlesbrough; (1997-2000) Ipswich; (2001-02) Eastbourne; (2004) Belle Vue; (2005) Exeter, Poole.

SWIST, Piotr   BORN: 20 June 1968, Gorzow, Poland.

BRITISH CAREER: (2005) Arena-Essex.

TACEY, Shaun   BORN: 27 November 1974, Norwich, Norfolk.

BRITISH CAREER: (1992) Ipswich; (1993) Ipswich, Arena-Essex; (1994-96) Coventry; (1997) King's Lynn, Isle of Wight, Bradford, Coventry; (1998-2000) Coventry; (2001-02) Arena-Essex; (2003) Hull; (2004) King's Lynn, Coventry; (2005) Workington.

TERENZANI, Simone   BORN: 23 June 1978, Udine, Italy.

BRITISH CAREER: (2005) Hull.

THEOBALD, James   BORN: 31 December 1985, Ashford, Kent.

BRITISH CAREER: (2002) Rye House (CL), Carmarthen; (2003) Rye House (CL), Sheffield (CL), Newport (CL), Peterborough (CL); (2004) Sittingbourne (KOC), Wimbledon, King's Lynn (CLKOC); (2005) Sittingbourne.

THOMPSON, Ben   BORN: 10 September 1990, Lincoln, Lincolnshire.

BRITISH CAREER: (2005) Buxton.

THOMPSON, Mark   BORN: 8 July 1979, Orsett, Essex.

BRITISH CAREER: (1996) Sittingbourne, Linlithgow, Mildenhall, Eastbourne (CL); (1997) Anglian Angels; (1998) Mildenhall, Newport (PL), Stoke; (1999) King's Lynn (CL), Mildenhall, Newport (CL); (2000) St Austell, Arena-Essex; (2001) Peterborough (CL); (2002) King's Lynn (CL), Mildenhall; (2003) Boston, Peterborough (BLC); (2004) Weymouth, Swindon (CL), King's Lynn (CT); (2005) Mildenhall.

THORP, Paul   BORN: 9 September 1964, Macclesfield, Cheshire.

BRITISH CAREER: (1980) Birmingham; (1981) Birmingham, Scunthorpe, Workington; (1982-83) Berwick, Birmingham; (1984-85) Stoke, Wolverhampton; (1986) Stoke, Sheffield, Belle Vue; (1987-88) Belle Vue; (1989-92) Bradford; (1993) Newcastle; (1994) Bradford; (1995-96) Hull; (1997) Belle Vue; (1998) Hull; (1999) Hull, Stoke; (2000-03) Hull; (2004) Hull, Belle Vue; (2005) Hull.

TOMICEK, Lubos   BORN: 14 March 1986, Prague, Czech Republic

BRITISH CAREER: (2003) Oxford (BLC); (2004) Newcastle; (2005) Newcastle, Oxford.

TOPINKA, Tomas   BORN: 5 June 1974, Prague, Czech Republic.

BRITISH CAREER: (1993-95) King's Lynn; (1996) Oxford; (1997-98) King's Lynn; (1999) King's Lynn, Ipswich; (2001) Belle Vue; (2002) Coventry; (2003-04) King's Lynn; (2005) King's Lynn, Coventry.

TRESARRIEU, Mathieu   BORN: 2 March 1986, Bordeaux, France.

BRITISH CAREER: (2002) Isle of Wight (YS); (2003) Isle of Wight; (2005) Reading.

TRESARRIEU, Sebastien   BORN: 10 January 1981, Cenon, France.

BRITISH CAREER: (2001-03) Isle of Wight; (2004) Isle of Wight, Eastbourne; (2005) Swindon, Exeter.

TULLY, Andrew   BORN: 26 May 1987, Douglas, Isle of Man.

BRITISH CAREER: (2003) Armadale (CT); (2004-05) Armadale.

TUTTON, Matt   BORN: 19 June 1982, Newport, South Wales.

BRITISH CAREER: (2000) Rye House; (2002) Swindon (CT), Wimbledon; (2003) Mildenhall, Buxton, Carmarthen (CT), Newport (CL); (2004-05) Newport (CL).

ULAMEK, Sebastian   BORN: 20 November 1975, Czestochowa, Poland.

BRITISH CAREER: (2000) Wolverhampton; (2002) King's Lynn; (2003-04) Oxford; (2005) Coventry.

VEDEL, Henrik   BORN: 1 January 1981, Denmark.

BRITISH CAREER: (2005) Newport.

WALASEK, Grzegorz   BORN: 29 August 1976, Krosno, Poland.

BRITISH CAREER: (2000-02) Poole; (2004) Arena-Essex; (2005) Poole (CS).

WALDRON, Shane   BORN: 26 October 1989, Swindon, Wiltshire.

BRITISH CAREER: (2005) Rye House (CL), Weymouth.

WALKER, Simon   BORN: 19 February 1980, Bristol, Avon.

BRITISH CAREER: (2001) Newport (CL); (2002) Newport (CL), Swindon (CT); (2003) Swindon (CL), Trelawny (CT); (2004) Somerset, Swindon (CL), King's Lynn (CT); (2005) Boston, Somerset.

WARWICK, Carl   BORN: 7 October 1981, Poole, Dorset.

BRITISH CAREER: (2002-03) Newport (CL); (2004) Weymouth; (2005) Newport (CL).

WARWICK, Danny   BORN: 21 November 1983, Poole, Dorset.

BRITISH CAREER: (2002) Newport (CL); (2003) Newport (CL), Poole (BLC); (2004) Weymouth, Swindon (CL), King's Lynn (CT); (2005) Newport (CL).

WATSON, Craig   BORN: 6 August 1976, Sydney, New South Wales, Australia.

BRITISH CAREER: (1997-99) Newport; (2000-01) Poole; (2002) Newport; (2003) Newport, Belle Vue; (2004-05) Newport.

WATT, Davey   BORN: 6 January 1978, Townsville, Queensland, Australia.

BRITISH CAREER: (2001) Isle of Wight; (2002) Newcastle; (2003) King's Lynn, Poole; (2004) Rye House, Poole, Eastbourne; (2005) Eastbourne.

WEBSTER, Tim   BORN: 26 May 1989, Walsall, West Midlands.

BRITISH CAREER: (2004) King's Lynn (CT); (2005) Weymouth (KOC), Scunthorpe.

WERNER, Brent   BORN: 15 April 1974, Los Angeles, California, USA.

BRITISH CAREER: (1995-97) Long Eaton; (1998) Newcastle; (1999-2000) Workington; (2001) Eastbourne; (2002) Rye House; (2003) Rye House, Peterborough; (2004) Rye House, Belle Vue; (2005) Rye House, Oxford.

WESTACOTT, Jamie   BORN: 9 April 1988, Newport, South Wales.

BRITISH CAREER: (2003) Newport (CL), Stoke (CT); (2004) Newport (CL), Reading; (2005) Newport (CL).

WETHERS, Matthew   BORN: 30 May 1985, Adelaide, South Australia.

BRITISH CAREER: (2003) Armadale (CT), Wolverhampton (CL), Edinburgh; (2004) Edinburgh, Armadale; (2005) Glasgow, King's Lynn, Edinburgh.

WHITE, Karl   BORN: 1 December 1987, Thurrock, Essex.

BRITISH CAREER: (2004) Rye House (CL); (2005) Rye House (CL), Boston, Wimbledon.

WIDMAN, Chris   BORN: 25 March 1990, Leicester, Leicestershire.

BRITISH CAREER: (2005) Scunthorpe.

WILKINSON, Carl   BORN: 16 May 1981, Boston, Lincolnshire.

BRITISH CAREER: (1997) Peterborough (AL); (1998) Norfolk; (1999) King's Lynn (CL); (2000) Boston, Newcastle, Glasgow; (2001) Boston; (2002-03) Newport (PL & CL); (2004) Newport (PL); (2005) Boston, Berwick.

WILSON, Ben   BORN: 15 March 1986, Sheffield, South Yorkshire.

BRITISH CAREER: (2001-02) Sheffield (CL); (2003) Sheffield (PL & CL), Buxton (CT); (2004) Sheffield (PL & CT), Carmarthen; (2005) Sheffield.

WILSON, Dean   BORN: 19 January 1988, Boston, Lincolnshire.

BRITISH CAREER: (2004) Weymouth (CT), King's Lynn (CT); (2005) Boston (CT).

WILSON, Sean   BORN: 7 November 1969, York, North Yorkshire.

BRITISH CAREER: (1986-88) Sheffield; (1989) Coventry; (1990) Coventry, King's Lynn; (1991-93) Bradford; (1995-96) Bradford; (1997) Coventry; (1998) Belle Vue; (1999-2005) Sheffield.

WOLFF, Richard   BORN: 12 June 1976, Prague, Czech Republic.

BRITISH CAREER: (2001-03) Trelawny; (2005) Reading.

WOODWARD, Cameron   BORN: 8 January 1985, Mildura, Victoria, Australia.

BRITISH CAREER: (2003) Poole (BLC); (2004-05) Edinburgh.

WRIGHT, Charles   BORN: 26 October 1988, Stockport, Cheshire.

BRITISH CAREER: (2004-05) Buxton.

WRIGHT, James   BORN: 13 June 1986, Stockport, Cheshire.

BRITISH CAREER: (2002) Buxton; (2003) Buxton, Belle Vue (BLC); (2004) Workington, Buxton; (2005) Workington, Belle Vue.

WRIGHT, Matthew   BORN: 19 November 1985, Harlow, Essex.

BRITISH CAREER: (2002) Boston, Mildenhall, Carmarthen, Wimbledon (CT); (2003) Mildenhall, Ipswich (BLC); (2004-05) Wimbledon.

YORKE, Keith   BORN: 20 September 1961, Crawley, Sussex.
  BRITISH CAREER: (1995) Stoke; (1996) Sittingbourne; (2005) Sittingbourne, Stoke (CL).
ZAGAR, Matej   BORN: 3 April 1983, Ljubljana, Slovenia.
  BRITISH CAREER: (2003) Trelawny; (2004-05) Reading.
ZETTERSTROM, Magnus   BORN: 9 December 1971, Eskilstuna, Sweden.
  BRITISH CAREER: (1996) Poole; (1998-99) Poole; (2000) Peterborough; (2001) Poole; (2002) Poole, Peterborough; (2003) Poole (BLC); (2004) Poole; (2005) Somerset.

STOP PRESS

The speedway world was saddened when the tragic news came through that twenty-three-year-old Ashley Jones had lost his life on 13 November 2005, following a track accident the previous evening at Myrtleford Speedway, Victoria in his native Australia. The youngster, who had helped King's Lynn to their Knock-Out Cup and Young Shield double, unfortunately sustained serious facial injuries after picking up drive and crashing heavily in the last ride of the meeting while representing home state Victoria against New South Wales. He was rushed to the local hospital before later being airlifted to the Royal Melbourne Hospital, where he was placed on a life-support machine. After consulting with medical specialists, his family faced the hardest decision anyone is ever likely to have to make and the machine was switched off. King's Lynn co-promoter Buster Chapman led the tributes, stating: 'Our deepest sympathies go out to Ashley's family and closest friends. It's at times like these when you realise just how dangerous our sport is.'

Ashley Jones

COMPLETE
YOUR COLLECTION
OF THE TEMPUS SPEEDWAY YEARBOOK

Previous editions now available for only **£5.99**

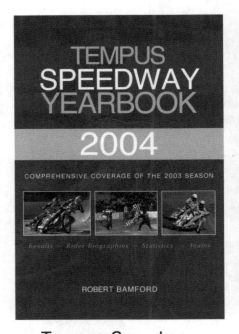

Tempus Speedway Yearbook 2004
ISBN 07524 29558
RRP £17.99

Tempus Speedway Yearbook 2005
ISBN 07524 33962
RRP £19.99

To order your back copies please contact the Tempus Sales Department
on **01453 883300** and quote SHYB06.

To find out about other Tempus speedway titles visit
www.tempus-publishing.com